D0597058

Jim Bawden
24 Bain Ave.
Toronto 6

SURVEY OF BRITISH COMMONWEALTH AFFAIRS

Problems of External Policy

1931 — 1939

The Royal Institute of International Affairs is an unofficial and non-political body, founded in 1920 to encourage and facilitate the scientific study of international questions. The Institute, as such, is precluded by the terms of its Royal Charter from expressing an opinion on any aspect of international affairs. Any opinions expressed in this publication are not, therefore, those of the Institute

SURVEY OF BRITISH COMMONWEALTH AFFAIRS

Problems of External Policy 1931 – 1939

BY

NICHOLAS MANSERGH
B.LITT., M.A., D.PHIL.

Abe Bailey Research Professor of British Commonwealth Relations at the Royal Institute of International Affairs

Issued under the auspices of the Royal Institute of International Affairs

OXFORD UNIVERSITY PRESS
LONDON NEW YORK TORONTO
1952

Oxford University Press, Amen House, London E.C.4
GLASGOW NEW YORK TORONTO MELBOURNE WELLINGTON
BOMBAY CALCUTTA MADRAS CAPE TOWN
Geoffrey Cumberlege, Publisher to the University

PRINTED IN GREAT BRITAIN

TO
THE MASTER AND FELLOWS
OF PEMBROKE COLLEGE
OXFORD

ACKNOWLEDGEMENTS

PROFESSOR ALEXANDER BRADY of the University of Toronto, Sir William Clark, formerly United Kingdom High Commissioner to Canada and to the Union of South Africa, Lord Hailey, Professor W. K. Hancock of the University of London, Mr. Paul Hasluck, M.H.R., and Mr. Gavin Long of the Australian Official War History Branch, Senator Michael Hayes, Mr. J. D. O'Shea of the New Zealand War History Branch, Professor C. H. Philips of the University of London, and Professor K. C. Wheare of the University of Oxford have read parts of this book in typescript and I am grateful to them for their many criticisms and suggestions. I am indebted also to Sir Charles Dixon of the Commonwealth Relations Office who has answered many questions from his store of detailed and surely unrivalled knowledge of the constitutional development of the Commonwealth in recent years; to Lord Hankey, Mr. L. S. Amery, and Mr. Malcolm MacDonald for the opportunity of some illuminating conversations; to many others whose anonymity in no way reflects upon the value of the assistance they gave me, and to my wife who helped me in the arrangement of my material. I should also like to pay tribute to the generous co-operation of my colleagues at Chatham House, among whom the Hon. Mrs. Collier and Miss Ann Hurley, who in turn acted as my research assistants, and Miss H. G. Oliver of the editorial department should be mentioned by name. Finally, I should like to record my deep sense of gratitude to the Carnegie Corporation, whose generosity made possible the writing of this book. It should be particularly emphasized that no responsibility rests with anyone but the author for the opinions expressed, or the facts included, in this book.

N. M.

CHATHAM HOUSE
September 1951

CONTENTS

PART I

FROM EMPIRE TO COMMONWEALTH: THE YEARS OF TRANSITION

PART II

THE EXTERNAL POLICIES OF THE DOMINIONS

1931–9

CHAPTER IV. CANADA: THE SEARCH FOR UNITY

CHAPTER V. AUSTRALIA: THE PACIFIC OUTPOST

CHAPTER VI. NEW ZEALAND: IMPERIALIST AND INTERNATIONALIST

PART III

THE COMMONWEALTH AND THE WAR

ABBREVIATIONS
USED IN FOOTNOTE REFERENCES

UNITED KINGDOM AND COMMONWEALTH PARLIAMENTARY DEBATES

United Kingdom Debates are referred to as 'H. of C. Deb.' (Commons) and 'H. of L. Deb.' (Lords), respectively. All Commons Debates are those of the fifth series, unless otherwise stated. Abbreviations used for the Debates (always referred to as 'Deb.') of the Commonwealth countries are as follows:

Australia, H. of R. (House of Representatives), or Senate.
Canada, H. of C. (House of Commons), or Senate.
New Zealand, H. of R. (House of Representatives), or L.C. (Legislative Council).
South Africa, H. of A. (House of Assembly), or Senate.

The Debates of Eire and the Irish Free State are referred to as Dáil Debates or Eire (or Irish Free State) Senate Debates, respectively. Dáil Éireann, *Debates on the Treaty between Great Britain and Ireland, December 1921 and January 1922* (Dublin, Talbot Press) is referred to as *Treaty Debates*.

IMPERIAL AND PRIME MINISTERS' CONFERENCES

These are referred to by their Command numbers only, as follows:

Cd. 5745: Imperial Conference, 1911, *Minutes of Proceedings.*
Cd. 9177: Imperial War Conference, 1918, *Extracts from Minutes of Proceedings and Papers Laid before the Conference.*
Cmd. 1474: Conference of Prime Ministers and Representatives of the United Kingdom, the Dominions, and India, held in June, July, and August, 1921, *Summary of Proceedings and Documents.*
Cmd. 1987: Imperial Conference, 1923, *Summary of Proceedings.*
Cmd. 2768: Imperial Conference, 1926, *Summary of Proceedings.* This contains the Report of the Inter-Imperial Relations Committee, generally known as the Balfour Report.
Cmd. 3717: Imperial Conference, 1930, *Summary of Proceedings.*
Cmd. 3718: Imperial Conference, 1930: *Appendices to Summary of Proceedings.*
Cmd. 5482: Imperial Conference, 1937, *Summary of Proceedings.*

BRITISH COMMONWEALTH RELATIONS CONFERENCES

B.C.R. Conference, 1933: *Proceedings of the first unofficial Conference at Toronto, 1933*, ed. by A. J. Toynbee (London, Oxford University Press, for Royal Institute of International Affairs, 1934).

B.C.R. Conference, 1938: *The British Commonwealth and the Future: Proceedings of the second unofficial Conference . . . Sydney, 1938*, ed. by H. V. Hodson (London, Oxford University Press, for Royal Institute of International Affairs, 1939).

BOOKS AND PERIODICALS

These are cited in full at the first reference but thereafter abbreviated. The following abbreviations are not self-explanatory:

Canada in World Affairs: Canadian Institute of World Affairs, *Canada in World Affairs: the Pre-War Years*, by F. H. Soward, J. F. Parkinson, N. A. M. MacKenzie, and T. W. L. MacDermot (Toronto and London, Oxford University Press, for C.I.I.A., 1941). The later volumes in this series are not referred to in this book.

Carter, *British Commonwealth*: Gwendolen Carter, *The British Commonwealth and International Security* (Toronto, Ryerson Press, for Canadian Institute of International Affairs, 1947).

Churchill, *The Aftermath*: W. S. Churchill, *The Aftermath: being a sequel to The World Crisis* (London, Macmillan, 1941).

Churchill, *Second World War*, vol. 1: W. S. Churchill, *The Second World War*, vol. 1, *The Gathering Storm* (London, Cassell, 1949).

Contemporary New Zealand: New Zealand Institute of International Affairs, *Contemporary New Zealand: Survey of Domestic and Foreign Policy* (Auckland, Whitcombe & Tombs; London, Oxford University Press, 1938).

Crisp, *Parliamentary Government*: L. F. Crisp, *The Parliamentary Government of the Commonwealth of Australia* (London, Longmans, in association with the Wakefield Press, Adelaide, 1949).

Documents on German Foreign Policy, 1918–45: *Documents on German Foreign Policy, 1918–45, from Archives of the German Foreign Ministry*, published jointly by the U.S. Department of State and the British Foreign Office, Series D (1937–45), vol. 1: *From Neurath to Ribbentrop (September 1937–September 1938)*; vol. 2: *Germany and Czechoslovakia (1937–8)*: vol. 4: *The Aftermath of Munich (October 1938–March 1939)* (Washington, U.S.G.P.O., and London, H.M.S.O., 1949–).

Dugdale, *Balfour*: Blanche E. C. Dugdale, *Arthur James Balfour, First Earl of Balfour, 1906–30* (London, Hutchinson, 1936).

Glazebrook, *Canadian External Relations*: G. P. de T. Glazebrook, *A History of Canadian External Relations* (Toronto and London, Oxford University Press, for Canadian Institute of International Affairs, 1950).

Die Grosse Politik: Germany, Auswärtigen Amtes, *Die Grosse Politik der Europäischen Kabinette, 1871–1914* (Berlin, Deutsche Verlagsgesellenschaft für Politik).

Hancock, *Survey*: W. K. Hancock, *Survey of British Commonwealth Affairs*, vol. 1: *Problems of Nationality, 1918–36*; vol. 2 (pts. 1 and 2): *Problems of Economic Policy, 1818–39* (London, Oxford University Press, for Royal Institute of International Affairs, 1937–42).

van den Heever, *Hertzog*: C. M. van den Heever, *General J. B. M. Hertzog*, trans. and abridged by the author (Johannesburg, A.P.B. Bookstore, 1946).

J.P.E.: *Journal of the Parliaments of the Empire*.

Keith, *King and Constitution*: A. Berriedale Keith, *The King and the Constitution, the Empire and Foreign Affairs* (London, Oxford University Press, 1938).

Keith, *Speeches and Documents*: A. Berriedale Keith, *Speeches and Documents on the British Dominions, 1918–31* (London, Oxford University Press, 1932; World's Classics).

Milner, *New Zealand's Interests*: I. F. G. Milner, *New Zealand's Interests and Policies in the Far East* (New York, I.P.R. Inquiry Series, 1940).

Shepherd, *Australia's Interests*: Jack Shepherd, *Australia's Interests and Policies in the Far East* (New York, I.P.R. Inquiry Series, 1939).

Skelton, *Laurier*: Oscar D. Skelton, *Life and Letters of Sir Wilfrid Laurier* (New York, Century, 1921).

Taylor, *Canada*: T. Griffith Taylor, *Canada, a Study of Cool Continental Environments and their Effect on British and French Settlement*. 2nd ed. (London, Methuen, 1950).

Wheare, *Statute of Westminster*: K. C. Wheare, *The Statute of Westminster and Dominion Status*. 4th ed. (London, Oxford University Press, 1949).

White, *O'Higgins*: T. de V. White, *Kevin O'Higgins* (London, Methuen, 1948).

QUOTATIONS

For the sake of consistency, certain minor typographical alterations have been made in passages quoted. These in no way affect the sense.

INTRODUCTION

THIS book is a study of the external policies of the Commonwealth countries from 1931, the year in which the Statute of Westminster was enacted and in which also the authority of the League of Nations was first openly challenged by a Great Power, to the outbreak of the Second World War in September 1939. It is concerned equally with relations between the self-governing members of the Commonwealth and with the exercise by the dominions of new responsibilities in the field of foreign affairs.

It has been my aim to make this book, which is one in a series the first two volumes of which were written by Professor W. K. Hancock, complete in itself. This has meant the comparative or even complete neglect of some topics whose intrinsic importance is not in question and to which detailed reference might be expected in a work of this kind. It is my hope, however, that for the reader such sacrifices will be more than counterbalanced by the advantages of unity of theme and presentation. It has also involved some disregard of chronology, but that seems unavoidable and it is in conformity with the pattern of Professor Hancock's earlier *Survey of British Commonwealth Affairs*, each volume of which was concerned with the study of one aspect of Commonwealth affairs over a comparatively long period. The first volume dealt, in the words of its sub-title, with 'Problems of Nationality, 1918–1936' and the second[1] with 'Problems of Economic Policy, 1918–1939'. This study of 'Problems of External Policy, 1931–1939' is intended to be complementary to both, and such duplication as exists may perhaps be excused on the ground that in so extensive a field more is generally gained than lost by analysing events and their causes in different contexts.

By 1931 the British Commonwealth of Nations, as refashioned by the reformist egalitarian sentiment of the post-war English-speaking world, had reached a certain maturity. The emphasis on theory, though still pronounced, was giving way to sober estimates of reality. The equality of status acquired by the dominions between 1926 and 1931 was felt in ever widening circles to be insubstantial and unsatisfying so long as there was lacking the requisite functional machinery for exercising the sovereign status enjoyed in principle. Independence in policy is after all conditional upon the existence of means for putting it into effect and power to back it; and the period 1931–51 is notable in the history of Commonwealth relations chiefly because these were the years in which, under the strain of crisis and the impact of war, the dominions acquired practical independence in external policy. The use they made of it tested the assumptions of the Balfour Report and the Statute of Westminster in the field of international politics for the first time.

[1] Published in two Parts.

The exercise of international responsibilities significantly developed the personalities of the individual member-states of the Commonwealth. Hitherto it had been the practice to speak of the dominions collectively as though the differences between them were subordinate to the characteristics they possessed in common. But with the definition of distinctive policies this convenient, comprehensive classification of 'the dominions' was emptied of much of its meaning. Because the factors that determined Canadian policy were so different from those that conditioned Australian or South African policy it became more unreal, and at times positively misleading, to generalize about dominion attitudes. Canadian, South African, or even Irish reactions to given circumstances may often have had a great deal in common, but nothing is more inimical to an understanding of recent Commonwealth history than the bland assumption that they had, or should have had, all things in common and that the dominions were a species of state which conformed, or should conform, to a certain pattern of behaviour. The emphasis placed in this volume on the emergence of individual dominion policies and on the long-term fundamental factors which necessarily condition them is intended as a corrective to a traditional approach which, it seems to me, has allowed insufficiently for that interplay of particular forces which has remoulded the character of the Commonwealth in recent years.

From 1931 onwards, the dominions were confronted ever more directly with the harsh realities of international politics, and though some were tempted to turn away in self-righteous isolation, none in the end could evade the responsibilities of independent nationhood. To meet these responsibilities external policies had, however tentatively or reluctantly, to be formulated. For contemporaries, even for those who were citizens of the dominions, the emergence of separate dominion policies was overshadowed by the continuing predominance of the United Kingdom within the Commonwealth. This was not surprising, for till 1939 these dominion policies for the most part lacked dramatic interest. Yet even where their content and aim were veiled in uncertainty they are deserving of analysis not necessarily because of their intrinsic importance at the time but because they reveal, often in instinctive, spontaneous reactions to world events, those unchanging essentials which will determine the external policies of the member-states of the Commonwealth in future years. Originality in foreign policy is something to which statesmen often aspire but rarely achieve, and in the dominions, as in older countries, the essentials of policy are predetermined by racial composition, by material resources, and above all by geographical situation. Deviations from the pattern may occur, but fundamental changes can be undertaken only at the risk of disaster. For these reasons, there is a great deal of lasting importance to be learned about the attitudes of the individual member-nations of the Commonwealth to world affairs from a study of this early phase in the evolution of their external policies.

An analysis of the attitudes of the dominions to world affairs is essential also to a just appreciation of United Kingdom policy before the war. What was the influence of the dominions upon it? This is an important question. While the role of the dominions in international affairs has tended to be overestimated in the Commonwealth overseas, it has been consistently underestimated in the United Kingdom. It is true that in its early phase constitutionalists delighted to expound the theory of individual dominion responsibility in foreign policy, but its later practical consequences have passed almost unnoted. In the detailed analyses of pre-war British foreign policy which have been published in recent years, the influence of the dominions upon it has been virtually disregarded. Even in the most comprehensive and authoritative of such works the reader will find at the most some passing reference to their views. Yet they were in fact strongly expressed and of no little importance. Such neglect of the part played by the Commonwealth overseas in the shaping of British policy may be attributed in part at least to the magnetic attraction which the problems of Central and Eastern Europe possess for the predominant school of contemporary English historians, leaving them curiously indifferent to the contribution of the new worlds which will one day surely more than redress the balance of the old. But in any event while historians have remained indifferent, politicians have not. They have made cryptic references to the attitude of the dominions, especially in 1938, which suggest at least that some share of responsibility for the policy, which reached its climax at Munich, is to be attributed to them. This is a field where a more exact examination of dominion policies may throw some new light upon a highly controversial phase in British policy and in so doing illustrate the working of the Commonwealth relationship in the field of external policy.

The title of this Survey excludes from its purview international affairs in the wider sense of the term and the domestic affairs of the member-nations of the Commonwealth except in so far as either directly influenced the development of Commonwealth relations. In the international field the line of demarcation presents no very formidable difficulties. In respect of detailed dominion policies at the League of Nations full account has been taken of the comprehensive analysis written by Dr. Gwendolen Carter under the title of *The British Commonwealth and International Security, 1919–1939*[1] and in the consideration of it these policies are examined here only in so far as the principal theme of this study demands. In the domestic field, however, the dividing line cannot be so clearly drawn. Inevitably greater attention must be paid to the domestic policies of those states in which membership of the Commonwealth itself was a controversial issue. In South Africa and in Ireland internal politics have, therefore, been closely examined because they had so direct and immediate an influence upon the attitude of these

[1] Toronto, Ryerson Press, for Canadian Institute of International Affairs, 1947.

countries to the Commonwealth. Yet here, as elsewhere, the attempt has been made to confine the study of domestic issues to what is strictly relevant to a survey of Commonwealth affairs as a whole. This book is intended to be, not a history of the Commonwealth, but a study in Commonwealth relations.

The purpose of this Survey is to interpret as well as to record. For that reason selection rather than comprehensiveness has been the aim. For that reason, too, chronological narrative has been sacrificed, where that seemed to be desirable, to the fuller analysis of a subject over a longer period. Yet fundamentally this book has been written as a study in history; not, it is true, a study in narrative history, but a study primarily in historical analysis. The aim throughout has been to apply the standards of historical scholarship to a field of contemporary history. This is no easy task. If there seems to the reader to be more than a hint of pedantry in the copiousness in the footnotes, that may be explained, if not excused, by a desire to ensure that neither the reliability nor the sources of the written evidence used should be left untested or unnoted. This caution is the more necessary because the evidence is incomplete. Where students of international affairs may rely more and more upon documentary evidence published in vast quantities by the principal belligerent states (excepting only the Soviet Union), the student of Commonwealth relations can draw upon few post-war revelations. He must depend very largely upon contemporaneously published statements of policy, upon parliamentary debates, and upon personal inquiries. The gap in written evidence is not likely soon to be remedied, for by a wise convention, communications between His Majesty's governments have not hitherto been made public. For the student this is a handicap, but it is one the seriousness of which may easily be overestimated. It is extremely doubtful if the publication of the communications between Commonwealth governments on matters of major policy would modify in many important respects the picture that may already be filled in from public statements or private knowledge. Certain of the dominion governments are known to have been cautious to the point of inaction in commenting about the great issues with which the Commonwealth was confronted in the years before the war. The more general aversion to formulae or specific commitments characteristic of all the dominions affords in itself a reasonable guarantee that there is little of major importance that remains unknown about dominion views or policies. In addition, some Commonwealth statesmen, among whom Mr. Mackenzie King was not to be numbered, have remained uninhibited by the conventional reticence in which the conduct of foreign affairs has been shrouded in the old world and have preferred indulgence in the refreshing candour of the new. Here, at least, the student of Commonwealth relations is in their debt.

Even at this time when documents are so very highly regarded by historians, critics of the writing of contemporary history will be less concerned about gaps in documentary evidence than about the possibility of surveying with detachment political issues which are not yet wholly removed from the field of controversy. It is, indeed, difficult to write about the last decade in the history of Commonwealth relations with the distant, even patronizing, unconcern with which the medieval historian may write about the colonization of Anatolia by Basil the Great or the rise and fall of the Norman Kingdom in the Two Sicilies. Any disposition to condemn the shortsightedness or the mistakes of Commonwealth statesmen with an air of clever condescension is checked by the recollection that the end of the story is as surely hidden from the historian of one short period in it as it was from the actors who for a brief while played their part upon its crowded stage. And may it not be hoped that the greater awareness, induced by such reflections, of the part which chance and the imponderable have played in Commonwealth history will help us to see it in less simple but in truer perspective? Yet even if so much be allowed, the difficulties of the task remain formidable. The historian of Commonwealth relations during a period of rapid and remarkable change is undertaking a task demanding that same delicacy of judgement required by the biographer of a living person whose most remarkable achievements may fall in the closing years of his life. Had John Morley written his biography when Gladstone had attained his allotted span of three score years and ten, how very different must have been the balance of his work. But while it is well to remind ourselves of the problems and the risks inseparable from the writing of contemporary history, it is well also to remember that not even the historian of his own time should abandon what Lord Acton called the historian's moral function. The historical approach demands detachment, but detachment can be achieved only too easily by merely recording passively what happened. Discrimination and judgement are also a part of the historian's duty.

PART I

FROM EMPIRE TO COMMONWEALTH: THE YEARS OF TRANSITION

The tents have been struck, and the great caravan of humanity is once more on the march.

JAN CHRISTIAAN SMUTS, 1918

A common interest in loyalty, in freedom, in ideals—that is the bond of Empire. If that is not enough nothing else is enough. . . .

ARTHUR JAMES BALFOUR, 1926

CHAPTER I

THE DEFINING OF DOMINION STATUS AND ITS CONSEQUENCES FOR COMMONWEALTH AND CROWN

THE IMPACT OF NEW IDEAS

AFTER 1919 the British Empire never regained the sense of unconscious security it had enjoyed in the past. Victory, made possible by the sacrifices of an Empire united as never before, brought with it neither a lasting settlement in Europe nor protection against the impact of ideas which had been so greatly stimulated in war. By these ideas the conception of imperialism was directly challenged. The nationalism that had fragmented the Habsburg Empire, the social revolution that had engulfed Tsarist Russia released powerful forces which recognized the frontiers neither of states nor of continents. Within the British Empire the triumphs of the one gave a sharper edge to the aspirations of Irishmen, Afrikaners, and Indians who inquired with unrelenting persistence whether the much vaunted principle of national self-determination was to be applied only to the inhabitants of the defeated European empires; the victory of the other prompted less immediate but even more fundamental questions about the ordering of human society and the place in it of imperialisms denounced by Lenin as the supreme manifestation of capitalist exploitation. These challenging ideas which influenced thinking far beyond the ranks of professed nationalists or the small community of avowed Marxists, exposed the foundations of the British Empire to the critical, questioning spirit of the age. Empires, indeed, were no longer fashionable and the British Empire had perforce to get to know itself, to explain its *raison d'être*, to justify its privileged position in the world. No longer could it presume simply to exist; it had to expound, to argue, to defend. For an unconscious way of life it had to substitute a conscious one.[1]

The search for a conscious way of life in harmony both with the spirit of equal partnership within the Empire that had flowered so splendidly during the war years and with the spirit of the age brought first the uncritical exultation of discovery and then more sober analysis. In the first phase the unique character of the British Empire was extolled by Empire statesmen. It was proclaimed to be an empire that had nothing in common with those discredited, absolutist empires of Central and Eastern Europe which had perished in the war. It had turned its back, too, upon the blatant, grasping imperialisms of a rather more distant past. It was no longer to be associated

[1] In this respect 1919 for the British Empire was what 1848 was for the Habsburg Empire. cf. A. J. P. Taylor, *The Habsburg Monarchy, 1809–1918* (London, Hamilton, 1948) p. 57.

with scrambles for Africa or the extraction of concessions in Asia. It was inspired by a new idealism and it represented a spirit hitherto unknown in history. 'We are', declared Mr. A. J. Balfour, 'still unconscious of the extraordinary novelty, the extraordinary greatness, and the extraordinary success of this unique experiment in human co-operation.'[1] But did not such glowing tributes in themselves suggest that in one respect Mr. Balfour was mistaken? Such praise is not bestowed by its own statesmen upon an empire of whose character and qualities they are unconscious but rather upon one of whose virtues they are becoming aware for the first time. It was the search for a conscious way of life that turned men's minds to a consideration of what the British Empire really was and what it might one day become.

The novel character of the British Empire after the First World War, which Mr. Balfour stressed, was a favourite theme both of statesmen and professors. It found one expression in a search for new names, which was in itself symptomatic of the disfavour into which empires had fallen. The British Empire of the post-war world must not be confused with other empires or even with the British Empire of pre-war days, and so it was given a distinguishing designation. Yet while the title British Commonwealth of Nations[2] happily reflected the spirit of equality and free co-operation which was the foundation of this new community of states, it was slow to gain general acceptance. Some disliked the implied breach with the past while others, who rejoiced in it and never doubted its reality, preferred not to discard but to amend the historic imperial title. Thus Sir Alfred Zimmern, who observed 'the British Empire of 1926 is not the British Empire of 1914' but 'something new—how new neither the outside world nor even its own citizens have yet adequately realized',[3] identified it as the Third British Empire. Yet however expressed, all this emphasis upon a great divide between present and past was indifferent history, if good psychology. The post-war world believed with a curious naïveté that all would be well if the relics of the bad pre-war world could be discarded. 'The Old World', 'the Old Gang', 'the Old Diplomacy', were the current terms of contempt. Yet it is a fact that the transformation of Empire into Commonwealth was both real and possible not on account of some great watershed that divided the present from the past, but because the history of the old British Empire, its evolution towards autonomy and equality, provided the solid, the indispensable foundation upon which the Commonwealth of the future could be built.

The emphasis upon novelty and uniqueness was symptomatic, but it was

[1] Cd. 9177, p. 19, quoted in Hancock, *Survey*, vol. 1, p. 1, and see generally pp. 1–3.

[2] For an account of the origin and implications of the term Commonwealth see Hancock, *Survey*, vol. 1, pp. 53 ff., and for a commentary on more recent usage of the terms Commonwealth and Empire see N. Mansergh, *The Commonwealth and the Nations* (London, Royal Institute of International Affairs, 1948) pp. 5–12.

[3] Sir Alfred Zimmern, *The Third British Empire* (London, Oxford University Press, 1932) p. 2.

neither particularly revealing nor in itself sufficient. The Union of Soviet Socialist Republics was also new and unique. The empire of the Habsburgs had, in the words of its English historian, 'a unique character, out of time, out of place'.[1] More than that the British Empire assuredly could not claim. Its spirit and its working needed to be explained and exposition in general terms was unsatisfying. Definition alone could reassure the restless and satisfy the sceptical. For them the structure of the old had to be brought into conformity with the spirit of the new. This process of redefinition was undertaken with the greatest reluctance. Conservative imperialists, ill at ease in this new Empire with its pronounced flavouring of intellectual idealism, could see neither the need nor the desirability of self-conscious analysis. On the contrary they thought it, and they continued to think it, dangerous. The Empire in the past had relied upon traditional loyalties and half-expressed convictions, and they were deeply disturbed at the prospect of sentimental ties being reduced to legal formulae. Their approach to Empire was essentially emotional and romantic, for they believed with Yeats in thinking 'with the marrowbone'.

The reluctance of romantic imperialists—and they were many—to define the nature of the British Empire rested not only on an instinctive distaste for an analysis of fundamental loyalties. Definition in any form was felt by them, and others besides, to be incompatible with the traditional spirit of English government. For English people it has been a long accepted article of faith that the predisposition of continental races to precise definition in political affairs has led to the most deplorable consequences. Their conviction received new and authoritative expression in the debate on the Anglo-Irish treaty of 1921 when Mr. Lloyd George, having asked himself the question, 'What does "dominion status" mean?' refrained from answering it, preferring instead to speak of the dangers of definition. He recalled the anxiety of all the dominion delegates at the Conference of Prime Ministers held earlier in the year that there should not be 'any rigid definitions'. 'That is not the way', he continued, 'of the British Constitution. We realize the danger of rigidity and the danger of limiting our Constitution by too many finalities.'[2] Yet in this he was fighting a stubborn rearguard action. Some definition of the Commonwealth system there had to be. It was directly demanded, as we shall see, by self-consciously nationalist dominions, and in a fundamental sense it was made necessary by the inquiring, destructive temper of the age. This indeed was generally recognized. None challenged, though many regretted, the need to define the nature of dominion status in 1926. In making their masterly definition of the imperial relationship as it then existed, the drafters of the Balfour Report could not, however, refrain from underlining how undesirable and how impossible definition was. The British Empire, says the Report,

[1] Taylor, *Habsburg Monarchy*, p. 9.

[2] 14 December 1921, H. of C. Deb., vol. 149, coll. 27–28.

'considered as a whole, defies classification and bears no real resemblance to any other political organization which now exists or has ever yet been tried'. That was certainly as true as it was gratifying, and was there not more than a reflection of insular mistrust of foreign ways about the Committee's conclusion that 'a foreigner endeavouring to understand the true character of the British Empire by the aid of this formula alone [the Balfour Report] would be tempted' to think quite the wrong things?[1] Yet for all its reluctance and its reservations, the Imperial Conference of 1926 implicitly and explicitly had gone a long way towards defining the essentials of the Commonwealth system. It was a first step to be followed by many others.

SELF-GOVERNMENT; THE FOUNDATION OF THE COMMONWEALTH[2]

The evident incapacity of foreigners to comprehend the structure, and still more the spirit, of the British Commonwealth of Nations was a source of abiding satisfaction to British constitutional experts who appeared to consider the infinite complexity of imperial relationships as evidence in themselves of a superior political wisdom. In this there was once again a tendency to discount history. It was not a deliberate act of policy but the pattern of past events which was responsible for the grouping of many states and many races at different levels of political consciousness, of civilization, and of material well-being within the British Empire. The essential contributions of British statesmanship were, negatively, a firm resistance to all suggestions for creating a greater degree of uniformity and, positively, a lively appreciation of the need for growth in living political organisms. While therefore there was no particular virtue in the complexity of the pattern, there was rare and undoubted political wisdom in the insistence that its flexibility be not sacrificed to the innate predisposition of twentieth-century governments to organize.

Of the states composing the British Commonwealth of Nations in 1937[3] some were wholly self-governing, many more were dependent colonial territories, while intermediate in status lay the great empire of India, its neighbour Burma, the lapsed dominion of Newfoundland, and the aspiring dominion of Southern Rhodesia; and on the circumference were to be found protectorates and mandated territories. They were formally united by a common allegiance to the Crown;[4] informally by history, by common interests and associations, and by a faith in parliamentary institutions; while inherent in the very conception of Commonwealth was the idea of progress down a road that led to

[1] A reluctant tribute from a German critic which appeared in the *Berliner Tageblatt* on 20 August 1938 conformed to the Englishman's most cherished beliefs about the nature of the Empire. He wrote: 'The Empire gives an impression of unsystematic genius in the Englishman who has no sense of structural beauty or systematic creation. To him nothing is wrong, however illogical, so long as the machine works.'

[2] For an illuminating discussion of this topic see Hancock, *Survey*, vol. 1, pp. 393 ff.

[3] The year of the last pre-war Imperial Conference.

[4] Except for the protectorates and mandated territories.

the full responsible self-government which the dominions had now attained. Here beyond question was diversity in unity and a rare complexity in constitutional relationships. Yet too much emphasis upon the diversity and the complexity is apt to obscure the essential, distinguishing characteristics.

At almost all times in the history of the ancient and the modern world there have existed empires ruling over vast colonial possessions. Some have administered their territories more efficiently or more humanely than others: some few have even contrived to associate the deeper aspirations of their colonial subjects with loyalty to the empire of which they were a part. Some, like the French in North Africa in our own time, have placed their faith in centralization; others, like the British, in the devolution of authority so as to promote a sense of responsibility among their subject peoples. But, significant though these differences in method may be, they do not in themselves constitute any fundamental difference in principle. The acquisition of colonies, made possible through some bygone mastery of the seas, reflected a spirit of adventure or of missionary zeal, or of lust for gold, but their retention is no proof of continued vigour or greatness. When the stormy precursors of change blew over Asia after the Second World War colonial empires, that might have long endured in untroubled times, were seen to have struck no roots deep enough to enable them to survive. And who can tell how the hitherto less exposed empires of Africa will meet the challenge of rising nationalism within and social revolution without that must surely one day confront them? If when that day comes the fate of the British Colonial Empire is different from that of other colonial empires, then the principal reason for it will be that fundamentally the British peoples did not believe in colonial rule at all. They believed in the government of men by themselves; and because of that faith in self-government they regarded colonialism as a stage necessary for the bringing of backward peoples to political maturity, but of its very nature transient. In the end Indians must govern India, Africans must govern Africa. What, therefore, was distinctive about the British Commonwealth of Nations was neither its extent nor the complexity of its internal relationships, but its reliance upon the principle of self-government. Sceptics who questioned whether the new Commonwealth, composed of equal and autonomous members, was more than the old colonialism writ large; Americans who with benevolent ignorance doubted whether Canadians or Australians were really free; Marxists who bitterly denounced self-government within the Commonwealth as skilful camouflage designed to facilitate the sinister purposes of capitalist exploiters were confronted not by a reassertion of theory but by its progressive application in a large though still very incomplete field. It was this that gave substance to the claim that the British Commonwealth represented something new in inter-state relations.

After the First World War the reputation of the Commonwealth suffered from the exaggerated claims of its more ardent protagonists. Often it was extolled as a model for the international society of the future. 'The British Empire', proclaimed General Smuts, 'is the only successful experiment in international government that has ever been made. . . .' Such claims cannot pass unquestioned. How far were the relations between the self-governing members of the British Commonwealth international? The number of the self-governing nations of the Commonwealth listed by name in the Statute of Westminster was seven, and those seven—the United Kingdom, the dominion of Canada, the Commonwealth of Australia, the dominion of New Zealand, the Union of South Africa, the Irish Free State, and the dominion of Newfoundland—were all European in government and outlook and five of them were predominantly British in racial extraction. Was not, therefore, the validity of the experiment in the wider international field qualified by the comparative racial homogeneity of the member nations as well as by their long historical association in one imperial community? Were not in fact most of the European peoples of non-British extraction within it, the French-Canadians, the Irish, and the Afrikaners, showing signs of increasing restiveness? Such sceptical inquiries did not lack substance. The experiment was being tried out under exceptionally favourable conditions. But the presumption was that this would not always be so. In 1931 it appeared only a matter of time before India and Burma would be associated as equal partners in the Commonwealth. Could that be done successfully, then the significance of the Commonwealth for a world of many races and many peoples seeking for an enduring pattern of international relationships would be immediate, for the Commonwealth would thereby have proved its capacity to extend a system buttressed by a common kinship and all that that implied in political tradition and symbolism into a truly international multi-racial system for friendly co-operation between equals. But until it was, the Commonwealth afforded an embryonic rather than an actual prototype for a wider international system.

The reliance of the British Commonwealth upon the principle of self-government was clearly understood by its statesmen and publicists, and it gave to their policies a coherence and a sense of direction without which the extent and complexity of the Empire's constitutional relationships and political responsibilities could have resulted only in a paralysis of will. But, if Commonwealth statesmen had discovered here a guiding principle which marked out clearly the road along which they should travel, that in itself did not make the journey less interesting or notably less exacting. Political principles, however enlightened, cannot alter the legacy of the past. History may not be ignored with impunity; and it was the task of reconciling fruitfully an old imperial order with a new conception of Commonwealth that confronted British statesmanship in the inter-war years. In appearance the task was primarily a constitutional one, because it was necessary to bring the forms of centralized imperial government into accord with the newer ideals of freedom and equality, but its inner meaning is to be found in a wider political context. How it was accomplished has often been recorded in the past, but as the perspective lengthens the outline of the story subtly changes. What were thought at short range to be great landmarks in the defining of the Commonwealth system have almost disappeared from view, while others hardly noticed before now loom large on a receding horizon.

THE PRESSURE TO DEFINE DOMINION STATUS

When in 1921 Mr. Lloyd George spoke of the dangers of definition he buttressed his argument, as we have already seen,[1] by referring to the anxiety of all the dominion delegates at the Prime Ministers' Conference lest there should be any rigid definition. Though factually correct this reference to dominion views was far from being the whole truth. In fact only the two dominions which were almost wholly British in extraction had unreservedly endorsed such misgivings. Mr. W. M. Hughes, the Prime Minister of Australia, had emphatically declared that there was 'no need' to set down in black and white the relations between Britain and the dominions.[2] New Zealand's reluctance to embark on a process of definition, which she foresaw could result only in a weakening of the formal bonds of imperial unity, was even more pronounced. But Canadian opinion was reserved, and in sharp contrast to the attitude of the Pacific dominions was the reaction of the Union of South Africa and of the Irish Free State when it came into being as a new dominion later in the same year. In the Treaty Debate in Dáil Éireann the protagonists of the Treaty settlement were hard pressed to reassure even their own sympathizers that the freedom and the equality implicit in dominion status would really be extended to the Irish Free State. Though the value of the specific association of its status with that of the dominion of Canada was not discounted altogether, it was felt to be insufficient to counterbalance the lessons of history and the implications of geography. Here the lack of any authoritative statement of the rights and the duties of a dominion was a severe handicap to the pro-Treaty party, defending themselves against the assaults of republican fundamentalists.[3] The endorsement of the Treaty by the narrow margin of seven votes served only to accentuate the need for convincing evidence of the freedom that dominion status conferred. Accordingly the Cosgrave government, far from thinking definition undesirable, were resolved to reinterpret in precise form the nature of the Commonwealth of which the Irish Free State was now a self-governing member. Only thus could they

[1] See p. 5, above.

[2] Cmd. 1474, pp. 22–27. Reprinted in Keith, *Speeches and Documents*, pp. 54–56.

[3] See Dáil Éireann, *Debates on the Treaty Between Great Britain and Ireland, December 1921 and January 1922* (Dublin, Talbot Press; hereinafter referred to as *Treaty Debates*). See particularly speeches of Mr. Erskine Childers, pp. 38 ff., and Mr. Arthur Griffith, pp. 20 ff.

demonstrate their independence and in so doing justify their reluctant acceptance of the Treaty and confound their critics.

The motives which impelled Mr. Cosgrave's government to press for redefinition of intra-imperial relations were powerful indeed. Yet it remains open to question whether the influence of the Irish Free State in bringing this about was in fact as great as some of the members of Mr. Cosgrave's Executive Council appeared to believe later, or even as some impartial commentators have suggested. 'In 1921 the immersion of a foreign body, the Irish Free State, disturbed the quiet waters of the conventional Commonwealth. Out of the ferment which it created the Statute of Westminster, 1931, emerged.' So wrote Mr. Latham in his brilliant essay on 'The Law and the Commonwealth'.[1] But was it really so? Were not the waters disturbed already, and did not the immersion of this 'foreign body' simply increase the disturbance to a marked degree? The distinction is not merely academic. If it be accepted that the immersion of the Irish Free State—and it was not a voluntary immersion—was the primary cause of the disturbance, then the wisdom of British insistence on dominion status for the Irish Free State in 1921 needs a more critical scrutiny in the field of intra-imperial relations than it has hitherto received. But was it really so? Did not South Africa play an even greater part in securing the formal redefinition of the Commonwealth relations, not because she had more compelling reasons for doing so, but because as a longer established member of the Commonwealth she had the greater influence? Moreover while South African secession from the Commonwealth would have been a serious, perhaps fatal, blow to its prestige and pretensions, Irish secession could have had no such disastrous consequences. The Irish Free State was a dominion in name, not in spirit, and the failure of the dominion experiment there would not necessarily have had disruptive consequences overseas.

This impression of the decisive role played by South Africa is materially reinforced by the recent publication of General Smuts's views. In 1921 he urged upon the United Kingdom and other Commonwealth governments that the theory of the Commonwealth should be brought into conformity with its practice. Too many of the old ideas, he complained, clung to the new organism. In a private memorandum entitled 'The Constitution of the British Commonwealth', which made a deep impression upon its readers, he pointed out that:

> unless dominion status was quickly solved in a way that would satisfy the aspirations of these young nations, separatist movements were to be expected in the Commonwealth. . . . The only way to meet such movements is not to wait until they are fully developed and perhaps irresistible in their impetus, but to anticipate them and make them impossible by the most generous concession of the dominion's nation-

[1] Printed in Hancock, *Survey*, vol. 1, p. 510, and reprinted separately in 1949 by the Oxford University Press for the Royal Institute of International Affairs, with an introduction by Professor W. K. Hancock.

hood and existence as a state. The warning against always being too late with a proper solution, of which Ireland is an example to the whole Commonwealth, is one which we can ignore only at our own peril.[1]

Among the practical steps which General Smuts considered essential in 1921 was the redefinition of the status of the Governor-General so that henceforward he would be the representative of the King and not in any way the agent of the United Kingdom government; this would mean as a necessary corollary direct access to the King by all his governments. General Smuts pressed, too, for a clarification of dominion responsibility in the conduct of foreign policy. With these views General Hertzog was in full agreement. Indeed he was pleasantly surprised, so his biographer records, to find on his accession to office that General Smuts's views (as set out in this confidential memorandum) accorded so nearly with his own. But Hertzog's resolve to secure an immediate redefinition of the Commonwealth relations was the more insistent. He was not concerned to forestall the demands of South African nationalism, but to fulfil them. He went to the Imperial Conference of 1926 with two alternative policies in his mind; the first to secure the recognition of full dominion equality, in which case South Africa would welcome a lasting co-operation with the Commonwealth, but if that were not secured, then he was resolved to advocate secession. This was no idle threat but a considered opinion, for General Hertzog still believed in 1926 that there were strong forces prepared to challenge dominion claims for equality. In this he was altogether mistaken, and even taking into account the contemporary South African political background from which his impressions were almost wholly derived, it is a matter for surprise that he should have entertained such unfounded views. None the less it underlines the fact that whatever the Irish attitude, the South African government was adamant in its resolve to secure an explicit definition of dominion status. What Mr. Lloyd George had considered unwise in 1921 could not in some form be avoided five years later without the serious risk of a major disruption of the Empire.

THE 1926 FORMULA

There is a pleasing anecdote that Lord Balfour, who presided so memorably over the Inter-Imperial Relations Committee of the 1926 Imperial Conference, after listening to the discussions of his colleagues, wrote out spontaneously on the back of a dirty envelope those classic phrases in which the Report that bears his name defines the status of Great Britain and the dominions as:

> . . . autonomous communities within the British Empire, equal in status, in no way subordinate one to another in any aspect of their domestic or external affairs, though united by a common allegiance to the Crown, and freely associated as members of the British Commonwealth of Nations.[2]

[1] Made public for the first time in van den Heever, *Hertzog*, p. 212.
[2] Cmd. 2768, p. 14.

But the reality was at once more exacting and more enlightening than the legend. There was in fact a great deal of discussion, some of it formal, much of it informal, and the final definition was agreed only after a number of drafts had been considered either at full meetings of the Committee or in more intimate gatherings of those particularly interested.[1] One draft was prepared by General Hertzog himself. Wordy and argumentative, it lends some colour to the characteristically ruthless verdict of Kevin O'Higgins, the principal Irish delegate, who described Hertzog as 'a very decent and likeable kind of man', who 'has not been a success—he talks a lot and none too clearly'.[2] Yet Hertzog knew, perhaps more clearly than O'Higgins, where he wanted to get to and how to get there, and his memorandum deserves quotation if only because a comparison between it and Balfour's well-known final draft brings out plainly the nature of the conflict between equality and freedom on the one hand and unity on the other. The memorandum reads:[3]

The Prime Ministers of the United Kingdom and the dominions of South Africa, Canada, Australia, New Zealand, Newfoundland and Ireland with their respective ministers met at the Imperial Conference, recognize that they are respectively the representatives of independent states, equal in status and separately entitled to international recognition, with governments and parliaments independent of one another, united through a common bond of loyalty to the King and freely associated as members of the British Commonwealth of Nations, and they acknowledge that (*a*) whatever surviving forms of inequality or subordination may exist in the mutual relations of one to another of the aforesaid states, either in regard to the legislative, executive or judicial power, such inequality and subordination are attributable to and dependent upon the voluntary agreement of the associated state concerned, and (*b*) that it is desirable that the constitutional relationship between Great Britain and the dominions be properly made known and recognized, and that the necessary steps be taken to make known formally and authoritatively the equal status of the associated states and their relationships, as here set out, to their own communities and the whole world.

These were no revolutionary ideas, but it is understandable that General Hertzog's anxiety to define them so comprehensively prompted renewed mis-

[1] Mr. van den Heever's narrative which is revealing on this point is not always easy to follow. See pp. 213–17. Lord Balfour's biographer merely remarks that the Chairman 'confidently allowed the discussion to proceed for many days' in the course of which 'drafts were amended and rejected'. See Blanche E. C. Dugdale, *Arthur James Balfour, First Earl of Balfour, 1906–30* (London, Hutchinson, 1936) p. 379. A short but authoritative analysis of the principal considerations involved is to be found in L. S. Amery, *Thoughts on the Constitution* (London, Oxford University Press, 1947) pp. 128–32. Mr. Amery was Secretary of State for Dominion Affairs at that time.

[2] White, *O'Higgins*, p. 221.

[3] This draft is printed in van den Heever, *Hertzog*, p. 213. A further reason for reproducing it here in full is that it was made public for the first time in van den Heever's book and remains almost wholly unknown to students outside South Africa. Likewise the account, pp. 213–18, of the subsequent efforts to reach agreement on a draft satisfying to all, contains much material not hitherto published.

givings on the part of Mr. Amery and Sir Austen Chamberlain, and even Lord Balfour, about the wisdom of issuing any declaration at all. Lord Birkenhead, of whose masterly and sympathetic speeches General Hertzog later spoke with appreciation, was, however, more encouraging. It was decided largely as a result of his intervention to continue the attempt to define. General Hertzog's draft was succeeded by one from Lord Balfour (first amended by Mr. Mackenzie King) whose opening sentence suffered little subsequent change but whose later emphasis on 'duties' and 'obligation' disturbed General Hertzog profoundly. Lord Birkenhead's succeeding draft reinstated the phrase 'freely associated as members of the Commonwealth of Nations' which had appeared in General Hertzog's original draft. Mr. Amery's two drafts introduced the phrase 'British Empire', but despite further contributions from Lord Balfour and Mr. Mackenzie King neither the Irish, who disliked the phrase 'common bond of allegiance', nor General Hertzog, who detected in the phrase 'common citizenship of the Empire' the intention to make the Empire into a super-state, nor Mr. Mackenzie King, who mistrusted the South African use of the word 'independence'[1] were to be satisfied easily. And yet the search for a formula was resolutely pursued if only because General Hertzog was politically committed to securing one. Despite his consistently helpful attitude in London he felt that failure to obtain it would have left him with no alternative but to sail for home and set the veld on fire with a cry for secession.

It was the genius of Lord Balfour, who had sat 'presiding over it all with a smile like moonlight on a tombstone',[2] which at last effected a final and positive reconciliation in the draft (already quoted) which will always remain one of the great landmarks in British constitutional history. The essence of the Commonwealth had been defined with the assent of all its self-governing members. At the one extreme New Zealand, who lamented the need for any definition, was reassured by the reference to the British Empire and by the emphasis on common allegiance to the Crown, while at the other Afrikaner nationalists welcomed the assertion of equality on the basis of free association, which was soon to be interpreted as implying freedom to dissociate. The Irish delegation led by Kevin O'Higgins, though equally determined to remove all the symbols of subordination, were somewhat less exclusively concerned with these negative considerations than the South Africans. Yet when General Hertzog was reported to have said on his return, 'we have brought home the bacon', Kevin O'Higgins commented drily 'Irish bacon'.[3]

The setting to the classic definition of dominion status was fittingly provided by Lord Balfour himself. In a loose-leaf notebook he wrote out in

[1] cf. van den Heever, *Hertzog*, p. 216, and Dugdale, *Balfour*, p. 379.

[2] The phrase was used by Kevin O'Higgins. See White, *O'Higgins*, p. 222.

[3] ibid. p. 223. It may be questioned whether an Afrikaner would in fact have used such distinctively Irish terminology, but the moral of the story remains.

manuscript a section that appeared without amendment in the Conference Report under the heading 'The Status of Great Britain and the Dominions'.[1] It was that section in which freedom and equality in status were balanced with diversity of functional responsibility which gave to the Report its quality of 'finely accurate description' of Commonwealth relations at that time, and its sense 'not merely of the form but the motion of a community'.[2]

In no respect may this be more aptly illustrated than by a reference to the apparently indiscriminate use by the Report of the terms 'Empire' and 'Commonwealth'. The dominions were described as autonomous communities 'within the British Empire' but they were 'freely associated as members of the British Commonwealth of Nations'. Yet such inconsistencies in terminology were neither accidental nor illogical. The British Empire symbolized tradition and past achievement, the British Commonwealth the hopes and aspirations of the future. The predominantly 'British' dominions tended to place the accent on Empire while the predominantly non-British dominions preferred Commonwealth. The use of both terms satisfied the reasonable demands of all, and in so doing faithfully reflected the state of Commonwealth opinion. Mr. Amery, moreover, has explained that the word 'Empire' was embodied in the Balfour Report to describe the British political organism as a whole because

> No other term, indeed, would be appropriate to the totality of autonomous states, dependencies, colonies, protectorates, mandated territories, feudatories, and allies which are comprehended within the orbit of our polity. Within that wider whole the relationship of certain of its members constitutes a definite political system whose character is appropriately designated by the fine old title of 'Commonwealth'.[3]

From this viewpoint the use of the terms Empire and Commonwealth faithfully reflected the distinction between the deserving, or fortunate, few who enjoyed autonomous status and the many who aspired to it within that wider unity of which both were part.

The pressure to define the nature of the Commonwealth came from no single source. The role of South Africa and of the Irish Free State has received prominence because they were the most active, though not necessarily the most influential, participants in the Imperial Conferences of 1926 and 1930. Had they stood alone the trend in Commonwealth relations might have been seriously modified when the Irish Free State ceased to be a dominion in any but a formal sense in 1936.[4] But this did not in fact prove to be the case. Here the influence of Canada was decisive. Her central position between the predominantly British and imperialist dominions of the Pacific and nationalist Ireland and South Africa, backed by her own particular status as the senior and most powerful dominion, enabled her to make a deep impression on the

[1] Dugdale, *Balfour*, p. 380.
[2] Hancock, *Survey*, vol. 1, p. 263.
[3] Amery, *Thoughts on the Constitution*, pp. 130–1.
[4] The Imperial Conference of 1930 was the last attended by Irish delegates.

character of the Commonwealth in these years.[1] Unresting in her efforts to remove the last and the least relics of subordination, Canada's continuing membership of the Commonwealth and her allegiance to the Crown were never in question. She spoke, therefore, for a great body of central opinion, within Canada and without, who upheld the compromise embodied in the Balfour Report against imperialists on the right and dissident nationalists on the left.

While the Balfour Report has subsequently been treated with respectful deference, Mr. Lloyd George's misgivings about defining have not proved altogether unfounded.[2] Definition in fact there had to be. The Empire had to conform to the temper of the age. But even the finely balanced phrases of the Balfour Report did not survive altogether unimpaired the minute textual examination, rarely surpassed in the hey-day of medieval theological controversy, to which they were subjected by constitutional lawyers and politicians. One of the risks involved was present in the mind of Mr. Amery when the Report was being drafted. The phrase 'freely associated' seemed to him to imply a right of dissociation from the Empire, and for that reason he would have liked to have had it modified. But his colleagues were unanimous in holding that the phrase could refer only to the freedom with which association within the Commonwealth was exercised and could have no bearing on the question of allegiance to the Crown. 'Freedom to break away from that allegiance', writes Mr. Amery,[3] 'may not be in dispute as a matter of practical politics, but was certainly not intended to be sanctioned by the framers of the definition. . . .' On this, Mr. Amery, the first Secretary of State for Dominion Affairs, carries unquestioned authority, but it was hardly in doubt that nationalists and even liberals would in time challenge this restrictive interpretation of free association. And yet despite troublesome questions of interpretation about the binding nature of the Commonwealth association and the exact implications of common allegiance to the Crown, who can doubt that much was gained in 1926? That fear of open conflict between nationalism and imperialism, whose shadow gave urgency to General Smuts's insistence on definition, had been not merely avoided but dispelled. The rival protagonists declined to take up 'the posture of gladiators'. Great Britain, far from fighting to the last ditch for the old imperial order, was forward in her desire to give substance to the new; and the dominions while insistent on liberty and

[1] On 2 May 1950 the Canadian Prime Minister, Mr. St. Laurent, remarked in Ottawa that 'Canadians have virtually shaped the Commonwealth as it exists today' (*The Times*, 3 May 1950). In substance this claim is justified.

[2] In the Pacific dominions many would argue that they had proved only too well founded. 'My criticism', said Mr. Menzies in 1937, 'is criticism of the whole 1926–1931 process, and that begins and has its roots in what I would have thought was a misguided attempt in 1936 to reduce to written terms something which was a matter of the spirit and not of the letter. . . .' (Australia, H. of R. Deb., 1937, vol. 159, pp. 85–94).

[3] *Thoughts on the Constitution*, p. 131. See also Dugdale, *Balfour*, p. 379, which shows that this was also Lord Balfour's view.

equality were far from wishing to make inroads on the unity of the Commonwealth, believing on the contrary that the reconciliation of form with political reality would not impair but rather strengthen it. The old Empire had been the outcome of British expansion overseas;[1] the new Commonwealth was created by all its self-governing nations, and they took a proper pride in their creation.

THE STATUTE OF WESTMINSTER

The recommendations of the Imperial Conferences of 1926 and of 1930 paved the way for the legal endorsement of the transformation that had taken place in the relations between Britain and the dominions. That endorsement was embodied in the Statute of Westminster which was enacted in 1931.[2] This one great legal landmark in the history of the Commonwealth has remained of preponderant importance not merely in defining Commonwealth relations but in determining their later development. Some account, therefore, of dominion reactions to the Statute of Westminster is essential to an understanding of Commonwealth relations in subsequent years.

The purpose of the Statute of Westminster was to state some of the constitutional conventions governing relations within the Commonwealth and thereby to give some of them the force of law.[3] In its Preamble, which has not the force of law, the new constitutional pattern of the Commonwealth was conveniently summarized:

> And whereas it is meet and proper to set out by way of Preamble to this Act that, inasmuch as the Crown is the symbol of the free association of the members of the British Commonwealth of Nations, and as they are united by a common allegiance to the Crown, it would be in accord with the established constitutional position of all the members of the Commonwealth in relation to one another that any alteration in the law touching the Succession to the Throne or the Royal Style and Titles shall hereafter require the assent as well of the Parliaments of all the Dominions as of the Parliament of the United Kingdom.
>
> And whereas it is in accord with the established constitutional position that no law hereafter made by the Parliament of the United Kingdom shall extend to any of the said dominions as part of the law of that Dominion otherwise than at the request and with the consent of that Dominion:

However creative in the political sphere, the Statute of Westminster marked no such positive advance in constitutional law. One authority in an illumin-

[1] Its history is well recorded in C. E. Carrington, *The British Overseas* (Cambridge University Press, 1950).

[2] 22 Geo. V, c. 4. The standard authority is Professor K. C. Wheare, *The Statute of Westminster and Dominion Status*, 4th ed. (Oxford University Press, 1949); see also R. T. E. Latham, *The Law and the Commonwealth* (Oxford University Press, for Royal Institute of International Affairs), 1949.

[3] The wording of this sentence may seem too precise. The facts are, however, that not all the conventions which were adopted at the Imperial Conference of 1930 were stated in the Statute, and not all of those which were stated were given the force of law.

ating overstatement has indeed described it as making 'a purely negative contribution in law'.[1] It constituted the legal endorsement of certain of the resolutions of the 1926 and 1930 Imperial Conferences.[2] It added little to them. None the less it would be a profound mistake to dismiss this formal ratification as being of no substance or importance. The mere fact of legal endorsement contributed powerfully to the direction of political thought about the Commonwealth and that in turn influenced both intra-imperial relations, and even in some instances, internal political attitudes. Its impact upon thought and practice was heightened because the Statute of Westminster constitutes all that there is of the Commonwealth in law.[3]

(*a*) *The Position of Newfoundland*

Just as the first steps towards a redefinition of Commonwealth relations had been regarded with varying degrees of enthusiasm, so, too, the dominions responded to the enactment of the Statute of Westminster in different ways. The reservations of the Pacific dominions and of Newfoundland were reflected in the Statute itself, for by express provision sections 2 to 6, which related to the transfer of full legislative authority to the dominions, did not at their own request apply to them unless and until they were adopted by their respective Parliaments. In the case of Newfoundland this never occurred. The replacement of parliamentary government by government by Commission in 1933[4] left Newfoundland a dominion in name[5] until her incorporation as the tenth province of the Canadian Confederation in 1949, but not in fact, for even if she possessed a Parliament competent to exercise the powers conferred upon 'the Parliament of a dominion' she could hardly have been permitted to use them. After 1933 Newfoundland lacked, as Professor Wheare[6] has pointed out, the fundamental element in dominion status—equality. Her inaction, therefore, is without general significance.

(*b*) *The Reactions of Canada, Australia, and New Zealand*

The protracted delay in the ratification of the Statute by Australia and New Zealand was, however, not without significance. In Australia Mr. Scullin's Labour government, which had been in office when the Statute was drafted, was defeated at a general election in December 1931 and the succeeding United Australia and Country party coalition under Mr. Lyons lacked any enthusiasm for the extension of the relevant sections of the Statute of West-

[1] Latham, *Law and Commonwealth*, p. 513.

[2] It was intituled 'An Act to give effect to certain resolutions passed by Imperial Conferences held in the years 1926 and 1930'.

[3] Latham, *Law and Commonwealth*, p. 513.

[4] 24 Geo. V, c. 2.

[5] Since section 1 of the Statute of Westminster in which she is listed with the other dominions was not amended.

[6] *Statute of Westminster*, p. 238.

minster to Australia. Mr. Menzies, who was appointed Attorney-General in 1935, was indeed a forthright critic of the decentralizing tendencies which the Statute reflected, and it was with evident reluctance that he introduced bills to adopt sections 2 to 6 in 1936 and again in 1937.[1] But on both occasions the bill lapsed. No further action was taken until Labour returned once more to power under Mr. Curtin in 1941 and a bill adopting these sections was again introduced and duly enacted in the following year.[2]

In New Zealand lack of zeal for the formal reconstitution of the old Empire into the new Commonwealth was even more marked than in Australia, and little interest was displayed by any section of opinion in the adoption of the relevant provisions of the Statute of Westminster till, as in Australia, war-time experience demonstrated some of the practical inconveniences of further delay. Even then Mr. Fraser readily concurred in the suggestion of the United Kingdom government that legislation should be deferred till after the war, and it was accordingly not enacted till 1947.[3]

The politico-psychological pressures which had been principally responsible for the enactment of the Statute of Westminster did not, however, alone determine the timing and the extent of its application. Here cogent constitutional considerations exerted their influence. Two of the dominions, Canada and Australia, possessed federal Constitutions and quite apart, therefore, from any desire to retain the British root for their constitutional law, some practical difficulties would have to be resolved before a wholly indigenous one could be substituted. This was a consideration which applied with particular force in Australia. As Mr. Latham,[4] himself an Australian, pointed out, should Australia at any time wish to sever her law from its imperial root, the nature of her federal system would create serious difficulties. The Constitutions of the Commonwealth of Australia and of the Australian states were not contained in a single instrument but in several separate acts of the Imperial Parliament, with the result that there was no measure within Australia defining the mutual status of the parties to federation. If, therefore, at any time the people of Australia wished to found their Constitution upon an original Australian source, a new constitutional foundation would first have to be laid both for the Commonwealth of Australia and for its component states. So formidable and far-reaching a reform would clearly never be undertaken save under the pressure of a most insistent public demand, of which there has hitherto been no evidence whatsoever.

[1] In his speech he took the view that the devising of the Balfour Declaration and of the preamble to the Statute of Westminster was open 'to grave criticism' and 'was in substance a grave disservice', and he recommended adoption of the Statute only because of the 'minor advantages' it would bring (Australia, H. of R. Deb., vol. 154, pp. 85–94).

[2] cf. Wheare, *Statute of Westminster*, pp. 216–216a. See also Australia, Attorney-General and others, *A Monograph on the Statute of Westminster Adoption Bill* (Canberra, 1942).

[3] New Zealand Constitution (Amendment) Act, 1947. See also Mr. Fraser's speech, New Zealand, H. of R. Deb., vol. 271, pp. 531–4.

[4] *Law and Commonwealth*, p. 526.

Like Australia, Canada too was a federal state deriving its basic law from an act of the Imperial Parliament, the British North America Act of 1867.[1] In the case of Canada, however, amendment presented fewer obstacles because this one act provided a broader constitutional foundation[2] and there was also a strong impulse towards the substitution of a Canadian source for her constitutional law.

The Statute of Westminster provided that neither in the case of Australia nor in the case of Canada should the constitutional *status quo* be disturbed. Section 8 of the Statute declared categorically that 'Nothing in this Act shall be deemed to confer any power to repeal or alter the Constitution or the Constitution Act of the Commonwealth of Australia . . . otherwise than in accordance with the existing law', and section 9 safeguarded the position of the Australian states by declaring that nothing 'shall be deemed to authorize the Parliament of the Commonwealth of Australia to make laws on any matter within the authority of the states of Australia, not being a matter within the authority of Parliament or Government of the Commonwealth of Australia'. Likewise section 7 explicitly provided that nothing in the Act should be deemed to apply to 'the repeal, amendment or alteration of the British North America Acts, 1867 to 1930, or any order, rule or regulation made thereunder'. No such amendment was contemplated until in 1949–50 the Canadian government, under the leadership of Mr. St. Laurent, took the necessary steps to transfer to the Canadian Federal Parliament final constitutional authority in respect of all matters that lay outside the field of provincial rights.

New Zealand, a unitary state, was in a different position. She had no practical reasons of equal weight for excepting her Constitution from the provisions of the Statute of Westminster. None the less partly on grounds of sentiment she asked that this should be done. Accordingly section 8 also provided that the New Zealand Parliament and government should be given no power to repeal or alter the Constitution Act of the dominion of New Zealand 'otherwise than in accordance with the law existing before the commencement of this Act'.

(*c*) *South Africa and the Status of the Union Act*

It was the hope of the drafters of the Statute of Westminster that this charter of the Commonwealth liberties should stand the test of time.[3] But then that is the hope of all who frame constitutional laws and rarely has it been fulfilled. In the years that followed 1931 it became more and more apparent that the codifying of existing constitutional practice in the Statute of Westminster had re-created, above all in South Africa, a demand for further

[1] See Wheare, *Statute of Westminster*, pp. 177 ff.

[2] It was not, however, comprehensive. The Constitutions of Ontario and Quebec alone derived directly from the B.N.A. Act, those of Nova Scotia and New Brunswick dated from an earlier period. See British North America Act 1867, 30 Vict., c. 3, sections 88 and 64.

[3] cf. Amery, *Thoughts on the Constitution*, pp. 128–9.

advance by way of further clarification. There was, however, after 1931, this important difference in emphasis. Where the earlier pressure had been for a positive assertion of equality, the later turned upon the need for a more precise interpretation of the exact meaning to be attached not as much to the provisions of the Statute of Westminster as to its Preamble, which did not possess the force of law. The nature of this demand needs to be clearly indicated. Australia and New Zealand had acquiesced, not without reluctance, in the changes which had received legal endorsement in 1931; Canadians, 'save for those few whose attitude to the Empire reflects an incurably antiquarian cast of mind',[1] welcomed the transition from the old Empire to the new Commonwealth, but South African nationalism was not wholly reassured and Irish nationalism remained unreconciled. It was, therefore, in these two dominions that centrifugal pressure remained strong, and even here the end in view was not identical. Predominant Afrikaner opinion desired further clarification in order to confirm and to reinsure South Africa's independent status within the Commonwealth. Only the left wing of the Nationalist party, then a small minority, desired to use this newly acquired status to carry through by constitutional means a policy of separation. But the great majority welcomed the opportunity of interpreting the Statute of Westminster in such a way that it could be used theoretically to justify such a policy. They did not wish to secede but they placed a high value upon recognition of their constitutional right to secede. Here curiously enough the Irish, after Mr. de Valera's accession to office, were not particularly interested. They were at that time revolutionaries, not legalists, who wished not to reinterpret dominion status but to create for themselves a relationship with the Commonwealth different in kind. Nevertheless by the mere fact of its being a dominion, the policies of the Irish Free State had a significance in the field of Commonwealth relations to which the Irish were themselves largely indifferent since they thought almost exclusively in terms of Anglo-Irish relations.

Let us consider South African reactions first. It had been the consistent aim of Afrikaner nationalists to secure for the Union first, full equality of status within the Commonwealth, and then an explicit recognition of the Union's full sovereign independence, symbolized in constitutional terms by the replacement of an uncongenial legal dependence on the United Kingdom by a South African source for the fundamental law of the Union. The Imperial Conference of 1926 realized the first of these aims, equality. For the moment that sufficed. On his return General Hertzog declared himself well satisfied. 'I can only state that I hope the epoch-making declaration by the Imperial Conference has brought to a happy close the century-old struggle for South African national freedom. . . .'[2] 'As a result of the work of the Imperial Conference the old Empire no longer existed. . . . Englishmen need not fear

[1] Vincent Massey, *On Being Canadian* (London, Dent, 1948) p. 73.
[2] *The Times*, 13 December 1926.

that they would say farewell to the Empire, because it was in their interests not to do so.'[1] For the moment it seemed as though republicanism in South Africa had been robbed of its *raison d'être*. Dr. Malan himself stated in those halcyon days of late December 1926 that 'instead of looking upon Great Britain as the conqueror, we look upon her now as the mother of our freedom'. The independence, he declared, 'which the Nationalist party has always lived for is now attained, and cannot well be more complete'.[2] But second thoughts were less reassuring. Was General Hertzog justified in the broad liberal interpretation he placed upon the Balfour Report? English-speaking South Africans were loud in their belief that he was not, and Afrikaner nationalists, their old suspicions revived, feared their hopes might prove unfounded. And so with undiminished asperity old controversies were revived in a new form, and for their revival English-speaking South Africa must bear no small share of the responsibility.[3]

South African controversies about the nature of the Commonwealth reappear in various contexts in succeeding chapters. Here we are concerned not with the many debatable issues but simply with the constitutional consequences which they produced. In that constitutional context the question turned on the location of sovereignty. Was South Africa a sovereign state? Could her Parliament decide every issue of policy? Could it amend the Constitution? Was it free from all external control? To these questions neither the Balfour Report, which had no legal sanction, nor a Statute of Westminster enacted, and therefore open to repeal, by the United Kingdom Parliament, afforded any satisfying answer. If their content could be introduced in South African legislation and made an integral part of Union law, then indeed misgivings would be removed and moderate nationalist sentiment reconciled.

The Statute of Westminster made the way clear for the transfer of the source of South African sovereignty from Westminster to Cape Town, for it conferred in principle the power to proclaim the ultimate constitutional sovereignty of the people of South Africa upon the government and Parliament of the Union. And since the Afrikaners constituted the majority of white South Africa, their desire that the South African system of law should have a foundation which acknowledged their Dutch (or at least their non-British) legal tradition, however uncongenial to their English-speaking compatriots, was not difficult to fulfil.

In itself the application of the Statute of Westminster to the Union of South Africa was not so simple as might appear at first sight. It is true that South Africa, which had the appearance of a federal, was none the less a unitary, state in which the provinces had no fundamental rights as against the central government, and in which there were not as a result either provincial

[1] ibid. 15 December 1926.

[2] S. G. Millin, *General Smuts* (London, Faber, 1936), vol. 2, p. 441.

[3] cf. B. K. Long, *In Smuts's Camp* (London, Oxford University Press, 1945) pp. 33 ff.

or state rights to be protected as in Canada and Australia. The difficulties arose from a quite different cause. Under section 152 of the South Africa Act[1] of 1909, the Parliament of the Union was empowered to repeal or alter any of the provisions of the Act subject to the reservations that certain provisions should not be amended unless the amending bill had been passed by both Houses of Parliament sitting together, and that at the third reading such amendments had been agreed to by not less than two-thirds of the total number of the members of both Houses. The general effect of these reservations was to ensure that those sections of the South Africa Act which fixed the proportionate representation of the original four colonies comprising the Union in the House of Assembly, which defined the native franchise in the Cape Province, and which guaranteed the equality of English and Dutch languages, should not be amended unless the representatives of both European peoples were in agreement that they should be, the assumption being that an artificial majority of two-thirds of the total membership of both Houses could not be obtained if the amendment were resolutely opposed by either of them. Section 152 of the Act which laid down these safeguards was itself safeguarded in the same way, so that it could not be repealed by a simple majority in each House sitting separately. So long, therefore, as the Colonial Laws Validity Act continued in force, the effective power of the Union Parliament under the existing political conditions to modify these 'entrenched clauses' was slight, since the measure of agreement demanded was difficult to obtain. But with the enactment of the Statute of Westminster the legal safeguard was no longer effective, since the Union Parliament could henceforward amend or repeal any section of the South Africa Act by simple majority at any time it saw fit. Any legal doubts that were entertained—and there were some—on this point, were removed by a decision of the Union Supreme Court in 1937, which ruled that with the repeal of the Colonial Laws Validity Act, the Union Parliament became a sovereign Parliament in the same sense as that of the United Kingdom, and that in particular the Union Parliament no longer remained bound by the provisions of the Constitution from which its powers were derived, nor was it compelled to exercise its power of amendment in accordance with the artificial majority provisions laid down in section 152 of the South Africa Act of 1909.[2]

In 1909 the safeguards contained in the 'entrenched clauses' had been a condition of Union itself. Clearly therefore any attempt by one party to take advantage of the new powers vested in the Union Parliament by the Statute of Westminster would have provoked a dangerous internal crisis. Of this none were more fully aware than the leaders of the principal parties, and accordingly they sought to establish by agreement a constitutional convention whose observance would in practice safeguard the rights entrenched in the South Africa Act as effectively as they had been protected in law before 1931. Nor

[1] 9 Ed. VII, c. 9.

[2] cf. Wheare, *Statute of Westminster*, pp. 239 ff.

was this 'entrenchment' by convention merely a matter of political expediency. It was also a matter of moral obligation since the 'entrenched clauses' had afforded safeguards which, in 1909, had been the condition of the co-operation of the four provinces within a single state. For these reasons both General Hertzog and General Smuts agreed to include in the resolution requesting the passage of the Statute of Westminster a phrase indicating that this request was made on the understanding that the proposed legislation would in no way derogate from the 'entrenched clauses' of the South Africa Act. It is true that this resolution had no legal or binding force, but its intention was respected and enforced[1] until Dr. Malan came to office in 1948, when he proposed by the process of ordinary legislation to repeal one of the 'entrenched clauses'—a proposal justly criticized on grounds not of law but of convention and moral obligation.[2]

The formation of the Coalition ministry in South Africa in 1933, followed by party fusion in 1934, made possible inter-party co-operation in formulating the relationship of the Statute of Westminster to South African law. The desire of South African jurists to underline the legal sovereignty of the Union Parliament was met by the inclusion of the Preamble and the relevant provisions of the Statute of Westminster in the Status of the Union Act[3] introduced into the House of Assembly in March 1934 and enacted later in the same year. The Preamble to the Status Act outlined the principal purposes of its enactment:

Whereas the delegates of His Majesty's governments in the United Kingdom, the dominion of Canada, the Commonwealth of Australia, the dominion of New Zealand, the Union of South Africa, the Irish Free State and Newfoundland, at Imperial Conferences holden at Westminster in the years of our Lord 1926 and 1930, did concur in making the declarations and resolutions set forth in the Reports of the said Conferences, and more particularly in defining the group of self-governing communities composed of Great Britain and the dominions as 'autonomous communities within the British Empire, equal in status, in no way subordinate one to another in any aspect of their domestic or external affairs, though united by a common allegiance to the Crown and freely associated as members of the British Commonwealth of Nations';

And whereas the said resolutions and declarations in so far as they required legislative sanction on the part of the United Kingdom have been ratified, confirmed and established by the Parliament of the United Kingdom in an Act entitled the Statute of Westminster, 1931 (22 Geo. V, c. 4);

And whereas it is expedient that the status of the Union of South Africa as a sovereign independent state as herein before defined shall be adopted and declared by the Parliament of the Union and that the South Africa Act, 1909 (9 Edw. VII, c. 9) be amended accordingly;

[1] e.g. when the Cape Native Franchise was abolished in 1936.

[2] Owing to the restraining influence of Mr. Havenga's Afrikaner Party, who held the balance of power in the House of Assembly, the proposal was temporarily shelved.

[3] No. 69 of 1934.

And whereas it is expedient that the said Statute of Westminster, in so far as its provisions are applicable to the Union of South Africa, and an Afrikaans version thereof, shall be adopted as an Act of the Parliament of the Union of South Africa;

The Preamble to the Status Act is expository and has not the force of law. It prepares the way for the main purpose of the Act which was to establish the doctrine that South African constitutional law had a South African and not an imperial root. On this point section 2 of the Act is categoric:

The Parliament of the Union shall be the sovereign legislative power in and over the Union, and notwithstanding anything in any other law contained, no Act of the Parliament of the United Kingdom and Northern Ireland[1] passed after the eleventh day of December, 1931, shall extend, or be deemed to extend, to the Union as part of the law of the Union, unless extended thereto by an Act of the Parliament of the Union.

Other provisions of the Act were concerned to define by South African legislation the constitutional relationship between the Union and the Crown which was the symbol of her free association in the Commonwealth. Accordingly it was laid down that unless otherwise stated, the King should be regarded as 'the King acting on the advice of his ministers of state for the Union'.[2] Further the South African position in respect of the succession to the Throne was explicitly defined by providing that His Majesty's 'heirs and successors in the sovereignty of the United Kingdom' as 'determined by the laws relating to the succession of the Crown of the United Kingdom'[3] should succeed by virtue of this South African legislation to the Crown of South Africa. Here the Status Act took one more step towards the creation of a separate sovereignty and a separate sovereign for the Union. While a change in the succession to the Crown in the United Kingdom would take effect in the Union, it would henceforward do so only because an act of the Union Parliament had so provided. Or to put it negatively and more precisely, the provision in the Status of the Union Act allowing that the succession would be determined by the United Kingdom Parliament did not admit that any law about the succession passed by that Parliament would have validity in the Union. On the contrary, it was the intention that while the United Kingdom legislation should be followed, it should have no validity in the Union except in so far as it was endorsed and embodied in South African law. In this respect legal formulation of a theoretical viewpoint was shortly and unexpectedly to be followed by its application in practice.

The terms of the Status Act provoked general questions susceptible of no very explicit answers. By asserting the legal sovereignty of the Union, the Act cast doubts upon the extent to which a Commonwealth, of which South Africa was a member, could any longer be said to possess an organic unity

[1] This phraseology is otiose since Northern Ireland is part of the United Kingdom.

[2] Section 4 (2).

[3] Section 5.

deriving from common allegiance to a common Crown.[1] Did not the act on the contrary implicitly enunciate the heretical doctrine of a divisible Crown? And if so, did that not mean that common allegiance could be used to carry through constitutionally a separatist policy and thereby establish that legal right of secession upon which South African nationalists had set their heart?

The desire to assert South African independence was also responsible for the enactment of the Royal Executive Functions and Seals Act[2] in 1934, which formally placed the conduct of the foreign affairs of the Union under the complete control of the Union ministers. Here South Africa did not blaze a new trail, but she was the first of the older dominions to follow a precedent set by the Irish Free State which had had its own Great Seal since 1931. Henceforward the Union no longer needed to make use of the Great Seal of the Realm in the conduct of foreign affairs and as a result she could dispense with the formal intervention of a United Kingdom Secretary of State. This step was wholly consistent with the pattern of Commonwealth, as well as of South African, constitutional development and was noteworthy chiefly in point of timing.

The South African legislation which followed upon the enactment of the Statute of Westminster was concerned to affirm South African sovereignty through the restatement with appropriate differences in emphasis of the established law and convention of the Commonwealth. That this restatement involved some deviation in spirit from the prevailing concept of Commonwealth unity is not to be denied. But more instructive than the measure of deviation was the resolve to bring about such modifications in Commonwealth relations as South Africa desired by strictly constitutional means. From this derives the South African concern to establish a legal right to secede, or to become a republic, without any immediate intention of seceding or becoming a republic. The means was to South Africa in many ways more important than the end. And that is precisely why South African influence on the evolution of Commonwealth relations has been so marked and why the South African, and not the Irish, heresy of yesterday has tended to become the Commonwealth orthodoxy of today.

(*d*) *The Irish Free State Discards Dominion Status*

Between the Union and the Irish Free State there was much in common and more at variance. Both welcomed the powers conferred upon the dominions by the Statute of Westminster; both resolved that those powers should be used to establish, or re-establish, unquestioned national sovereignty. But agreement about these immediate aims should not disguise differences about the purposes they were intended to serve. The legalism of Afrikaner nationalism, which was then concerned with establishing a right rather than with its

[1] cf. Wheare, *Statute of Westminster*, p. 314.
[2] No. 70 of 1934.

immediate exercise, found its counterpart in the more revolutionary outlook of Irish nationalism which, after Mr. de Valera's accession to office, was prepared to take advantage of concessions in the constitutional field by the Imperial Parliament, while at all times firmly repudiating the authority of its enactments within the Irish Free State. Irish lawyers consistently emphasized the constitutional authority of the Oireachtas deriving directly from the first Dáil, and ultimately from the inalienable national sovereignty of the people of Ireland which the first Dáil had proclaimed in 1919. For Mr. de Valera the end in view was a reassertion of popular national sovereignty, free from all ambiguity or reservation, and not a reinterpretation, on the South African model, of legislation enacted by the United Kingdom Parliament with a view to embodying it in Irish law and thereby making it subject to repeal or amendment by the national Parliament. Where South Africa's leaders were concerned to emphasize the new, particular relationship of the King to his Kingdom of South Africa, Mr. de Valera regarded him quite simply as an 'alien King' who, by virtue of being alien, could and should have no place in the Irish constitutional system. By reason of this sense of foreignness to the constitutional symbolism of the Commonwealth, the Irish reaction to the Statute of Westminster was of less importance in the context of Commonwealth relations than was the South African.

The distinction between the South African and the Irish attitudes to the Commonwealth is a useful corrective to much that has been written about the constitutional precedents established by the Irish Free State. In the nineteen-thirties Irish nationalism was in a revolutionary phase and an examination of the finer constitutional implications of Irish actions is as much a hindrance as an aid to understanding. Revolutionaries who respect constitutions, conventions, and legal precedents are not revolutionaries at all. This has been sufficiently understood by Irish and by English historians. But the fact that the Irish Free State happened to be a dominion has given to Irish constitutional developments and legal precedents a significance in the Commonwealth that they never enjoyed in Anglo-Irish history. What importance Irish reactions to the Statute of Westminster possess is to be found therefore not in Irish history, where it is negligible, but in the history of the Commonwealth.

The application of the Statute of Westminster to the Irish Free State was governed by one overriding factor, which was that under the Constitution of 1922 the Treaty of 1921 was vested with the force of law. The second article of the Constitution Act[1] provided that:

> The said Constitution shall be construed with reference to the Articles of Agreement for a Treaty between Great Britain and Ireland . . . which are hereby given the force of law, and if any provision of the said Constitution or of any amendment thereof or of any law made thereunder is in any respect repugnant to any of the

[1] No. 1 of 1922, Constitution of the Irish Free State (Saorstát Éireann) Act, 1922.

provisions of the Scheduled Treaty, it shall, to the extent only of such repugnancy, be absolutely void and inoperative, and the Parliament and Executive Council of the Irish Free State (Saorstát Éireann) shall respectively pass such further legislation and do all such other things as may be necessary to implement the Scheduled Treaty.

This 'repugnancy clause' invested the Treaty with the highest legal status in the municipal law of the Irish Free State,[1] with the result that its provisions overrode both the Constitution and all subsequent legislation. The aim of the United Kingdom government, on whose insistence the clause was inserted, was to make the Treaty which brought the Irish Free State into being the ultimate source of its constitutional law. This view, indignantly repudiated by Irish nationalists, was in any event hardly consistent with the explicit association of the status of the Irish Free State with that of Canada and the other dominions. It implanted an element of fixity in a settlement designed to guarantee an evolutionary growth in status. For this reason, quite apart from the strength of nationalist sentiment within the Irish Free State, the actual provisions of the Treaty were certain sooner or later to require reinterpretation if they were not to become plainly incompatible with a developing dominion status. It could indeed be reasonably argued that such reinterpretation was already overdue by 1931.

The geographical proximity of Ireland to Britain, reinforced by an intimate social and economic interdependence and still more by past history, encouraged many Englishmen to draw a distinction, not expressly but implicitly, between the status of the Irish Free State and that of the oversea dominions. It was this sense of difference, wholly inconsistent with the detailed provisions of the Anglo-Irish Treaty, which prompted amendments designed to exclude the Irish Free State from the general provisions of the Statute of Westminster in the House of Commons and in the House of Lords.[2] These amendments elicited a strong protest from Mr. Cosgrave,[3] ostensibly fearful lest the government at least in part might adopt them. In his protest Mr. Cosgrave was on strong ground because it had been agreed by the Imperial Conference of 1930 that no law enacted thereafter by the United Kingdom Parliament should extend to a dominion unless that dominion had requested and agreed that it should do so.[4] This convention, which, it is worth noting, did not in any way compel the United Kingdom Parliament to enact whatever a dominion might wish, did deprive her of the right to legislate specifically for a particular dominion except at the wish of that dominion.[5] The point is of little positive importance in respect of amendments which in fact enlisted no solid support in either House, but it had a negative bearing on what followed. The United Kingdom government, faced with actions by Mr. de Valera after

[1] For a fuller account see N. Mansergh, *The Irish Free State, its Government and Politics* (London, Allen & Unwin, 1934), pp. 46 ff.

[2] cf. H. of C. Deb., vol. 260, col. 303, and H. of L. Deb., vol. 83, col. 231.

[3] Reprinted in Keith, *Speeches and Documents*, p. 302.

[4] Cmd. 3717, p. 18.

[5] cf. Wheare, *Statute of Westminster*, pp. 255–8.

his accession to office which they regarded as breaches of the Treaty of 1921, contended that the Treaty, which had been accorded the status of fundamental law by the Constitution of the Irish Free State, froze her constitutional position to the extent that changes which other dominions were now free to make could be made by the Free State only if agreed to by the United Kingdom government.[1] In this view, therefore, the association of the status of the Irish Free State with that of Canada implied not an assurance of development as rapid as that of the senior dominion, but conformity to the status of Canada as it existed in 1921 except in so far as the United Kingdom government, as the other party to the Treaty, agreed otherwise.

In the Irish Free State the United Kingdom government's appeal to the sanctity of the Treaty and the existence of possible legal restrictions upon the authority of the Oireachtas were disregarded by the passage of the Constitution (Removal of the Oath Act)[2] in 1933 which deleted the 'repugnancy clause' from the Constitution. Subsequent legislation passed by the Oireachtas, abolishing the power of reservation in 1933[3] and the office of Governor-General in 1936,[4] in that they both conflicted with the provisions of the Treaty, widened the scope but did not alter the substance of the dispute. The act of 1933,[5] however, which abolished Appeals by Special Leave to the Judicial Committee of the Privy Council, posed the principal constitutional question most directly because in this case Canada had not only acquired but had actually exercised her right to abolish appeals in criminal cases before the government of the Irish Free State took similar action.

It was one of the curiosities of a complex situation that after the enactment of the Statute of Westminster the Irish Supreme Court continued to adopt a restrictive view of the effect of the Treaty in Irish law. In a judgement in the case of *State* (*Ryan*) v. *Lennon* in 1934 the Chief Justice maintained that the Irish government had acted *ultra vires* because no power had been conferred upon them by which they were entitled to repeal the 'repugnancy clause' in the Constitution. But if Mr. de Valera's government were disconcerted, though not surprised, by this pronouncement they were to be consoled by a subsequent judgement of the Judicial Committee of the Privy Council. In the case of *Moore* v. *Attorney-General for the Irish Free State*, the Judicial Committee, placing a liberal interpretation on the effect of the Statute of Westminster upon the constitutional authority of the legislature of the Irish Free State, held that it did in fact give power to the Oireachtas to repeal or amend the Constituent Act, and that as a result the amendments which had been enacted were valid even though they did not fall within the terms of the Treaty. 'The effect of the Statute of Westminster', they declared, 'was to

[1] cf. speech of Mr. J. H. Thomas, Secretary of State for Dominion Affairs, H. of C. Deb., vol. 260, col. 282, and of Lord Hailsham, H. of L. Deb., vol. 83, col. 240. Cf. Hancock, *Survey*, vol. 1, pp. 371 ff., for a detailed consideration of what was involved.

[2] No. 6 of 1933.

[3] No. 44 of 1933.

[4] No. 57 of 1936.

[5] No. 45 of 1933.

remove the fetter which lay upon the Irish Free State Legislature by reason of the Colonial Laws Validity Act. That Legislature can now pass acts repugnant to an imperial act. In this case they have done so.' The general effect of this judgement was clear beyond doubt. It allowed that the Irish Free State had acquired under the Statute of Westminster a power by which it could constitutionally abrogate the Treaty. It also would seem to have implied that any enactment of the Oireachtas to abolish the monarchy or to secede from the Commonwealth was valid in strict law after 1931,[1] and this implication afforded an interesting illustration of the possible significance of Anglo-Irish relations in the wider Commonwealth field.

It was, it is well to remind ourselves, Mr. de Valera's policy to take full advantage of the powers conferred by the Statute of Westminster, provided that that involved no recognition of the Imperial Parliament as a source of Irish law. For this reason, he was careful to justify his repudiation of the overriding authority of the Treaty and his consequent amendments to the Constitution as deriving their authority through the Oireachtas from the people. But at the same time the fact that the Judicial Committee of the Privy Council had placed a liberal interpretation upon the power which the Statute of Westminster had conferred upon the Oireachtas in the constitutional field eased the way for a future tolerant understanding based upon an agreement to differ about fundamentals. As a result the constitutional dispute was not reopened by the enactment of the new Irish Constitution of 1937.[2] It might indeed have been reasonably maintained, as Professor Wheare suggests, that while the Statute of Westminster empowered the Oireachtas to abolish the Constitution of 1922 and to substitute for it a new Constitution, that power had been conferred on the Oireachtas alone and not on the people of Ireland.[3] Yet it was in fact the Irish people who, in accordance with the nationalist tradition of popular sovereignty, approved the new Constitution, and in the Irish view it was their approval which was the source of its validity. This nice distinction between the authority of the people and of their elected representatives might indeed have provided an interesting point for jurists to examine had not the United Kingdom government, weary of profitless legalistic wrangling and for broad reasons of policy, agreed with the assent of the oversea dominions not to regard the new Constitution as affecting any fundamental alteration in the status of the Irish Free State. This was a step whose decisive importance lay in the political rather than in the constitutional field and therefore its wider implications are considered later.[4]

SOME GENERAL CONSEQUENCES OF THE STATUTE OF WESTMINSTER

For the Commonwealth as a whole the lasting interest of the constitutional legislation enacted in South Africa in 1934 and the constitutional issues raised

[1] cf. Wheare, *Statute of Westminster*, p. 270.

[2] Bunreacht na hÉireann, Constitution of Ireland, 1937.

[3] *Statute of Westminster*, p. 276.

[4] See below, pp. 305–7.

by Mr. de Valera's actions derived from the evidence they afforded of the ways in which the law and conventions which recognized the autonomy and equality of the dominions might be used to make serious inroads upon the unity of the Commonwealth. It so happened that Mr. de Valera was not much concerned whether or not his actions conformed to the law of the Commonwealth, but none the less the constitutional debate which he provoked, and more especially the judgement of the Judicial Committee of the Privy Council in Moore's case, giving a wide interpretation of the effect of the Statute of Westminster upon Irish status, reinforced the South African argument that 'free association' must imply a freedom to dissociate. Such, we know on the authority of Mr. Amery, was not the intention of the drafters of the Balfour Report, but the distinction, always a fine one, could not withstand the pressure of centrifugal forces nor even the implicit logic of the Balfour Report itself. That Lord Balfour himself well understood. 'A common interest in loyalty, in freedom, in ideals—that is the bond of Empire. If that is not enough nothing else is enough. . . .'[1] The aftermath of the Statute of Westminster testifies to the correctness of his conclusions more clearly than anything else. The countries which had grown by easy, co-operative stages to full autonomy could accept the positive ideal of an equality that strengthened unity. But those, Afrikaners and Irishmen, who had not grown to political maturity within the Commonwealth but had been brought by force within it were greatly concerned to know whether free association on a basis of equality meant that they could freely secede if they so desired. The question was inevitable, for there was an inner incompatibility between an enforced membership and the spirit of the Balfour Report which could be reconciled only by secession or by a recognition that secession was permissible. Which course was adopted depended on whether those common loyalties and common ideals of which Lord Balfour spoke were, or were not, enough.

The Statute of Westminster, all that there is of the Commonwealth in law, made no attempt to describe the whole complex of intra-Commonwealth relations or to codify its conventional procedure. In respect of the self-governing members of the Commonwealth the Statute merely set out in its Preamble, which has not, be it recalled once more, the force of law, three essential elements in the concept of dominion status.[2] They were free association, equality of status, and common allegiance to the Crown. But if all three were essential one was fundamental. That one was equality of status.[3] It supplied the dynamic of the Commonwealth as well as its most distinctive feature. Yet while equality of status alone was fundamental, the common allegiance to the Crown, which remained an essential element in full membership of the Commonwealth till April 1949, was of the highest importance.

[1] Quoted Dugdale, *Balfour*, p. 382.

[2] See Latham, *Law and Commonwealth*, pp. 595 ff., and Wheare, *Statute of Westminster*, pp. 293 ff.

[3] See ibid. p. 294.

After 1931 the Crown remained the one institution essential to the character of the Commonwealth.[1] The redefining of Commonwealth relations had thus implicitly exalted the role of the Crown in the Commonwealth by implicitly depreciating the status of all other imperial institutions. They might be important and useful but none could be described after 1931 as indispensable.

THE DECLINING ROLE OF IMPERIAL INSTITUTIONS

The Commonwealth had its roots deep in the past, and from the past it inherited many institutions of an imperial character whose earlier purposes had been outlived and whose form had become outmoded with the transformation of an empire into a partnership of equal states. Such institutions were not discarded but for the most part adapted to the new order, a task presenting no very formidable difficulties, for the gradualness of the transition from Empire to Commonwealth had at each stage modified their character and the duties they were called upon to discharge. They continued none the less to be very differently regarded by rival schools of thought. To the champions of unity the continued survival of institutions, imperial in form or in name, afforded a welcome reassurance of continuity with a great past and of a more closely knit co-operation in the future, while to impatient egalitarians these relics of imperial domination seemed to take a suspiciously long time in dying. The defining of Commonwealth relations that took place between 1926 and 1931, by sanctioning the progressive transfer of the initiative in policy and responsibility for its execution from the centre to the circumference, in itself diminished the role of the central imperial institutions. In particular the very nature of the achievements of the Imperial Conferences of 1926 and 1930 detracted from the authority of the Imperial Conference itself. By the success of its work it had prejudiced its own future.

The function of the Imperial Conference has always been consultative and advisory. In the course of its meetings, which began with the Colonial Conference of 1887, it had accomplished its work by agreement and not by the exercise of any superior, binding authority, with which indeed it had never been endowed. The character of its resolutions had always been that of honourable undertakings on the part of the governments which adopted them.[2] Its principal function, therefore, unaffected by the constitutional changes of the inter-war period, remained the promotion of co-operation through an interchange of view and discussion. For this task it was well fitted, and its periodic meetings could hardly have aroused much misgiving had not the Conference attracted to itself by its name, by its composition, by the comparative formality of its meetings in the capital of the Empire, and by the suggestion of executive government which, though wholly unfounded, it

[1] ibid. pp. 277–8.

[2] For a concise summary of the history and constitution of the Imperial Conference see Gerald Palmer, *Consultation and Co-operation in the British Commonwealth* (London, Oxford University Press, for the Royal Institute of International Affairs, 1934) pp. 11–13.

continued to evoke, the hopes of centralists thinking of the wider responsibilities which it might profitably undertake in a more closely knit federal Commonwealth. But in truth designation and function represented the two conflicting schools in imperial thought, one insistent always on the need for formal constitutional unity, the other on the freedom by which co-operation among equals could alone be made effective. Where the former strove constantly to enlarge the functions and the authority of the Imperial Conference, to make its meetings more frequent, to bridge the gaps between them by the creation of a permanent secretariat, the other defined ever more narrowly the limits of an authority which should not be permitted to grow. The Imperial Conference itself unquestionably suffered by over-much association with the school of thought which believed fundamentally in a highly centralized Commonwealth. As the tide of Commonwealth opinion moved steadily towards ever increasing decentralization, the Conference accordingly declined in prestige. Admirably though it had performed its task of transforming an Empire into a Commonwealth, some dominion Governments became more concerned about what it should not do in the future than about what it might do at the present.

The conflict of opinion about the proper role of the Imperial Conference emerged from the description of its functions given by Commonwealth statesmen at its meetings in 1930 and in 1937. In the earlier year Mr. R. B. Bennett, Canada's Conservative Prime Minister, underlined the importance of its role in imperial affairs:

> I think [he said] it is agreed that, since its first convocation, the value of the Imperial Conference in the effective adjustment of those Empire problems incident to the growth and development of its component parts has steadily increased until it has come to be acknowledged not only as the clearing-house of Empire ideas, but as well the instrument by which constructive Empire action is initiated and sustained.[1]

If here Mr. Bennett had fewer inhibitions than some of his colleagues in allotting a positive role to the Imperial Conference, his views were endorsed, though not without some reservation on the part of General Hertzog, by the other delegates. By 1937, however, the atmosphere had cooled. Mr. Mackenzie King, not Mr. Bennett, was the representative of Canada. He used studiously modest terms. 'An Imperial Conference is only a conference,' he told an anxious member in Ottawa, 'it is not a cabinet.' And he continued: 'unless the government permits it there is nothing that an Imperial Conference can do which can in any way bind the country without the knowledge and consent of its Parliament.'[2] To the Imperial Conference itself he elaborated later his views about the appropriate field for its activities. The role of the

[1] Cmd. 3718, p. 9. It is not suggested that there is anything new about Mr. Bennett's views or those of Mr. Mackenzie King which are quoted on the following page. Mr. Mackenzie King, indeed, had used almost identical language many years earlier.

[2] Canada, H. of C. Deb., 1937, vol. 2, p. 1056.

Imperial Conference was consultation and advice, its task being no more than that of considering

> whether the several governments represented, while preserving their individual rights of decision and action, can co-ordinate their various policies in such a way as to assist one another, and help forward the cause of peace. Its function is not to formulate or declare policy. The value of this, as of other Imperial Conferences, lies mainly in the free exchange of information and opinion; in furnishing the representatives of the several governments with more adequate knowledge of the problems, the difficulties, the aspirations, the attitudes of other members of the British Commonwealth of Nations; and in giving that direct and immediate understanding of the national and personal factors in the situation which cannot well be obtained by correspondence or indirect communication. With this further knowledge in their possession, the representatives of each government, in consultation with their colleagues and their respective parliaments, are in the best of positions to formulate policies on questions where co-operation is required.[1]

In this judiciously phrased commentary Mr. Mackenzie King, explicitly excluding from the sphere of the Imperial Conference any policy-making function, confined its activities to consultation and exchange of view. This was lamented by New Zealand and in less marked degree by Australia. Mr. Savage, who had come to London hoping for 'effective results', reported a trifle bleakly to the New Zealand House of Representatives on his return that it was 'just a case of talking matters over until we arrive at a common understanding'.[2] Yet that seemed too much to Dr. Malan, who opposed General Hertzog's participation in the Conference at all on the ground that 'our freedom' being now 'our own, the principal reason for the Prime Minister having to go to Imperial Conferences has passed'.[3] Mr. Mackenzie King's standpoint was therefore central, and it represented a practical compromise between conflicting views. It was in line with the historical evolution of Commonwealth institutions, not in any sense a departure from it. But if it was in conformity with the past it also foreshadowed the future. Since interchange of view was to be the principal purpose of such a conference, was there not ground for arguing that the formality of the Imperial Conference was not altogether in keeping with the tasks it had to perform? If Imperial Conferences were to be, in the words of Mr. Neville Chamberlain, 'family gatherings held at more or less regular intervals, at which members of the family assemble together in order to exchange information, to examine the events of the past and the prospects of the future',[4] might it not be that more personal, less formal meetings of the principal statesmen of the Commonwealth would

[1] Cmd. 5482, pp. 63–64.
[2] 29 September 1937, New Zealand, H. of R. Deb., p. 475.
[3] 6 April 1937, South Africa, H. of A. Deb., vol. 29, p. 3256.
[4] Cmd. 5482, p. 61.

be more in accord with normal family practice? It was this feeling, reinforced by a peculiarly Canadian mistrust of large and ostentatious imperial gatherings, which led to the discontinuance of Imperial Conferences after 1937.[1]

The Imperial Conference had long been regarded as the chief buttress of imperial unity and the tangible expression of imperial co-operation. The abandonment of its wider pretensions was symptomatic of the temper of the times. Other institutions of an imperial character suffered a corresponding decline in their range of actual responsibility or in prestige. By the mere fact of being 'imperial' in name or character they tended to be suspect. Equality being the one fundamental condition of dominion status, there was a constant anxiety lest its reality be impaired by the encroachments of imperial bodies upon dominion freedom of action. This anxiety, historical in origin, acquired contemporary reality because of the continuing preponderance of the United Kingdom within the Commonwealth. She might be equal in status with the dominions but in stature she far surpassed them. It was this almost as much as positive nationalist sentiment which precluded a calm indifference on the part of the dominions to the survival of institutions associated with an imperial order now outgrown. Unless they were watchful might not the Commonwealth prove to be no more than the old Empire writ large?

In the light of this psychological background it is easy to understand why the central institutions which aroused least misgiving were those devoted to severely practical or limited ends, while those which aroused most were those which by their function, their name, or their history inevitably raised questions of status. The list of bodies falling into the first category is a long one. It included the Imperial War Graves Commission, committees concerned with shipping and communications, institutes devoted to the advance of education and of technical knowledge in various fields.[2] In the second category were to be found, in addition to the Imperial Conference, the Committee of Imperial Defence whose name belied both its responsibilities and its composition,[3] and the Judicial Committee of the Privy Council. Though an object of recurrent suspicion both to more extreme nationalists and to isolationists, the technical nature and the secrecy which necessarily shrouded so much of the work of the Committee of Imperial Defence protected it from much overt criticism. The Judicial Committee, however, did not enjoy an equal measure of immunity. It was hardly to be denied that the continued existence of an appeal from dominion courts to the Judicial Committee constituted a restriction upon dominion judicial autonomy. Moreover, the composition of the Judicial Committee remained, despite endeavours at various times to broaden it, predominantly United Kingdom and it could not therefore claim in any

[1] But not of less formal meetings of dominion Prime Ministers.

[2] They are listed in Palmer, *Consultation and Co-operation*, pp. 164 ff., and their functions are briefly described in the revised edition of this book by Heather J. Harvey (London, Oxford University Press for the Royal Institute of International Affairs, 1951).

[3] See below.

strict sense to be a Commonwealth tribunal.[1] Perhaps for this very reason its judgements, particularly in Canadian constitutional cases, were open to criticism on the ground of their being restrictively legalistic and remote from actuality. In any event, save where there were strong reasons of sentiment as in New Zealand, or cogent constitutional arguments for maintaining the appeal to the Judicial Committee, dominion opinion hardened against it. In the two decades which followed the enactment of the Statute of Westminster the appeal to the Judicial Committee was abolished by the Irish Free State in 1933, by Canada in criminal cases in the same year, by South Africa and by India and Pakistan in 1950, and by Canada in civil and constitutional cases also in 1950.[2]

It would be very wrong to identify mistrust of central imperial institutions with reservations about membership of the Commonwealth. It is true that in the case of the Irish Free State secession was the ultimate goal, but such was not the case for the majority in South Africa or for any considerable body of opinion in Canada. It was indeed perfectly logical to maintain that the survival of imperial institutions of the more formal kind was not an aid but a hindrance to closer co-operation. Their continued existence fostered reservations about status which detracted from the spirit of freedom and equality on which the Commonwealth rested. Nor is it to be assumed that imperial bodies despite the normally high calibre of their personnel were necessarily well equipped for the tasks they had to perform. Mr. Swart, the South African Minister of Justice, in introducing a bill to abolish South African appeals to the Privy Council conveniently summarized dominion objections to it which have application in a wider field. Appeals to the Privy Council were, he said, incompatible with sovereign independence, they were expensive, they were heard by a tribunal over whose membership the Union had no control.[3] These are arguments in which the emphasis of a less pronounced nationalist might be different, but which have all to be taken into account in assessing the factors which determined dominion attitudes. Nor must it be supposed that the abolition of appeals to the Judicial Committee was regarded with general misgiving in the United Kingdom. At a ceremony in the House of Lords to mark the abolition of appeals from Pakistan, the Secretary of State for Commonwealth Relations, Mr. Patrick Gordon Walker, observed: 'Some people might say we are here to sever a tie. We are not. We are doing something to bind us closer together.'[4]

THE ASCENDING IMPORTANCE OF THE CROWN

It seems at first sight paradoxical that the egalitarianism which had swept away so many institutions of an imperial character should not merely have

[1] See Wheare, *Statute of Westminster*, pp. 87–99.
[2] For a summary see Harvey, *Consultation and Co-operation*, pp. 122–33.
[3] 8 February 1950, South Africa, H. of A. Deb., vol. 70, coll. 916–23.
[4] *Manchester Guardian*, 21 June 1950.

left unimpaired but should have actually exalted the position of the Crown. Yet the paradox is easily resolved. The self-governing members of the Commonwealth all stood in the same relationship to the Crown, for the Report of the Inter-Imperial Relations Committee had laid it down in 1926 that it was 'the right of the government of each dominion to advise the Crown in all matters relating to its own affairs'.[1] This direct dominion relationship with the Crown acquired substance by a recognition that the Governor-General of a dominion was the representative of the Crown 'holding in all essential respects the same position in relation to the administration of public affairs in the dominion as is held by His Majesty the King in Great Britain', and by a declaration in the Preamble to the Statute of Westminster to the effect that 'any alteration in the law touching the Succession to the Throne or the Royal Style and Titles shall hereafter require the assent as well of the Parliaments of all the dominions as of the Parliament of the United Kingdom'. What this meant negatively was vividly illustrated by Mr. Patrick McGilligan when, on the enactment of the Statute of Westminster, he told the Dáil that henceforward 'the King, acting on the advice of the British government, can no more contract for the Irish Free State than can the King of Italy or the Mikado of Japan'.[2] More positively this multiple relationship with the Crown symbolized the free association of the member states of the Commonwealth united by a common allegiance to the Crown. Canadians, observed Mr. St. Laurent many years later, have brought the King intimately into their national home as King of Canada.[3]

While the relationship of the dominions to the Crown was defined, the nature of the Crown was not. The Preamble to the Statute of Westminster spoke of 'common allegiance' but not of a 'common Crown'. In the absence of an authoritative definition, the conflict between imperialists and nationalists was renewed with metaphysical refinement in this pleasantly speculative field. The traditional view of the Crown, as a common Crown, has been most carefully expounded by Mr. Amery who wrote:[4]

> There is under our system no such thing as definite separation between Monarchy and Crown, no mere personal union of separate Crowns, such as once linked Hanover to England or Austria to Hungary. It is the same common Crown which is an integral part of the constitution of each part of the whole Empire. . . . This gives to the whole Commonwealth a constitutionally indissoluble unity which is as essential a part of its constitution as the absolute independence and equality of its several partners. The fact that, in practice, any dominion, or for that matter the United Kingdom, might disclaim all further connexion with or responsibility for the rest, and emphasize that decision by declaring itself a republic, without forcible interference, would not affect the fundamentally unconstitutional nature of such a step.

[1] Cmd. 2768, p. 17.
[2] 16 July 1931, Dáil Debates, vol. 39, col. 2303.
[3] *The Times*, 3 May 1950.
[4] *Thoughts on the Constitution*, pp. 151–2.

The emphasis upon 'one single, indissoluble body corporate composed of the King and his subjects' was provocative, and represents a view unacceptable in Canada, and directly challenged by South Africa. Nor indeed does its dogmatism seem in accord with the empirical approach to Commonwealth relations in recent years. By contrast South Africa, insistent upon the assertion of a dominion's right to secession and neutrality, maintained that the Commonwealth was linked together by allegiance to a King in whom were united several and therefore presumably separable Crowns, rather than to a King who wore the common Crown of the Commonwealth.[1] This theory of the divisibility of the Crown unquestionably made an inroad upon the conception of Commonwealth unity hitherto entertained, but equally it was not necessarily incompatible with the terms of the Statute of Westminster, and it received implicit vindication in the London declaration of 1949 admitting republican India to full membership of the Commonwealth. What is important to notice here is that the recognition of the unique position of the Crown as the only institution essential to the Commonwealth relationship did not impose an artificial uniformity upon the Commonwealth wholly foreign to its spirit, but allowed for changing views and for reinterpretation.

Dominion governments rightly attached much importance to the position of the King as King of each dominion. He was King of Canada, King of Australia, King of New Zealand, King of South Africa, as much as he was King of the United Kingdom.[2] When King George VI visited the Kingdom of Canada in 1939, and the Kingdom of South Africa in 1947, he discharged in person duties and responsibilities corresponding in all respects with those which he discharged as King of the United Kingdom. But despite the similarity of the constitutional relationship it would be mistaken to suppose that the role of the monarch in the dominions was, or ever could be, in practice identical with the role he fulfilled in the United Kingdom. Though constitutionalists often write of the institution of the Crown as divorced from the person of the monarch, in practice this divorce did not, and could not, take place. For the King himself, there could be no such separation between his personality and the symbolic office which he occupied.

The King normally resided in the United Kingdom. From this there followed important consequences. According to Bagehot's classic definition

[1] When the Royal Toast was proposed some Nationalist Ministers of the Crown used to make this clear by drinking not to 'The King', with its implications of a common Crown, but to 'Our King', i.e. the King of South Africa.

[2] King George V expressed concern lest the multiple responsibilities which as a result devolved upon him should prove irreconcilable. In a matter which affected two or more dominions he might receive conflicting advice from two or more Prime Ministers. Such an eventuality could not be disregarded. In 1939 General Hertzog might have given to the King, as King of South Africa, advice about the transfer of the High Commission Territories then under discussion in which the United Kingdom government could not have concurred. The only safeguard against such a situation is the exercise of the same prudent restraint by dominion Prime Ministers which General Hertzog displayed in 1939.

a constitutional monarch has the right to be consulted, the right to encourage, the right to warn.[1] Yet these are rights which can be exercised effectively only by a King who has intimate knowledge of the ministers with whom he is dealing and an experience of national affairs as long or longer than theirs. It is true that in respect of the dominions a King may acquire a wide knowledge of their affairs but he can rarely, if ever, hope to acquire an advantage in that respect over his dominion ministers, such as he may possess over his ministers in the United Kingdom. In a dominion, too, the King must inevitably lack that intimate day-to-day touch with the business of state which is an essential part of his influence in the United Kingdom. Indeed it is not normally likely that he would know personally more than the principal ministers of a dominion unless it had been possible for him to visit that dominion on more than one occasion. Anxious that theory and practice should conform more closely, constitutional lawyers have suggested that modern means of transport might allow the King to reside for a period every year in each of his realms. Such an undertaking would tax the physical endurance of a young monarch to the limit, and as the royal tour of South Africa in 1947 made clear, the strain of frequent royal visits overseas upon a monarch of middle age are too great to be contemplated with equanimity by anyone. Moreover, even if it were possible, it is open to question whether royal residence in different parts of the Commonwealth each year would be desirable. Over a period of years it would inevitably mean that the King would not be very intimately acquainted with the details of government or of political and social life in any part of the British Commonwealth. This might prove a serious disadvantage, for a broad but necessarily somewhat superficial view of the politics of many countries is often a less sure guide in the exercise of great influence than an intimate knowledge of the working of government in one. The English preference for education in depth as against the American practice of education in breadth seems best suited to the circumstances of that peculiarly English institution, constitutional monarchy.

At this point it may be suggested that since the King is represented by a Governor-General in each dominion, the direct relationship between a dominion and its King is satisfactorily established. Such indeed has been the theory, but here developments in constitutional practice have tended to deprive it of much of its reality. The Imperial Conference of 1930 recognized that:

> The parties interested in the appointment of a Governor-General of a Dominion are His Majesty the King, whose representative he is, and the Dominion concerned. . . . The Ministers who tender and are responsible for such advice are His Majesty's Ministers in the Dominion concerned.[2]

[1] Walter Bagehot, *The English Constitution* (London, Oxford University Press, 1928; World's Classics) p. 67.

[2] Cmd. 3717, p. 27. The *Proceedings* also spoke somewhat ambiguously of the responsibility of dominion ministers to tender advice to the King about the appointment of a Governor-

Once the Governor-General had thus become the nominee of the dominion government concerned, the royally representative character of the office declined. The Irish Free State,[1] the Commonwealth of Australia,[2] the Union of South Africa,[3] the Dominions of New Zealand,[4] of Pakistan,[5] and of India[6] have recommended the appointment of one, or more than one, of their own citizens as Governor-General. In most, but not in every, instance was the person appointed calculated to raise the prestige of the office, though only Mr. de Valera exercised his power of recommendation to secure the appointment of a person expressly designed to lower it.[7] In such circumstances the relations of dominion Prime Ministers with Governors-General have been very different from those of United Kingdom Prime Ministers with the King. The great Lord Chatham was said by Burke to be intoxicated 'by the least peep into the King's closet', but dominion Prime Ministers far less imperious in character have not and could not feel any such deferential awe towards a Governor-General who is the King's representative for a limited period of years. Mr. Mackenzie King conducted his controversy with Lord Byng without undue inhibitions and Mr. de Valera, in bringing about the resignation of Mr. James MacNeill, demonstrated that Governors-General were not irremovable. Nor is depreciation of the office an exclusive preserve of more extreme nationalists. Australian radicalism has never been easily reconciled to its usefulness. To Alfred Deakin the title of Governor-General appeared 'to be little better than a glittering and gaudy toy'. To John Cockburn the Governor-General whose highest function was 'to be a dummy' seemed, in filling that role, to be 'less than the least in the whole of the colonies, a useless image and bauble'. To judge by some appointments in recent decades, the disparagement of the office by the fathers of Australian Federation is not considered unjust by their political heirs. In general there has been a per-

General. So long as dominion Prime Ministers normally retained the External Affairs portfolio in their own hands the initiative rested very largely with them individually though it was customary to secure cabinet approval before a formal recommendation was made to the King. It is generally understood that Mr. Mackenzie King proposed the appointment of Mr. John Buchan (afterwards Lord Tweedsmuir) as Governor-General of Canada, and that his cabinet colleagues warmly assented. On the other hand, there is good reason to believe that Mr. John Curtin, then Prime Minister of Australia, was attacked in Caucus in November 1943 for not having consulted all his colleagues before recommending the appointment of the Duke of Gloucester as Governor-General of Australia. (See article by Ross Gollancz in the *Sydney Morning Herald*, 22 November 1943, and L. F. Crisp, *The Parliamentary Government of the Commonwealth of Australia* (London, Longmans, Green, with the Wakefield Press, Adelaide, 1949) p. 199.)

[1] Mr. T. M. Healy appointed in 1922, Mr. James MacNeill in 1927, Mr. Donal Buckley in 1932.

[2] Sir Isaac Isaacs appointed in 1930, Mr. W. J. McKell in 1947.

[3] Sir Patrick Duncan appointed in 1936, Mr. G. B. van Zyl in 1945, Dr. E. G. Jansen appointed in 1951.

[4] General Bernard Freyberg in 1946.

[5] Mr. M. A. Jinnah, in 1947, Mr. Khawaja Nazimuddin in 1948.

[6] Mr. C. Rajagopalachari in 1948.

[7] See below, p. 289.

ceptible decline in the prestige of the office and a corresponding enhancement in all the dominions of the position of the dominion Prime Minister.

> The history of the Governor-Generalship in the first forty-five years of federation [writes Professor Crisp[1] of Australian experience] is . . . a history of gradual but constant encroachment upon the initially very restricted personal initiative and discretion of its incumbents. In becoming ever more innocuous and politically unobtrusive it has provided an ever more satisfactory keystone to the constitutional arch.

Historically that has been the experience of all the dominions, but not everyone would assent without reservation to Professor Crisp's sanguine verdict upon it. The drafters of the Irish Constitution of 1937 and of the Indian Constitution of 1950, after some experience of dominion status in the traditional form, decided to invest their respective Heads of State with a wider measure of discretionary authority than that enjoyed in practice by a Governor-General.

The greater detachment of the King from the political life of the dominions is by no means necessarily a disadvantage in all respects. The symbolic role of the monarchy as the one remaining formal link of the British Commonwealth of Nations has imposed upon it a complex character which demands that the King should fulfil many roles. Here a certain remoteness lent verisimilitude to them all. For the colonial Empire, the majestic and paternal elements of the monarchy loomed large; in the Indian Empire the King assumed an imperial mantle unfamiliar to the tradition of British kingship, while in the dominions, on the other hand, particularly in Australia and New Zealand where radical sentiment has always been so pronounced, as well as in the United Kingdom itself, changes in social thought demanded an adaptation of the monarchy to the outlook of contemporary society. It was the contention of Mr. Attlee during the abdication crisis that the need for the monarchy to conform to the changing social outlook was of cardinal importance.[2] Nor should any clear-cut distinction be drawn between these contrasted views. There were many who at one moment delighted to see the King perform his 'majestic' functions and who at other times desired him, if one may parody G. K. Chesterton, to be

> The sort of King who might pass,
> For a member of the middle class.

The Crown has proved no mere colourless symbol of the free association of the Commonwealth; on the contrary it has been a powerful unifying force, particularly among people of British descent. They inherited the mystic reverence, the religious allegiance which Bagehot[3] discerned to be essential to a true monarchy. They are not feelings which a legislature can manufacture,

[1] *Parliamentary Government of Australia*, p. 236.

[2] H. of C. Deb., vol. 318, col. 2204.

[3] Bagehot, *English Constitution*, p. 3.

for they are, as Bagehot noted, semi-filial feelings which are inherited. 'You might as well adopt a father as make a monarchy,' he wrote, 'for the special sentiment belonging to the one is as incapable of voluntary creation as the peculiar affection belonging to the other.' These wise reflections help to explain the often misrepresented attitudes of non-British peoples within the Commonwealth towards the Crown. Among them respect rather than loyalty was predominant, but that respect did not modify fundamentally the convictions of Afrikaner or Irish republicans or the trend of the Indian Congress party towards republicanism. They felt unable to adopt the English monarchy. On the other hand, for many of the less sophisticated colonial peoples the appeal of the Crown was direct and profound. For them it represented something personal and intelligible in the elaborate mechanism of government; it carried with it an assurance of justice and impartiality; it was the dignified, the theatrical element in the imperial constitution and its contribution, as in Bagehot's day, was inestimable.

THE ABDICATION OF KING EDWARD VIII: THE ROLE OF THE DOMINIONS

The drafters of the Statute of Westminster, mindful of the high traditions of the monarchy since the accession of Queen Victoria, little expected that within a few years the relation of the Commonwealth to the Crown which they had elaborated in 1931 would be severely tested. By making the succession to the Throne a matter of concern to all the dominions, they had presumed that in the highly unlikely event of any disputed succession or other crisis all their Governments and Parliaments would agree upon a common course of action. In 1936 their confidence was shown to be well founded. It was a remarkable fact that in the difficult and controversial circumstances of the abdication there was no government within the Commonwealth which dissented from the course sponsored by Mr. Baldwin as Prime Minister of the United Kingdom. That it was so may reasonably be regarded as evidence both of an underlying community of outlook within the Commonwealth and of a resolve not to allow the unity, symbolized by the Crown, to be impaired by divided counsels about the succession to it.

The abdication crisis illustrated very clearly that whatever the constitutional theory, it was the United Kingdom government in fact, and its Prime Minister in particular, who was most directly concerned and almost wholly responsible for finding a solution for a problem touching so closely the succession to the Throne. Mr. Baldwin, in his speech to the House of Commons on 10 December 1936, made it clear that in the early stages he had consulted neither the dominion governments, nor even his own colleagues in the cabinet. In the second half of the preceding October Mr. Baldwin, not only as Prime Minister but also 'as a counsellor and as a friend', first advised the King of the gossip and criticism about his association with Mrs. Simpson which had spread from the United States to the United Kingdom. He told the King that he had two great anxieties; the first was the effect of American press comment in the dominions and particularly in Canada where it circulated most freely, and the second, the effect which it would have in the United Kingdom itself. He reminded the King that while the Crown had been deprived of many of its prerogatives it stood for far more than it had ever done in its history. The importance of its integrity was, Mr. Baldwin argued, beyond all question far greater than it had ever been, partly because 'the Crown was the last link of Empire that is left'. He feared that if the monarchy were exposed to criticism, the power that had been built up slowly over generations would be lost rapidly, and he doubted whether anything could restore it.[1]

Mr. Baldwin did not consult the cabinet after this conversation with the King in October, but merely reported it to 'about four of my senior colleagues'. He did not say categorically whether he had or had not consulted the dominion governments, but the presumption that he did not do so is strong. The King's own statement, 'you and I must settle this matter together; I will not have anyone interfering', was a direct discouragement to formal or even informal consultation with the dominion governments. On the other hand, Mr. Baldwin's initial concern about the damage likely to be caused to the monarchy by rumours spreading from the United States to Canada and the other dominions can hardly have been pure speculation and was most probably based on reasonably authoritative information informally received from official or quasi-official dominion sources. It so happened that Mr. Mackenzie King was on a private visit to the United Kingdom from 16 to 31 October 1936 and during that period he saw Mr. Baldwin. It is inconceivable that the subject of the King's proposed marriage was not discussed at their meeting. It is therefore possible, even probable, that Mr. Baldwin in the first instance was prompted to take the initiative as much by informal advice received from the dominions and particularly Canada as by concern expressed in the United Kingdom itself. But even if this were so, any such expressions of anxiety did not qualify the primary responsibility for the determination of policy which rested throughout the crisis upon the Prime Minister, the members of his government, and the Parliament of the United Kingdom.

The next meeting between Mr. Baldwin and the King took place on 16 November, at Buckingham Palace. The King said:[2] 'I understand that you and several members of the cabinet have some fear of a constitutional crisis developing over my friendship with Mrs. Simpson?' And Mr. Baldwin replied, 'Yes, Sir, that is correct'. Mr. Baldwin then went on to say that he did not think that a marriage with Mrs. Simpson would receive the approbation of the country. In his opinion marriage would certainly have meant that

[1] H. of C. Deb., vol. 318, col. 2179.

[2] Edward, Duke of Windsor, *A King's Story* (London, Cassell, 1951) p. 330.

Mrs. Simpson would become Queen, and he said that on this 'the voice of the people must be heard'. For his part Mr. Baldwin felt that the marriage was impracticable and so advised the King. In reply the King said: 'I am going to marry Mrs. Simpson and I am prepared to go.'

The importance of this conversation from the point of view of the Commonwealth overseas is that it underlined the overriding responsibility of the Prime Minister of the United Kingdom. It was he who put before the King, without formally consulting the dominion governments, the alternatives of giving up the idea of marrying Mrs. Simpson or abdication. It was at a later stage when the King, despite Mr. Baldwin's own feeling that Parliament would never pass the necessary legislation, expressly requested that the possibility of a morganatic marriage be considered, that Mr. Baldwin advised him that it would mean 'my putting that formally before the whole cabinet and communicating with the Prime Ministers of all the dominions. . . .'[1] The King requested him to do so. Accordingly on 27 November Mr. Baldwin telegraphed the dominion Prime Ministers giving an account of his interviews with the King and the alternatives of ordinary marriage, morganatic marriage, and abdication in favour of the Duke of York that had now to be considered. He recorded in the telegram the views he had already expressed to the King, and asked the dominion Prime Ministers for their personal opinions on the course that should be followed and also for their assessments of the likely views of their peoples.[2] Whether in this he was constitutionally correct is open to doubt. In theory the question should have been broached, as the Duke of Windsor later pointed out, by the King to the Governor-General in each dominion as his personal representative. But the King was himself loath to employ this course on so delicate and personal an issue and it is hardly to be doubted that the procedure adopted by Mr. Baldwin was best calculated to ensure unity of action by all the governments of the Commonwealth.[3] When Mr. Baldwin saw the King again on 2 December, the inquiries which he had thought proper to make had not been completed, but he told the King that they had gone far enough to show that neither in the dominions nor in the United Kingdom would there be any prospect of such legislation being accepted. The dominion governments were in fact united in their opposition to a morganatic marriage.[4] Mr. Mackenzie King told Mr. Baldwin that 'the

[1] H. of C. Deb., vol. 318, col. 2182.

[2] ibid., see also General Hertzog's speech to South African House of Assembly on 25 January 1937 in which he made public the personal nature of Mr. Baldwin's inquiry (H. of A. Deb., vol. 28, pp. 571 ff.), and Mr. Lyons's speech to the Australian House of Representatives on 11 December 1936 (H. of R. Deb., vol 152, pp. 2898 ff.).

[3] Lord Beaverbrook expressed much concern when the King told him that he had not seen the text of the cables to the dominion Prime Ministers before they were sent off. 'Sir,' he exclaimed, 'you have put your head on the execution block. All that Mr. Baldwin has to do now is to swing the axe.' See *A King's Story*, p. 347. It should perhaps be added that Lord Beaverbrook was generally not disposed to represent Mr. Baldwin's actions in a favourable light.

[4] It would appear, however, from a conversation of Mr. Baldwin with the Archbishop of

people of Canada would not approve of marriage to Mrs. Simpson whether she was to become Queen or not'.[1] Mr. Lyons warned him that 'the proposed marriage, if it led to Mrs. Simpson becoming Queen, must incur widespread condemnation' and that a specially sanctioned morganatic marriage 'would run counter to the best popular conceptions of the Royal Family',[2] while General Hertzog considered abdication to be a lesser evil than marriage to Mrs. Simpson. 'The one would be a great shock, the other would be a permanent wound.'[3] The Archbishop of Canterbury, Dr. Cosmo Gordon Lang,[4] recorded in his diary that Mr. Baldwin received a particularly strong telegram from Mr. Lyons, Prime Minister of the Commonwealth of Australia, stating that in his view King Edward VIII could not re-establish his prestige or command confidence in future as King. Mr. Baldwin did not hesitate to show this telegram to the King, and it is possible that any remaining doubts which Mr. Baldwin may have entertained about the course of action which he should adopt were removed by it. But support for a course of action already clearly chartered is not the same thing as the determination of the course. And there the initiative still rested with the Prime Minister of the United Kingdom, and indeed it is evident that however equal in theory may be the constitutional relationship between governments of the Commonwealth and the Crown, only the Prime Minister of the United Kingdom can normally establish the intimate personal relationship with the person of the King essential for advising in delicate personal affairs.

It was commonly said at the time that the abdication of King Edward VIII demonstrated once again the strength of the Nonconformist conscience in the United Kingdom. It may be added here that it also revealed the strength both of the Nonconformist and of the Roman Catholic conscience throughout the Commonwealth. Mr. Mackenzie King, a Presbyterian, and General Hertzog, a member of the Dutch Reformed Church, may be regarded as the spokesmen of dominion nonconformity. Australia, New Zealand, and the Irish Free State all at that time had Roman Catholic Prime Ministers, who viewed with equal disfavour a marriage with a woman who had been twice divorced and both of whose previous husbands were still living.[5] And while the responsi-

Canterbury that Mr. de Valera expressed no view on this point. See J. G. L. Lockhart, *Life of Cosmo Gordon Lang, Archbishop of Canterbury* (London, Hodder & Stoughton, 1949) p. 401.

[1] 18 January 1937, Canada, H. of C. Deb., vol. 1, p. 37.

[2] 11 December 1936, Australia, H. of R. Deb., vol. 152, pp. 2898 ff.

[3] 25 January 1937, South Africa, H. of A. Deb., vol. 28, col. 572. An enlightening summary of the abdication and dominion reactions to it is given in Latham, *Law and Commonwealth*, pp. 618 ff.

[4] Lockhart, *Cosmo Gordon Lang*.

[5] There is, however, no evidence that Mr. Savage expressed any strong opposition to the proposed marriage, and the terms of the statement he issued on the morning of 11 December alluding to 'the profound and universal regret' which would be felt at the news that every effort to find a solution 'suitable to His Majesty and acceptable to the British Commonwealth of Nations' had failed suggests that he had not entertained it. Mr. de Valera, whatever his personal views, felt on political grounds that the question was one for the United Kingdom and the older dominions to settle as they thought best.

bility of the dominion Prime Ministers is not to be unduly exalted at the expense of that of their cabinets, the prevailing practice by which the office of Prime Minister was associated with that of Minister for External Affairs meant in practice that the abdication crisis was dealt with mainly by the individual Prime Ministers themselves.[1]

The formal action required of and taken by the dominions consequent upon the abdication varied considerably, partly for reasons of policy and partly for reasons of law.[2] Because neither Australia nor New Zealand had adopted the Statute of Westminster by 1936, the Abdication Act[3] merely recites that the Commonwealth of Australia and the Dominion of New Zealand had assented thereto, and no special legislation was necessary in order that the Abdication Act should be extended to them as part of their law. In respect of Canada the Preamble to the Abdication Act declared that the dominion . . . 'has requested and consented to the enactment of this Act. . . .'[4] As a result the act extended to Canada as part of the law of Canada and the assent of the Canadian Parliament was embodied in an act passed when Parliament reassembled in 1937. The course followed by South Africa and the Irish Free State was influenced by political as well as constitutional considerations. While General Hertzog cordially endorsed the policy adopted in the abdication crisis, he wished to take advantage of the opportunity it afforded to underline the sovereign status of South Africa. He did not therefore desire that the United Kingdom Abdication Act should be extended to the Union as part of the law of the Union. He contended, on the contrary, that no legislation was necessary to make the abdication effective in the Union on the ground that the deed of abdication was effective in itself and did not need new legislation. Accordingly in his view the Duke of York succeeded to the throne automatically upon its vacation by King Edward VIII by the operative sections of the Status of the Union Act.[5] On this assumption King George VI succeeded in South Africa on 10 December 1936, the day on which King Edward signed the Instrument of Abdication, whereas in the United Kingdom, Canada, Australia, and New Zealand he succeeded only when the necessary legislation had been enacted by the United Kingdom Parliament, that is on 11 December. This difference in the date of King George's accession, retrospectively endorsed by the Union Parliament in 1937, was important to General Hertzog because it could be used as evidence of the personal nature of the link between South

[1] Mr. Mackenzie King replied to Mr. Baldwin's first communication 'entirely on my own', and consulted his cabinet colleagues only when Mr. Baldwin advised him that he had placed the matter before the United Kingdom cabinet (Canada, H. of C. Deb., 1937, vol. 1, col. 38).

[2] For a careful analysis of them see two articles on the abdication legislation in the United Kingdom and the dominions by Professor K. H. Bailey in *Politica*, March and June 1938. See also Wheare, *Statute of Westminster*, pp. 284 ff.

[3] 1 Edw. VIII, c. 3 (H.M.'s Declaration of Abdication Act, 1936).

[4] For a critical examination of the procedure adopted see F. C. Cronkite, 'Canada and the Abdication', *Canadian Journal of Economics and Political Science* (Toronto), 1938.

[5] See above, p. 24.

Africa and the other countries in the Commonwealth arising from their allegiance to the Crown. It was not to a common Crown, but to the King of South Africa who was by South African law the same person as the King of the United Kingdom that South Africa owed allegiance.

Mr. de Valera took advantage of the abdication to put into effect more far-reaching plans of his own. He introduced simultaneously legislation to remove from the Constitution all reference to the Crown and an External Relations bill which contemplated its continued use in external affairs.[1] The concluding subsection of this bill provided that:

> Immediately upon the passing of this Act, the instrument of abdication executed by His Majesty King Edward VIII on the tenth day of December, 1936 . . . shall have effect according to the tenor thereof, and His said Majesty shall, for the purposes of the foregoing subsection of this section and all other (if any) purposes, cease to be King, and the King for those purposes shall henceforth be the person who, if His said Majesty had died on the tenth day of December, 1936, unmarried, would for the time being be his successor under the law of Saorstát Éireann.

In accordance with this provision King George VI did not succeed to the Crown of the Irish Free State till the External Relations Act received the force of law on 12 December 1936. Thus, as Professor Wheare points out, between 10 December and 12 December 1936 the Commonwealth was partially disrupted by allegiance to different Kings, but it was happily reunited on 12 December by general agreement that King George VI was now King in all the dominions owing allegiance to the British Crown.[2]

SOME REFLECTIONS ON THE PLACE OF THE CROWN IN THE COMMONWEALTH

The consequences of the abdication for the Commonwealth were important in the field of doctrine and politics alike. Doctrinally it served to reassert the sovereignty of Parliament, or to be more exact, Parliaments, in their relations with the Crown; and in so doing made it increasingly difficult to maintain the older conception of a unitary Crown. Politically the crisis prompted misgivings lest the abdication should undermine the prestige of the monarchy and in so doing lessen its value as the symbol of Commonwealth association. These anxieties were the keener because it was clearly understood that the Crown was, as Mr. Baldwin had emphasized, the one remaining institution linking the countries of the Commonwealth together. Yet it was this very awareness of the unique position of the Crown that helped most to place the crisis of the abdication in perspective and to ensure to the new King abundant good will and a loyalty that was deepened in the succeding years by his high and exacting devotion to duty. Whatever, therefore, the loss in the prestige of the

[1] Constitution (Amendment No. 27) Act, 1936, and Executive Authority (External Relations) Act, 1936. See below, pp. 290–4, for a detailed discussion of their provisions.

[2] *Statute of Westminster*, p. 290.

monarchy in 1936, it would not appear to have been so great as some contemporary observers supposed,[1] and it was fully restored within a decade.[2] The abdication proved, as General Hertzog rightly forecast, a great shock rather than a permanent wound. Equally, however, it is not to be assumed that any second crisis of this kind would leave the position of the monarchy in the Commonwealth unimpaired. Nearly a century ago Englishmen, in the words of Bagehot,[3] had come to regard the Crown as the 'head of our morality'. The very virtues of recent sovereigns have placed a very special emphasis upon this aspect of the monarchy, and in this respect the Nonconformist conscience of the Commonwealth overseas is likely henceforward to reinforce predominant opinion at home.

The exaltation of the Crown as the one remaining institution symbolizing the association of the Commonwealth implied a high measure of confidence in the hereditary principle. In England the monarchy has not in fact consistently produced a succession of kings who could sustain the progressively more exacting standards required in modern times. It might, therefore, at first sight be supposed that a considerable risk was being taken in proclaiming the Crown the one symbol of the Commonwealth association. Did not that presume qualities of mind and character in the succession to the Throne more than could reasonably be anticipated over a long period of years? Was it not disturbing to think of a Commonwealth owing allegiance to a George IV, that 'model of family demerit', or even to a George III, who was for the greater part of his life a kind of 'consecrated obstruction'?[4] 'As far as experience goes', wrote Bagehot, 'there is no reason to expect a hereditary series of useful limited monarchs.'[5] Yet our experience has gone farther than that of Bagehot and has encouraged that very expectation. Upon its part-fulfilment at least much now depends in Commonwealth affairs. Once it was possible to distinguish between the symbol and the person of the King, but in the contemporary world publicity, prying and shameless, has made that well-nigh impossible.

In the Oath used at the coronation service of King George VI each of the dominions was mentioned by name so as to indicate that the King was equally King of Great Britain, Ireland, Canada, Australia, New Zealand, and of the Union of South Africa,[6] It was essential that the new relationship of the

[1] cf. *Political Quarterly*, January–March 1937.

[2] Professor Brady has commented, 'my impression is that in Canada the monarchy did not lose any prestige after the abdication. If anything, it gained in prestige in that many considered that the abdication had demonstrated how it was not made subservient to an individual's wish, even when that individual was already King.'

[3] *English Constitution*, p. 47.

[4] ibid. pp. 47–48.

[5] ibid. p. 74.

[6] In the form used in 1937 the King was asked: 'Will you solemnly promise and swear to govern the peoples of Great Britain, Ireland, Canada, Australia, New Zealand, and the Union of South Africa, of your possessions, and the other territories to them belonging or pertaining and of your Empire India, according to their respective laws and customs?'

dominions with the Crown should be so recognized, yet the exact form to be adopted proved, so the Archbishop of Canterbury recalled, 'a matter of the utmost difficulty and intricacy', with the result that 'for weeks the air was thick with messages' from London to the dominion capitals. Even when the agreement of South Africa and the Irish Free State on this point had been secured a further difficulty had to be solved.[1] In the coronation service the Oath was to be followed by a promise on the part of the King to maintain 'the Protestant Reformed Religion as by law established', and it was recognized in London that Mr. Mackenzie King, mindful of Quebec, Mr. Lyons, and Mr. de Valera would feel that their King must be required to make no such promise. Yet here again the search for a compromise congenial to all gave rise to protracted and even more intricate negotiations. Their outcome was that the King was required to maintain 'the true profession of the Gospel' (a phrase to which none could object) and only in the United Kingdom to maintain 'the Protestant reformed religion as by law established'.[2] Then the injudicious suggestion was made that the High Commissioners for the dominions might join the peers spiritual and temporal in paying homage, but 'fortified by a memorandum on the meaning of homage',[3] the Archbishop of Canterbury firmly declined to act upon it. But however intricate the reconciling of theology with constitutional convention, the coronation service of King George VI was symbolic of the reality of a Commonwealth unity that rested on the foundation of free and equal membership. The Coronation Oath, observed Mr. Mackenzie King, recognized

> that the relationships of the several peoples under the Crown, one with another, as well as with foreign states, have become interpenetrated by the ancient principles of freedom and the rule of law . . . [and so] it may be said that the new oath, preserving the old and finding place for the new, embodies in simple fashion our political faith, and mirrors the structure of this group of free, equal and autonomous states known as the British Commonwealth of Nations.[4]

[1] The new form of Coronation Oath was agreed by the Commonwealth governments but it was not embodied in any legislative enactment. Its legality has been questioned on this ground.

[2] Lockhart, *Cosmo Gordon Lang*, pp. 412 ff.

[3] ibid. p. 416.

[4] Cmd. 5482, p. 50.

CHAPTER II

INTERNATIONAL RESPONSIBILITIES A PERSPECTIVE VIEW

THE COMMONWEALTH AND THE UNNECESSARY WAR

THE countries of the British Commonwealth of Nations played a decisive part in the winning of the Second World War. But it is open to question whether they made as great a contribution to preventing it. Was there anything that individually or collectively they could have done and failed to do before September 1939 to avert its outbreak? If, indeed, one accepts a determinist interpretation of human history, believing that its course may not be deflected by human will, then this is a question that needs no answer other than that given in some haunting lines of *The Dynasts*:[1]

> Ere systemed suns were globed and lit
> The slaughters of the race were writ
>
> . . . . .
>
> And wasting wars, by land and sea
> Fixed, like all else, immutably.

But at all times the conscience of mankind has rebelled against the acceptance of such fatalism as this. It is true that in history there have been wars predicted by contemporaries which have followed inexorably from identifiable and unmistakable causes. But they have been few and no one has suggested that the world war of 1939–45 is to be numbered with them. On the contrary, statesmen and historians are at one in their belief that by resolute action at some earlier date the war could have been localized or could have even been averted. When President Roosevelt told Mr. Churchill that he was asking publicly for suggestions about what the war should be called, Mr. Churchill replied at once, 'The Unnecessary War'. Never, he observes, was there 'a war more easy to stop'.[2] The verdict of the historian, Professor Namier, is expressed in almost identical terms. At several junctures, he writes, the second German bid for world domination could have been stopped without excessive effort or sacrifice.[3]

The two world wars that took place in the first half of the twentieth century began in Eastern Europe. As the principal causes of their outbreak were European, so too, the chief responsibility rests firmly upon the peoples of Europe themselves. In 1939 it was, to quote Professor Namier once again, a failure of European statesmanship, of European morality that made possible the Nazi bid for domination.[4] But predominant European responsibility is not

[1] Thomas Hardy, *The Dynasts* (London, Macmillan, complete edition 1910, reprinted 1931) p. 47.
[2] *Second World War*, vol. 1, p. 8.
[3] L. B. Namier, *Diplomatic Prelude* (London, Macmillan, 1948) p. ix.
[4] ibid.

the same thing as exclusive European responsibility. The overseas dominions, in common with the greater part of the world, had by their actions implicitly accepted the view that peace was indivisible. As signatories of the Covenant of the League in 1919 and of the Briand–Kellogg Pact in 1928 they had assumed responsibilities for the maintenance of peace and for the outlawing of war in Europe as in every other part of the world. By the way in which they interpreted and proposed to enforce the general obligations which they had voluntarily assumed the dominions (with the outside world of which they were a part) either stiffened, or weakened still further, the resolve of peace-loving but vacillating European governments to resist aggression. The extent to which these opportunities for influencing the course of European and of world politics were seized or neglected is the broad measure of dominion responsibility for the coming of the Second World War. Sins of omission due, not to any lack of good intentions, but to irresolution, to a failure to concentrate upon the great essentials of policy are the counts upon which they may be charged before the bar of history. But whatever the verdict, it should be made clear at the outset that any proven neglect on their part cannot detract from the fundamental responsibility of Europe herself.

THE CLIMATE OF COMMONWEALTH OPINION

In the Commonwealth countries overseas the influence of public opinion on foreign policy tended to be greater than in the United Kingdom. This is to be attributed, not to a more exact or widespread knowledge there of the international problems of the time, which indeed did not exist, but to the inexperience of governments. While the Foreign Office in London had acquired in the course of centuries a vast accumulation of knowledge about foreign affairs and a traditional approach towards most of the problems they presented, the concern of dominion governments after 1919 was first to establish in principle the right to conduct a separate foreign policy at all and then to create the machinery for carrying it out. As a result, while foreign policy in the United Kingdom continued even in the new age of open diplomacy to be largely the preserve of experts secluded in the sobering precincts of Whitehall and highly mistrustful of popular enthusiasms, dominion policies, in so far as they were defined, reflected much more exactly the attitudes, if not of their peoples as a whole, at least of that intellectual minority which concerned itself with such things. Where tradition and expertness were of necessity lacking, governments were reluctant to take the initiative without unmistakable preliminary evidence of outside support, with the result that public opinion had there a more decisive role to play. This was not without a general importance in determining the approach of the dominions to international affairs.

Public opinion in democratic countries is always disposed to view international relations in simpler and more spacious terms than the sceptical officials of the chancelleries of the Great Powers and never more so than in the English-speaking world of the early inter-war years. Where in the dominions that public opinion was guided by an earnest intellectual minority the emphasis tended to be on principle, with the result that at times devotion to principle overshadowed the practical consequences of its application. This was in itself a wholesome corrective to the predominant preoccupation of the professional diplomats of the old world with consequences, but it was too simple to be always a safe guide. In the dominions the greater influence on policy exercised by public opinion, in the absence of an adequate counterbalancing professional authority, gave a more uncompromising political expression to the idealist sentiments of the early inter-war years.

'En politique', observed Prince Louis Napoleon in the days of his exile, 'on ne doit jamais dire jamais.' For him the saying was a confession of faith; for others it is a prudent maxim, a timely warning against final judgements, against despair and above all indulgence in excessive hopes. 'Never again' was the verdict of 1919, for had not 'the war to end war' been fought and won? How these phrases ring down the years with an irony the more bitter because they had once embodied the confident conviction of millions of generous-minded men and women throughout the English-speaking world! In the flush of victory, won after long endurance and bitter sacrifice, they had been taken by their leaders to the top of a high mountain and shown the promised world of plenty from which war had been outlawed by the creation of a new international machinery. A hundred and thirty years earlier Mirabeau had solemnly warned the Girondists of what must inevitably follow from so untimely and so unjustified an exaltation of a people's hopes, but they, like their successors in 1919, paid no heed and on the scaffold reaped their harvest. For the peoples of the Commonwealth it was a new world that victory had ushered in, a world that had discarded with righteous contempt the secret diplomacy, the competition in armaments, the international anarchy of the old. On the heights of political emotion it proved hard for them as for others to retain a saving sense of reality. And it was largely because that sense of reality was lost that the great enterprise in human government launched in 1919 so dismally failed. To those who had been shown a promised land the dull practical measures required to consolidate much that had unquestionably been gained were casually discarded because they seemed, after the broad vistas of 1919, either superfluous or insignificant.

It is often tacitly assumed that the mood of unwarranted optimism followed by the bitter revulsion and the too-late awakening was a phenomenon peculiar to Britain and not shared by the peoples of the more robust and realistic dominions overseas. But that is an illusion. Preoccupied by regional interests, influenced by their particular historical development, the dominant trends of dominion opinion on international affairs did not nevertheless depart in essentials from the corresponding currents of opinion in Britain, and indeed in many instances they were more pronounced overseas. Internationalist idealists in the Canadian prairies tended to be both more internationalist and more idealistic than their counterparts in the United Kingdom, partly no doubt because geographical security supplemented by the protection of a mighty neighbour stimulated a more uncompromising fundamentalism. Again, while history and their existing circumstances prompted Afrikaners and Irishmen to recommend the undeviating application of the principle of national self-determination as a solvent for the tensions of Central Europe, there was also a large body of opinion in the United Kingdom which advocated a revision of the Versailles settlement in accordance with this principle, even after the rise of Hitler to power. It was naturally in the predominantly British dominions of the Pacific that the trends of individual opinion and party policies most closely coincided with those in Britain, but generally the climate of opinion on international affairs throughout the Commonwealth showed differences in emphasis rather than any fundamental differences in approach. The lines of division between internationalists and imperialists were horizontal, not vertical.

The idealism of the early inter-war years had another important consequence for the Commonwealth countries. It encouraged them to believe, first that there would be no more major wars and then, when that belief could no longer be entertained, to imagine that the League of Nations could preserve peace without necessarily imposing exacting obligations upon its members. This conviction coincided with the desire, most pronounced among the nationally self-conscious dominions, to build up the League as an object of loyalty in the supra-national field which could be used as a counterweight to the hitherto exclusive loyalty to the Commonwealth. Membership of the League was thus for the dominions at once the symbol of their aspirations towards a world order and a satisfying hall-mark of their fully autonomous status. Just because it fulfilled so many of their needs in the international field, there was great reluctance to recognize the decline in its authority or, after 1935, to acknowledge its failure. When that failure could be disguised no longer, the disillusion among those who had aimed at a policy firmly based on principle was so great that many of the most ardent internationalists sought a temporary refuge in isolationism. In Canada, in South Africa, and even in Australia it was not impossible to cherish a belief that isolation presented an alternative to collective security. In this way, first the faith in the ability of the League to prevent war, and then the reaction when that faith was destroyed, led to a neglect of strategic considerations at a time when new methods of warfare endangered the security of the Empire as it had not been endangered since its foundation.

THE CHALLENGE TO SEA POWER

In the inter-war years the countries of the British Commonwealth were profoundly pacific in outlook. Hitler, who never doubted this, argued that it was to be attributed to satiety and decadence. The Commonwealth, he said, had no territorial ambitions in the twentieth century because they had all been fulfilled, and more than fulfilled, in the preceding three hundred years. Having acquired a spacious place in the sun by a nauseous mixture of force and hypocrisy, Britain was now concerned to retain with pious, pacific platitudes what her people could no longer defend by force of arms.[1] The theme was not unfamiliar. In more flamboyant but less strident tones it had been voiced by the Kaiser Wilhelm II, and a century earlier by the great Napoleon whose contempt for 'a nation of shopkeepers' has remained an integral part of the outlook of European militarists.[2] Hitler's (and Mussolini's) violent reassertion of distorted though not unfamiliar half-truths made little impression within the Commonwealth except to stimulate anxiety that the former German colonies, wrested from her at Versailles, should be restored as soon as possible in order to remove all ground for legitimate grievance. What was not clearly recognized was that the challenge of the Axis Powers to the British Commonwealth acquired its deadly menace from an intuitive and only partially formulated premise which neither the Kaiser nor Napoleon could reasonably have entertained. This premise was that the influence of sea power on history had passed its zenith and was declining rapidly and the conclusion derived from it was that German air and land supremacy sufficed to conquer the world.

The British Empire had been built upon sea power. In the nineteenth century the unchallenged supremacy of the Royal Navy, used for no aggressive purposes, was at once a sure protection for Britain's overseas Empire and a guarantee of security to large areas of the world outside.[3] Even by the close of the century the Kaiser's Germany, predominant in Europe, could not intervene in South Africa because the Royal Navy guarded the seas. It was indeed from that bitter experience that von Tirpitz derived his most telling argument for the building of a German high seas fleet. Germany must build, he told his imperial master, 'unless she is prepared hereafter to go the way of renunciation' and to leave the colonial field 'to the Anglo-Saxons and to the sons of Jehovah'.[4]

Since the close of the century two things diminished British security. The first was the relative decline in the power of the Royal Navy itself. In the face of the Japanese and German naval construction, and the parallel and astonishing growth of American naval strength, the two-Power standard could no longer be maintained. Of that the Japanese Alliance of 1902 was the first

[1] See *Mein Kampf*.

[2] A writer in the *Berliner Tageblatt* of 20 August 1938 observed: 'If the French Empire resembles a collection of military barracks that of England is a mixture of wholesale shops and schools.'

[3] cf. G. S. Graham, 'The Foundations of Imperial History', *Canadian Historical Review*, June 1950.

[4] A. von Tirpitz, *My Memoirs* (London, Hurst & Blackett, 1919) vol. 1, p 67.

implicit admission. Britain unaided could no longer patrol the Seven Seas. Yet this relative decline, whose consequences were mitigated for some twenty years by the Anglo-Japanese Alliance, was not in itself disastrous. Britain was replaced as the greatest naval Power, not by a European Power traditionally envious of her vast overseas possessions, but by the United States of America who cast, it is true, no approving eyes upon colonialism but with whom, none the less, 'war was unthinkable'.[1] Here indeed was a striking vindication of Bismarck's insight in discerning so early that the most important fact in the modern world was that the language of the United States was English. Had it been possible in 1921 to reconcile America to the renewal of the Anglo-Japanese Alliance, the security of the Commonwealth from attack by sea would have remained virtually unimpaired. But despite the bluntly expressed anxieties of the Australian Prime Minister Mr. W. M. Hughes, lest a failure to renew the Alliance would leave the Pacific vulnerable to Japanese aggression at a time of tension or war in Europe,[2] Canadian opposition to renewal decided the Commonwealth in favour of the American point of view.[3] There is no doubt, whatever the merits of the argument, that as a result the security of the Commonwealth, particularly in the Pacific, was sensibly diminished after 1921.

It has been remarked that war between the Commonwealth and the United States was unthinkable, but so long as their friendship could be correctly described in these negative terms, so long did the security of the Commonwealth without a first-class naval ally depend upon the ability of the Royal Navy to maintain a two-ocean fleet capable of maintaining its supremacy in war in the Atlantic and in the Pacific simultaneously. Could so formidable a duty be successfully discharged in the face of German naval rearmament, of vaunting Italian aspirations to control the Mediterranean, and of Japan's undisguised resolve to seize the first favourable moment to embark on a career of large-scale conquest in the Far East? That was the potential challenge arising from the relative decline in the power of the Royal Navy, which was of critical importance to the Commonwealth as a whole before the war, though it did not confront Canada or South Africa with the same directness as it faced the United Kingdom, Australia, and New Zealand. Its existence deprived British policy as a whole in Asia, as in Europe, of some of that freedom of manœuvre which it had enjoyed before 1914. For, corresponding with the decline in security, and deriving from it, was a decline in the capacity to influence the course of

[1] The phrase was used by Mr. W. M. Hughes, 20 June 1921, see Keith, *Speeches and Documents*, p. 49.

[2] 'I am strongly in favour of its [the Treaty] being renewed', said Mr. Hughes. . . . 'Should we not be in a better position to exercise greater influence over Eastern policy as an ally of that great Eastern Power, than as her potential enemy? . . . We will do well for the world's peace—we will do well for China—we will do well for the Commonwealth of British nations to renew this Treaty' (Keith, *Speeches and Documents*, p. 49).

[3] For a concise account of Canadian Policy see Glazebrook, *Canadian External Relations*, pp. 350–2.

events; or, to put it in another way, the contribution which the British Empire could make towards the maintenance of peace in a world in which the United States, her natural ally, remained isolationist, was imperceptibly, but none the less sensibly, diminished by the decline in her naval power.

The relative decline in British naval power since 1900 was due mainly to factors outside the control of the United Kingdom or indeed of the Commonwealth as a whole. Here the industrialization of Germany and Japan and the United States was fundamental. As the Great Powers became greater, the resources of a small island state whose economic strength was conditional upon favourable and, as it was to prove, transient economic circumstances, were wholly unequal in themselves to maintaining its naval strength at the level sufficient to safeguard its imperial interests throughout the world. Nor could any substantial reinforcement be expected from the overseas Empire, for, on grounds of policy, or in some cases of necessity, its resources were committed almost wholly to local defence until 1939. In these circumstances, while naval disarmament further narrowed the margin of safety without correspondingly reducing the risks, it is well to note that no conceivable measure of rearmament could have restored that measure of security which the British Empire overseas enjoyed until 1914.[1] Indeed there was only one way in which that could have been done in the world of the nineteen-thirties, and that was by assured co-operation between the navies of the United States and the British Commonwealth of Nations in the event of open aggression leading to a large-scale war.

Less tangible than the relative decline of the Royal Navy between 1900 and 1939, but of even greater importance for the future of the Commonwealth, was the decline in the influence of surface sea power itself. For some four hundred years sea power had been the decisive factor in the making of history. But in the second quarter of the twentieth century was not the balance being redressed at last? By 1939 air power was still in buoyant infancy. Astonishing as were the achievements to its credit, they were clearly only a foretaste of what was yet to come. Already it had deprived sea power of some of its short-range protective value. For Britain this was immensely important. Mr. Baldwin had earlier recognized that her strategic frontiers had moved back from the Low Countries to the Rhine, and even if those frontiers could be held, the heart of the Empire would still be exposed to a direct assault from

[1] This conclusion should perhaps be modified in one respect. Had British scientific resources been consistently devoted to the production of really effective anti-submarine weapons the naval challenge of Germany could never have assumed so deadly a form in 1941. But we know, on the authority of the American scientist Dr. Vannevar Bush, that despite the development in naval laboratories both in the United States and the United Kingdom of the very important means of submarine detection called 'asdic' at the time, and later 'sonar', the democratic world for a second time entered a major war underestimating the power of the submarine. In 1914 the power of the submarine came as a surprise; in 1939 there was over-confidence in the weapons developed to deal with it. See Vannevar Bush, *Modern Arms and Free Men* (New York, Simon & Schuster, 1949) Chapter VII.

which command of the narrow seas had safeguarded her for so long. The bomber would always get through.[1]

For the Commonwealth overseas the increasing vulnerability of the centre was in itself a matter of concern. But on a broad view even more important was the likely effect of air power co-operating with the submarine on those long and lightly defended lines of sea communication which were the arteries of Empire. Here the introduction of a comparatively new weapon in warfare instilled in the minds of Empire statesmen, already conscious of the decline in the relative strength of British naval power, the need for caution. It is a wise maxim of diplomacy that policy should not be allowed to outrun the strength that backs it. Before 1939 the existence of unknown factors, likely to make more difficult the defence of a scattered Empire hitherto dependent upon sea communications, strongly predisposed British statesmen to cautious policies. Some might argue that the coming of air warfare on a larger scale would not sensibly diminish the security of the Commonwealth, but about that there could be no assurance till the test of harsh experience came. All that was certain was that another world war would provide object lessons in the use of air power as striking as that which von Tirpitz learned about the use of sea power from German inability to intervene in South Africa at the close of the nineteenth century.

THE CONSEQUENCES OF DOMINION AUTONOMY IN EXTERNAL POLICY

If the uncertainty about the effect of new weapons of warfare was a major consideration in the approach of the United Kingdom government to the mounting tension in Europe and in the Far East, this was by no means the only uncertainty with which they were confronted. By 1936 it was still convenient, but no longer accurate, to write of an imperial or Commonwealth foreign or defence policy. There was no longer a common policy; the Commonwealth was an association of autonomous states each of whom was separately responsible for the making if its own policies. It is true that the United Kingdom remained the predominant partner both in influence and in actual power; she retained in her own hands full responsibility for the government and administration of the dependent colonial Empire, and she was also ultimately responsible for the defence and foreign policy of Burma and of her great Empire in India. But in external as in internal affairs the self-government of the dominions, that is to say, of Canada, Australia, New Zealand, South Africa, and the Irish Free State, was a reality. It was their freedom of action, newly acquired and hitherto untried, in a major international crisis that added a second imponderable which had to be weighed in the making of United Kingdom policy. At the Imperial Conference of 1911 Mr. Asquith's

[1] The phrase was used by Mr. Baldwin on 10 November 1932, H. of C. Deb., vol. 270, col. 632.

language revealed his clear understanding of the direction of Commonwealth development: '. . . we each of us are, and we each of us intend to remain, master in our own household. This is . . . the life-blood of our polity.'[1] Yet it was he also who stated categorically that high policy—foreign policy in supreme issues affecting all the members of the Empire—remained and must remain exclusively in the control of the United Kingdom cabinet. 'That authority', said Mr. Asquith in 1911, 'cannot be shared.' By 1936 it was being shared. That was the great difference between the Empire as it existed three years before the First World War and the Commonwealth three years before the Second. In the intervening quarter of a century the principle of separate responsibility had been established beyond dispute. But how would it be applied when tested by 'a supreme issue'? That was a delicate question within the Commonwealth in the pre-war years and its general implications may usefully be noted at this stage.

The United Kingdom, both as a European and as a world Power, could not escape the consequences of her position. She was bound to be involved in any major war arising out of Axis aggression in Europe or Japanese expansionist policies in Asia. Yet it was all important that she should not become involved in such a war without dominion support. Here their separate responsibility for policy produced a very proper concern in London that the cause of the outbreak of war should commend itself to all, or at least to the great majority, of the dominions. In itself this was no bad thing. It might at other times have acted as a prudent check upon quixotic impetuosity, but at this particular period when Whitehall was neither quixotic nor impetuous its effect, in so far as it was felt, was almost wholly negative—even to the point of providing an excuse for inactivity or lack of policy. Nor was the temptation to attribute responsibility for a paralysis of will in London to the inexperience or the obstinate isolationism of the dominion governments at all times firmly resisted.

In the past the great protagonists of the decentralization of the Commonwealth had proclaimed their confident conviction that the equality and autonomy of the dominions would constitute a solid foundation for Commonwealth unity. Yet even if this faith were to prove wholly justified, unity founded upon equality and freedom, unlike unity imposed from above, could never be assumed. It could arise only from a coincidence in aim and policy, and that coincidence could derive only from a unity of wills. For this reason the outlook of the dominions, their approach to international and imperial affairs, assumed in the later nineteen-thirties an importance it had not hitherto possessed. How did the dominions propose to exercise in practice the responsibilities they had lately acquired? On what lines, in the light of what dominant considerations, were their policies likely to be formulated? How would they relate equality to unity? These all-important questions are later considered in relation to the individual member-nations of the Common-

[1] Cd. 5745, quoted in Hancock, *Survey*, vol. 1, p. 3.

wealth; here it is in place only to set out some of the broad considerations which influenced the general approach of the dominions to international and particularly European politics.

In 1937 the self-governing dominions of the British Commonwealth of Nations, Canada, Australia, New Zealand, South Africa, the Irish Free State were, with the one exception of the Irish Free State, extra-European countries with no intimate knowledge of the stormy background of European countries. With the one exception of South Africa they were, however, predominantly European in origin and culture, and even in South Africa the European minority enjoyed a virtual monopoly of political power. Geographically far removed from Europe, but racially and spiritually akin to it, this inner conflict was reflected in a certain disequilibrium in their external policies. Alternately attracted and repelled by the troubles of Europe they could embrace wholeheartedly neither the isolationism of the Americas nor the full responsibilities of intervention. Moreover, quite apart from the inner conflict, neither extreme was well suited to their particular circumstances. They were all middle or small Powers and as such their attitude was faithfully reflected by Mr. C. J. Doherty, Canadian delegate to the First Assembly of the League, when he said: 'Let the mighty, if they will, guarantee the security of the weak' but let them not ask for reciprocal guarantees from 'young and undeveloped states' for whom the burden would be disproportionaly great.[1] At the same time through their membership of the Commonwealth the dominions were in a position to exert indirectly a greater influence in Europe than any other middle Powers outside the Continent. In theory, if not always in practice, they enjoyed the opportunity of expressing their views on the foreign policy of one of the Great Powers, the United Kingdom, while it was still in the making, and since the United Kingdom was a European Power effective, if concealed, dominion intervention in European affairs was thereby made possible.

The United Kingdom's dual position as a European Power and as an island state which was the heart of a great overseas Empire, confronted her statesmen at all times with the need for reconciling her continental and her maritime interests. Her geographical situation had decreed that she should fill an essentially balancing position between Europe and the world overseas, and the implications of it could be disregarded only at her peril. 'The general character of England's foreign policy', wrote Sir Eyre Crowe in his classic memorandum of January 1907, 'is determined by the immutable conditions of her geographical situation on the ocean flank of Europe as an island State with vast oversea colonies and dependencies, whose existence and survival as an independent community are inseparably bound up with the possession of

[1] League of Nations, Committee on Amendments to the Covenant, *Memorandum Submitted by the Canadian Delegation* (C. 215, M. 154, 1921, reprinted in Glazebrook, *Canadian External Relations*, Appendix C).

preponderant sea power.'[1] The attainment of self-government by the dominions introduced a new and complicating factor, for thereafter the United Kingdom, while still controlling the policies of its colonial territories, no longer decided those of the greater colonies which had since become dominions. Yet the sharing of responsibilities did not alter their character. The twin purposes of Britain's policy in 1937, as in 1907, remained the safeguarding of her position in Europe by ensuring at the least that neither the Low Countries nor France were controlled by an unfriendly Power, and by ensuring the safety and well-being of the Empire overseas. Neither could be neglected with impunity, and so long as the United Kingdom remained the predominant partner in the Commonwealth both were of direct concern to all its members. By 1937 the task of the United Kingdom government was, therefore, first to reconcile its sometimes conflicting responsibilities in Europe and in the Empire overseas to its own satisfaction and then, over and above that, to satisfy dominion statesmen that these responsibilities were being wisely reconciled from the point of view of their own several interests. It was a task the inherent difficulty of which, at a time of mounting international tension, was often accentuated by the placing of Britain's European and extra-European responsibilities in unreal anatagonism. Between the imperialist isolationists of the nineteen-thirties on the one hand, who saw salvation in a close knit self-sufficing Empire free from compromising continental entanglements,[2] and on the other, pan-Europeans oblivious of all that lay outside the frontiers of the old world, the United Kingdom government had to chart, with deviations now to the one side and now to the other, that middle course which its geographical situation had imposed upon it. In the redefining of this course dominion attitudes were important.

DOMINION DISLIKE OF COMMON POLICIES

The dominions for the most part deliberately refrained from taking full advantage of their opportunities for influencing United Kingdom foreign policy, and as a result it is not easy to assess its possible extent had their aim been more positive. What evidence there is suggests that, while it was comparatively easy for the dominion governments to exert a negative, restraining influence on United Kingdom policy, they would have had no small difficulty

[1] Memorandum on the present state of British Relations with France and Germany, in G. P. Gooch and H. Temperley, eds., *British Documents on the Origins of the War, 1898–1914* (London, H.M.S.O., 1926–38) vol. 3, p. 402.

[2] In 1936 Mr. Amery, for example, suggested that with a view to a 'peaceful reorganization of continental Europe based on the fully recognized equality of . . . Germany, France, and Italy' Great Britain should 'make it clear beyond doubt, not only to Germany but also to France, that we shall have no part in, and afford no encouragement to, any outside intervention in a Russo-German quarrel'. Such an assurance coupled with proposals for a 'European Ottawa' would, he believed, have satisfied Germany and incidentally enabled Britain to detach herself in large measure from European affairs. See *The Times*, 23 and 30 October 1936.

in persuading the United Kingdom to embark on new or unknown paths. The weight of knowledge, the fruits of long experience lay, all too heavily some dominion critics felt, with the Foreign Office, and so long at least as dominion representation in foreign countries was on a trifling scale, it was difficult to persuade the United Kingdom to take positive action against her own inclination. But while this is the only conclusion to be drawn from the evidence that is available, it is to be noted that there appears to have been no occasion on which all the dominion governments advocated a policy other than that which the United Kingdom government proposed to pursue.[1] In any event the all important factor in the determination of the external policies of the Commonwealth countries in the period under review was not the modest extent of dominion influence but the reluctance of the dominions to assume active obligations in any region geographically remote from them.

In the past it had been supposed that once the overseas dominions had acquired equality of status with the United Kingdom they would take advantage of the opportunities thereby afforded to them in order to redefine United Kingdom policies in accordance with their own outlook and interests. But this supposition proved to be almost wholly unfounded before 1939. New Zealand and Australia, it is true, tried intermittently to bring United Kingdom policies more into line with their own ideas, but Canada, South Africa, and the Irish Free State adopted an attitude of more distant reserve. All recognized that effective influence on United Kingdom policy could not be divorced from some degree of positive responsibility; and of positive responsibilities in Europe the dominions were exceedingly shy. Much concerned to give substance to their autonomous status, they felt that this could best be done not by their influencing as equal partners the policies of the United Kingdom, but by accepting no responsibility for them. The ideal of an imperial diplomatic unity deriving from an ever-expanding measure of joint responsibility for policy on the part of all the self-governing members of the Commonwealth which had been so fashionable in the closing years of the First World War, melted away in the cooler, more critical temper[2] of the post-war years. Indeed as the pendulum swung back sharply from imperial unity to the older tradition of dominion autonomy,[3] there arose in most parts of the Commonwealth a pronounced antagonism to the very conception of a common foreign policy. The phrase, like the terms 'specific commitment' and 'centralization' usually associated with it, acquired a wholly opprobrious connotation in the doxology

[1] Opinion was divided on the wisdom of renewing the Anglo-Japanese Alliance in 1921 when Canadian views certainly influenced United Kingdom policy. See also Glazebrook, *Canadian External Relations*, pp. 356 ff.

[2] cf. Hancock, *Survey*, vol. 1, pp. 267 ff.

[3] Mr. Mackenzie King, its principal protagonist, believed that he was carrying on the policy of Sir Wilfrid Laurier, and his deputy minister, Dr. O. D. Skelton, the biographer of Laurier, shared this belief. During their brief interlude of office the Conservatives, under Mr. R. B. Bennett, discarded this reserved attitude towards imperial co-operation in word though not always in deed. They, too, had to take into account the temper of the times.

of Commonwealth relations. This was as much a psychological as a rational reaction. Whether it was wise or unwise can be judged only when the part played by the Commonwealth in the pre-war years has been told, but the fact that such was the predominant attitude in the overseas dominions is a matter of cardinal importance, essential to any appreciation of their influence on United Kingdom policies.

The profound aversion of the majority of the dominions to a common imperial policy was most emphatically asserted in relation to Europe because it was in a Europe of which Britain was a part that the consequences of its adoption were likely to be most far-reaching. But dominion dislike of a common policy was not geographically restricted. In principle and in application it had no geographical limitation. Nor was it related to the merits of the policies which Britain pursued. The dominions fully recognized, for example, that Britain's traditional anxiety to ensure that the Low Countries were not controlled by an unfriendly Power was in their interests almost as much as her own. But that did not predispose them towards accepting common responsibilities in Western Europe. Just as common policies were believed to imply subordination, so freedom from commitments was felt to carry an incontrovertible assurance of the ending of colonialism and the assumption of the full responsibilities of independent nationhood.

The illusion persisted, especially among those to whom this dominion approach to foreign affairs was unpalatable, that improvements in machinery would suffice to modify dominion dislike of common imperial policies. It was, so the argument ran, because the dominions had little part in the making of policies that they declined to be committed to them. But once assured of an effective voice in the shaping of policy would not their attitude be very different? On this point Mr. Lloyd George had felt few doubts after the First World War. In December 1921, in outlining the meaning of dominion status in the debate on the Irish Treaty, he told the House of Commons that the foreign policy of Great Britain would henceforward be the joint foreign policy of the British Empire. While the Foreign Office he said, would inevitably remain the instrument of that policy, all the dominions would combine with Great Britain in controlling it. From this premise he advanced to spacious and invigorating conclusions:

> The advantage to us is that joint control means joint responsibility and when the burden of Empire has become so vast it is well that we should have the shoulders of these young giants to help us along. It introduces a broader and calmer view into foreign policy. It restrains rash ministers and will stimulate timorous ones. It widens the prospect.[1]

But the 'young giants' were not enthusiastic about this widening prospect. They might have argued, cogently enough, that while science had to its credit

[1] 14 December 1921, H. of C. Deb., vol. 149, col. 30, quoted in Hancock, *Survey*, vol. 1, p. 251.

many triumphs the elimination of distance was not among them. Speed in telegraphic communications made rapid consultation easy but it provided only the appearances of a solution to the problem of joint control. Here in the last analysis must not, and did not, final authority always rest with the man on the spot? Events lent substance to such doubts. The determination of policy at critical moments did not wait upon the expression of the views of five cabinets in five widely scattered capitals. But as the Chanak crisis and the Locarno treaty, those two landmarks in the evolution of dominion external policies, so clearly demonstrated this practical difficulty was important but not fundamental.

FROM CHANAK TO LOCARNO

It was in September 1922 that Mr. Lloyd George made his dramatic appeal to the dominion governments to support United Kingdom policy in the Middle East.[1] They had had no voice in the determination of this policy and the appeal from London was their first intimation that they might be called upon to back it by force of arms. The New Zealand government responded enthusiastically,[2] Australia, while resentful of the brusqueness of the invitation, replied in the affirmative, but Canada, followed by South Africa, reminded Mr. Lloyd George in friendly but uncompromising terms of the overriding responsibility of their respective Parliaments. The issue of peace or war, asserted the Canadian Prime Minister, could be decided for Canada only after the Canadian cabinet had had a full opportunity of considering the issues involved and submitting them if need be to the final judgement of the Canadian Parliament. '. . . it is neither right nor proper', declared Mr. Mackenzie King, 'for any individual or for any group of individuals to take any step which in any way might limit the rights of Parliament in a matter which is of such great concern to all the people of our country'.[3]

The attitude of Mr. Mackenzie King's Liberal government in the Chanak crisis remains of outstanding importance in the history of Commonwealth relations. The contention that the parliament of a dominion alone could decide the issue of peace or war explicitly asserted ultimate dominion sovereignty in the field of foreign affairs. In so doing it implicitly but fundament-

[1] For a full account see Hancock, *Survey*, vol. 1, pp. 251 ff., and also P. J. Noel Baker, *The Present Juridical Status of the British Dominions in International Law* (London, Longmans, Green, 1929) pp. 60 ff., and Keith, *Speeches and Documents*, pp. 367 ff.

[2] Some commentators would seem to have attached undue importance to the promptness of the New Zealand reply. It would seem that Mr. Lloyd George's telegram happened to arrive when the members of the New Zealand cabinet were gathered together for some festive occasion, and they decided to deal with it immediately. The Labour opposition disapproved of the unreserved commitment into which they entered. See *J.P.E.*, 1923, pp. 140–1.

[3] 1 February 1923, Canada, H. of C. Deb., 1923, vol. 1, p. 33. For a carefully documented account of the crisis see Gwendolen Carter, *The British Commonwealth and International Security* (Toronto, Ryerson Press, for Canadian Institute of International Affairs, 1947) pp. 84 ff. For an account of the Canadian viewpoint see Glazebrook, *Canadian External Relations*, pp. 358–60.

ally challenged the conception of an imperial foreign policy to which the experience of the later war years had given some substance and upon which Mr. Lloyd George relied in 1922. It challenged such a conception, moreover, not on grounds of practicability, but on grounds of principle. After all, had Mr. Mackenzie King wished to justify the negative Canadian response to Mr. Lloyd George's appeal for joint action by reference to the obvious breakdown of any semblance of joint control, he could have found no better opportunity for doing so. He could have argued that no self-governing state could accept part responsibility for the consequences of policies over whose making or execution it enjoyed no effective measure of control. But one logical conclusion to such criticism would have been that joint control over common policies must be made effective, and that was not a conclusion acceptable to the Canadian government. They were not concerned to establish the effectiveness of joint control over common imperial policies because they did not want imperial policies. On the contrary it was their predominant concern in 1922, and later, to disentangle their external policies from the broad pattern of imperial foreign policy. It was because this was so that Mr. Mackenzie King at all times emphasized the final authority of the Canadian Parliament, not in general, but in specific terms, maintaining that Parliament itself must decide on every major issue of foreign policy.[1] In this view South Africa generally and the Irish Free State by particular constitutional provision[2] concurred, while Australia moved by easy stages towards an acceptance of it. It was because the majority of the dominions did not want a common imperial foreign policy that recurrent proposals for the creation of machinery, whether in the form of an imperial council or an imperial secretariat working to the Imperial Conference, had no prospect of general acceptance. They were all designed to serve ends to which the majority of the dominion governments were firmly opposed.[3]

In the immediately succeeding years there arose disputes on nice points of procedure and refinements about the degrees of responsibility involved in the negotiation or the signature of treaties.[4] Behind them lay the fundamental problems of unity and freedom. Was the pursuit of separate foreign policies consistent with imperial unity? Did it not undermine imperial security and

[1] This was not the view of the Conservative opposition. Mr. Meighen declared that Mr. Mackenzie King should have replied to Mr. Lloyd George's appeal, 'Ready, aye, ready, we stand by you'. Quoted in Glazebrook, op. cit. p. 359

[2] Article 49 of the Constitution of the Irish Free State declared: 'Save in the case of actual invasion, the Irish Free State shall not be committed to active participation in any war without the assent of the Oireachtas.'

[3] cf. Hancock, *Survey*, vol. 1, p. 254. Cmd. 1987 contains a clear and instructive statement of the principles governing the relations of the various parts of the Empire in the negotiation, signature, and ratification of treaties, pp. 13–15.

[4] The Peace Treaty with Turkey is the outstanding example. See Hancock, *Survey*, vol. 1, pp. 253 ff., and Cmd. 2146 (1924), *Correspondence on the Subject of the Peace Settlement with Turkey*.

the authority of the Empire in the world at large? These were questions, anxiously debated, which continued in one form or another to constitute the dominant theme in all discussions on the role of the Commonwealth in world affairs till 1939;[1] though even by the outbreak of war the evidence allowed only of tentative answers to them.

The assertion of individual responsibility in principle did not for some time to come mean any great change in practice. It did, however, bring to the surface questions which would one day have to be resolved. It would have been easy to interpret the assertion of the principle as an indication that the dominions intended to pursue then and there foreign policies that diverged from, or even conflicted with, those of the United Kingdom. But this would have been incorrect. The general intention of the dominions was more negative. They wished to establish their right to pursue individual policies in order primarily to ensure that their agreement with United Kingdom policies should not be presumed.[2] They did not wish to depart from her policies in principle, still less to dissociate themselves from the United Kingdom on any major issue of common interest. At the same time the long-term significance of the dominions' assumption of responsibility for the conduct of foreign affairs was clearly not to be measured by its immediate consequences, and it was with these long-term implications that the United Kingdom was profoundly concerned.

The element of uncertainty imparted by separate dominion control over external policy could not be viewed altogether without misgiving in London, and as a result the search for some practical and generally acceptable way of co-ordinating external policies was not relaxed. Yet it was by no means easy to prescribe any satisfactory method. Even if Mr. Mackenzie King had not, for good reasons of his own, underlined the failure of the dominions to contribute to the shaping of policy in 1922, the fact remained that they had not had an opportunity of doing so. As long as the so-called Imperial War Cabinet[3] had continued in existence, it was possible to think realistically of a joint agreement reached by representatives of all the Commonwealth countries on the foreign policies of the Commonwealth. But once this symbol of war-time unity had dissolved under pressure of centrifugal forces there seemed no prospect of reconstituting a body, which might inherit some of its responsibilities in the field of foreign affairs, with the agreement of all members of the Commonwealth. As a result even the co-ordination of separate policies

[1] See *B.C.R. Conference*, 1933, pp. 163 ff., and 1938, pp. 264 ff.

[2] Professor Glazebrook observes: 'Canada's insistence on full rights in the League . . . was so coloured by the ambition to secure thereby recognition of status that the decision on acceptance of the Covenant was at least as much influenced by constitutional growth as by belief in the merits of the plan as such' (*Canadian External Relations*, p. 370). This is equally true in the case of South Africa and the Irish Free State.

[3] It was not a cabinet in the strict sense of the term because it was not collectively responsible to any one parliament.

through consultation between governments continued to present many of those practical difficulties which had confronted Mr. Lloyd George in 1922 in the pursuit of his more ambitious aim of a common imperial policy. The need for inter-governmental consultation between capitals meant that the forming of United Kingdom policies had to wait upon the elucidation and co-ordination of the views of six cabinets. For a Great Power close to the undying antagonisms of post-war Europe such protracted deliberations preliminary to the formulation of policy might well prove intolerable. Of that no one was more conscious than Sir Austen Chamberlain. It was impossible, he said in the debate on the Locarno treaty, to wait on the dominions.

> ... the affairs of the world do not stand still.... I could not go, as the representative of His Majesty's government, to meeting after meeting of the League of Nations, to conference after conference with the representatives of foreign countries, and say, 'Great Britain is without a policy. We have not been able to meet all the governments of the Empire, and we can do nothing.' That might be possible for an Empire wholly removed from Europe, which existed in a different hemisphere. It was not possible for an Empire the heart of which lies in Europe, ... and where every peril to the peace of Europe jeopardized the peace of this country.[1]

What Sir Austen Chamberlain said was tantamount to an admission that United Kingdom policy could not represent the formally co-ordinated views of all the countries of the Commonwealth but must be itself an individual policy. It was no doubt framed in the light of known dominion views, but it could not at critical times await their formulation. The attitude of some dominions and the absence of imperial machinery for the co-ordination of policies meant that the aim could be no more than the securing of the widest possible unity in foreign policy. It was only with the passage of time that it came to be realized that this modest yet practical objective to be achieved mainly through informal but constant consultation had many positive virtues to recommend it, not least among them being its conformity with the spirit of the Commonwealth itself. It is in the light of this new realistic approach that the precedent established at Locarno in 1925 and consistently adhered to by dominion governments in later years assumes its full significance.

Article 9 of the Locarno[2] pact stated that: 'The present Treaty shall impose no obligation upon any of the British Dominions, or upon India, unless the Government of such Dominion, or of India signifies its acceptance thereof.' None did so. Their inaction is not to be attributed to doubts about the value or the timeliness of this attempt to build up a system of regional security in Western Europe. On the contrary, the dominion representatives approved the policy which the United Kingdom had pursued, and the Report of the

[1] 18 November 1925, H. of C. Deb., vol. 188, coll. 520–1, quoted in Hancock, *Survey*, vol. 1, p. 260.

[2] For a general account of the negotiation and terms of the Treaty see G. M. Gathorne-Hardy, *A Short History of International Affairs*, 2nd ed. (London, Oxford University Press, for Royal Institute of International Affairs, 1938) pp. 63 ff.

Imperial Conference of 1926 records that 'from the standpoint of all the dominions and of India, there was complete approval of the manner in which the negotiations had been conducted and brought to so successful a conclusion',[1] and the Conference formally congratulated His Majesty's government in Great Britain on its share in this successful contribution towards the promotion of the peace of the world.[2] Dominion inaction at Locarno is, therefore, rightly to be interpreted as evidence of their resolve to keep their hands free. However much they might sympathize with the general aims of United Kingdom policy, they did not wish to bind themselves by underwriting the particular obligations into which she entered.[3] They did not consider that this was their duty or responsibility, and since their attitude in 1925 proved to be no passing phenomenon, dominion inaction at Locarno later came to be regarded, and rightly regarded, as an historic landmark in the evolution of their external policies. The precedent established in 1925 was followed with remarkable consistency up to the outbreak of the Second World War. In 1939 none of the dominions had any major treaty obligations in Europe or in Asia.

THE LESSONS OF LOCARNO

There was at least a superficial contradiction between a restrictive interpretation of the principle of separate responsibility in foreign policy expressed in the policy of no active commitments and the sense of common interest and common purpose uniting the Commonwealth. Yet neither the insistence of the dominions that ultimate responsibility in foreign policy rested with their individual parliaments, nor their aversion to commitments implied any lack of awareness that their interests were ultimately bound up with those of the United Kingdom. They well knew that they could not, even had they so wished, escape from the consequences of her policies, and the fact that they assumed no obligations under the Locarno treaty did not mean that they considered the pact to be merely of local concern to the United Kingdom. On the contrary they recognized that the fulfilment of United Kingdom obligations under the Locarno pact might at any time confront them with the issue of peace or war, just as they were in fact confronted with it as a result of the Polish Guarantee in 1939, to which likewise they had not subscribed. 'While we may not have anything to do with the treaty by express declaration,' commented Mr. Stanley Bruce in the Australian House of Representatives, 'we cannot escape from its con-

[1] Cmd. 2768, p. 28.

[2] For an analysis of the implications of their attitude see Carter, *British Commonwealth*, pp. 92–96.

[3] It is worth noting that it was not necessarily confined to commitments of an imperial character. In 1924 the enthusiasm of the first Labour government in the United Kingdom to close 'the gap in the Covenant' of the League by means of the Geneva Protocol elicited criticism from the dominions as stringent as any evoked by the prospect of being drawn into exclusively imperial obligations.

sequences should the malice of circumstances bring it into operation, otherwise than by leaving the Empire. . . .'[1] Since this view commanded general assent, the interest of the dominions in the course of United Kingdom policy in Europe was not in question. But it found expression outside the field of formal written obligation.

Between 1925 and 1939 the dominions recognized that the United Kingdom, the predominant partner in the Commonwealth, had direct and vital responsibilities in Europe. They were profoundly concerned with the direction and the outcome of her European policies; they welcomed the opportunities open to them as members of the Commonwealth for influencing those policies in the formative stage; but they were insistent that neither their concern nor the expression of their views involved any positive commitment on their part. That could be assumed only at their own specific request in accordance with the accepted doctrine that no member of the Commonwealth could impose any obligation on any other member. In practice the experience of Locarno made it plain that dominion governments would not desire formally to underwrite obligations in Europe even if they strongly approved of the cause they were intended to serve. For this there were many reasons: Europe was an unsatisfactory continent, a prey to reactionary militarists or revolutionary Communists, and it was highly undesirable for distant dominions to be intimately involved in affairs of which they lacked a sufficient knowledge to steer a safe course.

You may say [observed Mr. Newton Rowell, Canadian delegate to the First Assembly of the League] that we should have confidence in European statesmen and leaders. Perhaps we should, but it was European policy, European statesmanship, European ambition that drenched the world with blood and from which we are still suffering and will suffer for generations. Fifty thousand Canadians under the soil of France and Flanders is what Canada has paid for European statesmanship trying to settle European problems. I place the responsibility on a few: I would not distribute it over many; but nevertheless it is European.[2]

This was commendable frankness. The record of Europe did not inspire confidence overseas, and lack of confidence powerfully reinforced the arguments for a policy of cautious detachment. Nor was the Foreign Office itself above suspicion. High-minded dominions had no wish to become entangled in the web of its complex diplomatic activities. Mistrust of European politics on the part of idealists was strongly reinforced by isolationist, nationalist sentiment in Canada, South Africa, and the Irish Free State. But however important all this may have been in the 1920s and early 1930s it was not fundamental. Behind it lay the more settled conviction that while the interests of Britain in Europe were direct, the interests of the dominions

[1] See *J.P.E.*, 1926, vol. 7, p. 826.
[2] League of Nations, *Plenary Meetings*, 1st Assembly, 8 December 1920.

were indirect. Geographical situation made it appropriate and necessary for the United Kingdom to assume specific obligations in Europe and made it equally inappropriate for the dominions to do so. In this there is to be detected a disposition on the part of the dominions towards the application of a Monroe doctrine in reverse, with its corollary of a restrictive regional approach to international affairs.

CONSULTATION AND THE MACHINERY FOR ITS CONDUCT

Dominion detachment from Europe did not imply indifference to European affairs. Nor did it necessarily detract from the unity of the Commonwealth in external policy. Co-ordinated Commonwealth policies in a general sense, it is true, were made impossible by the dominion refusal to underwrite particular obligations, but community of aim was not thereby necessarily imperilled. It had, however, to be sought and to be expressed in other and less formal ways. It was this need which led to an ever greater reliance being placed upon informal intra-Commonwealth consultation.

It was in November 1924 that Mr. L. S. Amery was appointed Colonial Secretary in Mr. Baldwin's first administration. He made it a condition of acceptance that he should be allowed to break up the office and create an entirely separate office for Dominion Affairs. He considered the step essential in order to secure due recognition of the importance of dominion affairs and also to remove lingering suspicions that the dominions were still dealt with by officials 'accustomed to the bureaucratic control of subordinate dependencies'.[1] The title of the new Secretary of State was symptomatic of the new approach. He was not Secretary of State for the Dominions, which would have implied a measure of responsibility for them, but Secretary of State for Dominion Affairs. This was a nice refinement which had its importance, for it reflected accurately the nature of the duties with which the department was charged. Its work was similar in kind to that of the Foreign Office but the atmosphere was different, for relations with the dominions were conducted with a degree of intimacy that is not possible in relations with foreign countries, however friendly. 'A Foreign Office with a family feeling' was the happy description of Mr. Walter Runciman.[2] The Dominions Office had administrative responsibilities only for Newfoundland, between the lapse of self-government in 1933 and its incorporation in Canada in 1949, and for the High Commission Territories of Basutoland, Bechuanaland, and Swaziland, which were administered by the United Kingdom High Commissioner to the Union of South Africa in his separate capacity as High Commissioner for these native reserves. The representatives of the United

[1] Amery, *Thoughts on the Constitution*, p. 127.

[2] H. of C. Deb., vol. 187, col. 93, and see also vol. 184, col. 2239, for official statement by the Prime Minister.

Kingdom in the dominions and of the dominions in the United Kingdom were representatives of their respective governments and not representatives of the King. Their status was, therefore, different from that of ambassadors.

The principal duty of the Dominions Office was to give as much background information as possible about developments in foreign affairs to the dominion governments. In the ordinary course its contact in the dominions capitals was with the dominion Departments of External Affairs. Matters of the highest moment were, however, usually dealt with direct by Prime Ministers. It is, however, an illusion to suppose that a communication even from one Prime Minister to another necessarily disposed of a problem more quickly than was possible by other means. A Prime Minister in a dominion was a member of a cabinet collectively responsible to his Parliament, and he was in no position to take an important decision without consulting with his colleagues. Mr. Mackenzie King, in his speech to both Houses of Parliament at Westminster in May 1944, rightly laid emphasis upon the fact that Commonwealth consultation is part of 'a continuing conference of cabinets'.[1] That is an all-important fact. The machinery for consultation has been evolved and works in relation to the British conception of parliamentary government.

It was through this system that the sense of active partnership in international affairs was maintained and even strengthened. But its effectiveness always depended upon the spirit in which it was worked. While membership carried an obligation to consult, it was an obligation of the kind that could not be enforced. Indifference could impair its usefulness, mistrust was certain to destroy it. By itself consultation could not bridge differences in opinion, still less could it reconcile opposites; but it could achieve a great deal, providing that there was a desire to reach agreement.

Consultation as a means of reconciling separate policies with Commonwealth unity rested upon the assumption that there was both a basis and a will to co-operate. It was that assumption which was responsible for the assured confidence of the Balfour Report which declared that 'though every dominion is now, and must always remain, the sole judge of the nature and extent of its co-operation, no common cause will, in our opinion, be thereby imperilled'.[2] The extent to which this confidence was justified in the pre-war years is a principal theme of this book. Here it may be noted that no attempt was made in 1926 to define the 'common cause'. Indeed it defied definition. This in itself meant that the aims of the Commonwealth countries in the international field had to be stated in broad, general terms. On the other hand, more detailed policies were framed and reactions to particular events emerged in the process of discussion between Commonwealth governments. Therein lay its outstanding value.

[1] *The Times*, 12 May 1944.

[2] Cmd. 2768, p. 14.

THE PREDOMINANCE OF THE UNITED KINGDOM

The condition of free discussion is equality. But while equality was recognized to be an essential element in dominion status in 1926 no formal acknowledgement could confer equality in function or in structure. So long as there existed marked inequalities in these closely related fields of function and of structure, consultation on a basis of practical equality could not take place. So much indeed was implicitly recognized in the Balfour Report in 1926[1] when it declared:

> Equality of status . . . is thus the root principle governing our Inter-Imperial Relations. But the principles of equality and similarity, appropriate to *status*, do not universally extend to function. Here we require something more than immutable dogmas. For example, to deal with questions of diplomacy and questions of defence, we require also flexible machinery—machinery which can, from time to time, be adapted to the changing circumstances of the world.

The language of the Balfour Report reflected the difference in stature between the United Kingdom on the one hand and the individual dominions on the other, and it was paralleled by corresponding differences in stature among the dominions themselves. Though much emphasis was laid upon this difference by imperialists in the belief that a continuing functional unity would counterbalance in practice the inherently centrifugal theory of full equality of status, the Balfour Report gave no countenance to such afterthoughts, for it treated the position quite factually, recognizing that while major responsibility in foreign affairs and defence must remain for some time to come with Great Britain, this was not necessarily an enduring feature of the Commonwealth system. For the time being, however, its continuing existence did delay the full impact of equality upon unity, with the result that any assessment of its consequences had to await a substantial levelling up in the discharge of functional responsibilities.

The predominance of the United Kingdom derived from her larger population, her greater industrial resources and technique, the more organized character of her society, her longer experience of the conduct of war and foreign affairs, and her control over the policies of India and Burma as well as of a large colonial Empire. The progressive extensions of state planning, accepted with enthusiasm or reluctance by political parties, much increased her capacity to mobilize man-power and to organize resources for war under modern conditions. In this respect, though ill-prepared to exert its power by continental standards, the United Kingdom far outstripped the dominions, where the authority of the central governments for the most part continued to be jealously restricted.[2] Moreover, it was probable by reason of her geo-

[1] ibid. pp. 14–15.

[2] This applies with particular force to Canada and Australia, where some of the most important restrictions on the authority of the central governments derived from the nature of their federal constitutions.

graphical situation, and certainly by reason of her preponderant power and comparative preparedness, that the United Kingdom would have to withstand the first shock of war while the oversea members of the Commonwealth mobilized their strength. This unenviable distinction in itself unquestionably enhanced her authority in Commonwealth councils. Ultimate control over the policies of India and Burma, and direct control over those of the Colonial Empire further added to Britain's prestige, though it is not easy to determine whether in large areas of the Colonial Empire the extent of colonial resources outweighed the additional responsibilities of their defence.

The consequences of the predominance of the United Kingdom within the Commonwealth were most evident in diplomacy and defence. In 1926 the Balfour Report proclaimed the principle of separate responsibility in foreign policy, but even ten years later the exercise of it was narrowly restricted in every case by the inadequacy of the machinery to carry it out. In Canada, South Africa, and the Irish Free State, where the governments, unlike those of Australia and New Zealand, had no reservations about the desirability of exercising full independence in foreign policy, there were departments of external affairs,[1] but they were on a modest scale, their activities critically scrutinized in Parliament, and their growth conditioned by the meagre allocations of Finance ministers, notoriously unsympathetic to the claims of mushroom departments. Moreover, departments of state cannot be satisfactorily created. If they are to discharge their duties effectively they must gradually assemble knowledge and establish precedents to guide their actions. In the field of external affairs particularly, a wise judgement demands not only a study of the merits of the issue at stake but an accumulation of experience built up through many years. From the point of view of the dominion governments all this reinforced the desirability of proceeding slowly, of building up

[1] In Canada, the Department of External Affairs was established in 1909 and given a minister of its own when the Department was joined by Statute to the office of the Prime Minister in 1912. It was not until 1946 that any member was enabled to be Secretary of State for Foreign Affairs. The South African Department of External Affairs was constituted in 1927, and the Prime Minister was accorded the additional designation of Minister of External Affairs. See E. Rosenthal, *South African Diplomats Abroad* (South African Institute of International Affairs, 1949). The Irish Free State established its own separate Department of External Affairs in 1922. The Australian Department of External Affairs was set up in 1901 as a part of the Prime Minister's office. It became a separate functioning department in 1935–6. A Department of External Affairs with a Minister was established in New Zealand by an External Affairs Act, 1919, but the function of the Department was limited to the administration of New Zealand's island territories, foreign affairs being handled by the Prime Minister's Department with the Prime Minister as Minister of External Affairs until 1943 when a separate External Affairs Department was established. An instructive account of the building up of the Canadian Department of External Affairs is to be found in H. Gordon Skilling, *Canadian Representation Abroad* (Toronto, Ryerson Press, for C.I.I.A., 1945) pp. 260–7. The fact that these new or expanding dominion Departments of External Affairs tended to be staffed by comparatively young men with a pronounced intellectual background did not always inspire confidence among the more conservative members of dominion parliaments.

a cadre of experienced officials at home and diplomatic representatives abroad before assuming the full responsibilities of independence in foreign policy. But such sobering, gradualist considerations were not wholly congenial to nationalist opinion and they were counterbalanced by the urgency of international problems the resolution of which often demanded the immediate discharge of those fundamental, external responsibilities which dominion governments had now assumed.

In the seminal stage of dominion external policies the League of Nations had much to contribute. Mr. Amery has written disparagingly of 'the distraction created by the League',[1] where the dominions were enabled 'to assert their individual international status without, in fact, incurring any serious individual responsibilities', but for governments formulating international policies for the first time and training officials to discharge them the platform afforded by the League was of the utmost value. It was a training ground in the realities of international affairs. The decline in the authority of the League was an object-lesson in the dependence of ideals upon the power to uphold them; and it was a lesson from which the dominions, as a result of their first-hand experience, did not fail to profit. It is true that actual dominion policies were for the most part moulded in the inner councils of the Commonwealth, but that enhanced rather than lessened the value to them of full participation in the affairs of the League. It was at Geneva that they could test against an international background the correctness of policies endorsed in informal intra-Commonwealth consultation or at an Imperial Conference. This was by no means without importance.

By 1936, a full decade after the devolution of responsibility for foreign policy from the United Kingdom to the dominions had been formally sanctioned, public opinion in the dominions continued to hold London primarily responsible for policies of the whole Commonwealth in the broad field of international affairs. This seems at once paradoxical and unfair, yet this instinctive attribution of responsibility was not wholly mistaken. The Foreign Office had a long experience and a great tradition behind it; it had representatives in every capital of the world, and its knowledge of European affairs was intimate to a degree to which an extra-European Power could not hope to aspire. Moreover, the United Kingdom remained a Great Power, and power, as always, meant responsibility. On every ground of tradition, of realism, of knowledge, the direction and execution of the foreign policy of the Commonwealth rested with the United Kingdom. All this was well understood, if not always welcomed, overseas. Mr. Menzies summed it up when he observed: 'We may, as indeed some of our predecessors did, claim that we are equal in all things in point of foreign policy, but the fact will remain that the great issues of peace and war will be much more determined by the gentleman who sits in a room looking across the Horse Guards Parade than it will be by

[1] *Thoughts on the Constitution*, pp. 126–7.

my colleagues in Canberra or one of our colleagues in Ottawa or Pretoria.'[1] It was at Geneva that the dominions felt they could in some degree check this 'gentleman's' opinion.

The extent of dominion dependence on the Foreign Office was accentuated by their own lack of representatives overseas. By 1936 Canada[2] had established legations in three foreign capitals, Washington, Paris, Tokyo; South Africa in seven, the Hague and Brussels, Rome, Berlin and Stockholm, Paris, Lisbon; and the Irish Free State in six, Washington, the Holy See, Paris and Brussels, Berlin, Madrid; Australia and New Zealand continued by deliberate choice to make use of the Foreign Office and its representatives in all parts of the world. In general this scanty representation meant that the dominions did not have at their disposal the information on which to form an independent judgement of the trend of international affairs. That at once enhanced, in their eyes, the value of the machinery for intra-imperial consultation, and at the same time made them more sensitive about their dependence upon Whitehall. It was through the eyes of Foreign Office representatives that the dominions saw the onrush of events in Europe. It is not to be imagined that their own representatives, had they been in Prague, or Warsaw, or Moscow, would have seen or judged events very differently. But at least in the inner circle of civil servants and statesmen, independent confirmation would have involved a less anxious scrutiny and possibly imparted a greater degree of confidence in United Kingdom policy.

THE PREPONDERANT RESPONSIBILITIES OF THE UNITED KINGDOM IN DEFENCE

The predominance of the United Kingdom in foreign affairs was matched by her preponderant responsibilities for maintaining the security of the Empire in peace and its protection in war. The extent of her responsibilities was to some extent disguised by the frequent designation of United Kingdom forces as 'imperial forces' and by the designation of the Committee of Imperial Defence, which suggested the existence of an organization representative of the Empire as a whole deciding upon the duties and the responsibilities of its several members. Any such impression was in truth altogether mistaken. At the Imperial Conference which met in London in 1908 it was recognized 'that it is the sole responsibility of the several Parliaments of the British Commonwealth to decide the nature and scope of their own defence policy'.[3] Despite its name, therefore, the Committee of Imperial Defence corresponded in its own field to the machinery which existed in the political field for intra-Com-

[1] Speech at the eighth annual dinner of the Royal Institute of International Affairs, 21 June 1938, quoted in *B.C.R. Conference*, 1938, p. 219.

[2] Here again Skilling (*Canadian Representation Abroad*, pp. 234–60) gives an instructive account of the building up of the senior dominion's diplomatic service, and of the political indifference and the problem of staffing which delayed it.

[3] Cmd. 5482, p. 20.

monwealth consultation and co-ordination of policy. Lord Hankey, who had more experience of its working than any man then living, stated: 'The Committee of Imperial Defence is sufficiently elastic to enable the dominions and India to take part in discussion and preparation to the extent that each may decide.'[1] The main task of the Committee was, therefore, to co-ordinate plans for Commonwealth defence in accordance with the wishes of the member-nations of the Commonwealth.

The membership of the Committee of Imperial Defence normally comprised the Prime Minister of the United Kingdom as chairman, the Chancellor of the Exchequer, the Secretaries of State for Foreign Affairs, for Dominion Affairs, for India, for the Colonies, for War, and for Air, the First Lord of the Admiralty and the Financial Secretary to the Treasury; the chiefs of staff of the three fighting services, and experts both from the United Kingdom and from the dominions, as well as such other persons whom the Committee invited to particular meetings for advice on particular subjects. Dominion attendance in practice was irregular and infrequent. Canada and South Africa were unwilling to be regarded as permanently represented.[2] The Committee therefore was predominantly United Kingdom in composition, but dominion representation usually sufficed in times of crisis or impending war to allow for a not inadequate co-ordination of defence policies within the Commonwealth. The Committee, moreover, remained directly responsible for a great part of imperial defence through its control over the defence forces of the United Kingdom and colonies and the defence policy of India. In view of these preponderant defence responsibilities of the United Kingdom and of the weight of military experience on which the Committee could rely, its influence in the determination of strategic policies throughout the Commonwealth remained great. Its professional opinion, for example, would seem to have been decisive in vetoing from the outset any thought of military sanctions against Japan approved by the League and enforced largely by the countries of the British Commonwealth.[3]

The Committee of Imperial Defence promoted defence co-ordination among the self-governing members of the Commonwealth in various ways. It encouraged a free interchange of technical knowledge, the temporary exchange of service officers, and the use by the dominions of the Imperial Defence College in London for the education of their officers in the broader aspects of

[1] *Diplomacy by Conference* (London, Benn, 1946) p. 103.

[2] cf. Skilling, *Canadian Representation Abroad*, p. 173. Mr. Mackenzie King, however, normally attended meetings when he was in London, but he displayed a certain reserve in the delegation of this responsibility to his subordinates, whether ministerial or official.

[3] On this point see Carter, *British Commonwealth*, p. 164. More generally, too much importance would seem to have been attached to actual dominion representation at the Committee. Minutes were taken and circulated to dominion governments who were thus kept fully in touch with developments and were in a position to co-operate as closely as they wished. It is not, for example, to be supposed that Canadian co-operation was less effective because her government was comparatively rarely represented.

strategy. In 1934 its secretary, Sir Maurice Hankey, made an extensive tour of the Commonwealth which was of major importance both in informing dominion governments of the extended defence measures contemplated by the United Kingdom government and in suggesting ways and means by which defence policies might be profitably co-ordinated without impairing individual dominion responsibility for action. The Imperial Conference of 1937 noted all this 'with satisfaction', and felt that the emergence of common systems of organization and training and the use of uniform patterns of arms, equipment, and stores which had been, so far as practicable, adopted in Commonwealth countries, would enable each of them 'to ensure more effectively its own security and, if so desired, to co-operate with other countries of the Commonwealth with the least possible delay'.[1] Though recorded as always in modest terms these were practical achievements, whose value was shortly to become apparent. They did not, however, modify the fundamental pattern of individual dominion responsibility for defence. On the contrary they underlined it.

The preponderant defence responsibilities of the United Kingdom may be illustrated by a brief review of her actual commitments in respect of each of the three fighting services.[2] In every case the United Kingdom assumed responsibility for the overall defence of the Empire. In respect of army commitments this involved the maintenance of line forces in the principal colonies, protectorates, and mandates, the garrisoning of focal strategic points throughout the Empire, and an overriding responsibility for the defence of India. In the colonial field Britain's principal commitments included the stationing of forces in Gibraltar, Malta, Cyprus, Bermuda, Jamaica, Mauritius, Aden, Ceylon, Malaya, and Hong Kong. Her forces in these colonial territories were supplemented in most cases by local volunteers. Until 1938 there were British care and maintenance parties in the Irish ports. In addition, by treaty or concession rights the United Kingdom maintained forces in certain non-British territories: Egypt, the Sudan, Palestine, and Iraq in the Middle East, and Shanghai and Tientsin in the Far East. The dominions for their part were solely responsible for their own local defence, but their responsibility extended only in part to their areas of local security where responsibility for the necessary reinforcement devolved upon the United Kingdom. In general, the extent of the United Kingdom military commitments overseas may be gauged from the fact that one-half of its military strength was normally stationed outside the British Isles.

In the naval field Britain's preponderant responsibility was even more pronounced. It was assumed, Lord Chatfield has recalled, that the Royal Navy would 'always provide general sea security to the scattered dominions, to

[1] Cmd. 5482, p. 20.

[2] See Major D. H. Cole, *Imperial Military Geography* (London, Sifton Praed, 1936) pp. 24 ff.

India, and to the Colonies'.[1] While the contribution of the dominions to the total naval strength of the Commonwealth was increasing, the United Kingdom's predominant share in maritime defence in the middle nineteen-thirties is most clearly illustrated by the following table:[2]

Navy	*Bases*	*Battle-ships*	*Cruisers*	*Aircraft Carriers*	*Flotilla Leaders, Destroyers*	*Sub-marines*
Royal Navy	..	15	44	7	146	54
Royal Australian Navy	Sydney	..	4	1	11	..
Royal Canadian Navy	Halifax	..	..	..	..	..
	Esquimalt	..	..	..	4	..
Union of South Africa Navy	Simonstown	..	..	..	..	..
New Zealand Squadron	Auckland	..	2	..	..	..
Royal Indian Navy	Bombay	..	..	..	..	..

Before the Second World War Canada, Australia, and New Zealand possessed the minimum naval forces for their own local defence and the protection of coastal trade, but even they were in no position to supplement the battle fleet of the Royal Navy in the general defence of the Commonwealth. Neither South Africa, nor the Irish Free State, nor India (which for the purpose of defence is most usefully considered as a dominion) were in a position to assume responsibility for their own naval defence. In general, therefore, as in the military sphere, the United Kingdom assumed overall responsibility for imperial naval security. Once more this demanded the maintenance of key bases throughout the world, and in their naval context they possessed an even greater importance because the British Commonwealth, which had been founded on sea power, still depended on it.

The dominions contributed towards the provisioning and defence of some of the most important of the British naval bases. Under the Smuts–Churchill agreement of 1921, which transferred to South Africa responsibility for the defence of the Union, her government agreed to make the Simonstown base available for use by the Royal Navy. The port itself was to be garrisoned by the Union Defence Force. Likewise under a contractual agreement Canada allowed the use of the harbours of Halifax and Esquimalt to the Royal Navy while garrisoning the ports with her own troops. The arrangement made with the Irish Free State under the 1921 Treaty[3] was rather different inasmuch as the ports were not only made available to the Royal Navy but were garrisoned

[1] *It Might Happen Again* (London, Heinemann, 1947) p. 146.

[2] Compiled in 1935, the table is reproduced from Cole, *Imperial Military Geography*, p. 27.

[3] Articles 6 and 7.

by British, not Irish, forces. The great port at Singapore was established by the United Kingdom and maintained by it, though large contributions to its establishment (begun in 1925) had been made by the Malay States and Hong Kong, and annual contributions towards its upkeep were paid by New Zealand. Elsewhere in the colonial Empire the United Kingdom was solely responsible for the long-established naval bases at Gibraltar, Malta, and Hong Kong as well as smaller bases, defended ports, or coaling stations in other parts of the colonial Empire.[1] Canada alone of the dominions extended her naval responsibilities to a share in the defence of the Canadian–Empire communications and in 1938, in fulfilment of them, she kept her four destroyers in the Pacific area. New Zealand was the only dominion whose navy remained an integral part of the Royal Navy, under its supreme command in peace as well as in war.

In the newer field of air power the distribution of responsibility in its early phase accorded closely with the pattern already laid down for the older naval and land services. Royal Air Force contingents were stationed at Malta, Singapore, and Hong Kong to co-operate with naval and land forces in defence of these imperial bases. Units were also maintained in Egypt, Aden, Iraq, and India to assist in discharging Britain's responsibility for the safeguarding of imperial communications, and for this purpose as war approached a concentration of air power was built up in the Middle East.[2] A decisive step in Commonwealth air defence was taken in the summer of 1939 with the agreement to establish a training scheme for United Kingdom and Canadian airmen in Canada and under the control of the Canadian government. This was later elaborated into the Empire Air Training Plan with headquarters at Camp Borden and Trenton.[3]

There are two points to be particularly noted in the distribution of the defence responsibilities of the Commonwealth. The Commonwealth was most closely knit together in the field of naval defence. The dominions were all in a position to provide their own military defence in the unlikely event of direct aggression upon them and they were all conscious of the significance of air power, which was a development coinciding in time with their own progressive assumption of individual responsibility for defence policy. It was, as a result, at sea that the older tradition of imperial unity survived longest. Nowhere was the preponderance of the United Kingdom more pronounced, and nowhere was it less easy to break up defence responsibilities without endangering security. For the purpose of the limitation of naval armaments the British Commonwealth continued to be treated as a unit, after the dominions had in fact become individually responsible for their own defence forces and

[1] These included Cyprus, Aden, Bermuda, Colombo, and Freetown.

[2] Units were established in the Sudan, Palestine, and Transjordan.

[3] For an account of its establishment see C. P. Stacey, *The Military Problems of Canada* (Toronto, Ryerson Press, 1940) pp. 113–16.

policies. The London treaty of 1930, which restricted naval forces until 1936, treated Commonwealth naval forces collectively though it was signed by its members individually. The second notable feature in the pattern of Commonwealth defence was the disproportionate burden borne by the United Kingdom in relation even to the great resources she controlled. Its weight provoked doubts about her ability to discharge all her responsibilities effectively and exposed to some criticism dominion concentration on local defence which, it was argued, overlooked the essential fact that the safety of the dominions might well be decided on battlefields, or more probably, on seas, many thousands of miles away from their own shores.[1] Both misgivings and criticism were frankly expressed at the unofficial Conference on British Commonwealth Relations held in Australia in 1938.[2] It is of some interest to recall that while the extent and weight of the United Kingdom's defence responsibilities were not questioned by dominion delegates, some of them felt that the scale of her defence obligations was dictated mainly in the interests of her own security. In keeping the sea and its communications open, in making possible the movement of reinforcements to hard-pressed points, the United Kingdom was in part at least safeguarding her own local defence. This view was substantially confirmed later by Lord Chatfield, who pointed out that while the main cost of imperial defence was borne by the United Kingdom, this was 'not entirely an altruistic act. If the Empire did not exist, the mother country would still have to spend annually almost as much money on its own security. . . .'[3] This is a point the importance of which is not lessened by the fact that other members of the Commonwealth derived obvious advantages from the scale of United Kingdom defence expenditure. If the Commonwealth had not existed the dominions would certainly have had to spend far more on their own defence. It allowed them, too, a freedom of choice not otherwise open to them. To quote Lord Chatfield once more, the 'various parts of the Empire have accepted British defence as its basic safeguard in war. To it, each part has added either a small or considerable quota, according to its means, to the risks to its freedom it has envisaged, or its inclinations and sentiments'.[4] It is that freedom of action which particularly underlines the advantages which the dominions, all middle Powers, all intent upon the development of very considerable internal resources, derived from the security which membership of the Commonwealth afforded to them, particularly when the prospects of international security declined with the decline in the prestige and effectiveness of the League. From that point of view, therefore, while there was no unified control of imperial defence, there was a community of

[1] Cole, *Imperial Military Geography*, p. 36. The Australian Prime Minister, Mr. Lyons, showed clear awareness of this fact on his return from the Imperial Conference of 1937. (*J.P.E.*, 1937, pp. 854–6.)

[2] *B.C.R. Conference*, 1938, pp. 272–4.

[3] *It Might Happen Again*, p. 211.

[4] ibid.

interest in ensuring its effectiveness which contributed to the growing feeling of imperial solidarity between 1936 and 1939.

POWER AND RESPONSIBILITY

'We are free but we are not equal.'[1] In these words an Australian delegate to the unofficial British Commonwealth Relations Conference held at Sydney in 1938 summed up that distinction between status and stature, whose importance in the field of intra-Commonwealth relations has already been emphasized, and which was also a determining factor in the Commonwealth's relations with the outside world at that time. Yet though explaining much, this phrase does not explain all. Within the Commonwealth in those years there was a sense of movement, a feeling that equality in status was a prelude, in some instances a protracted prelude, to greater equality in stature. In the Commonwealth, too, the new world, the 'young giants' of whom Mr. Lloyd George had spoken so imaginatively, would come, though in ways very different to those he had foreseen, to redress the balance of the old. It was this sense of dominion capacity for growth that, within the Commonwealth, at least, qualified the undoubted differences in stature between the United Kingdom on the one hand and the dominions on the other. It was a qualification the importance of which was accentuated as the war clouds gathered. The coming of war, like war itself, does not alter the direction, but accelerates the pace of change. It makes a democratic state more democratic by imposing responsibilities upon, and demanding sacrifices from, all alike; it makes a dictatorial state more dictatorial by concentrating ever greater power in the hands of its absolute ruler; and it makes an egalitarian community of nations more egalitarian. It is this which gave to the foreign policies of the dominions in the pre-war years an importance not strictly related to their actual power or the functional responsibilities they discharged.

By 1931 foreign policy had become of paramount importance to the British Commonwealth. If the principal purpose of this society of free nations was not yet, it was soon to be, the conduct of foreign policy. In the international field alone the common purposes of the Commonwealth could be realized; and in the international field, too, its sense of community could be progressively strengthened by wise policies or dangerously imperilled by imprudent courses. Here preponderant power inevitably placed responsibilities upon the United Kingdom which were most difficult to discharge in the years of dominion transition from functional dependence to a fuller autonomy in fact as well as in name. Its leadership had to be related not only to the actualities of power but also to the direction of Commonwealth development, and during this transition period the United Kingdom was confronted with the need to reconcile its own policies in Europe and elsewhese, framed in the light of its own

[1] *B.C.R. Conference*, 1938, p. 274.

interests, with dominion policies and predilections.[1] This was by no means always easy. Yet it was an end that had to be pursued, for a failure to effect reconciliation meant either a sacrifice of United Kingdom interests or a weakening of the sense of Commonwealth unity. Had the problem thus presented been approached on either side in a doctrinaire spirit, there was a by no means negligible risk that in the British Commonwealth, as in the closing years of the Habsburg monarchy, the system would resolve itself 'into a system of political paralysis in which immobility became the only pledge of equilibrium'.[2] This risk indeed, as we shall see later, was not wholly avoided between 1931–9. There was a tendency, arising from the sharing of responsibility for foreign policy, to choose the easy way, to seek refuge in passivity, and to substitute the confident assertion of agreed negations for a declaration of policy. That it was no more than a tendency even in this difficult transition period is a tribute not to the excellence of the system for the co-ordination of the foreign policies of the Commonwealth countries, but to the spirit in which it was worked. The sense of community on which the Commonwealth depended was confronted by the most exacting tests in pre-war years, and had it rested upon nothing more than outworn conventions and loyalities it would, like the Dual Monarchy, have hastened to its doom and final disintegration.

In securing the widest measure of agreement on foreign policy it was essential that the machinery should reflect, not the predominant power and responsibility of the United Kingdom, but the spirit of equal partnership which was the foundation of the Commonwealth. At the unofficial Commonwealth Conference held at Toronto in 1933, delegates, so Dr. Arnold Toynbee recorded,

> invariably welcomed suggestions for more effective common action, whether through the Commonwealth or through the League, when these took the form of proposals for free co-operation between autonomous and equal partners. They invariably shied away from any proposals which savoured of a super-state or of super-national institutions. For example, the proposals to strengthen the diplomatic bonds between the members of the Commonwealth by giving the Dominion High Commissioners in London diplomatic functions and by exchanging representatives, charged with similar functions, between one dominion and another, were received with notable cordiality, while the atmosphere of the Conference room instantaneously chilled at the suggestion that there should be any kind of unitary conduct of Commonwealth foreign policy either through a secretariat corresponding to the Secretariat of the League of Nations at Geneva or through a committee constituted on

[1] This was a factor in the making of United Kingdom policy which did not escape the attention of the German Embassy in London. In March 1938 the German chargé d'affaires noted, in a telegram to the German Foreign Office, the emphasis which Lord Halifax had placed upon the need for conducting United Kingdom foreign policy so that 'it might command the support of the whole British Empire . . .' (*Documents on German Foreign Policy*, Series D, vol. 2, p. 173).

[2] H. Wickham Steed, *The Hapsburg Monarchy* (London, Constable, 1913) p. 211.

the pattern of the United Kingdom Prime Minister's Committee of Imperial Defence.[1]

But if a foreign policy is to command the assent of six governments with different immediate interests and particular local anxieties, it requires not only the right psychological approach and congenial methods for reaching agreement, but also a capacity for statement in general terms. Specific detailed proposals are from the outset at a discount, for by their very character they can hardly commend themselves equally to all. Nor again can policies designed to advance limited interests, whether national or even imperial, normally hope to win the unanimous assent that is so highly desirable. As a result it was not long before Commonwealth statesmen recognized that the cause which transcended exclusively Commonwealth interests was the cause on which the Commonwealth would be most firmly united. In the world of the twentieth century the Commonwealth neither did nor could have aspired to live to itself alone. But what was the great cause that would unite, direct, give meaning to this community of nations? It was—can it be doubted?—the preservation of world peace. Here was a cause to which internationalist, imperialist, nationalist could all whole-heartedly subscribe; an aim whose fulfilment would be the only fitting memorial to an Empire's dead. But if the goal was not to be disputed, the way that led to it, which had seemed so clearly marked out in the high emotional atmosphere of the early nineteen-twenties, was lost to view in the mists of doubt and irresolution fifteen years later. Peace in our time was still the theme of Commonwealth statesmen, but its attainment depended no longer upon the assertion of ideals but upon the correct diagnosis of an inflammable situation. In their diagnosis the Commonwealth doctors, to their own dismay, differed deeply.

[1] *B.C.R. Conference*, 1933, pp. 9–10.

CHAPTER III

THE COMMONWEALTH FAVOURS APPEASEMENT

THE IMPERIAL CONFERENCE OF 1937; SOME REFLECTIONS ON ITS COMPOSITION AND CHARACTER

THE statesmen of the Commonwealth assembled in London in May 1937 for what proved to be their last formal meeting before the war. Mr. Stanley Baldwin, to whose wise understanding of Commonwealth affairs due tribute should be paid,[1] presided at the opening sessions of the Conference, and upon his relinquishing the office of Prime Minister was succeeded as chairman by the new Prime Minister, Mr. Neville Chamberlain. General Hertzog, who had played so significant a part in the reshaping of intra-imperial relations, came from South Africa with Mr. Havenga, for long the most intimate of his colleagues, with the stated resolve of using his influence to promote conciliation in Europe. Mr. Mackenzie King was accompanied by Mr. Lapointe, Minister of Justice, a man of outstanding integrity and political courage; Australia was represented by Mr. Lyons and New Zealand by Mr. Savage, the only Labour Prime Minister in the Commonwealth and the only member of the Conference still resolved to give unyielding support to the principle of collective security. Newfoundland, a dominion in suspense, had forfeited her right to representation. The absence of Mr. de Valera was evidence of a breach in imperial unity, never to be healed; for Irish representatives were not to be met with again in the innermost councils of the Commonwealth. The Secretary of State, Lord Zetland, was the principal spokesman of a still dependent India, but in her delegation was Sir Muhammad Zafrullah Khan, then a member of the Viceroy's Executive Council, and a decade later to be the first Foreign Minister of Pakistan. The Prime Minister of Southern Rhodesia, Sir Godfrey Huggins, and the Chief Minister of Burma, Dr. Ba Maw, attended as observers. The delegates were supported by a long and impressive array of advisers.[2]

The composition of the Imperial Conference of 1937 certainly did not suggest that there was anything static about the British Empire. The representation through observers, of countries quasi-autonomous in status, was in full accord with that sense of upward movement which had always been rightly regarded as an essential element in the Commonwealth association.

From the point of view of the dominions [observed that distinguished international

[1] Mr. Mackenzie King spoke of Mr. Baldwin's contribution to the Commonwealth in the most eulogistic terms after his death in 1947.

[2] For a list of them see Cmd. 5482, pp. 6–7.

lawyer Sir Cecil Hurst] the important thing to note is the evolution from a position of independence to one of freedom from control. These great communities have all the time been climbing a ladder. Now they have reached the top; but the climbing practice is common to all the communities which form part of the Empire. Each of them . . . is gradually, as it develops in strength and capacity, passing upward from the stage in which the community is wholly subject to control exercised from London, to that in which the control diminishes, and so on to that in which the control has ceased entirely. . . . The Crown Colonies of today will be dominions in days to come.[1]

Yet while this conception of orderly upward progress explained something of the nature of a dynamic Commonwealth it certainly did not explain everything. The lapsed dominion of Newfoundland, the resentful dominion of Eire, the mounting impatience of India and of Burma for full self-government little conformed to such comforting theories of evolution which the professors so carefully expounded. Not all the dominions were convinced that, as dominions, they had reached the top of the ladder, while some of those who were not dominions seemed to be not at all satisfied that the ladder to dominion status was the right ladder to climb. The metaphor itself fell into no little disfavour overseas. It had an unpleasing restrictive implication. Was it perhaps possible that the professors were over-zealous to impart an air of orderly progression to an Empire which in the past had conformed to no pattern and would not in the future, under the newer name of Commonwealth, conform for long even to theirs? These were sobering reflections and they found expression in the balanced phrases of the Commonwealth statesmen who assembled in London in May 1937. They liked the new Commonwealth pattern which had been woven in the preceeding decade but they were conscious that its quality had yet to be tested. Gone were the days of exuberant rejoicing at its unique excellence; and gone, too, that assertive confidence in the lessons which the world might learn from a study of its working. What could be said was wisely said by Professor Coupland, who observed that 'if the nations of the Commonwealth, with so many of the advantages which make concord and co-operation easy, with so much common sentiment and common tradition, cannot live and work together, what chance is there for France, Germany, Russia, and the rest? . . . if the British league of nations dies, no other league can live'.[2] The exalted mood of creation had given way to sobering assessments of strength and cohesion. The romance of the Commonwealth was over; its history had begun.

In a very real sense Mr. Mackenzie King was the voice of the new age in Commonwealth relationships, an age less assured, but in many respects more realistic than the old. The note he struck at the Imperial Conference had an attractively modest ring.

[1] *Great Britain and the Dominions* (University of Chicago Press, Harris Foundation Lectures, 1927) pp. 12–13.

[2] R. Coupland, *The Empire in These Days* (London, Macmillan, 1935) p. 92.

> The experiment in ordered relationships between free countries, which we call the British Commonwealth of Nations, has, we may venture to hope, value for other countries as well as for our own. We are endeavouring to prove the enduring possibility of establishing peace and sharing the gains of progress among peoples situated in every continent, held together not by centralized control or reliance upon force, but by similarity of political institutions and political ideals, by common interests and common loyalties. Through the past three centuries Britain gave the world an example and a challenge in the political democracy and the individual liberty it achieved within its own borders. It should be the aim of the members of the wider Commonwealth of Nations which has been built upon that foundation so to order their relations and co-ordinate their policies that they, in their turn, in the twentieth century, by the success of this experiment, may contribute, in the peaceful ordering of international relations, something of equal value to the common stock of mankind.[1]

Faith in the Commonwealth might remain undimmed, but it now was balanced by a sense of limitation, by an awareness of other forces in the world which openly challenged the liberal ideas from which the Commonwealth system derived its inspiration. How was the Commonwealth to respond to this challenge? Would its member-nations find themselves at one in their reactions to it?

THE INTERDEPENDENCE OF CONSTITUTIONAL THEORY AND DOMINION FOREIGN POLICIES

In the two preceding chapters the constitutional development and the external policies of the dominions have been outlined. In the relation between them nothing is more significant than the concern of most of the dominions to assert in principle and to establish in practice their autonomy in external affairs. They felt that it was in the international field that the reality of each advance in status could best be tested. This was not surprising. In essentials, internal self-government had been long conceded, and it was a sure instinct which guided those dominions who aspired to full autonomy to concentrate their attention on the external field. Their first step, as we have seen, was to ensure that they could not be committed to policies without their positive assent, their second to establish the right to separateness in diplomatic representation and policy, and the third to assert that the final test of autonomy was the right to decide on the supreme issues of peace or war. The times had been superficially favourable for the advancement of the dominion claims to external independence. In the 1920s and early 1930s there appeared, save to the discerning few, no prospect of war on a large scale. During those years considerations of security did not therefore inhibit dominion demands for widening measures of responsibility in international affairs. Moreover, apart from the apparent unlikelihood of another major war, there existed the

[1] Cmd. 5482, p. 50.

cushion of collective security to soften its impact if indeed it were to come. As late as 1934 Mr. Gerald Palmer, in an introduction to his work on the machinery of intra-Commonwealth co-operation,[1] observed that 'the fact that the dominions are members of the League of Nations and signatories of the Briand–Kellogg Pact of 1928 for the renunciation of war as an instrument of national policy' has rendered any further definition of the problem of possible dominion neutrality in a war declared by the King 'academic'.[2] Since in this the author faithfully reflected the state of Commonwealth opinion at the time, it will be seen that the assertion of ultimate dominion sovereignty in the international field was first advanced in a context soon to be deprived of all meaning. Almost certainly this made little difference to its substance or even its timing, but it did to its form and the atmosphere in which it was discussed. The Beit Professor at Oxford would scarcely have regarded such speculative questions as a dominion right to neutrality as 'frankly boring'[3] had he been confronted with them in 1938 instead of 1935. Even by May 1937, when the Imperial Conference assembled, it was apparent that seemingly theoretical questions, hitherto discussed almost exclusively in a context of status within the Commonwealth, had acquired a direct, even vital, bearing on the shaping of British foreign policy. The emphasis had shifted implicitly from constitutional to political questions. What would dominion policies be in the event of a war originating in Europe in which the United Kingdom was involved? This question, though not directly discussed, formed a highly significant element in the background to the deliberations of the Imperial Conference of 1937.

While it is suggested that political questions had assumed predominant importance by 1937, constitutional issues arising from conflicting interpretations of the nature of the Commonwealth are not to be disregarded as of no practical importance at all. The traditional view of the Commonwealth, which may be termed 'imperialist' for lack of a better designation, denied absolutely any dominion right of neutrality. In this view the Commonwealth remained an organic unity owing allegiance to a common king, and, because of that allegiance, was at war when its King was at war. A dominion declaration of neutrality was an unconstitutional act equivalent to the expression of a deliberate intention to secede. British subjects owing a common allegiance could not remain neutral when their King was at war without denying their allegiance. Stated in this austere, uncompromising form the doctrine emptied dominion autonomy of much of its substance. A United Kingdom delegate to the unofficial Commonwealth Relations Conference at Sydney in 1938 recognized frankly that there was only one logical conclusion to be drawn from acceptance of this viewpoint, and he maintained with commendable

[1] *Consultation and Co-operation*, p. xliv.

[2] Professor R. Coupland makes precisely the same point writing a year later (*Empire in These Days*, p. 89).

[3] ibid. p. 90.

forthrightness 'that the official and universally accepted doctrine that the Balfour Declaration and the Statute of Westminster have, in fact as well as in law, given dominion governments, legislatures, and electorates control of the issues of peace and war, is a dangerous illusion'.[1] Welcome in a New Zealand which, in the words of her Prime Minister at the Imperial Conference, attached 'no particular importance to the theoretical basis of our association as members of the British Commonwealth',[2] and still acceptable to non-Labour opinion in Australia, such a conclusion constituted a frontal challenge to Canadian, South African, and Irish insistence on the ultimate responsibility of their individual Parliaments. For this reason indeed the implications of allegiance were rarely stated in so uncompromising a form. Allegiance might preclude neutrality but it was not generally held to preclude passive belligerency. The dominion Parliaments could at least in this view decide on the extent of their participation in any war, and it was cogently argued[3] that beyond this limit membership of the Commonwealth became meaningless in a war for survival. Yet even this restriction was unacceptable in Canada and South Africa, quite apart from the Irish Free State. Both insisted on the absolute responsibility of their respective Parliaments to decide the issue of peace and war. The South African government had pushed their opinion to its legal conclusion in the Status Act, by challenging the doctrine of the common Crown, and insisting that a South African citizen's allegiance was simply to the King of South Africa. It was this view that the more empirically minded Canadian government favoured; though not without reservations particularly on the part of Mr. Lapointe, its French-Canadian Minister for Justice.

Allegiance to the Crown influenced decisively the attitude of millions in all parts of the Commonwealth, yet it presented a question on which no absolute conclusions could be reached. Fundamentally it derived from an emotional and immensely potent non-rational source. This meant that everything turned upon attitude and interpretation, and in such circumstances the interpreter is apt to have the last word. In the Commonwealth the interpreter in each case could be only the dominion government and people concerned. Where allegiance was not spontaneous, the instinctive opposition of government and people to any restrictive interpretation of Commonwealth law or convention counted for far more than any theoretic conclusions about constitutional obligations. Psychologically this was very understandable. Dominions who claimed the right to remain neutral did not necessarily intend to exercise it. They were concerned to establish their full independence. The one member of the Commonwealth who did remain neutral in 1939 did not, be it noted, concern herself with the rights of a dominion as such at all, but simply with the removal of practical obstacles to the recognition of a

[1] *B.C.R. Conference*, 1938, p. 220. [2] Cmd. 5482, p. 57.
[3] e.g. Coupland, *Empire in These Days*, pp. 89–90.

state of neutrality by all the likely belligerents. It was, therefore, because the right of a dominion to remain neutral in a war in which Britain was involved seemed inseparable from dominion responsibility for external policy, that so much attention was focused on it. On the cynical hypothesis of Clausewitz that war is the natural continuation of diplomacy, was it not logical that responsibility for deciding when diplomacy was helpless and statesmanship bankrupt should be vested in the same hands as had been responsible for its earlier conduct? How could responsibility for foreign policy and for its conclusion be placed in different hands? If the doctrine of common allegiance were to be asserted in its full rigour, then common policies framed and enforced by representative imperial institutions were the only way in which equality of status could retain reality. Here at least the federalists were on strong ground. But, federation being unacceptable, was it not both illogical and psychologically unwise for imperialists to extol the virtues of autonomous status within the Commonwealth and to maintain at the same time that its exercise must be confined within limits conventionally or constitutionally prescribed?

The Imperial Conference of 1937 felt unmistakably the desirability of finding common political ground for agreed action in the face of continuing aggression in Europe and Asia, and the Report is scrupulously careful to avoid any suggestion not merely of obligation but even that agreement upon the main lines of policy in any sense committed the members of the Commonwealth in any circumstances unless they so desired. 'While no attempt', records the *Proceedings*,[1] 'was made to formulate commitments, which in any event could not be made effective until approved and confirmed by the respective Parliaments, the representatives of the governments concerned found themselves in close agreement upon a number of general propositions. . . .' In the section on defence there was a presumption of co-operation should war come, but no suggestion of obligation. The security of all was enhanced by co-operation, but it was carefully recorded that 'the Conference recognized that it is the sole responsibility of the Parliaments of the British Commonwealth to decide the nature and scope of their own defence policy'.[2] The implication was unmistakable. Responsibility for the means could not be divorced from responsibility for the ends they were designed to serve. In the supreme issue of peace and war the Commonwealth had henceforward to rely not, as in 1914, upon a unity constitutionally imposed from above, but upon a unity of wills. That unity rested upon the foundation of a common outlook and common ideals buttressed by ties of kinship, but more immediately it demanded from the statesmen of the Commonwealth a statement of objectives reflecting and reconciling the views of their several governments. It was the principal task of the 1937 Imperial Conference to define and to formulate such objectives.

[1] Cmd. 5482, p. 14.

[2] ibid. p. 20.

THE IMPERIAL CONFERENCE ENUNCIATES A POLICY OF APPEASEMENT

The nature of the Commonwealth after 1931 virtually precluded the issue of dramatic or decisive pronouncements by its assembled leaders, and this has been a source of recurrent disappointment to those who continued to hope for the impossible. Speculative ventures in and bold declarations on foreign policy are neither congenial nor ordinarily practicable for Commonwealth statesmen, often dependent as they are on uncertain parliamentary majorities at home. But decisions of the highest significance are by no means always dramatic. Certainly this was true in 1937. The Conference's report on foreign affairs,[1] widely criticized, especially in Australia and New Zealand, for its negative character, seemed almost platitudinous when it was published, yet in retrospect it has acquired a great and controversial importance. This derives from the fact that the report crystallized a trend, rather than indicated a new departure. As recently as May 1935 the Prime Ministers of the Dominions had been in London for King George V's Silver Jubilee and had participated in general discussions on the international situation. No doubt was then left that they were generally sympathetic to a policy of conciliation and, subject to evidence that 'full faith and confidence'[2] could be placed in Germany's future actions, favoured her restoration to a position of full equality in the European community of nations. A month later, in June 1935, the Anglo-German naval agreement was formally concluded, presumably with their cordial assent. For defence against dangers which could not be overlooked reliance was placed first on measures designed to strengthen the system of collective security and, secondly, on greater expenditure on imperial defence as outlined in the White Paper of March 1935.[3] By 1937 the situation had changed in that the system of collective security had broken down and Germany had given no indication that any confidence could be placed in her future actions, but, although the approach of the Commonwealth was modified somewhat in form, it varied little in substance.

The section of the *Proceedings* of the 1937 Imperial Conference dealing with foreign affairs opened by saying that for each member of the Commonwealth the first objective was the preservation of peace. In their view 'the settlement of differences that may arise between nations . . . should be sought by methods of co-operation, joint inquiry and conciliation'. They desired, too, to base their policies upon the aims and ideals of the League of Nations, and they 'found themselves unanimous in declaring that their respective armaments will never be used for purposes of aggression or for any purpose inconsistent with the Covenant of the League of Nations or the Pact of

[1] Section IX of the *Summary of Proceedings*, Cmd. 5482.

[2] *The Times*, 8 May 1935.

[3] *Statement issued in connexion with the House of Commons Debate on 11 March 1935*, Cmd. 4827, p. 5.

Paris'. They advocated the separation of the Covenant from the Treaties of Peace—a step which had long been favoured in South Africa and Canada. They desired to see a wide measure of disarmament but felt 'bound to adopt such measures of defence as they may deem essential for their security, as well as for the fulfilment of such international obligations they may respectively have assumed'. They agreed to continue the closest consultation in the conviction that the cause of peace was likely to be promoted by their using their influence in the same direction. What direction that was to be was indicated in the concluding paragraph:

> Finally the members of the Conference, while themselves firmly attached to the principles of democracy and to parliamentary forms of government, decided to register their view that differences of political creed should be no obstacle to friendly relations between governments and countries, and that nothing would be more damaging to the hopes of international appeasement than the division, real or apparent, of the world into opposing groups.[1]

The effect of this paragraph was if anything reinforced by the conclusion to the general review of Empire trade, included in the *Proceedings*[2] which recognized that a healthy growth of international trade, accompanied by an improvement in the general standard of living, was 'an essential step to political appeasement'. Faith in conciliation and appeasement thus permeated the *Proceedings* and indicated that by the early summer of 1937 these were the guiding principles of Commonwealth foreign policies.

It is not easy to dissociate appeasement from the controversies which later surrounded it or the general condemnation which overtook it.[3] The reasons, the very varied reasons be it said, which disposed dominion governments in favour of the conciliation of men who were to prove irreconcilable are recorded in the following chapters. Yet here it may be noted that, while the adoption or endorsement of the policy in each instance is understandable, the phrasing of the concluding paragraph of the section on foreign affairs in the *Proceedings* embodies sentiments hardly consistent with the dignity of a great Commonwealth confronted with the shameless aggression of European tyrants unmatched for their cruelty and faithlessness since the Dark Ages. The preservation of peace in Europe would indeed have been a great achievement, but it reflects little to the credit or the perspicacity of Commonwealth leaders that they should have suggested that the differences in political creed between the Nazis and the Commonwealth should be no obstacle to friendly relations between their respective governments and countries. It is known

[1] Cmd. 5482, p. 16. [2] ibid. p. 21.

[3] Mr. Glazebrook, in his *History of Canadian External Relations*, observes that the policy known to its supporters as 'peaceful change' was known to its critics as 'appeasement' (p. 396). This was not so. Appeasement was the word chosen by the protagonists of conciliation themselves to describe their policy. It was the policy that gave to the word its contemporary ill repute, not the word that stigmatized the policy.

indeed that some members of the Canadian delegation disliked the use of such servile language and that New Zealand was not in sympathy with it, but such attempts as were made to have it modified unhappily failed. Appeasement was, as a result, proclaimed to be the policy not only of the United Kingdom, but of the Commonwealth as a whole.

Fundamentally it was the failure of the League in the Abyssinian war that drove the members of the Commonwealth back upon the refuge of appeasement. New Zealand alone continued to hold fast to her faith in collective security and would have welcomed an assertion in the *Proceedings* that the members of the Commonwealth based their policies upon the principles laid down in the Covenant of the League. Mr. Savage's influence with his colleagues was, however, not great and his advocacy of collective security as an alternative policy to appeasement was weakened by his own lack of any detailed knowledge of international affairs, coupled with a somewhat doctrinaire approach to the problems they presented. To Mr. Mackenzie King any such declaration was in any event unacceptable because it implied willingness to fulfil obligations which Canada had always viewed with misgiving and now regarded as no longer binding. In this, General Hertzog was on the side of Mr. Mackenzie King, while the United Kingdom was disposed to adopt a rather more positive attitude to the League without, however, expressing support as unequivocal as that of New Zealand. The outcome of the divergencies of view was a footnote. It declared 'nothing in this statement should be held to diminish the right of His Majesty's governments in the United Kingdom, Canada, the Commonwealth of Australia, New Zealand, and the Union of South Africa, and the government of India to advocate and support their statements of policy as submitted to the Assembly of the League of Nations in September 1936'.[1] Relegation of League policy to this subordinate position was in itself a sign of the times. The majority of Commonwealth statesmen were no longer prepared to subscribe to an open profession of faith in the principles of the League because they feared that might be held to imply an acceptance of obligations which they no longer regarded as binding. If one accepts their premise, their conclusion was unquestionably sound.

The attitude of the dominions towards problems of foreign policy may be conveniently related to this approval of the policy of appeasement at the Imperial Conference of 1937. Hitherto they had played a pre-eminently negative role in the shaping of Commonwealth foreign policies. More concerned to assert their autonomy in the international field than to pursue particular policies, they were confronted with direct and dangerous responsibilities in which endorsement of policy at times carried far-reaching implications. How did they discharge them, how did they resolve the

[1] Cmd. 5482, p. 14. The individual statements of policy are considered in subsequent chapters.

delicate interrelationship between Commonwealth and international affairs, how far were their policies conditioned by their racial composition, by their history, by their geographical position, and how easily in practice were equality and autonomy reconciled with Commonwealth unity? In all this the Imperial Conference may be taken as a watershed dividing the years of disentanglement of policies and definition of responsibilities from the years of hard experience. Was the confident assurance of the Balfour Report, that while each dominion was thereafter to be the sole judge of its policy no common clause would thereby suffer, to be justified or not? Those in the best position to judge were uncertain and anxious. Little by little, observed Professor Coupland[1] in Toronto in 1933, those fellow members of the Commonwealth who were partners in the great war-time brotherhood in arms seemed to be drawing away. Confronted with a strain scarcely less burdensome, an outlook scarcely less anxious than that of 1914

> we are facing it by ourselves—or so it seems. One wonders, indeed, now and then, whether the dominions have any interest left in Europe except to keep out of it. Is it only the reassertion of the fact of distance? 'The ocean remains; you cannot pump it dry.' Or did something of the spirit of comradeship fade away with the smoke of the home-going transports? Is England more alone in the world than she was?

Such anxieties, seeming in retrospect inseparable from an age of transition in Commonwealth relations, were widespread in Britain and profoundly influenced her assessment of the role the dominions might play in an international crisis. Might it not be that the imperialist Jeremiahs would prove right in the end and that equality and autonomy were milestones on the road to disintegration? Such misgivings are not to be left out of account, for even when not over seriously entertained they reinforced other arguments for a postponement of the day of reckoning.

So long as the dominions were primarily concerned with questions of status they could justly be treated collectively as a category of state. Some might be enthusiastic, others dubious or frankly uneasy about the pace of constitutional advance, but however significant their differences in emphasis the advance was in essentials uniform. Even after the great phase of constitutional development the dominions remained constitutionally a category, but politically they emerged as individuals, with their individuality underlined with each advance in their industrial strength and political maturity. Thus while the dominions remained members of one Commonwealth, their attitudes to that Commonwealth, and still more to international affairs, were conditioned by distinct and often conflicting considerations. To understand the nature of a Commonwealth, composed of equal and autonomous member-nations, it is essential to understand the forces and the environment which

[1] *Empire in These Days*, pp. 94–95.

have moulded the outlook of each one of them. Once equality of status was firmly established in practice the character of the Commonwealth was necessarily determined by the contribution of each of its members to its common purposes. The initiative had passed from the centre to the circumference, and it is therefore timely now to consider these problems of external policy with which this book is principally concerned, from the perspective of the dominions and of India, that Empire which had not attained the status of a dominion. While it is true that the Commonwealth remained more than the sum of its component parts, it is also true that the nature of those parts determined the character of the whole.

PART II

THE EXTERNAL POLICIES OF THE DOMINIONS, 1931–9

The task of shaping foreign policy becomes a phase of the problem of building national unity. EDGAR J. TARR

In the attainment of this high object of world appeasement, at this moment of great international tension, the mission of the Commonwealth stands clearly defined.
GENERAL J. B. M. HERTZOG AT THE IMPERIAL CONFERENCE OF 1937

CHAPTER IV

CANADA: THE SEARCH FOR UNITY

THE OCEANS GIVE SECURITY

CANADA has been much favoured by geography. A continental state bounded by the Atlantic on the east, the Pacific on the west, and barren Arctic wastes to the north, she has only one land neighbour and that neighbour, the greatest Power in the contemporary world, underwrote the high measure of security Canada already enjoyed. Not only, therefore, was it highly improbable that Canada would suffer any direct large-scale attack before 1939 but, if by some unlikely chance she did, then she was assured of the support of the United States who, whatever her formal obligations, could not afford to stand idly by while a hostile power obtained a foothold on the North American continent. 'Our major defensive buffer on the Pacific coast', acknowledged Mr. Mackenzie, the Minister for National Defence in 1938 when on the eastern seaboard fears were entertained of Japanese attacks, 'is not the Pacific Ocean alone but the existence there of friendly fleets. There is no commitment or understanding in regard to these matters, but at this time, I think reasonable assumptions are justifiable.'[1] A further reasonable assumption was that in the event of a major war the Royal Navy would constitute a powerful protective force in the Atlantic. As a result even when the world stood on the brink of war the Canadian Prime Minister could observe with perfect justice that talk of aggressor nations planning to invade Canada was,

> to say the least, premature. It ignores our neighbours and our lack of neighbours; it ignores the strategic and transportation difficulties of transoceanic invasion; it ignores the vital fact that every aggressor has not only potential objects of its ambition many thousands of miles nearer . . . but potential and actual rivals near at hand whom it could not disregard by launching fantastic expeditions across half the world. . . . At present danger of attack on Canada is minor in degree and second-hand in origin. It is against chance shots that we need immediately to defend ourselves.[2]

Canada's well-founded sense of a security, without parallel in the British Commonwealth and indeed in the Western world, produced some complacency and enhanced the appeal of isolationism as a realistic policy. In 1924 Senator Raoul Dandurand told his less fortunate European colleagues at Geneva that Canadians lived 'in a fire-proof house, far from inflammable materials', and warned them not to presume overmuch on Canada's willingness to undertake obligations in the more troubled areas of the world.[3] There was

[1] Canada, H. of C. Deb. 1938, vol. 2, p. 1650. [2] ibid. vol. 3, p. 3179.
[3] League of Nations, *Plenary Meetings*, 5th Assembly, 2 October 1924.

a tendency, too, for Canadians to proffer to Europe platitudinous and at times irrelevant advice on how to settle their problems by the methods of conciliation and arbitration which had so happily disposed of all disputes arising from their own extended land frontier with the United States.[1] What remained remarkable, however, was not the extent to which a self-righteous and self-regarding isolationism determined Canada's pre-war policy, but the high sense of responsibility which brought this country of many cultures[2] united into a war against a European aggressor. For Canada, alone of the dominions, detachment from the struggle was a possible, seemingly realistic, policy. Before her people lay temptingly the primrose path of isolation, but it is to their lasting credit that after anxious doubts and protracted self-examination they chose, regardless of the policy of their greater neighbour, to tread the hard road of sacrifice in the common cause of freedom.

THE INFLUENCE OF REGIONAL AND CULTURAL TENSIONS IN THE MAKING OF POLICY

It might at first sight be imagined that the high degree of immunity from direct assault which Canada enjoyed would have sensibly eased the problems of policy-making. Yet such was not the case. Throughout her history Canada has been notoriously a difficult country to govern. Aristotle in his wisdom declared that the size of a state should have no bearing upon the principles and the form of its government, but Canadian experience suggested that vast size and sparse population greatly accentuated the strains to which every democratic government is normally subjected. Nor was this surprising. Canada, nearly 4 million square miles in extent, was far larger in area than any country of the Commonwealth,[3] ranking next in size to China and the U.S.S.R. among the states of the world. If her size was no true criterion of her strength, her comparatively small population spread out along her southern border gave no less exaggerated an impression of weakness. Yet the essential factor in her development is clear enough. Unlike the United States the Canadian nation did not grow naturally; it had to be deliberately created. And while the task of nation-building was eased by the natural resources with which Canada was so richly endowed, it was made more difficult by the regionalism to which a

[1] cf. Glazebrook *Canadian External Relations*, p. 377. 'The unguarded frontier and the century of peace', he observes, 'became too well advertised to be of further interest in Geneva.'

[2] This word is used deliberately to avoid further misuse of that much misused word race. As Professor Griffith Taylor has pointed out in his *Canada, a Study of Cool, Continental Environments and their Effect on British and French Settlement*, 2nd ed. (London, Methuen, 1950) p. 499, it is quite absurd to talk of a French and an English 'race' in Canada. Immigrants from the east of England and from north-eastern France, whence came most of the French settlers to Quebec, both belonged to the Nordic race.

[3] Australia is less than 3 million, the sub-continent of India about 2 million, and South Africa about 1 million square miles in area. For an analysis of the implications of Canada's vast extent see Griffith Taylor, op. cit. *passim*.

continental state is peculiarly liable, by cultural tensions, and by a dependence upon precarious overseas markets. These were factors cumulatively of great significance which no Canadian statesmen could afford to overlook in the making of external policy. Their impact was the greater just because there was no direct external danger to exert its traditional unifying force.

Canada is divided into six clearly defined regions: the Maritime Provinces on the eastern seaboard, Quebec and Ontario in the St. Lawrence valley, the Prairie Provinces in the Middle West, British Columbia lying between the the Rocky Mountains and the temperate Pacific waters, and the virtually uninhabited Northern Tundra.[1] The Maritime Provinces, static in population and separated from the remainder of Canada by the Appalachian Barrier, have lain secluded from the main stream of Canadian development for the past half century. Poor in natural resources, having strong affinities with the New England states from whence many of their settlers came and went,[2] and flanked to the north and west by Roman Catholic French-Canadians with whose outlook they have little in common, their sense of separateness has not lessened much with the passing of the years. New Brunswick and Prince Edward Island remained in 1941 the two most rural provinces in Canada, though Nova Scotia with its coal pits at Glace Bay has become comparatively more urbanized.[3] Only in New Brunswick was there by 1941 a comparatively large French-speaking minority,[4] the remaining two provinces being overwhelmingly British in extraction, and by contrast with the western provinces, they were descendants of early, not recent, British migrations.

The separateness of the Maritimes in the east found some parallel in the situation of the two regional groupings in the west. The Prairie Provinces of Manitoba, Saskatchewan, and Alberta were cut off from Ontario on the east by a thousand miles of virtually uninhabitable swamp and forest, and from British Columbia still farther to the west by the Rockies. Despite a rapid increase in numbers through immigration in the early years of the century, these great wheat-growing lands remained but thinly populated even within their areas of settlement. For material and psychological reasons there developed among their people a certain antagonism to their wealthier eastern neighbours. From the outset the cultivation of the Prairies was conditional upon the influx of capital from Ontario and from overseas which in turn created what Professor Brady has aptly termed 'the restless mentality of a

[1] This is no more than a convenient politico-geographical classification. For a geographer's more detailed description see Taylor, op. cit. pp. 5 ff.

[2] Interchange of population with the United States was by no means confined to the Maritimes, but they were peculiarly conscious of the southward drain on their population. The United States census figures for 1850 showed 100,000 persons who had been living in the United States born in the British provinces of Canada, and by 1860 the figure had risen to a quarter of a million. See Glazebrook, *Canadian External Relations*, pp. 11–12.

[3] See *Canada Year Book 1943–4*, pp. 120–30, for statistics of rural and urban populations in each province at each decennial census from 1871 to 1941.

[4] According to the census of that year it amounted to some 36 per cent. (ibid. p. 104.)

debtor community'.[1] For the export of grain overseas the prairie farmers also had to rely upon railway systems controlled from eastern Canada, and they found frequent occasion to complain that their interests were neglected or overruled. Again their reliance upon overseas export markets fostered a predominantly free-trade outlook in sharp contrast to the economic nationalism of Ontario's industrialists, anxious to protect their markets behind high tariff barriers.[2]

While broad divergencies in economic interests underlay the regionalism of the Prairies, the influx of settlers from Central Europe was producing a cultural pattern which one day may be neither predominantly French nor predominantly British in extraction. The United States, observes Professor Griffith Taylor,[3] in its days of early settlement had not such a polyglot mixture as the Canadian prairies in the early twentieth century. By 1941 there were, for example, 241,000 Ukrainians, mostly in group settlements, in the three provinces and in the same year their population of European origin, other than French and British, was nearly 290,000 in Manitoba out of a total population of 730,000; 421,000 in Saskatchewan out of a total population of 896,000, and 327,000 out of a total population of 796,000 in Alberta.[4] These new settlers were little disposed to accept uncritically the traditional loyalties of either English or French-speaking Canada.[5]

Beyond the Rockies lay British Columbia, the most 'British' in race and outlook of the Canadian provinces. It, too, formed a distinct region, far removed from Ottawa, and easily disposed to believe that distance led to neglect. Its outlook on the Pacific and the existence of an immigrant Asiatic population numbering 42,000 in 1941 made British Columbia more conscious of the problems of the Pacific than other parts of Canada.

Both the Maritimes to the east and the Prairie Provinces to the west were at one in regarding with some mistrust the concentration of population and industry in the St. Lawrence valley where 60 per cent. of the Canadian people lived and where 80 per cent. of her manufacturing production was to be found. There lay the great cities of Toronto and Montreal and the federal capital, Ottawa. It was in this great, prosperous heart of Canada that there was to be found the politico-cultural division which constituted a barrier to the emergence of a sense of national community more formidable than any erected by distance or the conflict of material interests.

The descendants of the French settlers, who number 80 per cent. of the

[1] cf. Alexander Brady, *Democracy in the Dominions* (Toronto, Oxford University Press, for Canadian Institute of International Affairs and R.I.I.A., 1947) p. 29, and generally for an illuminating analysis of the political and economic consequences of Canadian regionalism.

[2] The Liberals were traditionally the low tariff party and this in part accounted for their comparative strength in the west.

[3] *Canada*, p. 506.

[4] See *Canada Year Book 1943–4*, pp. 103–6. The percentage of Canadians of European extraction other than French or British in the country as a whole was just under 18 per cent.

[5] See Brady, *Democracy in the Dominions*, pp. 30–31.

population of the province of Quebec, and the descendants of the United Empire Loyalists in the neighbouring province of Ontario have been partially but never wholly reconciled. The slow but sure processes of democracy have healed many wounds, but neither the victors nor the vanquished can overlook the consequences of that decisive battle fought on the Heights of Abraham nearly two centuries ago. In England the name of General Wolfe, whose statue stands so proudly on the village green of his native Westerham, recalled the treasured memory of a soldier who, on the eve of his last battle, declared that he would rather have written Gray's *Elegy* than have conquered Canada. But in Quebec, as the French-Canadian glanced at that monument which, with a magnanimity unique in commemorative sculpture, pays tribute both to the vanquished and the victor, to Montcalm and to Wolfe, he could hardly fail to be reminded of less sentimental realities. Wolfe, not Montcalm, was the victor and his victory ended for ever French rule in Canada.

The psychology of defeat long survives the generation that experienced it, and in twentieth-century Quebec it was still discernible in a defensive provincial separatism. To the French-speaking minority the jealous safeguarding of provincial rights seemed to supply a very necessary protection against intellectual or social absorption. From behind their provincial barriers French-speaking Canadians followed their chosen course with unyielding conviction and impressive consistency. In some measure their outlook was influenced by the social composition of their community. With defeat the *grands seigneurs* for the most part returned to France while the peasants remained, and having lost their secular leaders they leaned ever more heavily on their spiritual pastors, even for guidance in secular politics. The small white churches to be seen on either bank of the great inland waterway of the St. Lawrence with the countless little townships of Quebec clustered around them, symbolized an influence which had long sustained and reinforced the tenacious conservatism of the soil.[1]

The French in Canada form an isolated group in a continent dominated by Anglo-Saxons. Their numbers have not been replenished from their homeland since the eighteenth century, and after the revolution the descendants of emigrants from the France of the *ancien régime* recoiled in dismay from the new France that was born in 1789. Thrown back upon its own resources, this small community, which numbered some 300,000 souls at the close of the eighteenth century, resolved to survive; to preserve in the New World what remained of the heritage it had brought from the Old. To a natural conservatism was added thereby a suspicious defensiveness towards

[1] The influence of religion upon the daily life of a rural community in Quebec is well described in Horace Miner, *St. Denis, a French-Canadian Parish* (University of Chicago, 1939; Ethnological Series) Chapters V and VI. St. Denis is a characteristic small French-Canadian parish in rural Quebec and this detailed sociological survey of the life and outlook of its people throws a good deal of light upon the cultural traditions moulding the French-Canadian outlook.

the advances and the reproaches alike of their English-speaking neighbours in Ontario. It was absorption, whether political, cultural, or religious, that would spell final defeat. Therefore the French-Canadian was determined to preserve the heritage of his fathers by every means in his power. 'We bore overseas', wrote Louis Hémon, 'our prayers and our songs; they are ever the same . . . all we brought with us, our faith, our tongue, our virtues, our very weaknesses, are henceforth hallowed things which no hand may touch, which shall endure to the end.'[1] Such is the faith of the *habitants* of Quebec; sustained at once by racial consciousness and by the influence of the Church which has always recognized that to keep the people French is to keep them Catholic.[2]

While the French-Canadians retain to this day a good deal of the sensitiveness of a minority, they are well aware that the rapid growth in the population of French-Canada may yet once more make them the rulers of Canada. The descendants of the 300,000 French-Canadians of the early nineteenth century numbered in 1941 little less than 3½ million and comprised 30·27 per cent. of the total population of Canada.[3] And though the upward population curve has shown a tendency to flatten out with growing urbanization, the Quebec birth-rate in 1939 remained as high as 24·8 per thousand in comparison with 17·1 per thousand in Ontario, and in 1942 it rose to 28 per thousand, one of the highest in the world. In British Columbia, almost wholly British in extraction, the comparable figure in the same year was 19·3.[4] It is precisely this contrast in the relative rate of increase in the population of French and English-speaking Canada which has given a sharper edge to the misgivings of the predominantly Protestant population of Ontario still deeply attached to the traditions of the United Empire Loyalists who founded it. Their emphasis upon the imperial link, their resolve to stand with Britain in peace and war, stood out in sharp contrast to the negative, often isolationist, outlook of the *habitant*.[5] In war-time, or at moments of international tension, this divergence of outlook has assumed menacing proportions, but it was always present, a latent source of friction, in knowledge of whose existence all Canadian policies had to be framed.

INTERNAL UNITY: THE GUIDING PRINCIPLE IN EXTERNAL POLICY

Throughout her history Canada's external policies have been conditioned by the need to maintain unity at home, yet the reconciliation of divergent

[1] Quoted in Brady, *Democracy in the Dominions*, p. 28.

[2] ibid. p. 27.

[3] *Canada Year Book 1943–4*, p. 103.

[4] See Taylor, *Canada*, p. 502. It is interesting to notice that while the French-Canadian birth-rate was one of the highest in the world the French birth-rate at 13·0 per thousand was one of the lowest.

[5] The Federation of Catholic Workers of Canada, which reflected the views of organized labour in Quebec, was opposed both to radicalism at home and internationalism in external policy. See Glazebrook, *Canadian External Relations*, p. 329. The influence of the Federation subsequently declined.

regional interests and loyalties has not been easy and has often been bought at the price of a positive, coherent attitude abroad. In particular, policies which promoted co-operation at home have not always promoted close co-operation with the wider community of the British Commonwealth. Had there been any direct conflict between the claims of internal unity and Commonwealth membership the hard decision would long since have had to be made. But it has not been so. Commonwealth membership on the contrary has been in itself a condition of Canadian unity. But it has not been a membership free from inhibition or tacit reservation. In imperial affairs Canadian statesmen have trodden with wary circumspection. Conservative-imperialists from Sir Robert Borden to Mr. R. B. Bennett laid a more marked emphasis upon imperial unity than Liberal-nationalists whose eyes were firmly fixed upon the need for racial unity, and incidentally upon the need for the electoral support of Quebec. But from neither, when in office, came those carefree, rapturous eulogies on the surpassing excellence of Empire familiar in the Pacific dominions. A Canadian politician in power, whether his predilection was imperialism or Canadianism, found it necessary to voice his sentiments with a watchful reserve. Of this history provides many instructive illustrations very relevant to a study of more recent Canadian policies.

At the close of the nineteenth century the South African War confronted Sir Wilfrid Laurier with a challenge which, different in form but constant in character, was to recur in succeeding decades and to impress ever more deeply upon Canadian statesmen the virtues of compromise. In 1899 English-speaking Canada urged active Canadian participation in South Africa on the side of the mother country, French-speaking Canada resolutely opposed it. Laurier fearing, as he later observed, 'a cleavage in the population of the country on racial lines',[1] compromised by issuing an Order in Council announcing that the government would not send a contingent to South Africa but would equip and transport a thousand volunteers. With English-speaking Canada 'blazing for action' and French-speaking Canada 'silent in hesitancy' Laurier thus adopted the middle course that seemed most likely to avert an open breach at home, even if it exposed him to attack from both extremes.[2] Ten years later he summed up in the light of his experience the essentials of his own policy and that of the Liberal party. 'We are', he wrote in 1909, 'divided into Provinces, we are divided into races and out of the confused elements the man at the head of affairs has to sail the ship onwards' and to do this safely often means not the adoption of 'the ideal policy' but of the policy 'which can appeal . . . to all sections of the community. That has been my inspiration ever since I assumed leadership of the party'.[3] A

[1] Quoted in Oscar D. Skelton, *Life and Letters of Sir Wilfrid Laurier* (New York, Century, 1921), vol. 2, p. 107.

[2] ibid. p. 98. See also Glazebrook, *Canadian External Relations*, p. 185.

[3] Skelton, *Laurier*, vol. 2, pp. 331–2.

year later in a debate on naval defence he underlined the fundamental Canadianism implicit in the Liberal approach. 'I am', he said, 'Canadian first, last and all the time. I am a British subject by birth, by tradition, by conviction. . . . I want to speak from that double standpoint for our policy is our expression of the double opinion.'[1] But where to Laurier and to his party it was loyalty to Canada that was fundamental, with Conservative statesmen the scales were more evenly balanced. This was apparent in 1914 when Sir Robert Borden[2] sponsored unquestioned and immediate backing for the mother country, while Laurier argued in words often to be echoed by his successor, Mr. Mackenzie King, that it was for the 'Canadian people, the Canadian Parliament, the Canadian government to decide'.[3] But both Liberals and Conservatives were becoming increasingly aware that their particular predilections could be pushed to extremes only at the risk of dangerous division among their people. Here the sombre lessons of 1917 were never forgotten. In June of that year a conscription act was introduced into the Canadian Parliament by Sir Robert Borden. The Liberal opposition split, some remaining loyal to Sir Wilfrid Laurier who believed that conscription would do more harm than good, that it would divide the country on racial grounds, and that it would hand over Quebec to the extremists; others supporting the Prime Minister's efforts to form a Union government pledged to an all-out war effort. There followed the conscription election in December 1917. It was contested in an atmosphere of tense, overwrought emotion, which strained national unity almost to breaking point and, while its outcome was a clear verdict for conscription, the Union government securing 153 seats against the 82 of the opposition Liberals, more than 60 of the opposition were returned from Quebec constituencies. In other words Canada had divided on cultural lines and Confederation was subjected to a test which threatened its very survival. Professor Lower has gone so far as to say that there was then 'introduced into Canadian life a degree of bitterness that surely has seldom been equalled in countries calling themselves nations';[4] a verdict which an Irishman, an Indian, or a South African might question from his own experience, but which is perhaps the more enlightening for that very reason. Certainly Canadian statesmen of all parties were resolved that the events of 1917 should not be repeated. The latter-day experience of two nations warring 'within the bosom of a single state' had therefore notable consequences in the determination of inter-war policies. The Liberals, hopelessly divided

[1] ibid. p. 327.

[2] For his attitude see *Robert Borden, His Memoirs*, ed. by Henry Borden (London, Macmillan, 1938).

[3] There was no division of opinion about the action Canada should take. Everywhere, even in Quebec, there was virtually unquestioned agreement that Canada should actively participate. 'From the staunchest Tories of Ontario', records Mr. Glazebrook, 'to the nationalists of Quebec there was hardly a dissenting voice' (*Canadian External Relations*, p. 295).

[4] A. R. M. Lower, *Colony to Nation, History of Canada* (Toronto, Longmans, 1946) p. 466.

in 1917, had very particular reasons for keeping in mind the dangers of disunity to country and to party. In their view the first criterion by which any Canadian policy had to be judged was—did it help to preserve national unity? If it did not, however attractive on other grounds, it should not be pursued. That was the consideration which above all others guided Mr. Mackenzie King in the twenty-nine years of his leadership of the Liberal party[1] and his twenty-one years as Prime Minister of Canada.

During Mr. Mackenzie King's long tenure of power the influence of French-Canada in determining the external policies of the government was negatively very great. Unlike both his predecessor and his successor in the leadership of the party he could not count upon French-Canadian sentiment in his favour. He had to win the confidence of Quebec, with the result that he had to make the greater concessions. Where Laurier and St. Laurent could assess instinctively the reaction of their compatriots in Lower Canada, Mackenzie King had to rely on his judgement. The penalty of a major miscalculation during the whole of the period from 1935 to 1949 was the defeat of his government, for French-Canadian support was the condition of Liberal retention of office, even when they enjoyed apparently secure majorities in the House. In 1935 the Liberals, swept to office on a wave of reaction against Mr. R. B. Bennett's 'depression government' and, loosening even the traditional Conservative hold on Ontario,[2] returned no less than 180 members (including Independent Liberals) as against an opposition made up of 39 Conservatives and 26 Social Credit, Co-operative Commonwealth Federation, and Independent members. Yet despite this overwhelming victory at the polls Mr. Mackenzie King remained dependent on Quebec, for no less than one-third of the Liberal members returned represented French-speaking constituencies. At any time their estrangement could not have failed to endanger the government. And in 1936 the defeat of the Liberals in the province of Quebec and their replacement in office by the Union Nationale, whose militant local patriotism had so greatly commended it to the electorate, was a forceful reminder to the Liberal administration in Ottawa that the loyalty of Quebec could not be assumed.

The dependence of the Liberal government upon the vote of a province fundamentally conservative in outlook was the paradoxical outcome of the tensions between Quebec and Ontario. Both provinces were conservative by temperament, both were profoundly jealous of provincial rights which safeguarded their way of life against the encroachments of a possibly progressive and certainly bureaucratic federal government, but cultural feeling drove them into opposing political groups. There were, of course, important differences in the character of their conservatism. The conservatism of Quebec

[1] He was elected to the leadership at the Liberal Convention in 1919 and an important factor in his election was the impression that Laurier had favoured his claims to the succession. He was only forty-five.

[2] In 1930 the Conservatives returned 60 members from Ontario: in 1935 26.

was the deep-rooted, traditional conservatism of a profoundly religious peasant community, whilst the conservatism of Ontario was the confident, thrustful conservatism born of great industrial wealth and achievement and convinced of the supreme virtues of private enterprise.[1] Externally the conservatism of Quebec found expression in the demand for a cautious, non-committal, foreign policy which would safeguard Canada from war unless her interests were directly involved; while the conservatism of Ontario placed ever greater emphasis upon the bonds of Empire as the danger of war drew nearer. Neither, it will be noted, placed their faith in the League, whose most persuasive supporters were to be found among the English-speaking prairie Liberals.[2]

RELATIONS WITH THE COMMONWEALTH AND THE UNITED STATES

It is a commonplace to say that throughout her existence Canada has been subject to the conflicting pulls of history and geography, the one reflected in her membership of the British Commonwealth of Nations, the other in her intimate friendly association with the United States.[3] Canada is both a dominion and a North American nation. This is a fundamental factor in the determination of her foreign policy. Its importance is enhanced by the fact that it is the north-south pull that is geographically the more natural. The regions of Canada are linked both by the great waterway of the St. Lawrence and by the great east-west railroads and, in more recent times, by the trans-Canada air lines. But more than 90 per cent. of Canada's population lives within 200 miles of the American border and interchange of population has been easy, frequent, and at times disturbing. Between 1919 and 1930, when the average annual Canadian intake of settlers of European origin was about 123,000 a year, there was no comparable increase in her population, for in this same period in which Canada was thus gaining population from Europe she was suffering on balance a loss of over a million persons from her own potential population to the United States. And, as Professor Brebner has justly observed,[4] the character of these emigrants made their loss particularly hard to bear. In 1930 the number of Canadian-born citizens in the United States was about one-sixth of the population of Canada, though as partial compensation for this 'national deficit' there were some 345,000 American-born citizens living in Canada, and in 1931 they constituted the largest single non-British immigrant group in the country. After 1930 the movement of population

[1] This was coupled with no doctrinaire dislike of state services where their creation seemed desirable on grounds of efficiency. On the contrary, in Ontario public ownership of public utilities is extensive, and in this respect its provincial administration is as progressive as that of any province in Canada.

[2] It was no accident that Mr. John Dafoe, perhaps the most influential protagonist of League policies, was editor of the *Winnipeg Free Press*.

[3] This theme is fully examined in Professor J. Bartlet Brebner's *North Atlantic Triangle* (New Haven, Yale University Press for Carnegie Endowment for International Peace, 1946).

[4] ibid. pp. 298–303.

between Canada and the United States was on a far more modest scale, but the implications were always the same. Canadians and Americans did not regard the frontier between them as an insurmountable national barrier, nor did they look upon each other as foreigners. Their approach to world affairs had also much in common. Unremitting and unrelenting was the flow northwards of American ideas and American culture,[1] and it made its inevitable impact upon the Canadian mind. Even had they so desired, and the majority certainly did not, Canadians would have no opportunity of forgetting that they were a North American people.

Imperialists who liked to think of the British Commonwealth as a tightly knit economic and political organism viewed the southward pull with the gravest concern and not without reason. Canada's constant awareness of the extent of her common interest with the United States precluded, or at least was generally felt by Canadians to preclude, whole-hearted participation in imperial policies. When such policies were under consideration her representatives were for ever looking over their shoulders speculating whether Canada's greater neighbour was likely to regard her participation with approval or suspicion, and they generally decided 'better not'. Their attitude faithfully reflected Canada's predominant concern that the United States and the United Kingdom should keep in step in the essentials of their foreign policy, and it was because this rarely happened at a time when the one was a member of the League and the other almost aggressively isolationist in outlook outside it that Canada's attitude often tended to be depressingly negative in the councils of the Commonwealth. At Imperial Conferences Mr. Mackenzie King was the spokesman of Canada's 'everlasting no'. But it would be unwise to conclude that because the Canadian attitude was negative it was therefore mistaken. In later years Canada's insistence that Anglo-American co-operation should be the supreme objective of the Commonwealth was warmly endorsed by many who were most critical of her pre-war insistence on it.

The intimacy of Canada's friendship with the United States prompted speculation about her future place in the Empire. Would her dual ties to North America and to the Commonwealth in the long run prove irreconcilable, and if so would not the southward pull prevail? Such reflections called forth some pungent comment in 1930 from Mr. John Dafoe, a great editor and a great personality, which reproduced something of the atmosphere in which Anglo-Canadian relations were generally discussed at that time. He said:

> The Americanization of Canada, implying ultimate absorption by the United States, becomes a profound conviction with many visitors from Great Britain after

[1] An interesting appraisement of the extent and limits of American cultural penetration is to be found in Massey, *On Being Canadian*, and in Walter Herbert, 'The Cultural Pattern', in G. W. Brown, ed., *Canada* (Berkeley, University of California, 1950; United Nations Series).

they have been in our country two or three weeks. Clergymen, bishops especially, seem particularly prone to this delusion. They come to Canada in the expectation of finding a replica of England and, when they discover the Canadian variation from English customs and standards and note their resemblance to the habits of the American people, they at once jump to the conclusion that Canada is about to be lost to the Empire, and come home to impart the sad news to the English people. Often they accompany the announcement of this startling discovery with demands that Englishmen should rush out to Canada to save the country from the Canadians and keep it on the true path of Empire.

It is the hope of some of us that we are near the end of these fears and misconceptions. The characteristics of Canada, social, political, business, linguistic, journalistic, religious, are our own affair. They are what they are because they suit us; they are integrated with the whole life of the nation; they help to produce that national whole called Canada.[1]

On the longer perspective it was in fact apparent to most Canadians that their unity and their independence in world affairs rested upon their continuing membership of the Commonwealth and their continuing friendship with the United States. If as a North American nation Canada neither could nor wished to pursue exclusively Commonwealth policies, so, too, as a member of the Commonwealth she neither could nor desired to follow exclusively North American policies. For this there were both sentimental and practical reasons. Membership of the Commonwealth was not only part of the living heritage of English-Canadians but also a reinsurance for French-Canadians against absorption in the United States. Quebec had little wish to be submerged in a vast Anglo-Saxon North American community indifferent to her *ethos*, heedless of her views. With this in mind a French-Canadian member of Parliament who looked with no great favour upon the Commonwealth connexion observed in the House in 1937: 'I think that American imperialism is not any better, nor any brighter, nor any more desirable than British imperialism.'[2] It is possible to go further and say that had a choice to be made between membership of the Commonwealth and absorption in the United States, Quebec in her own self-interest could opt only for the Commonwealth. By the great majority of Canadians, whatever their racial origin, membership was seen to be a condition at once of unity and of independence. But the very fact that it was as much a matter of reasoned policy as of sentimental attachment gave to the Canadian attitude a distinctive flavour. By 1939 Canada—and this is very important—was no longer a predominantly British country. The 1941 decennial census revealed that for the first time slightly less than half of her population were of British extraction. So gradual had been the changes in its composition that their full significance was little appreciated outside the dominion.

[1] *International Affairs* (Journal of the Royal Institute of International Affairs), November 1930, p. 725.

[2] Canada, H. of C. Deb., 1937, vol. 1, p. 956.

Culturally Canada was composed of three important groups, the first two of British and French extraction, and the third mostly of Central European origin. The relative decline in the British element in the population is brought out by the decennial population statistics for the first half of the twentieth century.[1]

	1901	*1911*	*1921*	*1931*	*1941*
British . . .	57·03	54·07	55·40	51·86	49·68
French . . .	30·71	28·51	27·91	28·22	30·27
Others . . .	12·28	17·40	16·68	19·93	20·05

The significance of these figures from the point of view of Canada's relations with the Commonwealth, and especially with the United Kingdom, is accentuated by a corresponding and progressive decline in immigration from the United Kingdom between the First and Second World Wars. The figures were as follows:[2]

1908 . .	55,727	1926 . .	48,819	1936 . .	2,197
1911 . .	144,076	1927 . .	52,940	1937 . .	2,859
1913 . .	156,984	1928 . .	54,848	1938 . .	3,389

This decline meant a steady diminution in the number of Canadians with personal ties in Britain, and a corresponding weakening of emotional attachment. In 1914 no less than 64 per cent. of the first Canadian contingent that went overseas had been born in the British Isles, while in 1939 the comparable figure was less than 10 per cent.

While Canada remained in outlook and in government a British country, the origins of its population precluded an exclusively British foundation for national loyalty and national unity. It was largely a subconscious awareness of this which led Canadians to seek in what for lack of a better term may be called Canadianism, a more generally satisfying basis of unity. Old-fashioned imperialists were distressed when in 1937 Lord Tweedsmuir declared bluntly that Canada was a sovereign nation who could not 'take her attitude to the world docilely from Britain, or from the United States, or from anybody else. A Canadian's first loyalty is not to the British Commonwealth of Nations, but to Canada and to Canada's King, and those who deny this are doing, to my mind, a great disservice to the Commonwealth.'[3]

He might have added that they were doing a disservice to the cause of Canadian unity. 'A strong and dominant national feeling', said Mr. Mackenzie King, 'is not a luxury in Canada, it is a necessity. Without it this country

[1] See *Canada Year Book 1943–4*, pp. 103–4, where the racial origins of the Canadian population are shown from 1871 to 1941. See also Canadian Institute of International Affairs, *Canada in World Affairs: The Pre-War Years* (London, Oxford University Press, 1941).

[2] *Canada Year Book 1941*, p. 111.

[3] Speech at the Canadian Institute of International Affairs, Montreal, 12 October 1937; the speech is reproduced in *Canada in World Affairs*, pp. 274–5.

could not exist.'[1] In view of her varied racial origins, her regionalism, and her balancing external associations this was no more than a sober statement of fact. 'Canada, like Belgium', M. André Siegfried noted '. . . remains a precarious creation.'[2]

To say that the character of Canada's relationship with the Commonwealth was changing is not to say that it was weakening. It is true that at times the emphasis on Canada, a nation, tended to obscure the sense of partnership in a wider community. But fundamentally the concern of Canadians before the Second World War was to assert their full nationhood within, not without, the Commonwealth. 'I know of no large group anywhere', observed Dr. R. J. Manion, leader of the Conservative opposition, in March 1939, 'which does not want to remain in the Empire.'[3] The years of transition between the wars demanded adjustments in outlook unwelcome to some, but no break with history or traditional loyalty. Mr. Mackenzie King, who was not disposed to sentimentalize about attachment to 'the old country', described it in 1939 as 'still a very strong and determining factor' in Canada's policies. But it was an attachment not shared in equal measure even by all of British origin, because for most people as the years pass the 'centre of political gravity tends to shift from the land of their fathers to the land of their children'.[4] Psychologically very true, this is something that goes far to explain why the policies of the Liberal government, which its Prime Minister described as lying midway between those of a 'thorough going imperialist' and a 'regardless nationalist',[5] not only reflected faithfully the predominant Canadian attitude to the Commonwealth but also won wide acceptance from many descendants of earlier settlers of British extraction.

In the determination of the balancing, middle-of-the-road policies which Canada pursued between the two world wars, economic considerations played an important, if contributory, role. Throughout her history Canada has depended economically upon her export trade. In the decade beginning 1930 no less than 25 to 30 per cent. of her total production was exported overseas. In a world of competing economic nationalisms this meant a dangerous degree of dependence upon overseas markets, particularly upon those of Canada's two principal customers, the United Kingdom and the United States. The risks involved were accentuated by Canada's historical concentration upon a few commodities, notably wheat, which in 1935 made up almost one-quarter of her total exports. Between 1929 and 1933 the Canadian economy staggered under the force of the economic blizzard, and the plight to which the primary producers of the west were then reduced left an indelible mark upon Canada's outlook. The government's first concern was to weather

[1] Canada, H. of C. Deb., 1939, vol. 3, p. 2419.
[2] *Canada*, trans. by H. H. and D. Hemming (London, Cape, 1937) pp. 304–5.
[3] Canada, H. of C. Deb., 1939, vol. 3, p. 2437.
[4] ibid. 30 March 1939, p. 2422.
[5] ibid. 1937, vol. 1, p. 250.

the storm and then to seek some basis for future economic stability in assured markets and stable prices for Canadian exports. To Mr. Bennett the development of trade within the Empire, especially by means of preferential tariffs, afforded the one gleam of light in a world which, careless of the needs of exporting countries, sought refuge behind ever higher national trade barriers. The Ottawa agreements of 1932, successful in increasing trade between the Empire countries, did not, however, substantially modify Canadian dependence upon other external markets and above all upon the American market. This fact is clearly brought out in the following table:[1]

Trade of Canada with British and Foreign Countries (in percentages).

Exports	*United Kingdom*	*Other British Empire Countries*	*United States*	*Other countries*
1928–9	31·4	7·8	36·8	24·0
1932–3	34·9	7·2	37·4	20·5
1936–7	38·4	8·3	41·0	12·3
1937–8	38·2	10·1	39·6	12·1
1938–9	35·1	11·1	40·6	13·2
Imports				
1928–9	15·3	5·0	68·6	11·1
1932–3	21·3	8·3	57·2	13·2
1936–7	19·3	10·2	58·6	11·9
1937–8	18·2	11·0	61·0	9·8
1938–9	17·6	9·9	62·7	9·9

These figures, in so far as they can be taken at their face value, show that the volume of exports to the United Kingdom and to Empire countries generally increased appreciably in 1931–8 as a result of the Ottawa agreements, the 1938–9 decline being attributable to the failure of the wheat crop. On the other hand, it will be noticed that over the same period exports to the United States tended to increase in almost equal proportion, even though imports did not keep pace with the increasing volume from the United Kingdom until the very end of the period. It may, therefore, be reasonably concluded that important though the Ottawa agreements were in stabilizing Canadian trade, and above all in retaining for Canada at a critical moment the vitally important United Kingdom wheat export market, they did not so far as its two principal customers were concerned vitally affect its direction.[2]

In 1937 the Ottawa agreements were renewed. Mr. Mackenzie King's approach was, however, very different, in theory at least, to that of Mr. Bennett's five years earlier. It is true that, in the words of his Minister of Finance, the main objective of the Liberal government was 'to hold the most

[1] Quoted in *Canada in World Affairs*, p. 183.

[2] Canadian trade with foreign countries other than the United States was, however, reduced.

valuable market this dominion has ever known'. But if in agreement with Mr. Bennett about the supreme importance of the United Kingdom market for Canadian exports, Mr. Mackenzie King displayed far more concern than his predecessor about the desirability of broadening the basis of Canada's export trade, and with the receding depression had greater opportunities for doing so. Immediately on the government's accession to office in 1935 a new trade treaty with the United States was negotiated, and was renewed three years later. It aimed at the restoration of trade between Canada and the United States to its former level. In the absence of any real prospect of securing international agreement for the removal of restrictions and the lowering of tariffs, the government indicated that there was no disposition on their part to discount the importance of regional trading agreements either with the United States or still less with countries of the British Commonwealth. On the contrary, with the successful negotiation of an Anglo-American trade agreement in 1938, 'the greatest triangular exchange of commodities in the world had thus been "frozen" in patterns of reciprocal advantage by three carefully drawn treaties'[1] to two of which Canada was a signatory.

CAUTION AND COMPROMISE

A precariously poised economy, regional tensions, cultural divisions, the conflicting southward pull of geography and the westward pull of history all combined to make the Canadian external policy a matter of balance, or nice calculation in which vehement conviction was a liability rather than an asset. Canada, at least in the early years of her existence as an independent force in international affairs, was ill fitted to lead imperial or internationalist crusades, not because her people lacked the crusading spirit but because they were unlikely to agree about the crusade in which their country should enlist.[2] The basis of unity had first to be sought and found. That was the task which Mr. Mackenzie King set out to accomplish, and for two decades no man contributed more to its successful achievement. By temperament he was predisposed not to heroic solutions but to cautious, often almost imperceptible, advances towards his appointed goal. Like Count Taafe who, confronted with the rivalry of many peoples within the Habsburg monarchy, aimed 'to keep all the nationalities in a balanced state of mild dissatisfaction', Mr. King developed unrivalled dexterity in making small concessions to different viewpoints but no large commitments. He accepted with composure the criticisms to which he was in consequence subjected from almost every quarter, for he believed that to satisfy wholly the claims of one section would assuredly involve the alienation of another. Here, too, his attitude had much

[1] Quoted in Brebner, *North Atlantic Triangle*, p. 309, and see also generally pp. 305–9.

[2] Mr. Mackenzie King on more than one occasion alluded to the undesirability of Canadian participation in crusades. e.g. his speech of 24 May 1938, quoted Canada, H. of C. Deb., 2nd session, 1939, p. 60.

in common with that of Count Taafe, who declared on his acceptance of office that under his régime 'none of the nationalities' was 'to obtain decisive predominance'[1] because that would make the existence of the others intolerable. For his part Mr. Mackenzie King was greatly assisted in the fulfilment of his aim by the central position of his party which enabled him to assume the role of arbiter. The right and the left, the nationalists and the imperialists, denounced him, but, as for themselves, they were united only in negation.

Mr. Mackenzie King would probably not have found comparison with Count Taafe altogether unwelcome. No man believed more implicitly than he that Canada was a difficult country to govern, and even if in that respect it could not challenge comparison with the multi-national monarchy of the Habsburgs, at least the methods adopted by Francis Joseph's one tolerably successful minister were not inappropriate or unwise in dealing with the lesser problems of Canadian unity. Mr. Mackenzie King, indeed, partly in order to justify his policy, or on occasion his lack of policy, delighted to emphasize the quite exceptional difficulties with which Canada was confronted. In 1936 he spoke 'of the unparalleled complexity of our position as a member of the League, a member of the British Commonwealth of Nations and one of the nations of the American continent'.[2] In this he was followed by many Canadian politicians and writers. It became fashionable to emphasize the precariousness of Canada's export markets, but not the value of her exports; to speak of regional and cultural tensions within but not of the growing sense of unity; of the conflicting pulls of geography and history to which indeed every 'settled' country is subject, but not of the immense strength of Canada's position in the heart of the English-speaking world. In truth the complexity of Canada's problems was by no means unparalleled even within the Commonwealth, where South Africa was confronted with issues greater alike in intensity and variety. But if Mr. Mackenzie King's insistence on the complexity of the problems he had to resolve might not bear too exact a scrutiny, his emphasis was none the less significant. It indicated his overriding preoccupation with the preservation of Canadian unity. 'I believe that Canada's first duty to the League and to the British Empire', he declared in 1936, 'with respect to all the great issues that come up, is, if possible, to keep this country united.'[3] And in September 1939 he restated this fundamental conviction which determined all his peace-time policies with a valedictory flourish:

I have made it [he said] the supreme endeavour of my leadership of my party, and my leadership of the government of this country, to let no hasty or premature threat or pronouncement create mistrust and divisions between the different elements that compose the population of our vast dominion, so that when the moment of

[1] See Taylor, *Habsburg Monarchy*, Chapter XIII.
[2] Canada, H. of C. Deb., 1936, vol. 4, p. 3862.
[3] ibid. vol. 2, p. 1333.

decision came all should so see the issue itself that our national effort might be marked by unity of purpose of heart, and of endeavour.[1]

The undeviating pursuit of this aim gave meaning both to the ambiguities in which Mr. Mackenzie King's detailed statements of policy were customarily veiled and to his unvarying insistence that when the time came the elected representatives of the Canadian people must be left free to decide on peace or war. Leadership in foreign policy was not possible for a government whose principal purpose was to conciliate conflicting opinions at home. In the meantime initiative abroad was sacrificed, deliberately sacrificed, to internal unity, for in Mr. Mackenzie King's view what had to be done was to mould Canadian opinion on foreign affairs in a formative period by making clear, through a slow, unheroic process of elimination, the path which Canada should follow. Whether the aims which Mr. Mackenzie King set before his country were too restricted or not will long remain a matter of debate, even though the balance of Canadian opinion, both at the time and since, was, and is, on his side. What is not in dispute is the patience and the remarkable skill with which he pursued his chosen course in the face of bitter criticisms so that in the end he might bring a united country into a war from which the United States remained aloof.[2] In 1939 he realized his goal with cool and measured assurance. It was an achievement which will always give him a high and honoured place in the annals of Canadian and of Commonwealth statesmanship.

CANADA AND THE LEAGUE

Canada's attitude to the League was remarkable for its consistency. From the first the League was welcomed as a means of furthering international co-operation, as a forum for debate and discussion, and for the opportunities it afforded to the smaller nations, and above all the dominions, to assert their personalities, to play a creative role in world affairs. But at no time was any Canadian government prepared to regard the League as a means for enforcing, as distinct from maintaining, peace. On the contrary, they sought, not to extend, but to limit national obligations to impose sanctions, whether military or economic, against an aggressor. In a frigid reply to the invitation to subscribe to the Geneva protocol the Canadian government observed that it did 'not consider it in the interests of Canada, of the British Empire or of the League itself, to recommend to Parliament adherence to the protocol and particularly to its rigid provisions for the application of economic and military

[1] 8 September 1939, ibid. 2nd session, 1939, p. 25.

[2] The measure of this achievement is best judged in the light of a remark by Mr. Bourassa who expressed the widely accepted opinion of politically conscious Canadians before 1939 when he said: 'there is not one single major problem of either internal or external policy which we can settle in Canada without reference to the policy of the United States.' Quoted in *Canada in World Affairs*, p. 21.

sanctions in practically every future war'.[1] On the other hand, but for much the same reasons, Canada enthusiastically welcomed the invitation to become a signatory to the Briand–Kellogg Pact in 1928 which, while pledging the contracting parties to renounce war as an instrument of national policy, contained no suggestion of sanctions for the enforcement of peace. The pact had, moreover, the added attraction of United States sponsorship and general Commonwealth participation. But it was not without significance that Canada, in accepting the invitation to subscribe to it, should have taken the opportunity to restate her objection to automatic League sanctions and to reassert her conviction that the permanent value of the League lay in the 'positive and preventive action' by which it built up 'barriers against war by developing a spirit of conciliation, an acceptance of publicity in international affairs, a habit of co-operation . . . and a permanently available machinery for the adjustment of differences'.[2] It was not long before events were to throw serious doubts upon both the permanence and the value of this machinery and in so doing undermine the foundations upon which Canadian policy rested.

It was from Japan, one of the victors in the First World War, that there came the first challenge to the comfortable faith, shared by most of the English-speaking world, that the existence of machinery for the adjustment of differences was sufficient to adjust them. With that challenge Canada did not feel very closely concerned. It is true that as a signatory both of the Covenant and of the Washington treaties of 1921–2 she had entered into certain general obligations to maintain peace and to defend the *status quo* in the Far East, but these obligations were considered to be related to her available resources and to her interests in that part of the world, both of which were limited. Despite her long Pacific seaboard, Canada traditionally looked not to the East but to the West, for to her people the Atlantic, not the Pacific, seemed the vital area of security. Yet developments in Eastern Asia could not be, and were not, altogether neglected. In 1929 Canada established a legation in Japan and it was understood that the Canadian minister there, while concerned primarily with questions of trade and immigration, would also seek to keep in touch with political developments not only in Japan but also in China.[3]

Confronted in 1931–2 with Japanese aggression in Manchuria at the height of the economic depression at home, the Canadian government reacted with exemplary caution. The Prime Minister, Mr. R. B. Bennett, pressed to define

[1] Dated 10 March 1925 and reprinted in R. A. Mackay and E. B. Rogers, *Canada Looks Abroad* (London, Oxford University Press, for C.I.I.A., 1938) pp. 329–30. See also Glazebrook, *Canadian External Relations*, pp. 376–8.

[2] Canadian government's note accepting the pact, 30 May 1928, reprinted in Mackay and Rogers, *Canada Looks Abroad*, pp. 330–2.

[3] An analysis of Canadian interests and policies in the Far East is to be found in Charles J. Woodsworth, *Canada and the Orient* (Toronto, Macmillan, for C.I.I.A., 1941); see especially Chapters V, VI, and VII.

Canadian policy, thought it would not be wise for the Canadian government to try 'with the slight knowledge that we possess . . . either to blame or praise this country or the other in connection with matters so serious as those involved in the . . . differences between Japan and China'.[1] When later the imposition of economic sanctions against Japan was urged upon the government, Mr. Bennett replied with the unmistakable approval of the House that no one in a position of responsibility could adopt such a course at a time when the Great Powers were so evidently unprepared for resolute action.[2] Nor would he commit himself to any forecast of future Canadian policy for 'the government should not make a declaration of policy, when the policy must needs be to some extent governed by considerations that will arise through discussions that will take place by the tribunal which ultimately has to decide the matter'.[3] Thus all responsibility for the settlement of the dispute was firmly attributed to the League and nothing was more evident than that the Canadian government, while prepared to accept its decisions loyally, was resolved to assume no significant share in their making. This may be attributed as much to lack of any clear-cut views as to general scepticism about the possibility of the League's enforcing peace in Eastern Asia. Even when the Lytton Report was before the Assembly the Canadian delegate, Mr. C. H. Cahan, a member of the cabinet, was only in a position to express views that were 'more or less personal', though he thought his colleagues would concur in them. Nowhere did he expressly endorse the terms of the Report, and while to one observer[4] it appeared that 'in a curious oration' he spoke 'strongly on both sides of the question', the more lasting impression was one of a disconcertingly sympathetic attitude towards Japan.[5] At a subsequent session of the League Assembly a carefully prepared statement of the Canadian attitude was submitted by her permanent delegate to the League, Dr. Riddell, and it corrected this impression in recording Canada's adoption without qualification of the recommendation of the Committee of Eighteen which had been set up to report on the dispute. In general it was clear that Canada was prepared, despite her dislike of entanglements, to follow a firm lead but not to give one. This is to be attributed mainly to a sense of the inappropriateness of advocating policies which other and greater Powers would be primarily responsible for carrying out, but also to a continuing scepticism about the desirability of seeking to enforce peace.

The Italian invasion of Abyssinia in 1935 compelled Canadians to examine

[1] 7 April 1932, Canada, H. of C. Deb., vol. 2, p. 1826. Mr. Glazebrook has commented on the odd admission that a country which was a member of the League and which had a Department of External Affairs, and a diplomatic mission in Tokyo, should have no more than a 'slight knowledge' of a major international crisis (p. 402).

[2] ibid. 1932, vol. 3, pp. 3438 ff.

[3] ibid. 1932–3, vol. 2, pp. 1369–70.

[4] Miss Freda White.

[5] See Woodsworth, *Canada and the Orient*, pp. 193–5, and also MacKay and Rogers, *Canada Looks Abroad*, pp. 101–2.

more carefully the foundations of their external policy. Once again Canada was little interested in the area of conflict. Alone of the self-governing members of the Commonwealth she was not in any way dependent upon the Mediterranean 'artery of Empire'. Her vital line of communications was the Atlantic, and even at a time when the power of the Italian navy was unduly exalted by friend and foe alike, there was no suggestion that Mussolini aspired to dominate the oceans. But, here as elsewhere, Canada's otherwise enviable detachment carried with it one liability. Her policy, unlike that of the Pacific dominions or of South Africa, had to be formulated, not in relation to vital interests, but in the light of principles that were variously interpreted within Canada and without. It is, therefore, not a matter for surprise that Canadian policy towards the Italo-Ethiopian war was at times confused and uncertain. Its occasional eccentricities, however, are less deserving of attention than the extent to which Canadian policies conformed to principles already clearly defined.

When the League met in September 1935 Mussolini's resolve to invade Abyssinia 'with Geneva, without Geneva, or against Geneva' was open and proclaimed. There was, therefore, as there had not been in 1931, no room for doubt about where responsibility for aggression would lie. Accordingly the Canadian attitude was correspondingly stiffer from the outset. Mr. G. H. Ferguson, the Canadian delegate, told the League Assembly on 14 September 1935 that Canada could 'not agree that any member is warranted in resorting to war to enforce its claims in violation of its solemn pledges to seek and find a peaceful settlement of every dispute';[1] and he gave the assurance that if the need arose Canada would join with other members of the League in considering how, by unanimous action, peace might be maintained. This assurance was implemented. On 7 October 1935 Italy was declared to be the aggressor, and on 11 October Canada accepted membership of the Committee of Eighteen appointed to initiate sanctions against her. At its first meeting Mr. Ferguson pressed for immediate action. 'Let them show the world', he said, 'that the League was no longer to be scoffed or laughed at, but that it meant business. ... If the delegations were not at Geneva to see that the Covenant was carried out, there was no purpose in their being there at all. ...'[2] In this outspoken support for the effective application of economic sanctions the Canadian government was wholly in step with the United Kingdom and with opinion at home outside Quebec. But it is worth noting that in the Canadian election campaign, which was proceeding simultaneously, all parties either implied or openly stated that they would not commit Canada to armed intervention in an African war even if it were sanctioned by the League.

Within six days of the accession to office of Mr. Mackenzie King's new

[1] Canada, Department of External Affairs, *Documents Relating to the Italo-Ethiopian Conflict* (Ottawa, 1936), quoted in Mackay and Rogers, *Canada Looks Abroad*, p. 103.
[2] Quoted in ibid. p. 103.

Liberal administration the Prime Minister issued a statement which, while reasserting the government's firm adherence to the principles of the Covenant and its intention to make 'participation in the League the corner-stone of its foreign policy in the general field', proceeded to make familiar but significant reservations. Successive Canadian governments, it was argued, have opposed the view that:

> the League's central purpose should be to guarantee the territorial *status quo* and to rely upon force for the maintenance of peace. . . . The absence of three Great Powers from the League, the failure of the repeated efforts to secure the disarmament contemplated in the Covenant, and the unwillingness of League members to enforce sanctions in the case of countries distant from the European scene, have increased the difficulty of making general commitments in advance to apply either economic or military sanctions.[1]

So while the government were willing to continue Canadian co-operation in the imposition of economic sanctions against Italy, they declared specifically that they did not recognize 'any commitment binding Canada to adopt military sanctions, and that no such commitment could be made without prior approval of the Canadian Parliament'.[2] Thus the doctrine of parliamentary responsibility which had been used so tellingly against Mr. Lloyd George in 1922 was turned against the wider pretensions of the League.

It is in the light of this statement of Liberal government policy that the 'Riddell incident' assumes some significance. Dr. W. A. Riddell, who had replaced Mr. Ferguson on the Committee of Eighteen, was convinced, as were many other members of the Committee, of the need for further sanctions if the Italian armies were to be checked in their hitherto victorious advance. On 2 November he telegraphed Ottawa for instructions with regard to strengthening sanctions by adding petroleum and its derivatives, coal, iron, cast iron, and steel to the list. When, however, the opportunity to speak came later that day, before any reply from his government could have been received, Riddell took the initiative in making the proposal. When on 4 November a telegram arrived from Ottawa instructing him not to take any action without specific authorization from his government, Dr. Riddell's already widely publicized initiative had acquired the embarrassing designation of 'the Canadian proposals'. Italy interpreted them as a deliberately hostile gesture which if carried out would be regarded as an act of war and, equally important in this context, Quebec was bitterly hostile to any such rigorous imposition of sanctions against the homeland of the Papacy. In some perplexity Mr. Mackenzie King decided against immediate disavowal but on 2 December, during his absence in the United States, the government discarded its reserve. On that day Mr. Lapointe, the acting Prime Minister, declared that Canada did not intend to take the initiative in any proposal for extending

[1] The text is printed in MacKay and Rogers, *Canada Looks Abroad*, pp. 346–8.

[2] ibid. p. 347.

economic sanctions, and that any views expressed by its delegate on the Committee of Eighteen were his own and not those of the Canadian government.[1] In Quebec this statement was hailed with enthusiasm, in large parts of English-speaking Canada with dismay. Conservatives lamented the breach in imperial solidarity; internationalists the ominous implication of a weakening in Canadian support for the League. In Rome the repudiation by the Canadian government of its delegate's sponsorship of oil sanctions produced 'un véritable optimisme',[2] Virginio Gayda observing with satisfaction that 'the granite block of imperial will here displays the most noticeable fissures'.[3] Confronted with these varied repercussions, Mr. Mackenzie King on his return explained that the disavowal of Dr. Riddell did not necessarily imply that the government was opposed to the imposition of oil or other sanctions but that they did not wish to take the initiative. 'It was', comments Mr. Glazebrook, 'only from the fame of leadership that the government backed with such rapid steps.'[4]

The pace of the retreat was quickened by the announcement of the Hoare–Laval pact on 8 December. The supporters of the League were dumbfounded, their criticisms of Mr. Mackenzie King's action deprived of force overnight.[5] The pact, and the abrupt change in Great Power policy constituted a sombre warning of the risks that leadership by the smaller Powers might entail for themselves in a world where the actions of the great were still decided not by a simple reference to declared principles but by nice calculations of probable consequences. Mr. Mackenzie King learned the lesson all too well, his habitual caution in international affairs being henceforward notably accentuated. In February 1936 he went so far as to tell the House of Commons that but for his action in disavowing Dr. Riddell 'the whole of Europe might have been aflame today'.[6] That was a reflection, capable neither of proof nor disproof, likely to give pause even to the most ardent crusaders.

The moral Mr. Mackenzie King drew from the Italo-Ethiopian crisis was that 'our country is being drawn into international situations to an extent that I think alarming'.[7] Accordingly the Canadian government quietly liquidated

[1] See Canada, H. of C. Deb., 1936, vol. 1, pp. 92 ff. for Mackenzie King's review of the incident. Dr. Riddell's own record of his actions should be read in his *World Security by Conference* (Toronto, Ryerson Press, 1947), Chapters XV and XVI. He thinks that the disavowal of his action was made on the initiative of Mr. Lapointe and that Mr. Mackenzie King was consulted about it but was not its author. He also believes that the Italian Consul-General in Montreal played a not unimportant part in the publicity that led up to it. See pp. 129–30. Cf. also Mackay and Rogers, *Canada Looks Abroad*, pp. 105–6; Glazebrook, *Canadian External Relations*, pp. 409–10; *Canada in World Affairs*, pp. 24–26, and Carter, *British Commonwealth*, pp. 217–23.

[2] *Le Temps* (Paris), 5 December 1935.

[3] *Giornale d'Italia*, quoted in Carter, *British Commonwealth*, p. 248.

[4] *Canadian External Relations*, p. 411.

[5] cf. *Winnipeg Free Press*, 7 December 1935.

[6] Canada, H. of C. Deb., 1936, vol. 1, p. 98.

[7] Quoted in *Canada in World Affairs*, p. 23.

outstanding commitments and withdrew from all semblance of active participation in European affairs. In June 1936 it decided to lift sanctions in the belief that 'collective bluffing cannot bring collective security, and under present conditions most countries have shown they are not prepared to make firm commitments beyond the range of their immediate interest'.[1] Nor was Canada prepared to urge those members of the League, upon whom the main burden of compulsion would rest, to resort to force, if they were not themselves convinced of its necessity. Here Canadian policy was in line with that of Australia and of the United Kingdom, though Mr. Mackenzie King carefully explained that the Canadian decision to end sanctions had been made independently and before information had been received in Ottawa about the intentions of the United Kingdom.[2]

CANADIAN REACTION TO THE FAILURE OF THE LEAGUE

The Italo-Ethiopian crisis has a lasting importance in Canadian history. For the government it afforded conclusive evidence that the League could not enforce peace, and in their view lesser Powers would henceforward neglect that self-evident fact at their peril. In the light of it Mr. Mackenzie King re-examined the foundations of Canadian policy and submitted his conclusion both to Parliament in June 1936[3] and later, on 29 September, to the Assembly of the League.[4] At Geneva he underlined Canada's 'less intimate knowledge of European affairs', he alluded with dismay to the violent recriminations, the feverish race for rearmament, 'the ceaseless weaving and unravelling of understandings and alliances' so completely in contrast 'to the friendly relations with our neighbours to which we are accustomed', and maintained that while Canadians could not reasonably expect their relations with the United States to be duplicated elsewhere, equally, Europeans should not expect 'a North American state to have the same international outlook, the same conception of interest, or of duty, as a European state facing widely different conditions'. To him it seemed as if confidence and good will between the nations of Europe could best be restored by the governments immediately concerned. Certainly Canada did not wish to be embroiled in their quarrels. Moreover, for long she had believed that emphasis should be placed more upon the conciliatory, and less upon the coercive, functions of the League, and by 1936 the difficulty of automatic intervention seemed to the Prime Minister to be increasing as conflicts tended to become as much struggles between classes, between economic systems, between social philosophies, as between states. Participation in such civil conflicts abroad would bring to Canada 'the hazard of strain and conflict at home'. While therefore she adhered to the principles professed by the League, there was general concurrence on

[1] Canada, H. of C. Deb., 1936, vol. 4, p. 3866.
[2] ibid. p. 3867.
[3] ibid. pp. 3862–73.
[4] Reprinted in Mackay and Rogers, *Canada Looks Abroad*, pp. 363–9.

the part of all her political leaders that automatic commitment to the application of force was not a practical policy. By unanimous resolution, so Mr. Mackenzie King reminded his audience in Geneva, the Canadian House of Commons had made the application of economic or military sanctions subject to the approval of Parliament. This did not mean, he continued,

> that in no circumstances would the Canadian people be prepared to share in action against an aggressor; there have been no absolute commitments either for or against participation in war or other forms of force. It does mean that any decision on the part of Canada to participate in war will have to be taken by the Parliament or people of Canada in the light of all the existing circumstances; circumstances of the day as they exist in Canada, as well as in the areas involved.

The pattern of Canadian policy drawn by the Canadian Prime Minister at Geneva in the autumn of 1936 underwent no significant variations in the succeeding three years. While the supporters of collective security rightly diagnosed, in the words of Mr. Dafoe, that the League of Nations, 'with assurances of the most distinguished consideration', was being 'ushered out into the darkness by Mr. Mackenzie King',[1] the great preponderance of opinion at home was with the government and not with them. For most Canadians support for the League has been at all times conditional, not absolute. At one extreme the backing of imperialists was dependent upon united action with Britain, at the other that of the French-Canadians was doubtful under almost any circumstances. The truth was that in respect of the League, as of most of the great issues of foreign policy, Canadian public opinion was in a state of some confusion. Mr. Mackenzie King attributed this to many reasons, to a slow emergence from the colonial attitude of mind; to a relative immunity from any serious danger of attack; to the real difficulties inherent in Canada's preoccupation with 'the tremendous, absorbing, and paramount tasks of achieving national unity'; and to the 'unparalleled complexity' of Canada's position in the world. It was not through hasty action, but through restraint from all but essential action, that the clarification of opinion would come most quickly. This attitude was less negative in fact than Mr. Mackenzie King was often anxious to make it appear. Concerned above all with the preservation of internal unity, he was convinced that only by a policy of no commitments, coupled with a corresponding emphasis on the consequent right and duty of Parliament to decide, could that unity be created. It was by bringing home to the representatives of the people an immediate sense of their responsibility that they could best be persuaded to give to international problems something of the attention they deserved.

The failure of the League and the disappearance of the protective barrier against aggression which it seemed to afford, stimulated some vigorous discussion of what Canada's foreign policy should be. It reached its greatest inten-

[1] Quoted in *Canada in World Affairs*, p. 40.

sity in intellectual and academic circles, it was conducted not always without asperity, and it was unrepresentative in that the radicals and the nationalists were more vocal than the conservatives, who in any case were disposed to believe that it was a topic better left unaired.[1] While it was apparent that the process of disentanglement from specific obligations to a now discredited League commended itself to most sections of opinion, more delicate and debatable questions derived from the undefined and undefinable nature of Canada's obligations to the British Commonwealth.

> The nations of the British Commonwealth [said Mr. Mackenzie King in his September speech at Geneva] are held together by ties of friendship, by similar political institutions, and by common attachment to democratic ideals, rather than by commitments to join together in war. The Canadian Parliament reserves to itself the right to declare, in the light of the circumstances existing at the time, to what extent, if at all, Canada will participate in conflicts in which other members of the Commonwealth may be engaged.[2]

Conservative sentiment demurred at so imprecise an interpretation of Commonwealth obligations, but the deeper cleavage lay between those who accepted the interpretation in principle but differed about the course Parliament should adopt in the event of a major war in which Britain was involved.

The hardening of isolationist sentiment as a result of the failure of the League to enforce its authority against Italy in 1935–6 was self-evident. In Canada the principal result of the Abyssinian crisis was not a recrudescence of imperial sentiment but the strengthening of isolationism coupled with renewed emphasis upon Canada as a North American nation.[3] This was an important fact which afforded further convincing evidence that imperialists who regarded the League as a distraction diverting loyalty and attention from the Empire were mistaken.[4] Some indeed feared that Canadian opinion was inclining towards an isolationism which would insist upon Canadian neutrality in any conflict in which North America was not directly attacked.[5] For their fears there was some foundation, for the deep disillusionment on the part of the few with the failure of the Great Powers to support the League coupled with the distaste of the many for undertaking obligations in a distant and

[1] An analysis of the time devoted to the discussion of foreign affairs in the House of Commons in the critical years 1936–9 is instructive. In 1936 foreign affairs were debated on two separate occasions in the House totalling 6 hours in the session February to June; in 1937 on 3 days—a total of 9½ hours from January to April; in 1938 twice, making a period of 7½ hours in the session from January to July; and in 1939 3 days (representing a span of 18 hours) were set aside to their discussion for first session January to June. These times do not include debates regarding defence or questions on foreign policy in the House.

[2] Quoted in *Canada in World Affairs*, p. 34.

[3] *Round Table*, 1936, vol. 26, pp. 599–602.

[4] For a critical analysis of their views see John W. Dafoe, 'The Imperial Conference of 1937', *University of Toronto Quarterly*, 1937–8, vol. 7, pp. 1–17.

[5] For a summary of conflicting Canadian viewpoints on international affairs see Mackay and Rogers, *Canada Looks Abroad*, pp. 249 ff., and *Canada in World Affairs*, pp. 41 ff.

inflammable continent about whose problems comparatively little was known, combined to produce, outside the ranks of conservatives and professed internationalists, an attitude unresponsive to any demand for concerted action, whether in the interests of international or of Commonwealth security. It received its more forceful expression not in French-Canada, but in the Middle West, where the nascent left-wing Co-operative Commonwealth Federation enjoyed growing support. At its 1937 annual convention the party favoured a policy of rigid neutrality in any 'imperialist' war regardless of who the aggressors might be and regardless of whether or not the other member-nations of the Commonwealth were involved. On 25 January the party's leader, Mr. Woodsworth, a Christian Pacifist, moved a formal resolution on these lines in the House of Commons. He maintained that in the face of the mounting international crisis Canada had slavishly followed the lead of Britain, and had thereby tried to escape responsibility for any active policy of her own. But if war came and Canada participated, the country would be split from 'stem to stern', for to French-Canada's traditional reservations must now be added the doubts of the Prairies, of whose inhabitants over 50 per cent. were not of Anglo-Saxon origin at all. If the British connexion were to be maintained, he concluded, Canada must have a voice in determining policies which vitally affected her people. For that reason she should at once take steps to make clear to the world her right to remain neutral when Britain was at war. Only in this way could the policy of keeping out of war almost at any cost be effectively put into practice.[1]

The government dealt firmly with the C.C.F. motion. Characteristically Mr. Mackenzie King did not openly challenge the possibility of Canada remaining neutral in a major war in which Britain was involved, but turned against the C.C.F. the doctrine that Parliament must decide. A commitment to neutrality was as undesirable as a commitment to sanctions, or to war, and stood condemned on identical grounds. Nor did the government accept the simple Marxist thesis of a world rent by the self-destroying struggles of rival imperialisms. There could be no denying, said Mr. Mackenzie King, that there were forces of evil present in the world, fighting against the forces of good. So long as this moral conflict continued those who wished to see the good triumph had to take every possible means to prevent the evil from gaining control. There was need for unity in Canada and between all the countries and the Commonwealth, for the Commonwealth was exercising a greater influence for peace than any other force in the world. Instead of talking about the danger of Britain dragging Canada into war, he believed that Britain was determined to exercise her power to avert a world catastrophe. And, he inquired,

What would be the effect, regardless of who the belligerents may be, of a declaration of neutrality . . . ? It would simply offer succour and support to those forces

[1] Canada, H. of C. Deb., 1937, vol. 1, pp. 237–43.

that are ready to oppose Canada, to oppose the British Commonwealth of Nations, to oppose the English-speaking peoples, and that have their hand out against democracy and democratic institutions. In the eyes of the world it would simply be a 'contracting out' of any endeavour to preserve all that we hold dearest in our national and in our individual lives.[1]

The government were therefore as rigidly averse to neutrality as a policy as they were to the adoption of other policies which would limit Canada's freedom of action at a critical moment.

But was Canada in a position to determine her policy in all circumstances? The Prime Minister, while careful to refrain from any detailed exposition of the nature of the moral obligations that bound the Commonwealth countries together, was satisfied that for practical purposes the answer was in the affirmative. What confronted Canada was a choice of policies, all of which she was free to adopt. The policy of the government, though assailed from the right and the left, had therefore a well-defined starting point, but from its very character an uncertain goal. There were, said Mr. Mackenzie King,[2] three different policies: that of the imperialists who took the view that the Empire was one and indivisible, and that therefore in matters of defence there should be a common policy: that of the isolationists who held with Mr. Woodsworth that a policy of rigid neutrality was the right course: and that of the government, who took up a central position, maintaining that foreign and defence policy should be decided in the light of Canadian interests, but that those interests demanded that the interests of all those with whom Canada might be associated should be taken into account. There is no doubt that this central position, with final responsibility vested in Parliament, had the support of the great bulk of the Canadian people. One of the most instructive lessons to be drawn from the 1937 debate on neutrality was that French-Canadian opinion did not favour the doctrinaire isolationism which adherence to such a policy would have involved.

DEFENCE AND THE IMPERIAL CONFERENCE

The Canadian government was too clear-sighted to suppose that freedom from all formal commitment carried with it any assurance of freedom from attack or of non-participation in war. On the contrary, final responsibility for the determination of policy demanded a greater measure of national self-reliance in every field than had hitherto been contemplated. This was particularly true in respect of defence. After 1919 Canada had carried disarmament as far as any country in the world. Mr. Ian Mackenzie, Liberal Minister for National Defence, confessed[3] that when the Liberal government took

[1] ibid. p. 252.

[2] ibid. pp. 250–1.

[3] No doubt not without some satisfaction, since a Conservative government had been in office for the preceding five years.

office in October 1935 'there was not a single fighting aeroplane in Canada; there was not a single bomb to be dropped by an aeroplane; there was scarcely any ammunition for guns'.[1] Nor did Canada possess 'adequate naval forces to guarantee her neutrality in a war in which she did not wish to be belligerent'.[2] The need for rearmament was, therefore, urgent, but the government were here the prisoners of their own policies. They could not justify and so accelerate rearmament in relation to any particular purpose other than national self-defence because that would necessarily have meant some definition of the causes for which Canada would fight; and the national self-defence of a country rightly considered to be virtually immune from attack was hardly a sufficient stimulus to action. The League might have supplied the deficiency. It met a real need in a country whose people were of diverse origins and diverse loyalties, but the League was moribund and Canada was not prepared to pretend, or to allow others to pretend, that any final authority was still vested in it. The Prime Minister carefully explained in May 1938 that so far as the Canadian government was concerned, the sanctions articles 'have ceased to have effect by general practice and consent, and cannot be revived by any state or group of states at will'.[3] The Empire, it is true, was far from moribund but the extent of Canada's obligations was controversial. Co-operation in imperial defence carried the unwelcome implication of predetermined co-operation in the Empire's wars. For this reason the greatest care was taken to dissociate Canadian rearmament from general imperial rearmament. Addressing the House on the much increased defence estimates for 1937–8, the Prime Minister stressed that the national estimates had 'not been framed with any thought of participation in European wars', and had

> not been framed as a result of any combined effort or consultation with the British authorities, beyond what would obviously be in the interests of all in the matter of gaining the benefit of expert opinion where expert opinion was obviously desirable. So far as policy is concerned . . . no request of any kind has come from the British government . . . with respect to a single item that appears in the estimates. . . .[4]

Whatever had been put there was there as the result of what the government thought necessary. But even so categoric a reassertion of Canada's resolve to keep her hands free from all obligations did not pass unchallenged by those who feared lest they should be drawn into the Empire's wars. To their criticisms the Prime Minister replied by declaring that all the government was doing was to ensure that Canada's forces would have the most modern and efficient equipment available for the defence of their country. It was on the defence of Canada that 'every cent.' of defence expenditure would be expended.

Mindful of the isolationism of the C.C.F., whose leader denounced in principle Canadian participation in all 'foreign' wars and still more Quebec's

[1] Canada, H. of C. Deb., 1937, vol. 1, pp. 894–5.
[2] ibid. p. 903.
[3] ibid. 1938, vol. 3, p. 3182.
[4] ibid. 1937, vol. 1, p. 246.

traditional and lively fear lest Canada be dragged into an imperialist war in which she had no interest, Mr. Mackenzie King went to London for the Imperial Conference of 1937 with his own inherent dislike of all binding commitments strongly reinforced by the need to quiet the fears of minorities at home.

In London representatives of the Commonwealth contented themselves with a statement of the general purposes of their foreign and defence policies[1] and refrained from entering into any particular obligations. It was this absence of commitment which prompted Mr. Dafoe to conclude that 'if we are to go by the report issued by the Conference itself, it can be said without hesitation that it was the Canadian view which prevailed'.[2] There was nothing in it about a common imperial defence policy but a lot about individual responsibility for local defence; nothing about full acceptance of League obligations but an admission that each member of the Commonwealth must determine its own attitude to the League. This was all very much in accord with Mr. Mackenzie King's well-known dislike of commitments either to Empire or to League. Yet the Conference was certainly not without its importance in the evolution of Canadian policy. In London Canadian statesmen were brought face to face with the dangerous reality of a rapidly rearming Germany openly challenging the ill-armed democracies of the West. In such circumstances the endorsement of a general policy of political and economic appeasement, coupled with renewed emphasis upon individual responsibility for defence, was of considerable importance, all the more so because Canadian insistence that the conclusions of Imperial Conferences possessed no binding authority did not mean in this particular case that their acceptability to Canada was in question. Since Mr. Dafoe was correct in thinking that in essentials it was the Canadian view that had prevailed in 1937, there was no ground for reservation on the part of the Canadian government about the opinions expressed in the Conference Report. In retrospect this is a fact of no little significance, for the reaction of the Conference to the mounting crisis in Europe foreshadowed and in principle endorsed the policy which culminated in the Munich settlement of 1938.

Mr. Mackenzie King had exceptional opportunities for assessing the risks of an early war in Europe, for on the morrow of the Imperial Conference he toured the capitals of Western Europe and visited the German Chancellor in Berlin. This was not in itself a matter of great moment. Eminent North Americans liked to meet Hitler for much the same reason that distinguished Europeans desired to see the Niagara Falls. No full account of what transpired at the meeting between the German dictator and the Canadian Prime Minister has so far been published, but it can be said with some assurance

[1] See Chapter III above.

[2] 'The Imperial Conference of 1937', *University of Toronto Quarterly*, October 1937, pp. 13–17.

that Mr. Mackenzie King, unlike some other British visitors to Nazi Germany, was not likely to have been unduly impressed by what he saw, for he was protected by his temperament against the tempting delusions to which not a few of them fell victim. Yet in some respects it would seem he was reassured, for he declared on his return that he was certain that neither the governments nor the peoples he had visited desired war.[1] On the other hand, he did not fail to seize the opportunity of warning the German Chancellor that in the event of aggression Canada would fight at the side of Britain. This is an important fact, which has hitherto received insufficient attention, and Mr. Mackenzie King's own account of what he said deserves to be quoted.

> If anyone thinks that Germany went into this war because Canada had not declared, months in advance, that she would go into the war if Germany started a war against any country, he has a very limited view of the factors that weighed in bringing about this attempt to conquer the world. . . . May I tell my hon. friends that Germany had a very definite knowledge of what Canada's attitude would be in the event of war. . . .
>
> I do tell this House of Commons today that my visit to Germany had as its objective to make it perfectly clear that, if there was a war of aggression, nothing in the world would keep the Canadian people from being at the side of Britain. That was known to the German government at that time, and my action in the matter was fully known to the British government; but I did not talk about it at the time, for it is just as well that some of these matters should not be spoken of until later years.[2]

What impression his words made in Germany is not so far known[3] but the incident at the least disposes of the idea that the Nazis had any reason to be misled about Canada's reaction to further aggression in Europe.[4]

It was against the background of the Imperial Conference and a growing awareness of the extent of Nazi ambitions that Canada's defence policy—'a reasonable and effective defence programme of its own', as the Prime Minister characteristically described it—was framed. In introducing the defence estimates for 1938–9 Mr. Mackenzie, the Minister for National Defence, restated the principles on which each dominion framed its defence policy. First, the Imperial Conferences of 1923 and 1926 had laid down that each self-governing dominion was primarily responsible for its own local defence; secondly, that the security of the Empire was a matter of concern to all its

[1] Broadcast from Ottawa, 19 July 1937.

[2] Canada, H. of C. Deb., 1944, vol. 6, p. 6275. Debate on Supply—External Affairs, 11 August 1944.

[3] The German documents concerning this period have not been published at the time of writing, but it may be that some record will be found among them.

[4] Mr. Mackenzie King's warning coming so soon after the Imperial Conference no doubt also suggested to the German government that the reaction of the other dominions would be similar. The warning was known to the United Kingdom government and in an address to the Canadian Houses of Parliament in 1943 Mr. Eden, who was Secretary of State for Foreign Affairs at the time, spoke with gratitude of Mr. Mackenzie King's action 'in telling the German government what he did'. Quoted in Canada, H. of C. Deb., 1944, vol. 4, p. 6275.

governments; thirdly, that military action in peace or war was a matter for individual decision on the part of each dominion. He then proceeded to discuss these principles on which defence policy might be based in relation to Canadian external policies. He further refined upon his Prime Minister's earlier definition of three principal schools of thought on foreign policy and defence by increasing their number to five. First, there was the imperialistic school, which regarded Canada as an integral part of the Commonwealth, bound to support every other member with military action, and to accept the foreign policy of the United Kingdom government, whether arrived at independently or through consultation.[1] Second, there was the isolationist or nationalist school, which held that Canada's geographical position and economic interest required that she should dissociate herself from responsibility for troubles in other parts of the world, especially Great Britain's imperial commitments. The third group consisted of League of Nations collectivists, who would have Canada participate in international obligations for peace. A very minor group was the North American collectivists, who would have Canada join the Pan-American Union and unite with all other American nations in taking only so much interest in European and Asiatic affairs as might be consistent with American interests. The fifth, or middle, group believed in no automatic commitments either for military action or neutrality. These would join with Great Britain or with the League in war for a principle or for the safety of the liberty of the world, if convinced that it was seriously threatened. But they refused to imperil Canadian unity by accepting in advance either of the two following propositions: that when Great Britain was at war Canada must automatically go to her support with all her resources; or that when the League ordered sanctions Canada was bound to action.[2] There was no doubt that this school represented not merely the largest but an ever expanding section of Canadian opinion.

Mr. Mackenzie went on to state categorically that every minister who had represented Canada at the 1937 Imperial Conference was himself bound by the declarations made in its report about national defence and foreign policy. It was this that gave the findings of the Conference a direct relevance to Canadian defence policy. What its *Proceedings* recorded was:

In the course of the discussions, the Conference found general agreement among its members that the security of each of their countries can be increased by co-operation in such matters as the free interchange of information concerning the state of their naval, military and air forces, the continuance of the arrangements already initiated by some of them for concerting the scale of the defences of ports, and measures for co-operation in the defence of communications and other common interests.

[1] Conservative members vigorously denied that such was the view of their party.

[2] Canada, H. of C. Deb., 1938, vol. 2, p. 1644.

Then this vitally important paragraph:

> At the same time the Conference recognized that it is the sole responsibility of the several Parliaments of the British Commonwealth to decide the nature and scope of their own defence policy.[1]

In principle the Prime Minister might not have agreed that defence policy must necessarily be so closely related to the recommendations of the Imperial Conference, but this cordial endorsement of them by his Minister for National Defence strengthened the presumption that in London the Canadian view had prevailed.[2]

The favoured strategic position which Canada enjoyed was brought out very clearly by the scale of the preparations which she felt it necessary to make to meet a potential threat, whether direct or indirect, to her own security. Priority was given to the development of the Royal Canadian Air Force and to sea defences, particularly in the Pacific. But the Minister pointed out that when the programme for 1938–9 was completed there would be adequate provision only for the partial organization of two additional Air Force squadrons, bringing the total up to ten in all, and that with the completion of the 1938–9 orders for aircraft there would be available no more than 102 modern service aircraft. Naval strength was to be increased notably by the addition of two new destroyers.

So modest an expansion in the defence services could be contemplated only because the main deterrent against a major attack on Canada by a European Power was, as the Minister pointed out, the existence of the Royal Navy in Atlantic waters and the existence of friendly fleets in the Pacific. The Conservative opposition were highly critical of the limited scale of Canada's rearmament. They maintained that since there was no more certain way to war than an unarmed Empire, Canada should play a much fuller part in its rearming and, in particular, should contribute more to the security of the Pacific by displaying greater interest in the fortification of Singapore. In their view, too, the scale of consultation and co-operation in the planning of military operations with other Empire countries should be quickly and greatly expanded. More significant in its impact on future government policy was the attitude of the French-Canadian members. While mistrustful of the purposes for which the Canadian air force was being enlarged, they were for the most part satisfied that Canada should take adequate steps to make herself effectively responsible for her own security. If they continued to believe that the moral commitments of Canada towards the Commonwealth were more considerable than the Minister had allowed, they did not challenge the need for

[1] ibid. p. 1645.

[2] In March 1939 Mr. Mackenzie King thought that 'perhaps the chief significance of the Imperial Conference of 1937' was to be found in its general recognition of diffusion and decentralization of responsibility for defence and the greater importance of local defence. (Canada, H. of C. Deb., 1939, vol. 3, p. 2424.)

some increase in Canada's armed forces. Of this the C.C.F. were the only outright opponents. Resolutely opposed to Canadian participation in any 'foreign' wars, they regarded with suspicion measures which seemed to them to indicate that the government considered that the defence of Canada might reasonably and properly involve active participation in a war in Europe or Asia.

Despite criticism from imperialists and isolationists the middle-of-the-road position which Canada took up in defence, as in foreign, policy was generally endorsed. Yet the nature of the criticisms makes it clear how agreement on the main lines of Canada's defence policy was delayed by her own comparative security. The absence of direct danger from without seemingly opened up fields for speculation barred to less fortunately situated lands. In particular it suggested to many members that the defence of Canada and the defence of Britain might be dissociated more easily than was in fact the case. Despite the assured protection of the United States the security of Canada was linked more intimately with that of Britain than was recognized at all times even by the government itself.[1] The North Atlantic community existed before it was given a name.

THE GROWTH OF CANADIAN-AMERICAN FRIENDSHIP

The failure of the League, which in itself brought Canada no closer to the Empire, stimulated a new awareness of her position as a North American nation. As she deliberately withdrew from almost all active participation in the affairs of Europe and of Asia, the eyes of her people, and more particularly of her government, turned southwards to the great neighbour who had never been a member of the League. This sense of a growing community of interest between the two North American members of the sundered Anglo-Saxon world received outward expression in a speech of President Roosevelt's at Chautauqua in August 1936. 'If there are remoter nations', he said, 'that wish us not good but ill they know that we are strong; they know that we can and will defend ourselves and our neighbourhood.'[2] This implied assurance of United States aid in the event of an attack upon Canadian soil was reiterated in explicit terms two years later. On 18 August 1938 at Kingston, Ontario, President Roosevelt said with deliberation: 'The dominion of Canada is part of the sisterhood of the British Empire. I give to you an assurance that the people of the United States will not stand idly by if domination of Canadian soil is threatened by any other Empire.'[3] In Canada this declaration of continental

[1] It is, however, to be noted that the Canadian government, in common with the other governments of the Commonwealth, co-operated in the preparation of plans for common defence through the Committee of Imperial Defence. Canada remained, however, the judge of when aggression had taken place and of the extent to which for her part such plans should be put into effect.

[2] *The Times*, 15 August 1936, quoted in Brebner, *North Atlantic Triangle*, p. 314.

[3] The speech is reproduced in *Canada in World Affairs*, pp. 270–1.

solidarity was received with general acclaim. Mr. Mackenzie King remarked later that the President's words made August 1938 as memorable a date in the history of North America as September 1938 was in the history of Europe.[1] The moral he drew from it was that while the assurance of United States assistance in the event of direct aggression greatly increased Canada's security, it demanded from self-respect, if nothing else, that Canada should develop her own capacity for self-defence.

Mr. Mackenzie King was careful to emphasize that the new sense of solidarity between Canada and the United States did not in any way detract from the particular relationship of Canada with the Commonwealth countries. He was indeed concerned throughout his life to bring the United States and the United Kingdom into closer accord, and far from thinking that the strengthening of Canadian-American friendship was incompatible with Canada's membership of the Commonwealth, he believed it to be a condition of its vigorous survival. Thus in 1939 he emphasized that the 'closer and more responsible relations with the United States have not in any way lessened the intimacy of our relations with the United Kingdom. On the contrary, this development has been paralleled by a clearer understanding by those two great countries of the ideals and interests they share together.'[2]

CANADIAN DETACHMENT FROM EUROPEAN POLITICS

Canada's interests in Europe or in Asia though real were for the most part indirect and general in character, and that made possible her progressive detachment from their affairs after 1936. Yet her detachment was not, and never could be, complete. It was qualified in theory by her continuing membership of the League and in practice by her participation in intra-Commonwealth consultation. But even within the Commonwealth circle this policy was not without effect. Over and above Canada's dislike of any semblance of formal commitment to the Commonwealth, as to the League, there was on her part growing restraint in using the opportunities she enjoyed for influencing the course of United Kingdom policy. Where Australia, New Zealand, and South Africa frequently expressed opinions on the information received from London about developments in international affairs and the United Kingdom's contemplated reaction to them, Canada believed that silence was golden. It was indeed Mr. Mackenzie King's considered view that the Canadian government should not seek to influence Britain's policy, still less try to work out a common policy through active consultation on each issue as it arose. It is true that at a time when Canadian diplomatic representation in foreign capitals was negligible, information from London was welcome

[1] The analogy was intended to be complimentary, but the subsequent ill fame of Munich has given it a double-edged flavour not intended by the Canadian Prime Minister. See Canada, H. of C. Deb., 1939, vol. 3, pp. 2417–25, and *Canada in World Affairs*, pp. 288 ff., where Mr. Mackenzie King's speech is reproduced.

[2] ibid. p. 293.

and provided most of the background essential to the formulation of foreign policy, but comment on it was felt to be both out of place and likely to lead, however indirectly, to moral commitments which would restrict Canada's freedom of action in time of crisis. The Prime Minister's reply to questions about consultation with the United Kingdom accordingly never varied in substance. The British government had informed the Canadian government of particular events or decisions, but no advice had been asked for and none had been given. Mr. Mackenzie King did not think it should be given. When on 2 November 1938 Mr. Neville Chamberlain announced in the House of Commons that Australia and South Africa had telegraphed their approval of the Anglo-Italian agreement, Mr. Lapointe explained Canadian silence by pointing out that as 'the agreement does not deal with any matters in which Canada has any direct interest, there has not been any occasion for the expression of the views of the Canadian government'.[1]

> So far as the Canadian Government is concerned [Mr. Mackenzie King had said earlier] it does not consider that it is in the interest either of Canada or of the Commonwealth to tender advice as to what policy the United Kingdom should adopt week by week, or become involved in British political disputes. We have expressed no opinion on that policy, and no one in London is authorized or warranted in interpreting us as doing so.[2]

So absolute a reserve was not, however, maintained throughout the critical summer months of 1939, and at all times, even when no comment was made and no advice tendered, the views entertained by the Canadian government were rarely in doubt.

In general the Canadian government was in full sympathy with the aim of the United Kingdom to preserve peace at almost any price. Not once but many times the Prime Minister and Mr. Lapointe, the Minister for Justice, bestowed the highest praise on the continued efforts of the British government to avert war. The reason is not far to seek. Not only did Canada passionately desire to be left in peace, but her government knew that if war came unity at home could be preserved only if it could be shown beyond all reasonable doubt that the war could not have been averted by any reasonable concessions and that the ultimate aims of the aggressor were not limited to some particular and local objective. Canadian support for a policy of conciliation in Europe in 1937–8 for this reason never wavered. Prompted by the overriding claims of internal unity it was sufficiently clear in origin and purpose to require no formal expression in London.

Detachment from the affairs of Europe and Asia not only precluded spectacular policies but demanded restraint. Of that no one was more conscious than the Prime Minister. In May 1938 he warned members of the House of

[1] *New York Times*, 3 November 1938.

[2] 24 May 1938, Canada, H. of C. Deb., vol. 3, p. 3189.

Commons that unless they wished to have it appear that Canada was anxious to participate in events overseas, to become a party to what was happening on other continents, they, in common with all persons in positions of responsibility, should refrain from making any representations which would appear to have a contrary aim and purpose.[1] But such restraint was in itself inimical to the clarification of Canadian public opinion, and outside Parliament at least the Prime Minister's appeals fortunately passed unheeded. Detachment on the part of a dominion which, in the words of her Prime Minister, had 'neither the power nor the knowledge to settle the destinies of peoples thousands of miles away' commended itself to the prudent but not to the enthusiastic. Yet it was not fairly represented as tantamount to a negation of all policy. In Spain the Canadian government supported non-intervention on an issue which deeply divided opinion at home; in November 1937 it was represented at the abortive Brussels Conference called in the hope of resolving the Sino-Japanese conflict by peaceful means. It refrained from expressing any views on the Anglo-Italian rapprochement, though it made a modest contribution to the policy of appeasement by recognizing the King of Italy as Emperor of Ethiopia in December 1938. But if Canada was thus prepared to follow she was not prepared with insufficient knowledge to attempt to point the way. In that she showed a prudent sense of limitation.

CANADA AND MUNICH

In the Czech crisis of 1938 the Canadian government apparently played an almost wholly passive role. While kept fully informed of developments from London the evidence suggests that at no time did the Canadian government offer any written observations about the policy pursued by the United Kingdom government. On the other hand, Canada was represented in London by Mr. Vincent Massey, a diplomat of experience and distinction, who is not likely to have refrained from the expression of views at the many meetings between the Secretary of State for Dominion Affairs and the Dominion High Commissioners.

As the crisis moved towards its climax in the late summer of 1938 Parliament was not in session, and until mid-September the government issued no statement of any kind. When, however, Mr. Chamberlain announced his intention of flying to Berchtesgaden to meet the German Chancellor, Mr. Mackenzie King personally telegraphed his 'deep satisfaction', adding that 'the whole Canadian people will warmly approve this farseeing and truly noble action'. Three days later, on 17 September, the official silence was broken by the issue of a not very informative statement saying that the government was giving its 'unremitting consideration' to the European situation and, should attempts at mediation fail, would summon Parliament and submit its recommendations.

[1] See ibid. pp. 2752–3.

In the meantime 'public controversy as to action in hypothetical circumstances' was discouraged on the ground that it would serve to promote neither Canadian nor Commonwealth unity nor the cause of peace itself.[1] This tepid statement was well calculated to reassure Quebec, but it failed notably to satisfy Conservative opinion in Ontario. The government, however, was not to be moved by demands for what its Prime Minister referred to disparagingly as 'red-blooded ultimatums'. On 23 September the cabinet held an emergency meeting at which defence measures were discussed and its hand was significantly strengthened by the pledge of the new Conservative leader, Dr. Manion, on 28 September to co-operate in whatever steps the government might take in support of Mr. Chamberlain and the Empire. The news of the Munich agreement two days later was welcomed with general enthusiasm, and elicited a further telegram from Mr. Mackenzie King eulogizing Mr. Chamberlain's work for peace.[2]

There is no doubt that the Canadian government approved the policy of the United Kingdom government in September 1938, and it is easy to understand why they did so. If the British people, comments Professor Soward, 'found it fantastic to be on the verge of war "because of a quarrel in a far-away country between people of whom we know nothing", as Mr. Chamberlain remarked in his famous broadcast of 27 September, how much more so did the prospect displease a French-Canadian *habitant*, a Maritime fisherman, or a Saskatchewan wheat farmer?'[3] The Canadian government, concerned above all with internal unity, was well aware that if a united country were to resist the aggression of the dictators, it must be clear beyond all possible shadow of doubt that their aim was not the redress of grievances or the rectification of frontiers but the domination of the whole of the free world by force. For Canadians therefore the supreme merit of Mr. Chamberlain's policy of appeasement was that, possibly at a great sacrifice of material advantage, it exposed the true character of Nazi ambitions. But if appeasement was essential to the political education of Quebec, it exacted an internal as well as

[1] See *Canada in World Affairs*, pp. 114–15, for a detailed narrative of events.

[2] The text was as follows: 'The heart of Canada is rejoicing tonight at the success which crowned your unremitting efforts for peace. May I convey to you the warm congratulations of the Canadian people and, with them, an expression of their gratitude, which is felt from one end of the Dominion to the other.

'My colleagues in the Government join with me in unbounded admiration at the service you have rendered mankind. Your achievements in the past month alone will ensure you an abiding and illustrious place among the great conciliators whom the United Kingdom, the British Commonwealth of Nations, and the whole world will continue to honour.

'On the very brink of chaos, with passions flaming and armies marching, the voice of reason has found a way out of the conflict which no people in their heart desired but none seemed able to avert. A turning point in the world's history will be reached if, as we hope, tonight's agreement means a halt to the mad race in arms and a new start in building a partnership of all peoples. May you have health and strength to carry your great work to its completion' (*Manchester Guardian*, 1 October 1938).

[3] *Canada in World Affairs*, p. 113.

an external price. For many younger Canadians it seemed as if with Munich the moral case against aggression had gone. Nor were they without their spokesman. Amid the cheers that followed Munich at least one sobering voice was heard asking 'what's the cheering for?'[1] It was that of Mr. John Dafoe. The dismemberment of a small state by a process of bloodless aggression seemed to the venerable champion of collective security a prelude not to peace but to war. After tracing the course of Hitlerite aggression he concluded by challenging and condemning the role of the democracies:

> The doctrine that Germany can intervene for racial reasons for the 'protection' of Germans on such grounds as she thinks proper in any country in the world which she is in a position to coerce, and without regard to any engagements she has made or guarantee she has given has now not only been asserted but made good: and it has been approved, sanctioned, certified, and validated by the governments of Great Britain and France, who had undertaken in this respect to speak for the democracies of the world. This is the situation: and those who think it is all right will cheer for it.[2]

At the time his prophetic words passed well-nigh unheeded; in later years they were remembered to his credit and in vindication of the cause he championed.[3]

The Canadian White Paper[4] on the German-Czechoslovak Crisis included no Canadian correspondence but merely duplicated the material contained in the United Kingdom White Paper. But none the less the government were, and felt themselves to be, committed to the support of the Munich settlement. In subsequent speeches Mr. Mackenzie King went out of his way to justify Mr. Chamberlain's policy. Thus in March 1939, when the policy of appeasement lay in ruins, the Canadian Prime Minister declared that in September 1938 the United Kingdom government had emphatically made the right choice 'in striving to prevent the outbreak of war'. For Mr. Chamberlain himself it 'required unusual courage, disregard of risks to his personal prestige, prompt decision and dogged persistence to carry through those last . . . efforts for peace' and he 'never lost his patience, his temper or his head'.[5] Such unwonted vehemence in the defence of a United Kingdom policy suggested that the Canadian government had influenced and strongly urged its adoption in London.[6] Yet had appeasement failed to avert war in September 1938

[1] The title of the editorial in the *Winnipeg Free Press*, 30 September 1938. [2] ibid.

[3] The bitter reaction of some of the younger generation to the politics of Munich is set out with force and moving conviction in F. H. D. Pickersgill, *Letters Written During the Period 1934–43*, ed. by G. H. Ford (Toronto, Ryerson Press, 1948). Frank Pickersgill was a young Canadian who travelled widely in Europe before the war, and anyone who wishes to understand the viewpoint of young English-Canadians will find his letters more enlightening and more readable than most formal studies of contemporary Canadian opinion.

[4] *Documents Relating to the German-Czechoslovak Crisis* (Ottawa, September 1938).

[5] 30 March 1939, Canada, H. of C. Deb., vol. 3, p. 2411.

[6] To do so would not necessarily have involved any written communications from the Canadian to the United Kingdom government.

there is no doubt what recommendation the Canadian government would have submitted to Parliament. It would have proposed Canadian participation in war at the side of Britain and it would have been assured of the support of the great majority in English-speaking Canada, even if the attitude of Quebec was likely to be uncertain.

GROWING UNITY AT HOME

The reaction of the Canadian people to the Czech crisis was reassuring to their government. There was in September 1938 a greater measure of unity than would have been thought possible two or three years earlier. As a result, when in the spring of 1939 it became apparent that Germany remained unappeased, the government utterances struck a sharper note. On 16 January Mr. Mackenzie King quoted from a speech of Sir Wilfred Laurier's made in 1910, saying that it represented Liberal policy 'as it is today and will continue under the present administration'.

> If England is at war [the extract read] we are at war and liable to attack. I do not say we will always be attacked; neither do I say that we would take part in all the wars of England. That is a matter that must be guided by circumstances, upon which the Canadian parliament will have to pronounce and will have to decide in its own best judgement.[1]

Subsequently the Prime Minister explained that Laurier's words were to be interpreted only as implying that other nations might not respect a declaration of Canadian neutrality, but it seems certain that he intended at the time to leave his audience with some more positive impression than that. In any event on 20 March Mr. Mackenzie King responded to Hitler's seizure of Czechoslovakia with an outspoken denunciation of 'this wanton and forcible occupation' and a recognition that it was necessary to prepare for all future contingencies. Nor did he conceal any longer his own view that in the event of direct aggression on Britain Canada would go to her aid. 'If', he said, 'there were a prospect of an aggressor launching an attack on Britain, with bombers raining death on London, I have no doubt what the decision of the Canadian people and Parliament would be. We would regard it as an act of aggression, menacing freedom in all parts of the British Commonwealth.'[2] Even more noteworthy was the language of Mr. Lapointe, the Minister for Justice, in the debate of 30 March. He dismissed as impracticable the idea of Canadian neutrality in a major war in which Britain was involved. Neutrality demanded an attitude of impartiality towards all belligerents.

> Can such an attitude of impartiality [he asked] be possible in Canada during a

[1] Canada, H. of C. Deb., 1939, vol. 1, p. 52; see also for commentary *Canada in World Affairs*, pp. 121–2.

[2] Ibid., vol. 2, p. 2043.

war in our present international situation? A neutral state . . . would have to intern British troops or war vessels. I ask any one of my fellow countrymen whether they believe seriously that this could be done without a civil war in Canada. . . . It is clear that under the circumstances the right itself [of neutrality] is meaningless.[1]

Any bombardment of London, continued Mr. Lapointe in support of his leader, would certainly create a wave of public opinion that would force any government to intervene, and he pleaded with his fellow countrymen in Quebec to recognize the realities of the situation.

From the speeches of the Prime Minister and his French-Canadian Minister for Justice, it was apparent that German aggression against Western Europe involving a direct attack upon Britain would bring Canada into the war. It is true that the decision would rest with this Canadian Parliament, but, assured of Conservative support, the Liberal government had no need to entertain any fear lest its recommendation to go to war in such circumstances would be seriously challenged. What was remarkable was the extent to which differences and doubts tended to disappear under the impact of discussion within and events without. In May 1939 the Minister for National Defence had no difficulty in persuading the House to approve defence estimates which involved an expenditure of $64·5 million compared with some $33 million in each of the two preceding years. None doubted now that Canada at the least must be prepared to defend herself by land, by sea, and in the air, and while there was a general reluctance to contemplate the possibility of sending a full-scale expeditionary force overseas once again and general agreement that conscription should not be applied, the principles which should determine Canadian action were no longer seriously in question. The growing unity of outlook was deepened in early summer of 1939 by the visit of King George VI and Queen Elizabeth whom Canadians of all provinces and classes delighted to welcome as their King and Queen, and in late August by the announcement of the Nazi-Soviet pact which went far to convince Quebec that a war provoked by a German attack on Poland would be a war against the forces of evil. Throughout their protracted course the Anglo-French negotiations for a military agreement with Russia had been viewed with grave misgiving by the Canadian government, and Mr. Mackenzie King made no secret of Canada's dislike of any rigid agreement with the Soviet Union even if its character were purely defensive. The failure of these negotiations was therefore accepted with equanimity, even relief, and the announcement of the Nazi-Soviet agreement was followed by a warning from Mr. Mackenzie King to the German Consul-General in Ottawa that in the event of a German attack on Poland, the Canadian cabinet had unanimously decided to recommend to the Canadian Parliament that Canada should participate to the limit of her capacity on the side of Britain and France.

[1] ibid. vol. 3, p. 2467.

THE ROLE OF MR. MACKENZIE KING

The overriding consideration which guided Mr. Mackenzie King in his conduct of Canada's foreign policy was that the maintenance and the strengthening of internal unity was the indispensable condition of its successful application. That, too, had been the aim of Laurier, and his political heir made it part of Canada's national tradition.[1] He did so with cool deliberation. Lord Chesterfield once boasted that for more than forty years he had never used a word without considering first if there were not a better one. In this Mr. Mackenzie King could bear comparison with the polished littérateur of eighteenth-century England.[2] Little that he said, even his apparent indiscretions, was not calculated, and he rarely advanced to a position he desired to attain without leaving open, with some nice inflexion of meaning or ambiguity of phrase, the way of retreat lest later the advance should seem untimely. This gave to his policy an air of indecision which misled even his friends, exasperated his opponents, and sowed doubts about his intentions in a wider world. Yet indecisive though he was in small things, Mr. Mackenzie King saw with an almost prophetic clarity the pattern of Canada's future external policy. What he could do, and what he did, was to ensure that in the early days of Canada's fully autonomous nationhood nothing should be permitted to weaken the foundation of unity upon which the greatness of all nations is built. The tribute that can be paid to his leadership in the difficult, dangerous years before the Second World War is that with a painstaking care that amounted almost to genius he fostered a unity of outlook which, when the hour of decision came, brought a united people into a war against aggression on the side of Britain, when no other independent nation of the Americas felt a call to action.

[1] It has already been noted that his Deputy Minister of External Affairs throughout those critical years was Dr. O. D. Skelton, the biographer of Laurier.

[2] Mr. J. W. Pickersgill, who was Secretary to Mr. Mackenzie King and for ten years helped him in the drafting of his speeches, has described his exacting method of composition. In preparing a speech, writes Mr. Pickersgill, 'Mr. King would spend endless time in searching for the phrase or word with precisely the shade of meaning he wished to convey, and he had great satisfaction in finding the word or phrase that really suited him'. Even on comparatively unimportant occasions the draft would be repeatedly revised and 'he was never satisfied with the text of a speech and said, over and over again, that if he had only had one more day it would have been just right'. Mr. Pickersgill's article incidentally contains many revealing sidelights on Mr. Mackenzie King's personality. Entitled 'Mackenzie King's Speeches', it is published in the *Queen's Quarterly* (Toronto), Autumn 1950.

CHAPTER V

AUSTRALIA: THE PACIFIC OUTPOST

ENVIRONMENT AND TRADITION

As two thousand years ago the city-states of Greece looked out with mingled curiosity and apprehension upon 'Asia's myriad-peopled lands', so in our time Australia, the outpost of Europe in far-distant Pacific waters, has looked to the north-west upon the continent of Asia, mysterious, not a little frightening, and populated by teeming millions who lived on the very margin of subsistence. Strategically the most exposed of the dominions of the British Commonwealth, Australia since the late nineteenth century has watched anxiously for signs on Asia's political horizon which might portend the emergence of a dominant maritime power. Till 1905 fears of Russian as well as of Japanese aggression were widely entertained; but after the destruction of Russia's Far Eastern naval strength at Tsushima they were focused almost exclusively on Japan.[1] Yet this popular preoccupation with the coming of the 'yellow peril' was not for long paralleled, even in political circles, by any close study or growing interest in the Japanese, and still less the Asian, political scene. Tradition still remained more powerful than environment in determining Australia's outlook. 'In Asia but not of it; of Europe but not in it', Australians, like Canadians, felt the conflicting pulls of geography and history, but for them the pull of history, strongly reinforced by economic circumstances, was decisive. Their greater neighbours were not fellow Anglo-Saxons but men of different race and colour with whom easy, intimate association seemed precluded. Australians, therefore, strangers among the peoples with whom their lot was cast, have had no friendship with a neighbouring state to balance, still less condition, their loyalty to the mother country, and as a result they have remained far more conscious than Canadians of the homelands of their race and culture. This disposition to look westwards was powerfully reinforced by the composition of Australia's population and by her strategic isolation. Her population, the most homogeneous in the Commonwealth, was almost 99 per cent. of British extraction,[2] the rigid

[1] See G. C. Craig, *The Federal Defence of Australasia* (London, Clowes, 1897), Ch. V, and C. Brunsdon Fletcher, *The New Pacific* (London, Macmillan, 1917). The risk of aggression in the Pacific at a time when Britain was engaged in war in Europe was not altogether overlooked.

[2] To be exact of 'British Isles' extraction, for the large minority of Irish immigrants has played a notable part in Australian politics and has counteracted any tendency towards an over-sentimental conception of relations with the mother country. The census figures of 1933 showed a total population of 6,629,839 of whom about 38 per cent. were Anglicans, 19 per cent. Roman Catholics, 11 per cent. Presbyterians, and 10 per cent. Methodists. Religion may be taken to reflect the origins of population, Anglicans being of English,

enforcement of the 'white Australia' policy having excluded immigrants of non-European descent even from the tropical north.

Hartley Grattan has spoken of Australian foreign policy as 'existing below the level of consciousness'.[1] This is a very revealing remark which rightly suggests that Australia's traditional outlook on the world, but not her deliberately formulated policy, has been decisive in determining her relations with other countries. But that outlook has itself been moulded by circumstances. Strategic isolation which in early times encouraged dreams of expansion, of a 'united Australia ruling the South Seas' or even of 'a mighty empire' in the Pacific under the banner of the Anglo-Saxon race,[2] later imparted a sobering note of realism into Australian thinking about world affairs. It was felt instinctively to preclude independence in foreign policy until Australia had resources both of man-power and industry sufficient to repel large-scale invasion from the north. By 1939 she still lacked both. Her population in relation to the area to be defended was inadequate; and while Australian industry had reached a stage when considerable and rapid expansion was possible, it was not yet supplying any reasonable proportion of the weapons and equipment demanded by defensive warfare in modern times. Acquiescence generally in Britain's foreign policy before 1939 was not, therefore, as Professor Bailey has been careful to emphasize,[3] the product of a Crown Colony attitude, but of a political necessity deriving from a strategic situation which made British naval strength the condition of Australian security. At the same time dependence on Britain was not irksome. Most Australians were proud of the Empire, proud that Australia should be a member of it, and the men who in such numbers voluntarily enlisted in the First and the Second Australian Imperial Forces were moved, irrespective of any immediate threat to the security of the Australian continent, to fight in the Empire's wars.

THE CHARACTER OF AUSTRALIAN NATIONALISM

Australia's acquiescence in Britain's policies was by no means passive. On the contrary, United Kingdom foreign policy was criticized in Australia with the greatest freedom almost as though it were a domestic issue.[4] Indeed as such it was not altogether unreasonably regarded; for as Australia aspired

Roman Catholics of Irish, Presbyterians of Scottish, and Methodists of Welsh and English descent (Hartley Grattan, ed., *Australia* (Berkeley, University of California, 1947) p. 326).

[1] Quoted by K. H. Bailey in Australian Institute of International Affairs, *Australia and the Pacific* (Princeton University Press, 1944) p. 5.

[2] The phrases were used by Sir Thomas McIlwraith, Premier of Queensland, and Mr. Thomson respectively, quoted in W. K. Hancock, *Politics in Pitcairn* (London, Macmillan, 1947) p. 61.

[3] *Australia and the Pacific*, pp. 6–7.

[4] Mr. R. G. Casey, the Federal Treasurer, explained why this was so in an address to the Australian Institute of Political Science in January 1938. The foreign policy of the British government, he said, 'is pursued after consultation with Australia and the other dominions, and British foreign policy may accordingly be regarded in a very real sense as Australian foreign policy' (*Sydney Morning Herald*, 31 January 1938).

in her own interests not to a separate foreign policy but to a Commonwealth or at least an Anglo-Australian policy, so she insisted that the voice of both countries should be duly heard in its formulation. By an easy transition criticism of the Australian government's acquiescence in United Kingdom policies merged into criticism of the policies themselves and of the government primarily responsible for them, with the result that general debates on external policy at Canberra tended to follow closely the pattern already set at Westminster. This was particularly true between 1932 and 1939, when the outlook of Mr. Lyons's administration had much in common with that of the National government in Britain and when in both countries the animosity of the Labour opposition was heightened by the spectacle of a Conservative administration formed and in Australia led throughout by a Labour renegade.[1] In Australia, moreover, the acrimony of party politics tended to accentuate party differences in external policy and in some measure to distort them. Confronted by a Labour opposition inclining towards isolationism and profoundly mistrustful of the 'capitalist-imperialist' government of the United Kingdom, Mr. Lyons perhaps began to see merits in Mr. Chamberlain's policies which might otherwise have passed unnoted. But, however this may be, it is important to recognize that it was Australia's sense of unity with the mother country that made United Kingdom foreign policy a matter of domestic significance in Australia where the presumption throughout, irrespective of party attitudes, was that British people in Australia and in the United Kingdom swam or sank together. About methods and policies there might be deep differences of opinion, but about ends there was no dispute. The overriding responsibility of any Australian government was to ensure that the United Kingdom government, with its manifold preoccupations nearer home, did not overlook Australian interests in the Pacific.

While the sense of unity between Australia and Britain was fundamental, the absence of a more pronounced emphasis on the individual character of Australian policy is to be attributed to many factors, some of transient, others of lasting importance. Mr. Lyons's administration, composed of the United Australia and Country parties, was temperamentally predisposed towards imperial policies and unsympathetic to the active extension of dominion responsibilities in the external field. Nor did Mr. Lyons encourage parliamentary discussion of foreign policy. When in 1938, as leader of the opposition, Mr. Curtin requested that Parliament be summoned to consider the threatening international situation, Mr. Lyons declined, observing by way of

[1] In Australia this was a by no means unfamiliar phenomenon, Mr. W. M. Hughes providing the outstanding example of it. For an analysis of some of the reasons which prompted Australian Labour leaders to transfer the allegiance to the more conservative parties see L. F. Crisp, *The Parliamentary Government of the Commonwealth of Australia* (London, Longmans, Green, in association with the Wakefield Press, Adelaide, 1949) pp. 107–12. It is relevant to notice here that the issue on which Mr. Hughes broke with his former colleagues was conscription for overseas service in a war in which the British Empire was engaged.

explanation, 'if Parliament were called together undue anxiety would be created in the minds of the Australian people. . . .' The acquiescence of members in this negative attitude of the government was less reluctant than it might otherwise have been partly because foreign affairs constituted a topic at once unfamiliar and seemingly remote and partly because its adequate discussion would almost certainly have protracted parliamentary sessions and thereby extended members' period of residence in Canberra. This was generally regarded as highly undesirable. 'Hon. Members assemble here unwillingly', observed Mr. Blackburn in the House of Representatives in 1941,[1] 'and leave gladly. . . . That is one of the disadvantages which arises from having the seat of government remote from the large centres of population.'[2] In practice the desire of the government not to debate too much or too often the discharge of their new responsibilities in the field of international affairs was questioned only by the Labour leaders, and parliamentary and therefore popular interest in foreign affairs remained narrowly restricted. This in turn probably further inclined the government to accept United Kingdom policies without over careful examination of their implications except where Australian interests were directly at stake.

The character of the Australian Constitution has had a more lasting effect in delaying the emergence of a strong sense of nationality seeking expression in external policy. The Commonwealth of Australia is a federation in which residuary powers remain with the states comprising it[3] and, perhaps even more important, a federation in which the bias of popular opinion has remained hostile to any extension of the federal power. Despite 'the crimson thread of kinship which runs through us all'; despite the emotional appeal of creating for the first time in the history of the world 'a nation for a continent and a continent for a nation' there was, as Professor Crisp has noted, no Damascus Road miracle about Australia's conversion to federation.[4] On the contrary nearly a decade of drafting and hard bargaining lay behind it. Free from external pressure Australia's founding fathers took their time, resolved that the states' representatives should be fully satisfied before committing themselves to federation. That meant that the powers transferred to the centre were restricted to those which could be shown to be indispensable to its effective existence. 'I hold it', said Richard O'Connor in the Convention at Adelaide in 1897, 'to be a basic principle of this Federation that we should take no powers from the States which they could better exercise themselves, and that we should place no power in the Federation which is not absolutely necessary for carrying out its purposes.'

[1] 25 June 1941, Australia, H. of R. Deb., vol. 167, p. 380.

[2] Within the British Commonwealth New Delhi afforded the nearest parallel, and even if Delhi was notoriously 'far away', history lent a weighty sanction to its claims as capital.

[3] See the Commonwealth of Australia Constitution Act, 63 & 64 Vict. c. 1, pt. 5, 'Powers of the Parliament', in which the powers vested in the Federal Parliament are listed.

[4] Crisp, *Parliamentary Government*, pp. 1–2.

Mistrust of the centre has been little modified by experience, and while the Commonwealth government can operate effectively within its defined field the atmosphere is unfriendly to any extension of it. Even in time of war legislative approval for the additional powers essential to enable the Federal government to discharge responsibilities which cannot be evaded has been conceded only with reluctance, while in time of peace any increase in the activity of the Federal government even within its own alloted field is generally viewed without enthusiasm, particularly if it seems likely to involve new and recurrent expenditure. Members, therefore, regarded the growth of the Department for External Affairs, which was separated from the Prime Minister's Department in 1935, with no friendly eye, and the reluctance of the Lyons administration to appoint representatives in foreign capitals[1] was in accord both with Australians' sense of the unity of the Empire and with the prevailing mistrust of a frontier people for entanglement in foreign affairs.

Against this background the role of Labour in the evolution of Australian policies was of particular importance, for in every dominion it was from the left that the urge to assume effective control of foreign policy was most pronounced. From 1932 Labour was out of office. Like Canada, Australia had reacted against a 'depression government', but ir her case the move was from left to right, not right to left, and on the wave of the reaction the conservative coalition of the United Australia and Country parties was carried into office. This contrast in the political complexion of the Canadian and Australian post-slump governments obscures a comparison that might otherwise have been highly instructive. In Canada the 'imperialist' party was in opposition before the war; in Australia it was in power. Yet making due allowance for the discrepancy in their fortunes and responsibilities, significant differences in their approach to external affairs are none the less discernible. Where Mr. R. B. Bennett, especially at election time, found it necessary to exercise judicious restraint in his references to the Empire and still more to practical methods of imperial co-operation such as the Committee of Imperial Defence,[2] Mr. Lyons and Sir Earle Page, the leader of the Country

[1] The need for some overseas representation, however, could not be altogether disregarded, and in 1936 the government announced their intention of appointing representatives in foreign countries as need arose, Mr. Menzies, the Attorney-General, explaining that such representatives would be 'in the nature of liaison officers' and would be attached to British Embassies. The first appointment, made on 10 February 1937, was that of Mr. Keith Officer to serve as Australian Counsellor in the British Embassy at Washington (*J.P.E.*, 1937, vol. 18, pp. 362–3).

[2] On the arrival of Lord Hankey (then Sir Maurice Hankey) in North America early in 1935 Mr. Bennett stated that the Canadian government had not authorized discussion of Imperial Defence problems with him during his visit. The impending election no doubt accounted for this strange edict. (See *Manchester Guardian*, 25 January 1935.) Whether it was observed is another matter. Lord Hankey himself records that 'in every dominion most of my time was taken up in discussing these matters with Prime Ministers, and other ministers, staff officers, government officials, and sometimes by request with opposition leaders—and in visiting defence establishments' (*Diplomacy by Conference* (London, Benn, 1946) p. 131).

party, needed to entertain no such inhibitions. The more they talked about the Empire and their plans for strengthening co-operation between its members, the more votes they were likely to receive. And when one considers the attitude of Australian Labour, the contrast is even more marked. However critical of 'imperialist' policies, the Australian Labour party was prepared to contemplate, should circumstances demand, a degree of imperial unity which Canadian Conservatives never ventured to advocate openly any time after 1931. While an emphatic repudiation of United Kingdom policies before the war suggested an incipient isolationism which might spread over from the international to the imperial field, Australian Labour's concern once in office was not to weaken but to tighten the bonds of Empire, as was strikingly illustrated by Mr. Curtin's proposals for the creation of an imperial council and secretariat in 1943. Labour leaders might speak in the accents of nationalism, but it was a nationalism whose spirit made it almost as incomprehensible to the Canadian Liberal of the Middle-West as to the *habitant* of Quebec. It was a nationalism practical rather than emotional, deriving from a conflict of classes rather than of peoples.

In Australia *laissez-faire* died young. There was no place for it. State socialism, historically the product of geographical conditions and the needs of an immigrant population in an industrial age, had all the weight of practical argument on its side. 'Distance, aridity, and an erratic alternation of seasons', writes Professor Hancock, 'imposed upon the state responsibilities which no voluntary associations could have performed.'[1] The urban population demanded their assumption to protect their interests against an embryonic oligarchy whose wealth derived from the land. And in the early days they received vociferous support from shearers, from labourers, and even small farmers. In the extension of that struggle for power between the workman and the master, between the landless majority and land-monopolizing squatters, from the economic to the political field, the Australian Labour party was born. It was frankly a class party whose principal purpose was to champion the cause of the masses against the classes. Its aims were practical and immediate. Unlike the English Labour party it reposed little confidence in intellectuals and while not lacking a formidable and militant industrial wing, it drew inspiration more from the deep springs of English radicalism rather than from the rationalized doctrines of continental socialism. Indeed the Labour party in Australia was not wholly or even predominantly socialist in outlook. Its rural supporters, still an important element, were a restraining influence with an unmistakable dislike of socialist planning in the country-side, while the Irish Catholic element, driven by force of circumstance into the party of the under-privileged, aimed at promoting social justice within the framework of a social democracy rather than at the realization of a socialist programme

[1] Hancock, *Politics in Pitcairn*, p. 93. Also see generally pp. 51–93 for instructive commentary on Australian political beliefs and attitudes.

which would be inconsistent with the doctrines of their church. Yet making due allowance for these moderating influences, Labour in Australia remained a class party and the political conflict in Australia was essentially a conflict between classes. Mr. Henry Bournes Higgins, a distinguished president of the Commonwealth Arbitration Court, gave it as his considered view

> that most of the friction in Australia arises from the fact that there are here just two classes of society, and that the members of each class have neither the knowledge nor the sympathy necessary to enable them to understand how facts present themselves to the other class. One class lives mainly by profit; the other class by wages. Some people, of course, are connected with both classes, but everyone tends to hold the opinion of the class in which his interests and his associations chiefly lie.[1]

This has been clearly reflected in the asperities of party warfare. Australian nationalism was the incidental product of this conflict between classes. Therein lay its essential difference from Canadian nationalism, which was the product of tension between peoples. In Australia, where kinship was the unifying bond and where all rejoiced in 'the consanguineous peopling' of their land, nationalism lacked an impelling motive force. Within the Labour party, to quote Professor Hancock once more, 'it was impossible to disentangle the passions of class and of nationalism, so inextricably were they intertwined'.[2] Hostility to the wealthier more privileged section of a community who could satisfy their dual loyalties to Australia and to Britain by frequent visits, or business associations, or by sending their sons to universities 'at home', accentuated Labour's emphasis upon Australian nationalism. The easy acceptance first of federation and later of dominion autonomy by the home government removed a possible source of antagonism to the British Empire and deflected Australian nationalism into more positive channels where the essentially 'British' composition of the Australian population exerted its natural influence. But however congenial the concept of the British Commonwealth to Australian Labour, it did little to dispel its traditional mistrust of 'imperialism' or of its suspicion of policies favoured by plutocratic imperialists in London. Radicalism at home thus had its counterpart in a radical approach to foreign affairs. In the years before the Second World War the Labour opposition eyed askance the policies of London, sometimes on their merits, but often because they seemed to be the policies favoured by the wealthy, the privileged, the aristocratic society which so many of their ancestors had left in search of wider opportunities in the free egalitarianism of the new Commonwealth.[3] Yet from negative mistrust

[1] Quoted in Crisp, *Parliamentary Government*, pp. 4–6. [2] *Politics in Pitcairn*, p. 58.

[3] It was characteristic that when in 1939 Mr. Curtin advocated direct diplomatic representation in Tokyo, Washington, and other capitals where Australia had large-scale interests, he was motivated not by national sentiment but by practical considerations and a deep-seated mistrust of the outlook of Whitehall. It was the supposed bias of the Foreign Office which he feared and only incidentally dependence on Britain. (Cf. *J.P.E.*, 1939, vol. 20, p. 684.)

Australian Labour for the most part did not pass, as did Labour in New Zealand, to insistent positive support for the League and the ideal of collective security. Here a characteristic pragmatism in outlook was partly responsible. Emotional, or intellectual, support for the ideals of the League was never pronounced in a party which had always been empirical in its approach to socialism and undisguised in its dislike of intellectuals. A minority, it is true, mostly on the extreme left sought to harmonize the views of Australian Labour with international working-class resistance to Fascism, but the majority preferred a qualified isolationism to bold, imaginative policies whose consequences could not be foreseen. There was in these years no settled Labour party opinion on international affairs. There was tension between the views of internationalists and national isolationists; between a militant left and a conservative, Roman Catholic right; and out of the conflict of their views a compromise in respect of a particular situation could sometimes, but by no means always, be found.[1] So it was that the lukewarmness of government support for the League afforded useful opportunities for Labour criticism, but produced no positive assertion of faith accepted by all sections of the party. On the contrary nothing was more apparent, as the League entered upon its period of crisis and decline, than that nowhere in the British Commonwealth did it enjoy less assurance of support than in Australia. Her nationalism neither sought nor found an outlet in an international organization; to emotional internationalism her people were for the most part temperamentally disinclined, and experience suggested to them that it was the Royal Navy and not the League that in the last resort would afford them protection.

AUSTRALIAN REACTIONS TO THE RISE OF JAPAN

It has already been suggested that Australia did not make for herself a foreign policy. Even in the later nineteen-thirties most Australians preferred to be without one. Yet a foreign policy was thrust upon her, not by the imperial association which conditioned her outlook, but by her Pacific environment. It was the reawakening of Asia that compelled Australia to take a more active part in world affairs. Here the Anglo-Japanese alliance of 1902 was an important landmark. Expressly designed to ensure that in the event of a Russo-Japanese war Russia would fight alone, it made possible Japan's spectacular victory in 1905 and in so doing indirectly stimulated that great renaissance of Asian nationalism whose fruits were gathered in India and South-East Asia forty years later. Moreover the Japanese victory at sea brought nearer the prospect of successful Japanese aggression along the south-eastern perimeter of Asia. In the course of a conversation on develop-

[1] See an illuminating article by Lloyd Ross, the Labour party historian, in *The Australian Outlook*, March 1949, pp. 32–45. He states categorically that because of its background and composition there never is a Labour view on international affairs.

ments in the Far East with President Theodore Roosevelt in 1907, the German ambassador in Washington observed that Japan was 'doubtless aiming at control of the Pacific Ocean, extension of her territory southwards, and domination in China'.[1] When Japan was ready for another big war, which in the opinion of German military authorities would not be for many years, the interests and possessions of her English and French allies in South-East Asia could hardly, he thought, remain untouched any more than those of the United States. In this the German ambassador was a true prophet, and in the working out of his prophecies Australia was deeply concerned. A Japanese advance towards South-East Asia would imperil her security; Japanese control of the Pacific her existence as an independent state. And even if the perspicacity of the German ambassador was exceptional, the direction of Japanese ambitions, fixed by the events of 1902-5, was evident. Nor could a treaty of transient convenience indefinitely contain them, though it could, and did for a time ensure, at the price of a consolidation of Japanese power, that Japan's anxiety to relieve the pressure of population upon her resources would not lure her southward to the temptingly thinly populated, northern territories of Australia.

During the First World War, when Britain was dependent upon Japanese naval power in the Pacific, Australia had no alternative but to acquiesce in the Japanese occupation of the islands in the Pacific north of the Equator.[2] Their occupation brought Japan half-way to Australia and greatly improved her position should she decide at any time to embark on a career of conquest. It was this that largely accounted for Australia's resolute opposition at Versailles to the extension of the mandates system to former German possessions in the Pacific, because any such extension would have left the mandated islands open to the goods and to the nationals of all countries and would have debarred Australia, as a mandatory Power, from fortifying the territories allotted to her. She pressed, therefore, for outright annexation, maintaining that 'under foreign or international domination' the islands might become crowded 'not with their own islanders, whom no-one feared', but with 'immigrants from China and Japan'. In this she failed, but the choice of a 'C' class mandate under which restriction of imports and of immigration by the mandatory Power was permitted, went some considerable way towards meeting her point of view. Mr. Hughes, however, yielded reluctantly in the face of 'overwhelming odds' against annexation and only on the understanding that the 'C' class mandate would be 'the equivalent of a 999 years' lease as compared with freehold'. He could never, he remarked afterwards, agree that an open-door policy should be maintained. 'There could be no open door in regard to the islands near Australia. There should be a barred and closed

[1] *Die Grosse Politik*, vol. 25, p. 72.

[2] *Official History of Australia in the War of 1914–18*, vol. 11, *Australia During the War*, by Ernest Scott, Chapter XII.

door—with Australia as the guardian of the door.'[1] Action followed quickly upon words, and Australia's first ordinance for the territory for which she was made responsible barred the door to Asiatic immigration by extending to Asiatics the application of the Commonwealth Immigration Act. This action evoked a protest from Japan, who maintained that the principle of the 'open door' should be applied in all fairness to 'C' class mandates. Only after protracted and acrimonious debate did the Japanese government, prompted by 'a spirit of conciliation and co-operation, and their reluctance to see the question unsettled any longer . . .', concede the issue, carefully recording that their assent was not to be considered 'as an acquiescence on the part of His Imperial Japanese Majesty's government in the submission of Japanese subjects to a discriminatory and disadvantageous treatment in the mandated territories'; nor as discarding their claim that 'the rights and interests enjoyed by Japanese subjects in these territories in the past should be fully respected'.[2]

In a wider context Australian immigration policies contributed less than is generally supposed to the deterioration in Japanese-Australian relations. The Japanese government at no time openly questioned Australia's right to determine her own immigration policies, though it did often complain about the inconsiderate, or even offensive, way in which these policies were expounded and applied. In October 1897 Mr. Joseph Chamberlain, in a dispatch to the Governor of South Australia, explained that Japan had protested vigorously and repeatedly against the colonial legislation of 1896 chiefly because the colonies classed her people indiscriminately with the 'coloured races'.

> The point [wrote Mr. Chamberlain] which had caused a painful feeling in Japan was not that the operation of the prohibition would be such as to exclude a certain number of Japanese emigrants from Australia, but that Japan should be spoken of in formal documents, such as colonial acts, as if Japan were on the same level of morality and civilization as Chinese or other less advanced populations of Asia; the relief which they desired was not the modification of the laws by which a certain number of the Japanese population were excluded from Australia and New Zealand, but the abandonment of the language test which classed them with others to whom they bore no real similarity, and inflicted upon the nation an insult which was not deserved.[3]

In subsequent years the Japanese 'distinctly recognized' the right of the government of Australia to regulate the numbers and the type of immigrants permitted to enter the Commonwealth. Later Japanese acquiescence was qualified by her increasing pressure of population upon resources and her

[1] Quoted in *Australia During the War*, p. 787. See also Jack Shepherd, *Australia's Interests and Policies in the Far East* (New York, I.P.R. Inquiry Series, 1939) p. 19.

[2] *Australia During the War*, p. 796.

[3] Quoted in Myra Willard, *History of the White Australia Policy* (Melbourne University Press, 1923) p. 114, who refers also to a speech by Hon. J. H. Want in New South Wales Legislative Council Debates, vol. 92, p. 459.

sense of grievance accentuated by implied Australian assertion of racial supremacy. It is not to be doubted that relations between Australia and Japan were far more exacerbated by Australia's opposition, again astringently voiced by Mr. Hughes, to Japanese attempts to insert an affirmation of race equality in the Covenant of the League than by Australian immigration laws. That opposition was the less easily forgotten because it proved decisive. Even though Australia was in a small minority at Versailles, President Wilson's ruling that unanimity was the condition of acceptance left her with a Pyrrhic victory which fanned resentment against immigration policies henceforward popularly associated not only in Japan, but throughout Asia,[1] with doctrines of race supremacy even though they had in fact an economic justification which could not be lightly dismissed or easily controverted. Nearly thirty years later Mr. Justice Lal, the Indian member of the International Military Tribunal which delivered judgement on the Japanese leaders of 1941–5, observed that Australia, by her opposition to the principle of racial equality, had greatly contributed to Japan's psychological preparation for war and concluded that for his part he was unable to condemn the Japanese leaders who might have thought that they, too, were justified in inculcating the idea of racial superiority among their own people.[2]

Despite acrimonious dialectical dispute between the representatives of Australia and Japan at Versailles, the Australian government had no desire to see the Anglo-Japanese treaty lapse. On the contrary, at the Prime Ministers' Conference in 1921, Mr. Hughes was in favour of its renewal. This was not because of any confidence in Japanese intentions but because a renewal of the alliance would give the British Commonwealth favourable opportunities for influencing Japanese policies. 'To renew this treaty', he said, 'is to impose on her [Japan] some of those restraints inseparable from treaties with other civilized nations like ourselves.'[3] But while Mr. Hughes believed that the renewal of the treaty, which for Australia had 'special significance', would help to promote world peace, he was not disposed to discount the Canadian misgivings lest renewal should constitute a barrier to the growth of Anglo-American friendship. It was a question of approach even more than a question of policy. Where Canada, despite her Pacific seaboard, looked out on world affairs across the Atlantic, Australia first judged events in their Pacific context. To her the Pacific seemed of decisive significance. 'The war and the Panama Canal', declared Mr. Hughes, 'has shifted the world's stage from the

[1] It is, however, to be noted that in 1925 at the Honolulu Conference of the Institute of Pacific Relations a Japanese delegate allowed that Canada particularly but also Australia had shown more tact and wisdom in the immigration legislation than the United States, and that Australian legislation, enacted when the number of Japanese emigrants was still insignificant, 'was not openly offensive although the real purpose of the law was easily perceivable'. (Institute of Pacific Relations, Honolulu Session, 1925, *History, Organization, Proceedings* (Honolulu, 1925) pp. 77–8.)

[2] *The Hindu* (Madras), 15 November 1948.

[3] Cmd. 1474, p. 20.

Mediterranean and the Atlantic to the Pacific. The stage upon which the great world drama is to be played in the future is the Pacific.... Peace in the Pacific means peace for this Empire and for the world.'[1] In part mistaken, this sense of the importance of the Pacific greatly influenced Australia's policy between the wars.

When in 1921 the balance of opinion within the Commonwealth came down against renewal of the Anglo-Japanese Alliance, Australia actively assisted in the substitution for it of the collective security system built up at the Washington Conference. She was a signatory to the Four-Power treaty sanctioning the maintenance of the *status quo* in regard to island possessions in the Pacific and to the Nine-Power treaty binding the contracting partners to respect the territorial integrity of China. As a member of the British Empire, she was associated with the agreement for the limitation of naval armaments and with the restriction of fortifications in the Western Pacific embodied in the Five-Power treaty. With the general outcome of the Washington Conference Australia was well satisfied. The limitation of naval armaments averted the prospect of an armaments race for which the British Empire was far less well equipped than the United States; agreement on the part of Japan not to fortify islands in the Western Pacific temporarily, at least, removed the threat of Japanese expansion southwards; while the basis of Anglo-American co-operation in the Pacific was placed on a formal and broader foundation.[2] Australian armaments were accordingly reduced and compulsory military training was later abandoned. Few noted, as Sir Frederick Eggleston has reminded us,[3] that while the measure of disarmament agreed at Washington reduced the vulnerability of the imperial Powers in the Pacific, it equally incapacitated them from rendering adequate aid to China should she be attacked. The sequel soon showed how important this incidental result was destined to prove. Nor is it to be overlooked that henceforward relations with Japan were defined in terms of negative restriction and not, as hitherto, in terms of positive co-operation.

In succeeding years Australian policy towards Japan oscillated uneasily between a desire for more intimate relations and fear lest growing power should tempt Japanese militarists into aggressive courses. It was in fact with Japan that the initiative lay. From Versailles Australia had emerged not without serious liabilities. Her wider claims, particularly for the whole of New Guinea, had been rejected and at the same time the antagonism of the Japanese had been aroused. Thereafter Australians were for the most part only too content to think in terms of co-operation with Asian countries and of a rigid avoidance of adventure. Japan, on the other hand, had acquired both opportunity and renewed self-confidence.

[1] ibid. p. 21.

[2] For a detailed account see Carter, *British Commonwealth*, pp. 50–64, and Shepherd, *Australia's Interests*, pp. 20–22.

[3] In Grattan, *Australia*, p. 141.

In 1931, when Australia and New Zealand were concerned only with markets which might sustain their collapsing economies, Japan made her first move. Not only the time but also the place was well chosen. Against a background of disorder in China and disputed treaty rights in Manchuria, a preoccupied Commonwealth was slow and unwilling to understand that the imposing edifice of collective security was threatened at its foundations. When the realities of the situation could no longer be disguised, particularly after the Japanese naval action against Shanghai in January 1932, Australia, the dominion most likely to be immediately affected by a League challenge to Japan, showed significant restraint in defining her attitude. While the government was anxious to find an early and peaceful settlement, the Labour opposition was openly hostile to active Australian participation in the imposition of sanctions. Economic sanctions, they argued, would be so costly and complex as to be impossible of application and military action was unthinkable. Australian naval and military forces should not be permitted to engage in active service beyond the shores of the Commonwealth, declared Labour senators from New South Wales in March 1932, and they would never consent to Australian participation 'in what is nothing more than a sordid trade war'.[1] The government was almost equally averse to open conflict with Japan, and the Prime Minister had already assured the House of Representatives in February 1932 that he would do everthing in his power 'to avoid the Commonwealth becoming involved in any war'.[2] Other countries farther removed from the probable scene of conflict might assert that the time had come to enforce the authority of the League, but Australia, conscious of dependence on her trade with Japan and still more of her exposed strategic position, was in no mood to embark on any such enterprise in the absence of resolute Anglo-American support for it. The caution and the realism which were later to mark Australian policy in the Pacific were already in evidence in 1931–2. Ever mindful of 'the vulnerability of our empty north' and her 'virtually unprotected' position 'except for the strength of the British Empire',[3] she sought close co-operation with Britain and firmly discouraged provocative policies which might endanger the prospect of a peaceful settlement in Asia. It was doubtless regrettable that Japan had embarked on a career of aggression, but some Australians at least consoled themselves with the thought that Manchuria would take long to digest and that Australia was in no danger of attack 'because of the responsibilities' Japan had assumed there.[4]

The events of 1931–2 dispelled whatever slight confidence had hitherto existed in Australia about the capacity of the League to maintain peace in the Pacific Ocean area. The League 'is useless' declared Mr. Hughes at Geneva;

[1] Australia, Senate Deb., vol. 133, p. 561. See Carter, *British Commonwealth*, pp. 135–67.
[2] Australia, H. of R. Deb., vol. 133, p. 276.
[3] ibid. p. 1086.
[4] 3 November 1932, Australia, Senate Deb., vol. 136, p. 1823.

it 'is impotent' echoed Senator Dunn in Canberra.[1] But neither had ever rated it highly, and while many hitherto sincere supporters of collective security were disillusioned because sanctions were not applied, and others, isolationists at heart, were dismayed at the realization that support for the League might mean war, final judgement was still withheld. 'The advantage we gain from membership is not commensurate with the amount we contribute' was the banal comment of the Prime Minister. He might have added, what many thinking Australians felt, that League action, however effective it might prove in maintaining peace among comparatively well-organized European states, had no prospect of success in the Far East, particularly in relation to China, rent by faction and by civil war; and that any attempt to impose its will there could lead only to disaster. It was tempting for an Assembly sitting in far Geneva to try to assert its authority in Eastern Asia, but if and when force had to be used was it not likely, with the United States outside the League, that Britain and Australia would have to use it?

ECONOMIC FACTORS IN AUSTRALIAN POLICY

While broad considerations of policy and strategy determined the character of Australian reactions to events in Asia, as later in Europe, economic factors played a contributory role of no small importance. The United Kingdom has consistently been the greatest market for Australia's primary produce. Australia for her part, as an official memorandum published in 1938 recorded,[2] was not only one of the largest customers of United Kingdom goods, but was 'also the domicile of the largest amount of United Kingdom capital invested in any single overseas country'. The Ottawa Agreements had encouraged the idea that this complementary economic relationship might profitably be extended, but subsequent hard experience had shown that exclusive dependence on an imperial preferential system was liable to have disconcerting consequences. Since Ottawa, observed Professor Hancock, Australia[3]

> had bumped in turn against Great Britain's agricultural protectionism, against her interest as a world creditor and trader, against Lancashire's will to keep on living, against Japan's will to keep on growing, against would-be autarkies like Italy, against liberal traders like Belgium, against protectionist America, against the boomerang-return of their own protectionist excesses.

Attachment to imperial preference survived all this virtually unimpaired even if thereafter qualified by a recognition that a healthy economy could not be fitted comfortably into an exclusively imperial pattern. Trade with other nations was indispensable to an expanding Australian economy.

[1] Australia, H. of R. Deb., vol. 136, p. 1516. cf. Senate Deb., vol. 136, p. 1824, quoted by Carter (*British Commonwealth*, p. 156) who would seem to attach more importance to these observations than is warranted.

[2] Cmd. 5805 (1938). *Memorandum of Conclusions* (of trade discussions between representatives of the United Kingdom and Australia) p. 2.

[3] Hancock, *Survey*, vol. 2, pt. 1, p. 256. A full analysis is to be found in section v, pp. 260 ff.

In this wider pattern of Australia's external trade no country had a more important part to play than Japan. Between 1929 and 1936 Australian trade with the Far East was one of the principal factors which enabled her to weather the economic blizzard of the early nineteen-thirties. Because of her dependence upon the export of primary products, Australia was peculiarly vulnerable to the drop in world prices which followed immediately upon the economic collapse in the United States. Thus the average export value of a bushel of wheat fell from 5*s.* 9*d.* in 1929–30 to 2*s.* 5*d.* in the following year, while the export value of wool was almost exactly halved between 1928 and 1931. This sensational decline in the value of those primary exports, upon which the Australian economy rested, was coupled with an inability to borrow in London sufficient to cover even the normal excess of imports over exports. As a result it became essential to redress the traditionally unfavourable balance of Australian trade, and here Japan had an important contribution to make.

Japan was profoundly affected by the collapse in world trading conditions, but her response was different both to that of Australia and of the United Kingdom. Instead of a policy of restrictions on imports, Japan relied upon the expansion of exports and a rapid development of her production of cheap industrial goods. The result was that she became for the moment, not a dangerous competitor but an invaluable outlet for Australian produce. At the moment when the Australian need for additional export markets was greatest Japan doubled her total imports of raw wool, and of this total Australia supplied an average of 96 per cent. Thus in 1933 Japan imported 225,600,000 lb. of raw wool as compared with 108,200,000 lb. in 1928, and the percentage of the total wool exports shipped to Japan from Australia, which was 13·2 per cent. in 1928–9, increased to 20 per cent. in 1933–4. Japanese imports of Australian wheat showed a still more remarkable advance, and even if the total value of Australian exports to Japan did not increase significantly, at least it remained steady at a time when exports to other countries were rapidly contracting. This is clearly revealed by the increase in Japan's percentage of Australia's total exports which rose from 8·3 in 1928–9 to 12·1 in 1931–2.[1] Simultaneously exports to China showed a parallel increase, even though the Chinese market remained of very secondary importance to the Japanese.

Throughout the slump years the balance of trade between Australia and Japan remained favourable to Australia. There was none the less a marked increase in the volume of cheap textiles imported into Australia from Japan. At first these imports were welcomed by those sections of the community most hit by the fall in world prices, and above all by producers anxious to reduce the cost of living so that it might be brought once more into some relation with the reduced value of their products. As the demand increased so did the volume of Japanese imports. By 1935 the import of cotton-piece goods

[1] Figures quoted by Shepherd, *Australia's Interests*, pp. 24–27, where the reader will find a more detailed analysis of the direction of trade.

had risen more than 350 per cent. above the 1926 figure. An even more rapid expansion was seen in the import figures for rayon-piece goods. None the less the balance of trade continued to favour Australia, a factor of much importance in determining both the official and popular attitude at a time when much emphasis was being placed upon a bilateral assessment. Judged by this criterion, Japan remained a 'good' customer.

In Australia the protectionist manufacturing interest viewed the expansion of trade with Japan not without understandable anxiety, but the policy of Mr. Lyons's government was clear enough. It was to encourage trade with Japan. Its wisdom was generally endorsed. In a report published by the Bank of New South Wales in 1934 it was stated that:

> The industrialization of Japan promises to bring with it great possibilities for the development of markets for Australian foodstuffs and raw materials.... Australia needs markets for her primary products. The great potential markets for those products are the Far Eastern countries. Of these countries, China is at present the largest buyer of our wheat and Japan the largest buyer of our wool, but if Japanese living standards are allowed to improve, there is the possibility of selling more foodstuffs to Japan in the future.[1]

In 1935 a study of diplomatic and trade relations between Australia and the countries of the Far East recorded the view that: 'Australia has a very real interest in the progress of Japanese industry and the material welfare of the Japanese people. It is not too much to say that the future prosperity of Australia will to an increasing extent be dependent on that of her great neighbour in the Far East.'[2]

Such considerations, even if not of decisive importance, undoubtedly confirmed the direction of Australian policy in the Far East. In 1931–3, when Australia's economy was threatened with collapse, she could not afford to disregard the steadying influence of an expanding outlet for her exports and her desire to preserve it unquestionably increased her reluctance to support economic sanctions the enforcement of which against Japan at that time might have entailed for Australia not merely hardship, but serious, perhaps even disastrous, economic consequences.

Despite the benefits which Australia's trade with Japan brought to both countries in the depression years, it was destined to have an abrupt and disconcerting end. In 1934 Mr. Lyons's government sent Mr. (later Sir) J. G. Latham on a 'goodwill mission' to the Far East. Preliminary discussions for a trade agreement with Japan were begun in 1935, and public opinion welcomed an approach which, by way of economic co-operation, might lead to friendlier

[1] 'Australia and Industrial Development in Japan', Bank of New South Wales, *Monthly Circular*, March 1934, quoted ibid. pp. 28–29.

[2] I. Clunies Ross, ed., *Australia and the Far East; Diplomatic and Trade Relations* (Sydney, Angus & Robertson, 1935) p. 185, quoted ibid. p. 29.

political relations.[1] There was therefore both surprise and concern when, without warning, the Australian government suddenly changed course. On 22 May Sir Henry Gullett, who enjoyed the portentous designation of Minister Directing Negotiations for Trade Treaties, announced the government's decision to divert a portion of Australia's existing trade from 'bad-customer' to 'good-customer' countries 'with the object of increasing exports of primary produce, expanding secondary industry, and bringing about an increase of rural and industrial employment'. The United States and Japan were the countries principally affected. The United States, with whom the trade balance had tended in recent years to become progressively more unfavourable, was a 'bad customer' by the standard of a bilateral trade balance, but Japan most certainly was not. Why then was the importation of Japanese goods, especially textiles, so drastically curtailed? There is no single answer, but the dominant consideration was unquestionably the interests of Australia's 'best customer', the United Kingdom. Fears that the Japanese advance in the Australian market would prejudice the traditional British interests overrode all counterbalancing considerations.[2] Already by 1934 Japan had displaced Britain as the largest supplier of textiles to Australia, and the low price of Japanese goods lent substance to the prevailing anxiety lest the Australian market once captured by Japan could never be regained by Britain. It was on this that Mr. Lyons placed most emphasis in explaining his government's abrupt change of course. He maintained that Japanese competition was unfair; that during recent years Japanese manufacturers and exporters had 'reduced their prices to levels against which no European country or the United States of America could compete except upon a diminishing and insignificant basis in this Australian market.'[3] Japan, he argued, had the great advantage over all other countries of much lower wages, longer working hours, cheaper raw materials, a substantial advantage through currency depreciation, as well as lower freight rates because of her proximity to Australia, so that unless positive steps were taken to check Japanese dumping long-established and valued customers who maintained a tolerable standard of living, they would find their economic existence seriously imperilled through loss of overseas markets. And how would they react to such a situation? Britain was still the largest market for Australian wool, and, as Professor Hancock has underlined, 'the only market for the "difficult selling commodities" of the close-settlement areas'.[4] Might not Japanese competition in the Australian market stimulate or compel more valued customers to reduce their imports from Australia? The most significant reaction to the trade-diversion policy was its cordial welcome in Manchester.

Even if the view be accepted that the aim of the trade-diversion policy—the aim of maintaining and positively assisting the 'best customer'—was fully

[1] cf. Shepherd, *Australia's Interests*, pp. 34–36.
[2] cf. Hancock, *Survey*, vol. 2, pt. 1, p. 253.
[3] Quoted in Shepherd, *Australia's Interests*, p. 47.
[4] *Survey*, vol. 2, pt. 1, p. 253.

justified, the brusqueness with which it was carried out and the extreme form in which it was adopted had nothing to recommend them. What was achieved, to quote Sir Frederick Eggleston, was 'a maximum of irritation with a minimum of benefit'.[1] The policy did not in fact long survive without modification in principle and in practice. But its political consequences were not unimportant. In Japan there was much resentment and renewed emphasis on the imperative need for economic self-sufficiency, since no reliance could be placed on overseas sources of supply.

LEAGUE AND EMPIRE

More than any member of the Commonwealth Australia was conscious of the interrelation between events in Europe and in Asia. Neither her people nor her government doubted that peace was indivisible. War in Europe almost certainly meant war in Asia. That indeed was the opportunity for which Japan was so evidently waiting. In November 1933 the *Sydney Daily Telegraph* declared that war with Japan was certain. 'Americans, New Zealanders, Australians, Englishmen and Dutch', it recorded, 'are convinced they must inevitably fight the Japanese.'[2] But equally it was generally believed that Japan would not embark on a career of large-scale aggression unless and until the Western Powers were heavily committed in Europe. It was not in the East but in the West that war was likely to break out and the one hope of delaying or indefinitely postponing it lay in the preservation of peace in Europe. Australian influence on British policy was therefore generally a restraining influence. For her Europe was by no means of exclusive, even predominant, importance, and it was her constant anxiety lest Britain's overriding preoccupation with European affairs might lead her to overlook the probable consequences of her European policies in Eastern Asia. This anxiety was strongly reflected in Australia's attitude to possible British co-operation with the Soviet Union, the one European Power other than Britain herself which was also a Great Power in Asia. It was Australia's fear that any rapprochement between Britain and Russia would compel Japan to align herself militarily with the Axis Powers and thereby make peace in Asia directly dependent on peace in Europe. Accordingly the Australian government between 1935 and 1939 generally favoured a policy of conciliation in Europe effected through direct negotiation with the Axis Powers and independently of the Soviet Union.

While the principal aim of Australian policy was to preserve peace, its secondary objective was to ensure that if war came the Empire was well prepared, for it was not in the League but in the Empire that Australia trusted. This led to a pronounced concern with the safety of imperial communications through the Mediterranean, Suez, and across the Indian Ocean. On the maintenance of this life-line the safety of Australia largely

[1] In Grattan, *Australia*, p. 137.
[2] Quoted in Shepherd, *Australia's Interests*, p. 37.

depended and awareness of it gave her government a very particular interest in Britain's relations with Italy, Egypt, and Turkey.

From the outset of the Abyssinian crisis Australian emphasis was not upon the need to assert the authority of the League but upon the need to preserve the unity of the Empire and to safeguard its communications. In the view of her government a single-handed conflict between Britain and Italy in the Mediterranean should be avoided at almost any price. Australia, said Mr. Lyons on 25 August 1935,[1] was pledged 'to the hilt' to support Britain's efforts to maintain peace. There was no surer way, declared Mr. W. M. Hughes, Minister of External Affairs, on 26 August,[2] 'of unleashing the dogs of war . . . than a single-handed attempt by Great Britain to intervene between the Italians and Ethiopians'. Anti-imperialist in outlook and openly favouring a qualified isolationism the Labour opposition supported the government from a variety of motives in its insistence on the supreme need of preserving peace. In September the New South Wales Labour party recorded its 'unflinching determination not to allow Australia to become involved in war', while on 23 September Mr. F. M. Forde, deputy leader of the opposition, asked the House of Representatives to declare that it would not support sanctions or war, declaring that 'Labour wanted no war on foreign fields for economic treasure. It wanted Australia to be kept free of entanglements leading to a repetition of the horrors of 1914–18.[3] Nor did overwhelming League endorsement of sanctions against Italy make the use of force more justifiable or more respectable in the eyes of Australian Labour. They did not want 'war camouflaged as sanctions' nor did they consider the League's endorsement as sufficient to dispel deep-seated suspicions about the selfish motives of imperialist Powers seeking to gain their own ends under pretence of enforcing international law.[4] In this negative reaction the militant industrial left wing of Australian Labour supplied the dialectic, while the Irish Catholic element acquiesced because of their traditional sympathy with Italy. While, therefore, at the outset the government conformed without enthusiasm to the policies adopted at Geneva and the opposition suspected or disliked the purposes that lay behind them, no influential body of opinion desired that the full rigour of sanctions should be applied against the transgressor.

The success of Italian arms somewhat modified earlier Australian reactions but did not fundamentally alter them. On 5 October Mr. Lyons stated that Australia was 'greatly disappointed' at the failure of Britain and of the League to settle the dispute peacefully, and he declared that 'all our efforts will be directed towards confining the trouble within the narrowest limits and simultaneously giving the League the fullest support to effect a peaceful settle-

[1] *The Times*, 26 August 1935, quoted in Carter, *British Commonwealth*, p. 191.
[2] *New York Times*, 27 August 1935, quoted ibid.
[3] *J.P.E.*, January 1936, vol. 17, p. 59.
[4] ibid. p. 60.

ment'.[1] Sanctions were imposed[2] after a debate which reflected the tepidness of the government's convictions and the strength of Labour opposition. While not without sympathy for the victim of aggression, Labour was convinced that economic sanctions would lead to war and that their enforcement by Australia would plunge her 'into the perilous vortex of European conflicts'. This view was supported by the All-Australian Trades Union Congress which recorded a vote of 78 to 41 against the imposition of sanctions on the ground that they 'committed organized labour to sending armed forces overseas to take part in a capitalist war'. But within the Labour movement, and without, opinion was uncertain and divided.[3] What gave coherence and direction to Australian policy was the overriding determination to stand by Britain. When Labour asserted Australia's right as a dominion to decide on peace or war the Attorney-General vehemently denied 'Australia's right to go mad'.[4] Even those who desired in principle a formal exercise of the rights of autonomous status did not for the most part question the need for imperial solidarity.

Australia's desire, irrespective of party, to restrict the area of conflict and to keep the Empire out of war predisposed public opinion to thoughts of a compromise settlement. In Australia alone of the dominions opinion was not therefore outraged by the publication of the Hoare–Laval plan. True its terms were generally regarded as unwelcome, but the proposals themselves were not generally condemned as morally reprehensible. Thereafter predominant opinion hardened in favour of an early settlement. The maintenance of world peace was of greater importance than the reputation of the League, and Australia was the first and the most pressing of the dominion governments in urging upon the United Kingdom that sanctions should be raised. On 18 June 1936 Mr. Lyons formally announced that he had instructed Mr. Bruce to support the lifting of sanctions and the re-examination of the Covenant.

AUSTRALIAN REACTIONS TO THE FAILURE OF THE LEAGUE

For Australia the failure of the League to save Abyssinia was not in itself of major significance. She had long recognized that the writ of the League did not run in the Pacific, and it was a matter for little surprise that its authority could not be enforced effectively in Africa or in Europe. None the less the successful defiance of the Western democracies by Italy at a time

[1] *The Times*, 5 October 1935, quoted in Carter, *British Commonwealth*, p. 203.

[2] A bill to impose sanctions was introduced into the House of Representatives on 2 October 1935 and H.M.A.S. *Sydney* on its way from England to Australia was diverted to the Mediterranean where H.M.A.S. *Australia* was already serving, with the result that two of the three cruisers then in commission in the R.A.N. were in the Mediterranean for the period of the crisis.

[3] Mr. Hughes was compelled to resign in November 1935 because his support of sanctions against Italy notably failed to coincide with disparaging views he had expressed about their probable effectiveness in a recently published book. He returned to the cabinet in February 1936, having duly retracted part of his earlier views.

[4] *J.P.E.*, January 1936, vol. 17, p. 68.

when German reoccupation of the Rhineland portended a major threat to European peace exposed more clearly the extreme vulnerability of Australia in the event of Japanese aggression in the Far East coinciding with a European war. Widely expressed doubts about the ability of the Royal Navy to retain control of the Mediterranean in a war with Italy served at least to dispel some illusions about the margin of British resources that would be available in the Pacific should the United Kingdom become engaged in war against Germany and Italy. 'The Italo-Abyssinian crisis', wrote Mr. Shepherd, '. . . emphasized the possibility that Britain's line of communication to the East and to Australia through the Mediterranean might be cut and the bulk of the British navy fully occupied in European waters. For the first time the faith of the Australian public in Britain's naval supremacy was badly shaken.'[1] Equally sobering was the failure to find a new basis for agreement in the Pacific after the denunciation of the Washington naval treaty by Japan in 1935. With its denunciation the non-fortification agreement was held to have lapsed, and while the United States seemed more concerned to withdraw from than to develop its Pacific bases, that was very evidently not the intention of Japan. Yet the fortification by Japan of her mandated islands was in itself a matter only of secondary importance; what was of first importance was continued Japanese naval superiority in the western Pacific which made the invasion of the Australian mainland a possibility that had seriously to be considered in the making of Australian policy. Its effect was to deepen Australian concern with the safeguarding of imperial communications, to encourage the government to explore the possibility of some new agreement to maintain peace in the Pacific, and above all to focus attention on the need to strengthen imperial defence. There was no disposition, be it noted, to think with New Zealand in terms of a revived and strengthened League. In his speech to the Assembly in September 1936 Mr. Bruce argued that the principal lesson to be drawn from the Abyssinian war was that for a non-universal League 'to attempt to implement in full the Covenant involves the danger of spreading the areas of conflict', thereby negating 'the ideas embodied in the Covenant by its founders'. The argument was not new but it had a very particular relevance to the Pacific. A League which included neither Russia, Japan, nor the United States among its members could not restrain aggression in the Pacific because it lacked the power to do so. League intervention in such circumstances, certain to be ineffective, was likely only to extend the area of conflict and to lure the victim of aggression to even greater disaster. Australia favoured, therefore, not a reformed League or a League 'with teeth', but a League guided by a realistic recognition of its own impotence. If peace in the Pacific was to be preserved it could only be by agreement among the Great Powers with interests there, and accordingly an effective contribution to the general principle of collective security contained in

[1] *Australia's Interests*, p. 73.

the League would be for states, in regions where their national interests are directly involved, to agree to some form of regional pact subsidiary to the Covenant, by which they would be obliged to render military assistance . . . if one or more of them should be attacked by an aggressor.[1]

The Australian government, therefore, favoured 'a regional understanding and a pact of non-aggression by the countries of the Pacific' in conformity with the spirit, but outside the authority, of the League.

Australian proposals for a Pacific pact were carried a stage further at the 1937 Imperial Conference when on the initiative of Mr. Lyons they were discussed in general terms. On his return Mr. Lyons declared that the idea was received with sympathetic attention and was generally approved by the Conference as a desirable objective.[2] That view was not shared by the Labour opposition, who came out against partial pacts or treaties which would commit Australia to support or oppose groups of Powers with whom they had no quarrel as things stood.[3] Nor was such a pact generally considered practicable. In June Mr. Eden told the House of Commons that while the Imperial Conference had examined the possibilities in some detail and had considered the various forms which the pact might assume, they had also noted 'a number of difficulties which would have to be overcome'. It was a matter which needed to be approached with some circumspection.[4] This was diplomatic understatement. Growing mistrust of Japan in the United States and increasing tension between Japan and Russia deprived the Australian proposal of any prospect of success, and Mr. Lyons himself was in fact much concerned lest any negotiations with Russia about it should have the effect of alienating Japan. As a result, despite an apparently sympathetic response in Moscow and a qualified acceptance of the idea in Tokyo, the project for a Pacific pact had no prospect of realization even before renewed Japanese aggression in China made further discussion of it meaningless. It is, however, worth noting that the tentative soundings for a Pacific pact revealed the determination of the Dutch not to depart from their traditional policy of strict neutrality in respect of the East Indies, and therefore of their *non-possumus* attitude in relation either to a broad regional agreement or, in the event of its non-realization, to participation in defence talks designed to facilitate co-operation against possible Japanese aggression. But while Dutch-Australian co-operation in defence measures was thereby precluded, community of interest and a common fear of Japanese imperialism brought the East Indies and Australia into progressively closer association in other fields.[5]

The breakdown of the League and the failure to re-establish an effective guarantee of security in the Pacific increased Australian interest in the Eastern Mediterranean, for the greater her dependence upon the Royal Navy,

[1] Quoted in Shepherd, *Australia's Interests*, p. 77.
[2] *J.P.E.*, 1937, vol. 18, p. 853.
[3] cf. speech by Mr. Curtin, ibid. p. 856.
[4] H. of C. Deb., vol. 325, col. 1602.
[5] cf. Shepherd, *Australia's Interests*, pp. 123–6.

the greater her anxiety to ensure that the sea-lanes should be kept open in time of war. Alone of the dominions she was separately represented at the Montreux Conference in 1936, the Minister for External Affairs later justifying her separate participation on the ground that it was highly desirable for Australia to play her part in any international conference likely to lead to stability in the Near East',[1] while the fact that the Conference successfully carried through treaty revision by negotiation was convincing proof of its effectiveness. More important, from the point of view of Australian security in any future war, was the signature of the Anglo-Egyptian treaty in the same year. Here again Australia played a more positive role than any of the other dominions, making her views known at every stage in the negotiations. Her contribution was described by Sir George Pearce, the Minister for External Affairs, in these terms:

> In view of Australia's vital interest in the security of British Empire communications by way of Egypt, the Commonwealth government were in the closest touch with the government of the United Kingdom both before the initiation of the negotiations and throughout the proceedings, and each detail of their development was carefully followed. In London there were frequent discussions between the Secretary of State for Foreign Affairs (Mr. Eden), and the Minister for Commerce (Dr. Earle Page), the Attorney-General (Mr. Menzies) and the High Commissioner (Mr. Bruce).
>
> I shall not attempt to summarize the provisions of the Treaty. It has received wide approval both in Great Britain and in Egypt, and the general opinion is that it will have the effect of converting a most uncertain and difficult relationship into a friendly alliance. Everything has been done to ensure the continued security of those Empire communications through Egypt which meant so much to us in Australia.[2]

Nor was Australian interest confined to the Eastern Mediterranean. The desire for a restoration of traditionally friendly Anglo-Italian relations was a marked feature of Mr. Lyons's policy between 1936 and 1939, and while his own attitude was probably influenced by his Catholicism, Anglo-Italian understanding was a matter of undoubted importance to Australia. For similar reasons the Australian government gave consistent support to the United Kingdom's policy of non-intervention in the Spanish civil war. Despite the deep emotions which this conflict aroused, their attitude was not seriously challenged largely because the Labour opposition was deeply divided in its sympathies. Where the majority would have favoured more positive League backing for the Spanish Republican government, the Irish Catholic minority, sympathizing with General Franco, was strong enough to secure a compromise declaration in favour of virtual isolationism, not easily to be distinguished from the government's policy of non-intervention.[3]

In respect of Germany the Australian government was less disposed to be

[1] *J.P.E.*, 1937, vol. 18, p. 96. [2] ibid.

[3] cf. Crisp, *Parliamentary Government*, p. 87.

openly conciliatory. Mr. Lloyd George recorded that in 1919 'there was one dominion Premier and perhaps one British minister who held the opinion that Germany ought to and could pay the cost of the war into which her rulers had plunged the Allied Nations'.[1] The dominion Premier was Mr. W. M. Hughes. He was Minister for External Affairs in Mr. Lyons's administration from 1937 to 1939. There is no reason to suppose that the mistrust of German intentions which prompted his advocacy of a Carthaginian peace in 1919 had been wholly dissipated in the intervening years. Moreover, with the Anti-Comintern pact of November 1936 Germany re-emerged on the Pacific scene with Britain's former ally as her associate. This caused grave concern in Australia since it carried the threat of intensified pressure for the return of the Australian and New Zealand mandated territories. It was an issue on which there could be no compromise. From the outset Australia, while prepared to be conciliatory on economic questions, had no intention of returning her mandated territory to German sovereignty. In March 1936 Sir George Pearce, Minister for External Affairs, underlining the strategic importance of New Guinea, declared that 'the return of territories under Australian mandate is unthinkable', though Australia was prepared to consider practical proposals for economic adjustment and in fact approved the appointment of a committee for the study of the problems of raw materials set up on British initiative by the League Council early in 1937 in an attempt to meet the legitimate grievances of the 'have not' Powers. In June 1938 Mr. Hughes employed less diplomatic language: 'We have got our mandate on this rock (the Treaty of Versailles). We have built our church and all hell is not going to take it away. What we have we hold.'[2] Munich brought no modification in Australian policy, the deputy Prime Minister, Sir Earle Page, saying in October 1938, 'the League handed New Guinea to Australia as a sacred trust, and any talk of surrendering the territory can only be described as cowardly and unjust'.[3] Mr. Lyons was equally firm, saying, on 13 November 1938, 'the Commonwealth has no intention of handing back New Guinea'.[4]

In 1937–8 Germany was interested in furthering her general claim for the restoration of all her former colonies and not specifically in the return of the Australian mandated territory of New Guinea or of Nauru, a British mandated territory administered by Australia, or of the New Zealand mandated territory of Western Samoa. None the less her partnership with Japan in the Anti-Comintern pact afforded her opportunities for manœuvre which she attempted unsuccessfully to exploit. In February 1938 the colonial

[1] David Lloyd George, *The Truth About the Peace Treaties* (London, Gollancz, 1938), vol. 1, p. 457.

[2] *Daily Telegraph*, 3 June 1938.

[3] *The Times*, 15 October 1938.

[4] *Sydney Morning Herald*, 14 November 1938. See also for a useful summary of contemporary comment, Royal Institute of International Affairs, *Germany's Claim to Colonies*, 2nd ed. (London, 1939).

section of the German Foreign Office prepared a memorandum[1] on Japan's position in relation to the colonial question in which the desirability of a deal with Japan over her South Seas mandates was emphasized on the ground first that the recognition by one of the Allied and Associated Powers (in whose favour Germany had renounced her rights and claims to her former overseas possessions under Article 119 of the Treaty of Versailles) of an obligation to return them would be valuable in negotiation with other mandatory Powers, and secondly that direct negotiation with Japan would circumvent any disposition on the part of the mandatory Powers to deal with the colonial question through the League instead of by direct negotiation. However, despite German confidence that 'we could rightly expect our friends to render us assistance in this', the Japanese were prepared only for formal restoration to be followed forthwith by final German renunciation in return for financial compensation. On consideration this compromise proposal did not appeal to Germany since it would leave the way open to other mandatory Powers, notably South Africa, to maintain that their vital interests were also involved and that the same procedure should be followed in their case. But the Japanese were prepared to go no further, their ambassador informing von Ribbentrop on 22 February 1938 that 'the mandates held by Japan were vitally necessary for her defence' and that she could not therefore 'permanently relinquish' them.[2] Unknown though suspected in Australia,[3] these negotiations made timely her public refusal to contemplate the return of her New Guinea mandate to Germany. They indicated also a possible source of direct conflict between Germany and Australia which did not exist between Italy and Australia.

AUSTRALIAN REACTIONS TO RENEWED JAPANESE AGGRESSION IN CHINA

Renewed large-scale Japanese aggression in China in July 1937 evoked a sharper popular reaction in Australia than in 1931, but the government maintained the cautious, conciliatory course it had set six years earlier. It made no move either to help China or to hinder Japan, and indeed since collective security had broken down the imposition of unilateral sanctions was a dangerously provocative course, impossible of adoption by a small Pacific Power in the absence of a clear lead from the United States or the United Kingdom. Certainly no such imprudent step was contemplated by Mr. Lyons's government, which sacrificed all pretence at consistency in their pursuit of a balancing middle-of-the-road policy. Thus they permitted the continued shipment of tin and iron scrap, of which supplies were limited,

[1] *Documents on German Foreign Policy, 1918–45*, Series D, vol. 1, pp. 835–9.

[2] ibid. p. 841.

[3] Shepherd, *Australia's Interests*, pp. 73–74. Australia feared especially a deal between Germany and Japan in which Germany would be compensated in the East Indies for the Pacific islands held by Japan.

while prohibiting the large-scale shipment of ores to Japan from Yampi Sound. They were resolute, however, in combating the challenge of militant Labour, which claimed that they could and would impose 'working-class sanctions'. Legal action was taken against the waterside workers who, first at Melbourne in January 1938 and then at Sydney in May, refused to load cargoes of tin or iron scrap for Japan on the ground that they were likely to be used in the manufacture of munitions. In November the government, confronted with a more serious situation through the refusal of waterside workers at Port Kembla to load pig-iron for Japan, responded again with the threat to enforce its authority by law, Mr. Menzies, the Attorney-General, declaring that 'the persistent refusal of the men to load scrap-iron for Japan' raised 'an important issue'. 'The question', he said, 'is not whether the waterside workers are right or wrong in their views on what the international policy of Australia should be; it is whether that policy is to be determined by the duly constituted government of the country or by some industrial section.'[1] This time, however, public opinion took a less legalistic view than the Federal government and the waterside boycott of war materials for Japan won widespread sympathy. The government, however, remained firm both in its resolve to break the unofficial embargo of the workers, in which it was ultimately successful, and in its policy of detachment towards the war in China. In February 1939 it declared formally that it 'was not prepared to impose sanctions upon any country except in conjunction with other countries'.

The government's determination to check unofficial sanctions was paralleled by their conciliatory trade policy towards Japan. At the Imperial Conference Mr. Lyons had stressed the urgent need for wide policies of economic appeasement if their endeavours to bring about peaceful conditions in the world were to be successful,[2] and it is in the light of this general objective that Australia's later trade relations with Japan are to be judged. In its full rigour the trade-diversion policy, as has already been noted, was short lived. By an agreement, which took effect on 1 January 1937, tariff adjustments made possible a return to more normal conditions, but a limit was set to the exchange of wool and textiles which in effect rendered impossible any expansion of the trade in those key commodities beyond the level of 1935. This proved more to the advantage of Japanese than of Australian exporters. While Japanese textiles soon regained their position in the Australian market the Japanese demand for Australian wool had significantly contracted. The trade-diversion policy had helped to convince Japan that dependence on overseas sources of supply for materials essential to her economy was a source of weakness which must be remedied by seeking supplies nearer home and under her direct or indirect control. As a result the balance of trade, hitherto heavily in Australia's favour, slightly favoured Japan in 1937–8. Moreover,

[1] Quoted in Shepherd, *Australia's Interests*, p. 81, whom see generally, pp. 80–87.
[2] Cmd. 5482 (1937) p. 55.

while in 1935–6 14·15 per cent. of Australia's total exports went to Japan, in 1937–8 the percentage was only 4·16. The Australian government, however, remained 'conciliatory and obliging in its anxiety to smooth the way for a restoration of trade between the countries', and a new trade agreement came into force in July 1938. But the effect of Australia's policy of economic appeasement was seriously vitiated by her subsequent embargo on the export of iron ore to all countries in the interests of her own industrial development. This embargo provoked renewed indignation in Japan, to whom Australian supplies were of greater importance than the Australian government realized.

While the desire to conciliate Japan remained the predominant characteristic of Australian policy, renewed Japanese aggression in China brought home to the Australians for the first time the full dangers of their position. The government, though prepared to go to all reasonable lengths and beyond to propitiate her dangerous Asian neighbour, at the same time entertained few illusions about the direct dangers of unchecked Japanese militarism for Australia. 'A policy is being hatched abroad', warned Mr. Hughes in January 1938, 'which may shake Australia to her foundations.' 'For the first time in its history', said Mr. Lyons in December 1938, 'Australia might be in the war zone.' 'The bitter truth is', he repeated, 'that any time within the next few years we Australians may have to resist an attack on our country. . . . Would that you knew, while there is yet time, on what a slender thread the peace of Australia depends.'[1] Behind these veiled allusions to impending dangers, which for fear of giving offence abroad was all that the government ventured to tell an anxious people, loomed unmistakable the menace of Japan. Home defence assumed an importance it had never possessed before, and, however inadequate Australian preparations, there was at the least satisfaction that within Australia there was no minority prepared to act as a fifth column. The 'White Australia' policy acquired a new justification in Australian eyes. Mr. Shepherd, writing in 1939, observed that

> quite apart from the various historical and economic objections which would be raised, the recent course of Japanese policy has engendered so much suspicion in the Australian popular mind that any suggested modification of present immigration policy in Japan's favour would be generally denounced as madness comparable only to that of the Trojans who took the wooden horse within their walls.[2]

THE PROBLEMS OF DEFENCE

Until the middle nineteen-thirties it had been accepted as axiomatic that Australian security depended upon the protection of the Royal Navy. Naval policy remained on an imperial basis. Australia took part in the negotiations leading up to the London Naval Treaty of December 1936 and signed it

[1] Quoted by Shepherd, *Australia's Interests*, p. 115, from *Sydney Morning Herald*, 15 December 1938, and *Bulletin of International News*, 11 February 1939, p. 14.

[2] *Australia's Interests*, p. 196.

separately. Australian participation continued to be, as the Minister for External Affairs explained, on an imperial footing not because Australian interest was secondary or indirect but because naval armaments were regarded as imperial in scope.[1] However, the growing possibility of simultaneous war in Western Europe and in Eastern Asia, of which the United Kingdom government through Sir Maurice Hankey gave due warning in 1934, somewhat qualified this traditional view.[2] How effectively would the Royal Navy be able to safeguard Pacific waters while heavily engaged in the Atlantic or the Mediterranean? As early as November 1936 Mr. Curtin expressed his misgivings in forceful terms.

> If an Eastern first-class Power sought an abrogation of a basic Australian policy, such as the White Australia policy, it would most likely do so when Great Britain was involved or threatened to be involved in a European war. Would the British Government dare to authorize the dispatch of any substantial part of the fleet to the East to help Australia? . . . The dependence of Australia upon the competence, let alone the readiness, of British statesmen to send forces to our aid is too dangerous a hazard upon which to found Australia's defence policy.[3]

The moral Mr. Curtin drew was that greater emphasis should be placed on home defence, which meant a rapid expansion of Australian air forces, even at the expense of her naval forces.[4] The government, however, were for long unprepared to accept so radical a modification in traditional defence policy.

On 11 September 1936 the Minister for Defence, Sir Archdale Parkhill, had affirmed 'British sea power is our first line of defence . . . and non-participation in Empire naval defence by the Commonwealth would be a reckless disregard of its interests and security'.[5] 'In practice', commented Mr. W. M. Hughes, 'the Empire is an entity.'[6] And Mr. Lyons, the Prime Minister, on his return from the Imperial Conference, discounting altogether any assistance which the League might afford, told the House of Representatives, 'Our people are wise enough to realize that our defence rests on two pillars, one of which is our own maximum effort, and the other Empire co-operation.'[7] Since Australia was dependent for her security upon the command of sea communications the Royal Australian Navy should be maintained

[1] *J.P.E.*, 1937, vol. 18, pp. 361–2.

[2] 'After 1934 the *tempo* (of rearmament) in Australia, as in Great Britain, greatly increased.' In these words Lord Hankey has recorded what happened largely as a result of this warning. (*Diplomacy by Conference*, p. 139, and see also pp. 131–2.)

[3] 5 November 1936, Australia, H. of R. Deb., vol. 152, pp. 1547–8.

[4] This point, and the need for Australian self-reliance in matters of defence, had been emphasized by military commentators in recent years. For an analysis of the precarious Australian position in relation to the Far East see Col. J. D. Laverack, 'The Defence of Australia', *Army Quarterly*, vol. 25 (January 1933) pp. 209–17. An article in the *Round Table*, December 1935, entitled 'Australian Defence Policy', showed how unfounded was the belief that Australian security was safeguarded by the Royal Navy.

[5] Australia, H. of R. Deb., vol. 151, p. 70.

[6] See Carter, *British Commonwealth*, p. 253.

[7] *J.P.E.*, 1937, vol. 18, p. 856.

at a strength which constituted an effective and fair contribution to Empire naval defence. In London a most intensive expert examination of Australia's liability to invasion had been made, and it had shown that the safety of Australian and of imperial interests in the East depended mainly upon the presence at Singapore of a British fleet of sufficient strength to safeguard Pacific communications. 'It is an unavoidable geographical fact', said Mr. Lyons, 'that the first line of defence of the Commonwealth is naval, and if we expect a British Fleet to be based on Singapore as a safeguard to Australia, we must be prepared to co-operate and provide for the squadron necessary in our own waters.'[1] In reply to Labour criticism of dissipation of resources better devoted to home defence, Mr. Lyons observed cogently enough that in major wars the future of overseas territories was always decided in the main theatre. For Australia that meant that her fate depended on the outcome of the struggle between the British and enemy fleets for the control of sea communications.[2] The British government had assured Australia that all their resources were at the disposal of, and for the benefit of, any part of the British Empire that was attacked, while conveying at the same time warnings of the very real limits to their strength in Pacific waters.

In succeeding years the possibility of actual invasion of the mainland of Australia by Japanese forces caused some shift in emphasis and brought the government and opposition into closer accord on defence policy. On 27 April 1938 Mr. Lyons defined the defence policy of the Commonwealth in these terms:

> The scheme of Australian defence is related to a wider pattern of Empire defence, and its fundamental basis is Empire sea power and the Singapore naval base. Nevertheless, complementary to this conception of Empire collective security, we should do all we can to defend ourselves, and the new programme is claimed to be a substantial step towards this end. It will provide for the cruisers necessary for trade defence in our local waters; it will greatly strengthen the land, sea and air defences of the main ports and centres of population; it will strengthen the equipment and munitions reserves of the field army and increase the permanent personnel and the general standard of efficiency; and finally, it will provide greater resources for the local production of munitions, and complete the national planning of all phases of activity associated with the defence forces.[3]

This statement with its renewed emphasis on the need for efficient home defence[4] foreshadowed plans for a rapid increase in the strength of the air arm to be made possible by domestic production. By March 1939 the number of

[1] ibid.
[2] ibid. p. 27.
[3] Australia, H. of R. Deb., vol. 155, p. 561, quoted by Hankey, *Diplomacy by Conference*, p. 139.
[4] The measures taken by Australia for home defence before the First World War are apt to be overlooked. They were, however, very considerable. In 1914 Australia had a compulsorily enlisted citizen army of 45,000, planned to be increased to 120,000 by 1919; a navy including capital ships and five cruisers; and had even, in 1912, established a flying school.

first-line planes at the disposal of the Royal Australian Air Force was 132, and the Prime Minister announced the intention of the government to increase the permanent strength of the Force by 950 planes yearly, bringing the total to 5,600 by June 1941. In this way the second pillar of Australian defence was being strengthened with the cordial support of the main body of the opposition. More generally the new programme, as Mr. Shepherd has justly observed, 'seemed to envisage not only a large measure of self-reliance on Australia's part but also a positive contribution by Australia to the defence of imperial interests in . . . the Pacific. An effort was obviously to be made to transform Australia from an imperial liability to an imperial asset in matters of defence.'[1]

AUSTRALIAN EXTERNAL POLICY AFTER THE IMPERIAL CONFERENCE

It is in the light of Australia's exposed strategic situation that her external policies must be viewed. Long accustomed to think of Australia as 'an outpost of European civilization in a sea of colour', her people rightly sensed that while the dangers of direct assault upon her mainland came from Asia the future of Australia depended upon the fate of Britain, which would ultimately be decided in Europe. In practice this imposed a tolerably clear limit upon Australian initiative in foreign policy. In view of Australia's dependence on the Royal Navy it was a matter of common prudence that her government should pursue no policies in the Pacific unlikely to command the whole-hearted approval of the United Kingdom. Likewise, since the greatest risk of war would come, as in 1914, from Eastern Europe, Australia was easily persuaded that it was in her interest to support Britain's European policies which, with the agreement of the Imperial Conference of 1937, were directed to the one overriding aim of averting its outbreak.

The Imperial Conference had very considerable significance in the determination of the Australian attitude to international affairs. In the two critical succeeding years the Australian government accepted the conclusions of the Conference as a proper criterion by which to judge the correctness of United Kingdom policies and to decide their own. In particular, so long as United Kingdom policies could be defended as conforming to the general principles then defined, the Australian government was content to adopt and defend them. In this way the general conclusions about foreign policy and defence reached in London in May 1937 acquired an importance in Australia far surpassing that which they attained in any other dominion and in clear contrast to the tendency in Canada and South Africa to deprive the conclusions of the Imperial Conference of all binding authority. As a result, the Australian government after 1937 gave consistent support to the policy of appeasement. In particular Australia continued to display an active interest in Mr. Chamberlain's Mediterranean policies and especially in his attempts to bring about an

[1] *Australia's Interests*, p. 106.

improvement in Anglo-Italian relations. Throughout the negotiations for an Anglo-Italian settlement that took place early in 1938 Australia, alone of the dominions, displayed outspoken, positive interest in the development of British policy. In February 1938 Mr. Lyons telegraphed to Mr. Chamberlain saying: 'We agree that the present situation calls for action, and we feel that the reopening of conversations with Italy is of the utmost importance. I should be glad if you would continue to keep me fully advised as to the situation.'[1] Australia's confidence in the correctness of a policy, one condition of whose success was the recognition of Italy's conquest in Abyssinia, was not shaken by the criticism it provoked within Australia and still more without. Where Mr. Cordell Hull protested in January that a recognition of the Italian conquest of Abyssinia would 'rouse a feeling of disgust' and 'would be represented as a corrupt bargain completed in Europe at the expense of interests in the Far East';[2] where Mr. Eden, feeling that even the calamity of war with the dictators was to be preferred to the loss of American good will and British self-respect, resigned;[3] where Mr. Churchill, foreseeing the consequences that must follow, 'lay . . . consumed by emotions of sorrow and fear',[4] the Australian government continued to give loyal, painstaking support to a disastrous policy. The opposition detected disturbing contradictions between Mr. Chamberlain's professed devotion to League principles and his adoption of policies wholly inconsistent with them, but the government observed no such discrepancy. On the contrary they affirmed their belief that Mr. Chamberlain's policies were consistent with loyalty to the League. Mr. Lyons maintained that no major change in United Kingdom foreign policy would, or should, be undertaken without consultation with all the dominions, and not without some naïveté he replied to opposition charges that Britain was throwing, or had thrown, the League overboard by explaining that on 6 March he had secured the personal authority of Mr. Chamberlain to state that he still adhered to the policy which had been adopted at the Imperial Conference, and that in particular there had been no change in principle in the attitude of the United Kingdom towards the League of Nations and collective security.[5] Mr. Lyons endorsed Mr. Chamberlain's statement of the principles guiding British foreign policy made in his speech of 21 February and reasserted his conviction that Mr. Chamberlain's foreign policy had been in conformity with these principles. More significantly, the Australian Prime Minister appealed once again to the sanction of the Imperial Conference which had declared that 'differences of political creed should be no obstacle to friendly relations with other governments and countries'.[6] Fundamentally it was by reference to this

[1] 27 April 1938, Australia, H. of R. Deb., vol. 155, p. 536.
[2] Quoted in Churchill, *Second World War*, vol. 1, p. 197.
[3] Keith Feiling, *Life of Neville Chamberlain* (London, Macmillan, 1946) p. 338.
[4] *Second World War*, vol. 1, p. 201.
[5] *J.P.E.*, 1938, vol. 19, pp. 635–6.
[6] ibid. p. 635.

principle that the government defended their support of Britain's rapprochement with Italy.

THE MUNICH CRISIS

The Australian attitude to events in Europe was in essentials tolerably well defined before the Sudeten crisis confronted her with the possibility of imminent war in September 1938. From the outset it was evident that the whole influence of the Australian government would be directed towards securing a compromise settlement. Far removed from the probable scene of conflict, both government and people regarded the Nazi claim to the Sudetenland as not without some solid foundation, however much they mistrusted the way in which it had been advanced. In July 1938 Mr. Menzies, then Attorney-General and the most able of Mr. Lyons's colleagues, visited Germany as head of an Australian trade mission. This visit was not without importance. Australia had no diplomatic representation in Berlin or indeed in any other European capital, and the Attorney-General's first-hand impressions of the policy of Nazi Germany inevitably carried much weight with his cabinet colleagues when the September crisis came. Mr. Menzies was in fact deeply impressed with Germany's industrial strength but recognized that in some ways the German people did not understand 'either the British character or the British attitude'. He hoped none the less that 'mutual understanding will grow between two of the greatest and most virile nations on earth', and it is evident that he returned to Australia convinced that war between Britain and Germany on the Sudeten issue should at almost all costs be avoided.[1] From this view the opposition did not dissent. In 1938 it was still not proven, as Mr. Curtin implicitly allowed a year later, that Germany was embarking on a course of unprovoked aggression. Moreover, quite apart from the merits of a dispute about which comparatively little was known, Australia did not want a war for which she was almost wholly unprepared and which might have repercussions in the Far East which she was ill equipped to meet. Australia had fought one war in Europe to preserve the liberties of small nations, and only under extreme provocation were her people prepared to send the flower of their manhood overseas to fight again on Europe's far-distant battlefields. On that the Labour party were adamant.

From March to September 1938 the Australian government were in frequent communication with London about the Czech crisis. Before it was delivered Mr. Chamberlain's speech of 24 March 1938, in which he restated Britain's obligations in Europe and the Middle East and outlined the circumstances under which Britain would go to war, was agreed to 'on all vital issues' by the Australian government. Yet its implications were interpreted restrictively. On 25 May Mr. W. M. Hughes told the House of Representatives

[1] cf. Speech of 6 October quoted in *The Times*, 7 October 1938: 'It would be wrong had Europe drifted into a war in which the merits were not all one way.'

that Britain had 'assumed no new commitments in regard to Czechoslovakia' and he welcomed British and French representations to Czechoslovakia hoping that they might pave the way to 'a peaceful solution of this question which has so long been a disturbing factor in European politics'.[1] In general it is not in doubt that the Australian government fully endorsed Mr. Chamberlain's policy of appeasement at every stage of the Czech crisis, and at decisive moments encouraged Mr. Chamberlain to make further efforts to secure a settlement even at the price of greater concessions by the Czechs.

On 28 September Mr. Lyons informed the House of Representatives in some detail of the action he had taken.[2] Throughout the crisis, he said, his government had been in constant consultation with the United Kingdom government. In the belief that the rally of the Nazi party at Nuremberg on 5 September might herald some decisive German action, the Australian government had cabled the United Kingdom government on 2 September saying that 'it strongly supported' the policy outlined by Mr. Chamberlain on 24 March 'with special reference to that portion of the speech in which attention was drawn to the importance of saying beforehand what governments might become involved if Czechoslovakia were attacked'. At the same time the Australian government urged—and this was indicative of their attitude—'that the government of Czechoslovakia should not delay in making a public announcement of the most liberal concessions which they could offer, and that representations should be made to the Czechoslovak government with a view to securing an immediate public statement of such concessions'.[3]

Later, the Australian government strongly endorsed Mr. Chamberlain's efforts to avert war by his visit to Godesberg. Mr. Lyons telegraphed commending Mr. Chamberlain's decision to see Herr Hitler which, he said, had the support of the whole of Australia. This positive endorsement of Mr. Chamberlain's policy was defended by Mr. Lyons on the ground that it represented the implementation of the policy agreed at the 1937 Imperial Conference for preserving peace by conciliation so that 'if war is to come . . . our hands are clean'.[4]

Evidence of close and prompt consultation between the United Kingdom government and dominion governments in September 1938 was afforded by the fact that Mr. Lyons was able to place before the House of Representatives the text of all the most important documents which had passed between Mr. Chamberlain, Herr Hitler, and the Czechoslovak government up to 26 September, when he explained his own attitude on 28 September. Thereafter active consultation between the United Kingdom and Australian governments continued. On 28 September the Australian government sent a telegram suggesting a personal appeal to Signor Mussolini in the hope that

[1] Australia, H. of R. Deb., vol. 155, pp. 1375–6.
[2] His speech is fully summarized in *J.P.E.*, 1938, vol. 19, pp. 850 ff.
[3] ibid. p. 851.
[4] ibid. p. 854.

he would be prepared to persuade his Axis partner at least to extend the brief time limit given in the ultimatum to the Czechs. Mr. Lyons went on to say that Mr. Stanley Bruce, the Australian High Commissioner in London, would be made available to fly to Rome with a personal message if Mr. Chamberlain thought it would serve any useful purpose. 'We called Mr. Chamberlain out of his bed', said Mr. Lyons, 'in the early hours of the morning . . . to discuss this matter with him and to express our view.'[1] Mr. Chamberlain, however, had already contemplated an approach to Mussolini through the British ambassador in Rome, and therefore did not avail himself of this particular offer, though the importance attached by the Australian government to an appeal to the Italian dictator must at least have provided some reassurance to Mr. Chamberlain in the pursuit of his chosen course.

The intervention of Mussolini led direct to Munich, and Mr. Chamberlain's decision to fly there was hailed with joy throughout Australia. Mr. Lyons, speaking of 'the notable service which Mr. Chamberlain had rendered in the cause of peace', said he would like to

> assure honourable members that we have been in constant communication, both by cable and by telephone, over the whole course of the last fortnight, with Mr. Chamberlain and Mr. Bruce. We have been kept in hourly touch with the situation and with the many communications that have passed between the Prime Minister of Great Britain and Herr Hitler, and the heads of other states concerned in or affected by the crisis. We have made such suggestions as we believed would be helpful, and which we believe have been helpful, at various stages of the dispute.

It is apparent from Mr. Lyons's statements that the Australian government was closely associated with and fully approved Mr. Chamberlain's policy at Munich. When the agreement was signed on 30 September Mr. Lyons paid most cordial tribute to Mr. Chamberlain for the successful completion of his task. This was generally endorsed by public opinion.[2]

The Munich crisis prompted one important question. Had war occurred, would Australia have been committed? On this point Mr. Curtin, as leader of the opposition, cross-examined the government. He asked for more specific information about the communications which the government had sent to London and particularly about what had been said in them about Australia's attitude in the event of war. For his part, he argued that if the government had not committed Australia to support a war against Germany, then there was absolutely no distinction between the government and the opposition; but if they had, then there was a deep difference between them, for the Labour party remained opposed in principle and in practice to the recruitment of

[1] Australia, H. of R. Deb., vol. 157, p. 332.

[2] Throughout the crisis the *Sydney Morning Herald*, alone of all Australian papers, showed itself highly critical of the Czechoslovakian settlement and soberly reminded the public of the consequences of Hitler's 'unexampled diplomatic victory'. See in particular leading articles, *S.M.H.*, 23 September 1938, 3 October 1938, 4 October 1938.

Australians for the battlefields of Europe. Australia's duty was primarily to her own people, and they could not afford to become active participants in the disputes of another continent. Mr. Curtin therefore urged that Australia should not become tied to treaties which 'by a process of duplication and expansion, might lead them into the position of having to go to war in respect of developments with which they had no concern and for which they could not be responsible'.[1]

To all this the veteran Mr. Hughes, once more Minister for External Affairs, made a characteristic rejoinder. 'If war had occurred', he retorted, 'it would have required no committal. We should have been committed to war and no power could have saved us from it.' His categoric statement was generally accepted as a realistic recognition of the facts. Moreover, opinion within the Labour party, and still less in the country as a whole, was not prepared to give any final endorsement to Mr. Curtin's policy of limiting Australian participation in a war in which Britain was involved to home defence. On the narrower issue of the precise advice which the government had given to the United Kingdom, Mr. Hughes confined himself to saying that they had stood loyally and firmly behind Great Britain in the belief that in that way, and in that way only, could peace be preserved. Treaties had failed. The League of Nations had failed, not because the principles for which it stood were wrong, but because words could not secure peace. All were crushed into the dust, and against them were Powers whose creed was force. Was Australia to range herself with or against them? Or should they wait in perilous isolation until one by one the nations that stood for peace and who alone could save them from destruction were defeated? 'In this fateful hour the government stand with the British Empire because we believe that there is no other way in which we can be true and loyal citizens of Australia.'[2]

THE AFTERMATH OF MUNICH

Faith in the policy of appeasement dwindled slowly. As late as December 1938 Mr. Menzies felt that 'there was a great deal to be said for Germany rearming' in view of her geographical position surrounded by a ring of nations 'most of whom had armed or were arming to the teeth'. But he warned the Nazi leaders that if they wished their standpoint to be understood they must abandon the wholly mistaken idea that they could obtain justice by bullying and threats.[3] More important, the part played by Mussolini in September confirmed the Australian government in its opinion that a rapprochement with Italy might still be possible. Accordingly Mr. Lyons encouraged Mr. Chamberlain in his renewed attempts to detach Italy from her Axis partner. In October 1938 Mr. Lyons advised the United Kingdom

[1] *J.P.E.*, 1939, vol. 20, pp. 117–18. [2] ibid. pp. 116–19.
[3] *Sydney Morning Herald*, 12 December 1938.

government that in his view the sooner the agreement with Italy was implemented 'the better it would be for both Great Britain and Italy and probably for the peace of the world', and on receiving assurances from Mr. Chamberlain that this would be done immediately, Mr. Lyons expressed his appreciation of this further step in 'the general appeasement' of Europe.[1] No other dominion government so strongly favoured the conciliation of Italy, and the general Australian concern with the Mediterranean sea route which prompted it was also responsible for Australia's conciliatory attitude towards the Franco régime in Spain which she recognized, following the example of the United Kingdom, on 28 February 1939. Australia's continued support for a policy of conditional appeasement in the Mediterranean was useful to Mr. Chamberlain in dealing with criticisms at home even though it was in some measure counterbalanced by New Zealand's indignant refusal to sacrifice principle to expediency. On the other hand, Australia's influence on United Kingdom policy was slight because welcome though her backing undoubtedly was, the direction of that policy was already clearly determined.

While in the post-Munich period Australia continued to favour a policy of appeasement, there was a growing uneasiness, reflected in parliamentary debates, that it might fail. If that happened it was accepted almost without question that the only honourable and realistic policy for Australia was the closest co-operation with the United Kingdom in making adequate preparations for defence while peace continued, and participation at her side when war came. On 6 December 1938 the Minister for Defence warned the House of Representatives that 'events since Munich had not taken them very far along the road to peace', and he emphasized that while it was the instinctive hope of the Australian people that the policy of appeasement initiated by the Munich pact would succeed, they should not remain blind to the possibility that despite all the concessions that had been made, Australia might have to resist an attack, even upon her own mainland, within the next few years. What Munich above all had underlined was that time was not on the side of Australia unless her defence preparations were speeded up.[2] It was a recognition of that sombre reality which led Mr. Curtin to pledge the support of his party to the strengthening of the defences of Australia and to recognize the paramount responsibility of the government to make the most thorough preparations for the safety of the country.

For Australia, as for Britain herself, the Nazi annexation of Czechoslovakia on 15 March 1939 afforded decisive evidence that appeasement had failed. Mr. Chamberlain's speech at Birmingham two days later, recognizing that the day for conciliation was past and that if aggression were to be checked resolute action was imperative, expressed the reaction of the vast majority of the Australian people. Even the precipitate extension of unilateral guarantees to Poland on 31 March 1939 and to Greece and Roumania on 13 April 1939,

[1] *The Times*, 3 November 1938.

[2] *J.P.E.*, 1939, vol. 20, p. 427.

about which none of the dominions were consulted in advance, was greeted with satisfaction. Mr. Menzies, who succeeded Mr. Lyons as Prime Minister, reaffirmed on 26 April, in a broadcast speech to the nation, Australia's solidarity with Britain:

> The peace of Great Britain is precious to us, because her peace is ours; if she is at war, we are at war, even though that war finds us not in European battlefields, but defending our own shores. Let me be clear on this; I cannot have a defence of Australia which depends upon British sea power as its first element; I cannot envisage a vital foreign trade on sea routes kept free by British sea power, and at the same time refuse to Britain Australian co-operation at a time of common danger. The British countries of the world must stand or fall together.[1]

On 9 May the Minister for External Affairs, Sir Henry Gullett, explained, with the concurrence of Mr. Menzies, that the Prime Minister's words were not to be interpreted to mean that in any and every set of circumstances the foreign policy of a government of the United Kingdom, if it led to war, should or would automatically commit Australia to participate in that war. He admitted that it was conceivable that a policy might be adopted in London which would meet with strong disapproval or condemnation in Australia, but, he added, that in fact there was complete unanimity between the two governments at that time about the right policies to pursue. 'If, therefore, in pursuance of this policy, the government of Britain is at any moment plunged into war, this government will on behalf of the Australian people, make common cause with the mother country in that war.'[2]

There was subsequently a good deal of criticism both in Australia and New Zealand because Britain's unilateral guarantees to Poland, Greece, and Roumania were extended without prior consultation with dominion governments. These criticisms were not ill-founded. The accepted machinery for intra-Commonwealth consultation broke down because it was deemed in London that time did not allow of prior consultation. The dominion governments were as a result only informed *ex post facto* of the guarantees given by the United Kingdom government, and they had no opportunity of influencing a policy in whose consequences they were destined to be so deeply involved. The failure to consult was the more to be regretted in that the guarantees represented not the climax of a policy whose purpose was clearly understood, but a radical departure from it. Yet while such criticisms were forcibly expressed in Australia, it is not for one moment to be suggested that if consultation had taken place the Australian government would have advocated any very different course or, still less, wished to dissociate herself from United Kingdom policy. While not equally responsible her government had been equally committed to the Munich policy, and in March 1939 their reactions to its failure corresponded with those of the United Kingdom government, the

[1] Quoted ibid. p. 683.

[2] ibid. p. 684.

Australian Prime Minister expressing, as we have seen, positive agreement with Britain's policy of unilateral guarantees to the states most likely to be the next victims of aggression in Eastern Europe. While, therefore, Britain's failure to consult the dominions is to be carefully noted, it is also to be emphasized that it occurred at a time and on an issue in which the views of the Australian government were fully in accord with those of London. That this was so is one of the more important consequences of the Munich settlement. Without the experience of September 1938 and its disillusioning aftermath Australian opinion would hardly have acquiesced in, and still less endorsed, British commitments in Eastern Europe almost certain to involve the Empire in war.

While the failure of appeasement in Europe was fully recognized, Australia's leaders continued to cherish the hope that Japan might yet be conciliated. Deeply concerned to restrict the area of conflict they hoped that it might be possible to insulate the Far East from the repercussions of war in Europe. For this it was all important that any agreement between the Western democracies and Russia should be territorially restricted to Europe, lest any extension of its provisions to Asia should finally estrange Japan and drive her into open opposition to the democracies. In May 1938 the Prime Minister, Mr. Menzies, informed the House of Representatives that he had submitted the views of his government on the proposed Three-Power pact to the United Kingdom government and, whilst properly emphasizing 'the special interests of Australia in the Pacific', he had 'said nothing that would prejudice a better understanding, and a closer arrangement of a non-aggressive kind, with Russia'.[1] A little later, however, the Minister for External Affairs stated that from the time of the opening of the negotiations for the inclusion of the Soviet Union in the European non-aggression pact the Australian government had urged London not to overlook or disregard the effect which such an agreement might have upon Japan.[2] There was clearly a marked lack of enthusiasm for co-operation with Russia, and it is not to be doubted that Australian support for any such agreement was conditional upon its having no positive application outside Europe.[3] It was only acceptance of this territorial limitation as a basis for negotiation which partly reassured the Commonwealth government that such a pact would not act as a direct provocation to Japan.

On its own initiative the Australian government took what steps were open to it to ensure that the existing relations between Australia and Japan should not deteriorate. In May 1939 Mr. Menzies announced the government's intention, not only to establish closer diplomatic contact with Japan, but to do

[1] 23 May 1939, Australia, H. of R. Deb., vol. 159, pp. 604–5.

[2] 15 June 1939, ibid. vol. 160, p. 1926.

[3] ibid. It is not suggested that the Australian attitude was responsible in any way for the breakdown of the negotiations between the United Kingdom and the U.S.S.R., which is to be attributed to mutual suspicions and irreconcilable policies in Europe. For a brilliant analysis see Namier, *Diplomatic Prelude*, Chapter V.

everything possible to increase cultural relations and personal contact in the hope of reaching 'a real and permanent understanding with the Japanese people'.[1]

Australia's conciliatory policy in the Far East won only qualified approval in London. On 4 August 1939 Mr. Chamberlain issued a blunt warning to Japan. He acknowledged that Britain had not at the time a fleet in the Far East superior to that of the Japanese. But, he added, 'we have such a fleet here, and in certain circumstances we might find it necessary to send the fleet out there. I hope no one will think that it is absolutely out of the question for such circumstances to arise.'[2] This warning to Japan was intended to make it clear that while Great Britain would rather settle her differences with Japan by discussion and negotiation, she was not prepared to do so by the sacrifice of fundamental interests or principles. At Westminster such a stand was welcomed, the principal misgiving being the fear lest subsequent action might not be as resolute as the Prime Minister's language implied. Nor were Australia's probable reactions to a firmer attitude overlooked. On 3 August 1939 Lord Samuel, while recognizing Australia's interest in all questions relating to the Pacific, expressed doubts about the wisdom of her approach. He recalled that in the Manchukuo crisis of 1931–2 Australia had played an important part in influencing the thought of the United Kingdom government, and he trusted that in 1939 the government and people of Australia would recognize that a policy of constant retreat was neither likely to succeed in the long run nor consistent with the dignity or the interests of the British Empire; and that it resulted merely in loss of honour without buying safety.[3] This outspoken rebuke, which credited Australia with a more decisive influence in the determining of British policy than she had in fact exercised, while not unjust was not well timed. By August 1939 the most favourable moment for a resolute policy in the Far East had long since passed. The dispatch of the home fleet to Far Eastern waters would almost certainly have precipitated a European war. Britain no more than Australia could have contemplated with equanimity simultaneous war in Europe and in Asia.

In Australia the year that elapsed between Munich and the outbreak of war brought one clear gain. It narrowed the differences between government and opposition on major issues in policy even if it did not wholly remove them. What divided them now was not whether Australia should participate in a war brought about by further German aggression but the scale of her participation. Not till the German onslaught of April–May 1940 were all reservations on the part of the Labour leaders about the war effort to be dispelled. But none the less by September 1939 there were at least no remaining doubts about the principle at stake; it was a united nation that went to war. The common meeting ground was fairly reflected in Mr. Curtin's speech of May 1939:

[1] *J.P.E.*, 1939, vol. 20, p. 688.
[2] H. of C. Deb., vol. 350, col. 2863.
[3] H. of L. Deb., vol. 114, col. 831.

We say that our membership of the British Commonwealth of Nations gives to us a fraternity of national associations, that there is between the Commonwealth government and the governments of the United Kingdom and the dominions a common concern for peace, and a common interest in the security of the English-speaking race; but that the governments of the dominions must themselves decide, in the light of circumstances, how and to what extent they will be participators in a war.[1]

Mr. Curtin's language, so close to that of Mr. Mackenzie King, foreshadowed the outlook of succeeding years. The emphasis of the government was different. It rested firmly on imperial solidarity. But what was important was not these differences in approach but the wide measure of agreement about the action that should be taken. The events of September 1938, culminating in the Munich agreement, had played an important part in bringing this about. However great the differences of opinion that existed about the merits of that settlement, none doubted thereafter that if war came 'our hands are clean'.[2]

[1] *J.P.E.*, 1939, vol. 20, p. 685.

[2] The phrase was used by Mr. Lyons in September 1938. See above, p. 169.

CHAPTER VI

NEW ZEALAND: IMPERIALIST AND INTERNATIONALIST

'OCEANIA FOR THE ANGLO-SAXONS'

MACAULAY'S New Zealander, who stood looking across from Tower Bridge upon the ruins of St. Paul's, was an imaginative period piece. It belongs to the great age of robust Victorian self-confidence in all things British. States and empires might rise and fall, but against the inevitable day of decline Britain had reinsured herself by peopling with her own stock distant lands upon whom in the fullness of time the mantle of her greatness would fall. And of her overseas possessions none, as Macaulay sensed, was more fitted to inherit it than the island colony of New Zealand, peopled almost wholly by emigrants from the British Isles who had carefully and deliberately transplanted the social order, the beliefs, and the conventions of Victorian England to the far Pacific. Unlike Australia, New Zealand was populated, save only at the extremes of wealth and poverty, by a 'vertical slice' of nineteenth-century English society, by people who had gone out 'not in despair but in hope'. Their quest was for better opportunities of steady progress than they could find in Britain, but they nursed no grievances against the homeland they had left, nor were there numbered among them the landless dispossessed or the resentful, embittered misfits of the industrial revolution. If Wakefield's conception of a society dependent upon aristocratic leadership soon faded before the firm resolve of the colonists to be rid of the class distinctions and social inequalities they had known and to build up in place of them a predominantly classless society designed for the benefit of 'the common man', this departure from the English social pattern neither created nor implied any hostility to the mother country.[1]

From the first New Zealand's hopes for the future, despite passing moments of restiveness, were firmly set on the establishment and the extension of the British way of life in the Pacific. A century ago, according to New Zealand's historian, Professor Wood,[2] colonists of vision were calmly confident that New Zealand was destined to be the centre of a great empire. They believed that British culture and British enterprise would find new fields to conquer so that in ages to come the power, the political genius, the industrial skill of the British people might germinate and flourish a second time in an island empire of the South. Such expansionist ideas, in New Zealand as in Australia, were the

[1] cf. F. L. W. Wood, *Understanding New Zealand* (New York, Coward-McCann, 1944) pp. 61–63.

[2] F. L. W. Wood, *New Zealand in the World* (Wellington, Department of Internal Affairs, 1940) p. 1.

product of self-confidence, of an apparently unassailable security and a desire, for the most part subconscious but persisting to this day, to shift the centre of gravity of the Empire southward. They were materially reinforced in the last quarter of the nineteenth century by the desire to forestall a 'scramble for the Pacific' by the Great Powers of Europe. For New Zealand, as for Australia, the ideal was the implementation of 'a Monroe doctrine of the South' which would keep the South Pacific in perpetual peace under British hegemony. In the words of a sympathetic French observer, what began as 'Australasia for the Australasians' developed into 'Oceania for the Anglo-Saxons'.[1]

By 1870 the New Zealand vision of a Pacific Empire had already become part of the national tradition.[2] Forcefully expounded by Sir Julius Vogel, the thrustful protagonist of expansionist policies—a man who seemed to the Colonial Office 'the most audacious adventurer that perhaps has ever held power in a British colony'[3]—its realization was dependent upon the active co-operation of London. This was rarely unreserved or whole-hearted. Between 1870 and 1885 Vogel sought to impress upon the Colonial Office the desirability of annexing all the islands still unoccupied by a European Power and in 1874, acceding to pressure from both Australia and New Zealand, Britain annexed Fiji. The result was not altogether happy. Though the annexation had been prompted by the colonial governments, they were not given a voice in the administration of the island and they were affronted when asked to share its cost. Their reaction, not altogether unreasonable in the circumstances, none the less hardened opinion in London against further annexations,[4] and for the translation of an expansionist dream into practical reality the backing of London was indispensable.

It is easy to understand why Britain was generally reluctant to embark on the 'great national work' of extending British rule in the Pacific. The newly won predominance of Germany in Europe ushered in a dangerous phase in the age-old struggle for power, and England, without allies on the Continent, estranged from France, more than ordinarily disturbed by Russian advances towards the North-West Frontier of India, was little disposed for Pacific adventures which might well provoke angry counteraction nearer home. In retrospect it may be reasonably argued that preoccupations in Europe and Africa loomed unduly large, and that opportunities to establish security and good administration throughout the South-West Pacific, not destined to recur, were unwisely allowed to slip by. Certainly it was easy, temptingly easy, for Britain to preserve tolerable relations with Imperial Germany by making concessions in distant parts of the world. When in 1884 Germany occupied part of New Guinea and Samoa, London, anxious to retain the good will of Bismarck, and in disregard of violent protests from Australia and New Zealand,

[1] André Siegfried, *Democracy in New Zealand*, trans. by E. V. Burns (London, Bell, 1914) p. 351.

[2] Wood, *New Zealand in the World*, p. 63.

[3] Quoted ibid. p. 66.

[4] cf. ibid. pp. 66–70.

remained conciliatory. If Germany, observed Gladstone, 'is to become a colonizing Power, all I say is, God speed her! She becomes our ally and partner in the execution of the great purposes of Providence for the advantage of mankind'.[1] But for Australia and New Zealand the practical consequence was to establish in the Pacific a very unwelcome intruder who, in their opinion, should never have been allowed to secure a foothold there.

In 1899 German jurisdiction in Samoa was formally recognized. Like other 'incalculable losses' this was accepted in a spirit of loyal resignation in the antipodes. But Mr. Seddon, the New Zealand Prime Minister, advised Mr. Joseph Chamberlain, then Colonial Secretary, that 'some definite action of a forward kind is required in the Pacific at the earliest opportune moment, for the surrender of Samoa has disheartened the natives of the islands, disappointed the people of Australasia, and lowered the prestige of Great Britain in this part of the globe'.[2] But even as he wrote, the New Zealand Prime Minister must have recognized that the most favourable moment for a forward policy had passed. The reaction of the Great Powers in Europe to British reverses in South Africa left no room for any illusion that fresh entanglements or preoccupations would escape direct challenge.

THE PROTECTIVE ROLE OF THE ROYAL NAVY

Expansionist ideas which flourished in the age of security withered away when that security was undermined. The German foothold in New Guinea, her annexation of Samoa, the presence of a Russian fleet in the Pacific, and the rise of Japan to the rank of a first-class Power, combined to confront New Zealand in the early twentieth century with dangers which if still comparatively remote could no longer be ignored. As the rivalry of the Great Powers became more intense, this isolated British colony became more exposed to the changes and chances of that struggle for power which centred in Europe, but one of whose manifestations was to be seen in short-lived, but recurrent, crises about colonial territories in Africa and in the Pacific. These unwelcome developments underlined for New Zealand what indeed she had never desired to dispute, her dependence on Britain and above all on British sea power.

For a predominantly pastoral community lacking the mineral resources essential for rapid industrial development, and the man-power needed for successful defence in modern war, reliance on the protection of the Royal Navy was recognized to be a long-term factor decisively influencing her relations with the mother country. Nor was New Zealand content with passive acknowledgement of an indisputable fact. On the contrary, with courage and with remarkable consistency over the years, successive New Zealand governments made every contribution that lay within their power to the strengthen-

[1] Quoted in R. W. Seton-Watson, *Britain in Europe, 1789–1914* (Cambridge University Press, 1937) p. 555.
[2] Wood, *New Zealand in the World*, p. 91.

ing of the imperial forces by land and by sea. Their faith, their sense of an abiding imperial unity, was symbolized in the phrase 'one sea, one navy, one empire'. Not for New Zealand to hearken to those siren voices which urged that national self-respect demanded national control of all armed forces; not for them to follow the other dominions in establishing a naval force of their own. Rather was it their deliberate aim to contribute what they could to the strength of the Royal Navy, and to trust implicitly the wisdom of the Admiralty in the disposition of the forces placed at their disposal. When at the International Conference in 1909 Australia secured recognition in principle of the independence of the Australian navy in peace-time, New Zealand vehemently asserted that it was not independence but integration of naval forces that she sought. In the First World War the distinction disappeared in practice because the navies of the Pacific dominions both came by general assent under the unified command of the Royal Navy. But when the war was over the different aims of the two dominions in this respect were no longer to be disguised. This was symbolic of the different paths which Australia and New Zealand were destined to tread.

THE IMPORTANCE OF THE BRITISH MARKET

As in defence, so in trade, New Zealand's ties with the mother country have been peculiarly intimate. New Zealand is dependent for her livelihood upon the export of her agricultural products, especially dairy produce and fat lambs. Before the Second World War she was more densely populated with sheep than any country in the world. Aided by state planning and state intervention on a generous scale, her farming community developed a profitable export trade on specialized and scientific lines. But good as was the reputation and undoubted the quality of New Zealand's produce, the country's dependence upon exports placed a high premium upon assured and expanding markets and incidentally made her especially vulnerable to a fall in world prices such as occurred in 1929. For long the United Kingdom's apparently insatiable demand for cheap food of good quality made her the ideal customer. One virtue only she lacked. She could not assure stable prices over a long period, and stability in price was something much valued by the New Zealand farmer not only for economic but also for social reasons, for it derived in part at least from deep-seated trends in New Zealand life.[1] Yet the search for the stable or 'just'[2] as distinct from the 'market' price was full of frustration, but in times of surplus when bulk buying and long-term contracts did not supply any corrective to world price fluctuations, stability could be, and was, to a considerable degree assured by state intervention at home. As a result a widening measure of state control was a feature of New Zealand's economy

[1] cf. Wood, *Understanding New Zealand*, pp. 107–8.

[2] They were by no means the same, and for an illuminating commentary on the difference between them see Hancock, *Survey*, vol. 2, Part I, pp. 280 ff.

before 1939, and it was accompanied by measures designed to increase the country's economic self-sufficiency by expanding the internal market for her agricultural produce. Overseas a parallel search for supplementary markets in a world of rising trade barriers was not encouraging and served mainly to underline New Zealand's dependence on the British market.[1] Despite diversions therefore the aim of New Zealand's economic policy remained the cultivation and expansion of that all-important market in which sentiment and self-interest combined to afford her a favoured position. The measure of her success is best illustrated by the New Zealand trade figures for the first four decades of the century.[2]

Year	*Value of total exports* (£000)	*Percentage of total taken by United Kingdom*
1900	13,223	77·6
1910	22,152	84·1
1920	46,405	74·0
1925	55,243	79·8
1930	44,941	80·1
1932	35,610	88·0
1935	46,538	83·6
1937	66,713	76·0
1938	58,376	83·9

Despite the Ottawa Agreements New Zealand's trade with the countries of the Commonwealth, other than the United Kingdom, remained slight; and with foreign countries, other than Japan and the United States (where the balance of trade was unfavourable to New Zealand), it remained insignificant despite the efforts made to expand it in pre-war years. In this respect the 1937 figures shown overleaf are instructive.[3]

As this table illustrates, trade vitally influenced New Zealand's relations with the United Kingdom but not with any other country.[4] Trade policy thus materially reinforced strategic and political considerations, and in the late nineteen-thirties even more important than markets was money. In 1937 £157,600,000 of New Zealand's public debt was held in the United Kingdom as against £130 million in New Zealand itself. So long as the United Kingdom investors retained their confidence in the financial stability of New Zealand this was a formidable, but by no means an intolerable, burden. But Labour's home policies undermined that confidence, and produced a flight of capital. In the middle of 1935 New Zealand's net assets in London were £46 million; they were down to £28 million by the middle of 1938 and to £12 million by

[1] ibid. pp. 272 ff.

[2] Table quoted in I. F. G. Milner, *New Zealand's Interests and Policies in the Far East* (New York, Institute of Pacific Relations, 1940) p. 4. See also N.Z. Institute of International Affairs, *Contemporary New Zealand* (Auckland, Whitcombe & Tombs, 1938).

[3] N.Z. Institute of International Affairs, *Contemporary New Zealand*, p. 115.

[4] cf. ibid. pp. 114–38.

the middle of 1939.[1] The New Zealand government imposed exchange control in the hope of conserving their dwindling external reserves, but this proved no sufficient remedy and in 1940 United Kingdom investors refused to reinvest their money in New Zealand government securities on favourable or indeed on any terms without positive reassurance about the direction of New Zealand

New Zealand's External Trade
(N.Z. Currency)

Country	*Exports*	*Imports according to country of shipment*
	£	£
United Kingdom	50,724,550	28,186,958
Australia	1,824,183	6,943,838
Canada	1,667,449	4,549,802
India	135,730	569,964
Ceylon	1,074	812,267
South Africa	29,554	128,073
Fiji	95,214	122,473
Nauru Islands	4,354	169,285
Other British countries	299,890	517,652
United States	4,796,039	6,720,500
Japan	3,131,986	1,622,249
Dutch East Indies	4,053	2,237,468
Germany	918,171	868,995
Belgium	700,964	518,509
France	1,014,941	192,593
Sweden	92,765	351,427
Italy	10,322	154,995
Other foreign countries	1,020,484	1,503,647
TOTALS		
British countries	54,781,998	41,990,312
Foreign countries	11,689,725	14,170,383
All countries	66,713,379	56,160,695

policy and the future stability of her economy. 'By simply refusing to reinvest money originally lent decades ago, Englishmen deeply influenced the details of a distant dominion's domestic situation, and gave a convincing demonstration of the importance of economic, as opposed to constitutional power.'[2] But the demonstration provoked no resentment because it was recognized to be the natural and inevitable response of investors to a particular economic situation. More generally it was worth noting that the dominion most dependent upon the United Kingdom financially and commercially dissented more profoundly from Britain's pre-war foreign policies than any other member of the Commonwealth.

THE TIES OF KINSHIP

New Zealand's political links with the Empire have been notably reinforced by economic and strategic considerations. But New Zealand has been

[1] Hancock, *Survey*, vol. 2, Part I, pp. 283–4.
[2] Wood, *New Zealand in the World*, p. 126, and see generally pp. 123–7.

the model dominion of the Commonwealth not fundamentally because it is in her interest, but because membership of the British Empire is the expression of the deepest loyalties of her people. Like Australia, the great bulk of New Zealand's population is of British extraction. In the 1936 census the proportion was a little more than 94 per cent., and of the remainder some 5 per cent. were Maoris. This remarkable homogeneity has had more far-reaching political implications than it has in Australia, partly because of the predominantly middle-class origin of New Zealand's early settlers and partly because of the lack there of any strong Irish element mistrustful of the Commonwealth connexion. As a result in New Zealand there has been no barrier, no inhibition, against an easy and intimate relationship. Some recent New Zealand critics[1] have indeed expressed concern at the survival of a 'mother-daughter complex', which they feel should long since have been outgrown in New Zealand as it has been in the other dominions. But it may reasonably be asked whether the comparison is just. Has not New Zealand's attitude to Britain been conditioned by the origins of her people, by the smallness of her population, by her geographical isolation, by the nature of her economy, by her history; and only indirectly by the fact that she is one of the dominions? What would be surprising, and even artificial, would be a common approach to imperial affairs on the part of New Zealand and of those other dominions whose size, whose racial composition, and geographical situation inevitably make a different relationship natural and appropriate. Nor is the distinction merely of academic significance. Once accept the behaviour and attitude of the dominions collectively as a valid criterion of judgement, then the one logical conclusion is that New Zealand has 'in fact psychologically . . . remained a colony because economically it has remained a colony'.[2] But is not such an explanation altogether insufficient? Did the comparable economic dependence of the Irish Free State after 1921 make her psychologically a colony? It is indeed hardly to be doubted that hitherto, politico-historical circumstances, and not economic circumstances, have determined the character of New Zealand's relations with the mother country. But it would also seem probable that their influence is slowly declining. The Second World War stimulated a growing sense of nationality, and it is likely that any marked increase in New Zealand's population would have a similar effect inasmuch as a more populous community would tend to assert its distinctive identity more confidently than a people of less than two million.

NEW ZEALAND AND IMPERIAL FEDERATION

New Zealand's persistent advocacy of imperial federation has been, in one sense, the most characteristic expression of her approach towards imperial problems as, in another, it has been the most misunderstood. The idea of

[1] e.g. N.Z. Institute of International Affairs, *Contemporary New Zealand*, Chapter I.
[2] ibid. p. 3.

federation,[1] formally submitted to the Imperial Conference in 1911 by the New Zealand Prime Minister, Sir Joseph Ward, was designed mainly to ensure that New Zealand should have a small but sufficient voice in the determination of British policy.[2] The aim was not to merge New Zealand in a vast imperial unity, but to allow her the opportunity of informing herself at an early stage, and, if possible, of influencing the direction of imperial policy. 'We should be above all things', said Ward, 'strenuous to preserve our entity and individuality. . . .'[3] But, equally, New Zealand wanted 'to keep clear of being drawn into what one might term Continental troubles with England itself'.[4] At that time New Zealand was in fact dissatisfied and disturbed by the knowledge that the Foreign Office was in a position to take steps which would automatically involve the rest of the Empire in war without informing, let alone consulting, dominion governments beforehand. Federation from this point of view represented a revolt against tacit, uninformed dominion acquiescence in whatever policy Britain chose to pursue. Nor in New Zealand was it forgotten that she had not been consulted in the negotiations with Germany about New Guinea or Samoa, deeply concerned though she was with their outcome.

In principle the New Zealand claim for a voice in the determination of foreign policy was answered negatively in 1911 by Mr. Asquith's emphatic reassertion of the United Kingdom's exclusive responsibility in that field. But in practice after 1911, while responsibility remained with London, information about foreign, and especially defence, policies was thenceforward made more readily available to dominion statesmen. Sir Joseph Ward had himself suggested the separation of the Dominions Department from the rest of the Colonial Office as a step towards closer co-operation and a greater flow of information from London, and even if this suggestion did not bear fruit for some years the reasons which prompted it were not disregarded. But practical concessions in this field, however welcome, did little to satisfy the broader needs which had prompted New Zealand sponsorship of imperial federation. Yet here she has fought a lone and losing battle. In 1911 the heaviest blows were dealt by the two federal dominions, Canada and Australia. The newly constituted Union of South Africa was sympathetic to their viewpoint, and in 1921 the Irish Free State reinforced still further the anti-federal side. Yet

[1] It is worth recalling that the dominion which sponsored imperial federation had not itself any experience of federal government. To New Zealanders imperial federation was more an idea than a precise plan, whereas to Canadians and to Australians the term had precise and clearly understood implications.

[2] The resolution proposed by Sir Joseph Ward was in the following terms: 'That the Empire has now reached a stage of imperial development which renders it expedient that there should be an Imperial Council of State, with representatives from all the self-governing parts of the Empire, in theory and in fact advisory to the Imperial Government on all questions affecting the interests of His Majesty's dominions overseas' (Cd. 5745, p. 46).

[3] Wood, *New Zealand in the World*, p. 84.

[4] ibid.

while dominion opposition and the trend of imperial affairs have made abortive all New Zealand proposals for federation of the Empire, they have not disposed of the problems which such proposals were intended to resolve. For New Zealand, unlike the other dominions, in recognizing tacitly that in the foreseeable future she cannot by herself hope to play a major role in world affairs, has seen herself confronted with the choice either of passive acquiescence in the policies of Whitehall, or of an isolationism uncongenial to the temper of her people, or of participation as a unit in a closely knit imperial partnership; and of them only the last was satisfying.

NEW ZEALAND'S REACTIONS TO THE DECENTRALIZATION OF THE EMPIRE

The post-war years ushered in a revolution in the constitution of the Empire very different in scope and direction to that which New Zealand had consistently favoured. The several and separate signatures of the dominions to the Versailles Treaty were symbolic of its character, but the 'robust imperialism' of New Zealand's Mr. Massey was very reluctant to acknowledge the implications. He argued that the dominion delegates did not sign the treaty 'as independent nations in the ordinary sense of the term' but 'as the representatives of the self-governing nations within the Empire; we signed it as partners in the Empire—partners, with everything that the name implies'.[1] History and logic alike were, however, against him, and the developments of succeeding years left New Zealand lamenting each advance towards dominion status. By 1921 Mr. Massey was complaining that the Empire had gone backwards in the last two years, for while the dominions had gained in status they had lost the solid, organic structure of the Imperial War Cabinet. What use to New Zealand, he inquired, was an Empire united by 'consultation, and consultation only'?

Throughout the decade which followed New Zealand's attitude to imperial relations remained very much the same; it remained, in other words, unreconciled, though not in opposition, to the dominion advance towards full autonomy. This was most marked in the field of foreign relations, where the successive New Zealand governments made no secret of their reluctance to assume particular responsibilities. Where Canada and South Africa and the Irish Free State lost no opportunities of underlining their distinct personalities in the international field, New Zealand went out of her way to deny both the constitutional validity and the practical reality of dominion control of foreign policy. On his return from the Washington Conference of 1921–2, where he had represented New Zealand in the British Empire delegation, Sir John Salmond explained to the House of Representatives that

> the true significance of the presence of representatives of the dominions at the Conference is not that those dominions have acquired for either international or

[1] Quoted in Hancock, *Survey*, vol. 1, p. 71; cf. Keith, *Speeches and Documents*, pp. 59–62.

constitutional purposes any form of independent status, but that they have now been given a voice in the management of the international relations of the British Empire as a single undivided unity—relations which were formally within the exclusive control of the government of Great Britain. . . .[1]

This doctrine, so retrograde in the eyes of the other dominions, was wholly satisfying to New Zealand. What she wanted, as in 1911, was a voice in determining Empire policy, not the right to create a distinctive New Zealand policy. In practice her support for Foreign Office policies was whole-hearted. In 1923 the Attorney-General declared in the House of Representatives that he 'could not remember any instance in which we had been consulted . . . where the answer had not been in the stereotyped form: "New Zealand is content to be bound by the determination of His Majesty's government in London".'[2] During the Chanak crisis of 1922 the New Zealand government offered immediately, without consulting Parliament, to send a contingent to the Middle East. Likewise, New Zealand expressed her full support for the Locarno treaty and would certainly have been content to underwrite its obligations had this been considered desirable.

In 1925 Mr. Coates, the Prime Minister, explained the role New Zealand had played in imperial affairs since 1919 in these words:

The method that has been adopted is just this. The British government carry on the negotiations. We . . . express our opinions quite definitely. If the government . . . think that arrangements under consideration are likely . . . not to be in the interests of New Zealand, we say so. But if after that it is decided to go ahead, we say to the British government, after knowing all the facts of the case: 'Very well, if that is the arrangement to be made, we are prepared to stand by it.'[3]

On his return from the 1926 Imperial Conference Mr. Coates told the House of Representatives that he wished 'to make it quite plain that no suggestions or demands whatever were put forward on behalf of New Zealand. I feel sure I interpret opinion in this country aright when I say that we are entirely satisfied with our status and that we have no desire other than that our present association with Great Britain and with the British dominions may be maintained unaltered. . . .'[4] Where the South African and the Irish Free State representatives claimed much credit at the time for the advances that had been made, Mr. Coates was concerned to explain that he had neither part, nor lot, in the furthering of the process of disintegration. 'New Zealand', was Kevin O'Higgins's acid comment, 'must be rather like Northern Ireland—it produces the same type of Jingo reactionary.'[5] But Mr. Coates might here have retorted that he was no reactionary but a realist who understood the

[1] Quoted in Milner, *New Zealand's Interests and Policies in the Far East*, p. 9.
[2] Quoted ibid.
[3] New Zealand, H. of R. Deb., vol. 208, p. 772, quoted in Wood, *New Zealand in the World*, p. 103.
[4] ibid. vol. 216, p. 790.
[5] White, *O'Higgins*, p. 222.

implications of New Zealand's history and her geographical situation. His country was exposed to direct attack, the Irish Free State was not.

The New Zealand government noted with some satisfaction that the Balfour Report frankly recognized that in foreign affairs and defence the major share of responsibility still rested, and must for some time continue to rest, with the United Kingdom government. Nor had they any wish to hasten the process of transition. At the Imperial Conference of 1930 Mr. Forbes stated that New Zealand had not been concerned with recent developments in the constitutional relations between the members of the Commonwealth, and that 'we have felt that at all times within recent years we have had ample scope for our national aspirations and ample freedom to carry out in their entirety such measures as have seemed to us to be desirable'.[1] New Zealand sought no changes; and while she would place no barriers to the onward march of the other dominions, she could not, and was not, prepared to give practical effect to them herself. Not until 1939 did the New Zealand government limit the functions of the Governor-General (in accordance with the agreement reached at the Imperial Conference of 1926) by consenting to the appointment of a United Kingdom High Commissioner[2] to act as the channel of communication between the New Zealand and United Kingdom governments. And, as has already been noted, the New Zealand Parliament specially requested that none of the important sections of the Statute of Westminster should apply to New Zealand unless, and until, accepted specifically at a later date by her Parliament.[3] Equally the New Zealand government resolutely refused to exercise the powers in foreign affairs which the dominions now formally enjoyed. Here, deep-seated, lay the fear that the pursuit of separate foreign policies could only serve to weaken the foundations of Empire. Therefore, to quote Mr. Coates once again, 'such influence as New Zealand possessed was always used to the best of our wisdom in strengthening the bonds of Empire'.[4]

The policy of full support for Britain was coupled at that time with a not very tolerant contempt for the new-fangled machinery of the League of Nations. Welcome though the control of Western Samoa might be, New Zealand had little enthusiasm for the mandate system. She would have preferred outright annexation. Like that old-fashioned monarch the Emperor Francis Joseph, who thought in 1878 that there was something a little unworthy about the Austrian occupation of Bosnia-Hercegovina under international auspices, so it irked New Zealand in 1920 to think she would be responsible for her administration of Samoa to some council composed mainly of foreigners and, almost certainly, of impractical and inexperienced theorists sitting in distant seclusion in Geneva. In a wider field what reason-

[1] Cmd. 3718, p. 17, reprinted in Keith, *Speeches and Documents*, p. 209.

[2] The first United Kingdom High Commissioner was Sir Harry Batterbee, Assistant Under-Secretary of State at the Dominions Office, 1930–8.

[3] See above, Chapter I.

[4] New Zealand, H. of R. Deb., vol. 216, p. 790.

able hope was there that the League would in practice afford to New Zealand the protection which, in the past, she had derived from the Royal Navy? A comparatively defenceless island could not, in the opinion of the National government, afford to indulge in such dangerous illusions. Her concern was to strengthen the British Empire, the real guarantor of her security, by every means in her power. In the light of this conviction New Zealand contributed £1 million over a period of years to the building of the Singapore base, and continued to pay that contribution despite the extraordinary difficulties with which, as a primary producing country, she was confronted through the collapse of world markets after 1929.

DIFFERENCE IN PARTY ATTITUDES TOWARDS THE LEAGUE AND PROBLEMS OF INTERNATIONAL SECURITY

It is a paradoxical fact that New Zealand, a pioneer of an advanced social legislation, did not have a Labour government until 1935 and it illustrates the characteristically pragmatic approach of the New Zealand people towards political and social problems. In New Zealand the introduction of practical socialism was carried through with a profound mistrust of theory by parties not professedly socialist in outlook. Of the establishment of old-age pensions by the Seddon ministry in 1898 M. Siegfried observed that where the Frenchman's first care would have been to inquire by virtue of what principle such a momentous reform was being introduced, the New Zealanders were much more interested in doing than inquiring into the theory. 'They acted empirically', writes M. Siegfried, 'without theory or principles; without prejudice, . . . being ready to alter or even to repeal the law if it failed to give the results expected of it, and not worrying themselves in the least about the results that the law might have in fifty or a hundred years.'[1] This severely practical aim was coupled with a certain conservatism in outlook. There was no wish to disturb the existing social order but simply a desire to regulate it minutely so as to protect the weak against any possible injury from the strong. Here, the character and composition of the New Zealand population had a decisive influence. From the first it had included neither the very rich nor the very poor. Most of those who had come there came because, while New Zealand did not, in the words of Mr. Wood, 'offer vast wealth or even wild adventure, . . . it did seem to offer security and steady progress'.[2] This again helps to account for the slow rise of the Labour party. From the very nature of the society transplanted to New Zealand all parties shared the belief that 'man as such is entitled to a "fair" share of the world's wealth and privileges; New

[1] *Democracy in New Zealand*, p. 163. It is too early to say that this Anglo-Saxon approach was necessarily right and that the inquiring Frenchman would have necessarily been wrong. Mr. Reeves, about whom M. Siegfried noted 'something of the French Jacobin, with his devotion to principles and to closely-reasoned deductions' (p. 97), left New Zealand while the experiment was still in its formative stage with serious doubts on this point.

[2] *Understanding New Zealand*, p. 61.

Zealand is an experiment in the eighteenth-century idea of the rights of man, carried out with moderation and compromise'.[1] This has led to a general, if not uniformly enthusiastic, acceptance in practice of Labour principles, which greatly delayed the advent of the Labour party to power. The evolution of New Zealand politics is well illustrated in the following table:

Standing of the Parties in House after Elections

Year	*Reform (later National)*	*Liberal (later United)*	*Labour*	*Others*
1911	39	35	4	2
1914	40	33	7	..
1919	47	19	8	6
1922	39	19	17	5
1925	55	11	13	1
1928	26	27	19	8
1931	29	21	24	6
1935	19	..	55	6
1938	25	..	53	2
1943	33	..	45	2
1946	38	..	42	..
1949	46	..	34	..
1951	50	..	30	..

The accession of Labour to power in 1935 was due primarily to the desire of the electorate that Labour's remedies for the widespread social distress of the lean post-slump years should be put into practice. But the minority who were interested in international affairs also felt an urge to uphold the principles for which Labour stood in the wider international field. The Labour government were, therefore, temperamentally predisposed towards a renewed emphasis on the role of the League as the champion of the security of the weak and the comparatively defenceless, and upon its potential contribution to social welfare and the general raising of social standards. Nothing, indeed, was more characteristic of the attitude of the New Zealand Labour government in international affairs than its insistence that the reform of social conditions throughout the world was an indispensable preliminary to lasting peace.

The difference between the parties in their general approach to external affairs was reflected in a speech in 1930 by Mr. Mason, later to be Attorney-General in Mr. Fraser's Labour government, in the course of which he remarked that he could not understand the attitude of some people: 'that New Zealand has not quite grown up; that it has not yet acquired that stage of development when it can be granted full power and full charge of itself. I rejoice that the other dominions have a better idea of their status and I am sorry that in this country we should take pride in our insufficiency.'[2] Of little moment in relation to the Empire, the difference in party outlook was of importance in determining New Zealand's attitude to international affairs in the later nineteen-thirties. Both parties were concerned to maintain the traditional imperial connexion unimpaired, but where Mr. Forbes and Mr.

[1] ibid. pp. 75–76. [2] New Zealand, H. of R. Deb., vol. 178, p. 65.

Coates detected in the League a dangerous and disruptive rival which might win the people's loyalty to some visionary Utopia of perpetual peace and thereby dangerously weaken the one solid basis of security which the British Empire afforded, the Labour leader, Mr. Savage, saw in the League a buttress to imperial unity. Labour believed that the League was the first step towards the creation of that international system in which the Commonwealth itself must seek fulfilment, for only by embracing such wider loyalties could the Commonwealth be true to the spirit of the age and to the deeper impulses of its being.

Differences in party outlook were reflected in New Zealand policies at Geneva. In the nineteen-twenties New Zealand played an almost wholly negative role favouring the representation of her interests either through United Kingdom statesmen or through the Foreign Office, and her government even suggested that all New Zealand communications to the League secretariat should be directed through London so that New Zealand herself should have as little direct contact with Geneva as possible. She opposed plans for the strengthening of the League, condemning the Geneva protocol as 'mischievous', and contributed little or nothing, despite her own social achievements, to the work of the International Labour Organization. In the middle and later nineteen-thirties, when the prestige of the League was dwindling fast and when its capacity for effective action had virtually disappeared, New Zealand came forward as the uncompromising champion of its principles and its authority.

NEW ZEALAND'S RELATIONS WITH THE FAR EAST

The transformation in the attitude of New Zealand to the League would have been more easily comprehended by the outside world had it taken place in 1931 when the Manchurian crisis, with its implicit threat to her security, would have provided good reason for a departure from an attitude of aloof and critical detachment and a new emphasis on the need for an effective system of collective security. But in 1931 New Zealand, like Australia, was most concerned to find some shelter from the economic blizzard and thought little of that deterioration in the international scene which Manchuria so ominously reflected. Even apart from the temporary distraction of the economic crisis this was understandable enough. 'New Zealand', wrote Mr. Wood in 1940, 'thinks and acts as part of Europe, living in virtual isolation from the ancient cultures of the East and from the energetic modern people of North America.'[1] It was the completeness of her isolation from Eastern Asia socially and economically as well as politically that at root accounted for the failure of New Zealanders to assess events there in their full seriousness.

There exists a widespread but erroneous belief that New Zealand's attitude to colour questions, and particularly to Asiatic immigration, has been less

[1] *New Zealand in the World*, p. 1.

uncompromising than that of Australia. It is true that New Zealand has not been represented in the councils of the nations by so formidable and so aggressive a controversialist as Mr. W. M. Hughes, but New Zealand legislation against immigrants from Asia has none the less always run parallel to that of Australia. It elicited from M. André Siegfried early in this century the description 'draconian'. 'At the present time', he wrote, 'it can be said that the New Zealanders by their brutal action and their inflexible prejudices, have succeeded in removing from themselves the yellow peril.'[1] In the intervening years the prejudices softened, but for other reasons the principle of exclusion remained. Successfully though the Maoris' loyalties had been reconciled to the predominantly European state in which they lived, the fate of racially composite countries elsewhere was not one to encourage an attitude of easy tolerance towards the immigration of peoples not likely to be readily assimilated. It is, indeed, hardly to be disputed that racial or communal tension would have been the likely consequence of any considerable Asiatic immigration into New Zealand, and that was something for which no government could assume responsibility. It may well be, in fact, that starting from a doubtful premise founded both on racial prejudice and on a desire to preserve economic standards acceptable to a European community, New Zealanders reached a not wholly mistaken conclusion. But while the absence of any immigrant minority of dubious loyalty enhanced New Zealand's general security, it also in some measure contributed to her continuing feeling of detachment even after Japan launched out on her career of aggression on the mainland of Asia.

New Zealand's trade with China and Japan, always of very slight importance even in comparison with that of Australia, again reinforced the prevailing sense of detachment from the affairs of Asia. Mr. Milner, in an analysis of New Zealand's interests and policies in the Far East before the Second World War, shows that New Zealand imports from Japan, which were only 1·25 per cent. of her total imports in 1931 and which rose to a maximum of a little over 3 per cent. in 1935, were never of any major significance in her economic life.[2] Her exports to Japan were on an even smaller scale, the Japanese market offering no apparent opening for New Zealand surplus produce. In the early nineteen-thirties the total percentage of New Zealand's exports to Japan was considerably less than 1 per cent. New Zealand, therefore, unlike Australia, had little economic inducement to maintain friendly relations with Japan, a fact not without importance in 1937. But in 1931–2 the absence of any such restraining factors had no perceptible influence on her policy. Like Australia, she was not, officially, prepared to back any League resolution involving open or implied censure of Japan on the ground that it would make later conciliation difficult.[3] In February 1933 the Prime Minister stated that:

[1] *Democracy in New Zealand*, p. 228.
[2] *New Zealand's Interests and Policies in the Far East*, pp. 33–46 and 57–80.
[3] ibid. pp. 48–49.

While the government deplores the position that has developed it is of the opinion that no useful purpose would be served by raising this matter at the present juncture. New Zealand is a member of the League of Nations and the position of Manchuria is still under consideration by the League. The government earnestly trusts that a peaceful solution can still be found.[1]

For the rest she was ready to support unquestioningly whatever policy the United Kingdom government pursued in the Far East.[2]

In New Zealand, as in Australia, the public generally indulged in the comfortable illusion that Japanese preoccupations in China would prevent adventures in the Pacific at least for some time to come. As Dr. Arnold Toynbee noted in 1932, the predominant mental reaction in both dominions

appears to have been a sheer sense of relief that the Japanese tiger, now that he had made, at last, his long-expected spring, had chosen to leap the Yellow Sea and bury his claws in the flesh of China, instead of attempting to leap the Pacific and seek his prey in New Zealand or Queensland. They reckoned, apparently, that, for the moment, Japan had 'bitten off as much as she could chew', and that eventually she would emerge from her Chinese adventure either satiated or exhausted, and in either event less formidable to her other neighbours than she had been before.[3]

LABOUR AND THE LEAGUE

The year 1935 marked the parting of the ways in New Zealand's external policy. For this the coming to office of the first Labour government in November was primarily responsible, for the attitude of the new government towards the problems of international security was in marked contrast to that of its predecessor. A contributory factor was Italian aggression in Africa. New Zealanders were disposed to give greater heed to the probable consequences of successful aggression by a European, as distinct from an Asian, Power. Italy's invasion of Abyssinia accordingly made a much deeper impression in New Zealand than Japan's earlier attack on Manchuria. This was reflected in the attitude of the National government before its fall from office. In August 1935 the Prime Minister, Mr. Forbes, told the House of Representatives that if Britain were involved in war with Italy, New Zealand would also be at war.[4] In September he declared that 'the League of Nations is the hope of the future' and that 'its testing time had come'. New Zealanders, he said, were not going to shirk their obligations. Differences between the parties in their attitude to the League were, therefore, narrowing. In 1935 public opinion demanded at least lip-service to its ideals. The Abyssinian question, reported one observer in October 1935, 'had stirred New Zealand

[1] New Zealand, H. of R. Deb., vol. 235, p. 770, quoted ibid. p. 48.

[2] cf. Carter, *British Commonwealth*, pp. 147–8.

[3] A. J. Toynbee, *Survey of International Affairs*, 1932 (London, Oxford University Press for Royal Institute of International Affairs, 1933) pp. 532–3.

[4] *Daily Telegraph*, 23 August 1935.

from north to south' and 'it seems universally accepted that the League of Nations must be justified and supported by all nations even at great cost'.[1] On 23 October the government, in agreement with the opposition, introduced legislation to enable sanctions to be applied by Order in Council during the parliamentary recess. But the actions of the government in the past detracted from the weight of its assurances for the future. It was not only in New Zealand that an election was fought in 1935, in which all professed devotion to the cause of the League.

The Labour government supported the League and the ideal which it represented, not merely for reasons of expediency but also on moral grounds. It was that sense of the rightness of their backing the principle of collective security which persuaded them to persist in their support for the League even when it no longer seemed expedient to do so. Resolute support for the League, declared Mr. Savage, would bring them nearer 'to the principles advocated by the Prince of Peace'. What, therefore, most distinguished New Zealand's foreign policy in the years immediately before the war was a faith in international order and international morality at a time when the world was relapsing into anarchy, and the pacific and well-intentioned were persuaded that acquiescence, even connivance, in wrong was the tolerable price of peace. For this reason the general indignation which followed the public announcement of the Hoare–Laval plan in December 1935 received most pronounced expression in Labour circles.

In succeeding months as a discredited League attempted, first with some show of dignity and then without, to dispose of the Abyssinian affair, New Zealand like the other oversea dominions drew closer to the Empire, but unlike them did not in so doing draw farther away from the League. In March 1936 Mr. Savage suggested that a Commonwealth Conference be summoned to decide upon an economic and defence policy for the Empire as a whole. In June and July the New Zealand government, while themselves favouring the continuation of sanctions against Italy, subordinated their views to those of the United Kingdom.[2] But this concession in the interests of Commonwealth solidarity in no way implied any weakening in New Zealand's support for the League. On the contrary, when its Special Assembly in July 1936 invited member-states to submit proposals for the better application of the principles of the Covenant, New Zealand alone of the members of the Commonwealth made a positive response. By contrast with the prevailing Commonwealth opinion, she advocated not a watering down of the Covenant but its full enforcement. The Covenant, the government maintained, could not justly be characterized as 'an ineffective instrument until it has been applied'; and to ensure its effective application in the future they urged that it should be strengthened by the inclusion of the main provisions of the Geneva protocol,

[1] *Manchester Guardian*, 19 October 1935, quoted in Carter, *British Commonwealth*, p. 206.
[2] cf. Carter, *British Commonwealth*, p. 241.

once so rigorously denounced in all the dominions and not least in New Zealand. More particularly the New Zealand government expressed its conviction that unless sanctions were made immediate and automatic, unless economic sanctions took the form of a complete boycott, the League would prove as ineffective in checking aggression in the future as it had in the past. The probability of war arising from such rigid application of sanctions was not discounted, and New Zealand declared that she was ready 'to the extent of our power, to join in the collective application of force against any future aggressor'. Parallel with this New Zealand emphasis on the need to fortify the League against the challenge of the aggressor went a characteristic concern for the redress of injustices and the examination of the effect of economic conditions on world peace.[1] As a whole these proposals for the strengthening of the League were not, in the words of Mr. Eden, considered 'practicable at the present time'[2] by the United Kingdom government.

Recommendations for the reform of the League went hand in hand with New Zealand advocacy at Geneva of full use of its existing machinery against aggressors. It is true that in the summer of 1936 New Zealand reluctantly acquiesced in the raising of sanctions against Italy, but her action is to be attributed not to any modification in her own convictions but to deference to majority opinion within the Commonwealth and without. Her attitude was more clearly revealed in 1937 when New Zealand pressed for the consideration of the implications of the Spanish civil war by the League, arguing that the war in Spain fell clearly within the jurisdiction of the League and that the adoption of non-intervention procedure was equivalent to an evasion of responsibilities. In the following year New Zealand supported the contention of the Spanish government that the League should recognize that actual aggression by Italy and Germany had taken place in Spain, and recommended that the Spanish situation should be resolved by positive international action, including the holding of a plebiscite under international auspices. In respect of Japanese aggression her attitude in 1937 was very different from what it had been in 1931–2. At Geneva she advocated active measures against the aggressor, and in June that year she placed an embargo on the export of scrap cast iron to Japan and on 8 October extended the embargo to include all scrap metal. In recommending that the imposition of particular sanctions against Japan should be obligatory and not optional the views of the New Zealand government were in direct conflict with those of the United Kingdom government. Throughout 1938, and even as late as January 1939, New Zealand continued to support China's despairing appeals for positive League action.

The adherence of New Zealand to the principles of collective security and her sponsorship of positive League action in Italy, Spain, and China signified

[1] The memorandum, comprising twenty-one provisions, is reprinted in full in N.Z. Institute of International Affairs, *Contemporary New Zealand*, pp. 196–8.

[2] 16 December 1936, H. of C. Deb., vol. 318, col. 2431.

the growing divergence between New Zealand and United Kingdom policies. This fact, though it was profoundly regretted by the New Zealand government, did not restrain them, at least not until late 1938, from candid statement of their own opinions. Nor did they think it should be allowed to do so, for were not moral as well as political issues at stake? In reply to criticisms by the leader of the opposition, who declared that New Zealand's independent stand at Geneva had caused some weakening in the solidarity of the Empire at a time when there should be full co-operation and united action, Mr. Fraser, then Minister of Education, maintained that whether Britain, or France, or Russia did, or did not, agree with the New Zealand view, the righteousness of her attitude was not affected in the least. What mattered, he urged, was that New Zealand had to make up her own mind on international problems as a sovereign country, and that while working in the closest co-operation with the British government they should not 'be prepared to swallow everything the British government cared to put forward'. It was the duty of the New Zealand government to interpret the international situation in the light of the principles they professed and of their loyalty to the League of Nations, and even when the League of Nations was in retreat before dictatorship, New Zealand should never retreat from the defence of the principles that she had proclaimed, and should never acquiesce in crimes that had been committed.[1] Inevitably this created differences of opinion with the United Kingdom government the existence of which could not be concealed. In April 1938 Mr. Malcolm MacDonald, in reply to a question in the House of Commons, observed[2] that 'no communication has been received from the government of New Zealand or any other dominion expressing disagreement with the general policy in foreign affairs being pursued by His Majesty's government in the United Kingdom'. The emphasis was on the word 'general', which could reasonably be taken to allude to the conclusions of the Imperial Conference in which New Zealand had concurred. Mr. Savage implicitly confirmed this in a statement to the press in which he declared that New Zealand had disagreed with certain phases of British policy, 'but we have never allowed those differences of opinion to divide the British Commonwealth of Nations'.[3] It would seem therefore from the language used by the two participants in this family dispute that several detailed points of differences were involved, but until more documentary evidence is available their precise nature must remain uncertain. It is clear, however, that they derived from the different attitudes of the two governments towards the League and were specially concerned with the desirability or otherwise of attempting to appease Italy by a recognition of her African conquest.

[1] *J.P.E.*, 1938, vol. 19, p. 889.

[2] 12 April 1938, H. of C. Deb., vol. 334, coll. 913–14. See also coll. 1314–16 for later questions about Mr. Savage's press statements referred to in the next sentence.

[3] *The Times*, 14 April 1938.

New Zealand's resolute refusal to condone aggression left her isolated among the countries of the Commonwealth in the withholding of recognition of the Italian conquest of Abyssinia. Mr. Jordan, the New Zealand delegate to the League Council, declared categorically on 12 May 1938 that the British proposal that recognition of the Italian conquest was a matter for individual nations to decide was wholly mistaken. Individual recognition involved the undermining of the authority of the League.

> This return to the laws of the jungle is a direct denial of the League and another retreat from the principle of collective security. New Zealand stands for the non-recognition resolution, still considers it is most necessary that the Covenant should remain in force, and deplores anything that will weaken it. . . . The tragedy of retreat from collective security is today's compromise between leaving the League and remaining loyal to the Covenant.[1]

To that attitude New Zealand remained faithful, and by that attitude she would wish her record to be judged.

THE CONFLICT OF LOYALTY TO LEAGUE AND COMMONWEALTH

Adherence to principle in international affairs normally exacts a price, but for which, indeed, it might be more commonly practised. New Zealand's continuing devotion to the principles of collective action embodied in the League Covenant at a time when the United Kingdom was embarking on very different policies involved the risk of some weakening of the solidarity of the Empire. It was not possible for a member of the Commonwealth to dissent openly from United Kingdom policy in matters of such fundamental importance without in some degree weakening her capacity for resolute action. On that point the justice of opposition criticism is hardly to be disputed. But what if United Kingdom policy seemed to be mistaken, irresolute, or without any guiding principle? What in such circumstances was the right course for a dominion concerned at once with imperial unity and international order and morality to adopt? The answer of the New Zealand government to this difficult question was twofold. On the one hand there was Mr. Fraser's contention that whatever the price New Zealand could not modify her attitude. On the other there was the desire to convert the countries of the Commonwealth to the New Zealand point of view. At the Imperial Conference of 1937 Mr. Savage, as we have seen,[2] attempted this formidable task. He argued that international conciliation should not be bought by the sacrifice of League principles, and in order to make this clear he proposed that the countries of the Commonwealth should declare that their policies would continue to be conducted in accordance with the principles of the Covenant of the League of Nations. But this was farther than his Common-

[1] Quoted in *Contemporary New Zealand*, p. 195.
[2] See Chapter III above.

wealth partners were prepared to go,[1] and on his return to New Zealand Mr. Savage explained frankly how scant had been the measure of his success. At the Conference he had stated 'at some length the views of New Zealand on foreign affairs' with due regard to the fact that 'we are a small and isolated people, and that His Majesty's government in the United Kingdom are much more directly and immediately affected', and he had told his imperial colleagues that 'mistakes—and grievous mistakes—had in the past been made in the foreign policy of the Commonwealth. . . .'[2] This was plain speaking, but it made little impression and its influence on subsequent policies was negligible.[3] Mr. Savage was indeed advocating a course whose boldness he did not himself, perhaps, fully realize. His colleagues listened but they would not leap. Moreover, while the weight of Mr. Savage's main contention was reinforced by later events and would at the time have enlisted the support of Mr. Churchill, the more particular remedies he proposed, however admirable in principle, were not inspired by any exact knowledge of their probable consequences in Europe or Asia. What he advocated was an act of faith, not a course of action deriving from a cool and considered assessment of the determining forces in international affairs at that time. Nor does history lend justification to Mr. Savage's view that 'disputes between nations, leading as they have in the past to war, have invariably had an economic basis'. And was there not in 1937 an air of unreality in the confident assertion that once the general standard of living of the working man throughout the world had been raised so that 'he should be enabled to purchase to the same extent as he produced . . . the major possibilities of international conflict would have disappeared'?[4] Yet if it must be allowed that Mr. Savage's analysis was insufficiently related to hard facts at that time, the conclusion he reached was clear and still practicable. Until it was possible to remove economic causes of war it was essential, in his view, that the collective peace system established at Geneva should be made effective. He had no liking for regional substitutes, and indeed New Zealand did not take over-seriously Australia's intermittent pressure for the

[1] Their position was not unfairly summarized by Neville Chamberlain in his concluding speech when he said 'we declare . . . that never will our forces be used for aggression or for any purpose which is inconsistent with the Covenant of the League'. (Cmd. 5482, p. 62.)

[2] Quoted from the New Zealand press, 29 July 1937, in *Contemporary New Zealand*.

[3] The forceful expression of unfashionable views at an Imperial Conference by the Prime Minister of the smallest dominion of the Commonwealth, however, deserves notice. It discredits the general, but mistaken, assumption that members do not express their opinions frankly at such gatherings.

[4] Here the influence of eighteenth-century beliefs in the natural goodness of man is apparent. It was a short step from the categorical opening assertion of Rousseau's *Contrat Social* ('L'homme est né libre, et partout il est dans les fers') to an implicit assertion that in many parts of the world man was in economic chains, but could he be restored to his natural state of economic liberty and to the enjoyment of the fruits of his labour, his urge to war and conquest would disappear with the material reason for it. Christian teachers, with their insistence on original sin, however much in sympathy with the desire to bring about a greater measure of social justice, entertained no such illusions about the results that would flow from it.

negotiation of a Pacific pact. At root the New Zealand argument rested on the assumption that the wider interests and the unity of the Commonwealth would best be served by a foreign policy based on broad general principles, implemented through the League, and in that conviction they never wavered even when circumstances compelled them to modify their course in practice.

The weight of opposing opinion at the Imperial Conference left New Zealand with little freedom of action. In September 1937 Mr. Nash, the Minister for Finance, after noting that no group of nations, including the British Commonwealth, could enforce peace on the world went on to observe:

> If, however, the other nations of the world, dominated as they are by principles totally opposed to the principles that are associated with the government of the British Commonwealth of Nations, determine to use their coercive powers to dominate the members of the British Commonwealth, then at that point I think there is justification for defending the principles of the Commonwealth. If we are to defend the principles of the Commonwealth as a group, we in New Zealand as a unit of the group, with all the feelings we have as to the imperative, ultimate need of the League, and the imperative need of the League at the present moment, have to fit in, and, because of circumstances, must fit in, as best we can with something we know will not ultimately be to the permanent advantage of the world.[1]

This reluctant but realistic recognition of the considerations which would ultimately determine New Zealand policy faithfully reflected the opinion of the government. It has been recorded that some of the Labour leaders and a wider section of radical opinion felt that New Zealand could not maintain her assurance of aid to Britain in the event of war if Britain departed from a policy of strict adherence to the principles of the League and of collective security.[2] But attitudes adopted in hypothetical circumstances do not necessarily correspond with action undertaken when those circumstances materialize. And however strong in its support of the government's campaign to secure respect for the principles of the League, public opinion was most emphatically not prepared to contemplate any loosening of Commonwealth ties for the problematical security which a reformed League might afford. When, therefore, in the face of the fast-gathering storm in Europe, it was no longer possible to proclaim an absolute loyalty to the principles of the League without in some measure endangering the unity of the Empire, the New Zealand government decided that nothing should be said or done to embarrass the United Kingdom government, even though positive support could not be given to all the steps which it decided to take. Such considerations, reinforced by the imminence of a general election, account for the reserved attitude maintained by the government during the Sudeten crisis. Mr. Neville Chamberlain's flight to Berchtesgaden on 15 September elicited a warm tribute from Mr.

[1] New Zealand, H. of R. Deb., vol. 248, p. 490.

[2] cf. *Contemporary New Zealand*, pp. 180–1.

Savage as 'a historic gesture in the cause of peace'[1] and he added that New Zealand's attitude could be summed up in one sentence 'wherever Britain is, we must be'. On the eve of Munich Mr. Savage declared that the New Zealand government 'most earnestly' supported Mr. Chamberlain's continued and determined efforts for peace[2] and Mr. Fraser reiterated the categoric assurance, perhaps intended to encourage a stiffer attitude in London, that in the event of war New Zealand would give all possible support to the motherland. After Munich, while ministers in other Commonwealth countries vied in eulogistic appreciation of Mr. Chamberlain's contribution to the Munich settlement, New Zealand's congratulations were couched in more sober language and concluded with an expression of hope, but not of any confidence, that the basis of settlement would prove a lasting safeguard for world peace founded on justice and order between nations.[3]

NEW ZEALAND AND IMPERIAL DEFENCE

While after the Imperial Conference New Zealand felt reluctantly compelled to acquiesce in policies as a result of which, in the words of Mr. Savage, there was 'at times, not much left of principle',[4] there were no reservations about New Zealand collaboration in defence. In this respect her attitude was at no time substantially modified by devotion to the League. The New Zealand people generally did not share the illusion that peace could be preserved by the off-loading of national responsibilities on to a League without any force at its disposal, though it is true that many in the Labour party, who supported resolute action by New Zealand at Geneva, saw no inconsistency in at one and the same time opposing active rearmament at home. A year earlier Mr. Savage himself used language which suggested that he had not considered very carefully the full implications of the policies he recommended. Thus in October 1936 he told the House of Representatives: 'In the government's proposals to the League of Nations, the idea of sending a force to Europe was the last thing in its mind, but it was able to appreciate that, if a war was world-wide, New Zealand would have to play its part.'[5] But government defence policy was, in fact, determined throughout not in relation to the League but by the need for the closest possible co-operation with Britain. Of that the Imperial Conference had been reminded:

His Majesty's government in New Zealand . . . attached the greatest importance to close co-operation in defence matters. The government were anxious to make sure that expenditure in the three Services was properly balanced . . . so as best to enable the New Zealand forces to act in the most efficient way possible, not only in the local defence of their country but also in Commonwealth defence. . . .[6]

1 *Manchester Guardian*, 16 September 1938.
2 *The Times*, 30 September 1938.
3 ibid. 1 October 1938.
4 *J.P.E.*, 1938, vol. 19, p. 22, quoted in Carter, *British Commonwealth*, p. 308.
5 New Zealand, H. of R. Deb., vol. 247, p. 877.
6 Cmd. 5482, p. 18.

The importance of Singapore in this wider context was specifically underlined. On his return from London the Prime Minister declared that New Zealand did not wish to build up a defence system for the dominion alone. 'We want', he said, 'to play our part in doing that, of course, but we also want to play our part in the defence of the British Commonwealth, because that is the most effective way of doing it.'[1] Nor was there any difference of opinion within New Zealand about the essentials of her defence policy, though there was pressure from the opposition for its more rapid implementation.

The Minister for Defence pointed out in October 1938 that the most likely form of attack on New Zealand was by surface raiders. This also had been the opinion of experts at the Imperial Conference, and they felt confident that with an enlarged air force, and with the addition to the New Zealand navy of two cruisers, purchased from Britain, she would be able to repel any such attacks. But clearly the dominion could not resist a major attack by a Great Power 'any more than Australia could do so'.[2] There, indeed, for both the Pacific dominions lay the decisive argument for close co-operation with Britain.

In April 1939 the New Zealand government took the initiative in arranging a conference of British, Australian, and New Zealand technical experts at Wellington to discuss the co-ordination of defence plans in the Pacific. At this conference the New Zealand defence programme to date was approved, and she agreed to play her part in a general scheme for the production and distribution of aircraft among the British territories in the Pacific. The New Zealand government also arranged to buy a supply of modern aircraft of high speed and long range, and to obtain the advice of the United Kingdom military experts on the building up of its land forces. It was also agreed that New Zealand air personnel should be trained in Britain.

DEFENCE AND FOREIGN POLICY

Closer co-ordination in defence reinforced the growing reluctance to making public any differences of opinion with the United Kingdom on major issues of foreign policy. The silence on Munich set a pattern followed in subsequent crises, though there is reason to suppose New Zealand influence played its part in Mr. Chamberlain's abrupt realization that the policy of Munich had failed some days after the absorption of Czechoslovakia in March 1939. The terms of the Tokyo agreement of July 1939, on which the New Zealand government can hardly have looked with favour, were received officially from the United Kingdom the day after their publication in the press. Thus, though deeply concerned with British policy in the Far East, the New Zealand government were not consulted at the decisive stage in the negotiations and only after their conclusion were they made 'aware' of their outcome. Yet they

[1] New Zealand, H. of R. Deb., vol. 248, p. 476.
[2] 27 October 1937, ibid. p. 1158.

made no public protest. In response to questions from the Labour side in the House, voicing misgiving and disapproval, the government confined themselves to noting that the terms were in accord with the defence policy of the United Kingdom government and that discretion was necessary in any comment on United Kingdom policy in view of the threatening situation in Europe. But the episode was not forgotten and was held to indicate a fundamental weakness in the methods of intra-Commonwealth consultation.[1]

Behind New Zealand's restraint in commenting on policies she could not approve lay her fundamental loyalty to the Empire. The course that she would follow in the event of war was made clear beyond possibility of doubt in a number of official statements declaring that if Britain were involved in war New Zealand would be at her side. On 16 May 1938 Mr. Nash said 'if the Old Country is attacked, we are too . . . we will assist her to the fullest extent possible'.[2] In July 1938 Mr. Fagan stated: 'of course in one split second after Britain becomes involved in war this country also becomes involved'.[3] On 22 March 1939 Mr. Savage reaffirmed his faith in Britain and the determination of New Zealand to support her in meeting one of the gravest international situations in history.[4]

SOME CONCLUDING REFLECTIONS

There is some conflict of opinion about the extent to which New Zealand's support of the League between 1936 and 1939 had positive popular approval. Unquestionably the policy was the policy of the Labour government, and while the opposition for the most part dissented from it only when positive support of the League brought the New Zealand government into conflict with the views of the United Kingdom government, yet it is evident that throughout the New Zealand opposition's attitude to the League had about it a Laodicean tepidness. Professor Wood goes farther and suggests that only a minority supported the New Zealand government at Geneva, and it is his considered opinion that the vast mass of the people in New Zealand, as in the other dominions, lay between the League idealists and the imperialists who wished to follow British policy in all things.[5] Yet in a wider context New Zealand's support for collective security and world order reflected, as has already been suggested, something fundamental in the New Zealander's outlook. He was not content that the search for security should stop at home.

In any consideration of New Zealand's policy, it must always be remembered

[1] cf. Wood, *New Zealand in the World*, pp. 127–8.
[2] Quoted in *Contemporary New Zealand*, p. 184.
[3] New Zealand, H. of R. Deb., vol. 251, p. 343.
[4] *Daily Telegraph*, 23 March 1939.
[5] On the other hand, the far-reaching proposals made by the New Zealand government in July 1936 for the strengthening of the Covenant were considered by two of New Zealand's leading newspapers to have faithfully reflected the general reaction of New Zealanders to the failure of the League in Africa. See *New Zealand Herald*, 3 September 1936, and *Otago Times*, 5 September 1936. See also Carter, *British Commonwealth*, p. 259.

that in practice little time was devoted to its discussion either in the House of Representatives or outside. In the three sessions of Parliament held between September 1937 and October 1939 there were no debates devoted exclusively to foreign affairs, and though that on the Imperial Conference of 1937 dealt with the principal considerations which determined New Zealand's attitude towards them it occupied less than eight hours out of the total of some 405 hours in a session which lasted from September 1937 to March 1938. This small fraction of the parliamentary time allotted to foreign affairs faithfully reflected the meagre interest of members in them. The government themselves did little to foster it. From the time of Munich onwards their self-imposed silence left little scope for debate on the major issues of foreign policy, and thereby deprived Parliament and people of an opportunity of becoming better informed about world affairs. By 1939 New Zealand had still no representative in any foreign country, and the New Zealand High Commissioner[1] in London acted as representative at the League, where he enjoyed a wide discretionary authority in elaborating the views of his country. At home the Prime Minister was ministerially responsible for the conduct both of international and imperial policy, which were administered by a section of his department.[2] Since, in addition, Mr. Savage held the External Affairs portfolio, by virtue of which he was departmentally responsible not for external affairs generally, but for the administration of the island dependencies and the Samoan mandate,[3] the time he could devote to problems of foreign policy was necessarily limited.

New Zealand policy in the years before the war will be remembered not for what it achieved but for what it stood for.[4] It was in a sense the protest of the common man. It symbolized for him his aversion to the calculating inhumanity of *Realpolitik* and his instinctive belief that righteousness and the moral order should govern relations between states as between men. Alone of the countries of the British Commonwealth, New Zealand championed a strict adherence to the principles of the League and of collective security between 1935 and 1939. She was loyal to the League after the League had ceased to be loyal to itself. It may reasonably be argued that her action caused embarrassment within the Empire and achieved nothing without. It must be allowed, too, that there was a certain ingenuousness in the New Zealand reaction to the fast gathering storm. Her government believed in long-term remedies, particularly in economic and social reforms, when the greatest army the world had yet known was awaiting only a dictator's word to march.

[1] Mr. W. J. Jordan was New Zealand High Commissioner in London from 1936 to 1951, and he was President of the Council of the League of Nations in 1938.

[2] The Imperial Affairs Branch of the Prime Minister's Office was established in 1926.

[3] See *Contemporary New Zealand*, p. 187.

[4] In 1949 in conversation with the author a United Kingdom cabinet minister, reflecting gloomily on Commonwealth policies before the war, concluded more cheerfully: 'Thank God for New Zealand!'

Yet if the New Zealand government knew too little, it might with fairness be retorted that the United Kingdom government knew too much. They were weighed down by the burden of their knowledge, by anxieties which sprang from too great an awareness of the possible implications of every action. It was that burden of knowledge and of responsibility which led them into paths indefensible in principle, and into actions which, though they won acceptance from most governments of the Commonwealth, were viewed all too often with instinctive distaste, sometimes bordering on contempt, by its ordinary citizens. It is not to be denied that acceptance of New Zealand's policy of collective security would have resulted almost certainly in war, for strict adherence to League principles would assuredly have led through economic to military sanctions. But the policy of conciliation and appeasement did not save the peace.

CHAPTER VII

TENSIONS IN SOUTH AFRICA

THE LEGACY OF THE SOUTH AFRICAN WAR

WHEN James Bryce visited the South African colonies in 1897 he felt a certain confidence about their future. It might, he thought, safely be assumed that they would desire to maintain their connexion with the mother country, for strong as was the feeling of attachment to Britain in both Canada and in Australasia, Bryce felt that it was 'assuredly no less strong in South Africa'. There he found the English perhaps even more English than the people of Australia or Canada, whilst those of Dutch origin, 'warm as is their Africander patriotism, have never been hostile to the British Crown'. Sentiment moreover was powerfully reinforced by the need for the protection of a long and vulnerable coast-line by a great naval Power. At the close of the nineteenth century South Africa had as near neighbours in the South Atlantic and Indian Oceans two great European Powers bent on colonial expansion, to either of whom a strategic position such as Simon's Bay or Table Bay would be invaluable.[1] South Africa had therefore, so Bryce concluded, an interest in retaining her connexion with the mother country as strong as that which Britain had in retaining her association with the South African colonies.

This sanguine prospect of mutually advantageous and not uncongenial partnership was shattered by the South African War. Even by 1899 Bryce recognized that its one certain consequence was that the relations between the two European races in South Africa, far from being placed, as some still vainly imagined, on a better footing as the result of a bitter war between them, had suffered a grave, perhaps irremediable, setback. The war had sown 'a crop of dragon's teeth' which would produce in the course of time 'a harvest, if not of armed men, yet of permanent hatred and disaffection'.[2] Yet even in that discouraging hour Bryce firmly restated the principle which should guide Britain's policy. She must, he argued, still aim at retaining South African loyalties, if only because any colony which became disloyal and disaffected might give the signal for a loosening of the ties which bound the others, and she must use the opportunities which victory would one day give her with moderation and always with a full awareness that the Dutch and British races had to live together in South Africa, 'looking forward to a time, probably less than a century distant, when the exhaustion of mineral wealth will have made South Africa again a pastoral and agricultural country'.[3] To reconcile the two races, and so to pave the way for the ultimate fusion of Dutchmen and English-

[1] James Bryce, *Impressions of South Africa*, 3rd ed. (London, Macmillan, 1899) p. 476.
[2] ibid. p. xliii.
[3] ibid. p. xliv.

men in a common imperial, as well as a common South African patriotism, must, therefore, be 'the aim of every government that seeks to base the world-wide greatness of Britain on the deepest and surest foundations'.[1]

More than half a century has elapsed since Bryce surveyed the South African scene, but the corroding legacy of a war that had all the characteristics of civil strife has left not wholly reconciled the two European races now united in a single state. In this Bryce forecast the future aright. But the inevitable consequences of the war on subsequent relations between the two European peoples who fought it were mitigated by Britain's wise adherence in the peace terms to those generous and far-sighted policies to which Bryce had given his allegiance. They were indeed applied in full measure in the terms of the Peace of Vereeniging. Yet the not unpardonable satisfaction which that peace has commonly evoked in the English mind has found whole-hearted response only on the fringe of Afrikanerdom. To the great body of Afrikaner opinion the statesmanlike moderation of the victor constituted no full reparation to the vanquished for the loss of a cherished independence.

TWO CONFLICTING INTERPRETATIONS OF SOUTH AFRICAN HISTORY

The different attitudes towards the peace and the settlement which followed have given rise to two conflicting interpretations of the subsequent course of South African history. According to the first interpretation, the far-sighted and generous magnanimity of Sir Henry Campbell-Bannerman's Liberal administration had reaped its due reward in the progressive reconciliation of English and Dutch within a United South Africa and in the lasting and loyal co-operation of a South African dominion with the British Commonwealth of Nations. Thus to Campbell-Bannerman's biographer the Liberal policy of 1906 was 'an act of faith'[2] judged by the whole world to have been 'splendidly justified' when ten years later a Boer Prime Minister took it into his own hand to suppress a Dutch rebellion and fought side by side with the British Empire against its European enemies. Many South Africans have endorsed this eulogistic verdict. 'They gave us back in everything but name—our country', declared General Smuts in a memorable phrase. 'Has such a miracle of trust and magnanimity ever happened before?'[3] When Campbell-Bannerman died in 1908 General Botha, in a tribute sent to Mr. Asquith, wrote: 'In securing self-government for the new colonies he not only raised an imperishable monument to himself but through this policy of trust he inspired the people of South Africa with a new feeling of hopefulness and co-operation. In making it possible for the two races to live and work harmoniously together he had laid

[1] ibid.

[2] J. A. Spender, *Life of the Rt. Hon. Sir Henry Campbell-Bannerman* (London, Hodder & Stoughton, 1923), vol. 2, pp. 237–8.

[3] Quoted in Basil Williams, *Botha, Smuts, and South Africa* (London, Hodder & Stoughton, for English Universities Press, 1941) pp. 55–56.

the foundation of a united South Africa.'[1] Many years later, with an assured place in the councils of the victors at Versailles, General Smuts pondered again the lessons of Vereeniging when he, too, had felt 'the harrow' of defeat. Always the memory of what happened then prompted him to press more strongly for honourable and generous terms for the vanquished. 'My experience in South Africa', he declared at Versailles, 'has made me a firm believer in political magnanimity and . . . Campbell-Bannerman's great record still remains not only the noblest but also the most successful page in recent British statesmanship.'[2] That, too, was the verdict of Mr. Winston Churchill when in the late summer of 1950 he paid a last tribute in the House of Commons to the memory and the achievements of Field Marshal Smuts. 'No act of reconciliation after a bitter struggle', he said, 'has ever produced so rich a harvest in good will or effects that lasted so long upon affairs.'[3] From these tributes nothing can detract. No alternative British policy in 1906 could have achieved so much. Here indeed was one of the most remarkable illustrations that history affords of the truth of Edmund Burke's saying that magnanimity in politics is not seldom the truest wisdom. Yet appreciation of the imaginative generosity of Liberal England in one of the last and most lustrous periods in the history of a great party does not lessen the need for a cool appraisal of reactions in South Africa itself. No gesture, however well-timed and magnanimous, can alter the fundamentals of a complex political situation.

In retrospect the final success of the South African settlement would seem to have been over-lightly assumed by Englishmen with little knowledge or first-hand experience of the intensity of South African political life.[4] In the glow of post-prandial imperial oratory the peace of 1906 and the Union which followed in September 1909 were exalted beyond reasonable measure as the ultimate solvent of South Africa's ills. But at the time the settlement was more sensibly regarded as a significant and hopeful experiment. In December 1906 the Under-Secretary of State for the Colonies, Mr. Winston Churchill, earnestly besought the House of Commons to sustain the Vereeniging agreement on the ground that 'for the first time in many years the two white races in South Africa have found a common foundation . . . a foundation which they can both look to without any feeling of shame but, on the contrary, with feelings of equal honour and I trust with feelings of mutual forgiveness'.[5] But mutual forgiveness could not come easily. Lord Selborne recognized this and, on succeeding Lord Milner as High Commissioner, observed with justice: 'The white people of South Africa are committed to such a path as few nations have trod before them, and scarcely one trod with success.'[6] One of Lord

[1] Earl of Oxford and Asquith, *Memoirs and Reflections* (London, Cassell, 1928) p. 197.
[2] S. G. Millin, *General Smuts* (London, Faber, 1936), vol. 2, p. 211.
[3] 13 September 1950, H. of C. Deb., vol. 478, col. 1102.
[4] Botha's language at times lent substance to their too sanguine expectations.
[5] H. of C. Deb., 4th ser., vol. 167, col. 1072.
[6] Quoted in C. W. de Kiewiet, *History of South Africa* (Oxford, Clarendon Press, 1941) p. 141.

Milner's young men, Mr. R. H. Brand (afterwards Lord Brand), writing of the settlement in 1909, commented realistically, 'Hopeful, however, as is the future, it is useless to suppose that racialism will never trouble South Africa again. The new spirit animating the leaders of both sides has been generously welcomed by both the British and Dutch communities. But in the working out of the Constitution the differing ideals of the two races cannot fail to clash.'[1] And many years later another member of that famous 'Kindergarten', Mr. Lionel Curtis, declared, 'The South African question had not been solved by the grant of self-government to the conquered republics, as Liberals in England imagined.'[2] The reason why it has not been solved is to be found in the second and conflicting interpretation of South African history.

Among the Afrikaners whose ancestors had trekked northwards across the Orange River and the Vaal the desire for independence from all external control weakened little with the passage of time. They disliked government in general and British government in particular. Between 1906 and 1910 it seemed as though 'for a moment a new spirit had been poured out upon the people' and Afrikaner exclusiveness would break down before it. But the moment was short-lived. 'No sooner had the topmost peak of national sentiment been reached', wrote Senator F. S. Malan,[3] 'than the descent into the plain began. People began to realize that the past had not been obliterated by the magic wand of the National Convention, and that South African human nature remained very much what it had been before the Convention had met.' It was in this chill aftermath to Union that Afrikaner separatism re-emerged in an uncompromising form. Against the ideal of a united South Africa within the British Empire there was reasserted the ideal of an exclusivist Afrikaner republic deriving its inspiration, its pattern of government, its claim to the undivided allegiance of all true Afrikaners from the former republics of the Orange River Free State and the Transvaal. Fundamental to it was the belief that the Afrikaner alone was a true South African. For those who subscribed to this separatist republican ideal the dominant theme in South African history in the first half of the twentieth century was the gradual but irresistible advance of Afrikanerdom towards the realization of its aims. Defeat in war, followed by disastrous disunion within, brought about by the deviationist policies of the 'lackeys of imperialism', had delayed but could not divert the course of history. Afrikanerdom would be one day reunited, independent, republican; and for the hastening of that day all true Afrikaners must work unceasingly.

Between these two interpretations of South African history a great gulf is fixed. In an absolute form neither is historically true. Yet it is well, in study-

[1] *The Union of South Africa* (Oxford, Clarendon Press, 1909) p. 10.

[2] *Civitas Dei* (London, Macmillan, 1938) p. 619.

[3] *Cambridge History of the British Empire*, vol. 8 (Cambridge University Press, 1936) p. 641, and see generally Chapter XXIX.

ing the attitude of South Africa to Commonwealth and world affairs, to keep them both in mind, for out of the conflict between them South African policy has been born. And it is well also to remember that in white South Africa the Afrikaners were a majority of the population. Defeat and disunion might delay their effective exercise of power; it could not indefinitely prevent it were they resolved to act as a homogeneous group. By 1936 the descendants of the Voortrekkers were coming back again.[1] How much had they learned and how much had they forgotten in the century since the ox-wagons of their fathers rumbled northwards across the dusty veld?

THE GROWTH OF AFRIKANER NATIONALISM

While the Act of Union was accepted, though not without reservation, the pattern of government embodied in it seemed to Afrikaners in the northern provinces 'something imported from without and not the product of their national experience'.[2] The appointment of a Governor-General by the King as head of the state in place of a President chosen by the burghers, and the introduction of unfamiliar conventions of parliamentary government filled them with misgiving lest they be placed at a lasting disadvantage in relation to their English-speaking fellow countrymen. The Afrikaners, it is true, were in a majority, but the social and economic, even more than the political, environment of a modern state was altogether strange to them and, having no experience of the overriding power a well-organized racial majority may exercise under a system of representative parliamentary government, they feared for long that numbers alone would not compensate for their unfamiliarity with it. A sense of social injustice accentuated political anxieties. As a result partly of the South African War and partly of the agricultural depression of 1907 many of the Afrikaners had become impoverished. 'Poor whiteism' increased and, as Mr. van den Heever has observed, poverty creates 'many of the phenomena of inferiority'.[3] The Afrikaners, moreover, for the most part lived on the veld, while the government was carried on, as in other countries, by the men from the cities where the better educated classes, except in Bloemfontein and Pretoria, were predominantly English-speaking. In this way there was added to the racial feud the normal antipathy of the conservative countryman to the progressive and more sophisticated city-dweller. The Afrikaners were reluctant to recognize that in any event the trend of South African economy, and especially its dependence upon gold and diamonds, meant that their future influence was conditional upon their people taking a place proportionate to their numbers in the commercial and in the administrative life of the state. It was therefore a general sense of being 'a stepchild in

[1] cf. article on 'South African Commemoration of the Great Trek', by Professor E. A. Walker in *The Times*, 16 December 1949.

[2] van den Heever, *Hertzog*, p. 137.

[3] ibid. p. 138.

his own home', and the lack of assurance with which it was associated,[1] that led to an uncompromising Afrikaner insistence upon an explicit, formal, recognition of equality between the two races.

General Hertzog was from the outset of his political career the unyielding protagonist of equality.[2] In his long struggle to secure equality for his fellow Afrikaners Hertzog placed the greatest emphasis upon education. He regarded linguistic equality, particularly in the schools, as the essential step towards social and political equality. If the language were lost the distinctive traditions and way of life of Afrikanerdom would perish with it. If the language were recognized then all else would follow, for the language was the condition of a distinctive national existence.

On this, as on certain other issues, Afrikaner and Irish nationalists were at one. Both endorsed the opinion of nineteenth-century European nationalists on the supreme importance of language in a struggle for national survival, and General Hertzog at least regarded the safeguarding of the language as of greater importance even than the form of government. In the programme of the Nationalist party, formed late in 1912 with Hertzog as its first leader, 'South Africa first' was made a guiding principle and due emphasis was placed upon full equality in language. Republicanism was not included in the programme.[3] About the republic Hertzog and Malan after him were prepared to temporize, but about the language there was to be no weakening.

Republican separatism enlisted the loyalty only of some of the Afrikaner people. That was partly the fruit of Vereeniging. The Afrikaner leaders who were then convinced that the difficult path of reconciliation was the way of duty and of enlightened statesmanship no longer embraced the republican ideal. They believed on the contrary that republicanism and British-Afrikaner co-operation were incompatible. In their view the republic was the form of government which divided South Africans most, the monarchical symbolism of the British Empire what divided them least. As a result of these differences within Afrikanerdom the balance of opinion on the constitutional question for long came down on the anti-republican side, since English-speaking South Africa was monarchist to a man. Even when, towards the middle years of the century, opinion inclined more favourably to republicanism, the nationalist leaders recognized that the deep divisions within South Africa on the constitutional question demanded a cautious approach.

[1] In the economic sphere where English-speaking South Africans for long enjoyed a virtual monopoly, this sense of inferiority was especially pronounced, and it was reflected in a speech by Dr. Malan at the second National Economic Congress held in Bloemfontein in September 1950. He spoke of the 'remarkable success' of the Afrikaner in this field, adding that there was no need now for him to have an inferiority complex or 'to hang his head in shame' (*The Times*, 6 October 1950).

[2] It is interesting, however, to observe the implicit identification of 'Afrikaner people' with 'nation' in his speeches.

[3] E. A. Walker, *History of South Africa*, 2nd ed. (London, Longmans, 1947) pp. 542–4. For an account partial to Hertzog's point of view see van den Heever, *Hertzog*, pp. 158 ff.

The growth of Afrikaner nationalism during the First World War was slow but persistent. As it gained in strength and confidence its aims were defined more precisely. The leitmotiv of Nationalist party propaganda was summed up in the phrase 'we have a free constitution, we have an unfree government'.[1] Ultimate control rested not with South Africa but with London. What was in the interests, or the supposed interests, of England carried the day. Self-government had become 'a colossal piece of deception', for did not the right of peace and war lie beyond the power of the South African Parliament and had they not been dragged into a British war, thanks partly to the actions of renegade Afrikaners? Such were Hertzog's complaints. His remedy was complete freedom for South Africa in external as in internal affairs. He advocated a republican form of government, but being well aware of the practical difficulties involved, did not press it. His aim was unity, and he declared that independence was the means by which it might be fulfilled. There could not be cordial co-operation between the two Europeans races[2] till it was freely acknowledged and as freely accepted by all, that the interests of South Africa alone should determine her policy. In all this the tide of imperial affairs was flowing with him.

THE ROLE OF ENGLISH-SPEAKING SOUTH AFRICA AND OF THE PROVINCES IN PARTY POLITICS

It is a curious, even paradoxical, feature of South African political life that the bitter dispute between the parties about constitutional development, and South Africa's relations with the Commonwealth, was fought out between two sections of the Afrikaner people. Essentially the issue between them was the place of English-speaking South Africa in the Union, but in the protracted struggle first for the achievement of equal rights for Afrikaners and then, when the balance had tilted down the other side, for the maintenance of equal rights in the interests of English-speaking South Africans, the principal protagonists on both sides were Afrikaners. The leaders had fought as companions in arms in the South African War, and from 1910 to 1948 the post of Prime Minister was held successively by three Boer generals, the first civilian to hold the highest political office being Dr. D. F. Malan, a Cape Nationalist. In these years, therefore, leadership in politics was dependent upon a reputation acquired in active resistance to British arms. The political atmosphere which made such leadership appear not only right but inevitable

[1] van den Heever, *Hertzog*, p. 184.

[2] In these pages the terms 'race' and 'racial' are sometimes used in a sense that is common in South Africa, i.e. referring to the two European peoples who were in a position to exercise political power. The objections to their use in this way are as strong as in the case of Canada, where it has been deliberately discarded, but in the case of South Africa it has not always been possible to dispense with them, partly because South African leaders themselves have so often given them this meaning in the past.

excluded English-speaking South Africans from filling the highest position either in the parties or the state. For them prominence in politics was normally a liability to the cause they championed. Self-effacement was, therefore, the easy course and it was also the path of inclination, for preoccupation with mining and industry predisposed them to an ill-advised indifference to politics.

The English-speaking population had no option but to support the South African party led first by General Botha and then by General Smuts, and their allegiance was thus predetermined by the pattern of South African politics. This meant that while English-speaking South Africans were a very important element in South Africa's political scene they were also a constant element. They were not the deciding force. For that their numbers were insufficient and as a result in the analysis that follows comparatively little is said about them and much is said of the divisions within Afrikanerdom which were in fact of decisive importance in determining the Union's external policy between 1931 and 1939.

In the divisions within Afrikanerdom inter-provincial antagonisms played their part. From the time of the South African War the centre of political gravity moved gradually from the Cape to the northern provinces. From differences between the leaders in the two northern provinces, between Generals Botha and Smuts from the Transvaal, and President Steyn, Generals Hertzog and de Wet from the Orange Free State, the political cleavage in Afrikanerdom derived.[1] Where, after Vereeniging, the Transvaal leaders favoured co-operation with Britain and reconciliation with English-speaking South Africa their former colleagues from the Orange Free State, whose attitude faithfully reflected the stubbornly held prejudices of the backveld, were unprepared for compromise, disliked the efficient modern state that was being created with the wealth of the Transvaal, and lamented the days when their government had been in the hands of what Lord Milner once contemptuously described as 'Kruger's medieval race oligarchy'. In this conflict of personalities and ideas the Orange Free State, with its more homogeneous white population, could claim to be more truly representative of the deeper pulses of Afrikanerdom, but its numbers were small, and its political weight was insufficient to sustain its cause alone. As a result the political balance lay with the Nationalists in Cape Province, and it has been of no slight significance in the history of South Africa that some of the most intransigent leaders of the Nationalist party have come from south of the Orange River. In common with their compatriots in the Orange Free State they viewed askance the achievements of the 'bumptious north', and the rise of the wealthy cosmopolitan city of Johannesburg provoked self-righteous denunciations of this 'Monte Carlo superimposed upon Sodom and Gormorrah'.

The Cape Nationalists were not as heavily engaged in the South African

[1] cf. van den Heever, *Hertzog*, p. 115.

War as those in the northern provinces and their later intransigence has been attributed to a feeling that they should have played their part at the side of the northern republics, but unable or undecided at the time about the possibility of doing so effectively, they had endeavoured to compensate for their aloofness from the battle by passionate championship of the Afrikaner cause in politics later.[1] Perhaps, too, the stronger infusion of Huguenot blood contributed its full quota of logical intransigence. It was Dr. Daniel François Malan, formerly Minister of the Interior and at that time Superintendent-General of Education of Cape Province, who led the revolt of the Purified Nationalists in 1934 when at last the representatives of the Transvaal and the Orange Free State, Generals Hertzog and Smuts, had decided to allow the divisions of the past to be transcended by friendly co-operation for the future. But whatever the reasons, the contribution of Cape Nationalists to party warfare and, from their intellectual stronghold at Stellenbosch, to the enunciation of party doctrine has been both considerable and uncompromising.

THE GULF NARROWS, 1924–31

The differences between the Afrikaner leaders narrowed with the passage of time. All desired equal rights for their fellow countrymen and however much they might differ about ways and means they were at one in welcoming their progressive achievement. The surprise is not that the rival leaders ultimately agreed to co-operate but that their reconciliation was so long delayed. There the insurmountable obstacle was for long General Hertzog's continuing fears of veiled English intervention in South African affairs coupled with his deep-seated mistrust of the intentions of English-speaking South Africans. He condemned the policy of gradual reconciliation because he feared it might lead to a final loss of racial identity. If Englishmen were prepared to grant equal rights all—in his view—would have been well, but he was for long convinced that so far from that being the case, English-speaking South Africa was actively engaged in a conspiracy to destroy the way of life, the culture, and, above all, the language of Afrikanerdom. It was his contention that in such circumstances equal rights could be secured only by a frontal challenge, and he believed accordingly not in co-operation with the English-speaking South African but in his conversion.

In a world in which the English language and culture predominated, the Afrikaner would be unable to preserve his heritage unless he were watchful and insistent, even to the point of provocation, in the assertion of his rights. He had to wage an uphill struggle against great odds in which compromise spelt disaster. All thought of a fusion of the two races had to be rejected, because fusion meant absorption. 'Smuts', declared General Hertzog, 'was always the most hated enemy of national unity in a South African national sense . . . the national unity he urged, and urges today, is the unity we should

[1] Long, *In Smuts's Camp*, pp. 24–25.

have if we allowed the British lion to swallow the Afrikaans lamb.'[1] In the past intermingling of the two races at the Cape had led to better relations, but only by sacrificing the ideals of Afrikanerdom. Hertzog's policy was, therefore, in his own none too felicitous metaphor, a policy of 'two streams'. The two white races were to work together not in a mingling partnership but in a partnership in which each separately played its separate role. The streams must have two courses, and though they flowed forward together their waters should not mix.[2] Only by this rigid insistence on separation could the Boer hope to preserve his identity, his culture, and his language.

It was the same fear of submergence in a greater whole which made the Nationalists so mistrustful of the imperial connexion. It was the greatness of Britain, the expanse of her Empire, the universality of her language that made them feel that unless they safeguarded their own position zealously, intransigently, they would be swept forward in a great tide in which all would be lost. And they believed, moreover, that both the English-speaking South African and the Englishman at home wished for this to happen. To watchfulness was added suspicion. Every move in London, every outburst from the 'Jingoes' in Natal, must be scrutinized lest it portend a deep-seated plot to destroy Afrikanerdom. The English after all, whether within South Africa or without, did not believe in equal rights. They had no impelling reasons for doing so. As Hertzog once observed on a visit to Natal: 'the honest Englishman does not believe in a policy of 50-50 . . . only in 100 per cent. or nothing . . . Or else it is the 50-50 of the hotel chef, who made a hare-pie from hare's meat and horse-meat according to the 50-50 recipe, that is to say, one hare and one horse.'[3] Whatever happened to the English in South Africa, British culture and British civilization would survive not dangerously weakened. But it was upon the future of the Afrikaners in South Africa that the future of Afrikaans culture alone depended.

General Smuts's approach was less anxious, less mistrustful, and his vision was broader. He believed in conciliation because, with Botha, he had seen on a distant horizon a united South Africa making a positive contribution to the welfare not only of the Commonwealth but also of the world. A philosopher by temperament he saw beyond the nation-state of modern times to the more closely integrated society of a later age for which the Commonwealth might, and indeed should, endeavour to provide a pattern. The realization of his ideals involved unrelenting political warfare with doctrinaire Nationalists. But in that warfare the advantage did not lie on Smuts's side. The broader vision did not produce the more convincing election programme; its very latitude made it difficult to compress within that narrow gauge. On the European

[1] Quoted in van den Heever, *Hertzog*, p. 228.
[2] cf. Long, *In Smuts's Camp*, p. 15.
[3] Quoted in Michael Roberts and A. E. G. Trollip, *South African Opposition, 1939–45* (Cape Town, Longmans, 1947) p. 227.

racial issue Smuts's counterpart to Hertzog's 'two-stream' policy was in effect 'no policy'. He believed no policy was needed. It was an issue best left to the healing hand of time. As he had forgiven past wrongs, so must his fellow countrymen. How else could a South African nation be built? The broad humanity, the statesmanship of his approach was honoured by men in far-off lands; its electoral appeal at home while memories were still fresh, passions still inflamed, was indifferent. About this Deneys Reitz, his lieutenant in many a hard fought contest, had no illusions. 'Hertzog', he wrote of the 1919 election campaign, 'was supported by a large percentage of the Dutch whom we accused of intolerance and racialism but who knew their purpose, and their strong racial sentiment carried further than our humdrum appeal to common sense.'[1] Yet Smuts had much in his favour. With the increasing urbanization of Afrikaners social intercourse in the professions and, to a lesser extent, in business was growing. Intermarriage was becoming more frequent, and in this respect it was important that the two European communities were not separated as in Canada and in Ireland by a religious as well as a cultural and political barrier. The probable consequences of intermarriage are easy to exaggerate, yet its cumulative effect over the generations must surely be great.

The first Nationalist administration formed in 1924 (the Pact Ministry) was dependent on Labour support, but despite their restraining influence General Hertzog was able to take advantage of the tide in imperial affairs to remould imperial relations closer to his heart's desire. The achievements of the Nationalists between 1924 and 1930 in the constitutional field had results of decisive importance in bringing about equality of status for South Africa within the Commonwealth and, flowing from it, that equality at home between the two European races which General Hertzog had so consistently championed. The two languages, the two flags, the two anthems all belonged to the pattern, the pattern of full equality in South Africa between the two races, which Hertzog more than any single man had woven.

The achievement of equality within the Commonwealth and at home was only a stage and was insufficient as a goal. This was something that Hertzog was slow to realize. Attainment of his long-sought aims left him at somewhat of a disadvantage. What now should be the more distant objective for white South Africa? To such a question Smuts, with a gaze that ever and anon swept the far horizons, had long since returned an answer. The racial equality now attained should lead on, he felt, to close co-operation between the European peoples of South Africa, and that co-operation would be assisted—and the growth of South Africa as a nation fostered—by maintaining the close links with that great company of freedom-loving peoples which comprised the British Commonwealth of Nations. In Commonwealth affairs, decentra-

[1] Deneys Reitz, *No Outspan* (London, Faber, 1943) pp. 26–27; also Roberts and Trollip, *South African Opposition*, p. 182.

lization had long been his watchword, and he could therefore justly feel that the Balfour Report of 1926 and its sequel satisfied his sense of the appropriate condition for whole-hearted South African co-operation with the Commonwealth.

Despite the notable part General Hertzog had played in the transformation of Empire into Commonwealth, his attitude towards the Commonwealth remained less free from inhibitions than that of General Smuts. Yet in many of the great essentials they were now at one. 'The old British Empire . . . now no longer exists', General Hertzog told the Cape National Party Congress on his return from London in 1926. Its old 'domineering' system had been replaced by a free society of equal nations. Here was something both leaders could welcome. But a concern to demonstrate that the old order was discarded led Hertzog, under pressure of criticism from the left wing of his own party, to an almost exclusive preoccupation with important but none the less negative aspects of Commonwealth relations. What was the extent of the freedom accorded? For Hertzog, but emphatically not for Smuts, it implied freedom to secede and freedom to remain neutral in a war in which the British Commonwealth was engaged.[1] But even on these much debated questions of interpretation the views of the rival leaders in practice, as distinct from theory, were not so much at variance as might at first sight appear. In 1928 General Hertzog observed in general terms that the South African party was 'now so nationalist' that if it had always been 'like it is now the Nationalists would never have left it', that men were getting tired 'of the quibbling about unimportant things' and that 'the desire for unity and solidarity' was taking possession of the whole community.[2] Since 'the Empire's teeth had been drawn' even secession assumed a new complexion. The right had been claimed by the Nationalist party as an assurance and a test of freedom. It did not constitute, at least for its leader, a programme of action. Now that South Africa had acquired the right to leave the Commonwealth why should she do so? There were few convincing reasons. 'I believe', said General Hertzog, 'it would not be in our interests; it would be foolish and . . . if it were proposed not five per cent. of the population could be got to vote for it.'[3] The gulf was narrowing fast. By 1930 General Hertzog, with considerable political courage, was explaining to the Bloemfontein Congress of the Nationalist party that he had been feeling and working his way for a long time towards South African unity:

> After what has been accomplished at the Imperial Conferences of 1926 and 1930 there remains no reason whatsoever today why, in the sphere of politics and statecraft, Dutch and English-speaking South Africans should not feel and act in the spirit of a consolidated South African nation.[4]

[1] cf. van den Heever, *Hertzog*, pp. 218 ff.
[2] Quoted ibid. p. 220.
[3] ibid. p. 219.
[4] Roberts and Trollip, *South African Opposition*, p. 226.

The direction of his own thought was now unmistakable even though it was masked by reservations very proper to a party leader. In Hertzog's view the Nationalist party should accomplish the task of reconciliation in its own way, recognizing that 'English and Dutch-speaking South Africans are today, as never before ready to take each other's hand with mutual sincerity as equal and right-minded Afrikaners'.

By 1930 the way was clear for inter-party and inter-racial co-operation in South Africa, and it seemed as though the more sanguine interpretation of the consequences of Vereeniging and Union were about to receive a final vindication. Yet in truth any such vindication was dependent on two conditions: on the extent to which the extremists were prepared to follow the party leaders and on the care with which the foundations of co-operation were laid. Co-operation came, but neither condition was adequately fulfilled. The extremists were not converted, and under pressure of the economic crisis the bases of inter-party co-operation were hurriedly and insufficiently explored.[1] From this much was inevitably to follow.

Where political tension runs high and where past civil or racial strife has left deep scars a reconciliation between the leaders of rival parties rarely suffices to dispel the deep-seated antagonisms of their respective followers. Of this no one was more conscious than Mr. J. H. Hofmeyr, an intellectual humanist, sagacious and high-minded, who ploughed a lonely furrow in the bitter, unrewarding field of South African politics. Writing in 1931, nearly forty years after Bryce, he was confident that much progress had been made in the development of friendly social relations between the European races, and that while the advance on the political side had not kept pace it, too, had been considerable. But its continuance could not be assumed. Mr. Hofmeyr recognized that while the Nationalist party, through its leaders, had warmly welcomed the transformation effected in imperial relations which gave to South Africa full autonomy, their contentment with South Africa's status within the Empire was not shared by all their followers. General Hertzog might accept the British Crown as a bond of union, 'but', observed Mr. Hofmeyr,

> not all those who owe allegiance to the party, and whose allegiance to it was fired not so very long ago by an anti-British secessionist republican sentiment, are in their hearts in accord with their leaders on this issue. The spell of that sentiment upon them has not yet been destroyed.[2]

Like left-wing republicans in Ireland, the more extreme Nationalists wished

[1] It could, of course, very reasonably be argued that without outside pressure and the glossing over of unresolved and unexplored differences, co-operation would not have been possible. But even if that be allowed, and it is by no means proved, it is very questionable how far co-operation between the parties before the time was fully ripe has been to the benefit of South Africa in the long run.

[2] *South Africa* (London, Benn, 1931) p. 228.

to continue the struggle for a Boer republic, not connected with Britain. 'They could not stomach the idea of a common King, who was also the King of England; they wanted to be rid of the Union Jack and all English symbols and institutions.'[1] In their eyes, therefore, Hertzog was unprofitably occupied in reforming the machinery of an institution in which Afrikaners had no place. Such hostile reactions, while reflecting one of the more dangerous undercurrents of South African politics, were not in themselves of first importance. What was important was the general theory from which they derived. The premise of the more uncompromising Nationalists was that the English-speaking South African was not in the strict sense of the word a South African at all. He had another home, he had other loyalties. He thought first of Britain and of British interests. His loyalty to South Africa was and always would be secondary. He was therefore no true South African. The only true South Africans were those Europeans whose only conceivable home was South Africa. It was upon their single-minded loyalty that the South African nation must be built. A nation which could not count on the undivided allegiance of all its people would be no nation at all.[2]

From the extreme Nationalist premise only one conclusion was possible. It was not that embodied in Hertzog's concept of two streams which must flow separately till true equality was reached, but rather one of a united South African nation, the condition of whose emergence was that all white South Africans became in spirit, if not in culture, true Afrikaners. In logical and undiluted purity this doctrine was later enunciated by Professor L. J. du Plessis who wrote:

> We reject the idea entirely that all South Africans should together be considered as one people. For us, Afrikanerdom is the People of South Africa, and the rest of the South Africans are, as far as they are white, either potential Afrikaners or aliens.[3]

Here was Afrikaner exclusivism unrepentant and unashamed.

The ranks of the Nationalist party drank deeply of such disruptive doctrines, but General Hertzog would have none of them. The danger of English predominance within South Africa had gone and it should not be replaced by an Afrikaner predominance no less objectionable in principle. Moreover, he felt that, with the more or less equal division of races, the extremists pointed to an impossible goal. It was just not practical politics to think of absorbing 40 per cent. of the white population so completely that they would embrace the political and cultural ideals of another people. The aim, on the contrary, argued Hertzog, once equality was achieved in theory and practice, must be a drawing together on the basis of that equality. In 1931 the great weight of Afrikaner opinion was with him, but it was not destined always to be so. Had

[1] van den Heever, *Hertzog*, p. 225.
[2] cf. Roberts and Trollip, *South African Opposition*, pp. 14–15.
[3] Quoted ibid. p. 28.

he been able to feel his way towards inter-party co-operation by easy, well-planned stages it might have been otherwise, but he was caught and hurried onwards in the relentless grasp of twentieth-century economics which he did not pretend to understand.

THE SLUMP, MR. TIELMAN ROOS, AND COALITION

The irruption of unwelcome economic problems on to the political scene both provided the opportunity for a rapprochement between the parties and powerfully reinforced the arguments for it. By 1932 the Pact Ministry had a meagre majority of eleven in the House of Assembly. It had never enjoyed the support of one section of Labour and was fast losing the support of the other.[1] By-elections warned the government of its growing weakness in the country, the rigours of the economic blizzard showed no sign of abatement. At this moment Mr. Tielman Roos, 'an able lawyer and a jovial cynic',[2] who once remarked in a careless aside, 'I regard politics as a game', intervened. A Transvaal Nationalist leader, Mr. Roos had been mainly responsible for the formation of the Pact Ministry in 1924 in which he held the office of Deputy Prime Minister. Many believed the 'fabulous tales of his powers and his achievements in building up the Nationalist party and assuring its victory',[3] and even his critics could not deny that he was an attractive, even brilliant speaker. In 1929 Roos had deserted politics for the Bench and was commonly believed—though not by Hertzog—'to be desiccating respectably in the dignified *penetralia* of the Appeal Court', whence in 1932 he 'emerged upon anxious gaze of the public, tacking hither and thither in a fever of infectious energy'.[4] His target was the financial policy of the government reluctant to abandon the gold standard under pressure of what they regarded as non-national financial interests; his aim the formation of a national government. National governments were fashionable at the time, and the enthusiastic response which Mr. Roos elicited when he publicized his views indicated that he had judged opinion well. General Hertzog, who had reasons for mistrusting him, could not as a result afford to disregard him, much as he would have liked to.[5] In the country the idea of a national government gathered irresistible momentum and the question of its composition could not long be deferred. Mr. Roos, indeed, had no reason for desiring to do so. On the contrary, since the government enjoyed so slender a majority in the House of Assembly he explored at first the possibility of an arrangement with the South African party. He believed—and neither Hertzog nor Smuts were

[1] cf. Walker, *History of South Africa*, p. 622.
[2] Reitz, *No Outspan*, p. 167.
[3] van den Heever, *Hertzog*, p. 234.
[4] Roberts and Trollip, *South African Opposition*, p. 6. For a careful and illuminating study of the differences within the Nationalist ranks, the reader is referred to this work.
[5] cf. van den Heever for an instructive, detailed account of Hertzog's reactions, pp. 233 ff.

confident that he was mistaken—that he might hold the political balance himself with a following of some ten to twenty dissident members of the Nationalist party. This belief encouraged him to pitch his claims high.

I do not desire [he said at Cape Town early in 1933] to be Prime Minister but in the peculiar circumstances facing the country, I feel I am the only person who is capable of swinging over sufficient numbers of both sections to ensure the success of the policy I have enunciated.[1]

Later he observed more judiciously that the Prime Minister of a coalition 'would probably have to be a Nationalist', because the Nationalist party was in office, but the implication was the same.

General Smuts, his electoral prospects in the ascendant, was in a strong bargaining position. Yet when Mr. Roos proposed that if the South African party would support his candidature for the premiership he would break the Nationalist party through his control of some twenty seats, his offer was not rejected out of hand. On the contrary, as Colonel Reitz has recorded, the South African party leaders were deeply divided on this issue. They were confident of victory at the coming election and, having suffered much at the hands of the Nationalist régime, were prepared to go to almost any lengths to get rid of Hertzog. Though the evidence is inconclusive it would appear that Roos was offered, provided he could in fact bring over sufficient Nationalists to wreck the government, the deputy premiership and three other seats in a cabinet of ten,[2] an offer not easy to reconcile with Colonel Reitz's assertion that Smuts was at no time prepared to sacrifice principle to the advantage accruing from an unsavoury political bargain.[3] In any event Mr. Roos declined and Smuts pursued the idea of a coalition in a very different direction. He recognized that the only basis of a truly national government was to be found in collaboration with Hertzog. The national interest demanded agreement between the two major parties, and Roos's dramatic initiative which led to it proved the sorry prelude to the ruin of the political ambitions of its author.

FROM COALITION TO FUSION, 1933–4

The impetus once given, the end was not in doubt, even if the negotiations were detailed and often acrimonious. In 1933 a coalition government took office with Hertzog as Prime Minister and Smuts as his deputy. In the early stages the omens were all favourable. A wave of good will swept the country and in May 1933 the new coalition swept forward to a historic electoral triumph. But, tested at the last by the challenge of war, the experiment failed. In judging both the early success and the final breakdown of this

[1] Leslie Blackwell, *African Occasions* (London, Hutchinson, 1938) p. 227.
[2] ibid. p. 232, also pp. 232–5.
[3] Reitz, *No Outspan*, p. 168.

effort at reconciliation it is always well to remember its origins. Coalition was the product of external economic pressures and political manœuvre, not of fully matured design. The almost forgotten shade of Tielman Roos hung over the fateful debate of September 1939.

The Status Act[1] was an important product of coalition, and inasmuch as it represented in substance the legal endorsement of General Hertzog's conception of South Africa's place in the Commonwealth it enhanced his prestige. The immediate political consequences of coalition were not unexpected. On the right of the South African party, Colonel Stallard and the imperialists, assured of strong support in Natal, seceded to form the Dominion party, while among the more extreme Nationalists, Dr. Malan hardly troubled from the first to disguise his hostility to inter-party co-operation. When the Nationalist decision in favour of coalition was taken no fewer than thirty members of the Nationalist caucus abstained from voting. Though the abstentionists later stood on the coalition platform at the general election,[2] which gave the coalition no less than 138 members in a House of 150, their objections to a policy of co-operation were fundamental and lasting. It is possible, but not probable, that they could have been removed, for the time being at least, by concessions which Hertzog on his own might well have been prepared to make. But he was no longer on his own. Coalition from the outset had been and remained dependent upon the good will of the South African party. Its leader, General Smuts, was not prepared to enter a coalition government in which he would self-sacrificingly give first place to his old rival at a moment when all the electoral omens were favourable to his cause without demanding firm assurances of the policy to be pursued on controversial issues. Why should he? In the South African party General Hertzog's first overtures for a coalition had been regarded merely 'as a ruse to stave off defeat'.[3] 'By entering into a compact with the Nationalists', wrote Deneys Reitz, 'we deliberately gave up certain victory for the sake of peace and co-operation between the two white races in South Africa.'[4] And the condition of peace was acceptance of the constitutional status attained. This meant not only leaving aside the vexed questions of the right of a dominion to secede or to remain neutral and of the unity or divisibility of the Crown, but also positive agreement that there should be no substantial modification of South Africa's status within the Commonwealth, and above all that there should be a clear declaration that the coalition government stood for the maintenance of South Africa's constitutional position as defined in the Statute of Westminster and the Status Act.[5] To all this Hertzog assented. On the disputed constitutional

[1] See above, pp. 19–25.

[2] General Smuts actively intervened at Calvinia on behalf of Dr. Malan whose election till then had been much in doubt. See Blackwell, *African Occasions*, p. 235.

[3] Reitz, *No Outspan*, p. 168.

[4] ibid. p. 169.

[5] Roberts and Trollip, *South African Opposition*, p. 9.

questions neither side abandoned its interpretation but both agreed not to press it, while leaving their followers free to express their own opinions without endangering coalition or cabinet. By his agreement Hertzog made possible the further step of party fusion, and he made certain of the alienation of Malan.[1]

The formal separation of the dissident left wing from the Nationalist party took place on the question of whether the ministry was to remain a coalition ministry formed by two separate parties for particular purposes and for a limited period, or whether coalition should be regarded as a stepping-stone to party union or fusion, as it was termed. The practical arguments for fusion were strong. Here was the most favourable opportunity since Union for healing once and for all the fratricidal strife between the two sections of Afrikanerdom and reconciling English and Afrikaans-speaking South Africans, which, if neglected, might never recur. The people were weary of bitter party warfare. The South African party apart from their extreme right wing were ready, though not without misgivings, to follow Smuts's lead, and Hertzog, the unwavering champion of Afrikaner rights, was convinced of its wisdom and timeliness. But even his great prestige was insufficient to avert an open challenge to his authority from within his own party. The very air of finality which party fusion implied, and which was indeed its chief virtue in the eyes of its protagonists, made tacit acquiescence on the part of the extremists no longer possible. There followed, therefore, a struggle for power within the party, a struggle in which Hertzog's strength lay in the north, Malan's in the south. In August 1933 Hertzog won a notable victory when the Transvaal Nationalists accepted the principle of Fusion by 591 votes to 9. But at Port Elizabeth amid scenes of wild enthusiasm the Cape Nationalists rejected Fusion by 141 votes to 30. In the Orange Free State the issue was more open, but there General Hertzog's personal popularity sufficed to carry the day.[2] In the following year the Federal Council of the Nationalist party agreed to Fusion and to participate in the new United party by a majority of 13 votes to 7. The minority, led by Dr. Malan, thereupon seceded to form the so-called Purified Nationalist party.[3] This spilt determined the direction of South African party politics for the next two decades. What were its fundamental causes?

Why was Dr. Malan prepared to contemplate a coalition but ready to break with apparent finality, from his old leader, Hertzog, rather than contemplate party fusion which might do so much to heal old wounds? Was the break one which was brought about by personal incompatibilities, by the defects of Hertzog's aloof, autocratic leadership, or had it some more fundamental cause? And if it had a more fundamental cause, how was it that

[1] ibid. pp. 8–9, and Walker, *History of South Africa*, pp. 624–5.
[2] cf. Blackwell, *African Occasions*, p. 238.
[3] *Die Gesuiwerde Nasionale Party.*

Hertzog, whose political life had been one uncompromising, bitter struggle against the Botha–Smuts policy of conciliation, could contemplate fusion between his party and Smuts's if any sacrifice of principle were involved?

THE BREACH IN NATIONALIST UNITY; ITS CAUSES AND CONSEQUENCES

By 1933 Hertzog's political position had been weakened by the extent of his own achievements. What he had aimed at he had secured in full measure. To the theory of 'two streams' he clung with unwavering fidelity, but now that the Afrikaner was in a position of equal status and superior in influence as well as numbers, it provided a poor foundation for a positive political programme. To a leader of lesser calibre the moment might have seemed opportune for a programme, if not of actual domination, at least of racial exclusivism. But whatever Hertzog's faults, on this he was a man of deep conviction, and in the hour of victory he did not lose sight of the ideal of equality for which he had struggled for so long. It was because of this that he felt in 1933 that the time at last had come when the 'two streams' might safely be allowed to merge.

On this Dr. Malan, the leader of the extreme Nationalists, challenged him. The challenge had long been latent and was now brought to the surface by events. The extreme Nationalists maintained that the two streams could never merge for the simple reason that they did not believe there was a second stream. It was an illusion, in their view, to suppose that the English in South Africa were, and were ever likely to be, true South Africans. As some more extreme Irish nationalists believed in a Gaelic republic in which all ties with Britain, political, cultural, linguistic, were finally severed, so, too, Malan and his followers looked to the establishment of an Afrikaner republic wholly freed from the bonds and from the influence of Empire. That the English-speaking population comprised two-fifths of the white population was an awkward fact,[1] but it was regarded as constituting no argument for compromise. The extreme individualism of the Boer farmer, reinforced perhaps by an inferiority complex created during the years of English supremacy, forbade an acceptance of realistic policies. Moreover, once accept a policy of co-operation, as Hertzog had done, and, so it was argued, infiltration of ideas must follow, and much that Afrikanerdom treasured would be undermined and eventually destroyed. The aim was therefore the establishment not only of a republic, but of an Afrikaner republic.

It is easy to understand the misgivings of the purified Nationalists even where they seem exaggerated; it is less easy to regard as either practicable or

[1] The 1941 census figures showed that English-speaking South Africans numbered 875,541 and Afrikaans-speaking South Africans 1,226,382, while some 36,000 were wholly bilingual. See also footnote below, p. 253.

praiseworthy the conclusions which derived from them. Dr. Malan maintained vehemently that the English problem must be solved sooner or later by persuasion or by force. That he believed in persuasion was beyond doubt, but he was not hopeful of its results because he considered that the majority of English-speaking South Africans constituted what he termed 'unassimilable elements'. If they could not be assimilated, then they must be virtually disregarded in the building of a South African nation. Dr. Malan's policy was, therefore, directed towards strengthening Afrikanerdom by every means in his power so that in due course he would be able to establish an Afrikaner republic, with a dominant Afrikaner culture, with Afrikaans as the official language, and English 'tolerated for reasons of convenience' as 'a recognized language'. By unswervingly pursuing this course over many years he hoped that in time many of the English-speaking South Africans would come to believe that for a South African to be an Afrikaner was something inherent and natural. A dual allegiance they could not retain. They must have one allegiance, and in South Africa that allegiance politically, and ultimately culturally as well, could be found only in the Afrikaner heritage.[1]

The constitutional questions which divided the Nationalists, derived from these deeper differences and gave them concise but incomplete expression. The autonomy accorded in the Statute of Westminster alone made fusion possible. On that point General Hertzog was emphatic. On 8 May 1933 he said at Potchefstroom:

> The struggle was brought to an end by the passing of the Statute of Westminster, because thereby South Africa was recognized by statute as a free and sovereign nation. As to the equality of the languages in practice, that has been applied by the Nationalist Party ever since 1924, and as it has been accepted by the South African Party as a basic principle of co-operation, the struggle has been finally decided.[2]

Dr. Malan did not agree. Like Mr. de Valera, he had little faith in the evolutionary process, in 'the freedom to achieve freedom', which this transformation in Commonwealth relations in fact ensured and he pressed persistently for further definition. Familiar questions were asked once more. Could South Africa remain neutral when the Commonwealth was at war? Could she secede? Must not the divisibility of the Crown be recognized to allow for full freedom of action for a South Africa within the Commonwealth? Moreover, had not the time come to abolish 'constitutional anomalies', of which the office of Governor-General and the appeal to the Privy Council deeply offended Nationalist sentiment? With the implications of these questions Hertzog had, and could have, little quarrel. As a profession of aims he could himself willingly have subscribed to them. But experience had

[1] Roberts and Trollip, *South African Opposition*, pp. 186 ff.
[2] Quoted ibid. p. 227.

taught him to beware of over-much definition. In 1930 he warned his followers that 'to define is to limit'. And his participation in the Coalition government was an explicit indication of his willingness to let definition wait upon events. He was not, however, allowed to leave all Dr. Malan's questions unanswered.

While the negotiations for party fusion were proceeding in 1934 further attempts were made to heal the breach in the Nationalist party, and accordingly outstanding constitutional difficulties were once more explored in the hope of making reunion possible.

After a preliminary exchange of views the Cape Executive demanded that:

> In the definition of sovereign independence the fact will be admitted that the Crown is divisible, or that South Africa possesses the right of neutrality and the right of separation or else that the full meaning and substance of that sovereign independence shall be defined in some other unambiguous way.[1]

Hertzog responded in phrases redolent of Mr. Lloyd George's correspondence with Mr. de Valera in 1921. To define he argued, would be to restrict, and therefore it was in the interests of South Africa that he should not attempt to do so. But he did not refrain from elaborating his own view:

> that the British Crown, so far as the Union is concerned, is divisible; that we possess the right of neutrality; that we have the right of separation I have never doubted since 1926, and none of us dares to doubt it or give the impression of doubting it.[2]

This exercise in definition, which he had already described as imprudent, elicited an indignant protest from General Smuts. He was not prepared to ignore the Prime Minister's views merely because they were described as personal, and still less were many members of his party prepared to do so. While he whole-heartedly accepted South Africa's sovereign status, he did not admit that any such interpretation could be placed upon the provisions of the Statute of Westminster, and he was emphatic in his own opposition to anything that would weaken South Africa's links with the Commonwealth. General Hertzog, confronted with opposition both from the left and from the right, inclined perceptibly to the right. He reaffirmed the agreement to differ on the questions of constitutional interpretation, and he allowed that liberty to indulge in republican propaganda should be conditioned by a statement that the Coalition stood for the maintenance of the existing constitutional position. Smuts was appeased, Malan finally estranged.

THE CONSEQUENCES OF THE NEW PARTY ALIGNMENT IN INTERNAL AND COMMONWEALTH POLICIES

The Malanite secession left the balance of Nationalist opinion behind Hertzog and as a result the position of the Fusion government was unassailable

[1] Quoted in Blackwell, *African Occasions*, p. 240. [2] ibid.

in Parliament. But in the country, despite its decisive electoral victory in 1938, the foundations on which it rested were insufficiently secure to resist indefinitely the steady erosion of Nationalist propaganda.[1] What Nationalist Afrikaner did not lament in his heart the political division of Afrikanerdom or seek ways by which it might be ended? Remote though it seemed as bitter recriminations followed the final failure to reach a settlement, Afrikaner reunion was an ideal whose power of attraction remained an incalculable political force. But devotion to it did not inspire conciliatory courses. On the contrary, the impotence of the dissident Nationalists, numbering no more than twenty-seven members in the House of Assembly, tended to make them more than ever fundamentalists in politics. An exclusivist Afrikaner republic became their openly acknowledged goal. In 1936 a republican profession of faith became a condition of party membership, though it was freely recognized that the republic could be founded only 'op die bree grondslag van die volkswil'[2]—based broadly on the will of the people. In September 1939 Mr. van der Merwe, after observing that from 1934 to 1939 the republican ideal had become more deeply rooted in the souls of Nationalists,[3] went on to identify nationalism with republicanism. They would not, he told the Convention of the Purified Nationalist party, be nationalists 'if they were not republicans at the same time'.

The party [he said] is convinced that the republican form of government, separated from the British Crown, is the most suited to the traditions, circumstances and aspirations of the South African people and is at the same time the only effective guarantee that South Africa will no longer be dragged into the wars of Great Britain.[4]

By different people the republic was differently conceived, but as Irish Republicans appealed to the legend of 1916, so the Purified Nationalists derived much of their inspiration from the memory of the old republics which had fought so gallantly against odds in the South African War. In 1940 the Nationalist newspaper *Die Transvaler* described in uncompromising language the characteristics which the Afrikaner republic of the future should possess:

It will be a republic in which there will be no place for British public institutions. These things, which are foreign to the spirit and wishes of the Afrikander people, will be annihilated to the very foundations. It will be a republic with a government that is not subject to all sorts of foreign influences. General Smuts's holistic views, according to which the small Afrikaans culture must be dissolved in the great English culture, and South Africa be but a part of the great British Empire, will find no place in this Afrikaans republic. Mr. Hofmeyr's negrophilism and liberalism, which would wipe out all colour bars and would make the Afrikander a back-

[1] Even by 1938 its effects were apparent in political circles but not, as the voting showed, in the country at large.

[2] Roberts and Trollip, *South African Opposition*, p. 277.

[3] cf. ibid. pp. 22 and 228.

[4] ibid. p. 229.

boneless being, will have no place in this Afrikaans republic. Colonel Stallard's imperialism, which would make South Africa subordinate in all respects to British interests, will have no place in this Afrikaans republic. Mr. Madeley's socialism, and conceptions of the Afrikaans people, will have no place in this Afrikaans republic. The spirit of people who are too afraid to speak about a republic, will also find no entry in this republic. In economic policy this republic will be no milch-cow of Britain. It will be a republic in which the Chamber of Mines will not have authority. It will be a republic built up on ideals and views of such men as Piet Retief, Paul Kruger and Marthinus Steyn.[1]

To the backveld the emotional appeal of a revived Kruger republic was great, but to Afrikaners in the towns its attractions were more limited, its practicability even as a long-term political aim very much in question. So restricting an ideal could not reunite Afrikanerdom. Yet on the broad issue of the republic the Purified Nationalists had considerable advantages in their dialectical dispute with General Hertzog. He was a republican whose principles had been diluted by what the Purified Nationalists considered in their more generous moments to be a well-meaning but disastrously short-sighted desire for racial reconciliation. In 1933 Hertzog had in effect conceded that the republic was not an urgent or even a practical aim and had maintained as a matter of principle that conscious South African nationhood must first be created, and only if thereafter the people wished should a republic be declared. The Purified Nationalists would, in theory at least, have none of this. They wished, on the contrary, to reverse the democratic process altogether, insisting that in the first place an Afrikaner republic on the basis of *Afrikaner Volkseenheid* must be established, and then 'if the English behave themselves, their gradual assimilation and admission to civic rights would follow'.

The contrast in the approach of the Fusion and Purified Nationalists arose, as we have seen, not from a different concept of the ideal form of government but over the way and the manner in which the republic might come into existence, and particularly over the question of whether the large English-speaking minority, violently anti-republican almost to a man, should, or should not, be won over to it. For the Malanites republicanism tended to be exclusivist racially, secessionist so far as the Commonwealth connexion was concerned, and isolationist in foreign policy; for the followers of Hertzog, the republic was not an immediate objective, its coming into existence being thought of as conditional upon co-operation from the English-speaking South Africans, which in turn made it conditional upon the maintenance of friendly association with Britain. But all were nationalists and nearly all, including Hertzog himself, were republicans at heart.

The importance of these differences is not to be underestimated. The task confronting white South Africa in the first half of the twentieth century was no less than the building of a nation. It was about the way in which this

[1] Quoted in Brady, *Democracy in the Dominions*, p. 356.

formidable task should be approached that the Fusion government and its opponents differed so profoundly. Both recognized that success depended less upon material than upon emotional and psychological factors whose nature and complexity were well illustrated in protracted disputes about South Africa's national anthem. In 1938 General Hertzog asserted that the Union had no national anthem which was legally or officially recognized or generally esteemed and acknowledged as such in the hearts of the people of South Africa.[1] English-speaking South Africans, it was true, regarded *God Save the King* as the national anthem of the Union, but this had never been accepted by Afrikaans-speaking South Africans of any party, and was not correct. Yet a country without an anthem seemed to the Prime Minister, and all Nationalists, as something incomplete. But could an agreed solution be reached? General Hertzog had for long been feeling his way to the compromise solution of two anthems to match the two races and the two flags, but authoritarian by temperament, he took no pains to conciliate those who might entertain different opinions either about the desirability of the end he had in view or the way by which he proposed to reach it, and without consultation even with his principal colleagues in the government, he authorized the playing both of *God Save the King* and *Die Stem van Suid-Afrika* at the opening of the 1938 parliamentary sessions in the hope of establishing thereby a convention which could later be endorsed in law. The innovation introduced without warning greatly embarrassed General Smuts whose English-speaking supporters were profoundly disturbed by the incident to the point of questioning among themselves the wisdom of further support for the Fusion government. It elicited open and vigorous protests from the Dominion party on the right and also, for very different reasons, from the Purified Nationalists on the left. The Prime Minister as a result was compelled to effect a partial withdrawal. The playing of both *God Save the King* and *Die Stem*, he explained, had been sanctioned on this occasion simply because both seemed appropriate. To the leader of the Nationalist opposition, with whose criticisms he was the more concerned, he said,

> if my honourable friend [Dr. Malan] is of the opinion that the approval given to play *Die Stem van Suid-Afrika* with the official opening of Parliament . . . constitutes a recognition of it as the national anthem of South Africa, I am not prepared to dispute his conclusion, provided it be taken in the unintentional sense indicated by the facts.[2]

It was true that *God Save the King* had also been played but that not as an anthem so much 'as an invocation asking the blessing of God upon the King of South Africa'. The fact that it had been played before business began was not 'a question of precedence, but only a matter of order'.

[1] *J.P.E.*, 1938, vol. 19, p. 394. See generally pp. 393–6.
[2] ibid. p. 395.

Dr. Malan was not at all mollified by these explanations. In July 1938, while admitting that on the choice of a national anthem it was virtually impossible to obtain that racial unity which every well-disposed citizen of the Union would like to see, he argued none the less that South Africa could not continue without its own national anthem any more than it could have continued without its own flag. A national anthem was a symbol of nationhood, as much as the possession of a flag; and he regarded it as more important because an anthem appealed even more directly to national emotions. It should breathe the spirit and aspirations of the country and people, and it should also be *exclusive*. It could not be shared.[1] It was the right of that section of the community whose connexion with their original mother country had been cut off for generations, and who regarded themselves as wholly South African, to have the decisive voice in its selection. For was it not impossible, concluded Dr. Malan, for the English-speaking section, representing chiefly another race and speaking another language, to take root in South Africa and to express their national individuality in an anthem of their own?

The parliamentary disputes about South Africa's national anthem threw into relief, on a concrete issue, the fundamental differences between the Nationalists who had accepted Fusion and those who had rejected it about the way in which a South African nation should be built. Those who supported the government believed it must be founded on a comprehensive basis affording equality to both European races, and their leader, General Hertzog, was right in sensing that what was at stake in the vexed question of the national anthem was the conception of equal rights which he had championed for so long. He was therefore emphatic that he could not accept a solution which would place English-speaking South Africans in permanent subordination, and he denounced the Purified Nationalists because they did not want to have any co-operation with the English-speaking section but wished to act as though they were not there at all. For them the only logical course, he suggested, was 'to advocate a republic here and now' so as to show their complete disregard for the wishes of the minority. But for his part, the Prime Minister reiterated his determination to make one nation in South Africa by bringing English-speaking and Afrikaans-speaking people together, and by 1938 he ventured to believe that in the five years of the Fusion government that had been very largely accomplished. And as it had been achieved by conciliation, so, too, the issue of the National Anthem must be settled by co-operation and not, as the Purified Nationalists wished, by force and by ramming 'it down the throats of almost half the population of South Africa'.[2]

Differences on the republican issue between the two sections of Nationalist opinion appeared to English-speaking South Africans as little more than meaningless refinements about odious policies, but they had none the less long-term practical importance for the Commonwealth. Fusion, by making

[1] *J.P.E.*, 1938, vol. 19, p. 918, and see generally pp. 918–25. [2] ibid. p. 921.

the Purified Nationalists the principal opposition party, thereby rendered it virtually certain that in the fullness of time they would attain power. Since in South Africa, as in the Irish Free State, republicanism and secession were held to be synonymous terms, the hardening republicanism of the Malanites seemed to carry unmistakable implications about ultimate South African secession from the Commonwealth. More immediately it implied a suspicious antagonism to all imperial commitments. Here the impact of the Nationalist opposition on external policies in pre-war years, though indirect, was pronounced. Their existence, their bitter criticism of every step that could be interpreted as involving the subordination of South Africa to imperial interests, were a constant reminder that the political faith of the *platteland* remained predominantly what it had always been. Fusion might recommend itself for very practical reasons to the population of the great urban centres, but in the dorps scattered throughout a thinly populated country-side, in whose favour the electoral system was weighted, the Boer farmer did not easily accept the thought of reconciliation with traditional political opponents and still less with British imperialism. The uncompromising attitude of what for long was a small minority, coupled with an awareness of its deep roots in history, induced an extreme reluctance on the part of the Fusion Ministry to enlarge the field of South Africa's co-operation with the Commonwealth. It is true that in itself the persistent denunciation of Fusion policies by the Purified Nationalist mattered little, for in any event their alienation was final, but the tender consciences of many Fusion Nationalists, distressed as they remained by the continuing divisions of Afrikanerdom, had to be regarded.

SOUTH AFRICA'S LOYALTY TO THE LEAGUE IN THE ABYSSINIAN WAR

The fusion of the South African and the Nationalist parties prompted and facilitated the enactment in 1936 of two very important measures in the field of native policy, the Native Trust and Land Act,[1] the principal object of which was to remove from European-owned land all Natives not in the service of the owners, and the Representation of Natives in Parliament Act.[2] Under the provisions of this Act the existing Bantu voters at the Cape retained their individual votes but were to be entered on a separate roll and, voting in three constituencies, were to return three Europeans as members of the House of Assembly, while in the Senate the Natives as a whole voting in four vast constituencies were allotted four Europeans to represent their interests. At the same time there was set up a purely advisory Native Representative Council whose advice in subsequent years was more often than not disregarded. The provisions of both acts significantly implemented a policy of racial segregation and thereby constituted a landmark in the develop-

[1] Act No. 18, 1936; see Hancock, *Survey*, vol. 2, pt. 2, pp. 84 ff.

[2] Act No. 12, 1936; see Walker, *History of South Africa*, pp. 630–4.

ment of race relations within the Union. Their enactment was made possible by the existence of the Fusion government, whose great majority ensured that the necessary two-thirds majority in both Houses sitting together would be readily forthcoming.[1] But outside the field of Native policy, party fusion did not make for a strong government. In all controversial issues at home the policy of the Fusion government was of necessity one of letting sleeping dogs lie. Differences had been papered over, not resolved; and the unassailable majority of the Fusion government in the House of Assembly was no true criterion of its strength. Progress was by agreement between those who on many issues were in fundamental disagreement, and the result was little progress. With that white South Africa as a whole was well content. Fusion had been made possible by a deep desire for internal peace and it was not inaction, but imprudent action, that was likely to bring back party warfare with all its fruitless asperities. Because of a continuing anxiety for party peace it was not, therefore, from within but from without that the most dangerous challenges to this experiment in racial co-operation were likely to come.

General Hertzog was an ardent supporter of the League, General Smuts one of its principal architects. So long, therefore, as the strength and prestige of the League remained unimpaired agreement on external policy presented few difficulties. South African policy in the Manchurian crisis[2] of 1931 and in the Abyssinian war was indeed remarkable for its consistency and for the resolution with which it was pursued.

On 14 September 1935 Mr. te Water, the South African delegate to the League, speaking as the representative of 'the one permanent and indigenous white civilization in Africa', warned the Assembly of the danger of a new partition of Africa, 'danger to the adventuring nations themselves, danger to the black peoples of Africa, and menace to our own white civilization'. Above all, he declared, the Assembly should remember that 'the long memory of Black Africa never forgets and never forgives an injury or an injustice'.[3] Outspoken support for resolute action against the aggressor was followed by the prompt adoption of sanctions. On 9 October 1935 South Africa announced that she would put all the sanctions voted by the League into force against Italy. She was the first to take this decisive step. On Armistice Day 1935 General Smuts hailed the new spirit of action displayed by the League and believed that it 'would more and more stand forth as a determined foe to

[1] The majority on the third reading of the Representation bill was 169 to 11.

[2] In March 1932 Mr. te Water told the Assembly that 'we have no other name for the state of affairs in China today than that of war', and he asked of the Great Powers 'leadership which can be interpreted in terms of action and not in terms of words'. At that time no dominion, except possibly the Irish Free State, was so forthright about the need to assert the authority of the League.

[3] 13 September 1935, League of Nations, *Plenary Meetings*, 16th Assembly, pp. 66–67; quoted in Carter, *British Commonwealth*, pp. 195–6.

that imperialism, that spirit of aggressive expansion and annexation characteristic of the old pre-War order . . . which was once more showing its horrid head in world affairs'.[1] In the event of economic sanctions leading to military sanctions the government promised to consult Parliament before South Africa was committed to active participation, but ministerial language implied that in such an eventuality, which the policy of the Great Powers admittedly made highly improbable, the government would not have faltered in their resolve to support the authority of the League.[2]

The publication in December 1935 of the Hoare–Laval plan contemplating the cession to Mussolini of almost all the territory his armies had so far conquered provoked an outburst of indignation in South Africa.[3] The Africans who had watched with anxious concern the progress of the struggle in the north were above all deeply disillusioned with what appeared to them as the betrayal of a small independent non-European people by the Great Powers. The government, who had not been consulted by Britain in advance, were placed in a difficult, even embarrassing position which the later repudiation of the plan by the United Kingdom government did little to restore. 'The British government', observed the *Cape Times* on Sir Samuel Hoare's resignation, 'still base Britain's policy upon the League but there can be no sound basis for such a policy if the League is held together by compromises which in themselves come near to violating the Covenant.'[4] Dr. Malan alone had some cause for rejoicing. From the outset he had maintained that South Africa should in all circumstances remain neutral and that if membership of the League threatened to draw South Africa into war then South Africa should leave the League. When Parliament reassembled at the end of January 1936 he moved that no steps, 'including the application of military or economic sanctions, which may tend towards extending the sphere of operations' in the Italo-Ethiopian war, should be taken by the Union government, and he urged that 'subject to its duty of self-defence in case of attack, South Africa should strictly refrain from participating in any war between other nations'.[5] In his view the imposition of sanctions would have been justifiable only if the League had been a world-wide organization. But it was not; and one unpleasing consequence in the eyes of the Nationalists was the very unfortunate identification of South African with British policy. Thus Dr. van der Merwe, who seconded Dr. Malan's resolution, regarded collective security as no more than a cloak for concealing Britain's imperialist aims and, oddly enough, associated British imperialism with international Communism as the principal

[1] Quoted ibid. p. 207.

[2] Such a war, however, would have aroused little enthusiasm in the Union and lack of it would undoubtedly have seriously affected the war effort of a country dependent upon voluntary recruitment.

[3] cf. *Cape Times*, 10 December 1935; *New York Times*, 13 December 1935.

[4] *Cape Times*, 20 December 1935.

[5] 31 January 1936, South Africa, H. of A. Deb., vol. 26, coll. 30–31.

force favouring the full application of sanctions against Italy for their own sinister purposes.[1] Yet despite the shock of the Hoare–Laval pact, the criticisms it evoked, and the victorious advance of the Italian armies, the government never wavered in their policy of full support for the League. The day after the Abyssinian capital had fallen to the aggressor, General Hertzog maintained that the League should maintain sanctions even if they took years to achieve their purpose. 'The government became a member of the League of Nations for no other reason than to prevent international robbery, and the government wants to stand by that.' To withdraw sanctions would be to co-operate in killing the League, and in that South Africa would have no part. The choice, said Smuts, is between the League and 'chaos and destruction'.

These uncompromising views were perceptibly modified neither by events nor by the policies of other Commonwealth countries. On 10 June 1936 Mr. Neville Chamberlain denounced the continuance of sanctions as 'the very midsummer of madness'[2] and on 18 June the United Kingdom government, followed by the governments of Canada and Australia, announced its intention of recommending their withdrawal. But the Union government retracted none of its firmly expressed opinions, and when the Assembly met on 30 June with the evident intention of lifting sanctions Mr. te Water, unsparing in his condemnation of the policies of the Great Powers who had 'let down' the League, appealed on behalf of his government for the retention of sanctions. 'Where', cried Mr. te Water, 'are the Great Powers leading us, who have not the faith to persevere?'[3] But among great or small only New Zealand was found to give even qualified support to South Africa's demand. In Cape Town the failure of the League could no longer be disguised, though the hope was still cherished that it was not final.

THE SOUTH AFRICAN REACTION TO THE FAILURE OF THE LEAGUE

The failure of the League removed the only hope of agreement within the Fusion government on a positive external policy based on resistance to aggression. A world-wide system of security allowed a freedom of action which contracted sharply once resistance to aggression involved common action, not with the majority of peace-loving nations, but with the countries of the Commonwealth and of Western Europe. So long as there was any prospect of the League emerging as the effective guarantor of the rights of small nations, the South African government had given it unqualified and unwavering support. For South Africa, unlike the Irish Free State, Abyssinia was a good test case. Calvinist Afrikaners had no sentimental inhibitions about applying sanctions against Catholic Italy, and they had a direct material interest in

[1] ibid. coll. 46 ff.

[2] *The Times*, 11 June 1936.

[3] League of Nations, *Official Journal*, 1936, Special Supplement No. 151, pp. 31–33; quoted in Carter, *British Commonwealth*.

preventing an aggressive European Power from acquiring a firm foothold in north-east Africa. It was not to be doubted that the Italian conquest of Abyssinia brought the possibilities of a European conflict fought out on the African continent much closer, and that in any such conflict native troops would be armed. On grounds, therefore, both of defence and of racial policy, it was in the direct interests of South Africa to ensure that the authority of the League was resolutely enforced against the European transgressor in Africa. But while all the arguments for participation in collective resistance to aggression were, if anything, reinforced by the failure of the League, South Africa's complex, emotional relationship with the Commonwealth rendered the only possible substitute highly suspect. South Africa as a whole, unlike Australia and New Zealand, could discover no wholly congenial half-way house between a system of international security and reliance on national resources obviously inadequate to meet any major challenge. Nor could her government move ahead of public opinion, for by its very composition it reflected faithfully the divisions which precluded resolute action. In the case of South Africa, therefore, all the normal reasons for desiring to preserve peace were powerfully reinforced by an awareness of the highly unwelcome political problems that war would certainly bring.

After the failure of the League, which neither Hertzog nor Smuts recognized as final, Hertzog defined the guiding principle by which South African external policy should be determined as 'South Africa first'. South Africa would not concern herself with international issues, far-reaching though their implications might be, unless they were also of direct and immediate interest to her. Yet however restrictively the criterion of 'South Africa first' might be applied, South Africa's interest in the preservation of peace was beyond dispute. Her internal unity was dependent upon it. Therefore, was it not wisdom for South Africa to contribute so far as her influence allowed and without commitment on her part, towards the peaceful settlement of all disputes in which South African participation might be in question? A war in which the Commonwealth was involved would assuredly constitute a decisive test for the policy of Fusion, and a major war in which the Commonwealth was not involved was inconceivable. An isolationism qualified by a deep desire to secure the settlement of outstanding international disputes by conciliation became the essence of Hertzog's foreign policy.

To a general and well-founded anxiety not to expose the frail bark of Fusion to the stormy seas of contemporary world affairs, there was added a particular misgiving, should Germany for the second time in a generation prove the aggressor. The sinister machinations of international Communism were a favourite theme on Nationalist platforms, but comment on Nazi aggression tended to be more circumspect. The very fact that Afrikaners looked so much to the past kept fresh in mind the sympathy extended by Germany to the Boer republics at a time when Germany was the recognized counterpoise to

Britain in southern Africa. Nor were such friendly recollections confined to avowed Nationalists. At Versailles in 1919 Smuts had voiced the sentiments of the Afrikaner people in protesting against the harsher provisions of the peace treaties.[1] How could he, whatever reservations he made about Hitler's methods, in logic or sincerity denounce the steps which a renascent Germany might take to remove punitive provisions which he had condemned at the time of their imposition? And if such considerations weighed with Smuts, how much more did they determine the attitude of Hertzog. For him Versailles was the root cause of the mounting tension in Europe and for its terms the victors, not the vanquished, were responsible. By the later nineteen-thirties there were even to be found, on the fringe of the Nationalist party, open admirers of the Nazi régime while the main body of Nationalists supporters, whether Malanites or Hertzogites, were reluctant indeed to believe that Germany had embarked on a career of aggression. Sentiment thus reinforced internal political pressures, so that in the absence of an effective League which would have imparted an international sanction to resolute action against aggression, the arguments for the appeasement of Germany were so powerful that even in 1939 many believed they should still be pursued.

South African reluctance to oppose German denunciation of the peace terms imposed in 1919 was forcibly illustrated in March 1936 when German troops, in defiance of the freely negotiated Locarno pact as well as of the Versailles Treaty, entered the demilitarized zone of the Rhineland. All the influence of the Union government was exerted to prevent the adoption of military action by the Western Powers, for war on such an issue was as unpalatable to General Smuts as it was to General Hertzog and the Nationalists. Indeed Smuts made no secret of his opinion that every effort should be made by the dominions to convince the United Kingdom government that it had no obligation to go to war over the Rhineland, and that it would be sufficient if the League contented itself with a strong condemnation. It has even been stated on tolerably reliable authority that General Smuts felt that, if Britain had committed herself in support of France to military action in the Rhineland, it might well have meant the disruption of the Commonwealth as a military unit, since he believed rightly that all the dominions without exception were opposed to such action. In any event his appreciation of British restraint was expressed in unqualified language. At Cape Town on 22 March in a glowing tribute to the part Britain had played General Smuts said: 'We are tremendously proud of the way she has stood in the breach when the world looked like being precipitated into war.' As a result of her attitude 'a perfect peace' might be achieved, for the forcible reoccupation of the Rhineland brought to an end 'the spirit of inequality, subjection, and bondage in which the Peace of Versailles was concluded'.[2] Hitler, however, thought otherwise.

While the Rhineland crisis illustrated South Africa's anxiety to preserve

[1] cf. Millin, *Smuts*, vol. 2, pp. 208 ff.

[2] *Daily Telegraph*, 23 March 1936.

peace, even at the risk of condoning aggression, her policy in the Spanish civil war underlined her resolve to keep out of trouble in Europe. Throughout the whole course of the war South Africa gave consistent support to Britain's non-intervention policy. In April 1937 General Hertzog observed in the House that the question (of Spain) interested him vastly, but it was for that reason that his policy with regard to Spain was to have nothing to do with it.[1] In September the appeal of the Spanish government to the League for aid against Fascist intervention was strongly opposed by South Africa on the ground that any assistance would violate the principle of non-intervention, and the South African and Irish votes were partly responsible for its rejection.

THE COMMONWEALTH AND SECURITY

Isolation was the expressed policy of the Purified Nationalists, but it was also the state of mind of the Nationalists within the government and the inclination of the greater part of the country. Seven thousand miles afforded a satisfying sense of security behind which subconscious as well as deliberate isolationism flourished. The fact that the domination of Europe by one great military Power would leave the Union defenceless against any aggressor armed with modern methods of transport and modern means of warfare was but dimly recognized, even after the success of Italian aggression in Abyssinia. It was only the reflection of European tensions in an African setting afforded by Nazi activities in South West Africa, or defence problems arising from the existence of the British naval base at Simonstown, that attracted the attention of the House of Assembly, and seemed to link the fate of South Africa to that of Europe and of the Commonwealth.

General Hertzog could maintain with conviction, and not without justification, that South Africa was not interested in European politics and should refrain from active participation in them. There remained, however, a latent conflict between membership of the Commonwealth and isolationism, from which the formula 'South Africa first' afforded an easy but not a satisfying way of escape. The failure of the League to afford protection to the weak enhanced for South Africa the value of the Commonwealth. Without naval resources of her own she relied on the Royal Navy for the protection of a long and vulnerable coast-line, while improved methods of land and air transport deprived her northern frontiers of their old immunity from land attack by a major European Power. In South Africa, as in Australia and New Zealand, the logical answer to the failure of the League was a closer co-ordination of Commonwealth defence policies. The Fusion government did not shrink from it, though confronted with internal tensions of which the Pacific dominions had no experience, they advanced with circumspection both in deed and in word. 'We shall take part in no war except where the true interests of

[1] *J.P.E.*, 1937, vol. 18, p. 618.

South Africa make such a participation inevitable',[1] declared the Minister of Defence, Mr. Pirow, on 6 May 1936 before leaving for London for defence consultations with British Ministers and the Committee of Imperial Defence. But even such circumspect language could not disguise the evident fact of closer co-operation, and as a result a new astringency was henceforward to be detected in the defence debates in the House of Assembly, the opposition consistently challenging every modest increase in the defence budget on the ground that the Union's defence arrangements in themselves 'hitched them to the British dominion'. They suggested no alternative but argued that the Union could not expect, and need not reasonably make preparations against, an attack from overseas. It was inconceivable, emphasized Mr. Erasmus—later to be Dr. Malan's Minister of Defence—that a major European Power would invade the southern half of Africa, and therefore 'our policy should be a policy of neutrality . . .', but the Prime Minister who had once endorsed it had thrown it 'overboard and now calls it foolishness'.[2] 'We have broken with the Empire as a political unit', complained Dr. Malan, but now looming up in the foreground was the question of the Empire being a military unit, on the ostensible ground that the dominions, including South Africa, needed allies and could not stand on their own feet. Yet Dr. Malan conceded that complete isolation was hardly possible, for South Africa was 'so situated that they could not know what the most effective means of defence would be without learning from others'.[3]

The Minister of Defence, Mr. Oswald Pirow, an ambitious man with a liking for spectacular gestures, was then at the height of his reputation and considered by many as a possible successor of Smuts.[4] While Pirow was careful in his public utterances to delimit narrowly the area of defence co-operation with the United Kingdom and the Commonwealth, he was at that time convinced that in the event of a major war South African co-operation with British forces in East Africa and even in the Middle East theatre was possible, even probable.[5] Yet closely though he co-operated with the Committee of Imperial Defence, he entered into no commitments and could state with perfect justice in the House of Assembly that any arrangements made with the Chiefs of Staff in London or with the representatives of the dominions and India at the Imperial Conference amounted to no more than an agreement to discuss defence matters of common interest together. At all times, he explained, South Africa had insisted on the fullest freedom to decide whether

[1] South Africa, H. of A. Deb., 1936, vol. 27, col. 3117.
[2] *J.P.E.*, 1937, vol. 18, p. 168.
[3] ibid. p. 169.
[4] cf. Long, *In Smuts's Camp*, pp. 66–67.
[5] The progressive integration of South African land and air forces carried through under the active direction of General Sir Pierre van Ryneveld, South African Chief of General Staff from 1933, obviously greatly enhanced the contribution they could make to the defence of imperial communications in the Middle East.

she was going to take part in a war or not.[1] And in such circumstances co-operation could not but be of positive value to South Africa. It was essential for her to know what developments were taking place in arms and equipment. 'We have naturally taken part in discussions with other countries. We have taken part as interested parties, or we have followed the discussions as observers. . . . It is in the interests of South Africa to know what other nations are doing in connexion with their fleets and similar matters.'[2] Yet if Mr. Pirow's balanced language did not wholly suffice to dispel suspicions of undisclosed commitments in London, the defence policy of the government was hardly open to criticism by the criterion of 'South Africa first'. In essentials it recognized that the Union was wholly responsible for its own defence, but that its resources were inadequate to meet every challenge with which the country might be faced. Therefore, consultation and co-operation constituted a desirable reinsurance. Nor was it, in itself, inconsistent with a policy of non-intervention. 'Our policy', declared Mr. Pirow, 'is not to interfere beyond our borders'; and he added the categoric assurance 'that England has never requested us to go an inch further.'[3]

The resources of the Union whether on land or sea were wholly insufficient for its defence. Of its total population of 11¼ million little more than 2¼ million were European.[4] Since it was an unquestioned convention that the non-European should not carry arms, responsibility for the defence of South Africa's extended land and sea frontiers devolved upon her small European population. It was a responsibility they could not themselves adequately discharge. In September 1938, when war seemed imminent, Mr. Pirow admitted in the House of Assembly that in view of the extreme shortage of man-power the Union would have to rely mainly on volunteer forces for its land defence. Expansion of the armed forces at the expense of industry or mining, he maintained, would undermine the economy of the Union which in any event, despite its potential wealth, was in no position to spend unlimited sums on defence. Yet despite this comparative defencelessness the likelihood of land attack by better equipped and more numerous forces was sufficiently remote to be largely discounted, provided always that Nazi penetration of South West Africa were kept under strict control. An equal confidence in immunity from sea-borne attack depended, however, upon the continued supremacy of the Royal Navy. South Africa had no navy. Partly for this reason she considered it inappropriate that she should sign the London Naval Treaty of 1936 even though she had been represented both in the preparatory talks which had taken place in 1935 and at the conference itself.[5] With her long and vulnerable coast-line possessing harbours of the highest

[1] *J.P.E.*, 1937, vol. 18, p. 170.
[2] ibid. p. 905.
[3] ibid. p. 907.
[4] 1936 census figures.
[5] South Africa did not in any event welcome the comprehensive grouping of Commonwealth navies in the treaty.

strategic importance, South Africa would have been a tempting objective for enemy raiders were it not for the protection of the Royal Navy which under the Smuts–Churchill agreement of 1921 maintained a naval base at Simonstown.

Under the 1921 agreement South Africa was pledged to defend the base at Simonstown in time of war with land and air forces, and its obligation to do so was specifically reaffirmed by Mr. Pirow in a speech at Simonstown on 2 April 1937.[1] The effective defence of the naval bases was indeed in the direct interest of the Union, for unless Simonstown were held, an attack upon Cape Town from the rear would become a practical possibility. To that extent, therefore, co-operation between the Union and the United Kingdom in war-time was assumed, and as a result it could reasonably be argued that in the event of a war in which the United Kingdom was involved, the alternative to active belligerency on the part of South Africa was a policy of non-belligerency rather than one of strict neutrality. It is true that General Hertzog in 1935 dismayed some of his colleagues by claiming that in the event of war Simonstown could be treated as 'foreign territory',[2] but this was highly doubtful in law and inconsistent with the provisions of the agreement. In any event the obvious advantages to the Union of the protective guarantee afforded by the existence of a base for the Royal Navy at Simonstown more than counterbalanced the effect of such speculation. In March 1935 General Hertzog himself acknowledged that Britain was South Africa's greatest and most powerful friend and 'now that our freedom has been restored . . . the British navy means exactly the same to me as to an Englishman . . . because the freedom of my people and my country is just as dependent upon it as England is herself'.[3] Even by the Nationalists the Simonstown agreement was subjected only to oblique attack on the ground that it might be used to restrict South Africa's freedom of action in foreign affairs.

In September 1938 the government decided to include East London and Port Elizabeth in their coastal defence scheme.[4] The significance of this decision was considerable. The formation of the Rome–Berlin Axis carried the presumption that a war with Germany would necessarily involve Italy, in which case shipping might well have to be diverted from the Mediterranean to the Cape route and, as a result, Simonstown, the Cape, Port Elizabeth, and Durban might all acquire greatly enhanced importance, both as bases on the line of sea communications to the East and as naval stations from which raiding craft could be attacked. It was this possibility which was mainly responsible for a curious request made to the Admiralty by Mr. Pirow in 1938. He asked the Admiralty to lend the monitor *Erebus* to South Africa. For some

[1] *Round Table*, 1937, vol. 27, p. 561.

[2] *Cape Times*, 31 January 1935; the 'Gibraltar' of South Africa was an analogy commonly used.

[3] ibid. 15 March 1935, quoted in Walker, *History of South Africa*, p. 666.

[4] *J.P.E.*, 1938, p. 915, and see also 1939, p. 450.

reason he had formed the opinion that the main defences of Cape Town should include 15-inch naval guns, despite professional advice which considered 12-inch guns would fully suffice and which was reluctant to see anything more than what was absolutely essential committed to sedentary defence. Moreover, the principal anxiety of the experts was that the defences of Simonstown, which had been much neglected, should be repaired and modernized, and they can hardly have welcomed evidence of South African distraction from this essential task. But Pirow remained insistent, though whether that was due so much to a conviction that 15-inch guns were necessary as to a desire to secure the *Erebus* is open to question. In any case the Admiralty yielded to pressure, it being recorded that 'to please Pirow (we) agreed to lend *Erebus* until their defences (Cape Town) were modernized in view of his fear of attack from Japan', and at the expense of the Union government, the reconditioning and rearming of the *Erebus* was undertaken. She was not, however, ready to sail till 29 November 1939. Japan was not then at war and while the Admiralty allowed that defences of Cape Town were weak, there was actual danger only from the two German battle-cruisers *Scharnhorst* and *Gneisenau*, and if they attacked Cape Town 'the Royal Navy would pursue them until hunted down'. 'Therefore', wrote Mr. Churchill, then First Lord, to General Smuts, 'it seems to me you are unlikely to have the need of this ship. On the other hand she would be most useful for various purposes in the shallows of the Belgian coast, especially if Holland were attacked.' General Smuts was accommodating and the *Erebus* was returned to the Admiralty.[1]

The situation which the Union government contemplated in 1938–9 was one in which the Union might be involved in active home defence against sea raiders. In 1939 a Seaward Defence Force to patrol her own coasts was created. The emphasis was consistently on defence. At that time majority opinion felt strongly that South Africa should not take an active part in fighting beyond her own sea and land frontiers, even if this restrictive view did not pass wholly unchallenged. It was the conviction of General Smuts, and probably of Mr. Pirow, that the defence of Central and East African colonial territories was essential to the safety of the Union. The correctness of this view was not contested on strategic grounds, but it was challenged by the opposition because they feared that any extension of the area of defence would lead by easy stages to the Union's being involved in any major European war in which Britain was a belligerent. Dr. Malan complained in April 1937 that co-operation in the making of plans for the defence of colonial territories north of the Union carried the implication of joint defence co-operation with the country whose territories they were. The government in its more robust moments welcomed this practical necessity as a means of reconciling their policy of 'South Africa first' with membership of the Commonwealth. Even though there was no explicit agreement, did not consultation about the defence

[1] See Churchill, *Second World War*, vol. 1, p. 588.

of Southern and even Central Africa almost certainly mean, as Dr. Malan inquired, 'that you act together if war breaks out'?[1] Yet the prospect of active warfare between European peoples on the African continent could be viewed only with the most profound misgivings. Dr. Malan feared that any such conflict might undermine the whole foundation of European rule in Africa. The Union in its foreign policy must aim, he argued, at creating a position under which the African races should stand 'under the rule of the white races of Europe and be preserved for Western civilization', and for that peace was a necessity. The quarrels of the European Powers were of no concern to the Union, but what was of direct concern to them was that they should not make enemies of the Christian countries of the West because all were needed for the civilizing of Africa. In the long run only by such a policy of complete detachment would it be possible 'to keep the black nations out of the quarrels of the white'.[2]

The government were not unmindful of such considerations which had indeed profoundly influenced South African policy in the Abyssinian war, or of South Africa's general responsibilities in the African continent. But they came to a somewhat different conclusion about the way in which they should be discharged. 'We occupy', said Mr. Pirow, 'a special position' towards states with a European population south of the Equator. In the nature of things those people 'look to South Africa for the maintenance of white civilization even though there is no military bond or obligation on our part to assist', and they would not look in vain.[3] On the African continent isolation was hardly a practical policy on general grounds and there were particular dangers which deprived it of all reality. It was a growing awareness of their existence which prompted criticism from within the United party itself of the sufficiency of Mr. Pirow's defence measures, and still more of the extent to which effective action followed upon skilful exposition of needs and plans for meeting them.

THE SIGNIFICANCE OF SOUTH WEST AFRICA IN THE DETERMINATION OF SOUTH AFRICAN EXTERNAL POLICY

In one of the most unctuous pages of his brilliant, complacent memoirs, the former German Chancellor, Prince Bernhard von Bülow, recalled[4] how in 1904 the rising of the Hereros in German South West Africa had been quelled by the 'sustained endurance and valour of our men' which showed that 'despite a long peace our people still retained their military virtues'. After

[1] *J.P.E.*, 1937, vol. 18, p. 620.

[2] ibid. p. 170.

[3] This protective attitude on the part of the Union elicited no great enthusiasm among white settlers farther north who detected in South African references an underlying desire for their absorption. Whitehall therefore was not encouraged to enlist South African aid in the defence of Kenya, Uganda, or even Tanganyika.

[4] Prince von Bülow, *Memoirs, 1903–1909* (London, Putnam, 1931) p. 19.

the victory of South African forces in 1915 von Bülow continued to hope that 'South West Africa, the oldest of our Colonies—the great territory where, inspired by Bismarck, Germans first trod African soil shall be ours again, with its diamond fields, when this war is ended and for ever'. Two things, however, he refrained from mentioning. The first was that the Herero rising was suppressed with such unforgettable barbarity that a German return to South West Africa was unthinkable; the second that this 'great territory' which Bismarck acquired as a counter in the game of European power politics was recommended by his son Count Herbert Bismarck in 1889 as a suitable exchange for Heligoland because 'our South West African Company is stagnant, bankrupt, and hopeless'.[1]

While von Bülow's lack of candour is to be attributed mainly to a desire to safeguard his own reputation, it has to be acknowledged that any German government which was prepared to consider the future of any of Germany's former colonies on its merits was displaying rare political courage and a conciliatory spirit not likely long to survive defeat. To this South West Africa, despite the comparative lack of material resources, was no exception, as was well understood by the South African government to whom the territory was transferred in 1919 as a 'C' class mandate, which implied that the Union would have full powers to administer and to legislate for South West Africa 'as an integral part of the Union of South Africa'.[2] Wisely therefore General Smuts on behalf of the Union government sought agreement[3] with the representatives of the Weimar Republic about the future of the mandated territory, having previously prepared the ground by the appointment of a commission under the chairmanship of Mr. Justice de Wet, whose recommendations about the 'automatic naturalization' of Europeans was submitted to the Permanent Mandates Commission and approved by the Assembly of the League before Smuts met the German representatives in London in 1923. At this meeting agreement was reached about the immediate future. The Union government promised to accept the Germans of South West Africa 'as part of the people, with the same privileges and responsibilities as the other citizens' enjoying full cultural and linguistic freedom, while the German government, for its part, recognizing 'that the future of South West Africa is now bound up with the Union of South Africa' and 'that it would be a wise policy for German nationals in that territory to throw in their lot with South Africa', stated that it was prepared to use its influence to induce its former nationals to accept Union citizenship, under the proposed general naturaliza-

[1] cf. A. J. P. Taylor, *Germany's First Bid for Colonies, 1884–5* (London, Macmillan, 1938) p. 56.

[2] For a balanced short account of some technical problems of sovereignty involved see E. Hellmann and L. Abrahams, eds., *Handbook on Race Relations in South Africa* (London, Oxford University Press, 1949), Chapter XXXV.

[3] The agreement was signed on the 23 October 1923, and the text was published in a United Kingdom White Paper, Cmd. 2220.

tion. This indeed was a conciliatory, even sacrificial, gesture which had, from the point of view of the Union, the happiest results, for of a total of 3,489 Germans in the territory, only 221 refused naturalization. But the arrangement suffered from one severe handicap. It was made at the time of German prostration by a government for which Hitler felt nothing but profound contempt, and no reliance whatever could be placed on it as a guide to German policy after his accession to power. The Nazis, indeed, soon discovered that the text of the 1923 agreement was not free from ambiguity. 'The future of South West Africa is *now* bound up . . . ' was interpreted retrospectively to mean 'for the time being', and not as the Union government had supposed 'now and for the future'.[1] A speech by General Smuts at Bloemfontein in December 1937, in the course of which he emphasized the binding character of the 1923 agreement, 'based not merely on force or victory' but on obligations freely undertaken, elicited a sharp protest from the German government who maintained the agreement had said nothing about the future of South West Africa.[2] But such verbal quibbles were merely a convenient mode of expressing a new political orientation towards the colonial question. Lord Hailey correctly analysed it when he observed:[3] 'As Germany has grown in strength and self-confidence . . . the [colonial] question has left the fields of economics and ethics, and entered that of political dynamics.'

German claims might not have aroused so much misgiving in the Union had there not been a German population in the vast, thinly populated mandated territory[4] where without difficulty they could be surreptitiously organized so as to confront the Union in time of emergency with a direct threat on its own vulnerable frontiers. The danger was indisputable and the possibility

[1] The dispute turned on the exact meaning of the word 'gegenwärtig'. The German government, however, clearly contemplated that South West Africa would be administered by the Union for at least thirty years, for the last article of the agreement provided that 'Germans in South West Africa and their children will not be liable in any circumstances for military service against the German Reich for a period of at least thirty years from this date' (Cmd. 2220, article 11).

[2] See *Documents on German Foreign Policy, 1918–45*, Series D, vol. 1, p. 126. In a cipher telegram from the German Foreign Ministry to the German Legation in Pretoria, dated 14 December 1937, the latter was instructed to inform the Union government of this distinction. It reads as follows: 'Press reports of Smuts's statement at Bloemfontein have come to the attention of the German government, to the effect that the German government in the London Agreement of 1923 assented to the idea that the future of South West Africa lay with the Union. The German government cannot leave this view uncontradicted. Nothing is said in the text of the Agreement with regard to the future of South West Africa. The letter of the head of the German delegation annexed to the Agreement merely states as the opinion of the German government that the future of South West Africa *now*, that is at the time of the conclusion of the Agreement, was bound up with that of the Union. That merely recognized the state of affairs brought about by the granting of the mandate to the Union.'

[3] *The Times*, 1 December 1938; report of an address to the English-speaking Union.

[4] The European population, about 50 per cent. of German extraction, numbered 31,000 in 1937. Of this total 18,000 were Afrikaans-speaking; 2,400 English-speaking; 9,600 German-speaking; in 1939 the native population was estimated at 283,500. For a more detailed analysis see *Handbook on Race Relations in South Africa*, p. 746.

that in South West Africa the Union would once again be involved in direct hostilities with the German Reich not to be discounted. In 1933 the German members in the South West Africa Assembly asserted first, that in spite of their naturalization in 1924 they reserved to themselves their German nationality, and second that 'every decent German must now be a National Socialist'. The Germans set up their own Courts of Arbitration presided over by a German Consular officer, and resort to the official courts was discouraged. All non-naturalized Germans were compelled to swear allegiance to Hitler, and those who had taken British nationality were required to 'affirm' allegiance instead of taking the formal oath. All this caused grave disquiet to the Union government. Precautionary steps were taken. In 1934 the Administrator banned the Hitler Youth and other Nazi organizations in South West Africa, and expelled their leaders. But the latent danger was not removed. An influx of Germans from the Fatherland organized the *Deutsche Front* into which virtually all Germans, willing or unwilling, were conscripted by pressure, and in 1936 the government decided to give the Administrator emergency powers. General Hertzog, after pointing out that the Union was responsible for the government of the territory, for its security, as well as for that of South Africa itself, declared that they could not tolerate within South West Africa the formation of a group awaiting a favourable opportunity to impose their will by force. When Dr. Malan, who thought this step provocative, argued that the solution of the colonial problem depended upon an attitude of good will which would ensure the co-operation of Germany, the Prime Minister replied that in the circumstances good will was not enough[1] and that when the German minister plenipotentiary had protested, he had explained that while 'we are just as friendly disposed towards them [the Germans] as ever, and we shall try to live with the German government, as with any other government, on the most friendly footing', there was a limit beyond which he could not go. . . . 'I am not prepared, in this case, to advise the government to do anything more than can be expected of a government which has to fulfil its duties in a decent manner.'[2]

The solution South Africa would have most welcomed was formal incorporation of the mandated territory in the Union. In a technical sense the way for this was cleared by the provincial election of 1934 when the United party (alternatively known as the Fifth Province party) secured the two-thirds majority which was the prescribed condition for a formal request for incorporation. But the government, reluctant to challenge Berlin or to provoke discussion at the League, decided to procrastinate and appointed a Commission of Inquiry. The Report of this Commission did not, however, take matters much farther.[3] Union administration received its meed of

[1] See van den Heever, *Hertzog*, pp. 276–7, for an account of his views.

[2] *J.P.E.*, 1937, vol. 18, p. 613.

[3] Union government, 26 of 1936.

praise. In the north the tribal Ovambo had enjoyed something approaching indirect rule and the scattered, decimated Hereros in the south had been helped by the provision of reserves and agricultural aid.[1] But with a public debt which reached £3½ million by March 1937, the financial position of the territory was desperate and its government incapable of functioning effectively. In the light of the situation described in the Report, the Fusion government, still reluctant to recommend the decisive step of incorporation, decided that the existing Constitution should remain in force with renewed emphasis upon the need to make it work effectively by maintaining a balanced budget. The government agreed to recognize German as an official language, and to sanction purely cultural associations, but it limited membership of any 'public body'[2] to British subjects, who were forbidden to take an oath of loyalty to any foreign sovereign, government, or organization. Foreigners who indulged in illegal political propaganda were rendered liable to deportation. Finally, the government stated categorically 'that it was not prepared to consider the possibility of the transfer of the mandate to another Power'.

The firmness of the Union government for the time being lessened the risk of large-scale subversive activity in the territory. But it did not remove it. The *Deutsche Bund*, reconstituted as the *Deutsche Sud-West Bund*, promised obedience to the law, but infiltration of Nazis from Germany did not cease, nor did the training in Germany of young Germans from South West Africa who returned home once their period of service was completed.[3] The danger created by the existence of this seed-bed of Nazi influence and intrigue on the Union frontier therefore remained, and in the face of it government policy stiffened. On 31 March 1937 General Hertzog defined it in uncompromising language:

. . . the Union is not prepared to allow South West [Africa] to fall into other hands. . . . South West Africa must not go back to Germany . . . that has always been the policy of the government. . . . The leader of the opposition says that we can only solve the problem of South West Africa in a psychological manner, in co-operation with Germany. . . . I entirely share his opinions, and we share it to such an extent that it has always been the policy that I and this government have followed, and by which we hope some day to come to a compromise with Germany in solving the problem of South West. . . . It is a mandate, and we are going to remain loyal to the instructions of the mandate . . . but I hope that we shall eventually come to an arrangement . . . that South West will remain what it ought to be, namely, a portion of South Africa.[4]

In October that year the Deputy Prime Minister, General Smuts, declared that 'the Union stands or falls by the mandate over South West Africa' and

[1] See Walker, *History of South Africa*, p. 655.
[2] ibid. p. 656.
[3] ibid. pp. 656–7.
[4] South Africa, H. of A. Deb., vol. 29, coll. 3945–8.

later, in the aftermath of Munich, his language became yet more uncompromising. At Bloemfontein, on 2 November 1938, he said: 'We must keep what we have, and we are not going through weakness and unpreparedness to allow any country to pluck South West Africa as a ripe fruit.' And at Pietermaritzburg nine days later he declared: 'We must make it plain that we shall defend South Africa, including South West Africa, to the bitter end.'[1] Viewed in perspective, therefore, there is no doubt that the attitude of the government in respect of South West Africa grew progressively stiffer in the critical years 1937–9, and equally there is no doubt that this was a major factor in determining the attitude of some of its principal members to German expansionist policies elsewhere.

South West Africa posed a difficult problem for the opposition. Concerned above all to maintain South African neutrality in a European war, the Purified Nationalists none the less endorsed the view that South West Africa 'belongs naturally to the Union'. It should not, however, be retained by force. If German claims in respect of South West Africa were not pressed, that would be the most satisfactory solution, but if they were, then the policy of the Nationalist opposition was, in the words of Mr. Strydom[2] at the 1937 Transvaal Nationalist Congress, 'not to give back South West Africa to Germany; but we say we will not lift a finger to prevent Germany from taking it back if she insists'. 'Nationalists', said Dr. van der Merwe[3] in the same year, 'are not prepared to shed a single drop of Afrikaner blood to retain the country.' If war was necessary to keep South West Africa, the Union must not fight. Germany's colonial claims, said Dr. Malan, 'could not and should not be denied'.[4] But should they be pressed it would certainly raise awkward questions, for as Dr. Malan himself had observed:

> . . . in view of the fact that the majority of the people in South West [Africa] come from the Union it would create a new and serious racial problem in South West if we should return that territory to Germany. . . . We must try to obtain the co-operation of Germany with a view to a friendly solution under which the future of South West Africa will be vested in the Union. We must, through the League of Nations and by other means, give our moral support to a scheme that will satisfy Germany's colonial needs.[5]

'Moral support' was not altogether conceived as a substitute for material action, though the Purified Nationalists and some members of the government, notably Mr. Pirow, hoped that the material sacrifices necessary to compensate Germany for the permanent loss of South West Africa might be made by other Powers.

[1] Quoted in Royal Institute of International Affairs, *Germany's claim for Colonies*, 2nd ed. (London, 1939) p. 74. This booklet contains much useful information.

[2] *The Times*, 8 October 1937.

[3] ibid. 15 October 1937.

[4] *Daily Telegraph*, 10 November 1938.

[5] Quoted in *Round Table*, December 1937, vol. 28, p. 189.

THE SOUTH AFRICAN REACTION TO THE GERMAN DEMAND FOR THE RETURN OF ALL HER FORMER COLONIES

Opinion in the Union, particularly Afrikaner opinion, was much concerned with the ethical aspect of the colonial question. Germany's deprivation of all her colonial territories in 1919 seemed to many of them one of the crowning injustices of Versailles. When, therefore, Hitler raised the colonial question, he had many sympathizers in South Africa, all the more so since his language on this issue tended for the most part to be studiously moderate till the end of 1938. Thus in 1935, when Mr. Pirow, in welcoming German officers and men from the visiting cruiser *Emden*, expressed the hope that 'Germany will again become a colonial Power in Africa',[1] he was voicing a sentiment widely shared, though many would have wished his own addendum, 'how, where, and when this can be accomplished cannot at the moment be determined', to have been more precisely phrased.

There were indeed cogent reasons why the Union should consider very carefully how the colonial problem might be solved. Apart from its direct responsibility for the mandated territory of South West Africa, its future security was equally bound up with the ultimate fate of Tanganyika. German reacquisition of that territory would cut in half imperial air communications from north to south; it would drive a wedge between the Union and British colonial territories in East Africa; it would endanger sea communications in the Indian Ocean; it might involve the training and arming of coloured troops. All these considerations made the return of Tanganyika to an expansionist, militarist Nazi state something to be resolutely opposed on practical grounds. It was with this in mind that Pirow declared in 1936: 'In no circumstances can South Africa or Great Britain envisage the return of either Tanganyika or South West Africa to Germany. We are at work hand in hand with the rest of the British Empire in a common defence policy, and in this respect South Africa is to be elder brother to the rest of British Africa.'[2]

Yet such considerations of security were balanced at least until 1938 by the widespread Afrikaner sympathy with German claims. It was a desire to give practical evidence of good will without endangering South African security that prompted speculation about possible compensation for Germany elsewhere. Thus it occurred to not a few that if the smaller European Powers, and Portugal and Belgium seemed the obvious victims, were prepared for some redistribution of their colonial territories as a suitable contribution to the cause of appeasement, a way of escape satisfactory to South Africa at least might be discovered. But were the small colonial Powers prepared for such sacrifices? And even if they were would Germany be satisfied? These were not uncongenial avenues for exploration, satisfying to tender consciences, and yet precluding any sacrifice of South African security or territorial aspirations.

[1] *Manchester Guardian*, 24 January 1935.
[2] *The Times*, 13 August 1936.

The German government noted not without interest South Africa's conciliatory attitude in respect of Germany's colonial claims, but, while anxious to draw what advantage they could from it, were under no illusions about the capacity of the Union government to offer or to secure adequate compensation for any final renunciation on their part of their revived claims to South West Africa. This was brought out clearly in a memorandum dated 31 October 1937 from von Mackensen, at that time Secretary of State at the German Foreign Office, to Herr Leitner, German minister in Pretoria, instructing him none the less to encourage Union ministers to commit themselves to views favourable to Germany on the colonial question. In general this memorandum shrewdly assessed the determining factors in South Africa's attitude towards Germany, its author rightly sensing that in the conflict between sympathy and self-interest the scales were weighted against Germany. The relevant passages read as follows:[1]

The Union of South Africa, in contrast to other mandatory Powers, has repeatedly attempted to enter into discussion with the German government regarding Germany's colonial claims. It has taken the viewpoint that the German claim should be discussed not only for political reasons, but because it is also legally justified to the extent that Germany could bring a claim for compensation as a result of failure to recognize a part of its demands. . . .

Consequently the government of the Union first was of the opinion that it could, in a separate discussion with the German government, negotiate an advance renunciation of South West Africa in exchange for a promise of political support in the assertion of our other colonial demands. With the whole question still completely open, such an agreement would have prejudiced our legal standpoint over against the other mandataries—the aim of which is the re-establishment of the *status quo ante*. Furthermore, at the same time as it was seeking to draw us into a discussion concerning the future of the mandated territory of South West Africa, the government of the Union was preparing special measures against the Germans in South West Africa—measures which, in their origin, could not be separated from the desire of the Union to administer the mandated territory as a fifth province of the Union. It was therefore impossible to give any practical effect to the proposals of General Hertzog in 1936. But, quite apart from this, a discussion with the Union concerning such a *pactum de contrahendo* would not have had any practical result, since the Union would not be in a position to compensate us suitably from her own resources for the renunciation of South West Africa which they were seeking; since we refuse absolutely to let ourselves be fobbed off on to other colonial states which are not mandataries for our former colonies; and since the idea of a financial settlement for a German colonial territory with a considerable German population is a thing we cannot even discuss.

Recently there has been a change in the attitude of the Union which is obviously the result of the discussion of German colonial claims at the British Empire Conference. The Union is no longer thinking of separate negotiations with the German government but has permitted itself to be persuaded by the government of Great

[1] *Documents on German Foreign Policy, 1918–45*, Series D, vol. 1, pp. 22–23.

Britain that a discussion regarding the satisfaction of German claims should be conducted only in connexion with other unsettled questions. . . . The statesmen of the Union are evidently of the opinion that they could somehow play the part of the honest broker between us and the British government, for General Hertzog brings up the influence he is able to exert in London. Whether such influence exists and how far it extends in practice the Union has not yet demonstrated to us. It is also to be feared that the attitude of the London government would merely be rendered more obdurate, if it should get the impression that *we* were using the Union in the colonial question and attempting to play it off against London. Nevertheless, in view of the negative attitude of the other mandatory Powers, it would be a mistake if we failed to derive some advantage from the fundamentally positive attitude of the Union and did not get the Union to commit itself as much as possible to the views which we consider favourable. If the idea of a separate discussion regarding South West Africa is put aside by the Union in favour of a solution of the colonial question within a larger framework, we should not avoid the issue.

There are two points of especial interest in this memorandum. The first is the initiative taken by the Union government before 1937 in exploring the possibilities of a colonial settlement satisfactory to Germany. It is not clear how far the United Kingdom government was kept informed in detail of such conversations, but it may be presumed that they knew at least informally that they were taking place, and it is probable that they were not discouraged in the still comparatively favourable atmosphere of 1935–6.[1] The inherent danger of separate negotiations with a powerful and unscrupulous state loomed much larger in 1937. The second point of outstanding interest in the German memorandum is German awareness of the change in attitude of the Union government after the Imperial Conference of 1937. This is of great significance and forcibly illustrates the value of imperial consultation on foreign policy at the highest level.

The German government were right in concluding that South Africa had in fact little to offer except general good will. The first allusions to the possibility of some redistribution of colonial territory for the purpose of satisfying German claims elicited the most indignant refusals to contemplate the necessary sacrifices on the part of those who feared they might be the intended victims.[2] Even more fatal were the objections of Germany herself. She did not want compensation; she wanted her former colonies returned. In a dis-

[1] It is to be remembered that General Hertzog visited London in 1935 for King George's Silver Jubilee celebrations, and no doubt that visit afforded opportunities for discussion which were not neglected.

[2] cf. statement by Jonkheer de Graeff, Netherlands Minister for Foreign Affairs, 19 February 1936: 'Never, never will Holland cede one square inch of her territory, even to serve the claims for expansion of other nations'; and the declaration by the Portuguese Government on 29 January 1937: 'We will neither return, cede, lease, or partition our colonies, either conditionally or unconditionally. . . .' The Belgian Prime Minister, M. van Zeeland, in a statement made on 25 February 1936 was equally emphatic.

patch dated 16 December 1937 the German minister impressed upon Berlin the need for clarification on this point if Germany was to derive full advantage from South Africa's admittedly dwindling anxiety for a settlement of Germany's colonial claims.[1]

As far as the problem in general is concerned, the greater part of the public considers a settlement of the colonial question necessary. Only the liberalistic British elements maintain a negative attitude. Recently, however, the desire for a quick settlement has decreased appreciably. In view of the favourable developments in Europe, fears of warlike complications particularly have decreased and the primary motives for a colonial settlement, in order to prevent war, or to avoid participating in a British war, have faded into the background. At the same time, the nationalistic Boer elements, the very ones which are most strongly in favour of a settlement, are becoming more and more restrained in the course of the domestic political campaign.

As far as the specific aspects of the problem are concerned, on the other hand, the return of the mandated territory of South West Africa is rejected by the greater part of the public. Occasionally, the idea of a settlement by indemnification or compensation is entertained. Belief in the possibility of such a settlement has grown because there has recently been an increasing tendency to count on German readiness to compromise for a Central African colonial empire. There is a disposition on the part of some in the nationalist Boer camp to disinterest themselves regarding South West Africa. By leaning politically toward a German South West they believe they will obtain an unconditional guarantee of neutrality in the case of a British war, that they will facilitate a more independent position in relation to England for the Union and the incorporation of the protectorates, and that they will receive German support in the treatment of the race problem. But they do not like to admit this disinterestedness publicly and it might not be possible to put it into practice at the present time or in the near future, since in view of the present prosperity of the territory, the conviction of the economic value of South West Africa is growing, since there is widespread fear for military reasons of having Germany for a neighbour, and, last but not least, since the retention of South West Africa has now become a question of prestige for the Union. . . . The opposition here to the return of the latter territory [Tanganyika] has stiffened very much since Italy established herself in Abyssinia.

It seems to me that a clarification of Germany's intentions regarding South West Africa would be very desirable, in order to dispel from the minds of the people here the idea of German readiness to compromise, to strengthen the undercurrents in the nationalistic camp and, above all, to reactivate support for settlement of the colonial question and to restore the pressure on London by the Union to this end.

Two months later in his speech of 20 February 1938[2] the German Chancellor expressly declined to admit 'that certain definite natural demands are connected with political bargaining which has no bearing on them. In the year 1919 there was imposed on several nations a treaty which involved violent

[1] *Documents on German Foreign Policy, 1918–45*, Series D, vol. 1, pp. 128–9.

[2] At Augsburg.

interference with national communities and property rights to an extent hitherto inconceivable', and it was only by redress of the particular wrongs then done that Germany could be appeased. Even this was perhaps hardly so emphatic a declaration as the German minister in Pretoria desired, and the possibility of some general colonial settlement not involving the return of South West Africa or of Tanganyika to full German sovereignty was still widely entertained in South Africa, and indeed in official quarters in London. Yet it was the restoration of Germany's former colonies that the Reich intended one day to demand. On this point the German documents tell a clear and coherent story. When on 13 January 1938 the United Kingdom ambassador informed Baron von Neurath that Mr. Neville Chamberlain 'was firmly resolved to make a positive proposal' about the colonial question when he had had time to consider it and in particular for consultation with the dominions who were also concerned, the German Foreign Minister's response was unconciliatory in the extreme. He declined to relax pressure for the return of Germany's colonies, and 'could only advise Neville Chamberlain to hurry'.[1] In February information reached Berlin of an impending 'generous' offer from London offering Portuguese territory for Tanganyika, for which Portugal would be compensated by British concessions elsewhere, and the return of other erstwhile German colonies excluding, however, South West Africa.[2] On 3 March 1938 Sir Nevile Henderson in the course of a conversation with Hitler, in the presence of Ribbentrop, unfolded the ideas of his government in the colonial field as part of a wider plan for a détente in Anglo-German relations to be brought about by the settlement of outstanding points of difference.[3] The British ambassador opened the conversation by emphasizing its confidential character and the fact that 'no information would be given to the French, much less the Belgians, Portuguese, or Italians, concerning the subject of the discussion'. Then after dealing with vital European issues he went on to express 'the sincere willingness' of his government 'not only to examine the colonial question but to make progress towards its solution'. As evidence of this he submitted a written proposal on behalf of his government which was as follows:

A solution which seemed to them to have many attractions might be found in a scheme based upon the idea of a new regime of colonial administration in a given area of Africa, roughly corresponding to the conventional zone of the Congo Basin treaties, acceptable and applicable to all the Powers concerned on exactly equal terms.

Each Power, while solely concerned for the administration of its own territories,

[1] *Documents on German Foreign Policy, 1918–45*, Series D, vol. 1, pp. 173–4.

[2] ibid. p. 197.

[3] ibid. pp. 240–9. The conversation is also summarized in U.S.S.R., Ministry of Foreign Affairs, *Documents and Materials Relating to the Eve of the Second World War* (Moscow, Foreign Languages Publishing House, 1948) pp. 61–62.

would be invited to subscribe to certain principles designed to promote the well-being of all.

For instance, there would be the question of demilitarization as well as stipulations for the welfare of the natives, and for freedom of trade and communications. Also perhaps a commission might be formed consisting of representatives of all the Powers having territory in the area covered by the new arrangements.[1]

The ambassador explained that the territory in question was bounded on the north by the fifth degree of latitude and on the south by the Zambesi River approximately, and added that a commission might possibly be established to represent those Powers whose colonial territory was within this area. Finally he asked the two vital questions;

first, whether Germany was prepared in principle to participate in a new colonial regime as provided for by the British proposal, and

second, what contribution she would be prepared to make to the general peace and security of Europe.[2]

Hitler's interest in these proposals would appear to have been lukewarm and he may even have had some difficulty in following them. The ambassador, however, demonstrated first on a map, and then on a globe, what they would have involved, explaining that all Powers with colonies in this Central African territory would have to accept certain obligations concerning demilitarization, freedom of trade, and the treatment of natives. No doubt these conditions gave a sharper edge to the Chancellor's negative response. According to the German report which was sent to and agreed[3] to by the British ambassador:

The Führer replied that Germany was, of course, primarily interested in the question regarding the disposition of her former colonies. Instead of establishing a new and complicated system, why not solve the colonial problem in the simplest and most natural way, namely, by returning the former German colonies? He, the Führer, must openly admit, however, that he did not consider the colonial problem ripe for settlement as yet, since Paris and London had declared themselves much too firmly opposed to the return. Therefore, he did not want to press the issue either. One could wait quietly for 4, 6, 8, or 10 years. Perhaps by that time a change of mind would have occurred in Paris and London, and they would understand that the best solution was to return to Germany her rightful property acquired by purchase and treaty. The prerequisite for Germany's collaboration in a new colonial regime was, therefore, the return of the former colonies which were legitimately acquired and taken away by treaty.

This answer would seem to have been accepted by the United Kingdom government as final. The return of Germany's former colonies was the condition of her appeasement in the colonial field, and that was regarded as impos-

[1] *Documents on German Foreign Policy, 1918–45*, Series D, vol. 1, p. 242.

[2] ibid. p. 243.

[3] In respect of all that was said on the colonial question, see ibid. pp. 247–50.

sible. For South Africa the German attitude had equally decisive implications. It is known that the Union government were fully consulted in the shaping of the proposals put forward by the British ambassador, and it is reasonable to deduce from General Hertzog's speeches that the constant concern of the Union government to ensure sympathetic consideration for Germany's colonial claims had played no inconsiderable part in prompting them. Their rejection removed all possible ground for negotiation and friendly compromise. When, therefore, Mr. Erasmus, on behalf of the opposition, complained in September 1938 that the German hand 'had been held out for negotiation' on the colonial issue 'but the government has not moved a finger towards it', the second part of his statement was substantially correct.[1] Where South Africa had nothing she was herself prepared to concede, and where Germany rejected all consideration of the compromise solution she favoured, the hand was one which it was dangerous to grasp. Yet Mr. Pirow at least was not wholly convinced either of the danger or even that all possibility of compromise was gone.

SOUTH AFRICA AND THE MUNICH CRISIS

The Union's interest in all matters affecting the future of Africa south of the Equator was direct and in consequence conditioned her policies in a wider field. The revival of German colonial ambitions in Africa, the existence of the Simonstown agreement reacting upon internal strains to which the Fusion government was subjected, combined to determine, almost to predetermine, her reactions to successive crises in Europe. In the councils of the Commonwealth General Hertzog's influence was thrown consistently on the side of conciliation. As early as 1935 he is believed to have impressed upon the United Kingdom government his belief that the Anschluss between Germany and Austria was inevitable and that, therefore, it was wise for Britain and France to rescind the treaty bans against it before they were confronted with irresistible pressure. At the Imperial Conference of 1937 he is recorded as having observed that England and France had no more right to say that Germany and Austria should not coalesce than Germany, for example, would have the right to say that Northern and Southern Ireland should not unite. He is also said to have expressed privately similar views about Germany's claims to the Sudetenland. In a speech in Pretoria in 1937 he attributed the chief responsibility for the persistence of war psychology in Europe to the terms of the Versailles Treaty, and declared that the next European war would be the 'child of Versailles'. In his attitude, therefore, is to be detected a disposition to concede the substance of the German case. German claims to the Sudetenland seemed to him to represent no more than a natural desire to reunite the German *volk* within a greater Reich. With Italy he was less

[1] *J.P.E.*, 1939, vol. 20, pp. 196–7.

concerned, but there, too, he favoured a policy of conciliation. When he was asked in February 1938 to comment on Mr. Eden's resignation, he replied that he was not concerned with it, but expressed full support for Mr. Chamberlain.[1]

General Hertzog's attitude to the Sudeten question reflected the instinctive reactions of Afrikaners irrespective of party allegiance, for the traditional sympathy of some with German aspirations was in this particular instance strongly reinforced by the doctrinal approach of others to questions of racial unity, and by the memories of almost all of their own struggle for racial and linguistic equality.[2] This was a fact of no small importance, for whatever reservations English-speaking South Africa rightly entertained about so sympathetic an interpretation of German aims the composition of the Union European population, with the majority Afrikaans-speaking, meant, as Mr. Pirow rightly observed in September 1938, that no foreign or defence policy would command the support of the bulk of the people unless its scope was explicitly confined to the protection of South Africa and her vital interests.[3] They were not prepared to believe that her vital interests were at stake in the Czech crisis of 1938. But equally it was only too apparent that in the event of a war arising from it in which Britain was involved, the division of opinion on the action South Africa should take would be so sharp that the Fusion government could not survive and internal peace might be endangered. General Hertzog spoke of war, 'the great divider', as 'the thing most to be avoided by South Africa, whose great task was unity'.[4] To this end he was firmly resolved that South Africa should 'never forget that it is not a part of Europe', and that it should not be a protagonist in European quarrels since any identification of South Africa with European causes would be fatal to South African unity and therefore to her own national interests.

In the general election campaign in the spring of 1938 discussion of the implications for South Africa of the drift to war in Europe could not be wholly avoided. The electorate were anxious to know where South Africa stood, and reluctant though many members of the government were to express any considered or detailed opinion, it was not possible to remain altogether silent. Moreover, the Deputy Prime Minister, a man not easily to be restrained either from the expression of his own convictions or from commenting on the world situation, was at some pains to define his own position and the attitude which he thought South Africa should adopt.

[1] *The Times*, 25 February 1938.

[2] cf. *Round Table*, vol. 29, December 1938, p. 52.

[3] 7 September 1938, South Africa, H. of A. Deb., vol. 32, col. 2293. In 1941 it was estimated that the home languages of Europeans were as follows:

English	875,541	Nederlands	6,870
Afrikaans	1,226,382	German	16,506
English and Afrikaans	35,889	Yiddish (including Hebrew)	15,908

See *Handbook of Race Relations in South Africa*, p. 7.

[4] van den Heever, *Hertzog*, p. 275.

There was indeed a fundamental antagonism temporarily glossed over by agreement on particular policies, between General Smuts and General Hertzog. Both, it is true, agreed that relations with Britain rested on voluntary co-operation, not on binding obligations, but where Smuts felt that that co-operation should be deepened and extended in the best interests of South Africa, Hertzog, despite his recognition of the indispensable role of the Royal Navy in the defence of the Union, placed most of his emphasis on the negative aspects of external policy. 'South Africa's co-operation in Europe', he declared in September 1937, 'when and how she shall co-operate, either in peace or war, are questions for South Africa alone to decide.'[1] 'The Union', he said on another occasion, 'has nothing to do with England's defence. The Union is responsible for its own defences only.' Even though he admitted that there might be common interests in the event of war, his reluctance to acknowledge them was unmistakable. Very largely this was due to his continuing preoccupation with status. Through that narrow window he looked out upon the problems of foreign policy, and his constant fear was lest South Africa be drawn into war, not of her own free will, but as a part of the British Empire. For this reason he shied off any appeals to 'obligation' or 'honour' because if once their validity were recognized, what became of South Africa's sovereign independence? By contrast General Smuts, his Deputy Prime Minister, went out of his way during the 1938 election campaign to underline the abiding community of interest between Britain and South Africa. In December 1937, in language reminiscent of Mr. Mackenzie King's, he argued that a binding declaration of neutrality as recommended by Dr. Malan was a fantastic absurdity. 'Can we', he asked, 'remain neutral if attacked? What if we are menaced and involved in great danger? No country in the world makes such declarations or takes such blind strides into the darkness of the future.'[2] On 4 May 1938, at Port Elizabeth, he declared:

If one part of the Empire is in danger the other parts will all stand by the one that is in danger. The policy of South Africa is to stand by our friends loyally and truly. If England is attacked I think that our position is clear. There can be no doubt whatever that if England is in danger all the free dominions will do their duty as they did in 1914. . . .[3]

Later Smuts laid yet more emphasis on this point when he said: '. . . if England should be involved in war, then South Africa will not allow herself to be waited for, and will grant assistance just as she did in 1914, not because we are obliged, but by our decision, from free choice . . . I do not doubt but that that would be the case if such a condition of things arose again.'[4]

The declared policy of the government as the Czech crisis approached its

[1] *Daily Telegraph*, 29 September 1937.
[2] *The Times*, 3 December 1937, report of a speech at Bloemfontein, 2 December 1937.
[3] Quoted, South Africa, H. of A. Deb., vol. 32, col. 1094.
[4] Quoted by Dr. Malan, *J.P.E.*, 1938, vol. 19, p. 907.

climax was that South Africa was free to decide herself whether she would or would not participate in a war in which the other members of the Commonwealth were involved. Ministers were categoric in their assurances that South Africa accepted no responsibility for the policy pursued by Mr. Chamberlain, and that the country remained free to determine its own policy should war come. In reply to Dr. Malan, General Smuts stated in the House of Assembly on 25 August 1938 that:

The policy of the government so far as participation by South Africa in any war was concerned has been repeatedly laid down by the Prime Minister, by me and by other ministers, viz., this, that South Africa will not be involved automatically in any way in a war, that South Africa will only take part in any war when the Parliament of the country has passed a resolution to that effect in the interests of South Africa.[1]

He allowed that a policy of non-commitment in the event of Britain becoming involved in a war over Czechoslovakia was both possible and justifiable: 'We are not in any way bound to take part in such a war if it should break out.' Again he stressed that his election speech of May 1938, from which some sentences have already been quoted, had no relation to a war in which Britain became involved under such obligations as the Locarno pact but applied only to a war where Britain herself was directly attacked.[2] On 6 September General Hertzog stated that the South African government had not consulted or negotiated with the British government to determine what policy Great Britain should pursue over the German-Czech dispute and had not, in consequence become obliged to support Great Britain if she became involved in war as a result of her policy. The preservation of peace was South Africa's aim, and the exercise of restraint by members 'at this critical juncture' was the course of wisdom.[3]

From what has been said it might appear that there existed a substantial measure of agreement between the two partners in the Fusion government on the policy to be adopted should the Sudeten crisis result in war. It is therefore all the more important to define its limitations. Agreement about the issues on which South Africa would not go to war and on the absolute right of her Parliament to decide freely if and when she should go to war did not extend to agreement on what would constitute a *casus belli*. 'It is very clear', said General Smuts in his speech to the House of Assembly in September 1938, 'that if Great Britain is attacked and comes into actual danger . . . not merely that she goes to war in Central Europe as an ally of France—but where England herself is attacked and is in danger . . . that South Africa will help her.' And he added that if he were a member of the government that is the course he would recommend.[4] But would General Hertzog or Mr. Pirow?

[1] South Africa, H. of A. Deb., vol. 32, col. 1677.
[2] ibid. coll. 1677 ff.
[3] ibid. col. 2198.
[4] See *The Times*, 7 September 1938.

Their attitude suggested, at the very least, that it would not be easy to prove to their satisfaction that a direct attack on Britain, even if the phrase were susceptible of precise definition, was a *casus belli* for South Africa, to be justified by reference to the direct interests of South Africa. On 24 September, the morning after Mr. Chamberlain's visit to Godesberg, when the prospect of war seemed imminent, General Hertzog threw little light upon what his own reaction might be if it came. He underlined carefully the fact that General Smuts's assurances referred only to an aggressive attack on Great Britain herself, by which she was endangered, and then expressed his own agreement with them, adding rather cryptically if only because South Africa is a member of the League of Nations. 'As if our obligations under the League of Nations had ceased to exist.'[1] Was his agreement then dependent upon the continued existence of the League?

The emphasis that was placed both by General Hertzog and by General Smuts upon the constitutional aspect was an indication that this at least was a point upon which they could agree without reservation. Both were satisfied that the decision about South Africa's participation in any war should rest with the South African Parliament, and constant reiteration of this view served to underline their agreement in this one, and certainly not unimportant, respect. For the rest the government preserved unbroken silence about its intentions should the Czech crisis lead to war. When on 24 September Dr. Malan complained that the Prime Minister was not, as was his duty, responding positively to requests for some definition of the government's policy, General Hertzog contented himself with the observation that the government did not anticipate things in any way.[2] Within the Fusion party as well as without there was unrest at the continued lack of leadership at so critical a moment. Even on 24 September, the last day of the session, Dr. Malan failed altogether to move the Prime Minister from his resolve not to commit himself to any definite statement. 'This juncture', observed General Hertzog, 'is such a delicate one . . . that I surely may not say anything here which might give cause to making the state of affairs worse.'[3] It is indeed a remarkable fact that a government composed of members holding sharply contrasted views should have been able to maintain its silence at such a time in the face of a militant opposition. In part it was made possible simply by the government's large majority in the House of Assembly, but, as was surmised in political circles at the time, the essential condition was that a private agreement had been reached between the principal leaders of the United party on the policy they should adopt if war came on the Sudeten issue.

In the Munich crisis the role reserved for the cabinet was almost as uninspiring as that permitted to the House of Assembly, which perforce adjourned without any statement of government policy. It was not till 28 September

[1] South Africa, H. of A. Deb., vol. 32, coll. 3585–6.
[2] ibid. col. 3585.
[3] ibid. col. 3583.

that General Hertzog called a formal cabinet meeting, and then he did not invite discussion but placed a declaration of policy before his colleagues. The declaration, which was in his own handwriting, was as follows:

Statement of the attitude to be adopted by the Union of South Africa in the event of war in Europe with England as one of the belligerents: The existing relations between the Union of South Africa and the various belligerent parties shall, so far as the Union is concerned, remain unchanged and continue as if no war were being waged, with the understanding, however, that the existing relationships and obligations between the Union and Great Britain and any other of the members of the British Commonwealth of Nations in so far as those relationships and obligations are the result of contractual obligations concerning the naval base at Simonstown; or of its membership of the League of Nations; or in so far as the relationships, etc., must be regarded *impliciter* as flowing from the free association of the Union with the other members of the Commonwealth, shall remain unaltered and shall be maintained by the Union; and that nobody shall be permitted to make use of Union territory for any purpose calculated to infringe the said relationships and obligations.[1]

General Hertzog informed his colleagues that in the event of war in Europe the Union should adopt the attitude indicated in this declaration, and this was agreed by all the members of the cabinet present. General Smuts, Mr. Havenga, and Mr. Pirow were already in the confidence of the Prime Minister, and it was the assurance of their support which enabled him to deal so summarily in the House with Dr. Malan's persistent inquiries for information about government policy. General Hertzog was indeed on firm ground once he had secured the agreement of General Smuts to a policy certain to command widespread support among Afrikaners.

General Hertzog carefully preserved in Afrikaans and in English the text of the statement agreed by the cabinet, for he attached great importance to it.[2] This was clearly justified, even though the declaration was more an indication of intention than a practical policy. It ignored the question whether the maintenance of South Africa's relations with the British Commonwealth and the fulfilment of her existing obligations would be consistent with non-belligerency, and it presumed that all the belligerents in a major war would respect a declaration of policy, which some of them might have little interest in observing and no moral scruple in disregarding.[3] The agreement was in fact a device for shelving differences within the cabinet, not for resolving them. Did it not assume a localized war? And was not a localized war in fact highly improbable? And once the war engulfed Western Europe and involved

[1] Reprinted in van den Heever, *Hertzog*, p. 275.

[2] ibid.

[3] It is not, of course, to be doubted that even with the reservations set out in General Hertzog's memorandum a policy of non-belligerency would have been greatly to the advantage of Germany, and to that extent Germany would have had an interest in respecting it until she deemed herself sufficiently strong to adopt other courses.

Britain directly, General Smuts was committed to recommend a very different course of action in which he would presumably have been assured of support in the House of Assembly comparable to that which he received a year later. The one firm conclusion, therefore, to be drawn from South African reaction to Munich is that from the South African point of view, the Sudeten issue was far from an ideal one on which to take a stand. On that all South African political leaders were agreed.

General Smuts's agreement to the policy embodied in the Prime Minister's memorandum is surprising and deserves further examination. No doubt he was greatly influenced by a desire to preserve internal unity and the Fusion Ministry which was its symbol. But to a greater extent his attitude would appear to have been determined by his assessment of German aims. An analysis of his speeches in the years preceding the Munich crisis makes it clear that, like Hertzog, he did not anticipate an early war. In March 1936 he expressed the view that the nations were moving not towards war but towards a state of armed peace which would be without precedent.[1] In December 1936 he said he did not believe 'there will be war tomorrow or the following day', even though certain nations had elected to travel a dangerous path. 'The big dogs are only barking', he said, but 'big dogs do not like to fight one another.'[2] After Munich, while acknowledging how close war had come to Europe, his confidence remained largely unimpaired. 'While I do not say that there will be no trouble and no unrest for some time, I think we are in for years of peace and quiet.'[3] This sanguine interpretation of events derived fundamentally from a feeling that the Germans had been unjustly treated at Versailles, and while Nazi methods were to be condemned, their aims could not be so easily judged so long as they were confined to the recovery of what had been lost, or the union of the German people within one state. For these reasons Smuts was himself far from convinced that the German demand for the Sudetenland should be resisted by force. It was in itself a matter in which South Africa had no interests and no obligations. Yet even if this makes Smuts's acceptance of a policy of non-belligerency comprehensible, it leaves open the question of its wisdom. Had war come in 1938 the government was assured of the support of the opposition for its policy of non-belligerency, for in September 1938 the Nationalists crystallized their demand that South African policy should be one of rigid neutrality. Dr. Malan said that the Nationalists did not believe a word of the 'terrorizing tales', which they constantly heard, about South Africa being placed in danger if 'it did not put its nose into the disputes and wars of Europe'.[4] Opposition insistence on neutrality in itself would have made a subsequent departure from a policy of non-belligerency even in the event of direct German aggression upon

[1] *Manchester Guardian*, 22 March 1936.
[2] *The Times*, 3 December 1936.
[3] *Observer* (London), 30 October 1938.
[4] *J.P.E.*, 1939, vol. 20, p. 733.

Britain difficult in the extreme. By subscribing to such a policy Smuts, therefore, might have made active South African participation in a war arising from the Sudeten crisis virtually impossible under any circumstances.

SOUTH AFRICAN REACTIONS TO THE MUNICH AGREEMENT

The Munich settlement was received with wellnigh universal acclaim in South Africa. In October, after paying tribute to the courage, the persistence, the wisdom, and the tact of Mr. Chamberlain, to whom 'peace in Europe was due', Hertzog ventured the opinion that Mr. Chamberlain had brought peace to Europe 'for the next fifty years'.[1] Though more cautious than his chief, General Smuts, as we have seen, was also optimistic in public. At Johannesburg on 15 October he advocated that the existing 'favourable opportunity should be used to bring about a wider settlement including the colonial question'.[2] And of Mr. Chamberlain's contribution to peace he said: 'We are proud of his achievement. We are proud also that through him, Great Britain, the senior partner of our great Commonwealth of Nations, which appeared in recent years not to be pulling its full weight in world affairs, has once more assumed the moral leadership of Europe.'[3] Mr. Madeley, the Labour leader, was the only political critic of any eminence. He denounced the policy of appeasement, saying that the British Prime Minister's visits to Germany were humiliating to the British Commonwealth of Nations and to all freedom-loving peoples. He warned South Africans that Hitler would never be satisfied with the agreement reached at Munich but would make it a stepping-stone to further aggression.[4] His words provoked only resentment and denunciation. The press, with one exception, applauded the triumph of appeasement. Less fortunate than Mr. Madeley, whose parliamentary seat afforded at least provisional security, was the editor of the *Cape Argus* who in his leading article of 22 September strongly criticized the Munich settlement: 'a problem is not about to be settled, but about to be started.' He was dismissed by the chairman of the Argus Company.[5]

In the crisis of September 1938, all parties, other than the small Dominion party on the extreme right, emphasized South Africa's status as an independent nation and the responsibility which she had to decide her own course. Yet, throughout the pre-Munich debates the deliberate restraint of the government sufficed to discourage informed discussion of the wider issues involved in the European crisis and their significance for South Africa. This was to prove of no little importance a year later. The emphasis on the exercise of national responsibility was not matched by a corresponding emphasis on the need to ensure that it should be rightly exercised.

The Munich settlement confirmed General Hertzog in his opinion of the

[1] *The Times*, 21 October 1938. [2] ibid. 17 October 1938.
[3] ibid. 30 October 1938. [4] *J.P.E.*, 1939, vol. 20, p. 734.
[5] H. Lindsay Smith, *Behind the Press in South Africa* (Cape Town, Stewart, 1946) pp. 92–94.

wisdom of appeasement. By it peace had been maintained in September 1938, and by it it should be preserved in the future. When Mr. Neville Chamberlain informed the House of Commons in November 1938 of his intention to bring the Anglo-Italian agreement into force, he referred to a message received from General Hertzog which said that the South African government had noted the intentions of the United Kingdom government 'with much satisfaction', and had felt that the steps it proposed to take 'are wise and necessary and will contribute materially to appeasement in Europe'.[1] No such approval was, however, forthcoming for the steps which Britain took to rearm.

MR. PIROW'S VISIT TO EUROPE

It is difficult to understand how, after the conversation of 3 March between the British ambassador and the German Chancellor,[2] the substance of which was presumably reported by London to Pretoria, any member of the South African government could any longer have entertained the hope that Germany's colonial claims could be disposed of either by bringing colonies under some general form of international control in which Germany would participate, or even by some redistribution of them in Germany's favour. But so it was. In November 1938, as the false dawn of Munich was fading fast, Mr. Pirow set off on a tour of Europe's capitals still cherishing some such illusion, at least so far as South West Africa was concerned. On Pirow's arrival in London, the German ambassador advised his government that while Pirow was believed to recognize in principle that Germany's colonial claims would have to be satisfied by the return of her former colonies, he wished to see her claim to South West Africa settled by other means.[3] What exactly Pirow had in mind remains uncertain. Belgium and Portugal, their fears revived, reasserted their resolve to make no sacrificial gesture. Shortly before Pirow's arrival in Lisbon Dr. Salazar declared that 'no discussion of Portuguese colonial sovereignty is admissible'.[4] On 31 October the Belgian Minister of Colonies declared: 'We did not steal the Congo from anybody, and nobody will steal it from us.... The Congo is Belgian and will remain Belgian.' If these declarations were to be accepted as final, the only possible alternatives were either that Britain and France would make the necessary sacrifices in the interests of general appeasement in Europe or that Germany could be persuaded to accept some form of economic or financial compensation for the final abandonment of her claim to South West Africa. Pirow would appear to have excluded neither possibility.[5]

[1] *The Times*, 3 November 1938.

[2] See above, pp. 250–2.

[3] Telegram dated 15 November 1938 from Herr von Dirksen to the Foreign Ministry, reprinted in *Documents on German Foreign Policy, 1918–45*, Series D, vol. 4, no. 268, pp. 331–2.

[4] *The Times*, 17 October 1938. It is, however, worth recalling that in the previous March the British ambassador had expressed his belief that Portugal and Belgium would co-operate in a Central African Colonial settlement. See *Documents on German Foreign Policy, 1918–45*, vol. 1, p. 247.

[5] ibid. vol. 4, no. 268, p. 332.

In view particularly of Pirow's German extraction, his visit to Germany provoked much misgiving both in Britain and in South Africa. He maintained consistently that he had no colonial mission, but many believed that he favoured an 'African Munich'. The principal purpose of his visit, however, was consultation about South African rearmament and trade, but he was, as we know from the published German records of his conversations, rightly assumed to be not unwilling to embark on the discussion of broader issues and particularly of the nature of a possible colonial settlement. Here the atmosphere was not altogether encouraging. While his welcome by Herr Funk, the Minister for Economic Affairs, by General Keitel, by Herr von Ribbentrop, by Field Marshal Göring, and later by Herr Hitler at Berchtesgaden, left little to be desired, German press comment about the possibility of any modification of Germany's colonial claims was chill and forbidding. 'The German Reich in Africa', observed the *National Zeitung*, Göring's mouthpiece, 'will not come into existence at the expense of smaller European colonial nations, who, in the course of their history, have set themselves a task in which they must not be interfered with.'[1] The only plan acceptable to Germany was the unconditional surrender of all her former territories in Africa. In this the press faithfully reflected the views of the government.

When Pirow saw von Ribbentrop on 18 November the German Foreign Minister did not encourage any discussion of the colonial question, merely observing that the matter did not seem to him to be acute and could be considered in five or six years' time.[2] A more discursive conversation with Hitler[3] at Berchtesgaden on 24 November was no more fruitful. Pirow, who throughout his visit showed himself to be much concerned with the plight of the Jews, suggested that Germany should propose one of her former colonies as an area for their resettlement. This, he argued, would create a new situation in the international discussion of the colonial problem. It was not, however, an idea that appealed to the Führer, who said that the German people 'would not understand why areas in which the blood of so many German heroes had been shed . . . should be put at the disposal' of their bitterest enemies. He then inquired how it was that South Africa did not understand that South West Africa should be returned to Germany. Pirow replied that South Africa was willing to negotiate. 'We want Germany to get exactly what she had.' But South West Africa, though an economic liability to the Union, was of great military and strategic importance. 'South Africa did not want to go to war with Germany over South West Africa; she would rather obtain other areas for Germany in exchange.' Hitler then asked what was the position about East Africa. But here, too, Pirow was discouraging. East Africa he described as being already integrated, as a result of its internal relations, in the

[1] Quoted in the *Manchester Guardian*, 17 November 1938.
[2] *Documents on German Foreign Policy, 1918–45*, Series D, vol. 4, no. 270, p. 385.
[3] ibid. no. 271, pp. 336–41.

great stretch of territory of the European Africans, which extended in a chain from Abyssinia to the Cape. It was 'a community of a white master race as opposed to the negroes'. But when Hitler asked if Germany would constitute any exception there Pirow was commendably frank. He recognized that the Germans 'would represent and defend the view of the whites' but they would also certainly stand outside the community of white people. 'They would always be Germans first and Africans[1] second whereas the Africans had a feeling of independence.' At this point Hitler broke off the discussion on colonies with the customary observation that it was useless to go on discussing the colonial question now, and that it would have to be brought up in five or six years' time. It was this which no doubt prompted Pirow's subsequent comment that nowhere in Europe had he found 'any desire to regard this matter (the colonial question) as urgent'.[2]

Before Mr. Pirow left for Germany he had come to the conclusion, shared by many of his Nationalist colleagues in the Fusion Ministry, that in the event of a war arising out of German ambitions in Central or Eastern Europe, South Africa should not take any active part. At Berchtesgaden he emphasized 'the very great efforts for peace' which South Africa had made during the Czech crisis, and he urged Hitler to help 'such men of good will as Chamberlain and Halifax', upon whose continuance in office good relations between Britain and Germany depended, by a conciliatory gesture, all the more timely because Germany was now the leading world Power. When Hitler modestly demurred, saying he knew the limits of his power and would call Germany not the greatest Power in the world but in Europe, Pirow remained insistent that 'for him Germany was the greatest Power in the world', and it was because of that that she should take the initiative. 'Britain today was the second nation in Europe, Germany the first. The Führer should give Britain time to get used to this idea.' The gesture Pirow asked for was a positive contribution to the solution of the Jewish problem. This suggestion provoked a long tirade from Hitler which concluded with the assertion that in the 'whole terrible struggle' against the Jews he had no deed of violence on his conscience. 'What do you think would happen in Germany, Mr. Pirow, if I withdrew my protecting hand from the Jews? The world could not imagine it.' With this nauseating nonsense Pirow had perforce to remain content, for while Hitler allowed that Chamberlain and Halifax were 'dancing on a tight-rope', Pirow's anxious pleas for a more sympathetic German appreciation of the delicacy of their position left him wholly unmoved. But Pirow's concern affords none the less instructive evidence of the importance attached by Nationalists within the Fusion Ministry to the continuing success of the policy of appeasement. In this respect he faithfully reflected the views of his Prime Minister.

[1] i.e. the European Africans, to adopt Pirow's terminology.
[2] *Manchester Guardian*, 27 November 1938.

From Berlin Pirow proceeded to Rome, where the colonial question was not discussed and where he made an unfavourable impression. 'It had been impossible', complained Count Ciano to the German ambassador[1] in Rome, 'to conduct any serious conversation with this man who was floundering about in world history.' Mussolini, for whom Pirow had proposed the unexpected role of mediator between Hitler and the Jews, spoke of him as 'an outstanding example of the rapidity with which a race living in another latitude could deteriorate'. 'Pirow', he remarked, 'was quite right when he always described himself as an African.' This was a hard verdict by a dictator on a man whose admiration for the dictators was soon to be openly proclaimed. But about essentials Pirow was not in fact deceived. He recognized that appeasement was likely to fail. On his departure from London early in December he said that he was leaving Europe 'with a feeling of almost unqualified anxiety'.[2] 'The only gleam of hope' lay in the fact that Mr. Chamberlain would spare no effort to secure a lasting basis for peace, and that 'his phenomenal success' at Munich might enable him to achieve the wellnigh impossible. But, he added in words that he had used to Hitler, Britain has made all the advances which can reasonably be expected, and a gesture should now come from one of the other parties to the Munich agreement. His views were dismissed by many in Britain and in South Africa as alarmist; they caused indignation in Germany. But this time, as least, Mr. Pirow was more clear-sighted than his critics.

Mr. Pirow's European tour did not lack a negative importance. It introduced a harsh note of realism into South African discussion of German colonial claims and served to dispel the comforting illusion that Germany might be satisfied with a redistribution of other people's colonies in place of the restoration of her own. When it was recognized beyond doubt that Germany could not be bought off in this way, the attitude of the Union perceptibly hardened.

Mr. Pirow's tour of Europe had other consequences. He returned as unimpressed with the state of British rearmament as he was impressed with the military might of Germany. If war came, he did not doubt that Germany would win. That was a fact of no small importance in the determination of General Hertzog's future policy. It was, however, partly counterbalanced by another unforeseen consequence of Mr. Pirow's visit to Europe. It discredited Mr. Pirow. His standing within the United party was thereby fatally impaired. Always an uneasy and difficult colleague, he had overplayed his hand and not a few welcomed the opportunity of undermining his influence. A fluent speaker, an able lawyer whose piloting of the Status Bill through the House of Assembly won general and deserved acclaim, ambitious, with a pronounced liking for spacious policies and the grandiose, he was ill fitted to sustain any check to his political ambition. The spectacle of

[1] *Documents on German Foreign Policy, 1918–45*, Series D, vol. 4, no. 272, p. 342.
[2] *The Times*, 9 December 1938.

dictatorship in Europe, which he had witnessed in the hey-day of its ruthlessness and its power, fascinated his authoritarian mind, and when in 1939 he found himself ousted from the exercise of power he had grown to love too well, he was fatally tempted to try to return by those same means which had brought Hitler and Mussolini to the pinnacle of personal greatness. But here he misjudged his country and his countrymen, and it was to be his melancholy destiny to spend succeeding years in fruitless intrigue on the sordid fringe of South African political life.

SOUTH WEST AFRICA: THE NAZI CHALLENGE ANTICIPATED

Events on South Africa's own borders after Munich did not suggest that Nazi Germany was finally appeased. The subversive activities of Nazi agents in South West Africa were not lessened but markedly extended in the winter of 1938–9 and when, in the early spring of 1939, the government received intelligence from overseas of the danger of a *Putsch*[1] to establish German control over the territory, the time for resolute action had clearly come. General Smuts, as Minister of Justice, with the approval of Parliament incorporated the South West African Police in the Union Police Force so that the latter might be used in the mandated territory. This action had a tranquillizing effect,[2] and if the Nationalists condemned it on the ground that the Germans in South West Africa were profoundly peaceful in outlook, they received from Mr. Burnside, a Labour member, the unanswerable rejoinder that if they were indeed a peaceful people, he would not like to see a warlike one.[3] Public opinion, including Nationalist opinion, was indeed sufficiently aware of what had happened under not dissimilar circumstances in Europe to welcome decisive precautionary action. A stiffening in General Hertzog's tone was symptomatic of this shift in opinion. He said:

> So far as South West is concerned, if the enemy were to come in and lay its hands on South West, notwithstanding the trust which has been imposed on us to see that South West is protected against injustice, the opposition would have us rejoice at having to hand over South West and to run away from it. I want to tell hon. members we will not run away from South West just as little as we will run away from the Union. We will protect our subjects there just as we protect the subjects of the Union; and whether he (the leader of the opposition) and his followers co-operate with us or not, that will not in the least prevent us, if the time comes, when we see that we have to defend our country and our people.[4]

However great, therefore, might be the Prime Minister's own anxiety to remain aloof from European disputes, by 1939 he was evidently convinced that such detachment was not possible in respect of dangers nearer home. There was indeed a growing contrast in the South African reaction to events in

[1] See *Round Table*, vol. 29, pp. 861–2.
[2] ibid.
[3] *J.P.E.*, 1939, vol. 20, p. 723.
[4] ibid. p. 725.

Europe and to the repercussions of those events in Africa. Consistently conciliatory in relation to the former, they were in practice progressively more resolute where South Africa's immediate interests were concerned.

SOUTH AFRICAN OPINION AND THE ABSORPTION OF CZECHOSLOVAKIA

The German destruction of an independent Czechoslovakia brought near to the surface the underlying differences in South African opinion on foreign policy. Here was aggression, naked and unashamed, to be condoned neither by reference to the iniquities of Versailles nor by a fundamental urge for the reunion of the Germanic people. General Smuts understood its significance. For him March 1939 was the decisive turning-point, but it was not so for General Hertzog. Only silence and inaction could thereafter preserve the unity of the government. It was in the streets of Prague that the Fusion Ministry received its mortal wound.

On 21 March 1939 the Prime Minister said he had not been asked by the British government whether the Union would support her policy following the Nazi occupation of Czechoslovakia, and he declined to allot a day for a debate on foreign affairs on the ground that it would not be wise. The Union government, he explained, had been kept informed by the British government of the more important facts about the European situation, but he was not prepared to make statements of policy with regard to any crisis in which the interests of South Africa were not more closely involved than they were at that time.[1] It was 'very vital and should not be lost sight of' that the government had to do with matters not directly concerning South Africa, but concerning European countries, of whom some were their most intimate friends; and for them to discuss any question which was life and death to those other countries could only be detrimental and do no good either to themselves or to those countries.[2] Yet the possibility of war could not be altogether discounted and in late March 1939 the Prime Minister outlined in carefully considered phrases the circumstances under which he felt the Union might have to define her attitude more positively.

> When and where the activities of a European country are of such a nature or extent that it can be inferred therefrom that its object and endeavour is the domination of other free countries and peoples, and that the liberty and interests of the Union are also threatened thereby, the time will then also come for this government to warn the people of the Union and to ask this House to occupy itself with European affairs, even where the Union would otherwise have no interests or would take no interest in them.[3]

In the opinion of the Prime Minister the time for such positive considered declaration had clearly not yet arrived, though it seems reasonable to conclude

[1] ibid. p. 719. [2] ibid. p. 718. [3] ibid. p. 736.

from his language that the danger from Europe appeared less remote than in the past. His comments undoubtedly led many United party supporters to believe that in the event of further Nazi aggression he would feel the time for action had come and his words were later quoted against him.[1] But it would seem that his language reflected a passing and not an enduring reaction to the absorption of Czechoslovakia. In April, by implication, he retracted earlier doubts in refusing a request from Dr. Malan for a debate on external affairs on the ground that it would be 'irresponsible'. 'At the present moment', he said, 'we are not concerned with them [events in Europe] and we have no interest in the matter, and our interests are not affected in any single respect.'[2] England, he observed, with reference to her guarantees to Poland, Greece, and Roumania, could enter into any treaty, could lay down any policy it desired with regard to Europe, and whether South Africa would approve or disapprove would depend upon whether it affected the interests of the Union.[3] The fact that South Africa had been informed about the guarantee to Poland did not mean that she accepted any obligations. She might, however, give advice as a friend: 'I am proud of the relation of friendship . . . a friendship as between friends and not allies who have entered into an alliance for a certain purpose. We are co-operating in times of peace, and we are trying to act in such a way that our interests coincide as much as possible with each other's.'[4] Yet how far co-operation went in practice was studiously left vague. The Prime Minister admitted, *so far as he could remember*, that he had written a letter to the South African High Commissioner in London to be communicated to the British government about the Polish guarantee, but its contents he was not prepared to divulge. And with this extraordinary half-admission, the House had perforce to remain content. But his views were not in doubt. He feared that the British guarantees in Eastern Europe would be interpreted in Germany as a threat of encirclement and thereby hasten the outbreak of war. For the same reason, but with a conviction sharpened by deep ideological mistrust, General Hertzog was opposed to the Anglo-French negotiations for a military pact with Russia. In this once again he was more concerned that Germany should not be provoked than that her expansionist ambitions should be contained. And so he remained faithful to the policy of appeasement after its principal architect had confessed its failure.

'South Africa first' remained the all-important principle determining the attitude of the South African government towards international affairs up to the outbreak of war. However much Smuts might dissent from its implicit

[1] See, for example, a United Party pamphlet, *South African Nationalism and the War, 1939–45*, pp. 12–13, where General Hertzog's speech of 23 March is described 'as a plain statement' which 'left no doubt in the minds of the United Party that South Africa would be found at the side of the Commonwealth if Hitler persisted with aggression'. (Compiled by the Head Office of the United Party, Pretoria, and issued by O. A. Oosthuisen, General Secretary.)

[2] South Africa, H. of A. Deb., vol. 34, col. 2714.

[3] ibid. coll. 2774–9.

[4] ibid. col. 2779.

isolationism, he had to recognize that it was an issue on which concession was essential if the Fusion government were to survive. As late as June 1939 he told the House of Assembly, 'there seems to be a pause in Europe and we all pray that the pause may be made permanent. It will not serve any useful purpose to indulge in wild declarations now. We are prepared to defend ourselves and South Africa's vital interests.'[1] Silence was the course of prudence, even if it became progressively more difficult to preserve. It was therefore not by those within the government but by those without that the choice the country would soon be called upon to make was stated in all its stark reality. In March 1939, after the Germans had marched into Prague, Mr. J. H. Hofmeyr[2] declared that a struggle was going on in Europe between the ideals of democracy and freedom on the one hand, and the ideals of authoritarianism and dictatorship on the other. He argued that it was futile to suggest that South Africa could avoid that issue; she would have to decide what action she would take. Not so, retorted Dr. Malan, for were not the issues artificial and merely designed to place South Africa in advance on the same side as England? South Africa should not say she would fight if England were attacked or in danger, since such a situation could easily be fabricated. 'We have nothing to do with the merits of this struggle; England may be right or Germany may be right.'[3] In this argument General Hertzog inclined perceptibly to the side of Malan. 'The question of Central Europe,' he said, 'of Czechoslovakia, or anywhere else, has nothing directly to do with South Africa today, and up to the present it has not affected the interests of the Union and the conduct of the Union in the least.'[4] That indeed was a sorry illusion destined to offer protection from realities for the space of six brief months and no more.

SOME GENERAL REFLECTIONS ON SOUTH AFRICA'S EXTERNAL POLICY

In principle the attitude of the Union government towards participation or non-participation in war appeared to approximate very closely to that of Canada. In reality it was very different. Both were insistent that the interests of their own country were paramount, and that Parliament must decide. In one sense South Africa, because of her less sheltered strategic position and more especially because of her liability to a direct challenge arising from a revival of German colonial claims pressed home by threat of war, had less

[1] *The Times*, 17 June 1939.

[2] With Mr. F. C. Sturrock he had resigned from the cabinet the previous September in protest against the blatant disregard of Native interests in General Hertzog's selection of Mr. P. J. Fourie as one of the four government-nominated senators supposed to be well qualified to represent them. cf. *Round Table*, 1938–9, vol. 29, pp. 176–8, for a contemporary reaction, and see also Walker, *History of South Africa*, p. 662.

[3] South Africa, H. of A. Deb., vol. 33, col. 2148, and see generally coll. 2142–8.

[4] ibid. col. 2230.

freedom of action and was more directly concerned to check Nazi aggression than Canada. It was with that in mind that Dr. Malan once criticized Mr. Pirow for sponsoring a defence policy 'in opposition to that of Canada', who wanted 'to maintain and protect her neutrality'.[2] But here Dr. Malan misread the signs of the times. In Canada the concern of Mr. Mackenzie King to ensure that a dissenting minority should not in any way feel that they had been rushed into a war which was not in Canada's interests was well designed, if need be, to serve his ultimate aim of bringing a united country into a war for the defence of Canadian interests or the liberties of mankind. In South Africa, on the other hand, the government could under no circumstances entertain any such hopes of unity in the event of war.

In respect of South African participation in war the guiding principles, to which all members of the Fusion government could assent, were set out by Mr. Pirow on 6 May 1938. He declared:

> We are not bound, directly or indirectly, to take part in any war in Africa or elsewhere. We shall take part in no war except where the interests of South Africa make such participation unavoidable. We, as a government, will not even take part in an inevitable war, except after the people, through their representatives in Parliament, have given us clear instructions to that effect with the utmost possible unanimity.[2]

In practice so long as German policy could be reasonably explained in terms of redressing the wrongs of Versailles or uniting all the German *volk* within one state, these restrictive principles of action afforded a not unsatisfactory basis for unity in external policy, as the agreement of the inner cabinet on the course to be followed in September 1938 had strikingly testified. But the events of March 1939 made the aim of 'the utmost possible unanimity' meaningless. Henceforward the members of the government differed fundamentally in their interpretation of events in Europe and about the attitude South Africa should adopt towards them. All prospect of an agreed national policy thereupon disappeared.

The division of opinion within the government after March 1939 placed ultimate responsibility for the determination of policy upon the House of Assembly. Only by testing the support which the conflicting policies commanded in the House of Assembly could South Africa constitutionally reach a decision. In consequence South Africa was unable to define her attitude in advance of the final crisis without risking the disruption of the government. So long as there existed the remotest prospect of peace in Europe, it seemed rash and unjustified to incur such a risk and so bring to an untimely end the great experiment of Fusion which in six years had achieved so much for the internal peace and prosperity of the Union. Even when in the summer of

[1] *J.P.E.*, 1937, vol. 18, p. 619.
[2] Quoted by Dr. Malan, H. of A. Deb., vol. 32, col. 1671.

1939 it was generally recognized that the issue would almost certainly have soon to be faced, internal political considerations argued strongly against facing it before it was absolutely essential.

The deliberate indecision of the South African government in the face of impending war has encouraged facile, retrospective condemnation on the part of those unfamiliar with the complex problems of this state which was not a nation. General Smuts's Fabian reaction to these problems, expressed in the phrase, 'let them develop', embodied a wise man's faith in the healing hand of time. But more than time was needed; peace was required as well. Not without reason many in South Africa feared the repercussions at home even of a war in a just cause; the awful consequences that might follow were the white man's madness brought to the black man's continent. What happened in Europe could not be viewed apart from its consequences in Africa, and they were incalculable. No country in the Commonwealth, and few outside, had deeper cause to try to weigh carefully the likely consequences of its actions; better reason to reflect long on those great imponderables which must in the course of the years determine the destiny of white civilization in Africa, before taking the decisive steps on the road that led to peace or war, even while also recognizing that in the end reason could be no sufficient guide. For that faith, faith in the future of South Africa, faith in the rightness of the cause she championed, alone would suffice.

CHAPTER VIII

IRELAND: THE TWILIGHT OF DOMINION STATUS

THE DOMINION EXPERIMENT

On 6 December 1921 the Irish Free State, consisting of twenty-six of the thirty-two counties of Ireland,[1] was born. Its constitutional status was that of a dominion. 'Ireland', declared Article 1 of the Anglo-Irish Treaty, 'shall have the same constitutional status in the Community of Nations known as the British Empire, as the dominion of Canada, the Commonwealth of Australia, the dominion of New Zealand, and the Union of South Africa, with a Parliament having powers to make laws for the peace, order, and good government of Ireland, and an Executive responsible to that Parliament, and shall be styled and known as the Irish Free State.' Article 2 of the Treaty provided that 'the position of the Irish Free State in relation to the Imperial Parliament and government and otherwise shall be that of the dominion of Canada, and the law, practice, and constitutional usage governing the relationship of the Crown, or the representative of the Crown and of the Imperial Parliament to the dominion of Canada shall govern their relationship to the Irish Free State'. In conjunction the two Articles at once explicitly assured the new state of the reality of the status conferred upon her by linking it directly with that of the oversea dominions and particularly of Canada, the senior dominion; and implicitly guaranteed by that same association that the status conferred upon her would not be static but evolutionary. In this way the final failure of the experiment of the Union which had lasted for 120 uneasy years was acknowledged, and in its place there was tried as a hopeful solvent of the conflicting loyalties, aspirations, and interests which made up the Irish Question, the experiment of dominion status. By 1936 its failure, less complete, less final, was none the less transparent.

Unlike the oversea dominions the Irish Free State attained dominion status not by a process of evolution but by an act of revolution. Unlike them she had not aspired to that status, and unlike them she was not peopled predominantly by immigrants of British stock. Unlike them, too, she was in her own right a mother country with an ancient and honoured civilization which in the dark centuries that followed the fall of the Roman Empire had helped to spread the Christian Gospel throughout Britain and Western Europe. 'The man', observed Dr. Johnson[2] when first he gazed upon what

[1] 13 Geo. V, c. 1, Articles of Agreement for a Treaty between Great Britain and Ireland, 6 December 1921, Articles 11, 12, 13, and 14. This was its extent in practice; in theory the Irish Free State included the whole of Ireland until Northern Ireland formally opted to remain out.

[2] *Journey to the Western Isles*, 1775.

remained a thousand years later of the great monastic foundation of St. Columba, 'is little to be envied whose patriotism would not gain force upon the plain of Marathon, or whose piety would not grow warmer among the ruins of Iona.' But Irish patriotism quite as much as Irish piety drew strength and inspiration from the memory of the great monasteries that spread from Clonmacnois to Iona, to Lindisfarne, and to the heart of the Frankish dominions. Were the heirs of the saints and scholars of early Christendom freely to acknowledge allegiance to the monarch of that neighbouring island to whose barbarian inhabitants their ancestors had long ago brought culture and civilization? The question was rhetorical, for who in Ireland save 'West Britons', educated in England or at Trinity College, and immigrant Scotsmen in north-east Ulster, could doubt the answer?

Dominion status was an admirable constitutional device which in nationalist Ireland lacked psychological appeal. For that reason it was not the obvious solution to Anglo-Irish relations which learned commentators were retrospectively so apt to assume. It was, on the contrary, a bold experiment whose success was dependent upon imaginative statesmanship upon both sides of the Irish Sea. It was an experiment from whose success or failure much incidentally was to be learned about the adaptability of dominion status to countries which were not *natural* dominions. Once dominion status had become in 1917 the declared goal of British policy in India, the lessons, both positive and negative, of experience in Ireland in guiding British policy in India were considerable. They were in fact almost wholly ignored, partly because the affairs of the Irish Free State were dealt with by the Dominions Office, those of India by the India Office,[1] and still more because the sense of experiment was soon lost. Once the Irish Free State had become a dominion it was all too readily assumed that she was, and should be, a dominion in spirit. Constitutional lawyers, with a deep affection for a well-marked pattern, noted that the Irish Free State often either conformed to it with reluctance or did not conform at all. This was generally attributed to temperamental eccentricities to which Irishmen were deemed to be peculiarly liable, or more rarely to deliberate malice. Yet was not some degree of deviation in form as well as in practice inevitable and even desirable? To Roman Catholic Ireland, nursed on memories of conquest and spoliation, of penal laws, rebellion, and famine, no easy, spontaneous attachment to the Commonwealth was conceivable. The legacy of the past could not in a moment be lightly cast aside. Where for Australians the common Crown was the natural focus of their allegiance, for nationalist Ireland it remained the symbol of alien rule. An imposed oath of allegiance might disguise such differences; it could not remove them. Moreover in disguising them it performed a disservice to Crown and Commonwealth. Resentment and friction followed,

[1] Between these two departments, divided geographically only by the width of a Whitehall quadrangle, there was surprisingly little contact and a marked difference in outlook.

and in their consequences both were in some measure involved. Thus the bold, imaginative outlines of the 1921 Treaty settlement which brought such great and unquestionable benefits to Ireland were prejudiced for the sake of a formula.

Important though the differences between the Irish Free State and the oversea dominions have been, and insufficiently though their implications were realized in the past, it is questionable whether they would themselves have sufficed to cause the breakdown of the experiment of dominion status. Between Britain and Ireland there existed a deep and lasting community of interest which supplied a solid, material basis for co-operation, and might well in time have counterbalanced the psychological difficulties in the way of a whole-hearted Irish acceptance of dominion status. But dominion status laboured under other and greater liabilities. The first was that it came too late, the second that it came as the result of violence, and the third that as a result of Partition it was deprived of strong, coherent support.

THE PRICE OF PROCRASTINATION

'The price of our successors' triumph was Partition—an Ireland divided into a state which is not coterminous with the country, and a province which is itself dismembered. They sacrificed Irish unity for Irish sovereignty and attained neither.'[1] Such is the lament of an unrepentant Redmondite over the victory of Sinn Féin. It is a sobering verdict which many outside Ireland have sincerely endorsed but which the majority inside Ireland have rejected out of hand. The old Nationalist party, to which in the hey day of the uncrowned kingship of Parnell all save the Unionist counties of the north-east gave unquestioning allegiance, was the principal victim of the Easter Rising of 1916, and between the members of that party and its political heirs 1916 fixed a great, impassable gulf. An Anglo-Irishman like Yeats could feel that in the Rebellion of 1916 'a terrible beauty is born';[2] the northern mystic A.E. could offer his more distant tribute:

> Here 's to you, Pearse, your dream not mine
> But yet the thought for this you fell
> Has turned life's waters into wine.[3]

But no romantic afterglow softened the sharp edge of the Redmondite verdict. If it be justified, then there is little need to seek much farther for the reasons why the dominion settlement of 1921 had so chequered and so short a life.

Between 1870 and 1914 Home Rule was the consistent demand of Nationalist Ireland. Though the 86 of '86 was destined to be the high watermark of Home Rule representation at Westminster, for more than forty years more

[1] John J. Horgan, *Parnell to Pearse* (Dublin, Brown & Nolan, 1948) p. 354.
[2] 'Easter 1916.'
[3] Quoted in John Eglinton, *Memoir of A.E.* (London, Macmillan, 1937) p. 119.

than three-quarters of the Irish electorate consistently demanded Home Rule. Yet despite the eloquence of Gladstone and the more wavering allegiance of Campbell-Bannerman and Asquith to the cause the greatest of Liberal leaders had so nobly championed, Westminster was not to be persuaded till too late. Was the hostility of Ulster the pretext or the cause of this prolonged procrastination? On that Irish Nationalists have never been in doubt. It was the pretext; it afforded to the Conservative party the most congenial and, as it proved, decisive argument against Home Rule. In that Nationalist opinion was correct on the admission of the Conservative leaders themselves, but the fact that Ulster opposition to Home Rule was a convenient focal point for Conservative opposition to Home Rule did not dispose of the awkward fact that Ulster Unionists were themselves resolutely opposed to Home Rule in any form.

The third Home Rule bill[1] which reserved to the Imperial Parliament not only full control over defence and foreign affairs but also over customs and the broad field of economic policy, and retained wholly unimpaired the position of the Crown, was bitterly opposed at every stage by the Ulster Unionists, who prepared for armed resistance should it come into force. In this they had the support of one of the historic English parties. At Blenheim on 27 July 1914 Mr. Bonar Law, after describing Mr. Asquith's cabinet as 'a revolutionary committee which seized by fraud upon despotic power', declared that 'in our opposition to them we shall not be guided by the considerations, we shall not be restrained by the bonds which would influence our action in any ordinary political struggle. We shall use whatever means seem most likely to be effective. . . .'[2] If a Home Rule bill conferring powers upon a Dublin government so restricted in scope evoked such violent opposition from Unionist leaders, is it surprising that Irish Nationalists concluded that no compromise short of the sacrifice of their aspirations to national self-government would qualify Unionist antagonism? To those in the Commonwealth who had forgotten the summer of 1914, dominion status, above all the symbolism of the Crown, always seemed to provide a foundation for co-operation between Northern Ireland and the Irish Free State. But to those who remembered—and what Irishman did not?—this conviction appeared to rest on that same illusion which in their day Asquith and John Redmond had cherished and for which they both paid so heavy a penalty.

By 1914, wrote Frank Pakenham,[3] only a miracle could keep Irish nationalism within the bounds of the Redmondite horizon. To many Englishmen John Redmond's gallant pledge to fight by England's side shone out as a

[1] 4 & 5 Geo. V, c. 90. The Act never came into force, its operation being suspended because of the war.

[2] Quoted in N. Mansergh, *Ireland in the Age of Reform and Revolution* (London, Allen & Unwin, 1940) pp. 170–1. For a general consideration of the issues involved see Chapter V, 'The Ulster Question'.

[3] *Peace by Ordeal* (London, Cape, 1935) p. 20.

gleam of light in a darkening sky, but in Ireland it worked no miracle. It brought Home Rule no nearer; it brought North and South no closer together. And for the party which John Redmond led it proved to be a step that led to irretrievable political ruin. The election of 1918 is something no Irish politician ever forgets. The party pledged to secure Home Rule by constitutional means was then wiped out, first because it had allowed itself in 1914 to be forced step by step to contemplate as the 'extremest limit of concession' the exclusion of Ulster for six years, and then because it had committed Ireland to participation in war on the basis of hopes which were not fulfilled. The first would have been forgiven had co-operation in war, to which on the Irish side there was an enthusiastic response at the outset, brought some prompt and tangible recognition of her claims to self-government. But it evoked instead further appeals to patience and delaying tactics which undermined all confidence in the good faith of the British government and, more fatal still, in the ability of the Nationalist party to attain their goal. The conclusion drawn in Ireland after 1914 was quite simply that constitutional action would never succeed.[1] Another conclusion less clear-cut but almost equally important for the future was that however good the cause, unconditional pledges of co-operation in war are a snare likely to lead the unwary to disaster. Mr. de Valera remembered the fate of John Redmond in 1939 and again in 1941; Mr. Costello remembered it in 1949 when Ireland was urged to join the Atlantic Treaty. In general such memories discouraged co-operation with the Commonwealth, by suggesting that the undoubted risks of co-operation were not to be balanced by any assurance that such co-operation was the high road that led to the reunion of Ireland.

In so far as the events of 1914–20 suggested that Irish membership of the Commonwealth would not one day lead to unity, they subtracted significantly from the appeal of dominion status. Nor, in succeeding years, was there any evidence that the Ulster Unionists had modified the grounds of their objection to a united self-governing Ireland. On the contrary, the Unionist objection remained an objection to rule from Dublin; the form of government there, its relation with the Commonwealth, while important factors in the argument, have not constituted the final issue. From the time of Lord Randolph Churchill's flamboyant phrases to the days of Sir Edward Carson's sombre warnings, the aim of the Unionist policy was not to secure special safeguards for Ulster but to defeat Home Rule. 'Ulster', declared Carson, 'will be the field on which the privileges of the whole nation will be lost or won.' Here was the great issue at stake. The Unionists believed in the economic, strategic,

[1] This is aptly illustrated in a story told by Colonel Maurice Moore, about the boy imprisoned after the suppression of the 1916 Rising whom Mr. Asquith visited in jail. The Prime Minister asked him what he thought of the rebellion now, and the boy answered that he thought it a great success. Asquith surprised said, 'How do you make that out?' 'Well, if not, what are you here for?' Socrates, as Colonel Moore observed, could not have answered more wisely. See Horgan, *Parnell to Pearse*, p. 293.

and political unity of the British Isles, and they were outraged at the thought that anything so precious should be sacrificed to appease a nationalist sentiment which, not mistakenly, they sensed as being at root separatist. The Nationalists, on the other hand, asserted in dogmatic, uncompromising language the indefeasible right of the Irish nation to be free and independent. On one point at least, therefore, Unionist and Nationalist were agreed. Their differences were fundamental and hardly to be resolved by a constitutional compromise of the kind to which Englishmen were by temperament so well disposed. If in this they were right, then clearly unity was not sacrificed, as the Redmondite critics have suggested, in a vain struggle for national sovereignty. Its cause had been lost before the Easter Rebellion took place.

THE EXTENT TO WHICH THE EVENTS OF 1920–1 PREJUDICED THE FUTURE OF DOMINION STATUS

When in 1919 Mr. Asquith boldly advocated Dominion Home Rule for Ireland, Mr. Lloyd George retorted, 'Whoever heard such nonsense?' Yet is it not clear in retrospect that it was Mr. Asquith who had displayed a statesmanlike sense of timing? Had the dominion solution been effected early in 1919, then dominion status and membership of a Commonwealth of free and equal nations would have escaped the taint which the two succeeding years of violence laid upon it. The election of 1918, which swept away the old Nationalist party, was a warning which a wiser statesman would not have disregarded. But Mr. Lloyd George, ever mindful of his dependence upon the Conservative members of the Coalition, affected to believe that this result did not reflect considered opinion in Ireland. When the Dáil, though it was unconstitutionally established, enlisted the allegiance of all the popularly elected representatives of Twenty-Six Counties, this interpretation wore a little thin. Yet Mr. Lloyd George was reluctant to depart from it. He proscribed the Dáil, and proceeded by means which outraged liberal opinion in England, to suppress the revolt. Once the small 'nest of assassins' had been wiped out all would be well. At the Lord Mayor's banquet in November 1920 he declared triumphantly, 'We have murder by the throat.' As late as May 1921 the Chief Secretary, Sir Hamar Greenwood, assured the House that the government would not rest till they had 'plucked the last revolver out of the last assassin's hand'.[1] A month later the policy of repression was abandoned with singular abruptness. 'No British government in modern times', commented Mr. Churchill later, 'has ever appeared to make so complete and sudden a reversal of policy. . . .'[2] The reversal achieved fruitful results. Within six months the Anglo-Irish Treaty was negotiated, and relations between Britain and Ireland were established on a new and happier

[1] Quoted in Pakenham, *Peace by Ordeal*, p. 73.

[2] *The Aftermath, sequel to the World Crisis* (London, Macmillan, 1941) p. 290.

footing. But from the wider aspect of Ireland's long-term relations with the Commonwealth the outcome was not so fortunate.

Dominion status was the essential feature of the settlement of 1921. But even after the opening of negotiations in June 1921 the offer was not unambiguous. In the protracted, astringent correspondence[1] between Mr. Lloyd George and Mr. de Valera which preceded direct negotiations, the Prime Minister expressed his hope 'that the Irish people may find as worthy and as complete an expression of their political and spiritual ideals within the Empire as any of the numerous and varied nations united in allegiance to His Majesty's Throne'. But for a self-conscious nationalist Ireland which claimed, in Mr. de Valera's words, that 'her right to choose for herself the path she shall take to realize her own destiny must be accepted as indefeasible', a dominion status which permitted 'no protective tariffs' made no very cogent appeal. As Mr. de Valera commented fairly enough, 'the principle of the pact is not easy to determine'. In subsequent negotiation the British government, by conceding full dominion status and safeguarding it in the Treaty by the direct association of the status of the Irish Free State with that of Canada, made it so. Yet the earlier use of the phrase 'dominion status' to gild something that was not dominion status at all, left its taint and instilled suspicions of which the republican dissidents were only too ready to take advantage.[2]

More far-reaching in consequence was the manner in which the negotiations which led to the signature of the Treaty were concluded. Mr. Churchill later maintained that in 1921 the British government had two alternatives before it in its Irish policy—'war with the utmost violence or peace with the utmost patience'. It is generally accepted that Mr. Lloyd George adopted each in turn. But is it true? Did he in fact wage war with the utmost violence? The answer is surely in the negative. Opinion at home did not permit him to do so. 'Persistence in the present methods of Irish government', protested *The Times*, 'would prove utterly irreconcilable with the ideals of this Christian country.'[3] 'If the British Commonwealth can only be preserved by such means', declared the *Round Table*, 'it would become a negation of the principle for which it has stood.' The 'utmost violence' was a policy public opinion would not tolerate. Again after the dramatic reversal in policy signalized by King George V's speech in Belfast in June 1921, did the British government pursue a policy of peace 'with the utmost patience'? The answer would seem

[1] Cmds. 1470, 1502, 1539, 1561.

[2] Even after 1931 Irish opinion was never persuaded that dominion status conceded full independence. Professor Denis Gwynn, for example, writing after the London Declaration of April 1949, observes: 'It is obvious that the special arrangement which was made in regard to India must be offered sooner or later, to the Republic of Ireland, or to any other Dominion which may desire to proclaim its full independence' (*The History of Partition, 1912–25* (Dublin, Browne & Nolan, 1950) pp. 13–14). If by 1950 Professor Gwynn believed that Canada and Australia did not enjoy full independence the opinion of the ordinary Irishman may well be imagined.

[3] Quoted in Pakenham, *Peace by Ordeal*, p. 62.

also to be in the negative. Patience was not numbered among Mr. Lloyd George's many qualities, and in negotiation with Mr. de Valera patience was most exactingly tested. In after years the question recurred; was Mr. Lloyd George, however prolonged the Treaty negotiations, however slow the Irish delegation to reach firm conclusions, wise in the end to impose a settlement by a threat of war? It was, as Mr. Churchill has recalled, at No. 10 Downing Street on the afternoon of 5 December 1921 that Mr. Lloyd George told the Irish that the British 'could concede no more and debate no further. They [the Irish delegates] must settle now; they must sign the agreement for a Treaty . . . or else quit . . . and both sides would be free to resume whatever warfare they could wage against each other.'[1] Though the Irishmen 'gulped down the ultimatum phlegmatically'[2] it was in its way as decisive as von Bülow's ultimatum to Russia in the last stages of the Bosnian crisis of 1909. It may be argued that so beneficial a settlement emerged that the use of the threat of force was well justified.[3] But even so it was not in accord with Mr. Churchill's policy of 'peace with the utmost patience', nor was it fundamentally in accord with the ideals of the Commonwealth. Mr. de Valera may have sketched too dark a picture with his familiar and frequent references to a threat 'of immediate and terrible war',[4] but it is a fact that the threat, however veiled or diluted, was a stigma from which the dominion settlement of 1921 never escaped. While Anglo-Irish relations after 1921 were placed on a new and friendlier footing, Irish relations with the oversea Commonwealth countries never acquired the intimacy which community of interest and outlook made possible, partly because her formal association with them was in some measure conditioned throughout by the inauspicious circumstances under which it began. More than a quarter of a century later the recollection of the consequences so profoundly influenced British policy in India and in Burma that it became almost a commonplace to say in Ireland that her struggle for independence had reached its climax too soon.

THE INFLUENCE OF PARTITION UPON THE WORKING OF DOMINION STATUS

The Government of Ireland Act of 1920[5] which brought into existence the government of Northern Ireland placed within its jurisdiction the counties

[1] *The Aftermath*, p. 305.

[2] ibid.

[3] An Irish writer, Arland Ussher, in a shrewd and discriminating book, *The Face and Mind of Ireland* (London, Gollancz, 1949) p. 3, is not critical. 'Ireland', he writes, 'by her brave endurance over two years showed that she was indeed in earnest; England by not hitting too hard, and by giving way at the right moment did the most a Great Power can be expected to do. It is the only way in which . . . such fateful bargains can be struck. And everything has worked together for Ireland's advantage in the end.' Mr. Ussher is a philosopher but he may none the less well be right in his assessment of the practical issues involved.

[4] cf. *Papers relating to the Parliamentary Oath of Allegiance in the Irish Free State and the Land Purchase Annuities*, Cmd. 4056 of 1932.

[5] 10 and 11 George V, c. 67.

of Antrim, Armagh, Down, Fermanagh, Londonderry, and Tyrone together with the cities of Belfast and Londonderry. The population of the Six Counties was a little more than 1¼ million and comprised 29·7 per cent. of the total population of Ireland.[1] Two-thirds of the population of Northern Ireland belonged to one of the Protestant denominations,[2] one-third to the Roman Catholic Church. Since in the north-eastern counties political and religious loyalties almost wholly coincided, the result was a stable system of local self-government with one party permanently in office and roughly a two-thirds majority against the reunion of Ireland at every election. Local self-government was not welcomed by the Ulster Unionists in 1920. On the contrary they wished to remain an integral part of the United Kingdom directly governed from Westminster. 'The Act of 1920', observed Captain Redmond later, 'was condemned in every corner of Ireland, and it had not even the support of a single Irish member, whether he came from the North or the South.'[3] But if Ulster Unionists regarded the Act without enthusiasm at least they had no doubts that a local, subordinate, parliament of their own was much to be preferred to government from Dublin. Self-government accordingly was accepted by Ulster Unionists as the 'supreme sacrifice', to quote Sir James Craig, because it could be regarded as 'a final settlement'.[4] In the course of time there has, however, been a discernible shift in emphasis. Less has been said about the sacrifice, partly because devolution of administrative power from Westminster has made for government more immediately responsive to the needs of the Six County area, and growing emphasis has been placed upon the finality of the 1920 settlement. By the mid-nineteen-thirties Partition had come to be regarded, not as a distasteful necessity, but as a positive and beneficent act of statesmanship. It was regrettable that one-third of the population of Northern Ireland remained unreconciled to Partition, but that was not felt to detract seriously from the merits of the settlement. 'We are determined,' said Mr. J. M. Andrews in 1936, 'come what may, to hold what we have got. We are determined to maintain our Parliament.'[5]

Even in the broad context of relations between the Irish Free State and the Commonwealth the delimitation of the Irish boundary has not been without importance. In 1914 it was proposed that 'veiled' or 'open' exclusion should extend to the whole province of Ulster for a stated period. At the Buckingham Palace conference of July that year Sir Edward Carson strongly appealed to

[1] 1926 census.

[2] Of this number, 31·3 per cent. were Presbyterians and 27 per cent. members of the Church of Ireland, according to the 1926 census figures. See *Ulster Year Book*, 1935.

[3] H. of C. Deb., vol. 151, coll. 1408–9. Here again is a significant contrast with the partition of India which, however reluctantly, was agreed by the Congress as well as the Moslem League to be the only practicable solution in 1947.

[4] Letter of 11 November 1921 to Mr. Lloyd George, Cmd. 1561.

[5] *Irish Times*, 6 February 1936.

Redmond to consent to the total exclusion of Ulster in the interests of the earliest possible unity of Ireland. He argued that if a smaller area were excluded, the reunion of Ireland would be delayed. In this he showed an admirable clear-sightedness which the nationalist leaders, anxious always to whittle down the area to be excluded, did not match then or later.[1] By 1920 the opportunity had gone. The Ulster leaders asked for no more than the largest area which would give them a secure majority over an indefinite period. Sir James Craig[2] told the House of Commons in 1920 of the reasons for this more modest demand.

> We had [he said] to take the decision a few days ago as to whether we should call upon the government to include the nine counties in the bill or be satisfied with the six. . . . The majority of Unionists in the nine counties' Parliament is very small indeed. . . . We quite frankly admit that we cannot hold the nine counties. . . . Therefore, we have decided that, in the interests of the greater part of Ulster, it is better that we should give up those three counties. . . .[3]

Mr. Lloyd George, by assenting to the Unionist wishes about the precise area to be excluded, in effect decided that Partition should be placed upon a quasi-permanent foundation. His action may be defended on grounds of expediency, but the method by which the conclusion was reached is not easy to justify on grounds of equity. When India was partitioned twenty-seven years later, the exact boundary was determined, with the agreement of the two parties concerned, by judicial arbitration. This was the only just and appropriate procedure,[4] for, as subsequent events in Ireland confirmed, no reservations or assurances about later arbitration are likely to prove satisfactory. Once a boundary is drawn, the arguments against any modification of it gather weight with every year of its existence.

In essence the problem of Irish unity has not a little in common with the problems of Canadian and of South African unity. In all three countries there is a large cultural minority. In both Canada and in Ireland the minority is concentrated in great strength in a tolerably well-defined area in which it forms a local majority, and spread thin elsewhere. Both the Protestant minority concentrated in the north-eastern counties of Ireland and the French-Canadian minority in the province of Quebec are kept apart from the

[1] See Gwynn, *History of Partition*, p. 119, where John Redmond's personal record of the Buckingham Palace conference is published for the first time. To understand Carson's attitude it is necessary to remember that he, unlike Sir James Craig and later Ulster Unionist leaders, was by upbringing and early association a Southern Unionist. The Union he wished to preserve at all costs, but the permanent partition of Ireland was never his aim.

[2] Afterwards Lord Craigavon, First Prime Minister of Northern Ireland.

[3] H. of C. Deb., vol. 127, col. 991.

[4] It is necessary to emphasize that it is the method of prompt judicial arbitration which is commended, since the consequence of its application on the Indo-Pakistan frontier was strongly criticized in Pakistan.

majority of their fellow countrymen by religious differences which have made intermarriage infrequent. In Canada the barrier is heightened by a difference in language and culture. In South Africa, where, as in Ireland, a recently dominant community is in the position of numerical inferiority, the province of Natal fills the role of Quebec in Canada and of Ulster in Ireland, and there is a linguistic barrier but there is no religious barrier, as there is both in Canada and in Ireland. It is the belief of some South African leaders that in the long run intermarriage, though discouraged by the Nationalists, will resolve the problem of relations between the two European peoples. In the meantime, however, it is a fact that the secession of Natal from the Union, often canvassed in the past, remains within the bounds of remote possibility. Were that to happen, then the parallel between a partitioned South Africa and a partitioned Ireland would be close, though it is to be noted that English-speaking South Africans who form a large minority in the Cape Province and in the Transvaal create an argument, possibly the decisive argument, against secession.[1] In some respects an even closer superficial parallel to the situation in Ireland was afforded by the partition of India in 1947, though nowhere else within the Commonwealth has there been propounded with equal vigour a theory of two nations which was the essence of Mr. Jinnah's argument for a separate state of Pakistan.[2] Moreover, both Pakistan and India are independent states, whereas Northern Ireland is an integral part of the United Kingdom.

These analogies and contrasts, not without interest in themselves, serve to throw a good deal of light on the consequences of the partition of Ireland in the field of Commonwealth relations. In both Northern Ireland and in the Irish Free State the settlement of 1920–1 created a homogeneity of outlook. This was even more pronounced in the Twenty Six than in the Six Counties because the Anglo-Irish minority there numbered less than 4 per cent. of the population. While this homogeneity afforded no little satisfaction to politicians on both sides of the Border, it has deprived Irish political and

[1] There is also the fact that Durban is the principal port for the Transvaal and parts of the Orange Free State, which means that these provinces would suffer materially from the imposition of trade or customs barriers.

[2] This distinction cannot, of course, be pressed too far. Irish Nationalists have often denounced Unionist claims to be part of another nation as 'the two-nation theory'. On 12 October 1913 Mr. John Redmond said: 'Ireland is a unit. It is true that within the bosom of a nation there is room for diversities of the treatment of government and of administration, but a unit Ireland is, and Ireland must remain.... The two-nation theory is to us an abomination and a blasphemy.' (Quoted in Gwynn, *History of Partition*, p. 64.) And in a leading article on 17 June 1950 the *Irish Press* denounced Sir Basil Brooke, Prime Minister of Northern Ireland, who, 'like the rest of the Orange politicians is for ever making great play with the two-nations theory', for seeking to persuade North American audiences that Ireland was not a unit politically or geographically. Not without justice they pointed out that if there are two nations in Ireland still more are there two nations in Canada and that in logic Sir Basil Brooke should have advocated national parliaments in Quebec and Toronto to match those in Dublin and Belfast.

intellectual life of much of its vitality. In South Africa, and more especially in Canada, the cross-fertilization of ideas and cultures, the need to reconcile divergent racial viewpoints, has, despite acrimonious disputes, enriched the life of their respective countries. But in Ireland, Partition has accentuated divergent tendencies by depriving the opposing groups of the need to resolve their differences in the interests of a wider national unity. Thus between 1932 and 1939 there was a pronounced trend in the Irish Free State towards the creation of an exclusivist Catholic Gaelic-speaking nation-state. It was an aspiration that did not pass unchallenged, for the older, more embracing ideals of Wolfe Tone and Thomas Davis were not to be easily overthrown, but its expression and its endorsement by a not inconsiderable minority was one consequence of Partition.

The existence of a state, virtually homogeneous in religion and race, fosters the belief that it can profitably be made yet more homogeneous. As in South Africa a natural anxiety to protect and encourage Afrikaner culture led on by easy stages to the more negative attitude of exclusion, so in the Irish Free State the positive aim of reviving and restoring the Gaelic language contracted in the minds of some of its most ardent protagonists into a cry for the exclusion of foreign books, of foreign newspapers, of foreign games.[1] In both instances the shift in emphasis was in some measure protective. Except on the western seaboard 'far and foreign', Gaelic was no longer a spoken language, and despite sustained official encouragement it had not been successfully revived. Again because of her geographical position in the very heart of the English-speaking world, with a large emigrant population in almost every part of it, the Irish Free State was exposed to Anglo-American cultural penetration more directly than South Africa, with the result that in her case the reaction had an even more markedly defensive character. But making every allowance, is it not clear that doctrines of exclusivism could not have flourished, and that even the force of the movement towards the re-Gaelicization of Ireland and all that it symbolized, would have been weakened in a United Ireland, in which more than 20 per cent. of the population would have constituted a hard, unassimilable core? As in South Africa realism would perforce have tempered doctrine. In Northern Ireland ministers of the Crown could talk of a Protestant Parliament for a Protestant people[2] because the Border had segregated a homogeneous group, while in the south Partition made meaningful attitudes and policies which in a United Ireland would have been meaningless. The Gaelic Republic was the dream of those who had been encouraged to forget the composite character of the Irish population because a barrier had been placed between the free mingling of

[1] With insignificant and passing exceptions none were in fact excluded on the ground of their 'foreignness'.

[2] cf. the Prime Minister's statement on 12 July 1932 at Dumbanagher: 'Ours is a Protestant government, and I am an Orangeman.'

the ideas and traditions of its two principal component strains. Behind that barrier each in isolation pursued its own way. Complete lack of contact between ministers in the Irish Free State and Northern Ireland ceased even to arouse comment and was accepted as part of the natural order of things. More far-reaching in its consequences was the progressive decline in social and intellectual contact[1] between 1921 and 1939. Northern Ireland and the Irish Free State each followed its chosen course, denouncing the outlook or the policies of the other in distant and rhetorical terms rarely introducing that note of reality which intimate knowledge of conditions and viewpoints could alone have supplied.

In the Twenty-Six Counties there has never been a Commonwealth party. It was a matter for surprise that after 1921 no party representing ex-Unionist opinion was formed, though the decision not to take the obvious course was in fact to be commended for its wisdom. The lack of any organized opinion in relation to the Commonwealth was, however, another matter and is to be attributed to more far-reaching causes. One possible merit of the 1921 solution of the Irish Question was that it might provide a common meeting ground for Unionist and Nationalist. But Partition having preceded the Treaty, there was no practical discussion of this possibility then, and there was very little later. For their part the Orange leaders never spoke of Partition as being an intermediate phase to be ended if and when the Irish Free State gave solid proof of loyal membership of the Commonwealth. On the contrary their emphasis has been more and more on Partition as the 'final settlement'. Within the Free State the pro-Treaty party inclined at times to positive support of the idea of the Commonwealth, but it had little inducement to sponsor it boldly and consistently in the face of republican critics and without encouragement from across the Border. There was no pro-Commonwealth vote to be wooed, only nationalist sentiment to be won. The fear of every government was lest it should be outbid or outmanœuvred on the national issue by those who stood to the left of it. The result was that relations with the Commonwealth were not debated in the Irish Free State as they were in the Union of South Africa, because secessionist assumptions and more widespread indifference were never challenged. The nature of the Commonwealth membership, never widely understood, was not assessed realistically after 1931 in the light of the changes which the Statute of Westminster had endorsed. This prevailing ignorance or indifference could hardly have survived in a United Ireland, where a coherent minority in the north might well have enjoyed much the same advantages as the French-Canadian minority in Canada in influencing, or even determining negatively at least, the direction of policy. It is highly improbable that in a United Ireland any professedly republican or secessionist party could have attained a majority between 1921 and 1939.

[1] The universities partially resisted the prevailing trend.

DOMINION STATUS AND EXTERNAL ASSOCIATION

Mr. Churchill regarded the negotiation of the Anglo-Irish Treaty 'as one of the most questionable and hazardous experiments upon which a great Empire in the plenitude of its power had ever embarked',[1] and by most Englishmen it was so regarded even if it was also welcomed by them as a generous and far-sighted attempt to bring about the settlement of an age-old problem. They appreciated the full force of the association of the status of the Irish Free State with that of Canada and, without inquiring too precisely into its exact implications, they were conscious that the evolution of the Empire into the full and equal partnership of the British Commonwealth of Nations would allow of the progressive advance of the Irish Free State towards autonomous status. What more could the Irish desire? In a sense they desired nothing more but rather something different. Dominion status had not been the Irish goal; it was something strange, unfamiliar, not easily grafted on to their political philosophy. It evoked no feelings of satisfaction or pride, and the full measure of freedom it accorded was perceived only by the few. It is against this background that the arguments used by the Irishmen who championed the Treaty settlement against the violent onslaught of the republican dissidents remain retrospectively so illuminating. It was, after all, the party who supported the Treaty in 1921 that proclaimed the Republic in 1949.

The classic summary of the position of the pro-Treaty party was made by Michael Collins, one of its signatories, when he said in the Treaty Debate 'that the Treaty gave Ireland freedom—not the ultimate freedom that all nations hoped for and struggled for, but freedom to achieve that end'. Mr. Kevin O'Higgins, then a younger member of the party and more conscious than his colleagues of the evolutionary character of dominion status, declared: 'I hardly hope that within the terms of this Treaty there lies the fulfilment of Ireland's destiny but I do hope . . . what remains may be won by agreement and by peaceful political evolution.'[2] Even Mr. Griffith on the right wing observed that he had signed the Treaty 'not as the ideal thing, but fully believing, as I believe now, it is a Treaty honourable to Ireland and safeguards the vital interests of Ireland'.[3] Their common text was that famous dictum of Parnell inscribed under his statue in O'Connell Street: 'No man has a right to set a boundary to the march of a nation.' The Treaty, therefore, was accepted not in principle but as a matter of expediency, as a stepping-stone to a goal that could not be attained in one bound. It was not the end, it was not a particularly congenial means, but it was a possible compromise and its merits were not to be lightly discounted. Above all it restored peace between Britain and Ireland.

While the Sinn Féin leaders did not regard dominion status as the natural

[1] *The Aftermath*, p. 296. [2] *Treaty Debates*, p. 42. [3] ibid. p. 38.

fulfilment of their political aspirations the majority, in 1921, were republicans but not separatists. They acknowledged that the common interests which existed between Britain and Ireland made desirable some close association between the two countries, and accordingly the Irish delegates to the Treaty negotiations in 1921 were instructed to press for a relationship which broadly corresponded to what was later known as External Association.[1] Its essential features were to be the recognition of Ireland as a sovereign independent state, the renunciation by Great Britain of all claim to legislate for Ireland (an anticipation of the Statute of Westminster), and Ireland's agreement to become 'an External Associate of the Commonwealth'. For Commonwealth citizenship, reciprocal citizenship was to be substituted.[2] Any suggestion of direct Irish allegiance to the Crown was to be resisted to the last, but there was a willingness to contemplate recognition of the King as the head of the Commonwealth. While the Treaty negotiations were in progress, Mr. de Valera suggested as a form of oath in which this might be expressed: 'I do solemnly swear true faith and allegiance to the Constitution of the Irish Free State, to the Treaty of Association, and to recognize the King of Great Britain as Head of the Association.'[3] External Association was regarded by its sponsors as a concession, as a compromise by which a republican Ireland could co-operate in external affairs with the members of the British Commonwealth. But its implicit republicanism, essential from the Irish standpoint, affronted the British delegation. Moreover, might not this concept, unfamiliar and disturbing, provoke questions outside the field of Anglo-Irish relations, more dangerous than any it resolved within? Such objections sufficed to preclude the Irish proposals from closer analysis. This is to be regretted on many grounds. In particular Irish willingness to allow that problems of defence and foreign policy might legitimately be approached as matters of common concern between the associated state and the countries of the Commonwealth deserved further examination. It is after all a remarkable fact that in 1921 the Irish leaders seemed prepared to contemplate close co-operation in external affairs, while attenuating the constitutional link in such a way as to make an Irish republic not a member of the British Commonwealth, but an independent nation outside, associated with it. Nor is it surprising in these circumstances that some of the earliest and sharpest criticisms of External Association came from the extreme left, who considered that the concessions contemplated in the external field were more than a true republican should be asked to swallow. Mr. Michael Collins, on the other hand, saw wide possibilities in the proposal and drafted a memorandum[4] suggesting

[1] It would seem that there was no detailed discussion among the Sinn Féin leaders about the nature of the association they desired. Many of those who subsequently supported the Treaty did not hear of External Association till after the Treaty was signed.

[2] Pakenham, *Peace by Ordeal*, pp. 111–12.

[3] ibid. p. 261, and Art. 6, Document No. 2.

[4] 'On the Wider International Aspects of an Anglo-Irish Settlement.' cf. Pakenham, *Peace*

that External Association might provide the pattern for a broader relation between the countries of the British Commonwealth and the United States of America, and he believed that at some future date some such loose constitutional link would provide an appropriate foundation for independent nations co-operating together for the preservation of peace.

In the years that elapsed between the signature of the Treaty and the enactment of the External Relations Act in December 1936, successive Irish governments pressed first for a loosening of the fabric of the Empire in such a way as to bring it more and more closely into line with their own ideas, and then, under Mr. de Valera's leadership, to move outside it. In the first phase the tide of dominion opinion was with them. Experience at the Imperial Conferences of 1926 and 1930 and the subsequent enactment of the Statute of Westminster did much to convince many of the leading members of Mr. Cosgrave's party that dominion status was a more acceptable solution than they had imagined in 1921. Familiarity indeed produced an attitude in which a tolerant, even mildly possessive, affection was a notable characteristic.[1] The leaders of the party, at least, were well pleased with their achievements at Imperial Conferences and liked to believe that their actions had not only placed the relationship of the Irish Free State and the British Commonwealth upon a more satisfying and a more enduring foundation but had also greatly contributed to the reshaping of the Commonwealth. For Mr. de Valera's ingenious constitutional devices they developed a bitter contempt, aggravated by the undying memories of the civil war.

In the second phase, which began with Mr. de Valera's accession to office, the views of the extreme left assumed a greater importance. The Irish Republican Army,[2] and that broader section of opinion always prepared to heed their claim to be the only incorruptible heirs of the revolution, believed that republicanism without final separation from England was a betrayal of the ideal proclaimed by those who had died for the republic in 1916. Had not Pádraic Pearse foretold that anyone who accepted as a final settlement 'anything less by one portion of an iota than separation from England will be repudiated by the new generation as severely as O'Connell was repudiated by the generation that came after him. . .'? Heavy were the responsibilities of the Fianna Fáil government to the living, but heavier still upon their shoulders 'lay the dreadful tyranny of the dead'.[3] When the young commandant who had been the last to surrender in 1916 came in middle age to the highest office in the Irish Free State he could not be unmindful of how far

by Ordeal, p. 281. It was submitted as a supplement to the Irish proposals for External Association on 28 November 1921.

[1] The author has been shown the desk in Dublin on which the Statute of Westminster is said to have been drafted.

[2] Often termed the new I.R.A. to distinguish them from the old I.R.A. who for the most part supported Mr. de Valera.

[3] Hancock, *Survey*, vol. 1, p. 99.

achievement fell short of the ideal so uncompromisingly proclaimed sixteen years earlier, nor could he entertain any illusions about the implacable hostility of the militant republicans to any compromise with Britain. Yet republican though he was himself by unwavering conviction, Mr. de Valera did not in 1932, any more than in 1921, regard the republic as necessarily involving a complete and final break with the British Commonwealth. In his 'Document No. 2', published after the signature of the Treaty, he had outlined his ideas of the right relationship between Britain and Ireland, and he did not in office depart from them. For matters of common concern Ireland should be associated with the British Commonwealth but should not be a member of it. He could, therefore, consistently adopt a reasonably flexible approach to the problems of Anglo-Irish and of Commonwealth relations, but the freedom of manœuvre which he might thereby have enjoyed was severely restricted by the strength of doctrinaire isolationist-republican opinion within his own party on the one hand, and by the *non possumus* attitude of the United Kingdom government on the other. Uncertainty about the reaction of the British government to the declaration of a republic, whatever its relationship with the Commonwealth, coupled with well-founded misgivings about its effect on the north, made him proceed judiciously and on the whole with moderation in deed, though not always in word, towards the realization of his aims. Their achievement by peaceful means had been made possible by the Treaty which he had so bitterly opposed.

In the Irish Free State, as in the Union of South Africa, there were two interpretations of recent history, and they were reflected in the attitudes of the two principal parties towards the problems of Anglo-Irish and Commonwealth relations. In the period before the Second World War during which Mr. de Valera was not only in office but in power in a sense rare in a democratic state, for by his personality he overshadowed his opponents and his colleagues alike, it was his interpretation that prevailed. But in examining how he applied it to the hard intractable problems of politics, it is not to be overlooked that there was another interpretation, another viewpoint, which had been in favour with the Irish electorate till 1932 and whose protagonists, after desolate years in the political wilderness, were destined after the Second World War to return to influence and power once again. It was their contention that while dominion status, as embodied in the Treaty, was not an ideal solution, it afforded a reasonable basis for peace with Britain and for the future political development of Ireland. They were for the most part republicans, but their republicanism was not dogmatic. In office they had worked for the transformation of Empire into Commonwealth, and they believed that by peaceful political evolution even Partition might be ended. They were not, for the most part, however, in principle supporters of the Commonwealth connexion though they were prepared to explore and to exploit the opportunities of membership and to learn by experience whether or not it held continuing advantage for their country. If there was to be an Irish General Botha, it was from their ranks he would have to come, but while some aspired to that role the omens remained unfavourable. In 1922 Mr. de Valera had, in the language of his critics, climbed back on to 'the rock of the republic', and from that wellnigh unassailable vantage ground he was not to be dislodged by any appeals to the attractions of a once hated Empire which had been refashioned in part by Irish hands into a more acceptable but still unexciting and suspected Commonwealth. Recognizing this, the pro-Treaty party, the realists of 1921 and of 1949, in the end abandoned the cause of the Commonwealth.

REPUBLICANISM AND UNITY

It was believed by some of the Irish leaders and by almost all outside observers that every step towards the republic diminished the prospect of a united Ireland. In logic incontestable, this view failed to have decisive practical influence on policy because there was lacking positive evidence that full dominion status would lead to unity. None the less it inspired Kevin O'Higgins's desire to resurrect the conception of a dual monarchy—'two quite independent kingdoms with a common king'—and apply it as a solvent both to Anglo-Irish relations and to the problem of Irish unity.[1] In theory this proposal had something to commend it, but it bore little relationship to practical politics. All the evidence suggests that Kevin O'Higgins had no chance of enlisting the support of his colleagues, let alone of the country at large. For while historians might engage in learned disquisition about the comparatively recent introduction of a republican ideology, and antiquarians might search the records of late Gaelic civilization to find convincing proof that its structure was in form and in spirit monarchical, the people remained curiously indifferent to the outcome of these intellectual exercises. It might well be that the republican doctrines which Wolfe Tone had brought over from revolutionary France were alien and even implicitly anti-clerical;[2] it had to be conceded that the High Kings in Tara would almost certainly have regarded them as odious; but appeals to traditional monarchical sentiment left the people of the Twenty-Six Counties unmoved. Despite the widespread Protestant belief that Roman Catholic peoples, believing in a hierarchical pattern of society, are natural monarchists, the strength of anti-monarchist sentiment in Roman Catholic countries has been a significant feature of the history of the first half of the twentieth century. By 1950 Belgium was the only Roman Catholic country which retained a monarchy. In respect of Ireland, Mr. Ussher has observed with wit and judgement:

[1] White, *O'Higgins*, p. 222.

[2] cf. J. J. Horgan in *The Tablet*, 2 April 1949: 'Republicanism, as such, has no traditional roots in Ireland and is a purely exotic growth dating from the end of the eighteenth century. Its spiritual fathers are those eminently secular political philosophers Rousseau and Tom Paine.'

the Irishman is a natural Jacobite—he prefers uncrowned kings. Moreover, unlike the Scottish Jacobite, he would keep them uncrowned; he would not submit them to the test of reality. A real Irish king, sceptred and gartered, would seem to the Irishman ridiculous, and probably would be ridiculous—a sort of glorified Dublin Lord Mayor.[1]

Certainly since 1916 the Irish conviction that the republican form of government was most congenial to them has never wavered. The British monarchy in their eyes was irremediably associated with oppression and exploitation; the revival of an indigenous monarchy appealed only to antiquarians. Moreover, though republican doctrines came from the Old World, their adoption by the New exercised a more profound influence. Countless Irish exiles extolled to families and friends at home the riches and the opportunities that lay open to all in the great egalitarian republic across the Atlantic. The United States, seceding from the British Empire, had advanced to wealth and world power under a republican Constitution, and it was by this achievement that secessionist sentiment, which meant after 1922 a preponderance of opinion within the Twenty-Six Counties, was mo t directly inspired. Moreover, the most intransigent Irish nationalists lived for the most part not in Ireland but in the United States, for, as not infrequently happens, it was the exile who was the fundamentalist in politics, and Irish-Americans had contemplated for wellnigh a century a republican goal.

Year by year after 1916 the republic widened the area of its allegiance till the majority no longer conceived any other form of government which would be acceptable to Irish opinion. If, to some extent, it remained as in France, the form of government which divided people least, it has also to be remembered that the republican form of government had in 1916 become a part of the Irish national tradition, and while nations may seem at times indifferent to their traditions, particularly in the reaction that follows on tense and dramatic years, they do not go back on them.

THE EXTERNAL RELATIONS ACT 1936

In 1936 the constitutional structure of the Irish Free State had at least the merit of simplicity. The state was governed by a unicameral legislature in which one party, Fianna Fáil, had a well-drilled and obedient majority. Mr. de Valera, in five years of office, had, one by one, removed the symbols of the monarchy from the Irish Constitution. The first to go was the oath, the oath which Lord Birkenhead did not describe as the 'greatest prevarication in history' but which none the less warranted that description, and there followed in quick succession the Appeal to the Privy Council, the Senate—

[1] *Face and Mind of Ireland*, pp. 106–7. History, of course, has helped to make him a natural Jacobite. The practical choice before him even after 1921 was the British monarchy or a republic. It was not an indigenous monarchy or an indigenous republic. But had this been the choice the weight of opinion would probably have still been on the republican side for the reasons Mr. Ussher suggests.

prejudiced in the eyes of Fianna Fáil less as a relic behind which ex-Unionist privilege was believed to be still entrenched than as a Chamber unsympathetic to their policies[1]—and finally, the office of Governor-General, first deprived of dignity and authority and later abolished.[2] The result of this process of constitutional elimination was that the Dáil, to which the Executive Council was responsible, remained the one effective organ of the people's will. In such circumstances misgivings about the emergence of authoritarian government were widespread. But Mr. de Valera, though unduly disposed to regard all opposition as captious, entertained no such aims. His intention was first to remove the Crown from the Constitution—and it was inserted in 1922 only by British insistence—and then to draft a fresh Constitution 'new from top to bottom', unquestionably indigenous in character, embodying the ideals of Irish nationalism in a republican form. The drafting of the new Constitution, very largely by Mr. de Valera himself, took time, with the result that the country entered upon a protracted interregnum, enlivened by judicious revelations of some of the principal features of the proposed Constitution. It was at this inconvenient moment, in December 1936, that the abdication of King Edward VIII confronted an unready ministry with the need for immediate decisions on fundamental constitutional questions.

The government of the Irish Free State, in common with the governments of the oversea dominions, was bound to take some action following the abdication, if only because of the express declaration in the Statute of Westminster that the order of succession to the Throne was a matter with which all the governments of the Commonwealth were concerned.[3] But what action was Mr. de Valera to take? The extremists hoped that this was the opportunity which would be seized either to declare a republic or better still to allow a republic to come into being by inaction. But Mr. de Valera remained convinced that the solution he had proposed for Anglo-Irish relations in 1921–2 remained the right solution for them in 1936. Already in November he had indicated his intention of trying to reconcile complete internal sovereignty in form as well as in fact with co-operation with the Commonwealth on a basis of external association. For this the prospects were somewhat less unfavourable than in the past, and Mr. de Valera's announcement of his intentions elicited a high tribute from Professor Berriedale Keith for the 'statesmanlike prudence which has marked so much of Mr. de Valera's

[1] For an astringent commentary on Mr. de Valera's relations with the Senate see Donal O'Sullivan, *The Irish Free State and Its Senate* (London, Faber, 1936).

[2] Mr. Donal Buckley, a faithful party man who laid no claims to political distinction and who was a defeated candidate at the general election of 1932 was, on Mr. de Valera's submission to the King, appointed Governor-General in 1932 to replace Mr. McNeill. During his period of office he lived in seclusion, his only duty being to sign bills when asked to do so. He himself signed the bill which removed from the Governor-General almost all his functions in December 1936.

[3] See above pp. 41–46 for an account of the general constitutional issues involved.

dealing with the British government'.[1] Confronted abruptly with the problems of the abdication Mr. de Valera did not modify in any essentials his earlier intentions.

On 11 December 1936 Mr. de Valera introduced two pieces of legislation[2] in the Dáil, the first designed formally to remove the Crown from the Constitution, and the second to reinstate the Crown in specific statutory form in relation to external affairs. The general purpose of the two bills was to replace dominion status by External Association, and it is from December 1936 that the implicit adoption of External Association is to be dated. The difference to be noted at the outset between External Association as contemplated in 1921–2 and as adopted in 1936 was that at the earlier date an indication was given of the matters of common concern in which foreign affairs and defence involving co-operation with the countries of the Commonwealth were specifically included, whilst by 1936 this positive content, not easily to be assimilated with the looser concept of dominion status that had emerged since 1926, was abandoned. The attenuated remainder was more negative both in conception and in approach than what had been earlier contemplated. Yet it is all important to remember, as Professor Keith almost alone recognized at the time, that the proposals made by Mr. de Valera were admirable in their moderation.[3] The Privy Council decision in *Moore* v. *Attorney-General for the Irish Free State* had not only asserted the legality of Mr. de Valera's earlier constitutional reforms but had in addition left it open to him to confer upon the head of the state 'the right to exercise every attribute of legal sovereignty'.[4] Yet a convinced, but not a doctrinaire republican, he refrained from so politically tempting a solution. What were the reasons for such restraint?

In December 1936 Mr. de Valera's declared purpose was to bring the law and the Constitution of the Irish Free State into accord with existing political realities by removing the Crown from the Legislature, the Executive, and generally from the Constitution. He assured Mr. Cosgrave that the Constitution Amendment Bill he introduced on 11 December did not contain any proposition to sever 'our connexion with the states of the British Commonwealth'. Article 1 of the 1922 Constitution, which provided that the 'Irish Free State is a co-equal member of the community of nations forming the British Commonwealth of Nations', remained untouched.[5] Nor did Mr. de Valera believe that the amending bill would jeopardize Irish membership of the Commonwealth. While there would be no reference to the King in the new Constitution, of which the draft was then nearing completion, he pointed

[1] *The King and the Constitution, the Empire and Foreign Affairs* (London, Oxford University Press, 1938) p. 53.

[2] Constitution (Amendment No. 27) Act 1936, and Executive Authority (External Relations) Act 1936.

[3] cf. Keith, *King and Constitution*, p. 54, and see above pp. 27–29.

[4] ibid. pp. 54–55.

[5] Dáil Debates, vol. 64, coll. 1232 ff.

out that any relations which existed between 'our State and Great Britain, so long as the people willed to have that connexion, would be maintained by the fact of co-operation and would be regularized . . . by law'.[1] He had not consulted other members of the Commonwealth about the terms of the legislation before the Dáil because he felt consultation to be inappropriate when the action to be taken by the Irish Free State was a matter to be determined by the Dáil and by the Dáil alone. He noted, however, that there had been 'a general desire expressed by the States of the British Commonwealth that there should be concerted action as quickly as possible' to dispose of the constitutional consequences of the abdication, and while he was unprepared to give 'any countenance to the idea that the British Parliament can in any way legislate for us' and maintained that 'if this thing has to be done it has to be done by our Parliament alone', he allowed at the same time that 'so long as there is any association at all . . . it is obvious that we ought to do our part to facilitate other countries in dealing with this situation'.[2]

Mr. de Valera's reluctance to consult the governments of the Commonwealth about the removal of the Crown from the Constitution was not surprising. A corresponding aversion to prior consultation about the provisions of the External Relations Act,[3] which embodied the positive aspect of his policy, was not altogether prudent, however discouraging the attitude of the United Kingdom government to departures from the constitutional pattern of Commonwealth relations had hitherto been. For the working of External Association demanded the co-operation of all members of the Commonwealth, and though that was obtained implicitly, the price was a tacit agreement to differ fundamentally in the interpretation of the constitutional link which it created.

The External Relations Act proceeded from the assumption that henceforward the Crown should have no place and should receive no recognition in relation to the internal government of the Irish Free State. Its purpose was, therefore, to define the place and the functions of the Crown in the external field. Articles 1 and 2 of the Act provided that the diplomatic and consular representatives of the Irish Free State were to be appointed, and every international agreement was to be concluded, on the authority of the Executive Council. There followed the all-important Article 3:

> It is hereby declared and enacted that, so long as Saorstát Éireann is associated with the following nations, that is to say, Australia, Canada, Great Britain, New Zealand, and South Africa, and so long as the King recognized by those nations as the symbol of their co-operation continues to act on behalf of each of these nations (on the advice of the several governments thereof) for the purposes of the appointment of diplomatic and consular representatives and the conclusion of international agreements, the King so recognized may, and is hereby authorized to, act on behalf

[1] ibid. col. 1233.

[2] ibid. col. 1234.

[3] Executive Authority (External Relations) Act, 1936.

of Saorstát Éireann for the like purposes as and when advised by the Executive Council so to do.

Immediately upon the passing of this Act, the instrument of abdication executed by His Majesty King Edward VIII on the 10th day of December, 1936 (a copy whereof is set out in the schedule to this Act), shall have effect according to the tenor thereof and His said Majesty shall, for the purposes of the aforegoing subsection of this section and all other (if any) purposes, cease to be King, and the King for those purposes shall henceforth be the person who, if His Majesty had died on the 10th day of December, 1936, unmarried, would for the time being be his successor under the law of Saorstát Éireann.[1]

It will be noticed that this Article allowed discharge by the Crown of specifically defined external functions, but did not make its use mandatory. Over and above this permissive element the use of the Crown was made conditional in the first place upon the continued association of the Irish Free State with the United Kingdom and the oversea dominions, and in the second upon the continued recognition of the King by these nations as the symbol of their association. This permissive and conditional character of the discretionary authority so conferred upon the Executive Council later acquired enhanced importance. In December 1936 the provisions of the Act were interpreted in the light of Mr. de Valera's statement that Article 1 of the 1922 Constitution, which declared the Irish Free State to be a member of the British Commonwealth of Nations, remained unaffected, but when the Constitution of 1937 was enacted, in which no such provision appeared, the implications of the External Relations Act became more far-reaching. In this way an arrangement made while the Irish Free State was a member of the Commonwealth by a provision of her own Constitution became within a year the one remaining link with the Commonwealth. It was not a link which, in the Irish view, acknowledged any allegiance to the Crown in the traditional sense. It did, however, allow an oblique recognition of the position of the Crown as the symbol of free association within the Commonwealth. In that respect it coincided almost exactly with what had been contemplated by the Sinn Féin leaders in 1921 and more particularly by Mr. de Valera in 1922.

The intention of the External Relations Act was to underline the final authority of the Parliament of the Irish Free State in external as in internal affairs, and in the exercise of that authority to allow certain functions to be performed by the Crown on the advice of the Executive Council so as to make possible the continued association of the Irish Free State with the Commonwealth in a manner acceptable at once to monarchist sentiment in the Commonwealth and to republican sentiment at home. Like other compromises it left neither side wholly satisfied and neither violently dissatisfied.

The principle on which the External Relations Act rested was unconditional

[1] See Great Britain, Foreign Office, *The Constitutions of All Countries*, vol. 1, *The British Empire* (London, H.M.S.O., 1938) p. 189.

Irish sovereignty derived from the people and exercised in their name by their elected representatives in the Dáil. This constitutional doctrine was alien to the fundamental concepts of the British Commonwealth of Nations which were extended to the Irish Free State by the Treaty of 1921 and given force of law in the Constitution of 1922. Yet the Act was not unconstitutional. The Statute of Westminster, as enacted and as interpreted in relation to the Irish Free State in *Moore* v. *Attorney-General for the Irish Free State* in 1935, had acknowledged that the authority and the power to enact such legislation was vested in the Irish Parliament. There was no suggestion, therefore, that the External Relations Act was *ultra vires* according to United Kingdom law, though there was a proposal to challenge its validity before the Irish Supreme Court who had hitherto taken a more restricted view than the Judicial Committee of the Privy Council of the powers conferred upon the Oireachtas by the Statute of Westminster. The legality of Mr. de Valera's legislation was, however, one thing, its conformity with the recognized conventions of the Commonwealth another. In that context the External Relations Act may be regarded as a first attempt to explore the possibility of establishing an intimate non-foreign relationship between a republic and a Commonwealth the symbol of whose free association was the Crown. For this reason alone the debate in the Dáil at the time of its enactment has a certain lasting importance.

The precise relationship with the Commonwealth established by the External Relations Act was not in fact very carefully considered by the Dáil in December 1936. That was partly due to some obscurity about its intention and its relation to the new Constitution which had not yet been promulgated, and partly to an unqualified refusal on the part of the opposition to allow that there could be any intermediate halting place between full dominion status and an independence which involved full and final secession from the Commonwealth. Mr. de Valera's first concern was to reassure his own followers by emphasizing that henceforward the King would act only in an external capacity so far as the Irish Free State was concerned, and that even in that capacity he would be only the instrument by means of which effect would be given to policies which were those of the Executive Council. It was in the Executive Council that authority was vested, and that was fully and formally stated to be so in the Act so that there might be no possible misrepresentation or misunderstanding.

> We propose [said Mr. de Valera[1]] to continue the King for the functions which he in fact directly exercises and for these only. The functions provided for here are the only functions which in fact the King exercises. We are providing for the continuance of these functions on the advice and authority—as in the past and in the future—of the Executive Council. We are clearing up the political, constitutional situation. . . . He [the King] is being retained for these [external] purposes because he is recognized as the symbol of this particular co-operation in the states of the

[1] Dáil Debates, vol. 64, coll. 1279–80.

Commonwealth. If the Irish people do not wish to continue him for these purposes, they can end that by legislation. They can end the whole situation by law or limit the exercise of these powers by law. What is given in the bill is permission to continue to use the same instrument.

As time went by this permissive element in the External Relations Act loomed still larger, and it was almost certainly the direction of Mr. de Valera's thought that the External Relations Act could remain indefinitely on the Statute Book as the symbol of co-operation with the Commonwealth whilst the actual use of the Crown in External Affairs might be allowed to fall into abeyance.[1]

Mr. de Valera resolutely maintained that the provisions of the External Relations Act and the removal of the Crown from the internal government of Irish Free State would make for better relations with Britain and the Commonwealth

because these relations between the people of this country and people elsewhere will be clearer. By these Bills, we are laying a foundation on which it will be possible to start at the beginning and establish relations in which all the friction that occurred just because of these symbols . . . will disappear.[2]

For this view there is more to be said than was allowed at the time. Whatever verdict may be passed on the particular form in which the legislation was drafted, it is clear in retrospect that the place of the Crown in the Constitution of 1922, where it was inserted against the wishes of the Irish provisional government, was a source of friction and of grave internal embarrassment, especially to governments which were themselves republican in outlook. If Mr. de Valera were to safeguard his own position against the extreme republicans who could still rely on armed backing, it was essential for him at the earliest possible moment to carry through amendments to the 1922 Constitution which would bring it into closer conformity with republican aspirations.

The militant republicans were a small but still politically dangerous group. The constitutional opposition consisted of the Fine Gael party led by Mr. Cosgrave and a small Labour party led by Mr. Norton. Both for different reasons were highly critical of Mr. de Valera's compromise solution. Mr. Norton felt that the External Relations Act conceded too much. Adopting the militant republican viewpoint, which held that if no action had been taken at the time of the abdication a republic would automatically have come into being, he argued that inaction was the course of wisdom now that the King had 'voluntarily relinquished his objectionable role here'.[3] This was at once indifferent politics and bad constitutional law. The opposition from Mr. Cosgrave's party was more sustained and more considered. Mr. Dillon contemptuously referred to the External Relations Act as yet one more

[1] Statement to United Press representative quoted in *Irish Press*, 18 April 1949.
[2] Dáil Debates, vol. 64, col. 1350.
[3] ibid. col. 1249.

exercise of Mr. de Valera's 'admitted gift' for bewildering and misleading the people'.[1] Dr. O'Higgins protested against this 'zebra legislation' which he felt was merely designed to

> undermine, to nibble away, to destroy as much as can be destroyed with safety, and to replace it by nothing—that type of legislation will get the respect of nobody, neither the person standing strongly for the republic nor the person standing strongly for the Commonwealth. They will join together in contempt not only for the legislation itself but for the unmanly way in which it is introduced.[2]

He went on to argue that there was no half-way house between Commonwealth association and separatism involving complete isolation, so that the alternatives were full membership of the Commonwealth or a republic outside it. The view of the Fine Gael party was that the Irish Free State should remain within the Commonwealth. Dr. O'Higgins went so far as to suggest that if the functions of the Crown were to be divided, it would be far preferable to retain the internal functions because the people would be generally concerned with these functions and would understand how they were being exercised, whereas the functions exercised by the Crown in relation to foreign affairs were not such as would be generally understood.[3] Mr. Costello, Mr. Cosgrave's former Attorney-General, and one day destined to be Prime Minister of the government which repealed the External Relations Act, disliked its provisions because he felt that it created 'a political monstrosity, the like of which is unknown to political legal theory, such a monstrosity as existed nowhere in any polity in the world'.[4] He doubted the value of Mr. de Valera's reassurances that the External Relations Act would not jeopardize the position of the Irish Free State in the British Commonwealth of Nations, but he laid most emphasis upon the work which Mr. Cosgrave's government had done in securing a redefinition both of the practice and of the law of the Commonwealth and maintained that that redefinition had secured for the Irish Free State a satisfactory position within the Commonwealth. He felt that 'we have under the Treaty as a member of the Commonwealth of Nations . . . a greater security for the freedom of this country' and an arrangement 'that secures greater freedom for democracy in this country than any other system that could be devised'. He went on to say that this principle of the Crown as the symbol not of Commonwealth co-operation as stated in the External Relations Act but

> of our freedom and of our free association is something that has never been thought of before in the history of political science and it would be difficult to find something that would replace it. That symbol, a symbol of our freedom, does not interfere in any way with the exercise by the people of this country of their completest freedom, with the exercise by the Irish people, through their representatives in

[1] ibid. col. 1254.
[2] ibid. coll. 1268–9.
[3] ibid. col. 1270.
[4] ibid. col. 1293.

Parliament, of any particular freedom that they wish to exercise. . . . Anything that is substituted for that scheme will inevitably eat into the freedom of the ordinary decent Irish person and take the ground from under democracy as we understand it at present.[1]

He then went on to observe:

we heard talk today about striking the shackles from the feet of this nation. The shackles which are supposed to exist on the feet of this nation can exist only, if I might mix the metaphor, in the minds of the people who talk about such shackles. There are not any such thing as shackles on our freedom at present. . . . The sooner we recognize that fact, the sooner we recognize that we are completely free, that we are freer, in fact, from outside interference than some of the greatest nations in the world under the system of polity in which we live, the better it will be for the material and for the spiritual prosperity of this country.[2]

Mr. Costello's arguments provide a curious commentary on his later actions.

THE CONSTITUTION OF 1937

The Constitution of 1922 was an essay in frustration. Embedded in it were the conflicting constitutional doctrines of the British monarchical system and Irish republicanism. Authority, both executive and legislative, which flowed nominally from the Governor-General as the representative of the Crown, was specifically declared to be vested in the people. 'All powers of government and all authority, legislative, executive, judicial, in Ireland', declared Article 2, 'are derived from the people of Ireland. . . .'[3] This inner conflict was resolved in the Constitution of 1937 wholly in favour of popular sovereignty, thereby making an undisguised and final break with the traditional pattern of dominion Constitutions. This was to be expected, but the way in which it took place was not without significance. Irish republican thought derived its inspiration through Wolfe Tone from the *Contrat Social* and revolutionary France, and while its origins were looked upon with some misgiving by the Catholic Church they none the less profoundly influenced the direction of Irish political thought. The successive republican Constitutions of France, and indirectly the Constitution of the United States, provided the channels through which the eighteenth-century notions of a sovereign people have permeated the minds of Irish constitutionalists. While Irish political thought has departed from the contractual conception so dear in one form or another to the eighteenth century, it has accepted as fundamental Rousseau's belief that the sovereign power resides in the people who may delegate but may not transfer it. Yet despite this background, popular sovereignty has not been

[1] Dáil Debates, vol. 64, col. 1437. [2] ibid. col. 1438.

[3] For a legal analysis of the Constitution of 1922 see L. Kohn, *The Constitution of the Irish Free State* (London, Allen & Unwin, 1932), and for an account of its practical operation see Mansergh, *The Irish Free State.*

conceived in Ireland as absolute and irresponsible but as something to be exercised with a full awareness that ultimately all authority derives from God. The Constitution of 1937 attempts, therefore, to reconcile the notion of an inalienable popular sovereignty with the older medieval conception of a theocratic state. Where the Declaration of the Rights of Man drawn up by the National Assembly in Paris in 1789, defining the aim of every political association as 'the preservation of the practical and imprescriptible rights of man', asserted that 'sovereignty resides exclusively in the nation . . .' which 'has the imprescriptible right to change its Constitution', the Irish Constitution of 1937, while affirming national and popular sovereignty in hardly less uncompromising terms, followed the Constitution of 1922 in reminding the sovereign people that all authority derives from them 'under God'.[1]

Under the Constitution of 1937 popular sovereignty, absolute in one sense, is conditional in another. It is declared to be the duty of the people and their responsibility to exercise their final authority in accordance with those moral laws proclaimed by the Founder of Christianity. This sense of an ultimate religious sanction which pervades the Constitution found expression in its Preamble.

> In the name of the Most Holy Trinity, from Whom is all authority and to Whom, as our final end, all actions both of men and States must be referred,
>
> We, the people of Eire,
>
> Humbly acknowledging all our obligations to our Divine Lord, Jesus Christ, Who sustained our fathers through centuries of trial,
>
> Gratefully remembering their heroic and unremitting struggle to regain the rightful independence of our nation,
>
> And seeking to promote the common good, with due observance of prudence, justice and charity, so that the dignity and freedom of the individual may be assured, true social order attained, the unity of our country restored, and concord established with other nations.
>
> Do hereby adopt, enact, and give to ourselves this Constitution.

It has been well said that the French ideal of self-government became, what it has never been in its British or American form, a challenge to every constituted government which did not recognize and embody the sovereignty of the people. That challenge was taken up by the Irish Constitution of 1937. Unlike the Constitutions of revolutionary France, the challenge was not directed against an absolute monarchy or a ruling class within the state, but against rule from without. The sovereignty of the people was asserted first of all as an insurance against the survival of alien domination in any form however diluted. The first section of the Constitution (entitled 'The Nation') reaffirmed the right of the nation to decide its form of government and defined its area. The relevant provisions read:

> 1. The Irish nation hereby affirms its inalienable, indefeasible, and sovereign

[1] Bunreacht na h'Eireann, 1937 (Constitution of Ireland), Article 6.

right to choose its own form of government, to determine its relations with other nations and to develop its life, political, economic, and cultural, in accordance with its own genius and traditions.

2. The national territory consists of the whole island of Ireland, its islands and the territorial seas.

3. Pending the reintegration of the national territory, and without prejudice to the right of the Parliament and government established by this Constitution to exercise jurisdiction over the whole of that territory, the laws enacted by that Parliament shall have the like area and extent of application as the laws of Saorstát Éireann and the like extraterritorial effect.

These were provisions which would no doubt have enlisted a warm benediction from Mazzini, that great nineteenth-century prophet of republican nationalism in Italy, who believed not only in the right of the people to decide their own form of government but also in their right to exercise their jurisdiction within the natural frontiers of the nation which had been so clearly indicated by geography. 'Nationalities', he wrote, 'appear to me to have been traced long ago by the finger of Providence on the map of Europe', and sceptical though he was of the authenticity of Irish nationalism, he might reasonably have acknowledged that, like Italy, Ireland had her 'sublime, irrefutable boundary marks'. In Northern Ireland, where transcendental interpretations of geography have not been much in favour, the bland assumption of the 1937 Constitution that the national territory would one day be reintegrated evoked an indignant reaction. Within the Twenty-Six Counties the continuing discrepancy between pretension and reality created problems in drafting not always very elegantly surmounted. At the head of the notice of assessment, income-tax payers were told that 'the word "Eire" throughout this form is to be interpreted, having regard to Article 3 of the Constitution, as referable to the area to which the laws of Eire have application'.

The second section of the Constitution defined the state. Its name was declared to be Eire, or in the English language Ireland, thereby creating a confusion which was not ended until the Republic of Ireland was formally proclaimed in 1949. In the intervening years the name Eire was commonly applied to the Twenty-Six Counties, whereas Ireland, a synonymous term, was applied to the whole thirty-two counties. This, however, was not a distinction of which Mr. de Valera could reasonably complain.

The 1937 Constitution described Eire as a sovereign, independent, democratic state,[1] and it was declared:

All powers of government, legislative, executive and judicial, derive, under God, from the people, whose right it is to designate the rulers of the state and, in final

[1] Article 5; this provision was adopted as it stood in the first draft of the Indian Constitution as promulgated in 1948, but subsequently the Indian Government was advised that the words sovereign and independent were redundant and therefore both need not be included.

appeal, to decide all questions of national policy, according to the requirements of the common good.[1]

The most surprising thing about these provisions was the failure to declare that the state was a republic. The omission was deliberate. Mr. de Valera admitted both at the time and later that he was reluctant to describe it as a republic because to him the republic was sacred, and its application to a state comprising only twenty-six of the thirty-two counties of Ireland was something akin to political sacrilege. Had not the martyrs of 1916 died for an All-Ireland Republic? To reasons of sentiment were added reasons of policy. The cautious reserve of the Constitution on this question was in conformity with the policy that inspired the External Relations Act. The declaration of a republic at that time would have finally estranged the North, and would thereby have notably lessened the ground for manœuvre in any negotiations designed to modify or to end Partition. Moreover, in 1937 it was reasonably certain that a republican Constitution would have involved secession from the Commonwealth, and that would have made much of Mr. de Valera's earlier policy meaningless. And if a precedent were required for silence in the Constitution about the form of the state, the hallowed example of the American Constitution was ready to hand.

While the state was not declared to be a republic, the Constitution was a republican Constitution. Not one syllable or comma of it, declared Mr. de Valera, would require to be altered were a republic to be declared the next day. At the head of the state was a President elected by a popular suffrage[2] for seven years and eligible for re-election only for a second term.[3] During his period of office, the President could not leave the country without the assent of the government.[4] He could be impeached for stated misbehaviour only if the charge were supported by a two-thirds majority of the House in which it had been preferred.[5] In him the supreme command of the Defence Forces was vested but its exercise was regulated by law.[6] Far more significant was the fact that the President was endowed with a discretionary authority which gave him wider powers either than the President of the Third Republic or than those which the Governors-General in the oversea dominions enjoyed in law or convention. The President was marked out as the protector of the rights of the people, and the method of election chosen, despite discouraging continental precedents, ensured that his representative status at least was unimpeachable. While the President was bound by the provisions of the Constitution to act, except as otherwise provided, in accordance with the advice of the Prime Minister, he was specifically given authority in his own absolute discretion to grant or to refuse a dissolution to a Prime Minister who had ceased to retain the support of a majority in the Dáil.[7] This provision con-

[1] Article 6. [2] Article 12 (2). [3] Article 12 (3).
[4] Article 12 (9). [5] Article 12 (10).
[6] Article 13 (4 and 5). [7] Article 28 (10).

ferred a potentially important discretionary authority upon him, the more so since the electoral system then in force and sanctioned by express provision of the Constitution[1] has tended to produce small majorities though not hitherto unstable governments. The other powers vested in the President were superficially of wider but actually of lesser significance. At any time he might, after consultation with the Council of State and with the approval of the government, send a message or address to both Houses of the Oireachtas or to the nation on any matter of national or public importance.[2] He was empowered also to refer a bill which he judged to be of substantial importance to the people for decision by referendum, if petitioned to do so by a majority of the Senate and not less than one-third of the members of the Dáil.[3] Likewise the President was invested with a certain discretionary authority in relation to money bills and to amendments to the Constitution, so that he might be in a position to safeguard the rights of the people against misuse of legislative power.[4] These provisions made it clear that the risk of conflict between the two arms of the Executive was deemed to be subordinate to that of abuse of authority by the government and the Dáil to which it was responsible. In introducing the draft Constitution in the Dáil, Mr. de Valera declared that

> if there is one thing more than another that is clear and shining through this whole Constitution, it is the fact that the people are the masters. They are the masters at the time of an election, and their mastery is maintained during the period from election to election through the President, who had been chosen definitely to safeguard their interests, to see that nothing that they have not in a general way given approval of is passed by the small majority which used to be threatened here as a danger to the country as a whole.[5]

The personal position of the Prime Minister, *An Taoiseach*, was enhanced in relation both to Dáil and cabinet by the power explicitly vested in him of recommending a dissolution in his own right. In this way formal constitutional sanction was given to the view of Mr. Baldwin, who maintained that in the United Kingdom the right to advise the dissolution rested with the Prime Minister alone, and that Mr. Asquith's insistence on collective cabinet responsibility for such advice was outdated.

An innovation in the Constitution was the creation of a Council of State composed of elder statesmen and designed to advise but not to control the President in the discharge of his discretionary powers.[6] The functions of the Council were confined to determining the temporary or permanent incapacity of the President and to advising him in the exercise of his residual authority in any unforeseen emergencies. In more normal times its effectiveness clearly depended upon the extent to which the government of the day was prepared

[1] Article 12 (2). [2] Article 13 (7). [3] Article 27 (1).
[4] cf. Articles 24 and 26. [5] Dáil Debates, vol. 67, col. 40.
[6] Articles 31 and 32.

to make use of a non-party body of elder statesmen. In the actual circumstances of Irish politics this in fact has proved to be very slight, largely because the long-continuing cleavage between the two main parties on the Treaty issue precluded co-operation between them in any field. The Council of State did, however, meet at the beginning of the Second World War, and its advice might have been more extensively used had the war involved Eire more directly.

The second Chamber[1] was reinstated. Mr. de Valera himself remained unconvinced of the need for a return to bicameral government, but he remarked, handsomely enough, 'if a large section of the people of the country think that there is something important in having a Senate, then, even if we ourselves are indifferent to it we should give way to the people who are anxious for it'.[2] Candidates were to be nominated by vocational bodies, except for eleven of its sixty members who were to be chosen by the Prime Minister. This elaborate method of indirect election and nomination in practice deprived the second Chamber of none of its predominantly party characteristics.

Of more particular interest were the provisions in the Constitution relating to fundamental rights and the directive principles for social policy arising from them. The fundamental personal rights guaranteed the liberties of the subject;[3] recognized the family 'as the natural, primary, and fundamental unit group of society'; and in a clause that aroused the wrath of ardent feminists declared that 'by her life within the home, woman gives to the state a support without which the common good cannot be achieved'.[4] There was an attempt also to reconcile individualist philosophy with the claims of the social order. It was acknowledged that the 'primary and natural educator of the child is the family', but that it was the duty of the state to provide for free primary education.[5] 'Man, in virtue of his rational being, has the natural right, antecedent to positive law, to the private ownership of external goods', but the state recognized the claims of social justice and might delimit their exercise in accordance 'with the exigencies of the common good'.[6] The recognition of 'the special position of the Holy Catholic Apostolic and Roman Church as the guardian of the faith professed by the great majority of the citizens' was noted with misgiving in Northern Ireland, though the specific recognition of the position of the various Protestant Churches in a subsequent clause and the assurance the state 'shall not impose any disabilities or make any discrimination on the ground of religious profession, belief or status' made it little more than the restatement of a self-evident fact.

The summary in the Constitution of fundamental personal rights was designed not so much to provide a guarantee of personal liberties as to create

[1] Article 18.
[2] Dáil Debates, vol. 67, col. 56.
[3] Article 40.
[4] Article 41 (2).
[5] Article 42 (1 and 4).
[6] Article 43 (1 and 4).

a broad framework within which the social system could develop. It was in that sense a reinsurance against sudden and disruptive social changes, and therefore conservative in intention. That is made more apparent when the 'Directive Principles of Social Policy'[1] are related to the broader enunciation of Fundamental Rights. These Principles, specifically excluded from the cognizance of any court, expressed Mr. de Valera's conception of the proper goal of social policy. The emphasis remained upon the individual. 'The state shall favour, and, where necessary, supplement private initiative in industry and commerce', and it would aim at establishing on the land as many families as in the circumstances 'shall be practicable'. The usefulness of these general directives has been much derided by lawyers, but this is a matter on which their verdict is not final. Recognition of aims is sometimes a help towards achievement, and it is instructive to notice that the provision both of Fundamental Rights and the Directive Principles of Social Policy contained in the Constitution were studied closely in other countries and were embodied either in whole or in part in the Constitutions of Burma and India after the Second World War. In the East this recognition of fundamental rights and the enunciation of directive principles of social policy at an experimental stage in the evolution of constitutional government had a potential importance far greater than they had had in Ireland a decade earlier. But it is largely because in this, as in other respects, the Irish Constitution of 1937 afforded a model for a written Constitution, republican in form, embodying the essentials of parliamentary government, that it had a wide significance in relation to those parts of the Commonwealth in which nationalist aspirations demanded a precise formulation of the political practices, aims, and ideals they were to adopt.

The student of Commonwealth relations is most directly concerned with the provisions in the Constitution relating to Eire's association with the British Commonwealth of Nations. In this respect the Constitution made no fundamental change in the situation created by the External Relations Act a year earlier. By confining itself to a general statement of principles, the Constitution, to quote Mr. de Valera, put 'the question of our international relations in their proper place—and that is outside the Constitution'.[2] Its relevant sections provided that executive power of the state in the external field should rest with the government, and it allowed that this power might by arrangement sanctioned through ordinary legislation be exercised in any other way that seemed advisable at any particular time.[3] The precise wording of this permissive clause was as follows:

> For the purpose of the exercise of any executive function of the state in or in connexion with its external relations, the government may to such extent and subject to such conditions, if any, as may be determined by law, avail of or adopt

[1] Article 45.
[2] Dáil Debates, vol. 67, col. 60.
[3] Articles 28 and 29.

any organ, instrument, or method of procedure used or adopted for the like purpose by the members of any group or league of nations with which the state is or becomes associated for the purpose of international co-operation in matters of common concern.[1]

Mr. de Valera admitted that this arrangement had been suggested by the 'exact circumstances in which we find ourselves at the moment',[2] but he argued that even if Eire was a wholly isolated state the facilities allowed by Article 29 would be appropriate and might be advantageous. He was insistent that such permissive authority contained nothing derogatory to the powers of the people or of Parliament or of the government. External relations would henceforward be in the position which they could be dealt with and handled as a matter of public policy without raising constitutional issues. Since the Constitution could be amended by referendum there was nothing to prevent an amendment which would delete Article 29 and, equally, nothing to prevent the Dáil passing by way of ordinary legislation an act which would supersede or repeal the External Relations Act. Moreover, as additional safeguards, the Constitution provided that every international agreement to which the state became a party should be laid before the Dáil[3] 'and that war should not be declared without the assent of the Dáil'.[4] This vital provision gave the force of law to what Mr. Mackenzie King was contemporaneously seeking to give the authority of convention in Canada.

The Constitution was approved by the people in a referendum held simultaneously with a general election in July 1937. The voting for the Constitution and for the election was entirely separate, and it was open to the electorate to reject the Constitution and yet return Mr. de Valera to office, or alternatively to reject the government and yet sanction the Constitution it had recommended. This dual vote, however, unquestionably encouraged a party verdict on the Constitution, which was regrettable. In the event both the Constitution and the government whose outlook it embodied secured the approval of the electorate.[5] In neither case was the majority large. This was not surprising in the case of the government because the accurate representation secured by the use of the single transferable vote has meant that Irish parties are virtually precluded from obtaining majorities comparable to those obtained in the United Kingdom by the Liberal party in 1906, the National government in 1931, or the Labour party in 1945. On the other hand, the

[1] Article 29 (2).
[2] Dáil Debates, vol. 67, col. 61.
[3] Article 29 (5).
[4] Article 28 (3).
[5] The voting was:

For acceptance of the Constitution	685,105
For the rejection of the Constitution	526,945

First preference votes at the General Election were:

Fianna Fáil	603,172
Fine Gael	460,086
Labour	135,758

ratification of the Constitution, the fundamental law of the state, was something for which wide approval on non-party lines might have been expected. But this was not to be. The Constitution touched too closely upon conflicting interpretations of recent Irish history to secure a general, as distinct from a majority, sanction.

The enactment of the Constitution in December 1937 was a milestone in the political evolution of the Twenty-Six Counties. Henceforward Eire was by her own fundamental law a republic in fact, though not in name, associated with the British Commonwealth of Nations, the symbol of whose unity was the Crown. However discreetly veiled, that was a development of far-reaching importance.

THE COMMONWEALTH AND THE CONSTITUTION

The new Constitution was inaugurated with high ceremonial in Dublin on 29 December 1937. That evening its architect, Mr. de Valera, broadcast to the United States on its significance:

> The Christian philosophy of life has determined the character of our people for over a thousand years, and the chief significance of the new Constitution, coming at the present time, is that it is in complete accord with the national conviction and tradition in these matters, and that it bears upon its face the character of the public law of a great Christian democracy.[1]

But important though the enactment of the Constitution might be, it aroused no general rejoicing in Ireland. Internally the familiar well-tried principles of British parliamentary democracy were retained in all their essentials, while the presidential superstructure was a tempting target for astringent humour. More important, the inauguration of the new Constitution marked no advance towards the reunion of Ireland. Its enactment served to throw into relief the widening division between North and South, for while the Constitution did not use the name of the republic, that was not because of any lack of conviction but because of the sense of inappropriateness. When Mr. Frank MacDermot asked Mr. de Valera what would have been the position if the boundary did not exist, Mr. de Valera replied categorically that 'if the Northern problem were not there . . . there would be a flat, downright proclamation of a republic in this Constitution'.[2] An awareness of the growing strength of the republicanism in the Twenty-Six Counties heightened misgivings in the Six Counties. It was Mr. de Valera's conviction that the Constitution had been studiously moderate. He might have made much political capital at home out of the dramatic declaration of a republic coupling it with final secession from the Commonwealth, but despite the occasional vehemence of his language, his actions were restrained. He had, he believed at considerable

[1] *Irish Press*, 30 December 1937.
[2] Dáil Debates, vol. 68, col. 430.

sacrifice, left the way open for reunion on a basis of close co-operation with the British Commonwealth. External Association, as embodied in the External Relations Act and authorized by the Constitution, was intended not only to recognize the community of interests between Britain and Ireland, but also to conciliate minority sentiment within Ireland. It is here that the measure of Mr. de Valera's misunderstanding of Unionist opinion becomes apparent. What he regarded as a concession, they viewed as a sinister measure designed to disrupt yet further the unity of the British Isles and thereby to undermine their own position as an integral part of the United Kingdom. The reactions to the Constitution revealed that with the passage of time the two sections of Ireland were drawing not closer together but farther apart. This might be a matter for regret; it was certainly not a matter for surprise. Partition, as C. P. Scott had foreseen, could have no other result. 'Its real objects', he wrote of the Government of Ireland Act in May 1920, 'so far as I can make out are, first to get rid of the Home Rule Act, and secondly to entrench the Six Counties against Nationalist Ireland. Its effect, one fears, will be not to make a solution easier but to make it harder, by creating a fresh and powerful obstacle.'[1] That was an accurate forecast to the realization of which politicians both north and south of the Border had made their own weighty contribution.

On the day when the new Constitution came into force, the *Irish Press*, the unofficial organ of the Fianna Fáil party, flamboyantly proclaimed:

> Eire is mistress of her own destiny. No foreign domination exists to thwart her plans, to invade her rights, to challenge her supremacy.
>
> The British connexion is a thing of the dead past. Its dark and blighting shadow has been forever removed from the face of the country. Another echo of the rattle of its chains and the memory of its misdeeds only serve to recall the gallant struggle which resulted in the overthrow of British rule.

In London, however, His Majesty's government, to whose ears the echo of rattling chains was clearly inaudible, adopted an attitude of judicious benevolence. Their views were embodied in a statement issued, with the agreement of the governments of the oversea dominions, which declared:[2]

> His Majesty's government in the United Kingdom have considered the position created by the new Constitution which was approved by the Parliament of the Irish Free State in June 1937 and came into force on 29 December. They are prepared to treat the new Constitution as not affecting a fundamental alteration in the position of the Irish Free State, in future to be described under the new Constitution as 'Eire' or 'Ireland', as a member of the British Commonwealth of Nations.
>
> His Majesty's government in the United Kingdom have ascertained that His Majesty's governments in Canada, the Commonwealth of Australia, New Zealand, and the Union of South Africa are also prepared so to treat the new Constitution.

[1] J. L. Hammond, *C. P. Scott of the Manchester Guardian* (London, Bell, 1934) p. 273.

[2] See *The Times*, 30 December 1937.

His Majesty's government in the United Kingdom take note of Articles 2, 3, and 4 of the new Constitution. They cannot recognize that the adoption of the name Eire or Ireland, or any other provisions of those Articles, involves any right to territory or jurisdiction over territory forming part of the United Kingdom of Great Britain and Northern Ireland, or affects in any way the position of Northern Ireland as an integral part of the United Kingdom of Great Britain and Northern Ireland. They therefore regard the use of the name Eire or Ireland in this connexion as relating only to that area which has hitherto been known as the Irish Free State.

Quietly and unobtrusively though this statement of policy was made from Downing Street, its importance was great. With a remarkable persistence Mr. de Valera had remained true to his conception of External Association over a period of sixteen years. Through the External Relations Act and the Constitution of 1937 he had put it into practical effect. This attainment of a once seemingly impracticable goal had been achieved only as a result of a constitutional revolution which had involved first the removal of the Oath, then the amendment or deletion of the clauses in the 1922 Constitution relating to the Crown, and finally the enactment of a new Constitution in which there was no reference to Crown or Treaty or to any relationship with the Commonwealth. All that remained on paper of the hardly negotiated constitutional settlement of 1921 was a provision, skilfully, if inelegantly phrased, which gave a permissive sanction to the government of the day to use the Crown for certain external functions. Mr. de Valera might well have felt not a little frustrated when in response to these drastic, even revolutionary, measures the government of the United Kingdom should feel that he had effected no 'fundamental alteration'.

This Commonwealth reaction to the new Irish Constitution avoided difficult questions by a resolute refusal to admit that they had been raised. Though it succeeded in its immediate purpose, its wisdom was doubtful, for it rested upon an interpretation of events and an estimate of the forces behind them not destined to be justified in the sequel. In 1937 the governments of the Commonwealth had a second opportunity of acknowledging frankly that the conception of dominion status was not well suited to a highly self-conscious national state whose history and tradition was quite distinct from that of Britain and of the oversea dominions. They were, however, more mindful of the risks of diversity in the Commonwealth pattern than of the dangers of a wholly artificial conformity. Accordingly they argued that the External Relations Act, by indirectly recognizing the Crown for certain limited purposes in relation to foreign countries, preserved the essence of the Commonwealth connexion because implicitly that was tantamount to paying allegiance to the Crown.

From a highly questionable premise—for was there not an element of absurdity in claiming that a state was paying allegiance when its rulers insisted that they were doing nothing of the kind?—many conclusions followed. If it were true that Eire remained a dominion after 1937 despite the Irish nationality legislation of 1935 and despite the provisions of the Constitution, Irish citizens were British subjects owing allegiance to the Crown. This interpretation, unacceptable both to people and to government in Ireland, was hardly conducive to good understanding. Persistence in it served to provoke not only irritation but also misunderstanding elsewhere within the Commonwealth, thereby obscuring and even modifying in some respects a relationship with the oversea dominions which rested on quite different and more solid foundations. At the time the view that Eire was still a member of the Commonwealth elicited no protest from Mr. de Valera, who had good reasons of his own for acquiescing in an interpretation which he did not wish to challenge. But subsequently he made it clear on many occasions that Eire regarded herself, not as a member of the British Commonwealth, but as a state outside it, externally associated for certain purposes with the countries of the Commonwealth. There existed, therefore, for no less than twelve years, a notable difference of view between the Irish government and the governments of the Commonwealth about the status of Eire. The one believed her to be not a member but an associate of the Commonwealth, while the others affected to discern no fundamental change in her position as a dominion. By so doing they committed themselves implicitly to the view that the relationship with Eire was not an inappropriate relationship between Britain and a dominion. From this, as we shall see later, consequences flowed which suggest that a less precipitate flight from reality in 1937 might have had some advantages. Tolerance and a generous moderation, which the Commonwealth governments displayed in marked degree, did not wholly compensate for lack of bold and imaginative statesmanship. Had not the time come to recognize that dominion status had failed, and to invite Mr. de Valera to expound his ideas of the relationship that should prevail between Ireland and the Commonwealth and to examine without prejudice how far they were practicable?

THE LAST PHASE OF THE ECONOMIC WAR

The enactment of the Constitution of 1937 and its acceptance by the United Kingdom government undoubtedly helped to ease Anglo-Irish relations by narrowing the area of dispute. Almost immediately conversations were begun to consider the ways in which the protracted economic war arising out of the non-payment of the land annuities in 1932 by the Irish government might be settled without leaving either party unduly dissatisfied. The prospects of such a compromise were greatly enhanced by the lessons to be drawn from the trade statistics for the preceding six years. As Professor Hancock[1] has so clearly

[1] *Survey*, vol. 1, pp. 351 ff., to which the reader is referred for an illuminating analysis of the causes and immediate consequences of the dispute.

shown, these statistics suggested that the economic interdependence of Britain and Ireland was so close that even deliberate policy could do little to break it down. Mr. de Valera had endeavoured to blunt the edge of the retaliatory economic duties imposed by Britain in 1932 on agricultural exports from the Irish Free State by seeking alternative markets for Irish products elsewhere. The search was pursued with diligence and imagination. Subsidies and bounties were paid regardless of strictly economic considerations in the hope of discovering and exploiting every alternative outlet. But the net result had been deeply disappointing to the Irish government. Six years of trial and experiment had resulted only in a very modest redirection of the Irish export trade. Where in 1929 some 6 per cent. of the Irish Free State's exports went to non-British countries, that proportion had increased only to just 7 per cent. by 1935 and to 8 per cent. in 1938. The economic argument was, therefore, from the Irish point of view strongly in favour of a settlement.

The report of the Banking Commission which was available to the government by the end of 1937 powerfully underlined the lessons to be drawn from the trade returns. The Commission laid much emphasis on the injurious economic consequences to the Irish Free State of the special duties imposed by the United Kingdom. The derangement caused to trade and vital economic activities constituted in their view 'a burden' on the economic life of the country which should be removed. They observed that

> the serious reduction in income of important branches of the Free State agriculture, rendering production unremunerative, tends to retard investment and improvement of efficiency. Moreover, when measures are taken to give compensation to agriculturists, one artificiality is often added to another; and these measures may often be a source of further dislocation.[1]

While it is true that the report of the Commission was to some extent discounted as being a masterly restatement of conservative economic doctrines in their Irish setting, the concern of the Commission both with the general deterioration in the economic position and with the growing artificiality of the price structure was too well founded not to exert some influence on government policy. Nor could the simple statement that 'a country gains an advantage by concentration upon those exports which are comparatively most profitable'[2] be fundamentally challenged. Yet acceptance of the report demanded some modification of economic nationalist policies as hitherto pursued by the Irish government and above all the lifting of Britain's retaliatory duties on Irish agricultural products. Mr. de Valera was himself not averse to profiting from economic experience provided always that his political objectives were not thereby sacrificed. If it were true that the farmers had shown 'great powers of resistance',[3] they could not be expected to withstand

[1] *Report of the Commission of Inquiry into Banking, Currency, and Credit, 1938* (Dublin Stationery Office, P. No. 2628) p. 50.

[2] ibid.

[3] ibid. p. 53.

adverse conditions indefinitely. Moreover, a reduced income for farmers meant less purchasing power in their hands, and that had wide and unwelcome repercussions.[1] Prohibitive duties, artificial redirection of trade through subsidy and bounty, had incidentally sheltered inefficiency. That was no part of Mr. de Valera's purpose. He recognized, too, the truth of the Commission's comment that social welfare was directly related to economic efficiency.[2] The raising of social standards had been one of the planks in the Fianna Fáil electoral platform. Yet, to take one important example, weekly agricultural wages had dropped from the low figures of 24*s.* 6*d.* a week in 1930, to 21*s.* in 1934, and by 1937 had recovered only to 22*s.* a week.[3] If Mr. de Valera's government viewed without disquiet the heavy losses incurred by the 'ranchers', regarded by the rank and file of the Fianna Fáil party as little better than parasites upon agricultural society, the plight of the agricultural labourer was something that concerned them more closely. It is true that in a country of small farmers actively farming their own land the number of agricultural labourers in the strict sense of the term is comparatively low. In 1926 their total numbered no more than 126,000 in the Twenty-Six Counties. But even on the basis of political calculation, the loss of their votes to Labour could not be taken lightly by a party which has always shown itself sensitive to opposition from the left. And more generally it was the hardships of the worker and the smaller farmer that most inclined the government towards a compromise settlement of the economic issues in dispute with Britain.

The failure to effect any substantial redirection of Irish trade should not be taken to mean that all the main objectives of the Fianna Fáil government in the economic and the social field had to be abandoned. On the contrary a substantial and lasting measure of success had been achieved in broadening the basis of Irish agriculture. New incentives were felt in the country-side. Irish farmers became more conscious of recent improvements in agricultural machinery and of the need to modernize their farm equipment so as to secure a higher level of productivity from the land. Hard times, the need for rapid readjustment, demanded the acquisition of new techniques. Fattening cattle on good land for a secure market in Britain unquestionably encouraged lazy farming, and Mr. de Valera and his colleagues were resolved that there should be no return to the days when the Irish Free State had been no more than Britain's 'kitchen garden'. The greater measure of self-sufficiency, attained after so exacting a struggle and such great economic hardship, had come to stay, and though the change-over from cattle-breeding to tillage had been carried too far, the growing of wheat, of sugar-beet, and other crops was to continue on a large scale. In such circumstances there existed no good reason why a policy of national self-sufficiency pursued with moderation should preclude a settlement with Britain, which would end the drain of the economic war and which might hold out hope of renewed prosperity to the country-side

[1] ibid. [2] ibid. p. 52. [3] ibid. p. 48.

after its lean years. National self-sufficiency remained the ideal of the government, but the unwelcome lessons of economic facts could not be indefinitely ignored.

The British government also desired a settlement of the trade war for both economic and political reasons. On the economic side Irish trade had always been profitable because it was roughly on a pound for pound basis. Irish imports of machinery and coal had been materially reduced at a time when growing economic austerity in the world at large enhanced the attraction of a close and secure market. In September 1934, two years after the beginning of the 'economic war', the *Manchester Guardian* protested that 'with a supineness without modern parallel', the government had allowed 'British commerical interests to be sacrificed because it has not the negotiating ability to settle a political dispute'.[1] In November of the same year *The Economist* inquired whether Britain was

> really to allow this suicidal 'economic war' to become a permanency? . . . The damage to Ireland is clearly large, though apparently by no means as catastrophic as the British government expected. The damage to Great Britain is no less. Our best customer has fallen to fifth place; our shipping, insurance, and other 'invisible' income has been diminished. . . . A trade war with Germany, France, or the United States would arouse insistent protests which the government could not afford to disregard. Trade with Ireland was, until two years ago, more important than trade with any of these Great Powers. If the British public allows the economic war with the Free State to continue, it does so in ignorance of the magnitude of the issues involved.[2]

But the economic argument did not prove decisive. More than three years elapsed with only slight modifications in the rigour of the economic war. It was only when the need for an Irish settlement loomed large on the political horizon that the deadlock was broken. By the end of 1937 it was apparent with the breakdown of the League of Nations that Europe had entered upon a period of crisis likely to culminate in war. Was it not folly at such a moment to persist in a highly technical legal dispute which both sides had agreed to submit to arbitration but in which neither would agree to the appropriateness of the tribunal which the other proposed? Mr. Neville Chamberlain's foreign policy was directed towards the reinsuring of Britain's position by removing one by one those points of friction which existed with potentially friendly nations. Did not this suggest not merely that the economic war with Eire should be ended but that any agreement with Mr. de Valera should seek also to remove as far as possible more fundamental sources of friction?

It is difficult to assess with any degree of exactitude what influence the over-

[1] *Manchester Guardian*, 13 September 1934.

[2] *The Economist*, 3 November 1934; quoted in Henry Harrison, *The Neutrality of Ireland* (London, Hale, 1942) p. 169.

sea dominions exerted on the course of United Kingdom policy in Ireland. It is certain that their interest was considerable, for one consequence of Eire's continuing status as a dominion was to keep alive an interest in the course of Anglo-Irish relations among the oversea dominions. Their approach, coloured by internal political considerations in Canada, Australia, and New Zealand where there existed Irish minorities, was by no means uniform, but in general their influence was exerted to secure a settlement of the issues in dispute between Britain and the Irish Free State. In April 1932 the Prime Ministers of Australia, New Zealand, and South Africa appealed to Mr. de Valera to observe the conventions which generally regulated the conduct of members of the Commonwealth one with another. Mr. de Valera did not accept the implied rebuke, and General Hertzog at once reassured him about his own motives by disclaiming any intention of expressing an opinion on the merits of the dispute. His intention was 'to promote the chances of a satisfactory solution of the dispute, a matter of interest to all of us'.[1] Mr. de Valera, moreover, may have remained a trifle sceptical at this stage about the spontaneity of dominion concern in the Anglo-Irish dispute. What evidence there is suggests, however, that in the early stages of the economic war the dominions felt that some measure of retaliatory action by the United Kingdom was not unjustifiable. But as the area of the dispute widened and as it dragged on without any apparent effort at a settlement, they became more restive. They could not indeed remain wholly indifferent to Mr. Neville Chamberlain's observation in the House of Commons to the effect that while the dispute with the Irish Free State had originated with the withdrawal of annuities it was 'really a political dispute' or rather 'an incident in a political dispute', for political disputes between one dominion and the United Kingdom had in the past generally affected the interests of all. Mr. J. H. Thomas, the Secretary of State for the Dominions, gave further ground for reflection when in 1935 he told the House of Commons:[2]

> No one assumes for one moment that the mere question of the annuities is the only difficulty. We could soon get over that difficulty if that were the only matter in dispute. But are the oath of allegiance, the Governor-General as the King's representative, 'a foreign King' as described by Mr. de Valera, not fundamental to any settlement? Of course these things are fundamental. Of course they have to be brought into review.

This was delicate ground, for the implications of Mr. Thomas's words provoked uneasy reactions overseas, particularly in the Union of South Africa, where the office of Governor-General was not free from controversy and where there existed among Afrikaner nationalists a strong bond of sympathy with the political aspirations of the Irish Free State. More widespread was the feeling that however provocative Mr. de Valera's actions might have been at

[1] See *The Times*, 2, 4, and 5 April 1932, and Hancock, *Survey*, vol. 1, p. 337 n.
[2] H. of C. Deb., vol. 304, col. 438.

the outset, this dragging dispute with a small neighbour reflected little credit on British statesmanship. It was not only in Dublin that Mr. Thomas's period at the Dominions Office was not considered outstandingly successful.

An invitation was issued to the government of the Irish Free State to send representatives to the Imperial Conference of 1937, but the invitation was declined. Mr. de Valera gave his reasons to the Dáil on 19 May:

> It may be that certain advantages might be derived for our country by our being represented at the conference . . . but . . . I do not think that it would make either for the settlement of the outstanding disputes between Great Britain and ourselves or for peace between the two peoples that our representatives should run the risk of being put in the same humiliating position in which they were put at Ottawa. Besides, our being there would be open to very grave misunderstanding.[1]

But even though the Irish Free State was not represented, the issues in dispute with the United Kingdom were informally discussed while the dominion Prime Ministers were in London. On the political side, and indeed generally, their influence was undoubtedly directed towards seeking a settlement. Their interest in restoring harmony within the Commonwealth was evident, and they were increasingly anxious to preserve its unity and solidarity in the face of mounting dangers in Europe and the Far East. For these reasons they encouraged the United Kingdom government to adopt a more liberal, forthcoming attitude towards Eire, and this expression of their views played a not inconsiderable part in persuading Mr. Neville Chamberlain to secure a settlement with Mr. de Valera at the first favourable opportunity.

THE AGREEMENT OF 1938 AND THE RETURN OF THE TREATY PORTS

On 17 January 1938 representatives of the governments of the United Kingdom and the Irish Free State met in London. The Irish Free State was represented by Mr. de Valera; Mr. Seán Lemass, Minister for Industry and Commerce; Mr. Seán MacEntee, Minister for Finance; and Dr. James Ryan, Minister for Agriculture. The United Kingdom was represented by Mr. Neville Chamberlain, the Prime Minister; Sir John Simon, Chancellor of the Exchequer; Sir Samuel Hoare, Home Secretary; and Mr. Malcolm MacDonald, Secretary of State for Dominion Affairs. That Mr. de Valera was not unduly sanguine about the prospects may be deduced from his remark that the approach of the two governments to the question of a settlement was diametrically opposed. In Mr. de Valera's view the reunion of Ireland alone could open the way to full and lasting Anglo-Irish friendship, and since the Partition of Ireland was an outrage for which the United Kingdom government was responsible, it was for them to undo it. On this question the United Kingdom government were not prepared to compromise. In their view

[1] Dáil Debates, vol. 67, col. 706.

Partition could not and should not be ended save with the willing assent of Northern Ireland.

Despite the divergence in approach of the British and Irish governments on the question of Partition and the clear impossibility of including it in any settlement at that time, the negotiations proceeded slowly but surely towards a more far-reaching agreement than had been generally anticipated. Its terms, set out in three parts, were announced on 25 April 1938. The first dealt with the arrangements for ending the financial dispute. The Irish government agreed to pay to the United Kingdom a sum of £10 million in final settlement of all claims by either government arising out of the previous dispute. The second part of the agreement dealt with the future development of Anglo-Irish trade.[1] Here the position established prior to 1932 was restored in essentials. The special duties imposed on Irish agricultural produce and livestock since 1932 were repealed, and likewise the retaliatory duties imposed by the Irish government on British coal and manufactured goods were removed. Irish agricultural produce was henceforward to be admitted to the United Kingdom market free of duties, while the British government secured a virtually complete monopoly of the Irish market for British coal. For the rest the formula accepted was the familiar one of equal opportunity 'as laid down in the Ottawa Agreements', and preferential duties on either side were re-established. The agreement was to last for three years in the first instance.

The financial and trade agreements reached in 1938 reflected credit on both governments. If they did not broaden the field of Anglo-Irish trade, at least they freed it from the shackles which had been imposed upon it since 1932, and while recognizing the desire of each country to protect certain of its own products, permitted most-favoured treatment on a reciprocal basis. The benefit to both countries was immediate.

The third part of the 1938 agreement has subsequently proved more controversial. It provided for the return of the Irish Treaty Ports to the control of the Irish government. Under the Treaty of 1921 it had been agreed that until an arrangement was made between the British and Irish governments whereby the Irish Free State undertook her own coastal defence, 'the defence by sea of Great Britain and Ireland shall be undertaken by His Majesty's Imperial Forces . . .'. This general principle was more precisely interpreted in Article 7 of the Treaty, which provided that

> The government of the Irish Free State shall afford to His Majesty's Imperial Forces:
>
> (*a*) In time of peace such harbour and other facilities as are indicated in the Annex hereto, or such other facilities as may from time to time be agreed between the British government and the government of the Irish Free State; and

[1] Cmd. 5728. *Agreements between the Government of the United Kingdom and the Government of Eire, signed at London on 25 April 1938.*

(*b*) In time of war or of strained relations with a foreign Power such harbour and other facilities as the British government may require for the purpose of such defence as aforesaid.

In an Annex to the Treaty the specific facilities required were enumerated. They included the Dockyard Port at Berehaven, the harbour defences at Queenstown and Lough Swilly, together with facilities in the neighbourhood of these ports for coastal defence by air, and fuel storage depots at Haulbowline and Rathmullen. In recent years Irish opinion had become increasingly restive at the retention of these ports and facilities by British forces. National sentiment demanded their return without any particular strategic end in view. The claim was advanced in absolute terms as deriving from an inalienable natural right to absolute control of all national territory. Mr. Churchill records his belief[1] that Mr. de Valera had included the return of the ports as a bargaining counter which could be dispensed with when other points were satisfactorily settled. This is not in accord with any available evidence. It was Mr. de Valera's contention throughout these years that the defence of Ireland should be wholly entrusted to Irishmen, if only because their co-operation in the defence of their country against any aggressor would be half-hearted so long as the responsibility was divided.

It might have appeared that the international situation had so greatly deteriorated by January 1938 that the United Kingdom government would be extremely reluctant to weaken its defensive system at that moment even for the most convincing political reasons. Mr. Chamberlain, however, thought otherwise. It is a remarkable fact that the son of Joseph Chamberlain, the man who had 'killed Home Rule' in 1886, should have approached the Irish question with so sympathetic an understanding of Irish aspirations. Even in 1921 he appears to have been prepared to contemplate a settlement that went beyond dominion status,[2] and by 1938 he was convinced that the settlement of the age-old dispute was essential to the safety of Britain and to her reputation for fair-dealing and good sense. Was it not absurd, at a time when Britain's policy was directed towards pacification and conciliation in Europe, not to take every advantage of the opportunities open to him to end tension nearer home which in recent years had grown dangerously acute, and which might have far-reaching repercussions within the Commonwealth as a whole? Even at a very early stage in the negotiations in January 1938 he entertained wide hopes of what might be achieved.

I shall be grievously disappointed if we don't get an all-round agreement, on everything except Partition. That is a difference that can't be bridged without the assent of Ulster, and her assent won't be given unless she has confidence in the government of Eire, and that cannot be attained except slowly and step by step. But if de Valera will heed the good advice I gave him, I should not despair of ulti-

[1] *Second World War*, vol. 1, p. 216.

[2] cf. Keith Feiling, *The Life of Neville Chamberlain* (London, Macmillan, 1946) p. 87.

mate agreement on unity, and in the meantime I am satisfied that, queer creature as he is in many ways, he is sincere, and that he is no enemy of this country.[1]

Not all his hopes were fulfilled, but in the course of negotiations Mr. Chamberlain and Mr. de Valera developed a mutual liking and respect which played no small part in bringing about the settlement, and particularly that part of it which involved the return of the ports. That was, in Mr. Chamberlain's words, 'an act of faith', and it was because he recognized the integrity of Mr. de Valera's character that he made it.

In view of the British resolve not to compromise in respect of Northern Ireland, Mr. Neville Chamberlain's policy of conciliation was from the first territorially limited to the Treaty Ports. For him the determining factor was the extent to which their return might improve relations between the two countries. But while this broad political consideration was predominant, strategic implications were at least not overlooked. The advice tendered by the Chiefs of Staff assured the Prime Minister that the political advantages to be gained were not likely to impose future strategic liabilities. From the British point of view a friendly Ireland freely negotiating a defensive alliance with the United Kingdom would have provided the ideal solution. But while Partition continued such a proposal had no prospect of serious consideration by the Irish government, though it was fruitlessly explored by the United Kingdom.[2] An alternative policy was the retention of the ports despite Irish protests. This was considered by the Chiefs of Staff in 1936 with the possibility in mind that such a policy might, in war-time, involve British forces in open conflict with a neutral, or even hostile, Ireland. Apart from the political risks of such a conflict, the military prospects were not altogether reassuring. In 1936 the Irish army numbered some 6,000 men not equipped with modern weapons, with a reserve of similar strength behind it, and in addition a territorial force of some 24,000 men. The Chiefs of Staff calculated in the light of these figures that a brigade at the least would be required merely to hold each port, and that if the ports were to be made safe for naval use a division would be needed since the occupation of a considerable hinterland against a probably hostile population would be essential. Anti-aircraft defences would be required as well. They concluded, in the words of Lord Chatfield then First Sea Lord, that

such a position, with 'a series of Gibraltars' scattered round the Irish coast, was, in view of our own meagre military position at that time, divorced from realities. It was natural, therefore, with their continental commitments to France in the event of war with Germany, that the General Staff should not only be strongly averse to accepting such a responsibility, but was anxious to free the army even of its existing task of guarding the ports in peace. . . .[3]

[1] Quoted in Feiling, *Neville Chamberlain*, p. 130.
[2] Chatfield, *It Might Happen Again.*
[3] ibid. pp. 126–7.

In a carefully considered letter to *The Times*[1] in 1942, when the return of the ports was the subject of severe criticism, Lord Chatfield reviewed the arguments used in 1938 in the light of the sequel and still felt that the conclusion then reached was the only one that had been possible.

> The hostility in Eire to the occupation of these ports by the United Kingdom was increasing and it was obvious that unless we were willing and able to hold them by military force they would be useless for naval purposes. To have made these ports secure against land attack, in time of war, by a hostile Eire would have required considerable military forces which we did not possess over and above those needed to fulfil our Continental obligations; nor was there any probability at that time that such forces would become available. It was obvious therefore to the Navy that whether these ports were handed over to Eire or remained under our guardianship there was little if any chance that the Navy would be able to use them.
>
> On the other hand, there were two considerations. First, the political opinion that if we handed back the ports, there would be a hope that an improved atmosphere would be created, that might enable the Navy under the circumstances of war to use the ports by consent. Secondly, a greater chance that Eire ports would be denied to the enemy for hostile action against us. Under these conditions the Admiralty preferred to trust in this matter to something reliable and to use non-Eire bases, trusting to improved anti-submarine measures and to the longer range of modern destoyers.

In the Dáil debate on the agreement, Mr. Cosgrave declared[2] that it would have been possible for his government to take over possession of the ports six or seven years earlier and that he had hesitated to do so because the cost involved would have meant expenditure by the Irish government of somewhere between £350,000 and half a million pounds. This interesting and instructive revelation suggests that the Admiralty view expressed by Lord Chatfield was not one lately formed but one that had been accepted over a period of years. That it was framed in the light of past experience and not of future needs seems, therefore, probable. Yet the Admiralty could hardly have been expected to foresee that enemy forces in the next war would control both the Norwegian and the French ports, and even if they had it is not at all clear, to judge by the substance of Lord Chatfield's argument, that they would necessarily have modified the advice they gave. All that is certain is that they would have had greater difficulty in reaching the conclusion they did.

The decision to return the ports did not escape severe strictures from Mr. Winston Churchill in the House of Commons at the time. He had been one of the architects of the 1921 Treaty and nothing had occurred in the meantime to modify his belief that under conditions of modern naval warfare, the ports, particularly those in the south-west of Ireland, were essential to the safety of

[1] *The Times*, 4 February 1942.

[2] Dáil Debates, vol. 71, col. 49. The offer would appear to have been made to Mr. Desmond Fitzgerald, the Minister for Defence, during a visit to London (ibid. col. 50).

the United Kingdom. On 5 May 1938 he confronted the House of Commons with the possible consequences of Irish neutrality in war-time and drew conclusions very different to those of the Chiefs of Staff. He asked:

But what guarantee have you that Southern Ireland, or the Irish Republic as they claim to be, . . . will not declare neutrality if we are engaged in war with some powerful nation? The first step certainly which such an enemy might take would be to offer complete immunity of every kind to Southern Ireland if she would remain neutral. . . .

. . . You cannot exclude this possibility of neutrality as being one which may well come within the immediate sphere of our experience. . . . the ports may be denied us in the hour of need and we may be hampered in the gravest manner in protecting the British population from privation, and even starvation. Who would wish to put his head in such a noose? Is there any other country in the modern world where such a step would even have been contemplated? . . . It would be an easy step for a Dublin government to deny their use to us. The cannon are there, the mines will be there. But more important for this purpose, the juridical right will be there. . . . You had the rights. You have ceded them. You hope in their place to have good will strong enough to endure tribulation for your sake. Suppose you have it not. It will be no use saying, 'Then we will retake the ports.' You will have no right to do so. To violate Irish neutrality should it be declared at the moment of a great war may put you out of court in the opinion of the world, and may vitiate the cause by which you may be involved in war. . . . You are casting away real and important means of security and survival for vain shadows and for ease.[1]

His later judgement upon Mr. Neville Chamberlain and his service advisers was harsh. He described the return of the ports as 'a gratuitous surrender' which was 'a major injury to British national life and safety', and as an 'improvident example of appeasement' endorsed by a House of Commons 'more completely misled' than any he had ever seen.[2] Yet despite such unreserved denunciation from so formidable a critic the return of the Irish ports is a matter on which judgement must be reserved until some of the war-time consequences of their cession have been examined. Two things, however, may be noted at this stage. The first is that Mr. Chamberlain may have been right in his political, Mr. Churchill in his strategic, judgement. If, therefore, the issue is considered strictly from the point of view of British interests, the historian may well hesitate before pronouncing a final verdict. The balance between political advantage and strategic liability may well be too fine to allow of any easy black or white judgement. The other point to be noted is quite different. How easy it was for a Conservative leader to pursue a policy of conciliation towards Ireland which if sponsored by his Liberal and Labour opponents would surely have elicited a storm of Conservative protest!

[1] H. of C. Deb., vol. 335, coll. 1101–5.
[2] Churchill, *Second World War*, vol. 1, p. 216.

IRISH REACTIONS TO THE RETURN OF THE PORTS

About the welcome accorded to the 1938 agreement by all parties in Eire there is no doubt. The agreement was the beginning of a better understanding between the two countries, and it was both at the time and subsequently regarded as convincing evidence of Britain's good faith. It is true that Mr. de Valera's language in the Dáil did not suggest a man appeased. It was unnecessary, he said,

to stress to anybody who has desired the independence of this country the importance of that agreement from the point of view of Irish sovereignty. The ports are handed over unconditionally. They belong to us as a matter of right, we have always held; we are glad that that right has been recognized and now we are to have them. Among the Articles of the Treaty of 1921 that gave most offence to national sentiment were these, because they meant that part of our territory was still in the British occupation.[1]

But he added, too,

there has been no bargain. There are no conditions. There is no secret understanding, but there is a belief, I am certain—a belief which I have tried, over twenty years, to get into the minds of the British governments and of the British people, . . .—that it is far better . . . and far more advantageous for Britain, to have a free Ireland by its side than an Ireland that would be unfriendly because of liberties which Britain denied.[2]

The agreement of 1938, he argued, was to the advantage of Britain as well as of Eire, because henceforward Eire would provide for her own defence and thereby would also of necessity be providing for the defence of Britain's interests.[3] But, he added, the 'full advantages' would accrue to Britain 'on the day on which the whole of Ireland is recognized as a completely independent state'.

The value of Mr. de Valera's assurances about the defence of the ports themselves was qualified by the lack of any Irish naval forces capable of defending their vital sea approaches. This was frankly recognized in London, but the strategic liability which it might involve in war-time was felt by the government to be more than counterbalanced by the acquisition of Irish good will in the effective land defence of the Twenty-Six Counties as a whole against foreign invasion.

Mr. de Valera's contention that it was good policy for Britain to have a friendly Ireland militarily responsible for maintaining its own independence against any aggressor was implicitly endorsed in guarded terms by Mr. Chamberlain who justified the surrender of the Irish ports, with their highly

[1] Dáil Debates, vol. 71, col. 35. [2] ibid. col. 36.
[3] ibid. col. 38.

doubtful availability, on the ground that thereby Britain obtained the assurance of a friendly Ireland.[1]

The return of the ports had important consequences on the direction of Irish policy. It had been maintained that so long as the ports were in British hands, the ultimate decision about peace and war was not effectively vested in the Dáil despite the explicit provisions to that effect in the Constitutions of 1922 and of 1937. Prior to the 1938 agreement, if Britain were at war, she was entitled to use not only the ports but their immediate hinterland and all such other facilities as were required for their defence. Had Britain availed herself fully of these rights it was hardly conceivable than an enemy engaged in a direct attack upon her would have been prepared to accept an Irish declaration of neutrality as valid. In principle the Irish situation until 1938 corresponded most closely to the South African, where Simonstown filled the role of the Treaty Ports. But in practice geographical situation, reinforced by the more far-reaching provisions of the Anglo-Irish Treaty, made the probable consequences of the existence of these naval facilities of more direct concern to Eire. Mr. de Valera had consistently argued that retention of the ports by Britain deprived the Irish Free State of independence in international affairs. In the course of his earlier correspondence with Mr. J. H. Thomas, he had declared that the defence provisions of the Treaty allowed Britain to claim in time of war or strained relations rights which if granted would make 'a mockery' of Ireland's right to neutrality.[2] Professor Keith acknowledged the force of the Irish arguments at the time, pointing out[3] that while the right of neutrality in a British war was asserted in the Constitution of 1937, nothing was done affecting the presence of British forces on Irish territory, and therefore the right of Eire to claim respect for her neutrality 'would doubtless be impaired' in the eyes of foreign states. This was precisely the reason why the return of the ports gave to Eire a new freedom of action in foreign policy. It was an important fact whose consequence we shall consider in relation to Irish international, as distinct from Commonwealth, policies.

A word, however, should first be said on the less controversial question of the long-term reaction to Mr. Chamberlain's policy in Ireland. Mr. Chamberlain felt, even as early as 1938, that he would be accused of making concessions to Eire from weakness. But he felt that the goal which he had in mind, the ending of a long quarrel, the beginning perhaps of better relations between North and South, and the co-operation of Eire with the United Kingdom in trade and defence justified the risks and counterbalanced any liabilities which his policies might incur. In one respect he was not mistaken. Mr. Chamberlain's policy of conciliation earned high tributes in Ireland. Mr. de Valera

[1] H. of C. Deb., vol. 335, coll. 1076 ff.

[2] Cmd. 4056, p. 4, reprinted in Keith, *Speeches and Documents*, p. 463.

[3] Letter to the *Irish Independent*, entitled 'The New Constitution, a British View', 7 May 1937, reprinted in *King and Constitution*, pp. 63 ff.

declared that Mr. Chamberlain's government had acted with a wisdom and generosity unsurpassed in British history, and it is perhaps fitting here to recall the letter which he wrote to the British Prime Minister on 15 May 1940 when, in a dark hour, Mr. Chamberlain fell from office:

> I would like to testify that you did more than any former British statesman to make a true friendship between the peoples of our two countries possible, and, if the task has not been completed, that it has not been for want of good will on your part. I hope that you may still be able to work for, and that we may both be spared to see, the realization of our dream,—to see our two peoples living side by side with a deep neighbourly sense of their value one to another, and with a friendship which will make possible whole-hearted co-operation between them in all matters of common interest.[1]

THE IRISH ATTITUDE TO THE LEAGUE OF NATIONS

Mr. James Dillon once illustrated, with characteristic over-emphasis, the undeniable fact that opinion in Eire was much more concerned with Anglo-Irish relations than with the affairs of the League of Nations, by observing that probably 999·9 persons out of every thousand were interested in the former, while only 0·001 were interested in the League and its problems in Africa and other parts of the world.[2] But that serves only to show how uncertain a guide public opinion may be, for the failure of the League was an event of critical importance for the Irish Free State and had a greater part in the determining of Irish policy before 1939 than it had in the case of any other member of the Commonwealth.

Ireland was a small country, geographically sheltered but none the less close to one of the great storm centres of the world. Her natural ally and protector, the United Kingdom, was her traditional enemy, and however much age-old antagonisms had been blunted Britain, in Irish eyes, still deliberately maintained Partition. That in itself made impossible the intimate association for security and defence which geographical situation, economic interdependence, and common sense demanded. It was reinforced by a widespread feeling which persisted even after 1938 that Eire was not wholly free to pursue her own policies. Here the imposition of dominion symbolism contributed materially to a feeling that while the dominions enjoyed freedom in all lesser issues, the supreme question of peace or war was still decided in London. This misgiving, prevalent, as we have seen, in some of the oversea dominions, could have been eradicated in Ireland only by the most convincing and conclusive evidence that it had no foundation in fact. That evidence could be supplied only by an Irish policy on the issue of peace and war which was different from that pursued and desired by Britain.

The emotions of Catholic Ireland were profoundly stirred by the League

[1] Quoted in Feiling, *Neville Chamberlain*, p. 311.

[2] Dáil Debates, vol. 62, col. 2661.

imposition of sanctions against Italy and by the course of the civil war in Spain, but the more usual atmosphere of indifference meant that it was Mr. de Valera, at once Prime Minister and Minister for External Affairs, who was responsible to an extent rare under a system of parliamentary government for the direction of foreign policy.

In September 1932 Mr. de Valera took office as President of the Council of the League, and addressed the Assembly as its acting President with memorable frankness. Within a year of the first Japanese aggression in China, he was convinced that the final testing time for the League had come. Ordinary people in every country, he said, were watching to see if the test would reveal 'a weakness presaging ultimate dissolution' or some assurance of a renewal of vigour and growth. He acknowledged that on all sides there were complaints, criticism, and suspicion, and he felt himself that the League seemed more and more to be devoting itself to matters of secondary importance while the great international questions of peace and war were being shelved and ignored. Worse still there was the suspicion that if 'the hand that is raised against the Covenant is sufficiently strong, it can smite with impunity'.

Let us make no mistake about it, the satisfaction with . . . the work of the League which we may feel in this Assembly is not shared universally by opinion outside. Blue books . . . and complacent resolutions cannot satisfy the general demand for effective action. We are defendants at the bar of public opinion, with a burden of justification upon us which is almost overwhelming.[1]

Mr. de Valera's outspokenness created more surprise overseas than at home. In so far as Irish opinion had been interested in the League, it had been throughout its existence concerned with two things. The first, with which Mr. Cosgrave was as much concerned as Mr. de Valera, was that the League should provide a system of international security which would allow the smaller nations to escape from their age-long dependence upon the will of greater neighbours. Every opportunity had been taken to underline Ireland's independent nationhood, which was felt to be guaranteed by full membership of the League, and reinsured by active participation in its councils. The other and the more general interest was that the League should in fact prove the instrument by which justice might be made to prevail over force. Mr. de Valera consistently argued that this organization which bore 'an appearance of a device for the continuance of the coalition which won the war, and for the effective domination of the world by that coalition,[2] should be transformed so as to allow not merely of the peaceful settlement of disputes but of the timely settlement of existing problems and the removing of existing injustices before they reached a dangerous point. The League, he argued, must be built up so

[1] The speech is reproduced in *Peace and War; Speeches by Mr. de Valera on International Affairs* (Dublin, Gill, 1944) p. 11.

[2] Broadcast from Geneva, 2 October 1932, quoted ibid. p. 19.

that it can lend effective material support to all those who, no matter what their nation, were striving to find a just and peaceful solution of urgent and difficult international problems. Settlement alone was not enough, for no settlement could endure which was not founded on justice. This was a theme to which Mr. de Valera consistently returned. After the Munich agreement, he spoke of the idea of collective assistance for the maintenance of wrong as a monstrosity which had to be replaced by the idea of collective assistance for the undoing of wrongs. The League should not shrink from raising a question simply because it had not reached a critical stage. It was, in his view, the function of the League to examine such problems before they reached that stage and so secure a settlement by consent, which being by consent might for that reason assume an air of finality. Just as emphasis upon the League as against the Commonwealth was regarded as a guarantee of real independence, so it was conceived that the League as the active redresser of existing wrongs might one day resolve the wrong of Partition. But this relation of international policy to a particular background did not lessen the force of Mr. de Valera's conclusion that the 'only alternative to competitive armaments is the security which an uncompromising adherence to the Covenant will afford'.[1]

The direction of Mr. de Valera's thought crystallized as the years went by. In 1935 he argued that the rights of the 'haves' and the 'have nots' needed to be adjusted from time to time in the case of states as of individuals within the states.

> . . . when a wrong cries out for redress or evil for a cure, there must be some means of providing them in time without waiting for a threat of war to compel attention. It is foolish to hope and extremely dangerous to expect that by any device, such as the Covenant of the League, one can freeze and keep for ever static any existing state system irrespective of how it came into existence.[2]

From this premise he reached the potentially dangerous conclusion that 'only what is fundamentally just has the right to last'. What is just? Who is to decide it? In his answer to the first question Mr. de Valera would certainly have placed high in the list of essentials national self-determination. His constant complaint was not that too much attention had been paid to that principle in 1919, but too little. Confronted with the difficulties its application involved he was prepared to contemplate drastic remedies. When the protection of minorities was discussed at Geneva, Mr. de Valera observed[3] that the ideal solution of minority problems was a transfer, where possible, of the minority back to its original home, but failing that the more practical solution was to give the minority, if it were homogeneous and inhabited a continuous area, the greatest amount of local autonomy that could be given consistent with the

[1] *Peace and War*, p. 11.
[2] 12 September 1934, quoted ibid. p. 42.
[3] 13 September 1934, quoted ibid. pp. 27 ff.

maintenance of the unity of the state. Either solution presupposed the existence of some tribunal by which the law should be interpreted and applied, and some means by which its judgements could be enforced against a recalcitrant state. How was it to be created? The League must not merely be strengthened, it must be radically reformed. There must be established, Mr. de Valera argued, 'an organ . . . for the making of the law and the changing of it'. The needs of international society demanded a flexible instrument to legislate for them and a tribunal to interpret and to apply the law. Thus Mr. de Valera, the unyielding champion of national sovereignty, advanced to the conclusion that no system of international government could be effective until 'the theory of the absolute state, interpreted to mean that a state is above all law, had been abandoned'.[1] In the meantime 'to destroy the League would be a crime against humanity'.[2] It must be maintained and strengthened by the fulfilment of its obligations in the spirit and the letter.

The Irish government did not shrink from the logic of its own conclusions. However indifferent might be the majority of the Irish people, the government—which for the purposes of external affairs meant Mr. de Valera—were insistent that the League's authority should be fully enforced. That was their view in 1931 when Japan invaded North China and occupied Manchukuo. That again was their view in the more critical case of Abyssinia. Mindful of the lessons of the Far East, which had made a deep impression on Mr. de Valera, there was no disposition to underestimate the issues involved.

In September 1935 Mr. de Valera declared in Geneva that no illusion should remain about the imperative need for the League to enforce its will. He recognized that for the Irish people there was no easy choice. 'To be thrown into a position of enmity with those with whom we wish to be on terms of friendship, to have to oppose those whom we admire . . .—what more heart-rending alternative can there be to the abandonment of duty and the betrayal of . . . our word solemnly given.'[3] But the price had to be paid. The 'final test' for the League had come. 'Make no mistake, if on any pretext whatever we were to permit the sovereignty of even the weakest state amongst us to be unjustly taken away, the whole foundation of the League would crumble into dust.'[4] Ultimate responsibility lay not with statesmen only but with peoples who had not yet been prepared to deny themselves the privilege of grasping opportunities to satisfy their own selfish ambitions, however much in theory they might assent to the principle that the rule of law should be substituted for that of force. As a result, 'after sixteen years of existence, the League would now appear to be in imminent peril of splitting on the the rock on which previous attempts at international organization . . . have perished'. Yet the policy of the Irish government would still be determined by its desire to see

[1] ibid. pp. 41–42. [2] ibid. p. 43.
[3] Speech in the Assembly of the League, 16 September 1935, ibid. p. 45.
[4] ibid. p. 46.

the League of Nations preserved as an effective guarantee of peace.[1] By October, when Italy had invaded Abyssinia and general hostilities had broken out, Mr. de Valera's conclusions were even more sobering. He warned the Irish people that Japan's successful violation of the Covenant had shaken the League to its foundations, and that if in Abyssinia 'a second similar successful violation takes place, the League of Nations must disappear as an effective safeguard for individual members. It becomes in fact, a source of danger—a trap for states trusting in it, leading them to neglect adequate measures for their own defence.'[2] Here was the principal lesson he was to draw from the Abyssinian crisis. It was a very important one.

Mr. de Valera's policy of support of sanctions against Italy was in itself courageous. Opinion in Ireland was deeply disturbed, and the Roman Catholic Church in particular was reluctant to see the full rigour of collective security applied against Italy. The imposition of sanctions was not opposed by the two principal opposition parties, but Mr. de Valera's strong support of the League evoked bitter recriminations. Some members of the opposition argued that the Italian invasion afforded an opportunity of making a bargain with Britain whereby Irish support for sanctions would be compensated by a deal over the ports or over Northern Ireland or preferably both. Others attacked Mr. de Valera for blindly following Britain's lead along a road which might lead to war with Italy. But Mr. de Valera's conviction, that here was an issue of principle on which compromise would be at once dishonourable and unwise, remained unshaken. He maintained that the Irish Free State had signed the League Covenant, that the League Covenant imposed the most solemn obligations, and that having undertaken these obligations the Irish Free State had no option about the imposition of sanctions against Italy. By signing the Covenant she had signed away her freedom of action, when the League by an overwhelming majority proclaimed a state to be an aggressor. All Mr. de Valera's emphasis throughout the crisis, therefore, was upon the need for full support for the League; to give it a last but a fair trial. If it failed it would, he made absolutely clear, fundamentally affect his own approach and presumably also that of his country towards international affairs. In October 1935 he said that 'we have consistently held that the obligations of the Covenant should be enforced', and Irish criticism of the League was not that the obligations it imposed 'are too strict but rather that they are not strict enough to be effective'.[3] And for those who denounced his subservience to British policy was reserved the crushing rejoinder, 'if your worst enemy happens to be going to Heaven by the same road you are, you don't for that reason turn around and go in the other direction'.[4]

When it was clear in the summer of 1936 that the League had failed in

[1] Broadcast from Radio Éireann, 4 October 1935, quoted in *Peace and War*, pp. 51–52.
[2] ibid. p. 50.
[3] ibid. pp. 52–53.
[4] Quoted in M. J. MacManus, *Eamon de Valera* (Dublin, 1944) p. 324.

Abyssinia, Mr. de Valera made no attempt to disguise the unwelcome fact. Of those who proffered consolation at Geneva, he inquired, 'is it not the height of folly to think we can go on just as if nothing had happened?'[1] He warned the Dáil that the all-important lesson to be learned from this sorry, tragic episode was that those who depended upon the League of Nations for security were depending 'upon a broken reed'. He dissented strongly from the view that the case was a bad one for the League of Nations. 'My view is that there was never a better chance for the League of Nations to be successful against a great power as there was in this case, and that if it failed in the case of Italy it was bound to fail in the case of other powers.'[2] So profound were his misgivings that Mr. de Valera considered whether the Irish Free State should withdraw from the League. It was not, he observed, possible or honourable for a country to withdraw when it was called upon to fulfil specific obligations, but when those obligations had been discharged, then it was fair and reasonable for a country to consider whether continued membership was an advantage or a liability. But he was reluctant to take so final a step. He still believed that the League had its value as a *milieu* in which statesmen could meet, as a debating society, as a means whereby lesser disputes might be quietly discussed. But on the major issue of peace and war he now concluded that the League had no further functions to discharge. He told the Dáil in June 1936 that he believed that 'the League of Nations as it is constituted at present, is a danger rather than a benefit'.[3] Because sanctions had failed, there was no use in a continuance of sanctions either in the particular case of Italy[4] or in future emergencies. Countries which committed themselves because of obligations under the League to take steps that would certainly fail to achieve their object were bound to provoke enmities which might have serious consequences for them, particularly if they were small Powers.

What then was left for a small nation to do? What was the prudent course for it to follow? After 1936 Mr. de Valera reluctantly answered: 'isolate itself from a world dominated by the greed and the ambitions and the selfishness of the Great Powers.' The reluctance was due to his own experience of the working of the League and his past hopes of strengthening it so that in the end it might become an effective instrument of world government. But when such hopes could no longer be reasonably entertained there was, for the Irish Free State, unlike Australia or New Zealand, no congenial grouping with which

[1] 2 July 1936, quoted in *Peace and War*, p. 55.

[2] Dáil Debates, vol. 62, col. 2726. An instructive analysis of Mr. de Valera's approach to the problems of the League and of Irish foreign policy will be found in the Dáil Debates for June 1936, vol. 62, coll. 2650 ff. The debate that followed is also of interest; see ibid. coll. 2661–784.

[3] ibid. col. 2735.

[4] Eire was among the first to recognize Italian sovereignty over Ethiopia, though Mr. de Valera argued in December 1937 that in accrediting the new Irish minister to the 'King of Italy and Emperor of Ethiopia' *de jure* recognition was not involved. 14 December 1937, Dáil Debates, vol. 69, col. 2260.

unreserved co-operation was politically possible. Mr. de Valera's experience of co-operation with the countries of the Commonwealth in the Italo-Abyssinian dispute had not been altogether happy. He had been criticized in Britain for underlining that the Irish Free State was acting independently. He was criticized at home, bitterly criticized, as we have seen, because he had co-operated with Britain in the general policy of sanctions against Italy.[1] Though his policy was carried through to the end without much open opposition, this criticism at home probably reinforced the conclusions which he had drawn in Geneva. Once the League had ceased to be a genuinely international organization for the preservation of peace, it was almost certain to become the mouthpiece of one group of Great Powers. That was a prospect which Mr. de Valera could not regard with equanimity, for, apart from the international implications, co-operation was bound sooner or later to place him in a false and vulnerable position at home.

There were, too, other considerations. Irish mistrust of Russia was deep and profound, and at Geneva Mr. de Valera voiced his frank misgivings about Russia's admission to the League.[2] They were reinforced by the course of the civil war in Spain. History and religion had created ties of sentiment and friendship between Ireland and Spain since the sixteenth century. While once more the Irish government responded to the crisis of the Spanish civil war by a correct and resolute adherence to a policy of non-intervention, Irish Catholic opinion came down heavily on the side of General Franco. Again there was no open challenge to Mr. de Valera's policy, but the United Ireland party urged in November 1936 and in February 1937 that relations with the Caballero republican government, 'the government of Anti-Christ', should be broken off and formal recognition accorded to General Franco. Again Mr. de Valera stood firm, maintaining that recognition should not be a gesture of sympathy but a response to a factual situation.[3] The ill-starred brigade enlisted by General O'Duffy to play its melancholy, inglorious part on the side of General Franco was important only as the symptom of the general conviction that General Franco was the defender of Christendom against the infidel from the East. Left-wing opinion might voice its dissent from so simple an interpretation of Spain's internal politics, but left-wing opinion in Ireland was neither strong nor particularly vocal. The Church came down with a heavy hand to discourage any opinions sympathetic to republican Spain, and more generally the adjective 'red' was freely employed to stigmatize and to discredit opinions that elsewhere might have passed as mildly liberal. In this atmosphere, from

[1] As late as 1938 these criticisms were commonplace. cf. Mr. de Valera's indignant comment: 'I resent very much the suggestion that our foreign policy is being dictated by Britain. That has never been true so far as I am aware and certainly it has not been true since I came into office' (Dáil Debates, vol. 72, col. 686).

[2] cf. Mr. de Valera's speech of 18 September 1934 on Russia's admission to the League. Quoted in *Peace and War*, pp. 32 ff.

[3] Dáil Debates, vol. 64, coll. 1220–4. See also Carter, *British Commonwealth*, p. 267.

which some members of the opposition tried to derive political advantage, Mr. de Valera's task was neither easy nor congenial.

Mr. de Valera was more and more convinced, as power passed from the League to the great states in Europe, that in matters of peace and war the small states were powerless.[1] Peace, he said, was dependent upon the will of the Great Powers, and all the small nations could do, 'if the statesmen of the greater states fail in their duty, is resolutely to determine that they will not become the tools of any Great Power; and that they will resist with whatever strength they possess every attempt to force them into a war against their will'. In the case of Ireland, the danger in that respect still came, in Mr. de Valera's view, from Britain. 'We hold', he said in 1936, 'that Britain, by the unrighteous continuance of aggression—and I regard the holding of our ports as an act of aggression against our people',[2] had made it difficult if not impossible for Eire to work in harmony with its greater neighbour. The condition of good relations and of co-operation with Britain in international affairs was dependent upon the reintegration of Ireland's national territory. In the meantime it was difficult to take any adequate measures for defence because 'we are liable, on account of the occupation of certain parts of our territory, to attack by any enemy of Great Britain'.[3] But even by 1936 the aim was clearly indicated. '. . . We have', said Mr. de Valera, 'no aggressive designs against any other people', and our desire '. . . is to strengthen ourselves so that we might resist any attempt to make use of our territory for attack upon any other nation', and 'so as to maintain our neutrality.'[4]

The agreement of 1938 produced a friendlier atmosphere but did not modify the essentials of Mr. de Valera's external policy. The European war, which he had long foreseen, remained for him, as for General Hertzog, a war between two groups of imperial Powers, a war between the victorious and the vanquished of 1914–18, in which a small people could play no decisive or even rightful role. Eire, in his view, had no territorial ambitions, for to him as to all Irish nationalists the claim to Northern Ireland being one of national right could not be legitimately so described; she had no commitments and, therefore, in the coming conflict she was not debarred from a policy of isolation. Indeed, it appeared to Mr. de Valera more and more that this was the only policy that could be pursued. Yet he rarely failed to remind his listeners that there continued, and would always continue, to be a community of interests between Britain and Ireland which, were Ireland a united country, might demand active co-operation. But no such co-operation could be considered so long as Ireland was partitioned, partly because it would be thereby rendered ineffective, but still more because it would run counter to the deeper springs of national feeling.

[1] Dáil Debates, vol. 62, col. 2658.
[2] ibid. col. 2741.
[3] ibid. col. 2660.
[4] ibid. col. 2659.

NEUTRALITY AS A POLICY

From 1936 onwards Mr. de Valera's aim, his declared aim, was a policy of neutrality in the event of a European war. Such doubts as he entertained were doubts about its practicability, not about its wisdom or desirability. He was entirely satisfied about the moral and the constitutional position. The Irish Free State had no commitments. In that respect, observed Mr. de Valera, her obligations, or rather her lack of obligations, differed

> in no wise from the position of Canada, Australia, New Zealand, or South Africa. The heads of governments in these states have very definitely stated that they cannot be committed to war and cannot be committed in advance to take any action, except whatever action may at the time be considered right and advisable by their Parliaments in all the circumstances of the time. We are exactly in that situation. There are no advance commitments on us to take any side in a conflict that may ensue or any action whatever, except such as, at the time, may commend itself to Parliament. In other words, the Parliament of that date . . . will be completely free.[1]

Here Mr. Mackenzie King and Mr. de Valera were wholly at one in their approach, though Mr. de Valera could reinforce his argument by reference to an express provision of the Constitution while Mr. Mackenzie King relied upon the established conventions of English parliamentary government.

Mr. de Valera equally had no doubts about the wishes of the Irish people. They would wish, he said, in 1938, to keep out of war if they could. Modern wars 'are not luxuries, they are not things which people desire to have'. But allowing the desire to remain neutral and allowing the constitutional right to do so, Mr. de Valera had very considerable doubts about its practicability. He was quite clear, as we have seen, that so long as the provisions of the 1921 Treaty in respect of the ports remained in force, neutrality was not a practical policy. As he pointed out to the Dáil in July 1938, it was not merely the occupation of the ports but the rights which Britain enjoyed under the Treaty to make a claim for any facilities she might require for the defence of Britain and Ireland by sea that was likely to make effective Irish neutrality impossible.[2] That was why he felt that any Irish government which acceded to demands made for additional facilities over and above the ports would immediately 'forfeit the confidence of the majority of its own people'. What he had feared, therefore, until the 1938 agreement had been successfully negotiated was that the government might find itself confronted with the dilemma of acceding to British demands, and thereby losing the confidence of its own people, or of rejecting them and being as a result drawn into hostilities with Britain. The return of the ports from the Irish point of view, therefore, not only made neutrality a more practical policy but removed the risks of open conflict between the British and Irish governments in a contingency not unlikely to arise.

[1] Dáil Debates, vol. 72, col. 697.

[2] ibid. col. 695.

It was, Mr. de Valera explained later, a sense of responsibility for home defence in the event of an early European war which he believed probable that was the immediate reason for his sending the dispatches which initiated the negotiations for the 1938 agreement.[1] It was a fundamental part of Mr. de Valera's conception of Irish policy in war-time that under no consideration would his government permit any part of Ireland to be used as a base for an attack on Britain. This was a negative but not negligible gain from the point of view of the Commonwealth as a whole. It assured Britain for the first time in modern history of a friendly neutral responsible for the defence of nationalist Ireland.

Co-operation between the British and Irish governments during the Czech crisis was close and continuous. The aims of Mr. Chamberlain and Mr. de Valera were to a large extent identical in that they both believed that almost any peaceful settlement was preferable to the disaster which would overtake Europe in the event of a second major war within a generation. Both, too, were deeply conscious of the dangers of Russian domination should a conflict arise involving the Great Powers of Western and Central Europe. These broad considerations transcended differences in outlook between Mr. Chamberlain, who regarded the future of Czechoslovakia with cool detachment, and Mr. de Valera who never for one moment forgot the problems of minorities under alien rule and the evil of the partition of a country. It was also a sense of common interest which accounted for Mr. de Valera's extreme caution about defence and foreign policy in the summer of 1938. While he assured the Dáil that so far as he knew there was no such thing as common Commonwealth foreign policy or common Commonwealth defence policy, and that each member of the Commonwealth decided its foreign and defence policy in accordance with its own interests, none the less each would naturally take into account 'what other states with which it is closely associated may be doing'.[2] He declined to give any assurance that he would not consult with the other members of the Commonwealth. Consultation he argued, might well be of great advantage to the Irish Free State, and if it were so, he certainly would not wish to be debarred from entering into it. That consultation would always be with a view to Irish interests was axiomatic, but Irish interests and those of other members of the Commonwealth might well coincide, and consultation might further common aims. But however useful, Mr. de Valera let it be clearly understood that the final decision in the case of any positive action would rest with the Irish government and the Irish Parliament alone.

The impression of a new Anglo-Irish accord was heightened when, as the Czech crisis moved towards its climax, Mr. de Valera was once more elected President of the Council of the League on Britain's initiative and with general acclaim. No one was more conscious of the fact that by 1938 power had passed from the League, and that there was no effective action that the President

[1] ibid. col. 691.

[2] ibid. col. 688.

could take. But whatever influence Mr. de Valera wielded was used to encourage and support Mr. Chamberlain's policy of conciliation. On his way to Geneva, Mr. de Valera saw Sir Thomas Inskip, the Minister for Co-ordination of Defence in London, and throughout the whole period of the Munich crisis the Irish High Commissioner in London was, with the High Commissioners of the other Commonwealth countries, in constant consultation with the Acting Secretary of State for Dominion Affairs, Mr. Malcolm MacDonald. On 16 September Mr. de Valera at Geneva warmly commended Mr. Chamberlain's initiative in visiting Hitler and urged that even if a just solution were difficult to obtain, it was important to secure the best solution possible in the circumstances without war. On 27 September when even that seemed impossible, Mr. de Valera wired to Mr. Chamberlain a further message of encouragement:

> Let nothing daunt you or defeat you in your effort to secure peace. The tens of millions of innocent people on both sides who have no cause against each other, but who are in danger of being hurled against each other, with no alternative to mutual slaughter are praying that your efforts may find a way of saving them from this terrible doom.[1]

After Munich, Mr. de Valera was warm in his appreciation of Mr. Chamberlain's work, and he took the opportunity on 4 October of visiting him in London on his return from Geneva.

The relations between Britain and Ireland during the critical month of September 1938 are important because they indicate that Irish policy at that time was not one of aloofness. It was concerned to ensure settlement by conciliation, even when that meant appeasement of the dictators. It is, indeed, a matter for some surprise that Irish opinion remained so little disturbed by the dismemberment of Czechoslovakia. With a fine disregard for the realities of the situation, local dignitaries and organizations, apparently under the impression that it was Germany that had been partitioned in 1919, not Czechoslovakia that was about to be partitioned prior to being wholly engulfed, sought to enlist the good will of Hitler in undoing the partition of Ireland. Mr. de Valera entertained no such illusions, but none the less his concern that peace should be preserved at almost any price left him less sensitive than might have been expected to the wrongs done to small nations other than his own.

So long as the Commonwealth was resolved to pursue a policy of appeasement, Irish co-operation would appear to have been as cordial as that of the oversea dominions. But unlike them her government had expressly declared that if appeasement failed and war came its policy would be one of neutrality. At Geneva the Irish delegation declared categorically that until a satisfactory system of collective security was established, the Irish government reserved to itself the right to determine who was the aggressor, and would not accept any

[1] *The Times*, 28 September 1938.

obligation to take action on the basis of the League's decision alone. Munich if anything reinforced Mr. de Valera's conclusions about the danger of full League membership for small nations. The settlement had been achieved outside the League. It had done nothing to revive the League; rather it had exposed its complete ineffectiveness, and in so doing it had confirmed Mr. de Valera's own view that the League was moribund. After Munich he advocated an attempt to secure a general settlement of European grievances. There were other questions that had to be settled before a lasting peace could be established. 'To adopt an ostrich policy towards these questions will not remove them . . . nor will the advice to let sleeping dogs lie keep the dogs indefinitely asleep.'[1] But with the collapse of the League there was no active part Eire desired to play, for, unreconciled, largely through the continuance of Partition, to co-operation with the Commonwealth for defence, she moved back into a position of isolation.

The considerations that influenced Irish policy in the year that elapsed between the Munich settlement and the outbreak of the world war, were stated by Mr. de Valera in a lengthy press interview in October 1938 in the course of which he said:

> Quite obviously, the existing Partition would be a grave danger to England in the event of that country becoming involved in a European war. Discontent, particularly along the border, is widespread, and if a new war were to come whilst Partition lasts the sentiments of the majority of the Irish people would be exactly those of 1914 and after.
>
> We have definitely committed ourselves to the proposition that this island shall not be used as a base for enemy attacks on Great Britain. It is possible to visualize a critical situation arising in the future in which a united free Ireland would be willing to co-operate with Britain to resist a common attack.
>
> Let me say clearly that the chances of such co-operation in the event of a European war are very, very slight while Partition remains. If such a war occurred while British forces were in occupation of any part of Ireland, Irish sentiment would definitely be hostile to any co-operation.
>
> Let England—who, to assist a settlement of this question has only to convert her friends in the North—help us to get a united Ireland on fair terms, and we shall have something to fight to maintain—a united, free, independent Ireland. . . . I want to bring about good feeling between the two countries, but I state categorically that no Irish leader will ever be able to get the Irish people to co-operate with Great Britain while Partition remains. I wouldn't attempt it myself, for I know I should fail.[2]

Mr. de Valera's language implied, though not unambiguously, that in the event of aggression a united Ireland would be prepared to co-operate with

[1] Quoted in *Peace and War*, p. 72.

[2] It is quoted more fully in Gwynn, *History of Partition*, pp. 30–31. Mr. de Valera's practice of making important statements of policy to foreign journalists or in broadcasts to the United States occasioned some passing resentment in the Dáil.

Britain. If this was intended to lead to some discussion of the possibility of reconciling Unionist sentiment to the ending of Partition by the negotiation of a defence agreement between Britain and Ireland, it evoked no positive response. Thereafter Irish emphasis on neutrality became more pronounced. 'We do not know', said Mr. de Valera in March 1939, 'whether a great war will break out' between the two groups of Powers, but 'if we can help it we will not be in that war at all.' In April he reaffirmed the policy of neutrality in more absolute terms. 'I have stated here in the House, and I have stated in the country, that the aim of government policy is to keep this country out of war, and nobody, either here or elsewhere, has any right to assume anything else.'[1] And again, 'there is no reason for any nation to think that our attitude would be other than that of neutrality'.[2] In May 1939 Mr. de Valera repeated that Article 16 of the Covenant was no longer regarded by Eire as 'at all in force under present conditions'[3] and that his government did not regard the imposition of sanctions against an aggressor as practical politics. It would refuse to accept 'any definition of aggressor' by the League as binding, and whatever advantages there might be in continued support for the League as a rallying point for those who believed in peaceful methods of settling disputes, Mr. de Valera made it abundantly clear that he considered it to be not a help but a positive danger when issues of peace and war arose.

The outline of Irish policy in the years before the Second World War was clearly drawn. It is probable under any circumstances that history would have strongly inclined Irish opinion towards neutrality in the first great war in which Britain was engaged after independence had been won. In that sense neutrality was almost a psychological necessity. It is probable that the form of the Irish Free State's relationship with the Commonwealth accentuated this need to prove to the world, and more important to the Irish people themselves, that Eire was an independent country exercising that final attribute of sovereignty which is to be found in free exercise of a choice between peace and war. Hence there arose what Lord Rugby[4] later called 'the great imperative of neutrality'. As a policy it commanded the assent of all parties, and at no time were Mr. de Valera's clear statements of his intentions challenged in the Dáil by the opposition. Till 1937 Irish fulfilment of her League obligations was unreserved. To strengthen the League was her declared policy. After 1937 the failure of the League was accepted as final, and it was believed that any weak or small nation which put its trust in it would be betrayed in a moment of crisis and might be led into disaster, as China and Abyssinia had been in turn. Thereafter, Irish policy had one aim, and that was the peaceful settlement of disputes so as to avoid war into which Eire might be drawn

[1] Dáil Debates, vol. 75, col. 1161. [2] ibid. col. 1160.
[3] ibid. col. 1469.
[4] Sir John Loader Maffey, first Lord Rugby, United Kingdom Representative to Eire, 1939–49. See *Irish Times*, 7 April 1949.

against her own wishes. But conciliation itself was a means to an end and not an end in itself. Mr. de Valera had recognized that often enough when he said no settlement would prove final which was not based on moral right and justice. But in fact reliance upon the policy of conciliation alone inevitably led to the conclusion that any settlement which preserved peace was better than none. That conclusion Mr. de Valera reluctantly accepted. But he recognized that 'not always will we have someone to do what Mr. Chamberlain has done, and we shall find that we shall have had one crisis too many'.[1] And it was only the Great Powers that could resolve the questions of peace and war. A small nation could only at its peril assume responsibility for any positive action or enter into commitments. In the case of Eire there existed over and above this general objection particular and formidable obstacles to the acceptance of commitments. They would incur the risk of civil war at home. So long as the republicans were unappeased, so long had any Irish government to tread warily in respect of co-operation with Britain and with the Commonwealth. But fundamentally Mr. de Valera's position, and his was the decisive voice, was that another great war in Europe would bring incalculable suffering and would create at least as many problems as it would resolve. Therefore almost any alternative which would avert such a calamity was to be preferred, and if it came it was the moral responsibility of a statesman to save his own people if possible from being engulfed.

In the debates on external affairs which took place in the Dáil between 1937 and 1939 there are to be found few words in condemnation of aggression in Europe. This was partly due to the fact that a large section of Irish opinion was so conscious of the 'iniquities of Versailles' that they were oblivious of the methods adopted by which those so-called injustices were being removed. It was partly also due to the deep and profound mistrust of Russia's policy and Russia's intentions. That made Irish opinion see in Hitler, or at least in Mussolini and Franco, a bastion of Catholicism against Communism. At no price should that bastion be weakened. But still more was it due to a failure, partly deliberate, and arising out of the very real difficulties of Ireland's internal situation, to acknowledge that ruthless unprincipled aggression was taking place in Europe. Had the facts been frankly and fully acknowledged by all parties it is highly unlikely that any alternative course would or could have been pursued. The failure to recognize them and to name them for what they were, therefore, did no more than impart a certain air of unreality to official Irish reactions to the approach of war and detract somewhat from the moral and intellectual integrity of a standpoint otherwise clearly and logically defined.

[1] Quoted in *Peace and War*, p. 71.

CHAPTER IX

INDIA: DIVISION AND PROCRASTINATION

PROBLEMS OF INDIAN GOVERNMENT AND THEIR IMPLICATIONS FOR THE COMMONWEALTH

BETWEEN 1919 and 1947 India filled an anomalous position in imperial and international affairs. She was not a fully self-governing member of the Commonwealth but she was none the less represented on the Imperial War Cabinet in the concluding years of the First World War and later at Imperial Conferences. In international affairs India was both a signatory to the Treaty of Versailles and a member of the League of Nations. Yet her representation on Commonwealth and international bodies, membership of which was otherwise confined to fully self-governing states, did not modify in essentials her continuing dependence in defence and external policy. The government of India was responsible in these years not to any Indian legislature, but through the Secretary of State for India to the government and the Parliament of the United Kingdom, and it was that government and Parliament which determined India's defence and external policies. In these matters, therefore, India, unlike the dominions, remained dependent. Indian membership of the League of Nations 'is a farce', complained Pandit Jawaharlal Nehru in his address to the Indian National Congress at Faizpur in 1936, 'for the selection of delegates is made by the British government'.[1] Yet, though certainly true, that was not the whole truth. At international and imperial conferences India's nominated representatives were for the most part Indians, and they acquired at these gatherings a knowledge and an experience that in many cases was to be used to advantage when independence came to India and Pakistan. They were mostly men of liberal mind with the temper and outlook of distinguished public servants, who stood for all that was best in India administration but who neither claimed to be, nor were in any way, representative of the political forces which were to determine India's future.

India's representation without any final responsibility for policy in the councils of League and Commonwealth fairly reflected the period of protracted transition from dependence to independence through which she was passing. Since 1917 responsible self-government had been the proclaimed goal of British policy in India, and independence within or without the Commonwealth the aspiration of the overwhelming majority of the Indian people. Neither aim nor aspiration was fulfilled before the outbreak of the Second World War, but it was apparent to most observers that India's advance to full

[1] *Presidential Address, Indian National Congress, 50th Session, December 1936* (pamphlet, Faizpur, Choudhri, 1936).

sovereign status could not be long delayed. It is because this was so that some consideration of India's relations with the Commonwealth and the world is not out of place in this study of the external policies of the self-governing members of the British Commonwealth of Nations.

The future of India confronted the Commonwealth with one question of outstanding importance. Could the peoples of India, the heirs of two of the ancient civilizations of the East, find a congenial and satisfying realization of their political ideals within the hitherto almost exclusively European circle of the self-governing countries of the Commonwealth? Or would they, as much perhaps by the logic of history as by their own volition, be compelled to seek it without? Upon the answer depended not only future Anglo-Indian relations but also the extent to which full membership of the Commonwealth would be regarded later by colonial peoples as the natural goal of their political development.

Whether Indians ultimately decided to remain within the Commonwealth or not was recognized to depend largely on certain broad considerations of self-interest; of community or diversity of outlook, especially towards the ideological conflicts of the twentieth century; upon the extent to which there existed a sense of affinity with the older members of the Commonwealth, and not least upon the personal relations established between Indian and British people. But if such general considerations formed the background against which India's future attitude to the Commonwealth would be determined, there were in the foreground practical questions not only of self-government but of the appropriate forms of Indian self-government which were rightly held to have a direct bearing upon these wider issues.

In all the self-governing dominions, including the Irish Free State, British parliamentary institutions had been adopted with only minor modifications and it was not altogether easy to conceive of membership of the Commonwealth by countries which were governed under some different system. But would a free India conform to these precedents? Was it really possible for the British parliamentary system to be successfully transplanted and to flourish in the very different social conditions and cultural traditions of the East? Could it be successfully reconciled with the Hindu caste system, or could it transcend Indian communal divisions? The majority of politically minded Indians were confident that it could, and in this the faith of the Congress in particular never wavered. But less sanguine views prevailed in the home of parliamentary democracy itself.

In 1912 the Liberal Secretary of State for India, Lord Crewe, discounted the possibility of attaining in India 'something approaching the self-government enjoyed by those colonies which have of late years received the name of Dominion'; and he added: 'I say quite frankly that I see no future for India on those lines.'[1] Five years later another Liberal Secretary of State, Mr.

[1] H. of L. Deb., vol. 12, col. 156.

Montagu, in 'the most momentous utterance ever made in India's chequered history',[1] saw no future for India on any other lines. He spoke of the goal of British policy as 'the gradual development of self-governing institutions with a view to the progressive realization of responsible government in India as an integral part of the British Empire.'[2] The analogy he drew with the pattern of development in the dominions was deliberate and exact. Professor Coupland has described the phrase he used as 'a terse and accurate description of the rise of the self-governing colonies to dominion status'.[3]

The Government of India Act, 1919, in which the substance of the Montagu-Chelmsford Report on Indian constitutional reforms was given its legislative sanction, afforded evidence not only of Britain's intention of divesting herself by stages of her imperial authority in British India, but also of her desire to foster there representative parliamentary institutions. In the provinces, to which the most important provisions of the Act related, self-government was brought a step closer by the introduction of a measure of ministerial responsibility which, under favourable circumstances, might be progressively enlarged so as to include the whole field of provincial government. At the centre no comparable advance was deemed possible, but measures were taken to further Indian unity and to pave the way for the introduction of responsible government by the creation of a central legislature consisting of an Assembly and of a Council of State, the majority of whose members were elected. If they could not determine policy they could debate it; and in fact the Legislative Assembly became a forum for the criticism of an executive whose actions were almost wholly outside its control.[4]

The Act of 1919 represented a substantial advance which ten years earlier would have been welcomed by most sections of Indian opinion.[5] But in the very different atmosphere of post-war India it received no such favourable reception. At its session at Amritsar in 1919 the Congress condemned 'the Reform Act' as 'inadequate, unsatisfactory and disappointing',[6] and demanded that the British government should take early steps 'to establish full responsible government in accordance with the principle of self-determination'. It asked, too, that a statutory guarantee be given that full responsible government 'should be established in the whole of British India within a period not exceeding fifteen years'.[7] Since it was apparent that the United Kingdom

[1] This was the description used in the first chapter of the Montagu-Chelmsford Report, Cd. 9109, p. 5. [2] 1917, H. of C. Deb., vol. 97, col. 1695.

[3] R. Coupland, *The Indian Problem, 1883–1935*, pt. 1 (London, Oxford University Press, 1942) p. 54.

[4] The working of the Act of 1919 is carefully examined by Dr. A. Appadorai in *Dyarchy in Practice* (Oxford University Press, Indian Branch, 1945).

[5] This is the opinion of Professor C. H. Philips, *India* (London, Hutchinson's University Library, 1948) p. 115.

[6] Quoted in A. C. Banerjee, ed., *Indian Constitutional Documents, 1757–1939*, 2nd ed. (Calcutta, Mukherjee, 1949), vol. 3, p. 83.

[7] Quoted in Coupland, *The Indian Problem*, pt. 1, p. 66. It could be argued that the United

government had no intention of committing themselves to this, or to any other, rigid time-table, the Congress decided not to await self-government but to win it by 'non-violent non-co-operation'. The amended Congress Constitution adopted at Nagpur in 1920 described the principal objective of the Congress, which had hitherto been defined as the attainment by the people of India of a system of government similar to that enjoyed by self-governing members of the British Empire by constitutional means, as 'the attainment of *Swarajya* by the people of India by all legitimate and peaceful means.'[1] Continuing Indian membership of the Commonwealth was thus no longer assumed as the Congress passed from its reformist to its revolutionary phase.

The Congress equipped itself for its new role by extending its appeal from the narrow circle of educated opinion to the illiterate masses. The mantle of leadership passed from the politicians to the prophet. Gandhi was the spokesman of the new age. The organization which looked to him for leadership and inspiration was popular, efficient, and in all respects, save one, remarkably comprehensive. Largely financed by Hindu big business it embraced within its fold socialists and communists, villagers and intellectuals, planners with a twentieth-century faith in technological progress, and disciples of Gandhi with a desire to return to the simple economy symbolized by the spinning-wheel. As in Sinn Féin before 1921, the co-operation of such diverse elements was secured by the rigid subordination of economic differences to the achievement of national aims. Remarkably successful in this the Congress, like Sinn Féin, failed to attract to itself the allegiance of the minority community which was the product of earlier invasion and settlement. Individual Muslims joined the Congress ranks as individual Irish Protestants had supported Sinn Féin. But individuals they remained; and the great bulk of their community stood suspiciously aloof. In both cases that community was a minority,[2] and in both cases as the day of the transfer of power approached they feared for their own future in a state in which they would be in a position of perpetual subordination so long as political life was dominated by religious differences and its government determined by the will of the majority.

Indian impatience for self-government revived those British doubts about the appropriateness of British institutions to Indian conditions which once had seemed to have been finally dispelled by Mr. Montagu's pronouncement.

Kingdom government would have been wise to have acceded to this request. By so doing they would at once have introduced an element of urgency and of responsibility into the Indian political scene.

[1] The Congress Constitution is reprinted in Banerjee, vol. 3, Appendix B. In an amendment of 1939 *Purna Swaraj* (complete independence) was substituted for *Swarajya* in the definition of aims.

[2] The 1931 census estimated the population of India at 353 million including 239 million Hindus, 78 million Muslims, 4 million Sikhs, and 6 million Christians.

The Indian Statutory Commission[1] of which the Liberal, Sir John (later Lord) Simon, was Chairman, entertained on this point far less confidence than Mr. Montagu had done.

> The British parliamentary system . . . has been fitted like a well-worn garment to the figure of the wearer, but it does not follow that it will suit everybody. . . . Many of its detailed contrivances work only because there is a will to make them do so, or because there is a general understanding that they will be used in moderation. British parliamentarism in India is a translation, and in even the best translations the essential meaning is apt to be lost.[2]

Filled with these misgivings the Commission concluded that there would be a serious danger inherent in the assumption that 'the only form of parliamentary government which can emerge is one which closely imitates the British system'. If Britain had been the size of India, and if communal and religious divisions so largely governed its politics, and if minorities had had as little confidence in the rule of others as they had in India, it seemed to them unlikely that popular government there would have taken the form it did.[3] Behind their misgivings, and in part inspiring them, lay mounting evidence of the weaknesses of the newly established democratic governments of Europe and a fear lest the introduction of parliamentary institutions in India might likewise prejudice stability of government. That fear explains why the feature of the British parliamentary system that appeared to the Simon Commission most unsuited to probable Indian conditions was the dependence of the executive upon the vote of the lower house, with its corollary that 'the government is liable to be brought to an end at any moment by a vote of the legislature'.[4] This largely accounts, too, for the sobering conclusion which the Commission reached about the need to take 'a long view of the development of Indian self-government' and to beware lest a premature endeavour to introduce forms of responsible government at the centre should result not in advance but in retrogression.[5]

The Viceroy, Lord Irwin, in commenting upon the Simon Report, was conscious of Indian dismay at this revival of doubts and fears all suggesting further delay in the transfer of power. Accordingly he reasserted his faith in the progressive realization of responsible self-government at the centre as in the provinces, arguing that caution about the ultimate form of the central government of India 'should not be carried to the point of allowing ourselves to be immobilized. . . .'[6] That indeed was the prevailing fear of nationalist

[1] It was appointed in 1927 to inquire into the working of the existing system of Indian government and to report to what extent it is desirable 'to establish the principle of representative government'.

[2] *Report of the Indian Statutory Commission, Volume II—Recommendations*, Cmd. 3569 (London, H.M.S.O., 1930) pp. 6–7.

[3] ibid. p. 146. [4] ibid. p. 146. [5] ibid.

[6] *Government of India's Dispatch on Proposals for Constitutional Reform*, 20 September 1930, Cmd. 3302 (London, H.M.S.O., 1930) p. 16.

India, the fear lest the government of the United Kingdom should be, if not immobilized, at least increasingly slow and reluctant to make concessions to meet the demand of British India for self-government, on the ostensible ground that British political institutions could not be successfully worked in India by Indians.

The Simon Commission alluded somewhat spaciously to the existence of forms of responsible government other than the British,[1] but it is very doubtful whether the British rulers of India, or indeed Indians themselves, trained under the British system, would have been well qualified to apply them. Moreover from the point of view of India's future relations with the Commonwealth the creation of a central executive on the American or the Swiss model would almost certainly have proved a handicap in intra-Commonwealth consultations.[2] Congress insistence on the adoption of British institutions had therefore an importance in the field of Commonwealth relations not wholly realized at that time. As the formal ties uniting the self-governing members of the Commonwealth dwindled the existence of common political institutions have assumed an ever increasing importance. In 1948 Mr. Liaqat Ali Khan, Prime Minister of Pakistan, speaking of the changed complexion of the Commonwealth since the addition of the Asian dominions, said: 'it is a Commonwealth of free nations who believe in the same way of life and in the same democracy.'

The attitude of most prominent nationalists, whether members of the Congress or of the Muslim League, towards future Indian membership of the British Commonwealth varied in emphasis but was well defined in essentials. They wished, when India had regained her independence, not to be under any obligation to remain within the British Commonwealth but to have themselves full freedom to decide whether to remain within or to secede. Thus at Nagpur in 1920 Gandhi told the Congress that while it was derogatory to think of the permanence of the British connexion at any cost, he did not wish to see it ended at all costs. 'If the British connexion is for the advancement of India', he argued, 'we do not want to destroy it.'[3] In 1924 his attitude was unchanged. 'In my opinion', he said, 'if the British government mean what they say and honestly help us to equality, it would be a greater triumph than a complete severance of the British connexion.'[4] In his presidential address at Calcutta in 1928 Pandit Motilal Nehru told the Congress that he was 'for complete independence—as complete as it can be—but I am not against full dominion status—as full as any dominion possesses it today, provided I get it before it

[1] Cmd. 3569, pp. 6–7.

[2] Statesmen, and more especially civil servants from the self-governing dominions who have sought to establish relations with the United States administration as close as those that exist with the United Kingdom, have found that differences in the form of government have created unexpected and formidable obstacles.

[3] Banerjee, *Indian Constitutional Documents*, vol. 3, p. 179.

[4] ibid. p. 180.

loses all attraction'.[1] Independence, said Sardar Vallabhbhai Patel at Karachi in 1931, does not mean 'a churlish refusal to associate with Britain or any other power.'[2] As time went on, however, and India awaited more and more impatiently the day of independence the attractions of dominion status faded. The opinion of the rank and file had always inclined markedly towards a final severance of all ties with Britain and by 1939 most members of the Congress, if not of the League, thought of 'complete independence', while not theoretically excluding a decision to retain Commonwealth membership, as meaning in practice an independent existence outside the Commonwealth.

PROBLEMS OF INTERNAL UNITY

Neither in Britain nor in India could India's future government be considered in the abstract. It was not a question simply of finding the form of government which Indians would find most effective and congenial: it was a question even more of finding a form of government which would make possible the continued unity of the subcontinent when the British Raj withdrew. Unity was the major achievement of British rule and successive British governments were loth to prejudice in any way its future. This in itself aggravated the problem of ensuring a peaceful transfer or power, for within India there were three major groups, the Princes, the Congress, and the Muslim League, whose views on the nature of the Indian successor government were in conflict. Broadly speaking the Princes, their authority buttressed by the paramount power, were prepared to enter a self-governing Indian Union only at their own discretion and on the assurance that in the states autocracy would be tempered to meet popular pressure for responsible government only as they themselves saw fit. The Congress, claiming to be 'the sole representative of Indian nationalism', demanded an early transfer of power to a responsible Indian central government whose first concern would be the drafting of a Constitution at least for British India; while by contrast the Muslim League, representing a minority community which in any system of popular election for a central legislature was bound to remain in a position of permanent inferiority, was not prepared to contemplate anything more than a loose federation in which the bias lay not in favour of the centre but of the constituent provinces, and in which the Muslim position would be safeguarded by separate electorates. In such circumstances there were endless possibilities for manœuvre about detail, but little ground for compromise on essentials. It was, too, a situation in which it was tempting, but not necessarily wise, for the imperial power to let action wait upon the reconciliation of views which could in the nature of things never be wholly reconciled.

The division within India that was most apparent was that between a British India which was by gradual steps advancing towards self-government

[1] Banerjee, *Indian Constitutional Documents*, vol. 3, p. 181. [2] ibid. p. 187.

in domestic affairs, and the Indian States comprising well over a third of the territory of the subcontinent and one-quarter of its population,[1] which were still governed by the older autocratic system of personal rule which had existed in India when first the British came. Yet this division though important was not fundamental. If the Indian States comprised a large part of India, they did not constitute a politically unassimilable element in it. It was not because of racial or communal cleavages but by chance and by the changing policies of the East India Company that the rulers of some states had retained their authority. With nationalism in the ascendant in British India they imparted an air of stability generally pleasing to the United Kingdom government, who perhaps hardly realized how completely the Princes were dependent upon British support for their survival, and who tended accordingly to exaggerate their importance as an independent force in the Indian scene.

In accordance with the recommendations of the Montagu-Chelmsford Report a Chamber of Princes was established by Royal Proclamation in February 1921 as a consultative body.[2] Its principal purpose was to bring the Princes at least formally within the framework of Indian government, but its establishment was also welcomed in official circles because it was hoped that the Princes would temper the ill-considered popular enthusiasms to which an elected Indian assembly might be susceptible. Indian nationalists, however, took a less kindly view of the likely contribution of princely India. The 1928 constitutional report drafted by an all-Indian committee presided over by Pandit Motilal Nehru stated that, while the Princes would be welcomed in an Indian Federation, their membership would necessarily involve some modification of their system of government and administration.[3] Nor was the pressure for change confined to admonitions from without. In 1927 an Indian States People's Conference was formed with the express purpose of stimulating the popular demand within the States for a grant of responsible government by their rulers. The Princes, observed Mahatma Gandhi, who described himself as their well-wisher and who saw for them a definite place in a free India, 'are British officers in Indian dress'. He warned them that they should be co-operative while the times were still favourable.[4] 'My successor, Pandit Nehru', he said, 'will be less patient with you than I am'; and this, indeed, to judge by Pandit Nehru's utterances, seemed probable enough. In 1939 he

[1] The total area of the Indian States and Agencies was 713,146 sq. miles with a population of 81,310,845 in the 1931 census. Of these Hyderabad covered 82,698 sq. miles with a population of 14,436,148; Jammu and Kashmir States 84,516 sq. miles with a population of 3,646,243; Mysore 29,326 sq. miles with a population of 6,557,302.

[2] Its meetings were held in private, its decisions were not binding upon the Princes either individually or collectively, and some of the most powerful of the Princes, notably the Nizam of Hyderabad, did not participate in its discussions. For an estimate of its importance see *Report of Indian States Committee*, 1928–9, Cmd. 3302 (London, H.M.S.O., 1929) pp. 20–21.

[3] See Coupland, *The Indian Problem*, pt. 1, pp. 87–94.

[4] Banerjee, *Indian Constitutional Documents*, vol. 3, pp. 463–4.

condemned the majority of the Princes as 'sinks of reaction and incompetence and unrestrained autocratic power, sometimes exercised by vicious and degraded individuals.'[1] Moreover, even when, as happened in some cases, the ruler was enlightened and his ministers progressive and efficient, Pandit Nehru's hostility was little modified, for he believed that the evil lay in the system itself. 'This system has vanished from the rest of the world', he said, 'and, left to itself, would have vanished from India also long ago. But in spite of its manifest decay and stagnation, it has been propped up and artificially maintained by British imperialism.'[2] Apart from imperialism, he believed that the Princes could not survive, and in this he was to be signally justified by events. The problem which the Princes presented, though formidable in its demands upon the tact and political ingenuity of the paramount power, which was bound to many of them by solemn obligations,[3] was not therefore fundamental, for its solution depended upon a change in a system of government and not upon a change in the outlook and tradition of a community.

In 1928 Pandit Motilal Nehru's Committee warned the Princes not to make an Ulster in India. But in fact it was not from the Princes that the danger of an enduring partition of the Indian subcontinent came. What imperilled future Indian unity was not their quasi-autonomous status outside British India, but the antagonism between the two principal Indian communities, between the Hindu majority and the Muslim minority, within. Religious and cultural in origin this antagonism was notably reinforced by differences in economic position and in educational standards. Hindus enjoyed a preponderance in economic power while in education the Muslims, having deliberately refrained from taking advantage of the educational facilities afforded by the British government, lacked the educational qualifications which were essential for executive and administrative positions in the government of India. These were facts which weighed heavily on the minds of the minority Muslim community as the days of British rule drew to their predestined close.

The Morley-Minto reforms of 1909 for the first time formally recognized that communal divisions transcended a sense of national unity by acceding to Muslim pressure for the creation of separate electorates for Hindus and Muslims. The decision to do so was final in the sense that while no specific pledge was given, the British government could not in honour go back on its concession to the Muslim separatism without the consent of the Muslim

[1] *The Unity of India* (London, Drummond, 1948) pp. 30–31.

[2] ibid. p. 31.

[3] The nature and extent of these obligations was set out in the Report of Indian States Committee (Cmd. 3302), which stated *inter alia* that 'the promise of the King Emperor to maintain unimpaired the privileges rights and dignities of the Princes carries with it a duty to protect the Prince against attempts to eliminate him and to substitute another form of government' (p. 28). This, however, was debatable.

community.[1] This was most unlikely to be forthcoming, for with the advance towards responsible government in which the will of the majority would necessarily prevail separate electorates were conceived of by the Muslim leaders as the one effective safeguard against the consequences of rule by a majority in whose intentions they had no confidence. Whether the creation of separate electorates, even in these circumstances, was wise is a debatable question outside the scope of this study; what is relevant here is the consequences which flowed from it and which, in the words of an Indian writer,[2] 'unfolded themselves with the remorseless march of a Greek tragedy'.

Separate electorates immeasurably strengthened the position of the communal extremist. The reservation of seats for Muslims was otiose unless those seats were to be filled by ardent protagonists of Muslim interests. It was indeed the constant complaint of the Muslim leaders that in a general or mixed electorate it was the moderate-minded, compromising Muslim who alone could hope to secure non-Muslim votes.[3] The effect of the 1909 reforms was, therefore, to ensure at once the more vigorous championship of Muslim interests, and in so doing to increase communal consciousness by strengthening the position of the communally conscious. For the same reason the representatives of the majority community were freed from the need to regard or to canvass for the votes of the minority, and the general result of separate electorates was to enfeeble 'the capacity of every group to throw the centre of gravity outside itself'.[4] Communal considerations thus tended to come first, and the general welfare second. The deterioration in relations between the two communities in subsequent years, marked before 1909, became more pronounced, despite the encouraging rapprochement signalized by the Lucknow Pact of 1916. Yet by no means all and perhaps not even the greater share of responsibility for this can be attributed to the decision to create separate electorates. They were as much a reflection as a cause of growing communal tension, but they had this result—that after their introduction the two communities were not only culturally but also politically distinguishable.

Among political organizations the Congress claimed to represent not one community but all India. This claim was not vigorously disputed by the Muslim League after the First World War partly because both Hindus and Muslims responded unfavourably to the Act of 1919. Thus at Lahore in 1924 Mr. Jinnah, presiding at a meeting of the Muslim League, came very close to the point of view of the Congress by demanding that the government should meet the universal demand 'to scrap the present Constitution

[1] cf. The comments in the Montagu-Chelmsford Report, pp. 185–8. Its authors saw no alternative to the retention of separate electorates and communal representation for Muslims, 'even at the price of slower progress towards the realization of a common citizenship'.

[2] Beni Prasad, *The Hindu-Muslim Questions* (Allahabad, Kitabistan, 1941) p. 45.

[3] Coupland, *India: a Restatement* (London, Oxford University Press, 1945) p. 105.

[4] Prasad, *Hindu-Muslim Questions*, p. 46.

and to devise a Constitution in consultation with the representatives of the people which will give them a real control and responsibility over their affairs'.[1] But differences about the future form of Indian government, deriving as always from Muslim fears of being placed in a position of perpetual inferiority through lack of numbers, soon re-emerged. While the Congress was prepared to concede the appearances of Federation they strongly favoured an essentially unitary pattern of responsible self-government. Thus in the Nehru draft Constitution of 1928, while the provinces were to be granted wide powers, ultimate residuary authority was to rest not with them but with the central government, and it was recommended, too, that separate electorates should be abolished. To neither would the Muslims ever give a free assent. It was a condition of their acceptance of any federal solution that the rights of the provinces should be fully safeguarded, that the centre should have no power to enforce the will of the majority in British India upon the Muslim majority provinces, and that separate electorates should be retained. Both Congress assertion and League reaction were understandable; they were not, however, easily to be reconciled.

CONSTITUTION-MAKING

The Montagu-Chelmsford Report contemplated a review of India's constitutional progress ten years after the enactment of the constitutional reforms of 1919. As that period drew to its close both Indian and British opinion became more and more preoccupied with the resolution of the complex problem of India's constitutional future. Constitution-making became itself at once an exercise in constitutional ingenuity and a test of political dexterity. 'The minds of all', commented the Simon Commission, 'were fixed on the future. Every community and every interest was thinking of what its position would be under the next Constitution. . . . Actions were calculated with a view to their effect on those who would have to deal with the next advance.'[2]

The first attempt to draft a new Constitution was undertaken, as we have seen, by an unofficial Indian committee under the chairmanship of Pandit Motilal Nehru. It left the Princes uneasy, the Muslims insistent upon a federal Constitution, and the majority of the Congress asserting with Pandit Jawarhalal Nehru, the Secretary of the Committee, that in contemplating co-operation with other self-governing members of the Commonwealth in external policy outside Asia the committee's recommendations ran contrary to the Congress insistence on full independence for India. The Simon Commission Report which followed aroused general protest in India. The exclusively British membership of the Commission had, from the first, prejudiced it in Indian eyes, and the nature of its findings were regarded as

[1] Quoted in Coupland, *The Indian Problem*, pt. 1, p. 74.
[2] Cmd. 3569, p. 6.

having more than fulfilled the worst Indian misgivings.[1] Not even the Viceroy's reassurance that dominion status remained the goal of British policy succeeded in removing the impression that continuing doubts about Indian capacity to work a system of responsible government were going to be used as an excuse for delaying indefinitely the transfer of power.

It was, therefore, against a discouraging background that the Indian Round Table Conference[2] assembled in London in 1930 to consider the work that had so far been done towards preparing for the government of an Indian dominion and to see how far agreement could be reached about the form that government should assume and the pace of the advance. The Congress, engaged in a campaign of civil disobedience, refused to send any representatives, and their absence[3] gave to the Conference something of the unhappy character of the Irish National Convention in 1917 which was similarly boycotted by Sinn Féin. Yet this discouraging analogy should not be pressed too far. Princely India was fairly represented,[4] and so, too, were the Muslims. Nor did the deliberations fail to reflect the trend of Indian opinion. The representatives from British India were virtually at one in demanding assurances that the claim for dominion status should receive a more constructive response than hitherto. 'India', said Sir Tej Bahadur Sapru, 'wants, and is determined to achieve, a status of equality—equality with the other free members of the British Commonwealth, an equality which will give it a government not merely responsive to, but responsible to the popular voice.' Provincial autonomy was not enough unless it were coupled 'with a decided and clear change in the constitution of the central government'.[5] Time was of the essence of the contract, urged Mr. Jayakar. 'What would have satisfied India in the year 1924 is not satisfying India today, and . . . what will satisfy India today will not satisfy India a year hence.'[6]

In the absence of any representatives from the Congress, the possibility of a unitary form of government was virtually discounted, and opinion came down with a surprising degree of unanimity in favour of an All-Indian Federation. Here the attitude of the Princes was unexpectedly forthcoming. 'We stand without compromise on our treaty rights and all that they involve', said the Maharajah of Bikaner,[7] but if they were respected the Princes would

[1] For a detailed examination of them see Coupland, *The Indian Problem*, pt. 1, ch. 8.

[2] Indian Round Table Conference, 1930–1, *Proceedings*, Cmd. 3778 (London, H.M.S.O., 1931).

[3] The resolution of the Working Committee of 31 January 1931 read: 'The Working Committee of the Indian National Congress is not prepared to give any recognition to the proceedings of the so-called Round Table Conference between certain members of the British Parliament, the Indian Princes and individual Indians selected by the government from among its supporters and not elected as their representatives by any section of the Indian people' (quoted Banerjee, *Indian Constitutional Documents*, p. 188).

[4] By sixteen delegates who included the rulers of Bikaner, Kashmir, Bhopal, and Patiala.

[5] Cmd. 3778, p. 28.

[6] ibid. p. 40.

[7] ibid. p. 35. See also pp. 36–37.

come into an All-India Federation. But, as he added later, 'they could not accept any position of the slightest subordination or inferiority to British India. . . . The Princes do not want to be levelled down from their present position of internal sovereignty.'[1] They would federate only with a self-governing and federal British India.[2] But even on such conditions this represented a clear advance.

The Muslim position in respect of the form of future Indian government had already been succinctly stated at an All-India Muslim Conference held in Delhi in January 1929, when federation alone was deemed tolerable.

. . . in view of India's vast extent and its ethnological, linguistic, administrative, and geographical or territorial divisions, the only form of government suitable to Indian conditions is a federal system with complete autonomy and residuary powers vested in the constituent states, the central government having control only of such matters of common interest as may be specifically entrusted to it by the Constitution.[3]

From that position their spokesman at the Round Table Conference never departed. Thus while the Muslims pressed for a rapid advance towards a federal goal, its attainment was for them conditional upon the full safeguarding of their rights by separate electorates and by their active participation in government both at the centre and in the provinces in which they were a minority. 'We have never on any occasion', said Dr. Shafa't Ahmad Khan, 'opposed any advance either in the centre or in the provinces. We have never tried to create an Ulster in India. . . . On the contrary, we have said we will fight shoulder to shoulder with our brethren for the cause of India, the cause of our common Motherland.'[4] But the majority community must not disregard the reawakening of Muslim sentiment. Muslims, too, were stirred by the political ferment of India.

The blood of the slave [declared Mr. Fazl ul-Huq] does not run in our veins. Until recently the Mussalmans held the sceptre of sovereignty in India. . . . I ask my brethren of other communities to remember that Muslim India has been deeply stirred, and will be satisfied with nothing less than the fullest recognition of their legitimate rights.[5]

In March 1931 the Viceroy, Lord Irwin, and Gandhi by personal negotiation reached an understanding which made possible Gandhi's attendance at the Second Session of the Conference which opened in September 1931. Gandhi confronted delegates with an assertion and a demand. As the representative of the Congress he maintained that he could speak for the whole of British

[1] Indian Round Table Conference, *Proceedings of Sub-Committees*, pt. 1, 70/249/1, pp. 4–5.
[2] These words were used by the Nawab of Bhopal. (Cmd. 3778, p. 447.)
[3] Quoted in Cmd. 3569, p. 84.
[4] Cmd. 3778, p. 432.
[5] ibid. p. 160.

India. 'The Congress', he said, 'claims to represent the whole nation . . .',[1] and its demand was that there should be complete responsibility transferred to India including control of the army, of the defence forces, and of external affairs.[2] 'If a nation's defence is controlled by an outside agency, no matter how friendly it is, then that nation is certainly not responsibly governed. This is what our English teachers have taught us times without number. . .'[3] Yet on one important question Gandhi did not differ fundamentally from the views of the Conference as a whole. While the Congress was resolved upon complete independence, the mandate which the Congress demanded did not necessarily mean that the Congress was contemplating the severance of all connexion with the British people. Gandhi himself contemplated a partnership with the British people such as could exist only between two absolute equals. 'I do not want to break the bond between England and India', he observed, 'but I do want to transform that bond.'[4] And for his own part he sought to such a partnership not merely for the benefit of India, nor for the mutual benefit of Britain and India, but in order that 'the great weight that is crushing the world . . . may be lifted from its shoulders.'[5]

In the light of the deliberations at the Round Table Conference the British government felt unable to contemplate any early grant of dominion status. Yet the results, if disappointing, were not wholly negative. At the end of the Second Session the Prime Minister reaffirmed the conviction of his government that an All-India Federation offered 'the only hopeful solution to India's constitutional problem'.[6] More important, he underlined at the same time the general agreement of delegates that in the future the provinces were 'to be responsibly governed units, enjoying the greatest possible measure of freedom from outside interference and dictation in carrying out their own policies in their own sphere.'[7] In both cases he foreshadowed the main provisions of the Act of 1935.

THE GOVERNMENT OF INDIA ACT, 1935,[8] AND ITS APPLICATION IN THE PROVINCES

The British government, having formulated its conclusions to the Round Table Conference,[9] proceeded to the appointment of a Select Committee of

[1] Indian Round Table Conference, Second Session (Sept.–Dec. 1931), *Proceedings of Federal Structure Committee and Minorities Committee*, 70/260, p. 530.

[2] ibid. p. 387.

[3] ibid.

[4] Cmd. 3997, p. 395.

[5] ibid. p. 394.

[6] ibid. p. 415.

[7] ibid. p. 416.

[8] 26 Geo. V, c. 2.

[9] *Proposals for Indian Constitutional Reform*. Cmd. 4268, 1933. The introductory sections on 'The Federation of India' (pp. 6–22) summarize briefly and cogently their opinions about the form the central government should take.

both Houses to examine them and to draft legislation for the future government of India. This formidable task was undertaken with conscientious thoroughness[1] and the Act which resulted was a model of careful, detailed, and effective drafting. As an essay in constitution-making it has not been surpassed in modern times; as a piece of constructive statesmanship it lacked boldness of conception and imaginative insight.

The banality of its opening descriptive phrase—'an Act to make further provision for the government of India'—suggested a lack of vision. The phrase, as Mr. Attlee observed,[2] might refer to 'any little bill' and not the comprehensive product of years of painstaking deliberation by Commission, Conference, and Committee about the best way to take the next great step on the road to full Indian self-government. By such cautious non-committal understatement the mind of India was not to be captured nor were its suspicions to be quieted.[3] Where Indians looked for some bold pronouncement on their future status they found a draftsman's hackneyed phrase.

The reticence of the Act of 1935 about India's advance to dominion status was deliberate. It was felt by the United Kingdom government that no further pronouncement was required. Sir Samuel Hoare, the Secretary of State for India, said in debate that the government stood 'firmly by the pledge contained in the 1919 Preamble, which it is not part of their plan to repeal, and by the interpretation put by the Viceroy in 1929 . . . on the Preamble that: "the natural issue of India's progress as there contemplated, is the attainment of Dominion status." '[4] Later he referred to 'the wide road that has been opened for Indians', and declared that it depended 'principally on their success as to how and when they reach their journey's end'.[5] But this did not satisfy either Indian or British critics. Neither the pace of the advance nor the principle involved was acceptable to Indian nationalist opinion, which was insistent that Indians should decide for themselves the form of their own Constitution. Both pace and principle were also sharply criticized by the Labour Opposition at Westminster, who advocated explicit recognition of India's right to dominion status and provision for its attainment.[6]

It is not [said Mr. Attlee] merely a matter of saying in a Preamble that dominion status is the goal. Dominion status means much more than that. It means the recognition of the right of India to dominion status. It means an admission that the Indians have the right to deal with their own constitutional affairs, and that is

[1] Joint Committee on Indian Constitutional Reform (Session 1933–4), vol. 1, pt. 1, *Report* (London, H.M.S.O., 1934).

[2] 6 February 1935, H. of C. Deb., vol. 297, col. 1168.

[3] cf. Professor Berriedale Keith's contemporary verdict: 'Whatever excuses are available, the failure to mention dominion status in the preamble . . . is a profound error' (*Letters on Imperial Relations*, p. 347).

[4] 6 February 1935, H. of C. Deb., vol. 297, col. 1165.

[5] 4 June 1935, H. of C. Deb., vol. 302, col. 1717.

[6] See the terms of the amendment moved by Mr. Attlee, 6 February 1935, H. of C. Deb., vol. 297, col. 1167.

not done . . . in the deeds which are embodied in this Act. There is nowhere any recognition of right. We on this side hold that you must recognize, as we recognize, the right of the Indian people to self-government, and that no Constitution can possibly be worked which . . . does not admit that claim.[1]

The sequel showed that, while the criticisms of the Act of 1935 were not without foundation, they applied, with by no means equal force, to all its provisions. Nor did they detract from its greatest achievement, which was the placing of all future discussion about Indian government on a higher and more realistic level. The real danger in India, observed Sir Samuel Hoare, was irresponsibility.[2] After the passage of the Act, that danger was sensibly lessened because at the least it afforded a starting-point for constructive criticism.

The Act had two principal objects—first the setting up of a Federation of India which would include both British India and, with the consent of their rulers, the Princely States; and secondly the provision of new Constitutions for the provinces of British India which would make their governments responsible to popularly elected assemblies for the ordinary purposes of administration. The provincial part of the Act came into force on the day appointed by Parliament, 1 April 1937, and its contribution to Indian political thought was lasting and fruitful. For all their defects, wrote Mr. G. V. Mavalankar, the first Speaker of the Parliament of the Indian Republic, the legislatures set up in the provinces under the Act of 1935 'made a beginning with the parliamentary system of rule by means of a Council of Ministers responsible to the legislature',[3] and experience in the provinces after 1937 unquestionably contributed to the later decision of an Indian Constituent Assembly to embody the British system of responsible parliamentary government in the Constitution of the Indian Union.

The detailed history of the experiment of responsible government in the provinces, despite its wider significance, belongs not to the history of Commonwealth relations but to that of India's constitutional development. By contrast with it the recommendations of the Act of 1935 for a form of Federal Government for India[4] were still-born. The Act proposed that the executive government of the Federation should be vested in the hands of the Governor-General assisted by a Council of Ministers not exceeding ten in number;[5] and that its legislature should consist of two Houses. The Upper House, or Council of State, was to comprise 156 representatives from British India, their seats being distributed among the provinces mainly on a population basis, with six seats to be filled by the Governor-General in his discretion and ten to be distributed among the smaller minorities; and not more than 104

[1] 6 January 1935, H. of C. Deb., vol. 297, coll. 1168–9.
[2] ibid. col. 1162.
[3] *Parliamentary Affairs*, 1950, vol. 4, no. 1, p. 111.
[4] 26 Geo. V, c. 2, pt. 2.
[5] ibid. art. 9.

members of the Princely States to be appointed by their rulers, with the smaller States grouped together as units for this purpose.[1] The Lower House, or Federal Assembly, was to consist of 250 members of British India and not more than 125 of the States. The members for British India were to be indirectly elected on a communal basis by members of the provincial Legislative Assemblies, while the representatives of the States were once again to be nominated by their rulers.[2] The House was to be re-elected every five years unless dissolved earlier.

The Federal executive was to be responsible to the Federal legislature except in such matters as were vested exclusively in the hands of the Governor-General. These matters specifically included defence and external affairs.[3] The Governor-General was also to have the right to advise the Governors on the exercise of their discretionary authority and, if it seemed to him necessary, to intervene in provincial affairs. In time of emergency the power thus vested in the Governor-General was extended so as to cover the preservation of law and order in the provinces of British India. Moreover, so as to ensure that his authority should not be the subject of dispute, it was expressly provided that should any question arise whether any matter was or was not a matter in which the Governor-General was required to act in his discretion or to exercise his individual judgement, the decision of the Governor-General in his discretion was final, and the validity of anything done by him could not be called in question on the ground that he ought or ought not to have acted in his discretion or ought or ought not to have exercised his individual judgement.[4] In this way the introduction of dyarchy at the centre left the Governor-General with a residuary authority which, if used, could virtually nullify the responsibility of the Council of Ministers to the legislature. It is true that it was the clearly stated intention of the United Kingdom government that this should not occur, and that the Governor-General's residuary authority should be exercised only under exceptional circumstances. Professor Coupland lends his weighty authority to the view that what was given was far more important than what was withheld, and that by the constructive use of their opportunities Indians could have ensured that the restrictions ceased to operate in fact.[5] Neither British Labour nor the Muslim League, however, quite apart from the Indian Congress who objected fundamentally to a Constitution imposed from without, formed so sanguine an estimate. To Mr. Attlee the keynote of the Act was mistrust, a mistrust of the Indian people, which was responsible for the introduction of a Constitution 'with restrictions of every kind all the the time'.[6] Mr. Jinnah spoke of '98 per cent. of the safeguards

[1] 26 Geo. V, c. 2, pt. 2, art. 18 (2) and (3), and First Schedule.
[2] ibid.
[3] ibid. art. 11 (1).
[4] ibid. art. 9 (3).
[5] *India: a Re-Statement*, pp. 146–7.
[6] 6 January 1935, H. of C. Deb., vol. 297, col. 1169.

and 2 per cent. of responsibility', and alluded ironically to the position of the Governor-General and 'his powers as to the interference in legislation, his extraordinary powers, his special responsibility . . . what do they leave us?'[1] Indeed, while few outside the Congress questioned the need for some safeguards in the transitional period, their scale affronted even moderate Indian liberal opinion.

There was a further and substantial source of misgiving about the federal provisions of the Act. They were dependent upon the will of the Princes and were not to come into effect until a proportion of the Princely States had agreed to join the Federation.[2] The British government, exercising no direct authority over the States, could not, of course, compel them to enter an All-India Federation but, in the light of the views expressed by their representatives at the Round Table Conference, may reasonably have hoped that they would be prepared to do so. After all, the status and the authority of the Princes in their own States were carefully safeguarded in the Act, and their representation through nominated members in both Houses of the Federal legislature would have given them an influential voice in the conduct of affairs. The British government, moving to the right under pressure of 'diehard' criticism, regarded the participation of the Princes at the centre as an essential stabilizing influence, for the autocratic rulers of the States, enjoying a highly privileged position in the Indian social system, were not likely, however susceptible to national sentiment, to be carried away by heady reformist zeal.

Though gratifying to the National government in London, the dependence upon the will of the Princes for the coming into force of the Federal provisions of the 1935 Act and their privileged position at the centre should they decide to participate aroused no enthusiasm in British India. Mr. Jinnah, in moderate language, and affirming that he was not against the Princes but 'for British India', described the conditions laid down for their entry into the Federation as being 'on the face of them most detrimental to the vital interests of British India. . . .'[3] The Congress, with its pronounced democratic-socialist outlook was less restrained. It will be a kind of federation, observed Rajendra Prasad in his Presidential Address to Congress in 1934, 'in which unabashed autocracy will sit entrenched in one-third of India and peep in every now and then to strangle popular will in the remaining two-thirds'.[4] 'The only kind of federation that can be acceptable . . .', declared the Congress at Haripura in 1938, 'is one in which the States participate as free units, enjoying the same measure of democratic freedom as the rest of India.'[5] The Congress would have preferred to see British India advance towards responsible self-govern-

[1] At Patna, 7 February 1935 (Banerjee, *Indian Constitutional Documents*, vol. 3, p. 231).
[2] Art. 5 (1).
[3] At Patna, 7 February 1935 (Banerjee, ibid. p. 230).
[4] Quoted in Banerjee, ibid. p. 238.
[5] Quoted in ibid. p. 466.

ment without the States rather than to find autocracy and capitalism strongly established in the Federation. Their open challenge to Princely autocracy in itself helps to explain why in fact none of the Princes joined the Federation, which accordingly never came into being.[1]

The first practical test of the 1935 reforms came with the provincial elections of 1937, which were contested both by the Congress, whose declared intention was 'not to co-operate in any way with the Act but to seek the end of it',[2] and by the League, who welcomed the emphasis placed in the Act upon provincial autonomy and was prepared to see the provincial scheme 'utilized for what it is worth'.[3] The results, disappointing to the League, more than fulfilled the highest expectations of the Congress. They obtained outright majorities in five of the eleven provincial Assemblies and they constituted the largest party in two more.[4] The Muslim League, on the other hand, appeared at a disadvantage owing to its lack of any effective mass organization. Before the elections this had caused its leaders comparatively little concern. Conservative and autocratic, they had no great liking for popular movements and in any case they contemplated the formation of coalition ministries in those provinces where the Muslims were in a large minority. But the Congress had other views. They disliked the idea of coalitions, and where they had obtained a majority they felt that they should, in accordance with British parliamentary practice, form the government. They might invite prominent Muslims to accept office, but only on an individual basis and on condition that League membership was renounced. By the League this was interpreted as the deliberate rejection of proffered co-operation, and when, after some doubts as to whether it was right or not for Congressmen to accept office in view of the safeguards still retained in the hands of the Governors, the Congress High Command decided that they should do so and without League co-operation, the League was mortally affronted. Protagonists of communal co-operation, among whom Mr. Jinnah was to be numbered, became the advocates of mass Muslim resistance.

An Indian writer has observed that it was an old attachment to parliamentary orthodoxy and a new sympathy with socialism that brought the Congress into antagonism with the Muslim League.[5] Certainly 1937 marked the parting of the ways. Nor is it to be doubted that the Congress outright rejection of the idea of Congress-League coalition ministries seriously impaired the prospect of an independent, united India, which was the declared goal of all their endeavours.

[1] The Princes, in fact, thought their position insufficiently safeguarded by the Act. For a statement of their views see Cmd. 4843.

[2] cf. also the resolution of the Congress at its Lucknow session, 1936, quoted in Banerjee, *Indian Constitutional Documents*, vol. 3, p. 325.

[3] ibid. p. 350.

[4] For a detailed account of the elections and the work of the provincial governments see Coupland, *The Indian Problem*, pt. 2, pp. 22–154.

[5] Prasad, *Hindu-Muslim Questions*, p. 65.

The Congress brought a new stimulus to provincial administration. Though the majority of its members was probably conservative in outlook, its able and energetic left wing determined policy, and Congress provincial governments accordingly pressed forward with long overdue social reforms. In a critical analysis[1] of Congress government in the United Provinces, Sir Harry Haig, who was their Governor from 1934 to 1939, numbered among its virtues a rapid response to public grievances, a new spirit of enterprise, courage to experiment and to take measures from which governments under the earlier Constitution would have shrunk. Reform was stimulated by members who were in close touch with their constituencies and was made possible by the existence of a large and disciplined parliamentary majority on which ministers could depend. It was indeed this assurance of organized support which constituted the strength of the Congress in the provinces as in the country as a whole. In the words of Sir Harry Haig, 'they monopolized the machinery of popular appeal'.

The strength of the popular position of the Congress, so dramatically illustrated in the elections of 1937 and in their conduct of provincial administration when in office, caused general consternation among Muslims, who did not fail to notice that the Congress provincial governments were, in fact, not independent governments individually responsible to their own electorates, but Congress governments whose acceptance of office and whose later resignation was decided by the All-India Congress Working Committee sitting at its headquarters at Wardha. Such centralized control, deemed by the Congress High Command to be essential for the advancement of the national aims which were its *raison d'être*, dismayed the League by exposing the comparative weakness of its own position.

THE RISE OF MUSLIM SEPARATISM

It was in the early nineteen-thirties that the name of Pakistan was adopted by Indian Muslim students at Cambridge to symbolize the ideal of an autonomous Muslim state.[2] It was not taken over-seriously even by the League, whose representatives told the Joint Select Committee in 1933 that Pakistan was 'only a student's scheme' that could be dismissed as 'chimerical and impracticable'.[3] The Muslims, in fact, like the Hindus, still presumed that unity, the greatest achievement of the British Raj, would survive its passing. In the provincial elections of 1937 the League, united with the Congress at least in qualified opposition to the Act of 1935 and in a common demand for independence, favoured a policy of communal reconciliation. In a phrase to which later events gave ironic immortality, Mrs. Sarojini Naidu described Mr.

[1] *Asiatic Review*, July 1940, pp. 427–9.

[2] cf. Richard Symonds, *The Making of Pakistan* (London, Faber, 1950) pp. 14 and 56n. and Coupland, *India: a Re-Statement*, p. 191.

[3] Quoted by Coupland, ibid.

Jinnah as 'the ambassador of Hindu-Muslim unity'.[1] But after the elections the situation was transformed by the Congress refusal to co-operate with the League. Not only was Mr. Jinnah driven into violent opposition to the Congress, but he became for the first time the unquestioned leader of Muslim India.[2] At the same time the once ridiculed idea of a separate Muslim state acquired prestige and growing popular support. For this the coming into existence rather than the actions of the Congress provincial ministries was the primary cause. While it is not to be denied that the Congress rebuff to the League was a major political error, it remains questionable whether greater wisdom and tolerance on the part of its leaders at this critical moment would in the long run have sufficed to quiet Muslim fears. In any event, the actual exercise of authority by the Congress in the provinces brought Muslim India face to face with the reality of the Hindu Raj, and thereby revived all their traditional fears and animosities. The faith and culture of Islam seemed to be in danger and, scrutinized with deep suspicion, every Congress action seemed to bode ill for Indian Muslims. With particular misgiving they looked, as we have seen, upon the control exercised by the Congress High Command over the Congress ministries. Was not this a foretaste of the Hindu dictatorship which would follow the British withdrawal? In his presidential address to the All-India Muslim League at Lucknow in October 1937 Mr. Jinnah declared the Congress provincial governments 'by their words and deed and programme' had shown that Muslims could not expect any justice or fair play at their hands. 'On the very threshold of what little power and responsibility is given, the majority community have clearly shown . . . that Hindustan is for the Hindus.'[3] A year later at the League meeting at Patna Mr. Jinnah's language was even stronger. The Congress High Command, he said, had demonstrated beyond doubt that they wanted 'the Mussalmans to be a mere understudy of the Congress, mere foot pages of the Congress leaders. . . .' They had 'killed every hope of Hindu-Muslim settlements in the right royal fashion of Fascism'. And there followed a list of particular charges, the singing of *Bande Mataram*, 'a hymn of hate against the Muslims', by Congressmen as the national song, the parading of the Congress flag as the national flag of India, the use of Hindi at the expense of Urdu, and the general imposition of the Hindu mentality and Hindu ideals upon the minority.[4] It was a cherished and traditional way of life that was felt to be in danger.

In this atmosphere of suspicion and fear it was difficult to disentangle fact from fiction. The weight of impartial evidence suggests that the Congress

[1] This phrase has been attributed to Pandit Nehru, but it is apparent from his own *Jawaharlal Nehru: an Autobiography* (London, Bodley Head, 1941) that it was coined by Mrs. Naidu (p. 67).

[2] Mr. Fazl ul-Huq in Bengal, and Sir Sikander Hyat Khan in the Punjab, who had earlier been opposed to Mr. Jinnah, now declared for the Muslim League.

[3] Address reprinted in Banerjee, *Indian Constitutional Documents*, vol. 3, pp. 349–54.

[4] Reprinted in ibid. pp. 354–6.

ministries for the most part sought to deal fairly and impartially in communal disputes.[1] After all it was the *raison d'être* of the Congress to unite all Indians in a secular national movement for liberation, and its leaders at least were well aware that communal bias on the part of Congress provincial governments would destroy it. But in a sense the facts were irrelevant. It was not so much what the Congress governments did as what they represented that mattered. And however much its leaders had sought to make the Congress all-embracing, it continued to be overwhelmingly Hindu in its membership and its ethos. Congress rule, therefore, meant Hindu rule, and it was simply that which to Muslims seemed unbearable. Safeguards that once seemed satisfying now appeared illusory. Muslim criticism of the federal provisions of the Act of 1935 was directed no longer against their failure to transfer effective power into Indian hands, but against the establishment of Hindu control at the centre which they would bring about. Indeed so long as there was a centre, might not Muslim majority provinces, even if enjoying virtual freedom from central control in theory, find in practice that their position was being undermined by the inevitable predominance that derived from greater numbers? Was not the only sufficient safeguard the creation of a separate Muslim state? Here logic was reinforced by emotion. The separatist ideal once proclaimed evoked from the Muslim masses, well prepared to believe that Islam was in danger, an enthusiastic response. Thereafter there was, and there could be, no going back. It was as the spokesman, not of a minority community, but of a separate and equal nationality that Mr. Jinnah henceforward demanded to be heard.

In September 1939 the Working Committee of the League urged the British government to abandon once and for all the federal part of the 1935 Constitution. Muslim India, it declared,[2] was 'irrevocably opposed to federation in any form'. When in December that year the Congress ministers resigned, in accordance with the policy of non-co-operation in Britain's war-time policies, Mr. Jinnah called upon all Muslims to observe Friday, 22 December 1939, as a Day of Deliverance from 'the tyranny, oppression, and injustice' from which Muslim India had suffered in the two and a half years of Congress rule in the provinces.[3] In March 1940, at its annual meeting at Lahore, 'the League unanimously resolved that no constitutional plan would be . . . acceptable unless . . . the areas in which the Muslims were in a majority were grouped together to constitute "independent states" in which the constituent units shall be autonomous and sovereign'.[4] 'Pakistan is our goal today', said Mr. Jinnah

[1] On this point see the impressive testimony of Sir Harry Haig in the *Asiatic Review*, July 1940, pp. 428–9. For an outspoken statement of Muslim grievances see Mr. Jinnah's statement to the press on 'Deliverance Day', 22 December 1939, reprinted in *Some Recent Speeches and Writings of Mr. Jinnah*, ed. by Jamil ud-din Ahmad (Lahore, Ashraf, 1943) pp. 97–104.

[2] *Indian Annual Register*, 1939, vol. 2, p. 351.

[3] M. A. Jinnah at Bombay, 2 December 1939, *Speeches and Writings*, pp. 95–97.

[4] *Indian Annual Register*, 1940, vol. 1, p. 312.

later in the year, a goal 'for which the Muslims of India will live and, if necessary, die.'[1]

To what extent the long delays in the transfer of power, long that is to say in relation not to dominion precedents, but to the actual situation in India itself, accentuated existing communal rivalries is a matter likely to remain in dispute. It was in 1917 that responsible self-government was proclaimed to be the goal of British policy; it was in 1931 that it was finally decided that independent India should assume a federal form; it was not till five years later that the outlines of that federation were drafted, and by the outbreak of war the federal part of the scheme had, under the pressure of Indian opinion, been virtually discarded.[2] Great, therefore, as had been the advance in provincial self-government and in the transfer of administrative power, the transfer of political power at the centre lagged far behind. This was doubly unfortunate. Indian nationalists were peculiarly sensitive to their status in the world, and they judged the pace of India's advance towards self-government far less by what happened in the provinces or any part of domestic government or administration than by the status which India enjoyed in the world at large. In this Hindus and Muslims felt alike. Delay, therefore, served to sharpen the edge of Indian nationalist sentiment. This made a compromise solution of a kind likely to reassure minorities progressively less easy to devise. The majority, disillusioned and frustrated, reasserted the demand for national independence in a fundamentalist form, while the minority, and especially Muslim, fears about the consequences for them of Hindu domination assumed a sharper edge, so that by 1939 a partitioned India came into the realm of practical politics. For this communal tensions within India were the principal cause, and it is questionable whether under any circumstances they would have permitted the emergence by consent of a free united India. 'The Hindus and Muslims', said Mr. Jinnah at Lahore in 1940,[3] 'belong to two different religious philosophies, social customs, literatures. They neither inter-marry nor inter-dine and, indeed, they belong to two different civilizations. . . .' If he was right—and he himself had earlier entertained less categorical opinions —then to yoke these two nations in a single state could have resulted only in disaster. If he was mistaken, then the slowness of the transfer of effective power, for which the British government must bear chief responsibility, was a contributory factor of no small importance in the sequence of events that led to the partitioning of India.

INDIA AND THE APPROACH OF WAR

Before the Second World War India's political contacts with the neighbouring peoples of Asia were neither so extensive nor so intimate as might

[1] At New Delhi, November 1940, *Speeches and Writings*, p. 178.
[2] cf. Prasad, *Hindu-Muslim Questions*, p. 56.
[3] *Speeches and Writings of Jinnah*, p. 153.

have been expected. This was in part the outcome of a geographical situation which gave to India a sense of affinity with other maritime countries and thereby counterbalanced the natural pull of her continental environment; in part it was the consequence of imperial rule which encouraged Indians to look westward for their political ideas and their higher education; but to a greater extent it was the result of the policies of Britain, and more especially of France and Holland, who feared the growth of a sense of Asian solidarity and accordingly discouraged too close an association between the non self-governing peoples of South and South East Asia.[1] The existence of these barriers was not, however, without some compensation. Precluded from active participation in regional affairs, Indian attention was the more readily attracted to broader world issues. Thus, while opinion was most deeply stirred by events in the Middle and the Far East, the greater struggle between the democracies of the West and the dictatorships of Central Europe was followed with anxious interest by the politically self-conscious minority, who realized that it was largely by its outcome that the political destiny of India would be determined.

For Indian Muslims the Middle East remained their natural area of interest, and for them Palestine was the touchstone by which they were disposed to judge British policies elsewhere. It was the Congress, on the other hand, who displayed the greater concern with developments in the Far East. From 1931 onwards the resolutions of the Congress Working Committee, while affirming as a matter of principle that India could not allow 'her man-power to be used as pawns by others' even in a cause they themselves deemed good, became progressively more outspoken in their denunciation of Japanese aggression and more critical of the Western democracies and particularly of Britain for her failure to give whole-hearted support to China. Thus at Wardha in August 1937 the Working Committee declared that 'our sympathies are inevitably with China', and they wished the Chinese people success 'in maintaining their freedom against imperialist aggression'.[2] At the meeting of the All-India Congress Committee at Calcutta in October the terms of the resolution moved by Mr. Sarat Bose reflected the hardening of anti-Japanese feeling in India. 'The whole of India', said Mr. Bose, 'has been moved by the events in China', and he desired to give expression 'to the great indignation which had swept India from end to end against Japan.'[3] Nor did he feel that this was a mere formal registration of a protest; on the contrary it was an expression of the deep sense of community that existed between India and China. China's struggle against Japanese imperialism 'was India's struggle'. In February 1938, at Haripura, Congress denunciations of Japanese aggression were in the strongest terms.[4] They condemned 'the aggression of a brutal (Japanese)

[1] This was much emphasized at the Inter-Asian Conference held in New Delhi in March–April 1947.
[2] *Indian Annual Register*, 1937, vol. 2, p. 318.
[3] ibid. p. 360.
[4] ibid. 1938, vol. 1, p. 296.

imperialism and the horrors and frightfulness which have accompanied it', and feared that this 'imperialist invasion' would have the gravest consequence for world peace. As a mark of sympathy for the people of China the Congress called for a boycott of Japanese goods.[1] On the eve of the Second World War Pandit Nehru visited China to express the moral support of the Congress for China's struggle for national survival.

It was, however, not in relation to events in the Far East but to events in Europe and in Africa that India's approach to world affairs was most clearly defined. India's hostility to Fascism and to Nazism was never in question. It was instinctive and fundamental. The prevailing misgiving was lest the British government should be driven through fear of Russia into making some unprincipled bargain with the dictators. Indian anxiety on this score was accentuated by British policies in the Italo-Abyssinian war. For almost all Indians, Abyssinia was the criterion by which both the power of the League of Nations and the resolve of the Western democracies to resist aggression, not merely against a small power, but against a small non-European power, was to be judged. Neither the authority of the one nor the reputation of the other survived the test unimpaired. In his presidential address to the Congress at Faizpur in December 1936,[2] Pandit Nehru declared that the League had now 'fallen very low and there are few who take it seriously as an instrument for the preservation of peace'. For British foreign policy he reserved a harsher judgement. By the negotiation of the Naval Treaty with Germany, Britain had thrown France into the arms of Italy and had thereby left the way open for Mussolini to march into Abyssinia. Britain's responsibility for the outbreak of war, if indirect, was heavy and her later actions gave no ground for reassurance. 'Behind all the talk of sanctions against Italy . . .', said Pandit Nehru, 'there was the refusal by the British government to impose any effective sanctions.'

Congress mistrust of Britain's foreign policy assumed a more emotional tinge during the Spanish civil war. 'In Spain', said Pandit Nehru, its principal spokesman on foreign affairs, British imperialism by a policy of non-intervention had 'hindered and obstructed the Spanish in their fight for freedom',[3] and his own visit to Spain in June 1938 gave a sharper edge to his desire to dissociate India from the British foreign policy. 'We cannot', he said, 'be tied down by any foreign policy of the British government. We are so strongly opposed to that policy that we cannot tolerate being associated with it.'[4] Yet India's enforced association with Britain's policy through the nomination of her representatives at international conferences by Whitehall and the determination of her foreign policy by the British government remained an ever growing source of grievance to the Congress. What could be done was done

[1] *Indian Annual Register*, 1938, vol. 1, p. 296.
[2] Presidential Address, Indian National Congress, 50th Session, December 1936, p. 8.
[3] *Unity of India*, p. 266.
[4] *Manchester Guardian*, 24 June 1938.

to make known to the world the views of the Indian National Congress on the great questions of the day, and when possible some positive course of action was adopted in order to give tangible evidence of India's detestation of Fascism, of Nazism and of her sympathy with democracy whether in Spain or Czechoslovakia or China. In all this Pandit Nehru was the spokesman of the Congress and the mentor of his colleagues, and in so far as a body so composite in political background as the Congress may be said to have had an attitude to foreign affairs it was faithfully reflected in his speeches.

Among Commonwealth countries New Zealand alone was felt to champion with vigour and with consistency the views which the Indian Congress entertained. In September 1937 when the Congress was distressed by renewed Japanese aggression in China and disturbed by rumours of the impending recognition by the democracies of the Italian empire in Abyssinia, Pandit Nehru, as its President, appealed to Mr. Jordan, the New Zealand representative at Geneva,[1] urging him to take the same bold stand as that adopted by New Zealand delegates in the past, for the cause of justice and the maintenance of international law. 'India', he said, 'is powerless to register a protest at the League Assembly through representatives who are nominated by the British government', but she did not wish to allow her views to pass unrecorded, and it was through New Zealand she hoped they would find vicarious expression.

The Czech crisis played an important part in clarifying Indian opinion on international affairs. Pandit Nehru visited Czechoslovakia as the crisis was approaching its climax, and he was present in the gallery of the House of Commons in Westminster in the historic debate which preceded Mr. Chamberlain's flight to Munich. His impressions of the scene were not favourable.[2] Of Mr. Chamberlain he had little good to say. The British Prime Minister's appearance was not striking, there seemed to be 'no nobility in his countenance', he looked 'too much like a business man', and he seemed too 'excited and proud about his personal intervention' and 'the part he was playing in world affairs' so that

> the intoxication of the adventure fills him. A Palmerston or a Gladstone or a Disraeli would have risen to the occasion. A Campbell-Bannermann would have put some fire into what he said. A Baldwin might have gripped the House, so would Churchill in a different way. Even Asquith would have spoken with a dignity suited to the occasion.[3] But there was neither warmth nor depth of intellect in what Mr. Chamberlain said. It was very evident that he was not a man of destiny.

Nor did Mr. Chamberlain seem to his Indian critic to be a man of force. Hitler 'for all his evil bent and distorted intent has something elemental

[1] *Manchester Guardian*, 10 September 1937.
[2] They were published at the time and later reprinted in *Unity of India*, pp. 290–3.
[3] Admirers of Mr. Asquith will not relish that 'even'.

about him', while Mr. Chamberlain was 'of the earth, earthy'. Pandit Nehru concluded, therefore, that in any clash of wills Mr. Chamberlain would go down before Hitler. But what troubled him still more was whether there had been or even would be a clash of wills. Where Pandit Nehru would have liked the emphasis laid on principle,[1] Mr. Chamberlain laid it on the possibilities of settlement by negotiation. Did not that mean collaboration between Fascism and imperialism designed to isolate Russia and to crush all progressive forces? These proved to be unfounded suspicions but they were important, for in India they were deeply and widely entertained. At its Tripuri meeting in March 1939 the Congress recorded

its entire disapproval of British foreign policy culminating in the Munich Pact, the Anglo-Italian Agreement, and the recognition of rebel Spain. This policy has been one of deliberate betrayal of democracy, repeated breach of pledges, the ending of the system of collective security and co-operation with governments which are avowed enemies of democracy and freedom.[2]

Pandit Nehru admitted that there was a distinction between Fascism and imperialism, and allowed that Britain and France at least spoke in terms of freedom, self-determination, and democracy. But he feared that their conception of freedom at best was limited to Europe. If he sensed rightly that the majority of the people in Britain would have welcomed immediate self-government for an Indian dominion, it was none the less in the light of British government policy that the Indian leaders had to define their own attitude. And as war approached the emphasis of the British government was more and more upon the need for a cautious advance, whose pace would be conditioned by external dangers and internal tensions, towards the declared goal of dominion status. In this the Congress was not prepared to acquiesce. While its members recognized that resistance to Fascism could come only from the West, they felt as strongly that it was from the West that Indians, who were passionately anti-Fascist, had first to win their freedom. In such circumstances their anti-Fascism came, as we shall see, to take second place to their anti-imperialist sentiments. Yet the Congress, while most emphatic in its resolve to dissociate itself from British foreign policy and in its refusal to sanction Indian participation in any war without the consent of its own representatives, did not fail to recognize that the victory of Hitler's new order in Europe would mean the most disastrous set-back to Indian hopes of freedom and national independence.

In a real sense the Indian dilemma was artificial. It derived not so much from any fundamental source of difference as from the delays that had occurred

[1] Little more than two years after Munich, when on trial for sedition at Gorakhpur, Pandit Nehru recalled his strong emotional reaction against Fascism and Naziism and maintained, not unjustly, that there were not many Indians or Englishmen who had so consistently denounced them (*Unity of India*, p. 397).

[2] *Indian Annual Register*, 1939, vol. 1, pp. 341–2.

in the fulfilment of the declared British policy of self-government for India. Responsibility for these delays might be variously attributed, but their consequence in relation to international affairs is hardly to be doubted. They made impossible free co-operation between equals, they sowed suspicions, and they accentuated divisions. Had a Federal Indian Government been established, as contemplated under the Act of 1935 or in some other form, at any time before 1939, India's co-operation with the Commonwealth in a war provoked by German and Japanese aggression could hardly have been in doubt.

PART III

THE COMMONWEALTH AND THE WAR

Once more we hear the word
That sickened earth of old:
'No law except the Sword
Unsheathed and uncontrolled.'

RUDYARD KIPLING

CHAPTER X

IN THE 'VALLEY OF DECISION'[1]

THE DOMINIONS FREE OF TREATY OBLIGATIONS IN EUROPE

DOMINION dislike of automatic involvement in the United Kingdom's European policies indicated in the Chanak crisis of 1922, implicitly re-affirmed in relation to the Locarno treaties, had hardened into settled policy ten years later. No dominion was a party to the Anglo-Egyptian Treaty of 1936, or to the renewed guarantee of Belgian neutrality in 1936, nor were any of them party to the ill-fated promise of a frontier guarantee made to the Czechs at Munich, to the Polish guarantee of March 1939,[2] to the Roumanian and Greek guarantees of April 1939, or to the Alliance with Turkey. In September 1939, therefore, the dominions had no particular commitments binding them to go to war in Europe. Their formal detachment from United Kingdom policy in Europe was accepted as part of the pattern of Commonwealth relations and it was assumed at all times that they would not wish to be associated positively with it. Where time allowed—and it had not in every case allowed—the dominions had been consulted about major developments in the United Kingdom policy; in every case they had been informed, and they were aware of the reasons that inspired United Kingdom actions. But neither information nor even consultation were regarded as tantamount to commitment even though it was recognized that the dominions could not remain unaffected by the consequences of British policies in Europe. This was a supremely important fact in 1939. On 3 September the United Kingdom declared war on Germany in fulfilment of the guarantee extended to Poland the previous March, but for the rest the issue of peace and war had to be decided in the light of broader considerations.

The statement that the dominions had no obligations of a specific character in Europe demands one qualification. All had been signatories to the Covenant of the League of Nations, and it might therefore be argued that a League declaration naming a particular country as an aggressor would oblige them to fulfil their obligations under Article 19 of the League Covenant. In practice this was no longer a consideration of first importance. While not all of the Commonwealth leaders had been so outspoken as Mr. Mackenzie King and Mr. de Valera, their conviction that the obligations accepted under the League

[1] 'Multitudes, multitudes in the valley of decision' (Joel iii. 14).

[2] Mr. Chamberlain announced that the United Kingdom would give all the support in its power to Poland in the event of a threat to its independence on 31 March 1939 (H. of C. Deb., vol. 345, col. 2415). This unilateral guarantee was given a reciprocal character in the Anglo-Polish communiqué issued on 6 April 1939. The Anglo-Polish Pact of Mutual Assistance, ratifying these arrangements, was signed in London in August 1939.

Covenant no longer possessed any binding force after 1938 was no less deep-seated. Nowhere in September 1939 was it seriously urged, as it had been in South Africa in September 1938, that the dominions or a dominion was bound to go to war because of its obligation under the League Charter. In substance, therefore, it remains true to say that the question of peace or war could be considered in each dominion on its merits without regard to any binding external obligations. This is a fact that lends an enhanced significance to the decisions taken in September 1939.

THE CHARACTER OF THE CONSTITUTIONAL AND STRATEGIC OBLIGATIONS OF THE DOMINIONS

The freedom of the Commonwealth countries from obligations to foreign countries did not in any way affect the existence or the non-existence of unwritten constitutional and moral obligations deriving from the nature of their membership of the Commonwealth. The predominant view in Australia and New Zealand was that the character of the Commonwealth made neutrality for any one of its member states in a major war in which Britain was involved incompatible with continued membership. It was acceptance of this view by the governments[1] of the Pacific dominions which led them in September 1939 to consider themselves automatically at war when the King was at war. This view also won some acceptance in Canada. Dr. Manion, the leader of the Conservative opposition, declared on 8 September 1939,

> we are bound to participate in this war. We are British subjects, we are part of the British Empire, and ... I do not see how we can possibly be in and out of the British Empire at the same time. ... I do not believe that there can be any neutrality for any part of the Empire when some other part of the Empire is at war.[2]

His conclusion received substantial support from Mr. Lapointe, the Minister for Justice, who argued on the following day that because the constitutional power in Canada derived, and continued to derive, from the Parliament at Westminster it was impossible to maintain that there was no organic bond uniting them. The existence of this bond, in the view of Mr. Lapointe, though not of his cabinet colleagues, constitutionally precluded Canadian neutrality.[3] But neither he, nor those who shared his view in Canada or elsewhere, contended that the existence of this organic bond deprived dominion governments and parliaments of all freedom of action in the making of peace or war. They could still decide the extent of their participation. Non-belligerency, though not neutrality, remained even in this view a policy consistent with continued membership of the Commonwealth. Yet no degree of automatic commitment, however slight, was easy to reconcile with the oft-

[1] The Labour opposition in Australia dissented from it.
[2] Canada, H. of C. Deb., Special War Session, 1939, p. 14.
[3] ibid. p. 66.

repeated assertions that dominion Parliaments in fact enjoyed an absolute constitutional power in the making of peace and war. The conflict between the older conception of a Commonwealth united in allegiance to a common Crown and the newer emphasis upon the unrestricted freedom of action of the dominions in external policy, which was squarely faced in the House of Assembly at Cape Town in September 1939, was characteristic of the age of transition through which the Commonwealth was passing. And the weight of opinion was still with those who urged that any constitutional restriction, open or implied, upon the freedom of action of the dominions must be removed in the interests not only of the dominions but of the unity of the Commonwealth itself.

No discussion of the constitutional position of the dominions in relation to peace and war could dissociate itself entirely from more practical considerations. Their defence policy (with the exception of Eire) was based upon the presumption that they would co-operate in the event of a major war. To that extent, therefore, their hands were by their own choice no longer wholly free in September 1939. There had entered into the picture a strategic obligation. Its weight is not to be exaggerated.[1] In the first place it applied with unequal force. South Africa had made it abundantly clear that in determining the extent of her participation she would be guided solely by consideration of her own interests, while Mr. de Valera stated in categoric terms the resolve of Eire to remain neutral, and he had taken no part in military discussions. Some of the dominions, too, had to take more particular considerations into account. The Simonstown agreement may or may not have created a constitutional barrier to South African neutrality; it certainly provided for co-operation of a kind that in itself might reasonably be held to preclude neutrality as distinct from non-belligerency. Equally, the United Kingdom contracts with Canada for the use of the docks at Halifax and Esquimalt constituted a practical obstacle to Canadian neutrality. Mr. Lapointe went so far as to suggest that they constituted an absolute barrier, and that only by their cancellation could Canada place herself in a position of being able to make an absolutely free choice. In the case of the Pacific dominions no such particular engagements existed, or were required, for the presumption of co-operation at sea was never questioned by them. More generally New Zealand initiative in the calling of a Pacific Conference on Imperial Defence at Wellington in April 1939 where Australia and New Zealand agreed to undertake measures for their common protection, including the establishment of a Defence Council to co-ordinate

[1] It is well to remember that on 31 July 1914 Sir Edward Grey maintained that 'our hands are free' even though military conversations between the British and French General Staffs had taken place at frequent intervals since 1906 and though joint Anglo-French naval dispositions had left the north-eastern coast of France unprotected by the French navy which was concentrated in the Mediterranean. Grey's attitude elicited from M. Cambon, the French ambassador, the bitter comment: 'I am waiting to see whether the word honour should be erased from the English language.'

imperial defence in the Pacific, meant that the general presumption of co-operation had passed into the realm of certainty.

The specific obligations of Eire until the 1938 agreement had been similar in kind to those of Canada and the Union of South Africa, though by reason of geographical situation and the uncertain limit of the rights of the United Kingdom in war-time they were more restrictive in their probable effect upon her liberty of action. After the return of the Treaty Ports, Eire was free from any contractual obligation towards the United Kingdom or the Commonwealth. It was, however, widely believed at the time that no part of Ireland could hope to avoid being involved in a prolonged war in which the United Kingdom was engaged. This view was very forcibly expressed, for example, by the Irish correspondent to the *Round Table* who maintained that Ireland's position on the map made neutrality impossible.[1] Mr. de Valera, however, also presumably looking at the map, drew very different conclusions.

Over and above the obligation to act in common where defence preparations had in greater or less degree been planned in common upon the assumption of co-operation in war-time, there was a sense of moral obligation implicit in membership of the Commonwealth itself which could hardly survive neutrality in a major war in which the United Kingdom or any of the dominions was engaged. This sense of moral obligation was felt most strongly by those of British extraction. By others its existence was disputed or denied, particularly, but not solely, by Afrikaners and by Irishmen whose inclusion in the Commonwealth was recent and enforced. Where for some, therefore, emotional loyalties demanded unhesitating participation in war in which Britain was involved, for others the appeal to emotion was widely suspect as a device by which hard-won concessions might lose their substance. An appeal to a widely questioned moral obligation, or to traditional loyalties in which many did not share was, therefore, insufficient to bring a united Commonwealth into war. The case for participation had to be argued on the hard basis of national self-interest. By 1939 the days of dominion knight-errantry were over.

It has long been recognized by jurists that the making of peace or war is the final test of sovereignty, and for that reason the action taken by the dominions in 1939 when confronted by it gives a new criterion by which to judge the practical consequences of the great reforms in the structure of the Commonwealth which were carried through between 1926 and 1931. These consequences were for the most part particular, not general, in character, for as the dominions developed in status and in stature the differences between them became more sharply defined. At the same time the crystallization of opinion in the hour of decision exposed more clearly the nature and relative strength of the forces which were to determine the character of the Commonwealth in succeeding years, and incidentally disposed by precedent of many

[1] *Round Table*, December 1938, vol. 29, p. 34.

hitherto vexed constitutional questions. For these reasons September 1939 was one of the great landmarks in the evolution of the Commonwealth.

HOW CANADA WENT TO WAR

Mr. Mackenzie King had made it clear in March 1939 that even if Canada were not *ipso facto* committed when the British Empire was at war, direct aggression upon Britain (or to take the example he normally used, if London were bombed from the air) would be regarded 'as threatening not merely the freedom of Britain but the freedom of the entire British Commonwealth of Nations'.[1] Since a war with Germany arising immediately out of Britain's guarantee to Poland and ultimately from Hitler's lust for domination would inevitably involve direct aggression upon Britain in the sense in which Mr. Mackenzie King used that phrase, there was no mistaking the nature of the Canadian reaction to the mounting crisis in late August 1939. On 23 August, Mr. Mackenzie King announced that the provisions of the War Measures Act of 1914, which had never been repealed, were to be put into force because of 'a state of apprehended war', and he also announced that Parliament would be summoned should the efforts for peace fail. On 31 August he announced that Parliament would be summoned for 7 September, and at the same time stated that the government would seek authority from Parliament to co-operate with the United Kingdom. He himself believed that by these and other actions he had made clear beyond question that the policy of the Canadian government would be co-operation with Britain and France in the event of war, and that therefore Germany should entertain no illusions about Canada's attitude to an invasion of Poland. On Friday, 1 September, Mr. Mackenzie King issued a statement declaring that 'in the event of the United Kingdom becoming engaged in war in the effort to resist aggression, the government of Canada have unanimously decided, as soon as Parliament meets, to seek its authority for effective co-operation by Canada at the side of Britain'.[2] Meanwhile it was pointed out that the necessary measures would continue to be taken for the defence of Canada and that consultation with the United Kingdom would continue. On 3 September Mr. Mackenzie King broadcast to the nation reaffirming the government's policy. In the course of his broadcast he alluded to the King's appeal to all his peoples to make the cause of freedom their own. 'Canada', said her Prime Minister, 'has already answered that call.' But no declaration of war had been made and, in conformity with Mr. Mackenzie King's assurance that Parliament should decide, it could not be made till after Parliament had reassembled four days later. The government of the United States, in its proclamation of neutrality issued on 5 September, listed the United Kingdom, India, Australia, and New Zealand as belligerents among the nations of the Commonwealth, but not Canada or

[1] cf. Canada, H. of C. Deb., 1939, 2nd session, p. 27.

[2] Quoted ibid. p. 30.

South Africa. As a result vast quantities of war materials were rushed across the border to Canada in the six days that elapsed between the United Kingdom and Canadian declaration of war. On the other hand, the Canadian government did not wait upon a formal declaration to detain some seventy German nationals as enemy aliens or to close down over a score of Nazi centres.[1] Some protested in righteous indignation at the undignified ambiguity of Canada's position[2] but the Prime Minister may well have felt that in their generation the children of this world are wiser than the children of light.

Mr. Mackenzie King was anxious not only that Canada should herself decide the issue of peace or war, but also that it should be apparent to her own people and to the world that she had done so. This insistence upon what many Conservatives considered to be a technicality had its importance, possibly a very great importance, in ensuring the support of French-Canadians, of Liberal radicals, and of the C.C.F., many of whose members were predisposed towards pacifist isolationism. The goal of Canadian unity was still the decisive factor in shaping Canadian policy. However pleasing imperial co-operation might be to Conservative sentiment in Ontario, the slightest suspicion that the war was being fought for any narrow imperial interest would at once have estranged the great bulk of the *habitants* in Quebec and left-wing opinion in the Prairies.

For many years Mr. Mackenzie King had proclaimed that Canada would not go to war just because the British Empire was at war, and equally that Canada would not go to war until her own Parliament had decided that in her own interests she should go to war. When the moment for decision did come Mr. Mackenzie King adhered faithfully to the views which he had expressed. If proof were needed that Canada was not committed to war just because the United Kingdom was at war it was supplied by the fact that the Canadian Parliament was not summoned to meet until 7 September 1939, and that in all Canada remained a non-belligerent for a period of six days after the United Kingdom declaration of war. When Parliament assembled, Mr. Mackenzie King explained how he had kept his promise that Parliament would decide.

I have said all along that as regards Canada's entry into war, and obligations ensuing therefrom, no commitments would be made until parliament met, that Parliament would decide the momentous question of peace and war; whether or not this country is to go into war. Now I wish to make perfectly clear at this moment, that Parliament has been summoned and is here today to decide that question. That question is not decided as yet. The government have reached their decision upon policy; they have announced their policy, and it is for the hon. members of this House to say whether or not they stand by the government's policy as it has been announced and as it is being announced today.[3]

[1] cf. *Canada in World Affairs*, pp. 152–3.

[2] e.g. *Toronto Globe and Mail*, 8 September 1939: 'We would . . . forfeit our self-respect were we to resort deliberately to such subterfuges to get supplies.'

[3] 8 September 1939, Canada, H. of C. Deb., 2nd session, p. 29.

The speech of the Governor-General indicated the policy of the government. It recalled that all efforts to maintain peace in Europe having failed, the United Kingdom had become engaged in war with Germany, and the Canadian Parliament had been summoned at the earliest moment in order

that the government may seek authority for the measures necessary for the defence of Canada, and for co-operation in the determined effort which is being made to resist further aggression, and to prevent the appeal to force instead of to pacific means in the settlement of international disputes.[1]

Mr. Mackenzie King then gave the House a detailed account[2] of the development of Canadian policy, in which he explained that he had made it the supreme endeavour of his policy

to let no hasty or premature threat or pronouncement create mistrust and divisions between the different elements that compose the population of our vast dominion, so that when the moment of decision came all should so see the issue itself that our national effort might be marked by unity of purpose, of heart and of endeavour.[3]

Far from expressing doubts about the wisdom of appeasement which the Commonwealth countries had endorsed at the Imperial Conference of 1937, he argued that had a stand been made against aggression a year earlier, the lack of preparation in different parts of Europe and overseas would have produced by 1939 'a situation which none of us . . . would care to contemplate'.[4] Moreover, the time gained had been, if not fully exploited, at least reasonably well used. From 1935–6 Canadian defence estimates had risen from $17 million to $34 million in 1938–9, and to $64 million in 1939–40. Whether they were sufficient to the need was another matter. Mr. Mackenzie King tacitly admitted that in all probability they were not, but he argued characteristically that 'had we gone further we would not have received the necessary support to get through our appropriations'.[5]

In the last months before the final crisis, Canadian initiative in foreign policy was restricted to the dispatch of messages to the German Chancellor, to the President of Poland, and to Signor Mussolini, seeking to persuade them to preserve the peace.

Mr. Mackenzie King justified Canadian participation in the war on a broad basis of principle. This was a war, he argued, in which the forces of good were ranged against the forces of evil, and Canada should take part at the side of Britain and of France and of other allied countries to defend the cause of good and of Christianity. His argument carried a greater conviction to many members because of the recent conclusion of the Nazi-Soviet pact.[6] In particular, Roman Catholic opinion in Quebec was far more prepared to identify

[1] ibid. p. 1.
[2] ibid. pp. 18–41.
[3] ibid. p. 25.
[4] ibid.
[5] ibid. p. 26.
[6] This pact was announced on 21 August and signed on 23 August 1939.

Nazism with the forces of evil when Nazism was in alliance and not in conflict with Soviet Communism.

Mr. Mackenzie King greatly reassured French-Canada by stating that in the opinion of the government, conscription of men for overseas service would not prove to be necessary. 'No such measure', he told the House, 'will be introduced by the present administration.'[1] Warmly welcomed by the great majority of the Liberal party as a necessary condition of continuing national unity, the wisdom of this categorical assurance was questioned by the Conservatives. Their leader, Dr. Manion, maintained that Canadian policy should be determined in the light of the very real dangers that threatened Canada. The western seaboard was vulnerable to attacks by heavy surface raiders, and should the democracies be defeated in Western Europe, the danger would be immediate. It was the Conservative contention that these risks would be best forestalled by an offensive in Europe in which Canada should whole-heartedly participate.[2] The Conservative doubt was, therefore, not whether Canada should participate in the war, but whether the Liberal government contemplated sufficiently whole-hearted participation.

Mr. Woodsworth, the veteran pacifist leader of the Co-operative Commonwealth Federation, felt unable to support the government,[3] and shortly afterwards resigned from the leadership of the party, which decided that with certain safeguards Canadian participation was not only justified but desirable. Mr. M. J. Coldwell, who succeeded Mr. Woodsworth, agreed with the Prime Minister in thinking that Canada must at all times choose the path that led towards national unity. That unity demanded participation in the war. But it was important to remember that Canada was a federation of provinces, a difficult country to govern, and one in which the dangers of undue centralization in war-time could not be disregarded.[4] The party's statement of policy, to which Mr. Coldwell referred, recorded its belief 'that the same struggle for trade supremacy and political domination which caused the last war, and was perpetuated in the Versailles Treaty, is again the primary cause of the present conflict'.[5] It restated, too, with undiminished confidence, some familiar half-truths of the inter-war period; the reversion of European governments to power politics and to secret diplomacy being held to be largely responsible for the outbreak of war. There was also a continuing fear of European entanglements.

The Canadian people have had no voice in the foreign policies of the European governments which have brought us to the present tragic position. Owing to the failure of our government to clarify our constitutional relations, Canada has been

[1] Canada, H. of C. Deb., 1939, 2nd session, p. 36; he had given a similar assurance on 30 March 1939. See above, Chapter IV.

[2] ibid. p. 15.

[3] See ibid. pp. 41 ff.

[4] ibid. p. 54.

[5] ibid. p. 55; the statement of policy was quoted in the H. of C. Deb. by Mr. Coldwell.

committed to a war policy even before Parliament has had an opportunity to declare its will.[1]

For these reasons the C.C.F. condemned the measures which the government had taken to place the country on a war footing before Parliament met, but then went on with sense but without logic to recognize that because Canada was thus implicated in a struggle which *might* involve the future of democratic institutions, she should support the cause of the Western Powers, whose peoples in part at least were waging a war against aggression. There remained, however, pronounced opposition to the dispatch of an expeditionary force overseas, Mr. Coldwell observing that any attempt to do so would not only deprive Canada of the man-power necessary for home defence and for production, but would also ultimately lead to conscription.

The contrasted views of the Conservatives and the C.C.F. both explained and in large measure justified the cautious deliberation of the administration. Attacked from the right because of the inadequacy of their war measures, suspected by the left of excessive zeal in preparing for war, the government, balancing judiciously between these conflicting views, were able to secure a qualified approval of their policy from both.

In the last analysis, Canadian policy was dependent less upon the attitude of the parties than upon that of the people of Quebec. It was there that isolationism was most deeply implanted, and it was buttressed by bitter memories of the enforcement of conscription in 1917. Much, therefore, depended upon the attitude of the French-Canadian leaders and above all on that of Mr. Lapointe. In a debate that was sober to the point of dullness his speech stands out for precision of argument and intensity of feeling.

Neutrality was not without its advocates. Mr. Raymond[2] from Quebec urged that Canada should remain aloof because she had no commitments in Europe. She was not bound by British guarantees to Poland, and she could not assume responsibility for a debt into which Britain should never have entered. He did not believe that the war was one for civilization and freedom. If it were, how could an alliance have been sought with 'barbaric Russia' that 'anti-Christian and materialistic state' of whose doctrines every French-Canadian was an enemy? Had not England and France witnessed unperturbed the inhuman and bloody experience of the Spanish war? They had not aided Franco's Spain at grips with the Bolshevist menace but instead had tried to force Italy to withdraw her troops. Another French-Canadian member who was no less outspoken in his denunciation of Communist Russia drew very different conclusions from recent events. He was Mr. Héon, who supported Canadian participation in the war just because the negotiations between the Western democracies and the Soviet Union had broken down.

[1] ibid.

[2] ibid. pp. 58 ff.

I do not mind stating here that had France and Great Britain concluded an alliance with Soviet Russia, I should have doubted their sincerity in the defence of Christianity, and would have opposed participation [by Canada] because I would have considered such an alliance a direct prostitution of all the Christian principles of freedom and individual liberty which we have now undertaken to uphold and defend.[1]

But while in his view Canada should go to war, Mr. Héon urged the government to exercise wisdom and tolerance in its prosecution. They should not attempt to force the pace in Quebec.

The French-Canadian has been mostly concerned, as were his ancestors before him, with clearing the forest, tilling the soil and providing food and shelter for the children with whom providence has blessed him from year to year. The practice of the golden rule, the presentation to the nation of stalwart intelligent sons and daughters, the defence of their territory against aggression, have been to my compatriots their main expressions of patriotism. The church, the little village, the large family, the soil enriched with their sweat, the peace and restfulness of the Quebec countryside, have drawn and kept their attention for three hundred years. . . . But let me assure hon. members that when Baptiste discovers that his freedom, institutions and essential rights which he prizes so dearly are really threatened, there will be no one who will fight more savagely to defend them. Meanwhile do not judge him harshly or impute to him motives that he never even conceived. Give him the British treatment of fair play and fair dealing, and his courage will not fail when an emergency arises.[2]

Mr. Lapointe had fewer reservations about the rightness of Canada's participation in the war than his compatriots or even than most of his colleagues in the cabinet. He argued that neutrality was not only constitutionally and politically impossible but morally wrong. A neutrality sympathetic to England and to Poland, such as was urged in many quarters in Quebec, seemed to him meaningless, for like faith, sympathy without works is a dead sympathy.[3] Moreover, neutrality on the part of Canada could not be other than favourable to the enemies of England and to France. He believed that the pressure from all parts of Canada for the dispatch of an expeditionary force would in fact be overwhelming, and he denounced another proposal which had been made to which he declared himself almost ashamed to refer.

Some say, 'Let volunteers go if they wish but let England pay for them, or let those who take the initiative in organizing regiments pay the cost'. They say, 'Go, but let England bear the cost, or pay it yourselves'. Well, Mr. Speaker, this is a shameless, dishonourable proposal. They say, 'You may give your life; you may shed your blood, but your country refuses to pay the expense incidental to your sacrifice'. I am too proud, too conscious of Canadian dignity, to discuss such a proposal. I am surprised that any man of whom it may be said, in the words of

[1] Canada, H. of C. Deb., 1939, 2nd session, p. 81.
[2] ibid. pp. 80–81.
[3] ibid. p. 67.

our national song, 'Il est né d'une race fière', could entertain this disgraceful suggestion. In the Middle Ages European countries were hiring mercenaries throughout the world to fight their battles. Canadians will never be mercenaries paid by any country—not even by Britain. If Canadians go to the front line of the battle they will go voluntarily as Canadians, under the control of Canada, commanded by Canadians and maintained by the Dominion of Canada.[1]

In that last sentence there spoke the voice of the new Canada.

The Address was adopted on 9 September without a division since fewer than five members rose to oppose it. Whatever scattered opposition there may have been to Canadian participation in the war on the part of a few members, the vast majority, reflecting faithfully public opinion throughout the dominion, declared their support for the government's policy of participation on the side of Britain. In the interests of Canadian unity, the policy of the government was a middle policy. Canada by the free choice of her representatives assembled in Parliament had endorsed Canadian participation in war, but they had not endorsed conscription for overseas service, they had not even specifically approved the sending of Canadian forces overseas. Mr. Mackenzie King felt that this distinction was vital because it sanctioned Canadian participation in war without sacrificing internal unity and therefore Canada's capacity to wage war effectively. It seems clear from his words that he himself believed that victory might be won without the need for oversea conscription.

The debate in the Canadian House of Commons in September 1939 suggests that the year of peace which was gained by the Munich settlement had helped to crystallize Canadian opinion. Only a few unrepresentative voices doubted by 1939 that Hitler's Germany was mainly responsible for the war in Europe. This hardening of opinion between September 1938 and 1939 was an important factor, whose significance is enhanced by the fact that the lessons it taught were accepted with great reluctance by isolationist opinion in Canada and were not accepted south of the border. In this context it is well to emphasize once again that the Nazi-Soviet pact was interpreted by almost all as final proof of Germany's desire to dominate the world by force. The great short-term advantages, therefore, which Hitler gained in Europe by the negotiation of the pact were in some measure counterbalanced by its destruction of comfortable illusions about his ultimate intentions till then entertained by a minority in Canada and in the other countries of the Commonwealth overseas.

Imperialist sentiment in its remaining strongholds in Ontario, and much Conservative opinion in England, viewed with misgiving the way in which Mr. Mackenzie King brought Canada into the war. They disliked its air of deliberation, and the doctrine of ultimate dominion responsibility in the making of peace and war by which it was inspired. Yet the historian may

[1] ibid. p. 68.

well be little concerned with their complaints, for to him the impressive fact remains that a united Canada pledged itself to resist aggression on far distant European battlefields when its great neighbour with all the responsibilities of power resting upon it considered a sympathetic neutrality the limit of its duty at that fateful hour in human history. If proof were needed of Canadian love of liberty and Canadian sense of responsibility here it was given in ample measure. For, unlike the other dominions, Canada was not threatened by direct assault; unlike them she was assured, whatever course she adopted, of the protection of the United States, and well might her people have decided that it sufficed for them, too, to wait upon events. The fact that her response was very different afforded in itself the most striking testimony that the faith of those who believed that the full freedom of the dominions would not weaken but would rather strengthen the unity of the Commonwealth was not misplaced.

THE PACIFIC DOMINIONS; 'ONE KING, ONE FLAG, ONE CAUSE'

The procedure adopted by the Pacific dominions in entering the war in September 1939 was in clear contrast to that followed by Canada and South Africa. Neither in Wellington nor in Canberra was there any disposition to conform to Mr. Mackenzie King's formula, 'Parliament must decide'. Almost wholly British in extraction and loyalties, untroubled by fears of internal disunity, Australia and New Zealand were free and anxious to pledge themselves to fight by Britain's side in resistance to further German aggression. The Empire was one and indivisible. Even if there were some reservations in respect of minor conflicts there was, in the view of their governments, no doubt that when Britain was involved in a major war they, as members of the Commonwealth, were at war too.

The contrast between the attitudes of the Pacific dominions on the one hand, and Canada and South Africa on the other, reflected more a characteristic difference in approach than in aim or aspiration. Both Australia and New Zealand had viewed without enthusiasm the progressive extension of dominion authority in the field of foreign affairs not because they wished to have their destinies controlled from London, but rather because they believed that they could influence the direction of British policy better from within than from without. It had been in particular the consistent aim of successive Australian governments to influence British policy by the expression of Australian views before final decisions on important issues of foreign policy were taken in London. It was with this in mind that Mr. Menzies remarked in 1938,

> Each time I have been in London and in contact with the High Commissioner for Australia . . . what has struck me most forcibly has been that if there is any dominion which has a mind of its own and expresses it quite freely and clearly it is Australia. If one were to go to British ministers today and say to them, 'Are not

these Australian ministers and the High Commissioner a lot of "yes" men', they would laugh and think it was a curious brand of Australian humour.[1]

So much was certainly true. Whitehall was well accustomed to the forthright expression of Australian views. In the successive crises that preceded the outbreak of war no dominion Prime Minister would appear to have telephoned Mr. Chamberlain more frequently than Mr. Lyons. Yet if influence were to be successfully exerted from within, time and opportunity were essential. The constant complaint from Canberra was that the Australian government were asked to ratify decisions already made, not to influence them in the making.

The Australian government did not shrink from the logical conclusion implicit in their approach. Their declared doctrine, qualified at times to meet Labour criticism, continued to be that when Britain was at war Australia was automatically at war too. In September 1938 Mr. Menzies stated categorically: 'My doctrine is that so long as the British Empire is constituted as it is today, it is not possible for Australia to be neutral in a British war.' In this Mr. Menzies had the support not only of politicians but also of the predominant school of Australian constitutional thought. But the very acceptance of an automatic Australian commitment when the United Kingdom went to war carried as a reasonable corollary the right of Australia to an effective voice in determining what obligations Britain should undertake. For that reason it was no sufficient answer to Australian complaints about the failure of the United Kingdom government to consult the dominions beforehand about Britain's guarantees in Eastern Europe to say that, regrettable though this was, the dominions were not thereby committed. So long as Australia and New Zealand took the view that they were automatically at war when the King was at war, this answer was irrelevant.

In Australia the doctrine of automatic Australian participation in a war in which the United Kingdom was involved was not accepted by the opposition. When in September 1938 it seemed likely that the Czech crisis would lead to war Mr. Curtin, the Labour leader, took 'the responsibility of going so far as to say that should war in Europe result . . . it will be a war that Australia would regret. But Australia . . . should not be involved in it.'[2] The implication in his words was that Australian participation in war was a matter for the Australian Parliament to decide. That was a viewpoint which Australian Labour increasingly adopted.

The Australian government left in no doubt their attitude should war come in Europe. On 1 July 1939 Mr. Menzies said that he was in 'hourly touch' with London, that he supported Britain's policies, and that Australia stood with Britain 'even if it means war'.[3] On 24 August, after the announcement of the Nazi-Soviet pact, Mr. Menzies said 'if Britain is forced to war she will not go alone', for Australia would be at her side. On 2 September,

[1] Australia, H. of R. Deb., vol. 157, p. 430. [2] ibid. p. 326.
[3] *Manchester Guardian*, 2 July 1939.

after the issue of the British ultimatum to Germany, Mr. Menzies expressed his conviction that 'the British nations throughout the world are at one. There is unity in the Empire ranks—one King, one flag, one cause. We stand with Britain.'[1] The next day Mr. Menzies broadcast a few minutes after Mr. Chamberlain's announcement that Britain was at war with Germany. He said: 'There was never any doubt where Britain stood and there can be no doubt that where Britain stands there stand the people of the entire British Empire. . . . Britain is at war, therefore Australia is at war.'[2] Though the Federal Parliament was in session, it was not summoned to ratify or endorse Australia's participation in the war because in the opinion of the government no separate declaration of war by Australia was required.

In Australia, as in Canada, the negotiation of the German-Soviet non-aggression pact if anything hardened the resolve to resist German aggression to the end, but the reasons were very different. In September 1938 it was, as we have seen, the possibility that war in Europe would mean a simultaneous war in the Far East that had greatly troubled well-informed Australian opinion. It was that fear which over a long period explained the Australian support for the policy of appeasement: it was that fear which prompted Australian misgivings lest the negotiation of a defensive pact between the Soviet Union and the Western Powers should extend the area of conflict by driving Japan, already a member of the Anti-Comintern pact, openly into the opposing camp. The breakdown of the negotiations between Russia and the Western Powers seemed to remove this fear, and the succeeding association between the Soviet Union and Nazi Germany was rightly interpreted as an assurance that the period of peace in the Pacific would at the least be prolonged.[3] Thus the situation was simplified for Australia. Yet if the risks of early aggression by Japan outside China were notably lessened by the events of August 1939, they were not dispelled, and Australia, the most exposed member of the British Commonwealth, was faced with the unenviable decision of risking her security at home by throwing all her resources into the European theatre, or of withholding her man-power to meet a potential threat in the Pacific and thereby prolonging the conflict in Europe, and in so doing incidentally giving to Japan extended opportunities for successful aggression in Asia. In the circumstances the government assured the House of Representatives that there would be no immediate conscription for overseas service, and that the extent of Australia's participation in the European war would be strictly governed by the consideration that the defence of Australia was their first and fundamental responsibility.[4] Both assurances were warmly welcomed by the opposition.

[1] *The Times*, 4 September 1939.

[2] *Sydney Morning Herald*, 4 September 1939.

[3] cf. *Round Table*, December 1939, vol. 30, pp. 190–1.

[4] Australia, H. of R. Deb., vol. 162, pp. 1133 ff., and see pp. 1194 ff. for opposition viewpoint.

'New Zealand will be found wherever Britain is, if Britain is in trouble.' In these words, spoken after the German seizure of Czechoslovakia in March 1939, New Zealand's Prime Minister summed up his country's attitude. In less dangerous days no dominion had been so critical of Britain's policies, but as war approached her one thought was to stand by the mother country in the common defence of freedom and of Empire. On 3 September 1939 the cabinet decided that New Zealand was in a state of war with Germany and timed their proclamation so that retrospectively it should be deemed to have had effect from the exact moment when Britain had declared war.[1] Mr. Savage, a sick man, broadcast from his home a stirring call for support for Britain in a war, not against the German people, but against Nazi domination. 'Not a moment too soon', declared the man who had always feared the consequences of appeasement, 'have Britain and France taken up arms against so faithless and unscrupulous an adversary.' New Zealand, 'with gratitude for the past and confidence for the future', ranged herself without fear beside Britain. 'Where she goes we go; where she stands we stand.'[2] It was a phrase that epitomized the loyalties of a people and that by itself alone assured its author of an honoured place in his country's history.[3]

In a formal message from the Governor-General to the Secretary of State for Dominion Affairs the New Zealand government declared that they entirely concurred

> with the action taken, which they regard as inevitably forced upon the British Commonwealth if the cause of justice, freedom, and democracy is to endure in this world. The New Zealand government wish to offer to the British government the fullest assurance of all possible support. They are convinced that the step that has been taken will meet with the approval of the people of this dominion, and they will give the fullest consideration in due course to any suggestion of the British government as to the method or methods by which this dominion can best assist the common cause.[4]

The motion approving and confirming the declaration of a state of war was passed without a dissentient voice and immediately afterwards the House rose to sing the national anthem. On 15 September the Acting Prime Minister declared that the whole of the man-power and the resources of New Zealand

[1] The text of the proclamation, published in a New Zealand Gazette Extraordinary the following day, read: 'His Excellency the Governor-General has it in command from His Majesty the King to declare that a state of war exists between His Majesty and the Government of the German Reich, and that such a state of war has existed from 9.30 p.m. New Zealand standard time, on the third day of September 1939.' (New Zealand, Department of Internal Affairs, *Official History of New Zealand in the Second World War*, Documents, vol. 1, p. 6.)

[2] *The Times*, 6 September 1939.

[3] No inscription has been written around the base of Mr. Savage's memorial statue which stands on a promontory overlooking Auckland's lovely bays. Would it not have been fitting to record there a saying that is already part of New Zealand's national tradition?

[4] *Round Table*, 1939–40, vol. 30, pp. 215–16.

would be organized for the protection of New Zealand and in support of Britain because New Zealand was 'indissolubly bound up with the United Kingdom and the other units of the Commonwealth'.[1] He told the House that the New Zealand government had been in constant consultation with the United Kingdom government since the outbreak of war and he stated explicitly that every single suggestion made by the United Kingdom government had been accepted and agreed to by New Zealand and was being put into operation as quickly as possible.

It will be noticed that while the New Zealand and Australian governments were at one in their sense of the fundamental unity of the Empire, the Labour government in New Zealand associated Parliament more closely with the making of war by asking for parliamentary approval of the action they had taken. In 1941, New Zealand adopted the same procedure as in 1939. On 11 December that year the Prime Minister told the House of Representatives, 'In common with the United Kingdom, the United States of America, Australia, Canada, South Africa, Netherlands East Indies, China, Free France, and other nations, New Zealand is at war with Japan'.[2] In Australia, however, there had been a change of government and Labour, now in office, were not disposed to follow the precedent set by Mr. Menzies in 1939. On learning of the Japanese attack on Pearl Harbour on 7 December 1941, Mr. Curtin summoned the Australian cabinet to meet on 8 December to determine Australian policy. There was no suggestion of automatic Australian commitment when Britain declared war on Japan. On the contrary, as Dr. Evatt later explained to the House of Representatives,[3] it was considered to be a necessary consequence of the fully autonomous status enjoyed by Australia as a member-state of the Commonwealth that the decision as to peace or war should be determined exclusively by the Australian cabinet and Parliament. And while the reaction of Australia was never in doubt, he argued that for that reason it was the more necessary to take special care to make the forms correspond to the facts lest otherwise the facts might later be disputed. Accordingly, the cabinet prepared a special instrument for approval by the King[4] which made it clear that there was an 'unbroken chain of prerogative authority extending from the King himself to the Governor-General', and which thereby enabled the Governor-General of Australia to declare a state of war when specifically authorized to do so by the King. The instrument conferring this authority upon the Governor-General was executed by the King on the advice of the Commonwealth Executive Council, and it was countersigned by Mr. Curtin so as to show that both the King and the Governor-General had acted exclusively upon the advice of the Prime Minis-

[1] New Zealand, H. of R. Deb., vol. 256, p. 155.
[2] ibid. vol. 261, p. 24.
[3] Australia, H. of R. Deb., vol. 169, p. 1088.
[4] United Kingdom ministers took no part in the arrangement which was made directly with the King through the Australian High Commissioner in London.

ter of Australia. Dr. Evatt maintained that this new insistence upon separate Australian responsibility implied no weakening of the tie of association between the British nations but merely indicated the proper basis on which the close co-operation in all matters affecting their common interest was and should be transacted. The story was completed on 16 December in the House of Representatives when the Prime Minister moved, 'That this House approves of the action of His Majesty's government in the Commonwealth in having advised the issue of proclamations declaring the existence of a state of war with Japan, Finland, Hungary, and Roumania'.[1] Thus while in 1941, as distinct from 1939, Australian emphasis was upon separate dominion responsibility in the making of peace and war there was no such insistence as there had been in Canada upon the exclusive right of Parliament to decide. Australia had no cultural minorities to conciliate. Yet in essentials, the procedure adopted by Australia in 1941 suggested that she had accepted the new pattern of Commonwealth relations, with its emphasis on ultimate dominion responsibility even in the making of peace and war, and thereby was helping to create a new uniformity.

SOUTH AFRICA, THE GREAT DEBATE

September 1939 is a memorable date in the history of Canada, Australia, and New Zealand, but for South Africa it is a landmark in the history of its two European peoples. Deep and bitter as was the division of opinion, all recognized the momentous significance of the occasion. For six years General Smuts and General Hertzog had worked together in the hope that by their co-operation the two European peoples of South Africa might be reconciled and ultimately fused into one nation. The experiment in Fusion was an experiment in compromise. From the outset it had one great handicap: the compromise evaded essentials. Differences had not been resolved; they had been recorded and the component parts of the United party were left free to 'differ'. By the late nineteen-thirties the prospects of final success were wearing thin. Within the cabinet there were strains and mounting friction. General Hertzog,[2] a great South African, a man of distinguished mind and appearance, a gentleman in politics who had done much to raise the standard of South African public life, was not temperamentally well fitted to reconcile conflicting forces. By nature he was secretive; he reached his decisions by instinct rather than by reason and so felt little need to consult his colleagues. Like Mr. de Valera he felt that he understood the deep fundamental aspirations of his people, and that conviction of intimate, natural understanding made him intolerant of all who differed from him. He had the virtues and the weaknesses of an autocrat. He did not shrink from respon-

[1] Australia, H. of R. Deb., vol. 169, p. 1068.

[2] van den Heever's *Hertzog* is the authoritative biography, and it is perhaps the more illuminating because of the author's bias in favour of his subject.

sibility; he was not afraid to lead. 'I hope', he once said at Vereeniging, 'that as long as I am leader and as long as the people need me, I shall have the right to speak my mind, whether it is to the taste of the people or not.'[1] He had the clarity of vision and the penetration of a man of narrow, inflexible mind and clear-cut principles of action. His views were maintained with a consistency equal to that of Mr. de Valera and within his own range they were for the most part just and moderate. He never preached a narrow nationalist doctrine of Afrikaner domination.

By 1939 General Hertzog had reached his seventy-third year. Age had not dealt hardly with him, though his colleagues noted with misgiving the growing authoritarianism of his leadership. What was more disturbing was the fact that his ideas of the world outside South Africa were set, and he was wholly unreceptive to new impressions. To him the new forces in Europe were to be explained by analogies with the stormy past of South African history. The rise of Hitler, the aggression of the Nazis, were they not simply the reactions of a people humiliated by the victors of twenty years ago? Had not he with his beloved Afrikaner fellow countrymen also been 'through the mill', and did not their experience of defeat enable them not only to sympathize with but also to understand the motives and the aspirations of a resurgent Germany in a way denied to the more fortunate members of the Commonwealth? Behind Hitler and all his actions stood 'the unholy Treaty of Versailles'.[2] On it, and on the victors who imposed it, rested ultimate responsibility for the plight of Europe. As in 1931 General Hertzog explained the economic blizzard sweeping across the world by a simple reference to 'the Versailles Treaty with its demoniac reparation demands' hanging 'like a curse over Europe' and preventing sound economic recovery,[3] so in the late nineteen-thirties he conjured away the monstrous tide of Fascist aggression abroad and inhumanity at home by reference to the 'iniquities' of Versailles. 'The next European war', he declared in 1937, 'will be the child of the Treaty of Versailles' unless the victors redressed the injustices it embodied. The onus was not so much on Hitler or on Mussolini (the leader, incidentally, not of a vanquished but of a victor state of 1919) to prove the fundamentally pacific nature of their ambitions as on Britain and France to give solid evidence of their readiness to return the spoils of war. They had preserved the Treaty of Versailles, and in so doing they had killed the League of Nations, and since the Treaty of Versailles was principally responsible for 'the war psychology' that prevailed in Europe, and since this war psychology had also 'to bear the responsibility for the gigantic arming which is driving Europe along the road

[1] Quoted ibid. p. 233.

[2] It may well be that the violence of Hertzog's feelings about Versailles was in part to be attributed to his own unhappy experiences there when he went to plead unsuccessfully for self-determination for the former republics.

[3] These phrases were used in a speech at Smithfield, quoted in van den Heever, *Hertzog*, p. 232.

to war',[1] Hitler emerged, not as the arrogant dictator resolved to dominate the world, but as a creature of circumstances which others had created. It was their responsibility to deal with the consequences of their own actions; it was not South Africa's. 'Let South Africa never forget', said General Hertzog, 'that it is not a part of Europe, and that it can never identify itself... with the spirit or aims of Europe' save to the detriment of its own interests.[2]

While Hertzog, in common with many Afrikaners, found it difficult to dispute Germany's claims to incorporate all Germans within the Third Reich, he neglected to carry his own tolerant interpretation of German actions to its logical conclusion. If the absorption into the Reich of Germans in Austria and the Sudetenland, who had never been part of the Kaiser's Empire, could be excused, no justification could be extended either on grounds of racial unity or of redress of past wrongs for the forcible incorporation of Czechoslovakia in March 1939. Yet Hertzog, imprisoned by his memories of the past, failed to observe that here was the parting of the ways.

General Smuts, a man very different in outlook and temperament, for the most part shared General Hertzog's opinion of developments in Europe until September 1938 and, as we have seen, he then agreed on a policy of non-belligerency should war come. He, too, had been 'through the mill'; he, too, was ever mindful of the severities of Versailles; but unlike Hertzog he retained with advancing years an impressionable mind. He suspected, even if he did not wholly understand, the forces that were at work in Central Europe. After Munich his suspicions slowly hardened into certainty. Thereafter behind the inconsistencies of his speeches on European affairs is to be detected a stiffening resolve that force and the lust for national and racial domination should not triumph in the world through any failure of South Africa to do what he conceived to be her duty.

Like Hertzog, Smuts was something of an autocrat at heart. Only an iron resolve that Fusion should not fail enabled him to serve for long years under Hertzog's leadership in the Fusion government, and throughout the two leaders remained on familiar but not on intimate terms. Smuts was not always an easy colleague. Not for nothing was he known in South Africa as 'slim Jannie', and he lacked, too, warmth of personality. It has been said of him that 'with far greater intellectual power than Botha, with equal tenacity of purpose and indefatigable energy, with the same ardent patriotism, the younger statesman is not so well endowed with the gracious patience that made the late Prime Minister's presence so winsome to all men'. Smuts was not unaware of his own deficiency by comparison with Botha, for he once said: 'I deal with administration, Botha deals with people'.[3] But if personal friction played its not unimportant part there were also deeper issues at stake. Smuts believed passionately in individual liberty. In the famous

[1] Quoted ibid. p. 274.
[2] Quoted ibid. p. 275.
[3] Williams, *Botha, Smuts, and South Africa*, p. 126.

lecture on Freedom which he delivered as his Rectorial Address at the University of St. Andrews in 1934, he had sounded a warning note about the new tyranny 'disguised in attractive patriotic colours, which is enticing youth everywhere into its service', and reaffirmed the foundations of his own political faith.

For me [he said] the individual is basic to any world order that is worth while. Individual freedom, individual independence of mind, individual participation in the difficult work of government seems to me essential to all true progress . . . Freedom is the most ineradicable craving of human nature. Without it peace, contentment, and happiness, even manhood itself, are not possible. . . . The fight for human freedom is indeed the supreme issue of the future, as it has always been in the past.[1]

It was this belief in human liberty which in the end made it impossible for Smuts to reconcile himself to the direction of Hertzog's foreign policy. It was freedom itself that was at stake in Europe and it is indeed a matter for surprise, not that the government broke on the issue of peace and war in 1939 but that it had not broken on this issue earlier.

In the recriminations which followed the break-up of the United party in 1939, General Hertzog declared that General Smuts 'lay in wait for a good chance to break'. This Smuts denied in the emphatic terms: 'I do not boast when I say the United party was, in a great measure, my work—my best work for South Africa, my pride and honour. It was the ideal for which I sacrificed everything, for which I sacrificed my personal interests. After I had done all that, why should I break down my own work?'[2] And if indeed he had so wished there were several occasions in 1938 when he could have advanced solid reasons for doing so. That he refrained is itself convincing evidence of persisting faith in the policy of Fusion. It is recorded that before making the great decision to join forces with the Nationalist party in 1933, General Smuts had climbed Table Mountain and there with two friends in serene detachment from the world he made his great decision, and having made it he never looked back until compelled by events outside South Africa to do so.

Fusion rested upon the stated assumption that the right of South Africa to remain neutral in a war in which the British Commonwealth was involved was an academic question. Dr. Malan had always maintained that it was not and never could be so. After Munich the correctness of his contention could hardly be longer disputed. The belligerency or neutrality of South Africa in such a war was the most vital issue before the country. It was also one well calculated to stimulate reviving prejudices between the two European peoples, and it so happened at this very time when issues of external policy thus

[1] J. C. Smuts, *Freedom* (London, Maclehose, 1934) pp. 26–32.

[2] At Bloemfontein, November 1939, reprinted in J. C. Smuts, *Plans for a Better World* (London, Hodder & Stoughton, 1942) p. 227.

threatened to divide South Africa that events at home helped to revive old antagonisms between Boer and British. It was as though some malign fate had decreed that the centenary celebrations of the Great Trek should fall in late 1938 to dispel the last hope of preserving South African unity in the event of war.

The government, full of good intentions, resolved that the celebrations should as far as possible be national in character, and so help to draw both peoples together in commemoration of an epic in South African history. But the Nationalist party had other aims. The centenary was for them a unique opportunity for reawakening the racial consciousness of Afrikanerdom, and in their hands lay all the trump cards. The Great Trek was, as a matter of history, a decisive event in the story of Afrikanerdom; emotionally at least, it was little more than a significant episode in that of English-speaking South Africa. The 'crowning mercy' of the victory at Bloedrivier recalled each year on Dingaan's Day, 16 December, had enabled the Afrikaner people to survive; when, a hundred years later, bearded Voortrekkers and their two ox-wagons slowly trekked northwards from the Cape,[1] one to the heights near Pretoria where the memorial was to be erected and one to the Blood River battlefield, antipathies were aroused, paradoxically enough almost as much against the British as against the Natives, with the result that in after years the memorial became less a symbol of a national unity founded upon the fusing of two traditions than the symbol of an undying Boer separatism which believed to the very depths of its being in an Afrikaner Republic, exclusivist in origin and in outlook. The centenary of the Great Trek revealed at once how thin was the crust of confidence upon which inter-European co-operation depended, and how deep was the fundamental emotional urge towards Afrikaner unity. From that time onwards the Nationalists, who had never compromised, were conscious of the growing strength of their position. It was General Hertzog who had erred by championing co-operation, and who would one day, humbled and repentant, return to the fold.[2]

It was with this background at home and abroad that South Africa was confronted in September 1939 with the challenge that was bound to bring all that divided the two races to the surface. Since 1934 party alignments had become so blurred that the outcome of this conflict remained incalculable. Before the great debate which began in Cape Town on 4 September 1939,

[1] The time taken by the ox-wagons was not without political significance. The protracted journey spread over months afforded opportunities for the intensification of an already highly emotional atmosphere. The Ossewa-Brandwag (ox-wagon picket), a semi-secret organization whose unconstitutional opposition to the war effort is part of a later chapter in South African history, was founded in connexion with the centenary celebrations of the Great Trek by van Rensburg, then Administrator of the Orange Free State.

[2] The Nationalists protested against General Hertzog's laying the foundation stone of the Voortrekker monument—a slight which he felt the more keenly because he had promised a state contribution of £150,000 towards its erection. In high indignation he refused to attend the ceremony.

none could say with assurance whether South Africa would remain aloof from a war in which the life of the Commonwealth was at stake or whether she would take her place actively with Britain and the other dominions in the fight against Nazi tyranny. In the light of this uncertainty, of the prevailing racial tension, and above all of the critical nature of the issue to be decided, which was bound to affect for generations the future of South Africa, it is greatly to the credit of the opposing leaders and of their followers that the debate in which the decision was reached was conducted with little sordid recrimination, with a high sense of responsibility, and with a dignity worthy of the traditions which South Africa had established in the thirty years of her existence as a united country.

It might have been supposed that the Prime Minister of a Fusion government would do his best to weld its component parts together by frequent discussion of policy. But such a supposition ignores the practice and tradition of South African politics. There, particularly among the Afrikaners, the old Boer concept of leadership dies hard. General Hertzog and General Smuts alike conceived themselves to be leaders, and during their premierships they were rarely content to act as chairmen of the cabinet over which they presided in the tradition of Prime Ministers of the United Kingdom. This authoritarian tradition was reinforced by the particular circumstances under which the Fusion Ministry had been brought into being. On both sides the leaders and their followers continued to entertain reservations or misgivings which in themselves discouraged any general discussion of the fundamentals of policy. The Prime Minister 'seldom consulted' cabinet colleagues not of his own way of thought, and issues of external policy were carefully avoided.[1] Why bring disagreements, which it was instinctively felt could never be resolved in argument, prematurely to the surface? There was, therefore, no sustained attempt to create a sense of cabinet solidarity and collective responsibility because any such attempt was felt to be foredoomed to failure.

In the last months before the war General Hertzog's critics detected behind his reactions to Axis aggression the sinister influence of Oswald Pirow.[2] But at the most Pirow's pro-Germanism confirmed views which Hertzog already strongly entertained. The agreement which Hertzog had reached with Smuts about South Africa's policy in the event of war in September 1938 was the formal expression of those views. It was General Hertzog's aim that that agreement should take effect in September 1939 on the presumption that in essentials the international scene had not changed, so far as South Africa's interests were concerned, in the intervening twelve months. It was a presumption certain to be bitterly contested by General Smuts. That was a further inducement to Hertzog to avoid discussion and to remain in seclusion from his colleagues at his farm at Waterval as the final crisis developed. Yet

[1] cf. Reitz, *No Outspan*, p. 236.
[2] cf. van den Heever, *Hertzog*, p. 277.

General Smuts, despite his conviction that South Africa should resist further Nazi aggression, which was made abundantly clear in his public speeches, did not at any time indicate to the Prime Minister and to the cabinet that the agreement on policy reached in 1938 no longer applied in the altered circumstances of 1939. This was a tactical error, in the light of which it was left open to General Hertzog not unreasonably to claim that he had been misled. General Smuts no doubt refrained from taking this formal step to make his position clear partly because he seems to the last to have hoped that war might once again be avoided, and also apparently because of the Prime Minister's repeated public promises that he would summon Parliament before he decided on war. But General Hertzog had never promised to consult Parliament if he decided not to go to war. This refinement, according to Colonel Deneys Reitz,[1] was lost on his colleagues, who supposed that the assurance of parliamentary consultation before going to war applied with equal force to a policy of neutrality. It was a refinement potentially of the utmost importance, for in fact General Hertzog's plan to proclaim South African neutrality without consulting Parliament broke down only because of a quite incidental and irrelevant factor. In South Africa as in the United Kingdom all laws have to be passed by both Houses of Parliament, and in the middle of August 1939 the government's law advisers noted that the life of the Senate would expire in a few weeks and that as a result, unless both Houses met to pass a law extending the period of its existence, no legislation passed by the House of Assembly alone would be valid.[2] It was, therefore, only to extend the life of the Senate that General Hertzog summoned Parliament to meet on Saturday, 2 September, and once that necessary task had been accomplished both Houses would have gone into recess. But on 1 September Hitler invaded Poland. It was this coincidence that deprived Hertzog of the opportunity of putting into effect his preconceived plan of action. Once Parliament had met, there was no possibility whatever of the government's being allowed to evade a full discussion of the course which the Union should pursue. None the less on 2 September General Hertzog still procrastinated and informed an anxious House that government policy would not be formulated till 4 September. It might be that he still hoped, as his biographer suggests, that Britain and France would not be 'so foolish' as to implement their guarantee to Poland after the non-aggression pact between Germany and Russia,[3] but this is hardly likely in view of the information the Prime Minister must have received from London.

On the afternoon of Saturday, 2 September, the cabinet were summoned to meet at Groote Schuur, the Prime Minister's official residence, and there

[1] *No Outspan*, p. 237. This is not very easy to understand. They were mostly experienced politicians and there had been no suggestion in September 1938 that Parliament should be consulted were the agreement, to which Smuts and Hertzog were both party, to be put into effect.

[2] ibid.

[3] van den Heever, *Hertzog*, p. 278.

between the mountains and the sea was held the most historic cabinet meeting in the history of the Union. At this first meeting General Hertzog was the speaker, his colleagues a patient though severely tried audience. At the outset the Prime Minister stated that he was going to recommend to Parliament a policy of neutrality. He spoke in all for some three hours, leaving no opportunity for any member of the cabinet to comment. His conclusion at least was clear: the war was of no concern to South Africa. If Hitler won, South Africa would not be molested, and if the Western democracies were victorious, South Africa would most certainly be secure. Therefore self-interest reinforced his own conviction that even at this late stage Hitler should not be opposed by force, for there was no conclusive evidence that he was bent on world domination.

The cabinet meeting was resumed at Groote Schuur on the Sunday afternoon. In the meantime the Prime Minister had received from Dr. Malan assurances of support for a neutrality motion, but he did not inform his colleagues about this.[1] Nor was he prepared to submit the issue to the party caucus. General Hertzog looked not for consultation or discussion of the issues involved but endorsement of the policy he recommended. This he did not get. General Smuts strongly opposed it. He went farther. He declared that he intended to test the issue in the House of Assembly and at that, as Colonel Reitz records, 'a hush fell on the room for we knew it meant the breakdown of the government and it meant many things still lying shrouded in the future'.[2] A few moments later the members of the government, knowing that at last they had come to the parting of the ways, said their farewells. Fusion was dead.

It would seem that neither side was at all certain of the reaction of the House when the issue came before it for a decision. In the cabinet General Hertzog was supported by five ministers, General Smuts by seven. The House of Assembly consisted of 153 members of whom 147 were in Cape Town at that time. The vast majority, 104, were members of the United party, 29 were Nationalists under Dr. Malan, 7 were members of the Dominion party led by Colonel Stallard, there were 4 Labour members and 3 Native representatives. It was clear that the decision would depend upon how the members of the United party itself divided. From all they had said and done during the past four or five years the Nationalists under Dr. Malan were certain to vote for neutrality. Had they not even advocated the return of South West Africa rather than see South Africa involved in war or strained

[1] cf. van den Heever, *Hertzog*, p. 279. Later General Hertzog was bitterly criticized for his 'deception' of his colleagues by failing to make known to them Dr. Malan's views. It would certainly have been better to have stated them, but who could possibly have been deceived about the attitude Dr. Malan would adopt? He had proclaimed it for years from the house tops. Cf., however, General Smuts's speech at Bloemfontein, 3 November 1939, reprinted in *Plans for a Better World*, pp. 221 ff., in particular p. 229.

[2] Reitz, *No Outspan*, pp. 239–40. See also van den Heever, *Hertzog*, pp. 278–9.

relations with Germany? It was equally certain that the Dominion party, the Labour members, and the Native representatives would vote for South African participation in the war. But could anyone say with absolute assurance how the 104 of the United party would vote? Sixty-six of them were in fact followers of General Smuts, and thirty-eight of General Hertzog, which suggested that if all Smuts's followers remained faithful to their leader on this issue, he would have a majority of thirteen. But was it so certain? It was at once a source of strength and a source of weakness to General Smuts that his followers were drawn from both European peoples. It is true that the great weight of English-speaking South Africans were behind him, but his majorities had always been dependent upon the support which he could muster from Afrikaans-speaking South Africans. It was their reaction that would decide the day. They could not feel with their English-speaking fellow countrymen that this was a war in which traditional loyalties obliged them to fight because their mother country was in danger. They knew, none better, that they would have to face bitter criticism from their fellow Afrikaners who would maintain that, as in 1914, so in 1939, General Smuts was seeking to sacrifice the true interests of South Africa to British imperialism. It was just because the issue of peace and war in 1939 was so deeply influenced by the memories of the past and was so susceptible to easy distortion by either side through excess of emotion that the arguments used in the debate and the way in which they were presented were of such cardinal importance.

On the morning of Monday, 4 September, the outcome still remained uncertain. By then much pressure had been brought to bear upon the waverers, though neither General Hertzog nor General Smuts played any part in the canvassing of opinion.[1] Indeed General Hertzog remained confident that he would carry the day, and though later he had doubts it was with confidence that he came to the House of Assembly that afternoon. The Prime Minister admitted in the opening of his speech that he was no longer the leader of a united cabinet, that he could no longer enunciate government policy. All he could do was to put forward as the nominal leader of a government still nominally in existence the policy which he himself had recommended to his cabinet two days earlier. Accordingly he read to the House a statement which his cabinet had already heard at Groote Schuur. It was as follows:

The existing relations between the Union of South Africa and the various belligerent countries will, in so far as the Union is concerned, persist unchanged as if no war is being waged, upon the understanding, however, that the existing relations and obligations between the Union and Great Britain or any other member

[1] General Hertzog in particular was accused of so doing, but the criticism seems quite unjust so far as he personally was concerned. As had already been noted, he had received an assurance of support for a neutrality motion from Dr. Malan before the cabinet meeting on Sunday (van den Heever, *Hertzog*, p. 279).

of the British Commonwealth of Nations, in so far as such relations or obligations resulting from contractual obligations relating to the naval base at Simonstown, or its membership in the League of Nations, or in so far as such relations or obligations would result impliedly from the free association of the Union with other members of the British Commonwealth of Nations shall continue unimpaired and shall be maintained by the Union, and no one shall be permitted to use Union territory for the purpose of doing anything which may in any way impair the said regulations or obligations.[1]

General Hertzog, speaking under considerable strain, maintained that while the first aim of his policy was to keep the Union out of the war, that was not inconsistent with the fulfilment of South Africa's existing obligations to the British Commonwealth whether arising from the Simonstown agreement or from the more conventional understandings between its members. What more could the Union be reasonably expected to do? With its small, limited resources and its population of some two million Europeans, it could in no circumstances assume greater responsibilities. 'It is the only support which . . . whether we participate in the war or not, can be given to the British Commonwealth of Nations.'[2] No one, he maintained, and as the debate proved quite correctly, suggested that South Africa should send an army away to take part in a war beyond its frontiers. We undertake, he said, to resist any attack on South Africa itself, and to preserve the situation precisely as it exists today. Such a policy was not only possible, it was also right. It was right because the great test of whether they should or should not decide to participate in war was the test of whether or not South African interests were concerned in that war and because 'our existence was at stake'. Deeply concerned, as always, with the forms as well as the realities of sovereignty, he argued that South Africa 'never may buy the friendly relations of the Commonwealth at the expense of our independence',[3] and it was because of that narrow concentration on national sovereignty that he condemned active participation in the war as 'an act of disloyalty' which would be 'a shock to the confidence of the Afrikaner people'. Viewed in that light South Africa's policy was clear. South African interests were not directly threatened by a war arising out of a German attack on Poland. 'It must not be forgotten', said Hertzog, 'that we are concerned here with a war in which the Union has not the slightest interest. We are not interested in the war between Poland and Germany.'[4] Britain was interested because Britain had undertaken obligations to Poland, but South Africa had no such obligations. The only ground on which it was argued that South Africa should enter the war was because Hitler had made it all too clear that he was determined on world domination. But where, asked General Hertzog, was the proof of this? There was no proof, for Hitler had

[1] South Africa, H. of A. Deb., vol. 36, coll. 18–19.
[2] ibid. col. 19.
[3] ibid. col. 21.
[4] ibid.

taken the action that he himself would have taken or that Britain herself would have taken in similar circumstances to undo one by one the injustices imposed by 'the monster of the Treaty of Versailles'.[1] He had long foreseen that Germany would react to the Treaty in this way. 'I know', he cried, 'what it is to be driven by humiliation and belittlement and insult to a point where you say "Come what may, everything is subordinate to the wiping out of that humiliation which we suffer from day to day".'[2] He, too, with the Afrikaans people, had been 'through the mill', and it was his own experience that enabled him to understand and sympathize with German feelings. South Africa had no part or lot in the war to resist Germany. Moreover, argued General Hertzog, the dangers of participation from South Africa were very great indeed. 'If it should happen that we should be dragged into war, it will be a catastrophe.' War would create a state of misery within the Union which would not be cured for fifty years. The Afrikaners had now made two attempts to bring together the Afrikaans and English-speaking sections of the people, to fuse them into one nation and

> . . . I say that this failure of the second attempt to weld them into one people is enough to shock the people so deeply that it will take years for us to recover. But if in addition this is to be followed by taking part in a war with which we have nothing to do, then I say that it will be something which will affect us for the next fifty if not hundred years, in our mutual relations.[3]

General Smuts took up the challenge.[4] He took it up on the main issue which the Prime Minister had raised, on the issue of whether or not there was to be active South African participation in the war. And he argued that that depended fundamentally upon whether Germany was or was not determined upon world domination. What the Prime Minister had proposed meant that South Africa was going to consider Germany as a friendly Power. To General Smuts that seemed impossible and intolerable—impossible because it was incompatible with the continuance of normal relations with the British Commonwealth, and intolerable because it would mean a compromise with something that was evil. 'My feeling', said General Smuts,

> my conviction is profound that although Danzig and the Corridor and the attack of Germany on Poland . . . is the immediate occasion of the war . . . [it] is simply the occasion, not the real cause. . . . To my mind the real issue in this matter reaches far beyond Danzig, far beyond Poland, and touches us vitally here in South Africa.[5]

Twelve months earlier General Smuts had allowed that the reunion of the German people within the German nation seemed to be the goal of Hitler's policy. So long as it was so, there was no ground for open opposition. 'We were prepared to take his word and to make concessions'; but since Munich the absorption of the Czechs within the German Reich by force, in spite of

[1] ibid. col. 22. [2] ibid.
[3] ibid. col. 20. [4] ibid. coll. 24–31. [5] ibid. col. 26.

repeated assurances, made that interpretation of German policy no longer tenable. Just as Chamberlain had revised his ideas of appeasement, so, too, in South Africa there was no alternative but to recognize that the goal of German ambitions was not a peaceful one. And if it were not, was not South Africa directly concerned? The question of colonies had been raised many times. The claim for the return of South West Africa would be presented to South Africa 'at the point of a bayonet'. If they stayed neutral in the war they would have to face that challenge alone, and alone against impossible odds. Therefore, argued General Smuts, it was in the direct interest of South Africa that they should participate in the war. South African neutrality would mean virtual dissociation of the Union from the British Commonwealth. That would be fatal to the Union, poor as it was in defence, rich as it was in resources, because it would then become a prey to every ambitious Power. All these practical considerations over and above the obligations of honour and the feelings of loyalty felt by many South Africans were decisive reasons for South African participation in the war. Accordingly he moved an amendment to the Prime Minister's motion in the following words:

To omit all the words after 'That' and to substitute 'this House declares that the policy of the Union in this crisis shall be based on the following principles and considerations, viz:

(1) It is in the interest of the Union that its relations with the German Reich should be severed, and that the Union should refuse to adopt an attitude of neutrality in this conflict.

(2) The Union should carry out the obligation to which it has agreed, and continue its co-operation with its friends and associates in the British Commonwealth of Nations.

(3) The Union should take all necessary measures for the defence of its territory and South African interests and the government should not send forces overseas as in the last war.

(4) This House is profoundly convinced that the freedom and independence of the Union are at stake in this conflict and that it is therefore in its true interest to oppose the use of force as an instrument of national policy.'[1]

It will be noted that in section three General Smuts stated categorically that the government should not send forces overseas.

The great debate once joined was protracted. There were moments when opinion wavered. One occurred when Mr. Heaton Nicholls, an English-speaking member of the United party, challenged the right of South Africa to decide the issue of peace and war. Mr. Heaton Nicholls maintained that the dominions were

linked together by a common allegiance to the Crown; that is, by an allegiance which all the states of the Commonwealth owe in common. You cannot [he said] owe anything in common and claim a right to act separately. Allegiance, sir, means

[1] South Africa, H. of A. Deb., vol. 36, coll. 30-31.

something more than a mere word to be bandied about on political platforms, it has a very deep, sacred significance, loyalty within the law to that common Crown. In the eyes of every English-speaking man in this country, South Africa is at war; and it does not require any vote of this House or any declaration by the government of this country to determine whether we are at war or not at war. The full right to determine the extent of our participation in that war is admitted. . . . But there is no doubt about the technical position of this country. We are at war in the eyes of every British subject and if we were not at war we cannot be British subjects.[1]

This was the language of the past, the concepts of an earlier age fighting a last rearguard action wellnigh fatal to the cause it cherished. For the speech 'shocked and startled the House'. In the great issues of peace and war, had there been no advance since 1914? Did not the dominion in fact enjoy the powers commonly held to be the final attribute of sovereignty? Were the interests of Britain to decide whether the Union of South Africa, of whose European population only some 40 per cent. were of British extraction, should or should not go to war? These were disturbing questions which required immediate answers. They came spontaneously and appropriately from another English-speaking United party member, Mr. B. K. Long.[2] He said bluntly that he did not agree with Mr. Heaton Nicholls; that he was convinced that there 'was no limit to our freedom under the Statute of Westminster as confirmed in our country under the Status Act'; that South Africa 'had the right to declare our neutrality', but that 'it is disastrously unwise in the interests of our country that we should take this course of action which the Prime Minister proposes'. By this rejoinder Mr. B. K. Long, in the opinion of those who heard the debate, stepped for a moment on to the page of history.[3]

It is instructive to recall that Mr. Hofmeyr, in a closely reasoned and convincing speech,[4] spoke in the same sense as Mr. Heaton Nicholls. He said that he, too, was one of those who as a matter of constitutional theory had consistently taken the view that when any part of the British Commonwealth was at war, the rest of the Commonwealth was automatically at war. He believed that that was implicit in the conception of common allegiance to the Crown which had been the basis of the declaration of the 1926 Imperial Conference, and of the Statute of Westminster. He had taken that view in the debates on the Status Act and he had not modified it since. But the impact of Mr. Hofmeyr's remarks was slight, partly because his approach was more legalistic and less emotional than that of Mr. Heaton Nicholls, and still more because he was an Afrikaans-speaking member and therefore could hardly be suspected of favouring constitutional doctrines designed to further

[1] ibid. col. 33.

[2] ibid. col. 37. See also Long, *In Smuts's Camp*, Chapter V, and Mansergh, *Commonwealth and the Nations*.

[3] Mr. Long, as befitted a former editor of the *Cape Times*, possessed a wider knowledge of foreign and imperial affairs than most members of the House.

[4] South Africa, H. of A. Deb., vol. 30, coll. 68 ff.

British imperialist interests. Moreover, he recognized that whatever the theory, the fact was that it was not a constitutional issue which was at stake in the debate. There was a time when constitutional theory gave way before political realities, and he acknowledged that in terms of political reality the decision did rest with the Parliament at Cape Town. For the rest Mr. Hofmeyr developed with deep conviction the arguments that General Smuts had advanced. He believed, too, that South African interests were directly affected. 'South Africa', he said, 'is a land of great resources with but a small body of men to defend its resources. South Africa has some of the Naboth's vineyards of the world. The Witwatersand is one of them. Here within the Cape Peninsula, having regard to its strategic importance, is another.'[1] Because of this South Africa needed friends and where should she get better friends than in the British Commonwealth of Nations? But it was not only on the ground of direct threats to South Africa that Mr. Hofmeyr believed that his country should actively participate in the war. He believed that South Africans were a freedom-loving people with a tradition of freedom on both sides.

We stand for freedom of parliamentary institutions. We stand for freedom of opinion and criticism; we have hitherto still stood by the ideal of tolerance. In Germany today parliamentary institutions have disappeared, there is no freedom of opinion, there is a servile standardized mass mentality; intolerance towards minorities, religious minorities, racial minorities and political minorities are rampant there. Our way of life, our attitude toward politics in South Africa is entirely different from all that kind of thing, but, sir, if Germany wins this war, these principles for which we stand to-day are going to be endangered. These ideals, these principles of Nazism are an article of export, and we have to face the implications of that fact. On that issue we cannot sit on the fence. We must assume our position, we must take our stand and take our stand now, I believe, sir, for the principle of respect for human personality, for the principle of freedom and for the principle of ultimate human brotherhood requiring us to approach international problems in the spirit not of the ethics of the jungle, but of the ethics of the family.[2]

The tight-lipped descendant of Huguenot exiles who with patience, with relentless purpose, and undoubted ability led the Purified Nationalists through their long years in the political wilderness looked out on the world from the narrower window of avowed racialism. That Dr. Malan would support, and would pledge the support of his party, to General Hertzog was a foregone conclusion. Not for a moment did he leave it in doubt. On the one hand he spoke with sympathy of Germany. He said he could well understand that a state with self-respect, a nation who loved liberty, could not permanently lie down under the injustices of Versailles. The League should have removed those injustices, but the League had not. Germany therefore sought redress by other means. What else could she do? And because the League had failed,

[1] ibid. col. 69. [2] ibid. col. 71.

therefore, argued Dr. Malan, it was the League, erected as a bulwark to maintain the Treaty of Versailles, that was really responsible for the war. How could South Africa for the sake of Danzig or the Corridor or the Sudetenland enter into a war with the German people? 'I say emphatically what I have said in other places lately, to draw us into a war, to fire one shot from a South African gun, to spill one drop of South African blood, would be a crime.'[1] But the real reason for Dr. Malan's sympathetic approach towards Nazi Germany is probably to be found in the appeal which the German ideal of racial unity had for him, and indeed for all Nationalists in South Africa. It was their aim to reunite all Afrikaans-speaking South Africans in one party just as it was the aim of Hitler to reunite all Germans within a single state. His ambition, therefore, seemed to them not merely unobjectionable but positively commendable. That which belonged together should not be kept apart. And still in 1939 Dr. Malan, despite the absorption of Czechoslovakia, which he explained away in language which Mr. Hofmeyr condemned as 'sinking to a level of sophistry' hitherto unsurpassed even by the Nationalist leader,[2] was not convinced that the fundamental aim of German policy was other than the reunion of the German people. Not without foreboding the House listened to Dr. Malan's more emphatic reiteration of General Hertzog's warning that participation in the war would mean a deeper division than ever before between the two European races in South Africa. Even in this prospect Dr. Malan found some cause for rejoicing because it seemed to him to bring nearer the day of Afrikaner reunion. Nothing indeed is more significant in his speech than the unconcealed jubilation at the proof, now so decisively forthcoming, that General Hertzog had been profoundly mistaken in entering into a Fusion government. He had been the victim of a dangerous illusion and now the folly of his ways was exposed for all to see. Once again the Afrikaner people were being betrayed and their powers of resistance had been sapped by General Hertzog's well-meant but ill-conceived efforts at reconciling what could not and should not be reconciled. To Dr. Malan, the debate afforded above all a golden opportunity to hasten the reunion of Afrikanerdom.

It was not till towards the close of the debate late in the evening that General Hertzog recognized that the balance of opinion was coming down against him. When the time came for the vote to be taken 'his face was ashen' and it seemed that then for the first time he realized that he was facing defeat and political ruin.[3] When the count was completed the Speaker announced the result. Sixty-seven members had voted in favour of the Prime Minister's neutrality motion and eighty had voted in favour of General Smuts's motion to enter the war. It is widely and almost certainly rightly believed in South Africa that Mr. Pirow, whose influence upon General Hertzog was still considerable, had advised him before the debate that he would secure a

[1] ibid. col. 51.
[2] ibid. col. 71.
[3] Reitz, *No Outspan*, p. 242.

majority for neutrality. Eye-witnesses agree that when the result was announced by the Speaker, General Hertzog turned with a gesture of angry rebuke upon the Minister of Defence who had so misled him.

That same night General Hertzog visited Sir Patrick Duncan, the Governor-General, and advised a dissolution. His request raised a delicate issue of constitutional convention and practice. Was a Prime Minister of a cabinet evenly divided on a major issue of policy entitled to advise a dissolution on his own responsibility and on that of the five ministers, Mr. Havenga, Mr. Fagan, General Kemp, Mr. Pirow, and Mr. Fourie, who supported him? The traditional view expressed by the Earl of Oxford and Asquith was that authority for advising a dissolution of parliament must rest with the cabinet as a whole. This view, so far as the United Kingdom was concerned, had since been modified in practice, notably by Mr. Baldwin who maintained that it lay within the discretion of the Prime Minister alone to advise a dissolution.[1] In the other dominions there were two precedents of some significance. In Canada the primacy of the Prime Minister in recommending a dissolution had been formally confirmed by an Order in Council in 1926, but his recommendation had to be put forward with the assent of the cabinet as a whole and not as an individual decision of the Prime Minister. In Eire, on the other hand, the Constitution of 1937 specifically allowed the President in his absolute discretion to refuse a dissolution to a Prime Minister who had ceased to retain the support of a majority in the Dáil.[2] It could therefore be argued that on balance constitutional thought in the English-speaking world remained firmly set against giving to the Prime Minister any absolute discretion in advising the Crown on a dissolution of Parliament.

The South African case was far from simple. No cabinet remained in existence, save in a formal sense, and therefore there was no possibility of securing its collective advice. It followed that the Prime Minister was not so much advising a dissolution without having consulted his colleagues as advising a dissolution when his cabinet was no longer in effective existence. Moreover, in so far as the opinion of his colleagues could be judged, the majority who voted with General Smuts presumably did not favour the request for a dissolution. More important still, it was known by the voting on General Hertzog's neutrality motion that he no longer enjoyed the support of a majority in the House of Assembly and that there was a majority prepared to support an alternative government under General Smuts. Least of all could the risk of widespread disturbance or even civil war be wholly disregarded were opinion to be inflamed by a bitter election campaign. In such circumstances the Governor-General would seem to have acted correctly and in the interests of his country in declining to accept the advice of the Prime Minister and in

[1] It is understood that he acted on this presumption in 1935 and did not consult his colleagues formally. Cf. Keith, *King and Constitution*, pp. 4–9.

[2] Article 13 (2).

seeking to form an alternative government with General Smuts at its head. Because of the controversial nature of the decision he had to take, the Governor-General wisely recorded in a letter to General Hertzog[1] the considerations which guided him in making it. They were as follows:

I have given careful consideration to the proposal you made to me last evening that I should dissolve Parliament with a view to a general election. There is a general feeling, which I share, that a general election at the present moment would lead to great bitterness and even violence. That situation must, however, be accepted if there is no constitutional alternative.

The present Parliament was elected in May last year. The question of South Africa's participation in a war in which England was involved was at that time clearly before the people, and the policy of the government, as proclaimed by you and your ministers, was that the question would be decided by the chosen representatives of the people in Parliament. When war broke out the government placed the question before Parliament for decision, but was divided on the recommendation that should be made to the House. Two opposing motions were submitted, by you and by General Smuts respectively, and the House decided by a considerable majority to adopt that of General Smuts.

In the circumstances I cannot see on what grounds I should be justified in rejecting the decision of the House and holding a general election if General Smuts, whose policy obtained the support of the House, is in a position to form a government which will have the support of the House. I have therefore asked him, if possible today, to inform me whether he can form such a government. If he is in a position to do so, I would not feel justified in accepting your proposal to dissolve Parliament.

The Governor-General's refusal to accept General Hertzog's advice to dissolve Parliament had important consequences. It is possible, even probable, that a general election in September 1939 would have returned General Hertzog to power by a narrow majority, or, to be more precise, he would probably have secured a majority of seats—because the heavy weighting of seats in favour of thinly populated rural constituencies would have told heavily in his favour—though not necessarily a majority of votes.[2] Be that as it may, not all Afrikaner Nationalists accepted the Governor-General's decision in good faith;[3] in any event Pirow, van Rensburg, the New Order group, and the Ossewa Brandwag sought to take advantage of it for their own unconstitutional ends. But General Hertzog behaved with dignified correctness. 'There must', he said, 'be no division of English and Afrikaans-speaking South Africans because that would make the building of a nation impossible.'[4] He advised his followers to maintain a strictly constitutional opposition to General Smuts's policy and he was consoled by the reflection that 'few other

[1] It was published on 5 September 1939.

[2] The South African correspondent of the *Round Table* thought he would have secured both in December 1939 (vol. 30, p. 211).

[3] It is hardly to be doubted that its general acceptability would have been seriously prejudiced had the Governor-General been, not a distinguished South African, but an English peer.

[4] van den Heever, *Hertzog*, p. 284.

things could so quickly or effectively have consolidated Afrikaans-speaking Afrikanerdom' as opposition to an imperialist war. Moreover, despite defeat, Hertzog was not discredited, and the long journey from Cape Town to Pretoria showed him that his place in the hearts of his own people was still secure. At the site of the Voortrekker Monument some 50,000 Afrikaners gathered to pledge their support to the new-found unity of Afrikanerdom. 'From the depths of the Afrikaner heart and soul we thank you, who have never been false to your nation',[1] they declared in tribute to the venerable figure who had so unflinchingly championed their rights in the past. But the future showed that these were empty tributes, that Afrikaner unity was not to be so easily restored, and for General Hertzog in his closing years there was yet reserved that last, corroding bitterness which comes from internecine strife within. He was too sure of the rightness of his actions and too proud to admit in 1933 he had been wrong; and because he would not retract his opinions or disown his past, he never regained the confidence or the good will of the Nationalists. Pursued by their unforgiving invective he withdrew, embittered and frustrated, to the lonely seclusion of his farm at Waterval and there he was haunted by the memories of Fusion to the end.[2]

When General Hertzog's request for a dissolution was declined, the Governor-General invited General Smuts to form a government. In this new government General Smuts himself took over the Departments of External Affairs and Defence and most of the key posts were placed in the hands of Afrikaners, Mr. Hofmeyr being given the portfolios of Finance and Education, Colonel Deneys Reitz, the romantic chronicler of the Boer Commandos, that of Native Affairs, while Mr. Colin Steyn was appointed to the Ministry of Justice. The Dominion party and Labour were also represented, and while the new cabinet had a pronounced English-speaking flavour, its composition underlined the support which General Smuts enjoyed among his own people. This was tactically sound, even if it could not altogether disguise the way in which the country had divided on the question of participation in the war. While it is true that the issue was not an issue between the two European races, virtually all the English-speaking names were to be found on one side of the voting-list.[3] Members who voted with General Smuts were both English-speaking and Afrikaans-speaking, but those members who voted with Hertzog were almost to a man Afrikaans-speaking. On the same day as the composition of the new cabinet was announced relations with Germany were severed.

General Smuts admitted later that the course which Parliament decided to take in September 1939 was 'a risky one because there might very easily have been a landslide in the opposite direction'. Some of his colleagues feared

[1] ibid.

[2] General Hertzog died on 22 November 1942.

[3] See South Africa, H. of A. Deb., vol. 36, coll. 95–98.

serious trouble at home and even regarded a rebellion on a larger scale than that of 1914 as not altogether improbable. But these fears proved unfounded. Within six weeks of the formation of the new United party government, General Smuts was satisfied that the South African people had accepted the challenge of war and that he was as a result assured of a steady support on the part of a sufficient and growing majority of the electorate.[1] He himself never doubted the rightness of the decision taken in September 1939, and subsequent events were to lend it their weighty justification. It was indeed partly as a result of the balance of argument in favour of the South African participation in the war that nationalist critics of the war policy could find no satisfying common ground for opposing it. The immediate consequences of the break up of the Fusion cabinet on the war issue was not, as General Hertzog and Dr. Malan so confidently predicted, an early reunion of Afrikanerdom but its further, if temporary, disruption through internal dissension among the Nationalist leaders.

The relative weakness of the Nationalists' position and their lack of a positive, popular programme in the early months of the war go far to explain their bitter denunciation of General Smuts's part in bringing South Africa into the war. Among their criticisms one retains a certain lasting interest. They argued that General Smuts's action in 1939 was wholly inconsistent with the course he had agreed to adopt had war come a year earlier. This argument cannot be lightly dismissed. It has already been suggested that by signing an agreement to support a policy of non-belligerency in 1938 General Smuts made at the least a tactical error. It is true that in the intervening months he made it clear in public speeches that he would advocate South African participation in war if Britain were directly attacked. But here again there was an element of ambiguity. What constituted a direct attack? The Nazi invasion of Poland was not a direct, but only an indirect attack upon Britain who was involved ostensibly because in April 1939 she had guaranteed the integrity of Polish territory. General Smuts, himself, felt that these criticisms demanded a considered reply. At Bloemfontein in November 1939 he explained that he had agreed to a policy of non-belligerency in September 1938 because in the first place South Africa had no interest in the Sudetenland, because in the second place 'we had no good reason at the time to suspect Hitler of his evil intentions', and finally because it was obvious that the United Kingdom and the French governments allowed that Hitler had a case in relation to Czechoslovakia.[2] But he went on to say that his agreement on a policy of neutrality was confined to that one particular question. It had nothing to do with any other problem that might arise, and he had never defined or agreed to a policy of neutrality for the future in general terms. On the contrary, as soon as it became apparent that Hitler's intentions were no longer the righting of the

[1] *Plans for a Better World*, pp. 223–4.

[2] This last was a very telling point.

wrongs of Germans, he had advocated a very different course and had urged on public platforms that in the event of an attack on Britain, South Africa's interests were directly involved and she would therefore be justified in going to war. Indeed in his view no other course was open to her consistent with her membership of the Commonwealth. These arguments cannot fail to carry conviction, though it may still be considered that General Smuts would have been wiser, even at the risk of provoking a major political crisis, to have informed General Hertzog that in his view the agreement of 1938 related only to the action to be adopted should the Sudeten crisis have led to war, and justified no inferences about his attitude in a later crisis which would be determined in the light of events in Europe at the time it arose.

The difference between General Smuts's attitude in September 1938 and September 1939 suggests that in respect of South Africa British policy at Munich was not without its justification. Had war come in 1938 it is certain that at the outset the South African government, representing as it did the two parties of the Union and the overwhelming majority of the electorate, would have decided on non-belligerency. A year later, convinced on the one hand that Mr. Chamberlain had made all reasonable, and even unreasonable, sacrifices in the cause of peace, and on the other that Hitler's absorption of Czechoslovakia in March 1939 afforded decisive evidence of his resolve to conquer and enslave the free peoples of the world, South Africa decided to go to war.

In the last analysis it was not the future of either European race that was most directly endangered in September 1939, but that of the non-European peoples who composed four-fifths of the population of the Union of South Africa. For them the triumph of the Nazi doctrines of race supremacy would have portended hopeless servitude. This was recognized by Mr. Molteno, one of the three European representatives of the Natives of Cape Province, who said that the issue was one between the forces of democracy and of liberty, as against 'the forces of aggression, of authoritarianism, and of intolerance and above all—and this is what concerns those of us who represent the constituents we do—the principle of race domination'.[1] But, no doubt deliberately, the theme was not developed and no other speaker concerned himself with the interests of the Natives, and their future would appear to have played no part in the decision that was reached. It may well be, therefore, that historians in later years reading the records of this historic debate in the South African House of Assembly will concern themselves as much with what was left unsaid as with what was said.

IRISH NEUTRALITY

Carefully, judiciously, balancing one consideration against another, avoiding every precipitate word or deed, Mr. Mackenzie King evolved a foreign policy

[1] South Africa, H. of A. Deb., vol. 36, col. 78.

for Canada designed above all to preserve internal unity; more autocratically and more secretively General Hertzog searched, in vain as it proved, for a policy which would keep South Africa united, while in Eire Mr. de Valera, with the greater assurance borne of a strong parliamentary position, defined Irish policy with the same end uppermost in his mind. In one sense his task was easier than that either of Mr. Mackenzie King or of General Hertzog. The people of the Twenty-Six Counties were a homogeneous people, predominantly Roman Catholic in religion, predominantly nationalist in politics. The whole tradition of their recent history marked out for them a course of action which might be interpreted with varying emphasis, but which was in essentials virtually unquestioned. In another sense, however, Mr. de Valera's task was more exacting. He was the heir of a revolution. He knew, none better, that revolutionary forces were still surging beneath the thin crust of ordered government. Within his own lifetime he had not only experienced a national revolution, guerrilla warfare, and civil war; he had himself been one of the principal protagonists in all three. He was no doctrinaire revolutionary. That last stand at Boland's Mill in April 1916, which had so nearly led to the scaffold, the strain of the fighting a few years later, and the envenomed wrangles that were at once the prelude and the sequel to the civil war, all left a deep impress upon his scholarly and inflexible mind. Never disposed to believe that he had himself been mistaken, the natural authoritarianism of his temper was softened by experience, and in internal politics his unchallenged ascendancy, a tribute at once to his nationalist record, to his outstanding political gifts, and to the integrity of his character, was maintained with a rare sense of what was possible in Irish politics.

Mr. de Valera was well aware that some of his former colleagues in the Irish Republican Army—and if he was ever disposed to forget there was Mr. Frank Aiken, former Chief of Staff of the I.R.A. and now his Minister for Defence to remind him—gave him an allegiance qualified by their unwavering faith in the uncompromising aims for which the I.R.A. had stood in the past. Their support was therefore always conditional upon a steady advance towards a republican-separatist goal and they were for that reason at the least not ill-disposed towards the re-established Irish Republican Army. At his accession to office Mr. de Valera had announced that since the Irish Free State at last had a government faithfully reflecting the deeper aspirations of her people, the Public Safety Acts introduced by Mr. Cosgrave, directed aginst the I.R.A. and giving to the government powers of arbitrary arrest and to military tribunals powers of summary jurisdiction, were to be repealed forthwith. Yet within the brief span of six years Mr. de Valera himself was confronted with the unwelcome duty of reintroducing measures as repressive as those which he had earlier so vigorously denounced. It was the recrudescence of the I.R.A. outrages of 1938–9 in Northern Ireland, Britain, and ultimately within the Twenty-Six Counties that confronted him with a challenge which he met with commendable resolution. He learned by experience that, whatever his sympathies might be, the head of a lawfully elected government could have no compromise with the forces of disorder without endangering the existence of the state itself. But though firm in action Mr. de Valera was only too well aware of the sentimental appeal of violent protests against Partition not only to the extreme republicans but also to opinion which on the surface had severed all connexion with revolutionary nationalist forces. The conception of a revolution still in being enlisted the loyalty of many young adventurous spirits who failed to understand why those who in the past had proclaimed an All-Ireland Republic as the goal of national endeavour should now stop short of it and first by pious exhortation and then by repressive legislation disavow the faithful militant few who believed that the methods which had served well in the past would reap an equal reward in the future.

The challenge from the left, promptly suppressed, within the Twenty-Six Counties inevitably forced Mr. de Valera into a more central position. Fundamentally, despite his aversion to compromise, Mr. de Valera was a man of the centre. But he was also an astute politician, and like Clemenceau before him he recognized that the critical challenge to his authority came not from the established opposition on the right with which he knew well how to deal, but from the subversive opposition of the left, which though small in numbers, might through some not altogether improbable concatenation of circumstances be placed in the position of undermining his authority or disrupting his government. It was here that the role of Mr. Frank Aiken, at the time Minister for Defence, was of some importance. His position was indeed not altogether dissimilar to that of Mr. Oswald Pirow in South Africa, his intentions as unpredictable. Both held the Defence portfolio and both exercised great, though not decisive, influence upon their respective leaders. Mr. Aiken's sympathies with the militant left[1] were not disguised and his ambitions were not narrowly circumscribed.

The recrudescence of the I.R.A. was one more protest, a violent protest, against the existence of the Border. But those who were familiar with the weapons employed by Nazi Germany and by Soviet Russia were not unaware that the often sincere and single-minded leaders of this subversive movement could be stirred on by *agents provocateurs* to actions which were in the interests neither of Ireland nor Britain but were designed to further the purposes of Nazi Germany or of Soviet Russia. Marx and Engels, and after them Lenin, had long since considered the interest of revolutionary Communism in Irish nationalism and that interest had not died in Moscow.[2] The Communist aim, as defined by Lenin, was to encourage and assist Irish nationalism in the first instance so as to undermine the strength of capitalist resistance within

[1] Left is used here in a national, not a social context.

[2] The writings of Marx, Engels, and Lenin on the Irish Question are analysed in N. Mansergh, *Ireland in the Age of Reform and Revolution* (London, Allen & Unwin, 1941), Chapter III.

the British Isles and then, when that first task was accomplished, to destroy Irish nationalism itself because the nationalism of small countries was recognized to be the fundamental obstacle to the spread of international Communism.

It is in this light of potential rather than actual tensions that Mr. de Valera's external policies must be considered. It is clear at once that the internal scene materially reinforced despairing conclusions about the course of international affairs that he had drawn at Geneva. The question that is perhaps not susceptible of a categorical answer is whether external or internal considerations proved decisive. Later the fear that active participation would almost certainly have brought about a civil war at home seemed uppermost in his mind, but in the years preceding the war his speeches suggest that the failure of the League carried at least equal weight. All that can be said with certainty is that in Mr. de Valera's mind the one powerfully reinforced the other in impressing upon him the necessity of neutrality. In the country at large nothing was more remarkable than the wellnigh universal acceptance of the view that Eire should if possible remain neutral in the event of war. It was indeed so widely and so generally endorsed that when war did come in September 1939 there was no discussion in the Dáil of the issues involved, or of the factors which should determine Irish policy. It was assumed that Irish policy had been determined, and the interest had shifted to how it might best be applied. It is true that Mr. Dillon, one of the leaders of the opposition, said that the Dáil should not disperse without placing on record that a policy of strict neutrality was not incompatible with the existence of strong sympathies with the cause of the Western Allies. But beyond that one statement, the policy was accepted by all shades of opinion from former Unionists[1] on the right to Fianna Fáil back-benchers on the left as being the only policy which the country could adopt in the circumstances and in the light of her recent history.

The Dáil assembled on 2 September 1939 and Mr. de Valera submitted to it two emergency measures designed to facilitate the maintenance of neutrality. The first of these measures amended the Constitution so as to enable both Houses of Parliament to declare that a state of emergency existed even though Eire itself was not actually at war.[2] The second was an Emergency Powers Bill vesting in the government wide powers to take such steps as seemed to them necessary or expedient for securing public safety, for the preservation of the state, for the maintenance of public order, and for the provision and control of supplies and services essential to the life of the community. Mr. de Valera explained that these measures implied a policy of neutrality which, he was sure, did not come either to members of the House or to the public as a surprise. He had stated on many occasions that in the event of a European

[1] There were at most only three or four deputies who could be so described and even of them not all would have welcomed the description.

[2] First Amendment of the Constitution Bill, 1939.

war, it was the aim of his government to keep Eire, if at all possible, out of it. The government had pursued that policy and they intended to pursue it though they recognized how formidable might be the difficulties which would arise.[1] But all the necessary steps had been taken to make Irish intentions known to the belligerent nations[2] and on 31 August the German minister in Dublin had informed Mr. de Valera that Germany would respect Irish neutrality provided that it was strictly enforced. Mr. de Valera had replied that the Irish government wished to remain at peace with Germany as with all other Powers.

Neutrality on the part of a state that remained in the opinion of other Commonwealth governments a member of the Commonwealth presented certain constitutional problems of greater interest than significance. One curious example of them arose from the fact that the newly appointed Irish minister to Berlin had had no letters of credence signed by the King before war was declared. Since the King's signature was required for such purposes by the provisions of the External Relations Act, the minister designate was unable to take up his appointment, for the King at war could hardly be expected to sign letters of credence for a minister of a neutral state owing a nominal allegiance to him. The outcome was that Eire was represented in Berlin throughout the war by a chargé d'affaires.

It was recognized by the Dáil in September 1939 that the interdependence of Britain and Ireland economically would mean an association of interest on the economic front which might, if the Nazi government so wished, be regarded by them as incompatible with neutrality. In peace-time over 50 per cent. of Eire's imports came from the United Kingdom and more than 97 per cent. of its exports were marketed there. This dependence upon the British for a market and for supplies could not be abruptly terminated even if that were so desired. It meant in the last analysis that the Irish economy would be dependent upon the ability of Britain to protect the essential shipping routes. Would she be able to do so? Would services across the Irish Sea remain normal, would the Germans be prepared to allow those shipping services to continue uninterrupted, or would they regard the supply of food-stuffs for Britain as a legitimate target for attack? On this question some deputies took a very gloomy view. Mr. Dillon, however, was more robust. He declared that 'there is no more danger of submarines dominating the Irish Sea than there is of my going over to Germany to cut the moustache of Adolf Hitler.' 'We have a perfectly safe sea around these islands', he continued, 'thanks not to ourselves, but thanks to God and the British Fleet, and across that safe stretch of sea we shall send all the bacon we can.'[3]

[1] Dáil Debates, vol. 77, col. 3.

[2] The published German documents record that on 31 December 1938 Mr. de Valera told the German minister in Dublin that Eire felt herself to be 'impartial' in respect of major policy questions concerning Germany. (*Documents on German Foreign Policy*, Series D, vol. 4, no. 285, p. 357.)

[3] Dáil Debates, vol. 77, coll. 286–7.

The aim of the government, endorsed by all parties, was that economic relations between Britain and Eire could and should continue on a basis most beneficial to both of them. The government itself took a legitimate satisfaction in the enhanced security afforded by the measures they had sponsored for the diversification of Irish agriculture. The extension of the area under sugar-beet was in the course of time to make Eire virtually self-supporting in sugar; while the encouragement of wheat-growing persistently pursued in peace-time in the face of determined opposition criticism, afforded a basis for more rapid expansion to meet war-time needs. On the declaration of war, compulsory tillage was enforced on the basis of 12½ per cent. of the area of suitable land on each farm.

Neutrality was a policy which demanded constant reinterpretation in the light of events. But from the outset the determination of the government to pursue it and the support which the policy enlisted in the country were not in doubt. It was that which accounted for the acceptance, despite protest, of wide censorship powers vested in the hands of the Minister for Defence under the Emergency Powers Act. The censorship, rigorously enforced, was designed principally to silence the extreme left. But it had the subsidiary object of keeping the general political temperature low. Since the main purpose of Mr. de Valera's policy was to maintain national unity, he felt that it was essential that all efforts to enlist the support of the people for either side must be rendered nugatory. That he deemed to be the first condition of the success of his policy. He recognized, it is true, that there were in the country sympathies, 'very strong sympathies',[1] but he did not feel that they should be freely expressed or be allowed to disturb public opinion in a country whose policy has been freely decided in the Dáil without a dissentient voice.

It is not in doubt that the weight of Irish sympathy was on the side of the Western Powers, especially after the announcement of the Nazi-Soviet pact in August 1939. But sympathy was one thing and positive action was another. And there most of those friendly to the Western Powers felt that the interests of their country should legitimately come first. In this they were in some degree influenced by the example both of the smaller democracies of Western and North Western Europe, all of whom remained neutral until attacked, and of the United States who, in September 1939, saw no sufficient cause to enter the war. It is also probable that the decision of the government to impose no restrictions upon the flow of volunteers to serve in the British forces removed a possible source of division within.

The coming of the war persuaded the United Kingdom government to take a step long overdue. In September 1939 they appointed Sir John Maffey, later Lord Rugby, as the first United Kingdom Representative to Eire. Hitherto British interests had been in charge of a trade commissioner. The delayed, but still timely, appointment of a diplomatic representative

[1] ibid. col. 4.

eased relations between the two countries from the outset of the war and enabled the United Kingdom government to secure wise and prudent counsel about the course of Irish policy and about Irish reactions to Britain's war-time measures.

Eire was a dominion in name but not in spirit, and as a result the decision of the governments of the Commonwealth taken in 1937 to continue to regard her as a dominion was virtually certain sooner or later to have some disconcerting consequences. So long as Eire was regarded as a dominion, every action of the Irish government was a matter of concern to the Commonwealth as a whole. In September 1939 General Hertzog argued that participation in the war 'will be the death so far as South Africa is concerned of the Commonwealth of Nations'. But the general view within South Africa and without was that the neutrality of a dominion in a war in which the Commonwealth was engaged would stretch, possibly to breaking point, that dominion's connexion with the Commonwealth. The risk of a final severance of ties with 'South Africa's best friend' was indeed a powerful argument on the side of Smuts and Hofmeyr. But in Eire that argument would have carried no weight, and since the question of neutrality was not challenged in the debate it was not in any event used. None the less just because Eire continued to be regarded as a dominion, her decision to remain neutral in a war in which the British Commonwealth was engaged established a precedent in Commonwealth relations that could not be ignored. If Eire remained neutral and the government of the United Kingdom and of the oversea dominions acquiesced in the view that her neutrality did not terminate her membership of the Commonwealth, then the question whether a dominion could remain neutral when Britain was at war and yet remain a member of the Commonwealth was answered in the affirmative. And by implication it was so answered. The United Kingdom government throughout the war continued to regard Eire as a member of the Commonwealth. It is true that Irish neutrality had practical consequences. It meant inevitably that full consultation could no longer be continued between a Commonwealth at war and a neutral dominion. But such practical consequences, however important, did not in any way diminish the significance of the constitutional precedent which the Irish action had established.

From the point of view of the Commonwealth as a whole it can and has been argued that the decision to accept Irish neutrality as affecting no change in her relations with the Commonwealth constituted the supreme proof of the full autonomy of the member-nations of the Commonwealth. Never again, it was urged, could it be questioned that the dominions were not fully free to decide their own course in foreign policy. The Irish decision might be widely regretted, but it was accepted without recrimination and without official reproof. That indeed is true, but it is also arguable that the precedent, however convincing as a debating point, was damaging to the spirit of the Commonwealth. It could reasonably be contended that the recognition of the right to neutrality and its practice were very different things, and that while the full freedom of the dominions in foreign policy implied their right to decide whether to participate in a war in which the Commonwealth was involved or to remain aloof, the actual decision to remain neutral in a major war in which the very existence of the Commonwealth was at stake suggested a lack of unity and a lack of a sense of moral obligation dangerous to its survival. The argument was not without importance for the future. After all the Irish government, at least since 1932, had indicated with provocative insistence that dominion status was uncongenial to them and that they wished to substitute for it an alternative relationship more in accordance with the historical facts and with the aspirations of the Irish people. It was the firm refusal of the United Kingdom not to contemplate any alternative relationship that was responsible for Eire's continuing status as a dominion.

Mr. de Valera was perfectly correct in saying that no one in Ireland received the announcement of the government's intention to remain neutral with any degree of surprise. His policy had been clearly enunciated and was clearly understood at home. It was not, however, so clearly understood overseas and particularly in the Commonwealth countries. Eire had continued to be called a dominion and had continued to be thought of as a dominion, a rather wayward dominion, but still a dominion. This fact in itself tended to create misunderstanding. As a result of it Mr. de Valera's declaration of Irish neutrality was regarded in some quarters of the United Kingdom and in many parts of the Commonwealth as a deliberate act of provocation. Yet unlike Prince Felix Schwarzenberg who, six years after the Czar had saved the Habsburg monarchy from dissolution, 'astonished the world by his ingratitude' in maintaining Austrian neutrality in the Crimean War, Mr. de Valera believed he was acting with a moderation that could scarcely be misunderstood. But misunderstood it was, and very largely because of the contrasting interpretations of Irish status which prevailed in London and in Dublin. That misunderstanding, coupled with the precedents which dominion neutrality established, called once more in question the wisdom of the British reaction in 1937. Might not the bolder course of inviting Mr. de Valera to expound his doctrine of External Association in the long run have been wiser?

One other consequence of Irish neutrality, which concerned Irishmen more closely, was plain for all to see. The partition of the country was underlined by the existence of a state of war north of the Border and the maintenance of neutrality south of it. The political separation was thereby reinforced by a growing sense of social and psychological separation deepening as the war intensified and auguring ill for the future reunion of Ireland.

INDIA COMMITTED

As war approached the continuance of the United Kingdom control over India's external policy became obvious and, standing out in clear contrast to advances in the field of internal self-government, it evoked a growing volume of protest from Indian nationalists. The dispatch in April 1939 of a small contingent of Indian troops to reinforce the garrison at Aden was condemned in strong terms by the All-India Congress Committee on the ground that it could only mean 'their employment for British imperialist purposes', and the Congress was determined 'to oppose all attempts to impose a war on India and use Indian resources in a war without the consent of the Indian people'.[1] The note of protest became still sharper when during the summer of 1939 more Indian troops were sent overseas to contribute to the defence of Egypt and of Singapore. At its meeting at Wardha in early August 1939, the Working Committee of Congress said that their dispatch was against 'the declared will of the Indian people', and recalled resolutions both of the Congress and of the Central Legislative Assembly to the effect 'that no Indian troops should be sent abroad without the consent of the Legislature'. In so doing, therefore, the United Kingdom government had 'flouted the declarations of the Congress and of the Assembly', and had taken steps which would inevitably 'lead to India's entanglement in war'. Accordingly the Working Committee decided to call upon all Congress members of the Central Legislative Assembly to refrain from attending its next session, and the Provincial Congress governments were reminded that they should 'assist in no way with the war preparations of the British government', though should war approach India, it was recognized that there would be a need for the encouragement of 'protective measures'.

In this atmosphere of growing tension differences of interest or aspiration were distorted and dangerously exaggerated. The British Commander-in-Chief in India, Sir Robert Cassels, was not, as some Indian critics supposed, guilty of any exaggeration when he said in a broadcast on 6 September 1939 that the loss of Malaya and Singapore would mean that the whole eastern coast-line of India would be liable to bombardment by sea and air, while a 'Burma in hostile hands would be a pistol pointed at the heart of Bengal'.[2] To the west, Egypt, Aden, and the lands bordering on the Persian Gulf fell equally within the natural area of India's defence interests. But this was not sufficiently recognized by Indian opinion at the time, mainly because the possibility of direct attack upon the subcontinent was virtually discounted. It seemed inconceivable to most Indians that Germany should overrun North Africa and threaten the western gateway to the Indian Ocean, while after the Nazi-Soviet pact of August 1939 a German advance to the Persian Gulf was ruled out altogether. To the east the danger from Japan seemed equally remote.

How can Japan come to India? [inquired Pandit Nehru]. Not overland. Deserts and the Himalayas offer an effective barrier, and not even air fleets can come that

[1] *Indian Annual Register*, 1939, vol. 1, p. 351. [2] ibid. vol. 2, p. 65.

way. By sea the route is long and intricate and full of danger in the narrow straits that have to be passed. A Japanese invasion of India could become a practical proposition only if China has been completely crushed, and if the United States, the Soviet Union and England have all been effectively humbled. That is a large undertaking.[1]

Such apparently reasonable, but in fact unjustifiable, notions of India's immunity from direct attack disguised the extent of her interest in the defence of the great West to East artery of the Empire and encouraged Indian nationalists to believe that all measures for defence outside the frontiers of India were taken exclusively in the interests of the Empire and were not in any way necessary to the security of the subcontinent. It was difficult in the prevailing atmosphere of suspicion, and in the absence of any apparent or immediate threat to India, to convince them that these complacent conclusions were mistaken and that India's self-interest demanded her co-operation in the wider imperial defence system. Yet it is hardly to be doubted that this was in truth the case.

In the field of foreign policy the situation was clearer. Domestic disputes could not disguise the community of interest and aim between Britain and India in world affairs. It had been the constant complaint of Congress India since 1931 that Britain's attitude to the dictators had been weak and compromising. The resolutions of the All-India Congress Committee in these years abound in denunciations of Fascist aggression in Abyssinia, in Spain, in Czechoslovakia; and the Congress demanded not the conciliation of the dictators but resolute opposition to them.[2] At the meeting of the Working Committee of Congress at Wardha in August 1939 it was once more recorded that Congress sympathies were 'entirely with the peoples who stand for democracy and freedom', and it was recalled that the Congress had repeatedly condemned 'Fascist aggression in Europe, Africa and the Far East of Asia as well as the betrayal of democracy by British imperialism in Czechoslovakia and Spain'.[3] The Working Committee indeed professed to doubt whether the British government's change of heart was sincere and whether even at this late hour it might not at any time betray the ideals of freedom and democracy. Yet such doubts were important not so much in themselves—for the prominence given to them was largely to be attributed to a desire to retain the left-wing dissidents within the Congress fold—as in their reflection of the dilemma with which Indian nationalists were confronted. Anti-imperialism was their *raison d'être*, anti-Fascism their passionate conviction, and yet the Power which must play, as Pandit Nehru freely allowed,[4] the leading part in resistance to Fascist aggression and in the overthrow of its totalitarian system of

[1] *The Unity of India*, p. 25.

[2] There is no evidence, however, that the Congress with its belief in non-violence would have been prepared to sponsor the use of force.

[3] *Indian Annual Register*, 1939, vol. 2, p. 214.

[4] e.g. *Unity of India*, p. 307.

government was the imperialist Power from whom Indian freedom must also be won. In the face of that dilemma only non-co-operation seemed a possible war-time policy. 'India', said the Working Committee at Wardha, 'cannot associate herself with such a government [i.e. the British] or be asked to give her resources for democratic freedom which is denied to her.'[1] India, in other words, could not fight for freedom unless she herself was free. This was an attitude which could be paralleled from the history of Afrikaner and Irish nationalism, and it was not to be modified in principle throughout all the vicissitudes of the Second World War.

In India the Nazi-Soviet pact of August 1939 dispelled many illusions. Hitherto the Soviet Union had been conceived of as fundamentally anti-imperialist, and above all—as distinct from the opportunist dictatorships and democracies of Central and Western Europe—as a Power whose policy was guided by principle. For that very reason its unprincipled indulgence in power politics deeply shocked Indian opinion.[2] In itself this helped to bring about a greater harmony of outlook between Indians and Englishmen, for many Indians recognized that the then fashionable denunciations of Britain's failure to co-operate with the Soviet Union might not after all be altogether well founded. Certainly there was no doubt about the indignation in India at the immediate sequel to the August pact. The invasion of Poland enlisted almost unanimous sympathy for the latest victim of Nazi aggression and for her Western allies. Yet such was the unhappy consequence of procrastination in the transfer of power that indignation and sympathy alike were deprived of almost all opportunity of positive and constructive expression. On 3 September 1939 it was the Viceroy who proclaimed that war had 'broken out between His Majesty and Germany', and who declared by virtue of the authority vested in him by the United Kingdom Parliament under the provisions of the Act of 1919 (which remained in force in respect of the central government because all the negotiations necessary to the practical application of the Act of 1935 at the centre had proved abortive) that in India a state of war emergency existed. By his proclamation India was automatically committed to war without reference to, or any consultation with, representatives of the Indian people. The failure to soften even by informal discussion the exercise of an imperial authority which in any event was acknowledged on all sides to be outdated must be accounted a grave error of statesmanship. It is true that any such discussion with the Indian leaders might have given opportunities for bargaining, which might in turn have confronted the government of India with formidable problems at a very critical moment. But in fact postponement did not resolve these problems but only accentuated them and made their discussion inevitable in circumstances that were yet more difficult. Moreover, in any event such reasons of dubious expediency

[1] *Indian Annual Register*, 1939, vol. 2, p. 214.
[2] cf. Pandit Nehru's reactions, *Unity of India*, pp. 308–10.

were insufficient to justify or to explain an exercise of authority which revealed above all a disturbing failure to understand not only the psychology of a nationally conscious but still dependent people but also the whole trend of Commonwealth development in recent years.

With the immediate outbreak of war Indians were united in common indignation against Nazi aggression, although party attitudes to the constitutional struggle were no less clearly marked. Princely India responded without hesitation to the call and pledged anew its allegiance[1] to the King-Emperor; and, faithful to their British protector, ally, and friend, the survivors of another age with their fabled wealth and their titles of far romance prepared to fight their last campaign. 'As for myself', declared the Maharaja of Bikaner, 'although I shall soon be entering my sixtieth year and my state is unhappily faced with famine of unprecedented severity I still hope to be permitted to have the privilege of fighting personally for His Majesty the King-Emperor.'[2] Nor did their loyalty fail to find its echoes in British India. 'I am certain', said Sir Muhammad Zafrullah Khan, law member of the Executive Council and leader of the Assembly, 'that everyone of us here fully realizes the gravity of the crisis and is determined to do his duty to King and country.'[3] But the high command of the Muslim League was more cautious. On the eve of the Nazi attack on Poland the Council of the Muslim League meeting in New Delhi had declared it to be 'premature at present to determine the attitude of the Muslims in the event of a world war breaking out'[4] and, despite the outspoken sympathy of individual members for Poland and the Western Allies, the League maintained official silence until the Congress formally defined its attitude to the war. That did not take place till 15 September. In the meantime Mr. Gandhi had conversed with the Viceroy. He had discussed the situation personally, without instructions from the Congress Working Committee and knowing, as he afterwards explained, that 'with my irrepressible and out-and-out non-violence . . . I could not represent the national mind'. But he made no secret of where his own sympathies lay. He told the Viceroy that he 'could not contemplate without being stirred to the very depth the destruction of London which had hitherto been regarded as impregnable. And as I was picturing before him the Houses of Parliament and Westminster Abbey and their possible destruction I broke down.' And Gandhi then went on to say that while he knew India's deliverance would come, he could not speculate what it would be worth 'if England and France fall, or if they come out victorious over Germany ruined and humbled'.[5] The sentiments of Pandit Nehru were no less sympathetic. Congress, he said on his return from China on 8 September, was not out to bargain.

[1] cf. *The Times*, 28 August 1939, and *Daily Telegraph*, 15 September 1939.
[2] *The Times*, 2 September 1939.
[3] Legislative Assembly Deb., vol. 5, pp. 279–80.
[4] *Indian Annual Register*, 1939, vol. 2, p. 348.
[5] *Harijan*, 9 September 1939.

We do not approach the problem with a view to taking advantage of Britain's difficulties. . . . In a conflict between democracy and freedom on the one side and Fascism and aggression on the other, our sympathies must inevitably lie on the side of democracy. . . . I should like India to play her full part and throw all her resources into the struggle for a new order.[1]

Inevitably the considered resolutions of the Congress and the League were less forthcoming. On 15 September, after five days of protracted discussion, the Working Committee of Congress published its conclusions. It took the 'gravest view' of the action of the British government in declaring India to be a belligerent country, in promulgating war ordinances and taking 'other far-reaching measures' which 'affect the Indian people vitally' without 'the consent of the Indian people whose declared wishes in such matters have been deliberately ignored by the British government'. At the same time the resolution recalled once more 'the entire disapproval' of the Congress of 'the ideology and practice of Fascism and Nazism and their glorification of war and violence and the suppression of the human spirit'. It condemned 'the aggression in which they had repeatedly indulged and their sweeping away of well-established principles . . . of civilized behaviour'. Then it proceeded to state its decision on the major practical issue involved:

The Congress had further laid down that the issue of war and peace for India must be decided by the Indian people, and no outside authority can impose this decision upon them, nor can the Indian people permit their resources to be exploited for imperialist ends. Any imposed decision, or attempt to use India's resources, for purposes not approved by them, will necessarily have to be opposed by them. If co-operation is desired in a worthy cause, this cannot be obtained by compulsion and imposition, and the Committee cannot agree to the carrying out by the Indian people of orders issued by external authority. Co-operation must be between equals by mutual consent for a cause which both consider to be worthy. The people of India have, in the recent past, faced great risks and willingly made great sacrifices to secure their own freedom and establish a free democratic state in India, and their sympathy is entirely on the side of democracy and freedom. But India cannot associate herself in a war said to be for democratic freedom when that very freedom is denied to her, and such limited freedom as she possesses, taken away from her.[2]

With this many in the Commonwealth, and not least Mr. Mackenzie King, could hardly fail to sympathize. The dominions in fact had demanded no less.

It was apparent from the resolutions of its Working Committee that the Congress intended to make its co-operation in war conditional upon the early achievement of independence. At a later meeting on 10 October the All-India Congress Committee passed a resolution clarifying this demand. 'India must be declared an independent nation', it read, 'and present applica-

[1] Quoted in R. Coupland, *Indian Politics, 1936–42* (London, Oxford University Press, 1943) p. 214.

[2] *Indian Annual Register*, 1939, vol. 2, pp. 226–7.

tion must be given to this demand to the largest possible extent.' Though the use of the words 'to the largest possible extent' left some room for compromise, the prospects of any advance towards self-government sufficient to satisfy the Congress were very slight. This was due not only to the risks inseparable from a war-time transfer of power of which the British government were necessarily mindful but also to the attitude of minorities within India and especially of the Muslim League. The conditions which the League prescribed as a basis for Muslim co-operation with the Government of India in fact proved to be irreconcilable with those laid down by the Congress. For, while the Working Committee of the League, meeting on 18 September, was forthright in its condemnation of 'unprovoked aggression' and expressed its deep sympathy with Poland, England, and France, it warned the British government that 'real and solid Muslim co-operation and support for Great Britain in this hour of her trial' was conditional upon 'justice and fair play' for Muslims in the Congress-governed provinces of British India and upon an assurance that 'no declaration regarding the question of constitutional advance for India' should be made without the approval of the All-India Muslim League.[1] Thus the principal protagonists on the Indian stage took up their respective positions and staked their conflicting claims. All were united in opposition to Nazi aggression but in little else.

The coming of war, which afforded final evidence of the independence of the dominions in external policy, underlined the dependence of India. Without discussion, without even consultation with her party leaders, India was committed to war.[2] Twenty-two years after the United Kingdom government had themselves declared 'the progressive realization of responsible government in India' to be the goal of their policy, such undisguised evidence of continuing subordination created general resentment in India and that resentment acquired a keener edge from the very contrast between the unfettered sovereignty of the dominions and the subjection of India in matters of external policy. Nor was it merely a question of symbolism or national pride. India, and particularly Congress India, believed that she had a distinctive and even a missionary role to play in world affairs: 'If we had been free', wrote Pandit Jawaharlal Nehru in September 1939, 'we might even have succeeded in preventing the war.' It was this very awareness of the contribution that a free India might make in world affairs that led him to deprecate too close an analogy between Indian and Irish national aspirations. Ireland was a small country 'geographically and economically tied to Britain', and in Pandit Nehru's opinion even an independent Ireland could not 'make much differ-

[1] ibid. pp. 350–2.

[2] The statement issued by the Governor-General of India on 17 October on *India and the War* opens with the sentence 'Since the outbreak of war, and more particularly during the last four weeks, I have been in the closest touch with the leaders of political opinion in British India. . . .' But not *before*, and the purpose of this consultation was not to decide policy but to carry out a policy already determined. See Cmd. 6121 (1939).

ence to world affairs'. But a free India with her vast resources could be of great service to humanity. 'India will always make a difference to the world; fate has marked us for big things. When we fall, we fall low; when we rise, inevitably we play our part in the world drama.'[1] But in 1939 while Eire gave a convincing, even dramatic demonstration of her enjoyment of the full rights of a sovereign state, India was left without a voice in the making of the supreme decision of peace or war. The contrast was too pointed to be overlooked and the sense of unfulfilled possibilities served only to accentuate a feeling of oppression.

[1] *Unity of India*, p. 307.

CHAPTER XI

COMMONWEALTH EXTERNAL POLICIES, 1931–9. A GENERAL APPRECIATION

'THE CHAOS OF THE MIND'[1]

THE making of policy in a democratic state, whatever subsequently published documents may suggest to the contrary, is rarely a matter only of calculation. Emotion and sentiment make their own highly important, though usually unrecorded, contribution. Not only are ministers, and even their professional advisers, responsive to the changing currents of public opinion but they are themselves moved by the spirit of the age in which they live. For this reason an understanding of the deeper impulses of action is to be sought as much in the writings of historians, poets, and philosophers as in the pronouncements of statesmen. This is perhaps particularly true of the English-speaking peoples in the period between the two world wars. In retrospect these seem to many to have been years of barren questioning and bleak scepticism, wasted years well described as 'the years which the locust hath eaten'.[2] The generation that succeeded to the dismal heritage of the First World War found much that was uncongenial in the values and the loyalties of their fathers, but never quite succeeded in finding a way of life satisfying to itself. Perhaps as a generation they were too critical to be constructive, perhaps they were just war-weary, or perhaps the pace of material change had undermined the moral foundations without which societies of free men lose cohesion. Whatever the reason, the fact remains that when the false dawn of the early nineteen-twenties faded the predominant reaction of the English-speaking world was not a resolve to master events, but to seek seclusion from their impact. This psychological reaction was of fundamental importance in the determination of Commonwealth external policies.

Twenty years later the catastrophe of 1914–18 was commonly considered in the English-speaking world to have been the consequence not of evil design but of a breakdown in the system of international relations. When those relations were institutionalized by the creation of a supra-national authority at Geneva, the risk of another major war was felt to be greatly diminished if not actually precluded. That the English-speaking peoples were tempted to accept such comfortable conclusions with easy complacency is no matter for surprise. When Prince von Bülow, the German Chancellor, visited England

[1] This sub-title is taken from a lyric by Michael Roberts entitled 'Midnight' which is included in *The Oxford Book of Modern Verse* edited by W. B. Yeats (London, Oxford University Press, 1936). In a few exquisite verses it reveals much of the spirit of the age.

[2] Joel ii. 25. The phrase was used by Sir Thomas Inskip, Minister for Co-ordination of Defence in 1939, and Mr. Churchill entitled Chapter V of *The Second World War*, vol. 1, 'The Locust Years'.

with the Kaiser in 1899 he noted that English politicians 'believe with difficulty that others have bad motives'.[1] This was equally true of Commonwealth statesmen of a later generation. When their faith in the capacity of the League to preserve peace was destroyed they were as much disposed to blame its institutional inadequacies as the actions of those who successfully challenged its authority. The risk of a war of deliberate aggression was discounted. On 25 September 1938, as the Czech crisis approached its climax, Mr. de Valera, then President of the Assembly of the League, said that in his opinion 'the war of sheer aggression, the war of the bully who covets what does not belong to him and means to possess himself of it by force, is not the war that we need fear most'.[2] In this he was wholly representative of Commonwealth opinion and he was also wholly mistaken. Commonwealth statesmen failed to read aright the riddle of German intentions. They could not excuse themselves by saying with Job, 'Oh . . . that mine adversary had written a book'. Hitler had written a book for all to read, but not many had read it and fewer within the Commonwealth accepted it as a serious declaration of intention. The spirit of *Mein Kampf* was so foreign to their traditional easy-going ways as to be almost incomprehensible to them. Yet we now know from the published German documents that nearly a year before de Valera broadcast from Geneva, Hitler in secret conference with his service chiefs had laid down the necessity of aggressive war by Germany.[3] Czechoslovakia was to be the first victim, and in the summer of 1938 the most favoured method for excusing a sudden and carefully prepared German attack upon her was the murder of the German minister in Prague, who little surmised the role for which he was cast.[4] These were things that were beyond the comprehension and the experience of all dominion ministers. Not till the absorption of Czechoslovakia in March 1939 were most of them persuaded that Hitler was bent on aggression, and even that did not suffice to convince General Hertzog and Mr. de Valera.

The reluctance of Commonwealth statesmen and peoples alike to think evil of others was important because it accentuated the slowness and the uncertainty of the Commonwealth reactions to dangers which threatened its existence. Yeats, a man of another generation who, perhaps because he had himself lived through a revolution, understood better the nature of the times, wrote:

> Things fall apart; the centre cannot hold;
> Mere anarchy is loosed upon the world,
> The blood-dimmed tide is loosed, and everywhere
> The ceremony of innocence is drowned;
> The best lack all conviction, while the worst
> Are full of passionate intensity.[5]

[1] *Die Grosse Politik*, vol. 15, p. 415.

[2] *Peace and War*, p. 72.

[3] *Documents on German Foreign Policy, 1918–45*, Series D, vol. 1, p. 29. This is the document known as the Hossbach Memorandum.

[4] ibid. vol. 2, p. 239.

[5] *Collected Poems* (London, Macmillan, 1934) p. 211.

It was that lack of hard conviction on the part of men of good will which virtually precluded any resolute response to the challenge of the dictators in its early phase. Within the Commonwealth some put their faith in isolationism, some in improved machinery for the closer co-ordination of Commonwealth policies, but in truth what was needed was something more simple and more fundamental, a firmer resolve and a clearer mind. To supply them was the essential task of Commonwealth statesmen as the authority of the League decayed.

The policies of the dominions were peculiarly susceptible to the *malaise*, to the divided counsels that were the affliction of the time, because their capacity for resolute action was directly dependent upon the will of their several peoples. If that will weakened or failed there was no superimposed authority which could disguise its infirmity. The control of external policy had been effectively decentralized. At the same time there did not exist in the dominions, as distinct from the United Kingdom and from states long accustomed to the exercise of full responsibility in the field of foreign policy, either well-established machinery for the conduct of foreign affairs or a generally accepted traditional approach to the problems they presented. As a result every major issue was to them a new issue, and that gave to dominion public opinion an influence in the making of external policy which it did not enjoy elsewhere. This was important, for despite all the uncertainties and the differences in dominion opinion, on one thing it was absolutely clear. It was not prepared, save in the last resort and in the light of the most convincing evidence that such was the hard condition of survival, to contemplate again the sacrifice of the flower of the Empire's manhood on the battlefields of Europe. Dominion peoples remembered that among the ancient memorials of cardinals and kings in the cathedral of Notre-Dame in Paris there was to be seen a newer tablet dedicated to the million dead of the British Empire who lay buried in French soil. It was that memory which was responsible for the resolve of the British peoples that peace should be preserved at almost any cost; which made so many in the dominions oppose on principle any commitment to participate in foreign wars; that gave isolationism its emotional appeal; and yet it was that memory, too, which bound even the most distant dominions most firmly to Europe. Something of the tension involved was reflected in a despairing protest of Mr. Mackenzie King on 30 March 1939 when the German occupation of Czechoslovakia had convinced him that Hitler's ambitions could be checked only by force and that Canada would soon be involved once more in a European war.

The idea [he said] that every twenty years this country should . . . take part in a war overseas for democracy or self-determination of other small nations, that a country which has all it can do to run itself should feel called upon to save, periodically, a continent that cannot run itself, and to these ends risk the lives of its peoples, risk bankruptcy and political disunion, seems to many a nightmare and sheer madness.[1]

THE REACTION AGAINST VERSAILLES

In the countries of the Commonwealth the reluctance to believe 'that others have bad motives' was extended from the present to the past. By an easy dialetical process, what had begun as a legitimate refutation of Germany's exclusive war guilt ended in an excess of impartiality with the even-handed attribution of responsibility for the outbreak of war in 1914 either to all the Great Powers or to some abstractions such as the armaments race, secret diplomacy, power politics, capitalism, which were held to be the causes of a war in which all alike were victims, and none, least of all Germany, aggressors. This perversion of history had very important consequences. It instilled not in the vanquished but among the Anglo-Saxon victors a sense of guilt.[2] At Versailles the Allied and Associated Powers had formally asserted the war guilt of Germany, but as soon as the once apparently self-evident fact of her aggression in 1914 began to be disputed in the light of documentary evidence so voluminous and contradictory that it could be used to support almost any interpretation of the causes of the First World War, or none, the moral foundation on which the Treaty rested and by which alone its terms could be justified was undermined. To this British opinion was peculiarly sensitive.

It is dangerous to generalize about dominion opinion and the Peace Treaty of 1919, for it varied greatly, but it can at least be said that the popular reaction against Versailles was even more pronounced and more decisive in its impact upon policy in the dominions than it was in the United Kingdom. The reasons for this are both general and particular. Among the former the distance that separated the dominions from Germany was not without its importance. It was easier to take an understanding view of the reasons which Germany gave for the unilateral repudiation of the provisions of the Versailles Treaty in Vancouver or Cape Town than in London, just as in turn London could afford to be less 'unreasonable' than Paris or Warsaw. In the late nineteen-thirties, however, the revival of German colonial claims directly affecting the interests of the Pacific dominions and of the Union of South Africa sensibly modified this attitude of tolerant comprehension. But it is doubtful if distance would have exerted so great an influence had not the moral foundation of the 1919 settlement been undermined. If the war of 1914–18 had been not a war to prevent German domination of Europe and to preserve the liberties of small peoples, but merely a continuation of an age-old struggle for power temporarily concluded by the imposition of a Carthaginian peace upon the defeated, then there was no moral claim upon countries outside Europe to

[1] Canada, H. of C. Deb., 1939, vol. 3, p. 2419.

[2] Their French allies never shared it. As M. Cambon observed, they were too logical to believe that Belgium had invaded Germany.

uphold the settlement by force. On the contrary, they were both well advised and morally justified in divesting themselves of responsibility for its maintenance. 'What we are witnessing in Europe today', wrote the Canadian Professor F. H. Underhill in 1936,[1] 'is a complete revival of the balance-of-power system of the nineteenth century.' That was the strongest argument of the isolationist in the Commonwealth overseas, and the fundamental assumption on which it rested was that the First World War had not been caused by deliberate aggression but by the inherent tensions of European society.

In 1919 two conflicting views about the proper treatment of Germany were expressed by dominion statesmen. The hard, unrelenting accents of Mr. W. M. Hughes demanded that Germany should make the fullest possible reparation for the catastrophe she had caused, while General Smuts pleaded in vain with Mr. Lloyd George for more generous terms for the defeated.[2] In the sequel it was the opinion of General Smuts that prevailed. Throughout the Commonwealth the peace which in 1919 had been widely criticized as too lenient was later generally regarded as vindictive and worthy to be stigmatized as 'Carthaginian'. If opinion in each of the dominions in the intervening years were analysed, differences in emphasis would have to be recorded, but the general trends would correspond closely to those in the United Kingdom which have been so well described by Mr. R. B. McCallum.[3] In a very real sense what was of lasting importance was what was held in common, for it was that which went far to determine the attitude of the dominions first towards German rearmament and later towards German aggression. If left-wing opinion in Canada and Australia and nationalist opinion in South Africa and Ireland condemned the Treaty on different grounds and in the light of their own preconceptions, what was important was that they agreed in regarding it not as the just and reasonable foundation for a European order, but as an iniquitous imposition of the victors upon the vanquished. Conservative nationalists and high-minded, progressive internationalists were alike anxious to be dissociated from the work of 'the hard-faced men' who, according to the Keynesian legend, had been responsible for the peace.[4] By a process of critical self-examination, which the Germans conscientiously encouraged, the onus of guilt was gradually shifted from the aggressors of 1914 to their victims. Throughout the Commonwealth a large and influential section of opinion felt that reparation to Germany was due. Canadian progressives believed it was 'the injustices of Versailles' which doomed the

[1] Quoted in Canadian Institute of International Affairs, *Canada in World Affairs: the Pre-War Years*, p. 38.

[2] Millin, *Smuts*, vol. 2, p. 283.

[3] *Public Opinion and the Last Peace* (London, Oxford University Press, 1944).

[4] J. M. Keynes, *The Economic Consequences of the Peace* (London, Macmillan, 1920) p. 133. It was not in fact Lord Keynes himself who described the House of Commons elected in 1919 as 'a lot of hard-faced men who look as if they have done very well out of the war', but he quoted the remark with approval and gave it a notoriety it would otherwise never have enjoyed.

League to failure.[1] Even in September 1939 Mr. Coldwell declared it to be the conviction of the Co-operative Commonwealth Federation that the struggle 'for trade supremacy and political domination' which caused the First World War 'was perpetuated in the Versailles Treaty' and 'is again the primary cause of the present conflict,'[2] while in Australia the leader of the opposition, Mr. Curtin, reflected on how different things might have been but for the terms of the Versailles Treaty.[3] These opinions were shared by the Working Committee of the Indian National Congress who, meeting at Wardha in September 1939, observed that in itself the coming of war signified 'the abject failure of the Treaty of Versailles and of its makers who . . . imposed an imperialist peace on the defeated nations'.[4] To them were added the more settled reactions of Afrikaners and Irishmen. Both had historic links with the defeated Empire, the one recalled by the Kaiser's telegram to President Kruger, the other by the landing of Sir Roger Casement's ill-fated expedition at Eastertide 1916. Both, too, by reason of their ardent nationalism were sympathetic to German aspirations for the union of all Germans within a greater Reich. Afrikaner opinion on the Treaty indeed never varied. 'My soul', said General Botha before going to Versailles, 'has felt the harrow. I know what it means.' In 1919, recorded Mrs. Millin,[5] 'Smuts could only see the Germans in the position of the Boers at Vereeniging.' This sympathetic understanding of Germany's reaction to defeat later proved an unreliable criterion by which to judge reviving German ambitions. There was a gulf between the outlook of the small, conservative, predominantly pastoral Afrikaner people and the highly organized, technically efficient millions of the Third Reich which a common allegiance to nationalist dogma concealed from the eyes of many Afrikaners. For General Smuts, as for General Hertzog, the repudiation of the terms of the Peace Treaty was only a matter of time, and their advice to Britain was to yield gracefully to the inevitable. In this dominion opinion generally was on their side. When, by unilateral action which violated both the Treaty of Versailles and the freely negotiated Locarno pact, Germany remilitarized the Rhineland in 1936, the dominions were united in their opposition to any military action by Britain in association with France, though nowhere was that opposition so pronounced as in South Africa. General Smuts was especially outspoken in applauding Britain's assumption of the role of peacemaker, and he excused Germany's treaty violations on the ground that they brought to an end 'the spirit of inequality, subjection and bondage in which the Peace of Versailles was concluded'.[6] The same arguments were advanced, though with decreasing

[1] *J.P.E.*, 1937, vol. 18, p. 307, and see pp. 303 ff. The speaker was Miss A. C. Macphail. Often expressed in varying forms in dominion parliaments this view was rarely, if ever, challenged.

[2] 9 September 1939, Canada, H. of C. Deb., p. 55.

[3] 6 September 1939, Australia, H. of R. Deb., vol. 161, pp. 36–37.

[4] *Indian Annual Register*, 1939, vol. 2, p. 227.

[5] Millin, *Smuts*, vol. 2, p. 283.

[6] *Cape Times*, 23 March 1936.

conviction, in all the dominions to explain German incorporation of Austria and of the Sudetenland. In this way a troubled conscience reinforced a desire to remain free of European entanglements and led to an infirmity of purpose of which the dictators were not slow to take advantage. How, in particular, could General Hertzog, who attributed responsibility for the economic slump of the early nineteen-thirties, for the failure of the League, for the aggression of dictators alike and indiscriminately to the 'monster of the Treaty of Versailles', and who had long since prophesied that the next war would be 'the child of Versailles', advocate resistance to any of Hitler's last demands in Europe?[1] Dominion refusal to defend what most of them regarded as the indefensible provisions of the Treaty of Versailles was an important factor in the determination of Commonwealth policies in the later nineteen-thirties. Appeasement was an acceptable policy at the Imperial Conference of 1937 largely because, rightly or wrongly, it was assumed that Germany had been too harshly treated in 1919.

THE ROLE OF THE COMMONWEALTH: DOUBTS AND MISGIVINGS

The reaction against Versailles had so decisive an influence on the evolution of Commonwealth policies largely because of the doubts that prevailed about the proper role of the British Commonwealth in world affairs. The transformation from Empire into Commonwealth was something that could be effected abruptly in theory and rapidly in law, but only slowly in practice. While it is true that the Balfour Report of 1926 recognized in felicitous language a relationship that had already been established, it also confronted the peoples of the Commonwealth with a challenge no longer to be disguised behind legal fiction or outmoded loyalties. It demanded above all an adjustment in outlook to correspond with the new distribution of responsibilities, and insistently though that adjustment had been asked for by Canada, South Africa, and the Irish Free State, it could not fail, once the first flush of enthusiasm had faded, to encourage a self-conscious analysis of the place of the Commonwealth in the world. Could allegiance to it be satisfactorily reconciled in principle with membership of the League of Nations? Was not its lesser loyalty a hindrance rather than a help to international understanding? Were the dominions really free or was the new Commonwealth of nominally equal partners anything but the old Empire writ large?

On these difficult and disturbing questions, inseparable from a period of transition, the misgivings of nationalists and radicals about the contemporary Commonwealth were by no means identical. The former, preoccupied almost exclusively with national independence, were concerned to ensure that the constitutional transformation of Empire into Commonwealth gave them an

[1] Hertzog's condemnation of Versailles was restrained by comparison with that of Malan, who spoke of the Treaty as having 'murdered' the League, its own child, as being 'the root of all evil, the source of unrest and danger in the world' and as 'the greatest, worst *hereditas damnosa* of world history' (South Africa, H. of A. Deb., vol. 32, coll. 574–5).

unrestricted right to control their own destinies in the field of external as of internal affairs. For them the forms of sovereignty were psychologically almost as important as their actual exercise. It was not enough that a dominion parliament should decide under what circumstances it should go to war; it should also remain free from all prior commitments so that when the hour for decision came it should exercise an unfettered and indisputable freedom of choice. Suspicious of continuing control from London, the dominions which were nationalist in outlook were apt to be irritated by appeals to the sense of moral obligation that sustained the Commonwealth system, not for the most part because they questioned its existence or necessity but because they felt that it might be exploited to make serious inroads upon their freedom of action. For the same reason they asserted their right to neutrality in a war in which Britain was involved, for its recognition seemed a necessary reinsurance against any veiled reassertion of imperial control over foreign affairs.

From the conflict between nationalism and imperialism, first the constitutional and then the political pattern of Commonwealth relations emerged. After 1931 the nationalists, satisfied in varying degrees in accordance with the intensity of their nationalism with what was so largely their own handiwork, were ready for the most part to acknowledge that it was good. Thenceforward the great constitutional debate subsided, and in September 1939 constitutional questions aroused no significant interest in any part of the Commonwealth. This was in itself an implicit tribute to the dexterity with which Commonwealth statesmen had refashioned the British Empire in accordance with the predominant sentiment of its self-governing peoples. Yet in recognizing the achievement it is important to recognize also its limitations. While Canadian opinion within Quebec and without, and the majority of Afrikaners were satisfied, separatist opinion in the Irish Free State remained in the ascendant even after the agreement of 1938. Of more general significance was the fact that success in reconciling the claims of nationalism with the conception of a wider community of free and equal states was not matched by a comparable measure of success in the superficially easier task of enlisting the positive support of progressive opinion behind the new idea of Commonwealth. In retrospect, indeed, it would seem that the risk of disunity within the Commonwealth in the years before the Second World War came as much from the dwindling confidence of the left as from the potentially disruptive challenge of nationalism.[1]

Within the Commonwealth the distinction between nationalist and socialist left-wing opinion was blurred both by pressure of events and by some preconceived notions about their supposed identity. It was for long the comforting illusion of many left-wing publicists that nationalists were socialists by temperament, if not by conviction, and that the national was inseparable from

[1] M. Halpérin in his *Lord Milner et l'Évolution de l'Impérialisme Britannique* (Paris, Presses Universitaires de France, 1950) pp. 184–9, has recorded Lord Milner's misgivings about the doctrinaire approach of the United Kingdom Labour party to imperial affairs.

the class struggle. In this view they were supported by most conservatives, who readily assumed that those who were to the left in one respect were to the left in all.[1] Yet within the British Commonwealth no belief was more ill founded. French-Canadians, Afrikaner nationalists, the old guard of the Indian Congress, the Muslim League, and Sinn Féin, all in greater or lesser degree inclined towards conservatism in social policy when they occupied positions of authority. In Quebec, the most nationally self-conscious province in Canada, the socialist C.C.F. made no headway; in the Union of South Africa it was Dr. Malan, first in opposition and then in office, who recommended the most reactionary racial and social policies within the Commonwealth. It was Mr. Jinnah, a conservative to his finger tips, who was the architect of Pakistan, and if in India after 1947 the balance was more evenly held, it is none the less significant that the principal opposition to Congress came from the Socialists on the left. Even in Ireland, where the old social system made inevitable a temporary alliance between the social and political revolutionaries, it was the political forces that were predominant after 1921, and they were either frankly conservative or, save for a brief period following immediately upon Mr. de Valera's accession to office, tepidly reformist in social policy. James Connolly, a socialist, embraced the nationalist cause in 1916. He was later remembered as a nationalist with left-wing sympathies. Kevin O'Higgins's remark that 'we are the most conservative revolutionaries who ever carried through a successful revolution',[2] evoked an echo from the earliest days of the Irish Home Rule party when its first leader, Isaac Butt, argued that Home Rule should be supported if only because a time might come 'when every Irishman would wish that we had in Ireland a Parliament and a government which an English revolution could not touch. . . .'[3]

The deep-seated conservatism of the most nationalist of the dominions is a phenomenon with far-reaching implications. In the year before the Second World War the nationalist dominions of South Africa and Eire, and the most strongly nationalist group within Canada, were most consistent in their support of appeasement, partly because for long they continued to hope that Hitler would provide a bulwark against the spread of Communism, and partly

[1] Lenin entertained no such illusion; see *On the Right of Nations to Self-Determination Collected Works* (London, Lawrence, 1929) vol. 17.

[2] The continuing conservatism of Irish nationalism was recognized by a special correspondent of the *Daily Worker* who, on 11 September 1950, reported that 'it required a considerable amount of courage to be a socialist in Ireland' but hoped that the ending of Partition might eventually 'improve the situation'.

[3] Some Englishmen were glad his wish was realized, as was evidenced by the post-1945 flow of well-to-do English settlers fleeing to Ireland from the austerities of Mr. Attlee's Welfare State. In Dublin this was known as 'the retreat from Moscow'. It is interesting to recall that J. A. Froude, who visited Melbourne in 1885, was encouraged by the steady progress and the easy social life he found there to believe that Australia would afford a last refuge for the English landed gentry. There they would be able to live as they wished 'without fear of socialism or graduated income tax', which he foresaw as the ruin of Old England. (Quoted in C. E. Carrington, *An Exposition of Empire* (Cambridge University Press, 1947) p. 59.)

because they feared so greatly the violent social upheaval which would almost certainly follow another world war. As a result the conservatism of Britain's foreign policy, which provoked radical and labour sentiment to indignant protest, afforded them considerable satisfaction. It was association with left-wing forces, above all with Russia, that they feared. In those parts of the Commonwealth where nationalism was predominant there prevailed also understanding of Hitler's desire to reunite all Germans within a greater Reich, and where nationalism was tainted with racialism his methods rarely evoked outspoken condemnation. Left-wing opinion in the dominions, as in the United Kingdom,[1] allowed itself easy indulgence in the fashionable denunciations of the iniquities of Versailles, but nationalists sincerely felt that where the Treaty of Versailles had departed from the strict application of the principle of self-determination in respect of Germany, it was in fact iniquitous. After the absorption of a non-Germanic people within the Reich in March 1939 the Nazi appeal to nationalism was exposed as a means to an end and not an end in itself. Within the Commonwealth nationalist sympathy for Germany was thereby alienated, save among those sections of Afrikaner opinion where Nazi doctrines of racial supremacy were not without their appeal. Yet if the illusions of most nationalists[2] were dispelled after March 1939, they were no more reconciled than before to any co-operation with the Soviet Union. To the great majority of them, whether in the Irish Free State or in South Africa or in French Canada, though not in India, any association with the Soviet Union was regarded as unwelcome in the extreme and even morally wrong. For strategic reasons Australia shared their views, with the result that the negotiation of the Nazi-Soviet pact in August 1939, which rendered impossible the dispatch of effective or timely aid to Poland, which tilted the balance of power heavily against the Western Allies and the British Commonwealth, and which made an early war certain, was none the less received with relief in almost all parts of the Commonwealth and significantly reconciled nationalist opinion in the dominions to co-operation in the struggle against Nazi Germany.

This interplay of nationalist and left-wing opinion was an important factor in the moulding of the external policies of the Commonwealth. Both disliked the prospect of automatic commitment in Britain's wars, and both were at one in their desire to assert each dominion's final responsibility in the field of foreign policy. But while for the nationalists the dislike was one of fundamental principle, for the left it derived less from principle than from passing circumstance. Labour was in opposition in the years immediately before the Second World War in the United Kingdom and in Australia, while in Canada the C.C.F. was still a mushroom growth, and opposition parties inevitably tend to

[1] cf. A. J. P. Taylor, *From Napoleon to Stalin* (London, Hamilton, 1950) p. 132.

[2] Mr. Curtin reflected the predominant reaction of British Commonwealth peoples and of many others besides when he said that from March onwards the policy of Germany had involved very much more than the rectification of injustices—to use the proper term—of the Versailles Treaty.

look critically at the articles of faith to which governments subscribe. Still more did the dislike derive from the deep mistrust of Labour and radical opinion for the policies of Mr. Baldwin and of Mr. Chamberlain, which were believed to be largely inspired by powerful vested interests in London. Canadians must be careful, warned Mr. Woodsworth in 1937, lest they lent themselves to carrying out the policies of a few industrial and financial groups in the motherland.[1] It was this same mistrust that prompted significant sections of Australian Labour to dismiss the war in Abyssinia as a 'struggle for markets' and the Sudeten crisis as the outcome of sordid trade rivalries. At the unofficial British Commonwealth Relations Conference at Sydney in 1938, Australian and New Zealand Labour delegates summed up their attitude in saying that whole-hearted working-class co-operation in Commonwealth foreign and defence policies was conditional upon the government of the United Kingdom working consistently for the establishment of a world order 'on a democratic basis' and resolutely opposing Fascism.[2] It was because the policies actually pursued by the United Kingdom government so significantly failed to satisfy these conditions that the trend towards isolationism in Australian Labour circles remained so pronounced. At root it reflected the suspicion that the destinies of the Commonwealth were still controlled by right-wing reactionary forces in London, in the direction of whose policies Australian Labour could repose no confidence. Prompted in some measure at least by the same misgivings New Zealand, where alone in the Commonwealth Labour was in office, formally questioned the wisdom of appeasement, and this was the only dominion government to do so. But while left-wing opinion in the dominions was critical of the readiness of the United Kingdom government to conciliate the dictators, its own aims were ill defined and often contradictory. If it was left-wing opinion which felt most keenly that with Munich the moral case against aggression had gone, it was that opinion also which had resisted most strongly the rearmament of the democracies without which aggression could not be checked.

The differences in approach between nationalists and socialists to problems of pre-war external policy were illuminating not least in that they suggest how difficult it was for the United Kingdom government to ensure general dominion approval for its conduct of foreign affairs. But such differences must not be pressed too far. Not all nationalists were conservative in social policy at home or conciliatory towards the dictators abroad, by no means all Labour supporters were averse to the appeasement of Nazi Germany or Fascist Italy. Mr. Winston Churchill and Pandit Jawaharlal Nehru, the two Commonwealth statesmen of the first rank who consistently denounced the policy of appeasement, constituted by their differences in outlook and party allegiance a timely reminder of the need to beware of all easy generalization. The one was a Conservative, the other a socialist; the one was an imperialist, the other a

[1] *J.P.E.*, 1937, vol. 18, p. 304. [2] *B.C.R. Conference*, 1938, pp. 249-51.

nationalist; both were excluded from all position of authority in their respective countries, and in matters of domestic imperial policy they were bitterly opposed. Yet the actions of 'the decent, easy men' who 'guided by wrong measurements' and 'inspired by feeble impulses' seemed to Mr. Churchill to have allowed themselves to be carried away on 'long, dismal, drawling tides of drift and surrender',[1] provoked Pandit Nehru also to passionate protest. To the Indian Congress leader British policy in Manchuria, in Abyssinia, in Spain, and in Central Europe seemed at the time not only consistently reactionary and anti-democratic but also a direct encouragement to Fascist and Nazi aggression.[2] Mr. Chamberlain's attitude towards the Czechs in 1938 produced in him 'a feeling of nausea', and he wondered 'how any Englishman with any trace of liberal instincts or decency' could tolerate it. Nor did he doubt before ever appeasement reached its climax at Munich that the policy it represented was 'an open invitation to war'. The common verdict of these two men on the events of those disastrous days tempts one to seek for some fundamental reason for it. But perhaps all that can usefully be said is that both were men of vision, both were lovers of liberty, and both had a high sense of the dignity of man. Mr. Churchill was more than an imperialist, Mr. Nehru more than a nationalist. Above all both understood the forces that move mankind.[3]

Indian reactions to British policies in Europe had a wider significance. Both Germany and Italy had colonial aspirations, and Germany proclaimed in strident terms her belief in a racial mission which decreed that Germans by virtue of belonging to a superior race had a right to rule. They left in no doubt their will to discharge it by the ruthless subjugation of other races. Whatever reservations Indians, Africans, and other non-European peoples within the Empire might entertain about British imperialism, they were under no illusions about what their fate would be under Hitler's New Order. For that reason their detestation of Nazism was unqualified. They did not, however, share in equal measure, or in some cases even at all, the fears of Soviet Russia which so deeply influenced the attitude of the dominions. From the point of view of India and of the Colonial Empire the war against Fascist aggression was, therefore, well calculated to elicit a response more wholehearted than a war against Communist aggression. But of the dominions this was less true, and that was one reason for their insistence that Hitler should be appeased till it became clear beyond question in March 1939 that the domina-

[1] *Second World War*, vol. 1, p. 201.

[2] Jawaharlal Nehru, *The Unity of India* (London, Drummond, 1941) p. 284. First published as a letter in the *Manchester Guardian*, 9 September 1938.

[3] It is interesting to speculate on what might have been the influence of an Indian dominion upon Commonwealth policies before 1939, especially in the light of Nehru's remarks already quoted (p. 413) that a free India might have been able to avert the outbreak of war. Exaggerated though this assertion must seem, the impact of ideological opposition to Fascism from within the Commonwealth might well have led to a much closer questioning of the wisdom of appeasement.

tion of Europe, and ultimately of the world, was his aim. In 1939 Nazi aggression united the Colonial Empire in support of Britain; ten years later the threat of Soviet aggression united most firmly the older dominions.

THE FAILURE OF THE LEAGUE AND ITS CONSEQUENCES

The enduring lesson of the years of transition in Commonwealth relations was that the Commonwealth could not live to itself alone. However firmly united in their fundamental loyalties, the outlook and the interests of its peoples were too diverse and scattered for their reconciliation even within its flexible framework. Unity had therefore to be sought without, and the value of the League of Nations to the Commonwealth lay in the fact that its appeal, though not its membership, was universal. It could unite conservatives and socialists, nationalists and internationalists, realists and idealists, because all were united in their desire for peace. The two dominions, South Africa and the Irish Free State, whose co-operation with the rest of the Commonwealth was in doubt in 1939, both strongly supported the League in Manchuria in 1931 and in Abyssinia in 1935. From this point of view the League, which was dismissed by many imperialists as a distraction on grounds that were convincing strategically but not politically, alone provided a sufficiently broad basis for united Commonwealth action in world affairs. At the same time it is true that under any circumstances the value of the League to the Commonwealth would have declined with the passage of time simply because its membership was not world wide. Australia, New Zealand, and above all Canada, were deeply conscious throughout this period that the United States of America was outside the fold, and that as a result the League could never assert its authority in the Pacific and that its effectiveness elsewhere would be seriously handicapped. None the less, even if it be allowed that the League, because of its restricted membership, was destined to go down before the challenge of an aggressor, the way in which this happened was of great importance to the Commonwealth. The conception of a world in which peace was enforced by a supra-national authority was no passing fancy to be lightly discarded in the face of changing circumstances but something which appealed to the deep urge of the peoples of the Commonwealth to establish the rule of law in the society of nations. It was for this reason that the Hoare–Laval pact proved so serious a set-back to Commonwealth unity. It suggested that the League had not merely failed but had been betrayed for dubious reasons of expediency with the open connivance of the country to which the Commonwealth looked for leadership. Even if the United Kingdom found it difficult to act on principle, it was essential that she should pay some regard to principle and to ideals so deeply and widely entertained by the peoples of the Commonwealth. She could not, after expressing whole-hearted devotion to the League and the cause of collective security, wantonly disregard it without seriously undermining confidence both in her leadership and in the integrity of her policy.

It was hoped by imperialists that the failure of the League in Abyssinia would lead to the closing of imperial ranks. In a limited sense this hope proved not unfounded. In the field of defence the failure of the League prompted closer co-operation with the United Kingdom. It was clear after 1936 that no small country could rely upon Geneva for its future safety, and even the dominions, who had reservations about the extent of their co-operation in imperial policies, none the less thereafter co-ordinated their defence plans more closely with those of the United Kingdom. Psychologically, however, the failure of the League strengthened not imperialism but isolationism. This was most marked in Canada; it was also pronounced in the Union of South Africa and in the Irish Free State. Indeed, in the case of the Irish Free State, history had decreed that only some supra-national authority of which the United Kingdom and the Irish Free State were both members could bring the Irish Free State into a war on the same side as the United Kingdom so soon after national sovereignty had been restored.

While the statesmen of the Commonwealth resolved to take active measures for their mutual defence after the failure of the League in Abyssinia, not all were prepared to abandon their allegiance to the ideals for which it stood. As late as 15 March 1938 General Smuts, one of its principal architects, said, 'There are only two alternatives before the world today, either to follow the way of the League, which is the way of consultation and understanding between peoples, or to fight it out to the end.'[1] But in fact with the resignation of Mr. Anthony Eden, in February 1938, the last chance of resolute British support for collective action against the aggressor disappeared. While the governments of the dominions for the most part accepted the fact of Mr. Eden's resignation, if not with equanimity, at least with no apparent dismay, public opinion sensed that here was a parting of the ways, and in this it was not mistaken. It was, it will be remembered, on the night on which Mr. Eden resigned, and on that night only, that sleep deserted Mr. Winston Churchill throughout all those anxious years. 'From midnight till dawn', he has written, 'I lay in my bed consumed by emotions of sorrow and fear.'[2] Yet public opinion was insufficiently well-informed to be able to express its instinctive reactions in a practical form. 'I am an ardent advocate of collective security', said Mr. J. H. Blackmore, the Canadian Social Credit leader, in May 1938, 'but I wish I knew with whom to "collect".'[3] That indeed was a difficulty to which dominion critics of Mr. Chamberlain's policies suggested no very convincing answer.

The failure of the League accentuated the caution of dominion governments and their preoccupation with problems of internal unity. They became in-

[1] *Daily Telegraph*, 16 March 1938.
[2] *Second World War*, vol. 1, p. 201.
[3] Canada, H. of C. Deb., 1938, vol. 2, p. 1938.

creasingly anxious not to become entangled in the affairs of Europe or of Asia. There developed as a result an exaggerated concern lest provocative or even careless words might either involve them in distant conflicts, or even themselves provoke a conflict. For Mr. Mackenzie King silence was golden, and at each of the great crises which preceded the outbreak of war he was to be found urging upon members in Ottawa the greatest restraint in word and deed. General Hertzog displayed no less anxiety to avoid all cause of possible provocation and even allowed himself to be prompted by the German minister in Pretoria into unprofitable dispute with the Mayor of Port Elizabeth who had denounced the 'deplorable and ruthless behaviour of the misguided celibate of Central Europe'.[1] In Australia Mr. Lyons interrupted a holiday in Tasmania to rebuke Mr. H. G. Wells for telling Australians that Hitler and Mussolini were enforcing in Europe a state of affairs similar to the days of the criminal Caesars, and that Hitler had acquired the capacity of 'making dastardly murder resemble today's good deed'.[2] Mr. de Valera, with perhaps better cause since he had subversive and militant opposition to fear at home, was already showing the concern, which became so marked during the war years, that the political temperature of Eire should be kept low. Such caution in retrospect may well seem exaggerated and even unworthy, but it was inspired by a prudent sense of limitation, not by pusillanimity. As the war-clouds gathered the dominions became increasingly aware of the limits of their strength and of the dangers of internal disunity. It was not only Canada that was a 'precarious creation'.

THE INFLUENCE OF THE UNITED KINGDOM ON DOMINION POLICIES

After 1935 dominion rearmament proceeded at an ever quickening pace and by 1939 their expenditure on armaments was generally more than twice what it had been three years earlier. At the same time it may be doubted whether this increased expenditure made adequate provision even for the local defence of each individual dominion by land and air. At sea the weakness of the dominions remained especially pronounced. By 1939 Australia alone had a more than negligible fleet, yet its heaviest unit was a cruiser of 10,000 tons. While this comparative weakness was in part counterbalanced in the case of Canada and Australia by a capacity for rapid expansion under pressure, the fact remains that in 1939 primary responsibility for imperial defence and virtually sole responsibility for the protection of imperial sea routes remained with the United Kingdom. That inevitably gave her government a leading

[1] *Manchester Guardian*, 11 April 1939. The Mayor was but little abashed and while allowing that his language had been a trifle strong added: 'When I recall the brutal murder of Dollfuss, the cruel imprisonment of Schuschnigg, and the way Beneš was hounded out of his country, I wonder whether you, sir, as head of a state protected by the British Navy are not being more complacent than you ought to be with the representative of a regime which apparently delights in treating Prime Ministers in this fashion'.

[2] *The Times*, 7 January 1939.

voice in all matters relating to the defence of the Empire. The rearmament of the dominions in its early phase itself would appear to have been stimulated by information given by Sir Maurice Hankey (later Lord Hankey) on his visit to the overseas dominions in 1934. At that time secretary to the cabinet and Committee of Imperial Defence and chairman of a standing sub-committee which had considered many defence questions referred to it by the governments of the dominions, Sir Maurice Hankey was intimately acquainted with the reasons which had persuaded the United Kingdom government itself to decide upon rearmament, and in all the dominions he discussed defence questions with ministers and staff officers. He has recorded as a matter of historical truth that every dominion from the time of his visit expedited its rearmament.[1]

In the conduct of foreign affairs the predominance of the United Kingdom remained as marked as in the field of defence. It is true that since 1936 dominion representation overseas had somewhat expanded, but by 1939 it still remained on a very modest scale. At the outbreak of war Canada had legations in Washington, Paris, The Hague, Brussels, and Tokyo; Australia had appointed counsellors to serve on the staffs of the United Kingdom ambassadors at Washington and at Tokyo; New Zealand had no diplomatic representation in foreign countries at all; South Africa had legations in Washington, Paris, The Hague and Brussels, Rome, Berlin, Stockholm, Lisbon, and Cairo; while Eire had legations at Washington, Paris, The Hague and Brussels, Rome, Berlin, Lisbon, and Madrid. None of the dominions, it will be noted, were represented in Prague or Moscow, and only South Africa and Eire were represented in Berlin. Diplomatic representation on so small a scale placed the dominions at a considerable disadvantage in attempting any independent assessment of the international situation. The fewer their legations overseas the greater of necessity their dependence upon the information which came out from London. While its value was never in doubt there were suspicions, particularly in Australia, that it was not wholly free from bias. How far this suspicion had any justification may not be determined unless and until the communications sent out from London to the dominion capitals are published in full, but clearly the degree of dominion dependence on London for the interpretation of events and policies in foreign countries left them exposed to the changes that took place in the conduct of United Kingdom diplomacy at critical moments. For example, the appointment of Sir Nevile Henderson to the Embassy at Berlin at the instance of Mr. Neville Chamberlain and despite the misgivings of the Foreign Office,[2] was a matter of considerable importance to those dominion governments who had no representative of their own in Germany. Sir Nevile Henderson was in fact appointed to further a

[1] *Diplomacy by Conference*, p. 132.

[2] cf. C. A. Murray, *Reflections on Some Aspects of British Policy Between the Two World Wars* (Edinburgh, Oliver & Boyd, 1946) pp. 33 ff.

particular policy, and his dispatches to the United Kingdom government, the substance of which was transmitted to the dominions, reflected the bias of his mind. In London this might be discounted, but in dominion capitals far removed from the scene of action, it was less likely. Yet the nature of the reports received from Berlin was a matter of major importance in the determination of dominion policies; and their dependence upon a source of information which they could not control underlined one of the more serious disadvantages of their position at that time. When separate diplomatic representation by the dominions was first contemplated it had provoked much concern among imperialists who feared lest it should make disastrous inroads upon Commonwealth unity. The establishment of the first Canadian legation in Washington filled Mr. R. B. Bennett with the gloomiest apprehension. Canada, he said, 'is entering on a great adventure, the last great adventure in our relation to the British Empire. I am wholly opposed to the establishment of this Embassy at Washington. It is but the doctrine of separation, it is but the evidence in many minds of the end of our connexions with the Empire. For that is what it means.'[1] But might it not be more reasonably maintained that once the dominions exercised separate control over foreign policy exactly the opposite was true? It was the failure to translate the principle of equality into practice more rapidly that imposed the greater strain upon the inner harmony of the Commonwealth. Had the dominions been more fully represented before 1939 in the danger zones of Europe and Asia they would have had the evidence of their own diplomatic experts on the course of events, they could have compared it with the reports they received from London and as a result they could either have expressed their dissent or they could have gone forward with greater confidence in the correctness of United Kingdom reactions. In the absence of such independent information suspicions of United Kingdom policies were fostered, and more important still, dominion reluctance to embark on positive policies was significantly and understandably strengthened.

There was another circumstance which increased dominion dependence on the United Kingdom in foreign affairs though it did not apply to them all with equal force. After 1926 when dominion Departments for External Affairs assumed control of the foreign policies of their respective countries a cadre of experts was slowly built up. This was excellent so far as it went. But the growing expertness of officials was not matched by a growing interest or knowledge on the part of ministers or members of Parliaments, who remained for the most part little interested in the details of foreign policy. For this one reason in particular may be suggested. Because foreign affairs and Commonwealth affairs were customarily dealt with by the same department, and because both were considered to involve issues of great delicacy, it became the practice for the Prime Minister in most dominions to assume ministerial re-

[1] 13 April 1927, Canada, H. of C. Deb., vol. 2, p. 2472.

sponsibility for the Department for External Affairs. In Canada, South Africa, and in the Irish Free State during Mr. de Valera's long period in power[1] this association of offices became almost a convention of government. Yet its consequences were not uniformly helpful. Dominion Prime Ministers, by the very nature of their responsibilities, were inevitably preoccupied with domestic problems and rarely had the inclination or the time to make any thorough study of foreign affairs. This lack of interest or knowledge was a handicap for which soundness of judgement and robust good sense could not wholly compensate. Its removal was conditional upon the appointment of separate ministers responsible solely for the conduct of external affairs, a step which was not generally taken till after the Second World War.

The influence of the United Kingdom upon dominion external and defence policy was in itself a reflection of the age of transition through which the Commonwealth was passing. It had been assumed in 1926 that equality of status would ultimately involve similarity of function, but it was unfortunate that this difficult period of functional transition coincided with years of unprecedented tension in the international field. In September 1939 the critical decision was in fact taken by the United Kingdom, and the dominions defined their attitude in relation to that decision. To this extent their participation in international affairs remained still at one remove. Lord Balfour had indeed indicated the essentials of the situation which prevailed thirteen years later in his opening address to the Committee of Inter-Imperial Relations in 1926 when he said:

> There are always moments in the conduct of fleets, of armies, and of negotiations, when decisions, if they are to be of any use, must be rapid, and when consultations if they involve delay are a danger rather than a strength. If this be so, it must be on one of the seven self-governing communities that the greatest share of responsibility must be thrown; and so long as the centre of difficulty is Europe, and the present distribution of population in the Empire suffers no overwhelming change, it seems impossible to ask any other portion of the Empire to bear the major responsibilities which devolve upon Great Britain.[2]

It was a situation never likely to recur in that form again.

THE INFLUENCE OF THE DOMINIONS ON UNITED KINGDOM POLICIES: SOME GENERAL CONSIDERATIONS

The influence of the dominions on United Kingdom policy remains a more vexed and difficult question. This arises largely from the very nature of the system of Commonwealth consultation. Dominion governments were rarely confronted with a direct question. They were not asked, as the false prophets of Samaria were asked by King Ahab, 'Shall I go against Ramoth Gilead to

[1] Before 1932 and after 1948 the two offices were ministerially separate, and at the Imperial Conferences of 1926 and 1930 the principal representative of the Irish Free State was the Minister for External Affairs and not the Prime Minister.

[2] Dugdale, *Balfour*, p. 381.

battle or shall I forebear?' They were sent a stream of information which, in the words of Lord Hankey, became 'a flood at times of crisis', but it was left to them to decide whether they would comment upon it or not. In fact they did so infrequently, and as a result the outgoing flood was answered only by an incoming trickle. But here again caution is needed in drawing conclusions. If comment or advice was comparatively infrequent, it would be unwise to measure its impact by its volume. Dominion governments for the most part preferred to exercise their influence informally. If it was Mr. Mackenzie King who had the most pronounced aversion to written communications on major issues of policy, only Mr. Lyons would seem to have been wholly free from inhibition in commenting on United Kingdom policies.

The very intimacy of intra-Commonwealth relations had always precluded any very precise allocation of responsibility for particular actions which are of interest and concern to more than one of its members. This has been especially true in the field of foreign policy where in recent years regular meetings of dominion High Commissioners with United Kingdom ministers have contributed much, not by recording decisions or particular points of view, but by eliciting what is in common in the attitude of the governments of the Commonwealth to important questions. Characteristically these meetings took place in the first instance, not because it was considered desirable in principle that they should, but in response to particular needs; and it is significant that their form became clearer and the frequency with which they were held increased as the international situation deteriorated. They had a dual origin. Before 1935 there had been one or two occasions on which the High Commissioners had met with the Secretary of State for Dominion Affairs in London to discuss some particular aspect of foreign policy, and it was the regular practice for dominion delegations at Geneva, which normally included their respective High Commissioners in London, to meet with the United Kingdom delegation during the sessions of the Assembly of the League to discuss matters of common interest. In 1935 during the Abyssinian crisis the meetings of Commonwealth delegations at Geneva were very frequent, and when the session of the Assembly concluded the discussions were continued in London at meetings of the dominion High Commissioners with the Secretary of State for Foreign Affairs. The value of the meetings was so evident that they were henceforward placed on a more regular basis, and by 1938 they had assumed their existing form with the Secretary of State for Dominion Affairs presiding at them. Their frequency was at all times related to the needs of the moment,[1] their proceedings were informal, and personality counted for a great deal. The dominion High Commissioner, who in his own right was a man whose judgement was respected in London, could influence a policy perhaps to a greater degree than a High Commissioner who had been given more explicit instructions

[1] In late September 1938 they sometimes took place more than once on the same day.

by his government.[1] It was the responsibility of the Secretary of State for Dominion Affairs to make known the views of dominion High Commissioners to the Foreign Secretary and to the cabinet,[2] and the personal element entered in again at this stage. At the Foreign Office and in the cabinet the weight that was attached to dominion views was to some extent dependent upon the degree to which the Secretary of State for Dominion Affairs commanded the respect and the confidence of his colleagues. The existence of these varying and imponderable personal factors, which undoubtedly played no inconsiderable part in determining the influence of dominion governments on United Kingdom policy at any given moment, normally precluded any very precise measurement of it.

With these reservations always in mind, an examination of the influence of the dominions on United Kingdom policy may usefully be approached by recording some United Kingdom ministerial statements which illustrate the extent to which dominion governments were informed or consulted and the nature of their reactions. In May 1936,[3] when the future of the League was being actively discussed, Mr. Eden, Secretary of State for Foreign Affairs, declared that the United Kingdom government proposed to engage at once upon a consideration of the problems involved with the dominion governments.[4] In the following month the Prime Minister, Mr. Stanley Baldwin stated in reply to a question in the House that while the fullest possible information had been given to the dominion governments about the attitude of the United Kingdom towards the continuance of sanctions against Italy, it was for the dominion governments themselves to make the announcements of what they would do in their own parliaments or at Geneva.[5] In November 1936 Mr. Eden[6] declared that he had had frequent discussions with the dominion High Commissioners during the negotiations leading up to the Anglo-Egyptian Treaty, and more particularly with Australian ministers in London and with the New Zealand government. Neither, however, were signatories to the treaty, and the New Zealand government emphasized that

[1] It is not without significance that Australia, who sought most consistently to influence United Kingdom policies, was represented in London in these years by Mr. Stanley Bruce (later Lord Bruce), a former Prime Minister.

[2] In 1950 Mr. P. C. Gordon-Walker, Secretary of State for Commonwealth Relations, described this aspect of the functions of his office in saying that the Secretary of State has 'the prime and special duty of seeing that the interests of the British Commonwealth and of every member of it are consistently present to the ministers of the British cabinet'. (Speech at Rotary International Conference at Southport, 21 October 1950, *Commonwealth Survey*, no. 58 (London Central Office of Information) p. 5.) In exceptional circumstances the dominion High Commissioners might also themselves wish to place their views before the Foreign Secretary or even the Prime Minister.

[3] The illustrations are taken from the later and more critical years under review for obvious reasons.

[4] 6 May 1936, H. of C. Deb., vol. 311, col. 1740.

[5] 18 June 1936, ibid. vol. 313, col. 1165.

[6] 24 November 1936, ibid. vol. 318, coll. 257–8.

their action amounted to advice only. In November 1937 the Secretary of State for Dominion Affairs stated that there had been no communication with any of the dominions about the future of Germany's former colonial possessions. In March 1938 the Prime Minister stated that the dominions had been kept fully informed by telegraph of the United Kingdom government's intention to reopen discussions with Italy, and he assured the House that they would continue to be kept informed of all developments and 'will, therefore, have every opportunity of expressing their views'.[1] Later in the same month the Prime Minister stated that the United Kingdom government was in close touch with the dominions 'on all important aspects of the present international situation'.[2] Such uninformative terminology, which glossed over the difference between the ordinary transmission of information and active consultation, was used on several occasions in the summer of 1938, but we know that during the Munich crisis events moved too rapidly for consultation, except on the long distance telephone. There was, however, a constant and rapid flow of information outwards from London. On 3 October Mr. Chamberlain told the House of Commons that throughout the discussions which preceded the Munich agreement the governments of the dominions had been kept 'in the closest touch with the march of events by telegraph and by personal contact. . . .'[3] In November 1938 Mr. Chamberlain stated that the Australian Prime Minister had approved the implementation of the Anglo-Italian agreement and that, in more general terms, General Hertzog had expressed his conviction 'that the steps that His Majesty's government propose taking are wise and necessary and will materially contribute to appeasement in Europe'.[4] There was, however, on that occasion no communication from Canada, New Zealand, or the Irish Free State. In December 1938 Mr. Chamberlain said that it was 'a source of continual satisfaction to His Majesty's government that our efforts to keep the dominions fully informed of the foreign situation, as we see it, have been rewarded by a general absence of criticism on their part'.[5] In March 1939 he assured the House that the dominions had been kept fully informed of developments in Europe and in particular about the guarantee to Poland.[6] But they were not consulted about this guarantee because time was not thought to allow of consultation. On 13 April 1939 Mr. Chamberlain said with reference to the guarantees to Greece and Roumania that 'the dominion governments were being continuously informed of all developments' but again they were not consulted.[7]

[1] 7 March 1938, ibid. vol. 332, col. 1508.
[2] 30 March 1938, ibid. vol. 333, col. 1995.
[3] H. of C. Deb., vol. 339, col. 48.
[4] 2 November 1938, ibid. vol. 340, col. 211.
[5] 19 December 1938, ibid. vol. 342, col. 2519.
[6] 31 March 1939, ibid. vol. 345, col. 2417.
[7] ibid. vol. 346, col. 13.

This brief summary illustrates the nature of the system of consultation and its limitations. The limitations arose partly from the nature of the system itself and partly from the attitudes of those who worked it. These attitudes, reflecting differences in the approach of dominion governments to Commonwealth relations, varied considerably. The Canadian government was reluctant to comment on United Kingdom policies partly because in many cases it did not feel competent to do so, and still more because it feared lest comment might be considered tantamount to commitment or at least the assumption of some share of responsibility. Australia, New Zealand, and South Africa used the opportunities which the system offered more fully and commented freely on those aspects of United Kingdom policy which were of particular interest to them. The procedure they adopted would not, however, appear to have been identical. The Australian government relied greatly upon direct communication from Prime Minister to Prime Minister reinforced by the intervention of their High Commissioner in London. The South African government, on the other hand, would appear usually to have transmitted its views through the South African High Commissioner in London by whom *aides-mémoire* setting out the views of his government were passed to the Secretary of State for Dominion Affairs. The inaction of the Irish Free State reflected the resolve of its government to dissociate itself from membership of the Commonwealth, though it is to be noted that the Irish High Commissioner continued to attend the High Commissioners' meetings with the Secretary of State for Dominion Affairs until the outbreak of war.

In Australia there were serious complaints about the inadequacy of the machinery of intra-Commonwealth consultation. Its most outspoken critic was Mr. W. M. Hughes, Minister for External Affairs, who in August 1938 complained that the Australian government could not exercise an effective voice in imperial policy because they were frequently not kept fully informed while a situation was still fluid and United Kingdom policy was still being formulated. He attributed to distance part of the responsibility for what he considered to be unnecessary delays, but more of it to the circuitous channels along which the information was passed. He singled out the Dominions Office as a particular cause of complaint. In his view it superimposed on the admirable machinery of the Foreign Office 'a creaking machine' which 'lagged superfluous on the stage'. He thought the Office a complete anachronism because the conditions which had warranted its creation had disappeared, leaving it 'as obsolete as the muzzle-loading rifle and the hansom cab'.[1] These forthright criticisms, which caused equal concern to London and to Mr. Hughes's Prime Minister, who hastily dissociated himself from them, were in substance wholly unjustified. In fact it was the Dominions Office which constantly reminded the Foreign Office of the need to send fuller information to the dominions and which, more rarely, was able to persuade it to delay

[1] *The Times*, 9 August 1938.

action for a time in order to give the dominions an opportunity to comment.[1] None the less Mr. Hughes's onslaught reflected a continuing sense of dissatisfaction in Australia. It was there, in the dominion which was most anxious to influence United Kingdom policy from within, that the system of intra-Commonwealth consultation was most severely criticized. This was understandable enough. Canada, who had little desire to influence United Kingdom policy and wished rather to disentangle herself from it, was well satisfied with a system which transmitted information effectively, whereas Australia, which was not interested in receiving information but in contributing positively to the making of United Kingdom policy, found her opportunities for doing so restricted by what seemed to be unnecessary delays. This was a fact which in later years prompted Australian proposals for the reform of the system. Yet in fact what many Australians desired was something which the machinery of consultation was not designed to give. It was intended to ensure the widest possible measure of agreement among the several governments of the Commonwealth about the foreign policies they intended to pursue, while its Australian critics at heart wanted something much closer to a co-ordinated and common imperial foreign policy. This was almost certainly administratively impracticable without some form of centralized machinery.

THE INFLUENCE OF THE DOMINIONS ON UNITED KINGDOM FOREIGN POLICY, SEPTEMBER 1938 TO SEPTEMBER 1939

There was no doubt about the support of the dominion governments, other than that of New Zealand, for a policy of appeasement in Europe. It received formal expression in the report of the Imperial Conference of 1937 but it dated back to an earlier period. There is evidence that all the dominion governments favoured the conclusion of the Anglo-German naval agreement in 1935, and it is certain that in 1936 they were strongly opposed to any armed resistance to the German reoccupation and remilitarization of the Rhineland. Indeed at that critical moment their restraining influence played its part in the determination of United Kingdom policy. At the same time this consistent early backing of a policy of appeasement in no way warrants the assumption that the policy which goes by that name originated with the governments of the dominions. They supported it, they welcomed it, they felt there was no alternative, but the initiative in almost every case and the ultimate responsibility always rested with the United Kingdom government.

The policy of appeasement reached its climax at Munich in September 1938. The dominions either actively encouraged or cordially welcomed Mr. Neville Chamberlain's successive attempts to reach a settlement with Hitler that would avert war, even if it involved very substantial concessions by

[1] ibid. 13 August 1938.

Czechoslovakia. This pressure from the dominions for a peaceful settlement was used by the United Kingdom to explain Britain's reluctance to commit itself to any explicit course of action in advance. On 20 July 1938 Lord Halifax, Secretary of State for Foreign Affairs, told M. Daladier, the French Prime Minister, and M. Bonnet, the French Foreign Minister, that he had received a visit from the Aga Khan who had stressed 'the responsibility that lay upon His Majesty's government to accept no commitment that might involve the British Empire in war', and he impressed upon them also that the attitude of South Africa would be the same.[1] On 10 September M. Bonnet asked the British ambassador, 'If Germany should attack Czechoslovakia, and France in discharge of her treaty obligations, should then mobilize and say to Britain: "We are going to march, come and march with us", what would be the attitude of the British Government?'[2] To this Lord Halifax, to whom the inquiry was transmitted by the ambassador, replied[3] that M. Bonnet's question, 'though plain in form, cannot be dissociated from the circumstances in which it might be posed, which are necessarily at this stage completely hypothetical', and then proceeded to explain that

> in this matter it is impossible for His Majesty's government to have regard only to their own position inasmuch as in any decision they may reach or action they may take they would, in fact, be committing the dominions. Their governments would quite certainly be unwilling to have their position in any way decided for them in advance of the actual circumstances of which they would desire themselves to judge.

These communications with the French government make it clear that dominion attitudes very properly weighed in the making of United Kingdom policy. But how great was their influence upon it? This is a very important question which the historians of Munich have hitherto strangely neglected.[4] In this they are surely mistaken, for no verdict on Britain's role in the Czech crisis which ignores altogether the attitudes and influence of the dominions upon it can lay claim to finality.

In September 1938 the Prime Ministers of Canada, Australia, South Africa, and the Irish Free State were in direct communication with Mr. Neville Chamberlain.[5] All of them sent messages encouraging him in his efforts to seek a peaceful settlement of the Czech crisis. Mr. de Valera, then

[1] E. L. Woodward and R. Butler, eds., *Documents on British Foreign Policy, 1919–39*, 3rd series, vol. 1, 1938, p. 602.

[2] Quoted in J. W. Wheeler-Bennett, *Munich: Prologue to Tragedy* (London, Macmillan, 1948) p. 98.

[3] Lord Halifax to Sir E. Phipps, 12 September 1938, published in Georges Bonnet, *Défense de la Paix* (Geneva, Bourquin, 1946) vol. 1, pp. 360–1.

[4] Mr. Wheeler-Bennett (op. cit.) alludes in one sentence (e.g. p. 184) to the strong pressure exerted by Canada, Australia, and South Africa upon the United Kingdom government; Professor L. B. Namier does not consider it at all in his *Diplomatic Prelude*. Nor does Mr. Winston Churchill refer to it in *The Second World War* (vol. 1).

[5] The attitude of New Zealand, as reflected in the documents that have been published, was throughout reserved by comparison with those of the other dominion governments.

President of the League Assembly, indicated his sympathy with Mr. Chamberlain's efforts to avert war by delaying the meeting of the Assembly while direct discussions with Germany were proceeding, and by offering to bring the Assembly into action if and when this seemed most desirable. On 3 October 1938 Mr. Chamberlain told the House of Commons that he wished to place on record 'how greatly I was encouraged on each of the journeys I made to Germany by the knowledge that I went with the good wishes of the governments of the dominions. They shared all our anxieties and all our hopes. They rejoiced with us that peace was preserved. . . .'[1] Lord Templewood, then Sir Samuel Hoare, a member of the cabinet particularly concerned with foreign affairs, later recalled that in September 1938 telegrams had 'poured in' from the dominions indicating unmistakably that they were 'not yet willing to approve the declaration of war'.[2] This was, if anything, an understatement. As we have seen, neither the Union of South Africa nor Eire would have gone to war in September 1938 had Britain intervened on behalf of Czechoslovakia. South Africa's pressure for a peaceful settlement at almost any price was strongly supported by Canada and by Australia. During September 1938 the meetings of the dominion High Commissioners with the Secretary of State for Dominion Affairs were very frequent and there is no doubt that the High Commissioners used the opportunity they afforded for underlining the supreme importance their governments attached to the avoidance of war on such an issue at such a time. Moreover, not only were their views made known to the Dominions Secretary and through him presumably to the United Kingdom cabinet, but also the High Commissioners who felt most strongly on this issue themselves sought and obtained an interview with the Prime Minister himself.

How great an impact did this pressure from the dominions make upon Mr. Neville Chamberlain's mind and policy? The answer would seem to be comparatively little because his own mind was already made up.[3] The actual policy Mr. Chamberlain followed in September 1938 owed little or nothing to dominion inspiration. He persisted in his attempts to find a basis of agreement, despite discouragements which to most men would have seemed final, because he was a man of peace and because he believed that no effort should be spared to preserve peace in Europe. It was suggested by Pirow in his conversation with Hitler shortly after Munich that General Hertzog's influence upon Mr. Chamberlain was considerable,[4] but for this there would seem to be little or no foundation. While among dominion statesmen General Hertzog was the most whole-hearted in his support of the policy of appeasement, he was not particularly intimate with Mr. Chamberlain, nor did his

[1] H. of C. Deb., vol. 339, col. 48.

[2] Viscount Templewood, 'The Lesson of Munich', *Listener*, 9 December 1948.

[3] Dominion influence upon the Foreign Secretary, Lord Halifax, would seem to have been more marked. See above, p. 438.

[4] *Documents on German Foreign Policy, 1918–45*, Series D, vol. 4, no. 271, p. 337.

views in any way inspire Mr. Chamberlain's actions. Mr. Chamberlain's biographer[1] makes no mention of the influence of dominion governments upon Mr. Chamberlain at this time. Mr. Chamberlain's policy was in fact in a very particular sense his own. The attitude of the dominions was important because it helped to confirm him in his own sense of the rightness of his policy and to secure for it the support of a virtually unanimous cabinet.

The role of the dominions is brought out most clearly if one inquires how was it that a policy destined to be so widely condemned in succeeding years gained the general approval of the United Kingdom cabinet at the time? Undoubtedly Mr. Chamberlain's personal predominance within the cabinet was important, the defencelessness of Britain was crucial, but supplementing both was the declared reluctance of the dominions to see Britain embark on any action which might provoke war on an issue not sufficiently clear-cut to enlist the support of their peoples. Lord Templewood later suggested that this dominion pressure for a settlement was a major consideration in the shaping of United Kingdom policy. Had war come in September 1938, he has said, 'we should have started with a broken Commonwealth front'.[2] So much indeed was true, but the implication that it was one of the considerations uppermost in the minds of the United Kingdom cabinet at the time is without solid foundation. Knowledge of the views entertained by dominion governments may well have exercised a restraining influence upon some members of the United Kingdom cabinet who might otherwise have questioned more closely the wisdom of continuing negotiations with Hitler, and it is perhaps not without significance that the one minister who resigned after Munich, Mr. Duff-Cooper, had greater intellectual and spiritual affinity with the countries of Western Europe than with those of the English-speaking world overseas. But discouragement of any departure from a course already set was the extent of the influence the dominions actually exercised. If, however, a more resolute course had been seriously contemplated, then their views might have been of decisive importance.

What would the dominions have done had war been forced upon the Western democracies in September 1938? Here we are on firm ground again. Canada, Australia, and New Zealand would have united with Britain in her resistance to Nazi aggression; South Africa, by agreement between the two principal leaders of the Fusion government,[3] Generals Hertzog and Smuts, would at the outset at least have remained non-belligerent, and Eire, as in 1939, would have remained neutral. In the case of French-speaking Canada and of wide sections of opinion in Australia, the lack of enthusiasm for war

[1] Professor Keith Feiling.

[2] 'The Lesson of Munich.' See also his letter in the *Listener*, 6 January 1949.

[3] The terms of this agreement were a close secret and almost certainly were not known in London in September 1938. The possibility of South African non-belligerency was not, however, overlooked. See Lord Halifax's remarks to M. Daladier and M. Bonnet quoted above (p. 438).

would have been very pronounced. The Australian Labour party for the most part failed to see that any major issue of principle was involved in the crisis of September 1938, and Mr. Curtin was emphatic that any war resulting from it would not justify the dispatch of a single Australian soldier overseas. Therefore, should the call have come, within two of the three dominions which were resolved to fight at Britain's side there would have been doubt and division. Had a more resolute policy been contemplated by the United Kingdom government at any time during the Czech crisis the divided opinions that prevailed within the Commonwealth would at once have assumed a major importance. It might well have been wiser and more honourable, as Mr. Chamberlain's critics contend, to have fought in September 1938, but it seems certain that at that time a united Commonwealth would not have gone to war.[1] South Africa as well as Eire would have remained neutral, and in two of the remaining three dominions there would have been no unanimity about the merits of the issues involved. Any such cleavage within the Commonwealth would at the least have represented a failure of Commonwealth, and especially of United Kingdom statesmanship, and it might have had more serious consequences. This in itself suggests that unqualified condemnation of Britain's policy at that time and in the circumstances should be treated with some reserve.[2] It may well have been a mistaken policy, but the situation was not so simple as some of its critics suggest. It is indeed hardly to be disputed that before the Commonwealth could unite whole-heartedly in resistance to Nazi aggression, it was necessary that there should seem to them to be conclusive evidence that the sole responsibility for the conflict rested with Germany. The peoples of the dominions needed unequivocal reassurance that in the bringing about of a second great war 'their hands were clean'. That reassurance Munich in fact supplied at a great price.

The major responsibility for the Munich settlement rests and must always rest with the United Kingdom government. It was they who were directly concerned, and all that the dominions could and did do was to proffer advice and indicate the likely reactions of their peoples. Here the all-important fact was that the dominions were psychologically as well as militarily unprepared for war. They were not yet convinced that Hitler was bent on the domination of Europe and ultimately of the world by force. They were far from satisfied that the retention of the Sudetenland by Czechoslovakia was a sufficient cause

[1] When it was suggested after Munich that the United Kingdom government should have given Czechoslovakia an assurance that once German troops crossed her frontier Britain would go to her assistance, Mr. Chamberlain observed that the dominions would have had a right to be consulted before the United Kingdom took a step which might have had 'such incalculable consequences for them'. And he added, 'although it is not for me to speak for them, I say it would have been difficult to convince them that we were justified in giving such an assurance. . . .' (H. of C. Deb., vol. 339, col. 546.)

[2] Dominion statesmen cannot be regarded as being wholly free from responsibility for those circumstances in which one important factor was the comparative defencelessness of their countries.

for war, the more so since from the outset of the crisis the Czechs seemed disposed to concede rather than to fight at any cost. Through their representation on the Committee of Imperial Defence the dominions were aware of the grave deficiencies in Britain's defence preparations, and while they could properly urge that every step should be taken to avoid war on an issue which did not seem to their peoples as a whole to justify war, they could hardly in any circumstances have pressed the United Kingdom government to adopt a more resolute course because it was the United Kingdom, not themselves, who would have to withstand the direct assault of the aggressor. It is perhaps for this reason that Munich, which both at the time and later assumed so great an emotional significance in the United Kingdom, has always been regarded with greater detachment in the dominions. They did not feel themselves to be morally implicated. It is true that, with the exception of New Zealand, their governments had pressed strongly for a settlement, but they did not, and were in no position to, suggest how that settlement should be reached. They were not directly responsible for any dishonourable pressure upon the Czechs nor for the discourtesy with which their representatives were treated. They were concerned with the broad objectives of policy, not with its detailed application.

After Munich the retreat from appeasement began. In respect of the further appeasement of Italy, New Zealand and Canada exercised a prudent restraint in not commenting on Mr. Chamberlain's ill-judged endeavours to detach Mussolini from his Axis partner, but South Africa and particularly Australia gave him direct and positive encouragement to overtures which were treated with supreme contempt. The decisive date for the Commonwealth was March 1939, after which General Hertzog alone retained his faith in appeasement almost unimpaired. For the rest, dominion statesmen recognized with the absorption of Czechoslovakia that appeasement had failed and that Germany could not be conciliated by concessions. Mr. Chamberlain's consequent abrupt change in policy, which was made known in his Birmingham speech of 23 March, was prompted in part, according to his biographer, by strong representations from the dominions.[1] The transformation in dominion opinion was indeed unmistakable, though there is no evidence to suggest that the dominion governments, with the possible exception of New Zealand, took the initiative in proposing alternative policies, and it seems unlikely that they did so. But equally they did not question the need for Britain's unilateral guarantees to Poland and later to Roumania and Greece, even though they were not consulted about them in advance or committed by their terms. This was the more remarkable when the implications of the Polish guarantee are recalled.

History [writes Mr. Churchill], which we are told is mainly the record of the

[1] Feiling, *Neville Chamberlain*, p. 400.

crimes, follies and miseries of mankind, may be scoured and ransacked to find a parallel to this sudden and complete reversal of five or six years' policy of easy-going placatory appeasement, and its transformation almost overnight into a readiness to accept an obviously imminent war on far worse conditions and on the greatest scale.[1]

Yet accepted it was in the dominions, as in the United Kingdom, as an unwelcome necessity created by now indisputable evidence of Germany's deliberate resolve to embark on a career of aggression. Noteworthy, too, was the fact that in accepting it dominion statesmen, and especially Mr. Mackenzie King, did not retract their earlier support of appeasement but went out of their way to justify it, on the ground that irrefutable proof of Germany's aggressive intentions there had to be before a united Commonwealth could fight once more on Europe's bloody battlefields.

The support of the dominions for the new course thus dramatically set acquired greater importance from the fact that their governments, with the possible exception of New Zealand, were reluctant in the extreme to see the Polish guarantee given reality by the negotiation of a military pact with Russia. To this General Hertzog was most strongly opposed on the ground that it would result in the encirclement of Germany and thereby provoke her to embark on an early war, while her chances still seemed favourable. But to Mr. Mackenzie King and to Mr. Lyons the conclusion of the pact was almost equally unwelcome. The former was deeply influenced by the fact that French-Canada would look askance at any association with this 'godless' state, whilst Mr. Lyons was fearful lest an open alliance with the Soviet Union would drive Japan, already a member of the Anti-Comintern pact, into the hands of the Axis Powers and thereby extend the coming war in Europe to the Pacific. For all these reasons the United Kingdom government received not encouragement but discouragement from the dominions (other than New Zealand) in its endeavours to negotiate a military agreement with Russia in the summer of 1939. Their failure to do so, followed by the announcement of the Nazi-Soviet pact of August 1939, hardened the resolve of the dominions to resist Nazi aggression against Poland.

From this analysis of dominion influence upon United Kingdom policy before the Second World War certain conclusions would seem to emerge. The first is that dominion governments were reluctant in the extreme to contemplate participation in war, however well justified its cause might seem or however great the provocation, unless and until they were satisfied that only by such action could a threat to the survival of Britain and to their own independent existence be removed. The second is that the dominions were unwilling to sacrifice principle, or prejudice, to *Realpolitik*. A military alliance with Russia might afford some chance of averting war and contain at the least some assurance of an early allied victory if war came, but it was no

[1] *Second World War*, vol. 1, p. 271.

more welcome to the dominions on that account. Finally, while the attitudes of the dominions were rightly an important factor in the making of United Kingdom policy, it would appear that at no time in this period was their influence upon it decisive, though at many times the views they expressed strongly reinforced the trend of United Kingdom policy, and in the Munich crisis they afforded a potent discouragement to any consideration of more resolute courses of action.

WAS GERMANY MISLED ABOUT DOMINION POLICIES?

It has been stated, more often in the United Kingdom than in Europe or in the Commonwealth overseas, that the indeterminate character of the dominion policies, arising principally from the reluctance of their governments to assume specific commitments in Europe, misled their potential enemies and so by default encouraged them in their career of aggression. It was argued after the Second World War that the fact that it had been possible for doubts to be entertained about united action by the Commonwealth had 'been a potent factor in tempting aggressors to launch two world wars in the present century'.[1] This is a far-reaching criticism which deserves the most careful consideration even though it can hardly be held to apply with as much force to the coming of the First as to the Second World War.

Before 1914 the dominions had no formal responsibilities in the determination of imperial foreign policy. That was the exclusive concern of the United Kingdom. Yet the trend towards decentralization in all fields of imperial policy was becoming pronounced, and in 1912 the German ambassador in London, Baron Marschall von Bieberstein, noted that the Canadian Prime Minister, Mr. (later Sir Robert) Borden, wished 'that the dominions shall possess a decisive voice in the deliberations upon which peace and war depend'.[2] But there was no suggestion in his dispatch or in other German documents that the dominions did exercise any independent voice in the making of peace or war or that their attitudes were of any importance in determining German policy. This is understandable. The plans of the Central Powers before 1914 by their very nature excluded any consideration of what smaller non-European states might or might not do. What the Schlieffen plan envisaged, what the German and Austrian Chiefs of Staff, von Moltke and von Conrad, discussed at Karlsbad in May 1914 was a war involving the knock-out of France within six weeks 'at least', to quote von Moltke, 'so far as to enable us to direct our principal forces to the East'. In such a war any action which the distant dominions of the British Empire might or might not take seemed to have no relevance, and was therefore not taken into account.

Twenty years later the position was different. The dominions had then become individually responsible for their own foreign policies and they had

[1] *Round Table*, September 1948, no. 152, p. 733.
[2] *Die Grosse Politik*, vol. 21, p. 241.

indicated unmistakably that they did not consider themselves in any way bound by Britain's treaty obligations in Europe. In particular they had not subscribed to the unilateral guarantee given to Poland in March 1939, nor were they a party to the later Anglo-Polish treaty. In September 1939 they had full freedom of action. But was there any reason for Germany to be misled about the action which any dominion proposed to take? The last word on this question necessarily lies with the German government. Here the evidence is not conclusive for the simple reason that it is mainly negative. But a reading of such official documents as have so far been published and of the press suggests that neither the German government nor the German people seriously miscalculated the reaction of the Commonwealth countries to continuing German aggression in Europe.[1] In November 1937 Hitler in conference with his chiefs of staff assessed the capacity of the Western Powers to resist him in his career of planned aggression. He did not share the view that the British Empire was 'unshakable'. On the contrary, he believed that the emphasis on the Crown as the symbol of imperial unity was in itself tantamount to an admission that in the long run the British Empire could not 'maintain its position by power politics'. Already in Ireland, in India, and in the Far East there were significant indications of its incapacity to impose its will by force. Yet he would seem to have entertained no expectation of internal divisions. On the contrary, he observed that 'opposition to the Empire was to be found less in the conquered countries than among her competitors'.[2] In August 1938 the *Berliner Tageblatt* in a well-informed article on British Commonwealth affairs suggested that while the old dependence of the dominions on Britain was ending, a new tie would take its place in which England's administrative and military needs would be equally well met. The article emphasized that the new agreements with Egypt, Iraq, and even with Eire did not exclude the possibility of satisfactory arrangements about defence or the possibility that the new treaties could become as valuable 'as the former overlordship'. It suggested, however, that while 'the dominions will stand by England through thick and thin in Western Europe' they would 'make reservations with regard to Eastern Europe'.[3] No one could complain that this was a misleading analysis. The distinction between the west and the east acquired its substance from the emphasis placed both by Mr. Mackenzie King and by General Smuts upon a direct attack upon the United Kingdom as an indisputable *casus belli* for their respective countries. Nor indeed is it to be doubted that a war arising from some dispute in Central or Eastern Europe was likely to elicit a less certain response from the dominions than a war arising from direct aggression in the West. In a dispatch from

[1] That they underestimated the capacity of the Commonwealth to wage war is undoubted, but that is a different point.

[2] *Documents on German Foreign Policy*, Series D, vol. 1, no. 19, pp. 32–33.

[3] *Berliner Tageblatt*, 20 August 1938.

London to the German Foreign Ministry dated 25 March 1938 the German chargé d'affaires specifically mentioned the possibility that Britain might not be disposed to intervene at least immediately in a war arising out of German aggression against Czechoslovakia because 'British policy is conducted in the closest agreement with the dominions'.[1] In general, while the German government confidently assumed that the weakness of the British Commonwealth would become apparent in war, they would not appear to have given much attention to the possibility of division within the Commonwealth in the making of war. In a long and competent review of his mission as ambassador to London from April 1938 to September 1939, Herr von Dirksen[2] did not examine such a possibility at all and the phrases which he used suggested that he assumed that the British Commonwealth would be united in war-time. His allusion to the Commonwealth as 'das englische Empire' in itself indicated the trend of German thought. German diplomats were only too disposed to believe that empires were controlled from above and that final authority was vested in the centre itself. This made less likely the harbouring of any major illusions about dominion policies in the event of war, and it was only in the case of South Africa that the German government would seem to have been misled by a belief that in the event of war the Union would not participate. In general, while the Nazis overestimated the unpreparedness and the military and political weakness of the Commonwealth, they underestimated the capacity of its component states for independent action. No evidence so far published suggests that doubts about the unity of the Commonwealth were a major factor in encouraging German aggression.

While it may reasonably be concluded that the Nazi government was not seriously misled about the degree of unity that would prevail in the Commonwealth in the event of a war brought about by German aggression, that is not tantamount to saying that a formal declaration of intention on the part of its members individually or collectively would have been without value. On the contrary, if well timed it might have been of considerable value as a dramatic reminder to the Nazi leaders of the opposition they would encounter if they persisted in their career of aggression. But was it possible? Was it not dependent upon a unity of outlook which did not exist? Mr. de Valera and General Hertzog could not have subscribed to it without abandoning strongly held views and carefully considered policies. Mr. Mackenzie King would have been temperamentally averse to doing so, for at all times and in all circumstances he was averse to throwing down challenges in public. He might also

[1] *Documents on German Foreign Policy, 1918–45*, Series D, vol. 2, p. 193; see also on a rather different point No. 383, p. 610, where Ribbentrop is recorded as having reassured the Hungarian Regent about possible British intervention by saying that she would not 'lightly risk the loss of her Empire'.

[2] U.S.S.R., Ministry of Foreign Affairs, *Documents and Materials Relating to the Eve of the Second World War*, vol. 2, *Dirksen Papers* (Moscow, Foreign Languages Publishing House, 1948) pp. 148 ff.

have questioned its usefulness so far as Canada was concerned, for had he not personally warned Hitler in 1937 of her probable reactions to further aggression? Australia and New Zealand it is true would almost certainly have willingly subscribed, but their attitudes in such an eventuality were hardly in doubt. Yet even where such a warning seemed superfluous, Commonwealth statesmen undoubtedly underestimated the risks of silence and inaction. In a broadcast in December 1938 Lord Hankey said that if he were the Chief of the General Staff of a country likely to become involved in war with the United Kingdom, 'I would warn my government—"Beware of underrating the dominions"'.[1] But no such warning was given by Keitel to Hitler, and the conclusion is surely justified that the opportunity of reminding the Nazi war-lords of the reaction of the Commonwealth countries to their continuing aggression should not have been neglected. No chance of confronting potential aggressors with the consequences of their actions should have been overlooked, even if slight hopes might be entertained of its probable effect.

SOME CONCLUDING REFLECTIONS

The leaders of the Commonwealth countries before the Second World War were predominantly liberal and nationalist in outlook. The discredit into which both liberalism and nationalism have subsequently fallen among intellectuals in the Western World has encouraged disparagement of their methods and achievements. In a retrospective verdict on Munich Mr. A. J. P. Taylor has described the Czech leaders, 'Beneš most of all', as 'liberals by historical background and social origin—men of bargaining and discussion. They could manœuvre and evade; they could not defy and perish . . . the Munich Conference was the last display of Liberal civilization.'[2] Such reflections are not without relevance to Commonwealth affairs. The Commonwealth system depended, too, upon consultation, upon bargaining, and upon compromise.[3] To its statesmen discussion seemed the great essential of the system they had contrived. It presumed fraternity; it assured liberty; it guaranteed equality, for no free discussion can take place save between equals. In internal relations this faith in discussion and in compromise served them well. The transformation from Empire to Commonwealth was carried through with an ease, an assurance, and a farsightedness which could be truly appreciated only in later years when equality of status was progressively matched with a growing equality of function. Yet extended into the field of foreign policy the system was not equally effective before 1939. There it was confronted by other and uncongenial forces. An approach which was well

[1] 'The Dominions and Rearmament', *Listener*, 29 December 1938.

[2] *From Napoleon to Stalin*, pp. 132–3.

[3] Characteristic of its outlook was the opening sentence of Mr. Mackenzie King's appeal to Hitler and to the President of Poland on the eve of the war. 'The people of Canada', he wrote, 'are of one mind that there is no international problem which cannot be settled by conference and negotiation.' (*The Times*, 28 August 1939.)

fitted to produce a right decision after careful consideration and discussion by statesmen well informed about the issues at stake was not equally fitted to reach a quick decision on matters of international policy about which many of its statesmen were without detailed knowledge or experience. Communications between seven governments, even in the age of telegraph and wireless, took time. That was rarely available in a period of mounting crisis when divided counsels most urgently needed to be reconciled. It was in such circumstances that the weakness of the system was exposed and the response to the challenge of the dictators became uncertain.

Mr. Mackenzie King, it has already been suggested, was in a very real sense the representative figure of the period. He was not, as General Smuts could justly claim to be after September 1939, a man who had changed the course of history, but one who had notably assisted its natural development. He was the solid, unromantic Hamlet of the Commonwealth, for ever refraining from leaping. Yet his characteristic reluctance to embark upon dramatic courses or to commit himself with finality to a particular policy carried with it long-term advantages, which perhaps outweighed its undoubted short-term liabilities. For the indecision of Mr. Mackenzie King was the indecision of a man who had a sense of distant perspectives, who saw the goal towards which the Commonwealth must move. If his critics were justified in their complaints about his irresolution, time has notably vindicated his constant insistence that an essential factor in the future of the British Commonwealth, and in the maintenance of world peace which was its great objective, was close co-operation with the United States of America.[1] In his preoccupation with healing the great cleavage of the Anglo-Saxon world he was not mistaken and by it he underlined a fact which has a wider application. To be true to itself and its destiny the Commonwealth had often in the difficult years of transition to sacrifice present advantages in order to safeguard long-term objectives.

Within the Commonwealth the critics of the system were most preoccupied with problems of organization. It was their constant complaint that the decentralization of responsibility in itself made quick decision and resolute action impossible. In this the correctness of their diagnosis may well be doubted. In retrospect it seems unlikely than any modifications in machinery involving even some central control of foreign policy would have essentially modified the attitude of the Commonwealth to events in Europe or in Asia. In September 1938, responsibility for Munich would have been wider but the policy of appeasement would, for good or ill, have none the less been pursued.

[1] The German ambassador in London was not mistaken in sensing that the Chamberlain government regarded such close political ties with the United States as at best an unwelcome necessity partly on grounds of supposed imperial interest. But he exaggerated in speaking of the resentment caused by the 'officiousness' with which Roosevelt had declared that the Monroe doctrine also applied to Canada and of 'the alarm' in London at the growing community of interests with America felt by Australia and New Zealand. (*Documents on German Foreign Policy*, Series D, vol. 4, no. 286, p. 363).

This is a point which deserves more thought than has usually been given to it. In a democratic society common action must spring from a common will, but the fact that it is common to many nations is no assurance that it will be resolute. The many are often as irresolute and as blind as the few. Yet the pre-occupation with machinery was not altogether mistaken. The fundamental cause of weakness derived from the fact that the Commonwealth was in a stage of transition. It was in practice neither centralized nor decentralized. Theory and practice did not as yet coincide. On the one hand this created exaggerated concern with questions of status on the part of many of the dominions, on the other it deprived them of independent sources of information and judgement on international affairs which might well have corrected some mistaken conclusions formed in London and would at least have made possible more informed and balanced discussion.

The forms and conventions which a society uses may conceal as much as they reveal, but in a questioning, dynamic age they will not long survive unless they are in harmony with the purposes they are meant to serve. It was the supreme merit of the Commonwealth system as it had evolved by 1939 that despite the weaknesses that were exposed when it was confronted with hard problems of foreign policy it reflected faithfully the inner spirit of the Commonwealth itself. A decentralized Commonwealth did not, and could not, enjoy the same freedom of manœuvre as a highly centralized military dictatorship. Reliance upon discussion is essential to democracy but it is rarely consistent with abrupt changes in policy. No free country, whatever its peril, could have performed the *volte face* executed by the Soviet Union in August 1939. This placed the Commonwealth countries at an inevitable short-term disadvantage. As Hazlitt said, 'the want of principle is power', and it is idle to pretend that reliance upon democratic, or any other, principles does not exact a price. It is not always 'prosperous to be just', though in free countries there is usually loud complaint when it is not. While the governments of the Commonwealth made some serious errors of judgement in their conduct of foreign policy before the Second World War, they remained true to the principles which were at once the indispensable foundation of their society of free and equal states and the condition of its future growth. Because they kept faith in the great essentials they were able, when the final crisis came, to astonish the world by their capacity for united and resolute action.

INDEX

PRINTED IN
GREAT BRITAIN
AT THE
UNIVERSITY PRESS
OXFORD
BY
CHARLES BATEY
PRINTER
TO THE
UNIVERSITY